HERMANN BECKH (187⁙ Sanskrit, becoming Profes⁙ University of Berlin. A mas⁙ guages, he wrote extensivel⁙ ical subjects, including Bud⁙ Alchemy and Music. In 1911 Steiner and was inspired to join the Anthroposophical Society, where he soon became a valued co-worker. In 1922, he helped found The Christian Community, a movement for religious renewal. His many books are gradually being translated from the original German and published in English.

RUDOLF FRIELING (1901-86) was born in Leipzig, Germany. He studied Theology and Philosophy and helped found The Christian Community, a contemporary movement for religious renewal, in 1922. He became the leader of The Christian Community in 1957, serving until his death. He is the author of several books on Christianity and the Bible.

# THE LANGUAGE OF THE STARS

ZODIAC AND PLANETS IN RELATION TO THE
HUMAN BEING

With a chapter on the Anthroposophical Soul Calendar

## by Hermann Beckh

*and*

## THE COSMIC RHYTHM IN THE CREED
## FOR READERS OF BECKH'S BOOKS

## by Rudolf Frieling

With an Introduction and Reviews by Rudolf Frieling and others
Translated by Maren & Alan Stott
Edited by Neil Franklin

TEMPLE LODGE

Temple Lodge Publishing Ltd.
Hillside House, The Square
Forest Row, RH18 5ES

www.templelodge.com

First published as a single volume in English by Temple Lodge 2020

A CIP catalogue record for this book is available from the British Library

ISBN 978 1 912230 53 2

Cover by Morgan Creative
Typeset by Symbiosys Technologies, Visakhapatnam, India
Printed and bound by 4Edge Ltd., Essex

# Contents

APPENDICES

# Foreword

by the General Editor of *The Collected Works of Rev. Prof. Hermann Beckh*

By 1930 Hermann Beckh had published well over a dozen major books which had investigated the divine-cosmic sources of Indo-European speech, Western music and the Gospels of Mark and John. As a Professor in Berlin he had produced scholarly works, especially concerning ancient Tibetan texts that were received with acclaim throughout European university departments. Totally devoted to Rudolf Steiner's guidance, he had continued tirelessly to work on himself in disciplined meditation, breaking through barriers to the dream, sleep and pre-natal states of consciousness, without which, he found, there was no meaningful access to the sacred literature of India, Iran, Egypt or Israel.

By 1930, The Christian Community and the seminary in Stuttgart, where Beckh was both priest and teacher, were facing hard times: there was total economic collapse (all banks and financial institutions were closed), Hitler's National Socialists were in the ascendant, and perhaps worst of all, Germany had been gripped by a popular fever for astrology, a travesty of all that Rudolf Steiner had worked for with regard to the stars. As Ellic Howe explains:

> ... the majority of some 400 astrological books and pamphlets were printed in Germany between 1921 and 1935; between 1926 and 1931 there were no less than 26 astrological year books or predictive annuals in production; by 1928 half a dozen specialist monthly or bi-monthly periodicals were available for practising astrologers in Germany (Ellic Howe, *Urania's Children*. London: William Kimber and Co., 1967, p. 102).

Then, in 1930, in his attic study in Urachstr. 41 or in his mother's house just around the corner, he took up his pen and started what was to be three years of *Contributions* to the Priests' *Newsletter*. Yet the higher value of Beckh's writing here is not the extent of his meditative knowledge, which had reached Intuition by 1930, neither his total faithfulness to the path opened up by Rudolf Steiner, nor his vast erudition. What is finally convincing about these hitherto forgotten pages is something infinitely more refined and delicate, almost elusive.

Between 1920 and 1930, Friedrich Rittelmeyer's books most consistently reveal the Christian pulpit: 'Not I, but Christ in me.' Emil Bock's slight publications during this decade rested on his grasp of Imaginative knowledge and broad background reading; Rudolf Frieling brought the most acute objective analysis to the structures of the gospels. A superficial reading of Beckh might suggest that his pioneering spiritual research into speech, music, the gospels and the heavens was his own major contribution to the upbuilding of The Christian Community and anthroposophy at large. But this is not quite the whole truth.

In these *Contributions*, more than anywhere among his publications, Beckh forges sentence after sentence with the wisdom of the stars and, naturally, instinctively, also offers himself as a mediator. It is this extraordinary, honest presentation of his own personal, authentic 'I' in the midst of gigantic astrological concerns which is utterly compelling.

Neil Franklin, Whitsun 2020

# Translator's Introduction

'Real Astrology properly understood is at the same time an understanding of the world, true understanding of the world.'

Hermann Beckh, Contribution No. 8.

Readers of Professor Hermann Beckh have become used to the self-effacing style and the scrupulous clarity of this universal scholar. All the more welcome, then, is the rarely-heard more personal, lecturing voice perceived, for example, in the memoirs 'From my life'.[1] This fragment narrates an almost fairy-tale childhood and youth that includes his struggles with the manner of his schooling, yet also the triumphs of a prodigiously gifted young man. The only other text to use the first person pronoun more frequently is the unique lecture held for the neo-Buddhists (1931) on 'Steiner and Buddha'.[2] Here the lecturer himself justifies the departure from his usual practice:

> At the suggestion of the editor of the *Zeitschrift für Buddhismus* ['Journal for Buddhism'],[3] while undertaking to write on this very topical theme, I deliberately choose to deviate from what is otherwise my usual form. For precisely with a presentation of 'Buddhism in the light of Anthroposophy' limited purely to the 'facts', as an anthroposophist and personal student of Rudolf Steiner I would all too easily meet with objections that this 'purely factual' account would somehow be personally coloured, given my personal relationship to Rudolf Steiner and anthroposophy as somewhat tendentious. Consequently, in this case I think it is right to allow everything personally-fated from the outset to feed into my presentation, hoping that just in this way it could succeed to help the reader most honestly in his own judgment to separate the facts from the personal element.

There is, moreover, yet another source where we may accompany the Professor on his researches. This is Beckh's *Contributions to Star-Knowledge* for the Priests' *Newsletter*.

> For me personally, if I may say this here, this musical subject of the keys was the starting point of all my zodiac and star research. From this I came much later to my gospel research—the cosmic rhythm in Mark's

Gospel and John's Gospel—and from there to everything that one understands in the narrower sense as 'astrology' (birth-horoscopes, etc.). And for all deeper understanding of astrology, the musical element is of very great significance (*Contribution* No. 12; see also *Contribution* No. 8).

It is worth emphasizing: Beckh's path was through music *to* the stars, not the other way around. The evidence shows that, like his teacher Rudolf Steiner, Beckh, too, works consistently with the holistic principle, 'from the whole to the parts', or, contrary as it may sound, 'from the centre', for a centre can only claim to be such through the existence of its surroundings, or periphery. Moreover, like his teacher and others, including J.S. Bach,[4] Beckh names that centre (*Contribution* No. 12):

> And what concerns the astrology governing today it seems everywhere important to draw it away from Anglo-Indian theosophy still controlling it today and to place it on the healthy ground of Rudolf Steiner's anthroposophy. This is the actual main reason and essential content of this whole study: to build astrology afresh on the Christian foundations of anthroposophy and for the great cosmic aspects which in astrology we have to gain in general for the revelation of the cosmic cross in the stars. For the centring of the entire astrology in the Mystery of Golgotha it is of decisive importance to perceive the three crosses in the zodiac as the crosses of the Father, the Son and the Spirit.

Today, 90 years on, we believe this unique text sketching a new star-wisdom should now appear where it belongs as the latest volume (not counting *Collected Articles*, forthcoming) in the *Collected Works*, translated here into English. Much of the material, it is true, already appears in Beckh's expositions of *Mark's Gospel* (1928) and especially *John's Gospel* (1930); many details are mutually explanatory. The younger colleagues were beginning to take note. In particular Rudolf Frieling, a fellow founder-priest of The Christian Community (1922)—who was to steer The Christian Community 1960–86—was inspired by the cosmic rhythm researched by the Professor to trace it in the 12 statements of the Creed of The Christian Community—to Beckh's complete satisfaction and approval. It seems appropriate to include Frieling's series of *Contributions* here; this work was the sign for Beckh to pick up his pen:

> In my *Contributions to Star-Knowledge* I have many things to say concerning this Uranus viewpoint, about Uranus in general, and I intend, since

the questions are directly stimulated by Frieling's contribution, to begin
with it already today... [See p. 357 below].

Professor Beckh repeatedly mentions *The Cosmic Rhythm in the Creed*;
he even claims Frieling 'so to speak supplies the highest and ultimate
viewpoint' (*Contribution* No. 12, p. 179).

Later, as Professor Beckh knew his end was approaching, he
fended away requests to revisit the spiritual past made by Dr Rittelmeyer (who steered The Christian Community from its foundation until his death in 1938), Emil Bock (who succeeded him)
and possibly others. The Professor had already explored that
realm at a consistently high standard in several publications and
innumerable articles. Now he wanted to write something directly
helpful for the future. He knew 'his theme' was to research the
Archetypes. And so he planned to rewrite these *Contributions to
a Spiritual Study of the Stars* for the public,[5] no doubt generally to
polish them and assume his accustomed self-effacing style. Rudolf
Meyer notes that Beckh's seminary lectures eventually all came
out in book form.[6] But time was running out, so he decided first
to revisit the musical language of tonality—as he thought, a more
popular, tangible approach to the theme of the cosmic rhythms.
Posterity, however, tends to regard *The Language of Tonality*[7] as
'specialist'. Does this show what general culture has lost over the
last 80 years since it was penned—or show unnecessary fear of
something 'unfamiliar'? However this may be, interest in the stars
has certainly increased, not to speak of space travel and what that
means for popular subculture. Alone the immense popularity of
the science-fiction, TV-series *Doctor Who* hints at the dim awareness of reincarnation and more; the Harry Potter phenomenon,
too, is drawing probably millions of souls amongst the coming
generations.

Today, alongside the popular creations as well as distortions—Beckh
was already aware of this tendency in his day (see his remarks in *Contributions* Nos. 7 and 17)—many people are now truly ready, indeed
actively *searching*, for an introduction to a *Christ-oriented astrology
for the twenty-first century*. Beckh, we can now appreciate, was
writing oriented to the future, which could be our present. He aimed
to research beyond mythology, which is apparent in an aside:

(Only out of astrology is one convinced of the eminent significance of
this Greek mythology of the gods, without which no really practical

psychology is possible. One does not arrive at human psychology with some kind of abstract notions, but only with a feeling for the real beings Mars, Jupiter, Venus, and so on, just as they are revealed in the human being). [*Contribution* No. 7.]

In addition to his monumental gospel studies, such monographs on astrology and the cosmic creation as revealed in Genesis also show the calibre of the man; aware of tradition, he wrote to renew it, knowing his work is unique.[8] His incentive to write on the stars was the Christened astrology sketched by Rudolf Steiner in his lecture-course *Christ and the Spiritual World: the Search for the Holy Grail.*[9] The lecturer hoped his stimuli would form the basis for a fresh study of the subject. Beckh saw this (see *Contribution* No. 1). When it did not happen immediately, he felt himself called to attempt to fill the gap with the present *Contributions* (see, too, his remarks in *Contributions* No. 7 and No. 19), while also realizing that such basic accounts as Rudolf Steiner's *Occult Science* [GA 13] and *Theosophy* [GA 9], textbooks of spiritual science, can be read at the same time as astrological texts.[10]

Alongside the study of universal, human symbolism regarding the cosmic rhythms, the profession of biographical counselling, as well as the arts of eurythmy, music and speech—and one could mention the use the film-industry makes of Joseph Campbell's research into myth and the stages of 'the hero's journey'; again, only a passing comment can be spared to mention the outlay of thousands—if not millions—of euros by top-ranking vine-growers who minutely follow the star calendar that is dependent on star knowledge to indicate favourable and unfavourable times in horticulture—all research the cosmic rhythms today in practical, artistic terms. What do we have at our fingertips? The basic thought, in varying degrees of clarity, is that if life within and around us is perceived as artistic, it implies the researching of that perceived creative process and its details—in the first instance, remaining with and employing to the best of one's intentions and abilities the perceived artistic process as method. Such contributions— runs the basic thought, shared by Hermann Beckh—ultimately lead to the heart and mind of the Creator Him/Herself; not only does it fulfil one's destiny, but at the same time benefits the race. Moreover, on the basis of the wisest known authority, it affects no less the expectant universe of Being: 'I will not leave you as orphans.'[11]

As an example, we choose here one of the arts mentioned above, that of English literature, and one piece of research. The 50-year-old secret of C.S. Lewis's *Narnia* (1950-56) has been discovered—this writer based his seven world-renowned children's stories on the moods of the seven planets. The love of the stars of this renowned author, an icon of present-day culture, has begun to be researched.[12] 'The astrological planets,' wrote Lewis, 'are spiritual symbols of permanent value.' Readers who prick up their ears at what Beckh reports at the end of *Contribution* No. 5, may want to reassess the artistic legacy of the renowned Oxford don and how deep his unacknowledged study of anthroposophy probably really was; for Lewis, though, this had to be tangibly *artistic*. The link is also there through George MacDonald (1824-1905) (to both C.S. Lewis [1898-1963] and G.K. Chesterton [1874-1936], the acknowledged master) to the early romantic poet Novalis himself. Mention has to be made, too, of Lewis Carroll's 'Alice' books, educational masterpieces on initiation (no less) disguised as 'nonsense', though the word 'fairytale' is used in the preface to *Alice's Adventures Under Ground* (1886). Carroll's literary relationship to MacDonald is one of the creative wonders of the nineteenth century.[13]

Scholars are revisiting children's literature and mythopoeia. Far from being cases of 'escapism', original writers are always preparing the future—the Bard himself (*MND*, V, i) points out the poet's prophetic imagination 'bodies forth the forms of things unknown'; furthermore, Jaques' 'seven ages of man' in his speech 'All the world's a stage' [*As You Like* It, II, vii] are concepts that have never been seriously contended. References to the planets and stars, their rhythms and influence both serious and humorous, abound in the Shakespeare canon; the subject forms the fabric of his creative thinking. Is, then, 'the discarded image' or 'Elizabethan world-picture' less a pretty fiction that serves the drama, but rather an experiential model of the spiritual universe, of a supreme cultural relevance? At the birth of modern times, Shakespeare did more than add immeasurably to the development of the language (coining over 3,000 words, we are told, and using a vocabulary approaching 21,000 words). At the same time, he basically founded modern English literature. The Bard knew the consciousness-soul has to be consciously developed.[14]

After promising to limit discussion here to *one* art, to forego a reference Leonardo's *The Last Supper* (mentioned by H. Beckh in *Contribution* 24) would be inexcusable. Several suggestions concerning the disciples and the zodiac have been made. Adam Bittleston (1911-89), who studied at the Priests' Seminary under Hermann Beckh and in conversation acknowledged his influence, contributed independent pastoral work on the stars and a searching article on Leonardo's *Last Supper*.[15] In his view, the alignment with the zodiac begins on the far left with Taurus, the Bull and from left to right follows the zodiacal order: Ram, Fishes, Waterman, etc. Michael Ladwein (*Leonardo da Vinci The Last Supper*, Temple Lodge 2006), in an endnote, is out of sympathy with the whole concept and thus dismissive. Ladwein does indeed mention a detailed study claiming to have found the definitive order, offering proof of the painter's intentions. This is an attempted East-West approach by Horst Lozynski.[16] Drawing on esoteric tradition and considerable geometrical evidence, Lozynski proposes that a path of *self*-development lies hidden in the painting. The geometric analysis based on circle, square and triangle certainly reveals much. The author weaves in measurements and relationships of the figure of proportions, of the elevation of the Great Pyramid (obviously, writing in 1987, with no reference to Robert Bauval & Adrian Gilbert, *The Orion Mystery*, 1994) and of the positions of the chakras and centres of the ideal human figure (based on C.W. Leadbeater). How far do the impressive discoveries in symbolism (derivatives of *Symbol*, and *Sinnbild* are used over 300 times), filtered through a Western mind, shed light on Rudolf Steiner's claim that a visitor 'from the planet Mars' (farther than, for example, India— some people consider a possible reference to the Buddha may also be contained here), seeing the painting, could 'understand the mission … the meaning of the Earth'?[17] Steiner saw that Leonardo portrayed the cosmic Sun-being and His deed for the Earth. Beckh followed Steiner's indication that anthroposophical study and—as he also mentions—'in a truly artistic way' is essential to pursue the subject of *cosmic* development. The 'cosmic rhythm' Beckh regarded as 'my theme'; the present volume, together with his work on music and the gospels, represent an achievement that has not yet been equalled.

Although written 90-odd years ago, *Contributions to a Spiritual Study of the Stars* clearly bears no sell-by date; its emphases address a pressing need of our time,[18] as August Pauli (*Die Christengemeinschaft*. 15. Jg. 12, März 1939), a fellow founder-priest of The Christian Community, wrote all those years ago:

> He spoke once for a whole week on his star-theme to an audience packed into the rooms of a private flat. His enthusiasm took his audience so strongly with him that they hardly felt the almost unbearable rising heat of the summer. The time will come when Beckh's 'Christened'

star-knowledge, which signifies a basic overturning of today's decadent astrology, will be appreciated for its significance.

Readers of Hermann Beckh are offered not one, but at least *three* approaches to the subject matter of the creative Archetypes: music, the gospels, and a 'Christened' star-wisdom itself. To speak accurately, all three 'esoteric' approaches interrelate. The subjects illuminate each other because all three draw on the same universal source, sometimes called 'logos philosophy' (not the same as what has been termed the 'perennial philosophy'). The reader can now answer such questions as, 'Whence did Beckh "intuit" his tone-zodiac?' This likewise confirms the 'cosmic rhythm' he traces in the gospel. The Professor's works on music are the 'travelling companions' for students of the gospel, and vice versa. Moreover, all three subjects interrelate because Professor Beckh was a remarkably integrated personality; the three approaches follow the writer's own progress (as mentioned at the beginning) to the creative origin of thinking. The possibility of a logos philosophy, or poet's philosophy, was already foreseen and sketched aphoristically by Novalis (1772–1801), with whom Beckh felt at home, and in the British Isles by the poet and seminal thinker S.T. Coleridge (1772–1834). For these seminal thinkers, as for Beckh, meditative work is seen as a veritable counter-pole to the increasing challenges. The laity—Coleridge's 'clerisy', the educated laity, of which J.H. Newman[19] expected so much—can offer inner support to those called to witness as ordained members of the Church.

Rudolf Steiner clinched the matter in his artistically faultless philosophical writings, where he naturally mentions musical composition:

> In composing, the rules of the theory become the servants of life itself, of reality. In exactly the same sense, philosophy is an *art*. All real philosophers have been *artists in the realm of concepts*. For them, human ideas were their artists' materials and scientific method their artistic technique [*The Philosophy of Freedom* [GA 4]. Preface to the first edition, 1894, rev. 1918, emphases original].

The number seven not only dictates the number of chapters (twice seven, plus a concluding chapter) of *The Philosophy of Freedom*, but also what I have called the 'seven-sentence chiastic rhythm' in (*sic*) *every* piece of written prose by Rudolf Steiner.[20] (Rudolf Frieling already pointed to one chiastic example in the Epistles (see below). In my own work on the Epistles (Anastasi 2013)—written 16 years before reading Frieling—I show how chiasm is the structural principle of them all.

With the 'seven-sentence rhythm' the evolutionary planetary rhythm is manifested, which we also live every week, not to mention the seven-year biographical periods. There is a rhythm of 12 at work simultaneously; there are likely to be additional rhythms at work. On the basis of firm principles, Steiner, for example, not only made use of these rhythms in all his *written* prose—even including his longer footnotes—but he left many details for further spiritual research, including (as mentioned above) the founding of a new star-wisdom itself.[21] In making use of these rhythms, I submit, Rudolf Steiner is following his own advice of practising Michaelic research right into 'administration', that is, the down-to-earth professional method—in his case (as his passport states) of a 'writer'.

In his life's work Beckh took up the call to research the details of what can now be appreciated less within different subjects, more as different approaches to central questions. In these pages, for example, the reader meets the born teacher on the theme (Beckh's 'my theme') which he felt as most important, inspiring his younger colleagues—and at the same time reaching twenty-first century readers also hoping to help herald a brighter future. It is apparent that a new generation, or rather generations, of priests and laity are unfamiliar with the work of the founder-priests who worked in the field before them, not only of Professor Beckh himself. In many respects, then, this matter is of topical concern.

> In the Christ-event lies that which the whole planetary development, to which these astrological *Contributions* are dedicated, signifies. It contains the key to the whole of astrology. Astrology is a concern of Christ [*Contribution* No. 9].

All this suggests that it is high time for readers—of children's literature as well as of the Bard himself, also students of human biography, not to speak of music-lovers (music, Beckh claims, was his starting-point) and those concerned with Service Music itself (to which Beckh also contributed), and several other subjects for which space here permits little or no mention—to judge whether Hermann Beckh is not fully to be recognized as one of the three spiritual leaders fostering the 'Movement for Religious Renewal'. This utterly generous human being was, and still is, *the* outstanding figure who inspired and encouraged seeking souls, 'leading from behind'. The 'case of Schult' is one precious example of how a passing complication was tactfully faced and solved at the time (1931) by a spiritual leader of impeccable integrity. If Beckh and Frieling are becoming unread and unstudied, the laity have to offer their meditative as well as practical help and support in the situation today where issues have become global.

Our grateful thanks to Herr Gaedecke and his helpers at the *Archiv der Christengemeinschaft*, Berlin, as well as all those priests who have given us moral support—all selflessly generous members of the profession—to see in print the *Collected Works of Rev. Prof. Hermann Beckh* in the English language, including his biography by Gundhild Kačer-Bock, *Hermann Beckh: Life and Work*. This project aims to be completed in good time for the centenary of the founding of The Christian Community (2022), and—more to the real point—in anticipation of the *next* hundred years.

All editorial additions are placed in the usual square brackets. Typos have been silently corrected, and only the brief notices of corrigenda were edited away; the publication details of the *Anthroposophical Soul Calendar* are simply updated. References to topical celestial phenomena are retained, e.g. remarks concerning Jupiter in the sky, as these references can still serve as examples. The 'case of Schult', though separate, is not at all irrelevant; here it forms an enlightening Appendix. One further detail: the Professor uses the word *Geheimwissenschaft* 'occult science', or 'esoteric science', which is both a subject and the title of the main textbook by Rudolf Steiner on the subject (GA 13, 1910), especially Chapter 4, subsequently supplemented by him in major lecture-courses. In practical terms, both meanings are probably contained, the subject and the book. *Geheimwissenschaft im Umriss* (spiritual science, as complementing natural science) appears in English translation under three slightly different titles: *Occult Science: an Outline*, tr. George Adams; *An Outline of Occult Science*, tr. Herbert G. Monges (most accurate in following the German original); and *Esoteric Science: an Outline*, tr. Catherine E. Creeger, which uses a more contemporary English. For the sake of simplicity, the choice fell to render the word in question mostly as: *Occult Science*.

My grateful thanks to my wife Maren Stott, MA.Eu., for much help in translating, also to Neil Franklin, Ph.D., for continuous editorial help, and very much more besides. From South Devon a steady, warm west wind of practical encouragement filled the sails of our little barque throughout the entire project of translating and publishing the *Collected Works*. Following the *Festschrift: Essays in Honour of Hermann Beckh* (2016), an organ for further research is there; a *Yearbook* is planned. Words become inadequate in trying to thank Tim Clement and Anastasi for the sterling support of an idealistic project. Tim's premature death in 2018 created a major change. The team are most fortunate in finding a sympathetic publisher in Sevak Gulbekian and his team.

To conclude this Introduction, we might briefly indulge in an English whimsy: If the reader should get up around 3 a.m. at Michaelmas (shortly before dawn, in the garden) with a clear sky he/she would see a panoply of stars, and perhaps recognize a good number of them—48 would be good, the founder members of The Christian Community. There's the Pole Star, Polaris (F. Rittelmeyer) providing solid orientation, the sparkling Rigel (Bock) still a young star, the musical Vega in the Lyre (Doldinger), the dubious variable star Algol (J.W. Klein) … and then Sirius rises (Beckh).

What remains to be said at the end of the whole translation-project has to take the first-person form: I was brought up to share. By initiating this project as a member of The Christian Community, I hope to return a little of the enormous help received, especially the privilege of a working life writing music and playing for its Services. If, as C.S. Lewis claims,[22] the planets are 'symbols of permanent value', how much more does the world of the stars itself present an ultimate subject of study? And consequently, what a loss if Beckh's and Frieling's work were to fall into oblivion through simple neglect! It is true, Frieling himself was embarrassed by the aphoristic state of his text, and in his day did not favour publication. Today, with all due respect for this writer's modest stance, we would nevertheless reverse the decision. The works of Frieling and Beckh belong together and are much needed! What, I wonder, would be the consequence if the Lost Word—discussed by Beckh in his gospel studies—were to be lost *again*? Humanity's principal help is fully engaged, original spiritual research, as Rudolf Steiner repeatedly emphasized, and again called for in his Last Address, the words which Prof. Beckh heard as a personal message. For this publication all remaining imperfections are mine. Above all I hope to have put nothing in the way of all three masters—Dr Steiner, Prof. Dr Beckh and Dr Frieling—who did their utmost to convey their own vision of the Master Himself, our Helper and Guide, 'the root and the offspring of David, the bright Morning Star' (Rev. 22:16), an image with which the New Testament concludes.

Alan Stott, Michaelmas 2019
alanstotty@gmail.com

# THE LANGUAGE OF THE STARS: ZODIAC AND PLANETS IN RELATION TO THE HUMAN BEING

by Rev. Prof. Dr Hermann Beckh

# I
# Introduction

Dear Friends,

## *Preliminary Remarks*

Since with many friends in the circle of priests an interest in many spiritual questions concerning the stars (astrology, etc.) has arisen, expressed in numerous conversations and questions directed to the author of these *Contributions*, the intention exists to deal with the mentioned realm in a manner serving the tasks and interests of the circle of priests with a loose sequence of short presentations to appear as an independent supplement to the *Newsletter*. These *Contributions* are *not* intended as a direct, didactic use of sharing with the members of the Communities and through Community meetings. It would not be fruitful there. Indirectly the content can be useful in Community work—especially in pastoral care. In this connection a reliable sense of tact of the individual priests is something on which to rely. Should any member of the circle of priests have no interest in these communications of star-knowledge, or later lose interest, such a member is requested to make his disinterest (or lapsed interest) known now, or later, to Herr von Wistinghausen, Stuttgart, in order that the *Contributions* are not copied beyond necessity, and no unnecessary costs arise.

I would like especially to emphasize that I am concerned with the *spiritual* wisdom of the stars (astrology, but not only birth-horoscopes, yet especially what has to do with gospel research, with a spiritual understanding of the Bible), not astronomy. The actual basic concepts of astronomy—the Copernican system, the planets (those inner planets nearer the Sun and those outer planets distant from the Sun—the seven planets and those beyond Saturn), the Moon, the fixed stars, the Platonic cosmic year (the movement of the first day of spring), the planetary sidereal [annual] courses—one would like to take [all this] for granted as known for the *Contributions* intended here.

Of course, anyone who is seriously interested in this realm has ample opportunity to inform himself. Others can explain it better than I can. In this regard I may point to Frl. Vreede's astronomical *Newsletter*.[23]

It does not always supply the final answer with regard to the 'spiritual' questions of the stars and the eminently desirable discussion of everything astrological with anthroposophy. In these *Contributions*, however, we proceed from Dr Steiner's insights in the various books and lecture-cycles, in the first place the lecture-cycle *Human and Cosmic Thought* [GA 151, 4 lectures, Berlin 20-23 Jan. 1914]. We shall attempt to bring those questions nearer to an answer that can arise for those priests carrying the anthroposophical 'I'-impulse in themselves within a contemporary religious movement out of their professional work, as well as out of their whole world-view and view on life of the human being in relation to the cosmos (the starry cosmos).

## *Introduction*

In contrast to many attempts striving today to remove everything astrological from anthroposophy, I seek to show how everything anthroposophical rightly understood leads precisely into *astrology in the higher sense*. Of course, many things that today appear as 'astrology' have little to do with it. '*Anthroposophy is a path of knowledge that would lead the spiritual in the human being to the spirit in the universe.*'[24] But this universe is the *cosmos of stars*. And so in my Foreword to my recently published book on *John's Gospel*,[25] I could write [p. 15] the sentences: 'Given in the form of people's thinking of today, anthroposophy would lead up to cosmic thinking, a *thinking relating to the stars*. A stellar impulse lives in it as the most inner seed for the future. To search in John's Gospel itself for this impulse was the concern of the present work.'

It is very important to see that anthroposophy is a *path* and not a *goal*. It shows in the form of thinking of today the path leading out of this thinking into the spiritual element and into the cosmic realm. One may pay attention how the word 'mysticism' is used in Rudolf Seiner's *Mystery Dramas*, in no way meaning a mere mysticism of feeling, of the 'mysticism of the Middle Ages' or of today's 'nebulous mysticism' in the style of many modern figures (Maeterlinck, Keyserlingk, and others). Rather in the sense of a highest esoteric spiritual life, in which knowledge connects with religion and art. To mysticism understood in such a way anthroposophy as we know it today is only the *path*. To come closer on this path of anthroposophy during the course of incarnations to such an experience of the cosmos, of the starry worlds, is a matter for the individual. In the future there lies before us an age when mysticism in this sense will be a concern of humanity. Such a mysticism understood in such a way still to be worked on today on the path of anthroposophy, which also encompasses astrology in a future form that today can only be imagined, will then in a coming age be the sublime religion and form of Christianity. For this we do not need to think of the sixth post-Atlantean epoch that still lies thousands of years ahead of us, but of an age the astronomical beginning of which lies only 100–250 years before us. The change of the cultural periods rests on the great ('Platonic') cosmic year of the precession, or more accurately 'regression', of the spring equinox during the course of the millennia. (The spring equinox on average lasts for 2,160 years in one zodiac-sign.) The new cultural period in the sense of the anthropo-sophical reckoning of history only begins when the Sun in the pre-cession of sign and constellation has already reached the middle of a constellation, or rather has already passed to a significant extent. Thus the year AD 1413 is given as the beginning of our present 'fifth post-Atlantean cultural epoch'.

Around Golgotha, at the beginning of the Christian era, the spring equinox, the position of the Sun at that moment moved over from the Ram to the Fishes. It is easy to calculate that in 1413 already the middle of the constellation of the Fishes was not only reached, but substan-tially passed. Today we are no longer so distant from the age when we shall find the spring equinox already in the first stage of the con-stellation, the Waterman. On the other hand a glance at the *astronom-ical* beginning of the present age of the Fishes—precisely the Christ-event—shows that in no way does it concern a mere astronomical fact, but in the most eminent sense also the beginning of a new spiritual era. This is indeed another viewpoint than that of the cultural epochs. In this sense, we again approach today a cosmic 'zero hour', as in the year nought [more correctly AD 1—*Tr. note.*], when with the Christ-era a new age began. Not only in the year 2,160, but quite a long time ear-lier, around 2000 if not before, the spring equinox of the Sun will lie in the Saturn-Uranus sign ♒, whereas today [1930] it still lies in the Jupi-ter sign (more correctly *zodiac*) of Pisces (with regard to the unequal size of the zodiacal signs ♒ is a large constellation, larger than ♓—all these expressions will soon be explained below). The wedding of Cana (John 2), already regarded in Rudolf Steiner's lecture-cycles from the viewpoint of future prophecy, points from its constellation ♒—♌ (♒ the sign of the etheric 'baptism by water', ♌ of the 'baptism of fire and the spirit', the baptism of the 'I') towards this future age (≈). (Further details in my book [*John's Gospel: The Cosmic Rhythm*].) Already then, that is, in a relatively near future, we have to reckon with the dawn of a new spiritual age. This already today casts its shadows ahead—in the same way as the event of Golgotha could be felt centuries before in the historical events and the thinking and religious hope of humanity. This Waterman-age (or Saturn-Uranus-age) no longer lies in such a far future. And because Uranus which is at home in ≈ is the significator[26] for astrology, *astrology in the sense of a Christened star-wisdom will have a future religious significance that today is only divined by a few.* The stage of Christianity of today still carries the signature of the age of the Fishes. Astrology will have become the new stage of the Christ-impulse, corresponding to the age of Aquarius (Waterman); it will have become the sublime religion of the future. The anthroposophical impulse to knowledge, to lead the spiritual in the human being towards the spirit in the cosmos (see the beginning of Rudolf Steiner's *Leading Thoughts* [GA 26]) is then brought one step nearer to realization. Astrology, wisdom of the stars, will again become a priestly concern, as it was millennia ago in early Egypt during the age of the Taurus, the Bull (spring equinox of the Sun in the Bull, governed by Isis-Venus). I add here a passage from Friedrich Creuzer's *Symbolik und Mythologie der alten Völker* (Bk. II, p. 122):

But as above in Sirius that primal genius, Anubis-Thoth-Hermes, seems to govern the whole planetary system, holding it in a ribbon of light, and to carry the universe from the pointed apex of the pyramid to its broad base; so stands the priest representing Hermes at the festive altar holding the magic lantern of Hermes. This is the picture of the world, of the drama the gods present, or of all the appearances of the gods and of all life. Above is the lamp with the sacred oil, like the lights in the heavens with the heavenly moisture: the source of all life and the seed, in the middle is the mirror, are the fruits and the plants and below is the chalice with the sacred water of the Nile. With the lantern the priest ignites the smoke [incense] offering, with the chalice he pours out the drink offering, and whoever looks into the mirror sees the universe; the priest prophesies out of the bright disc …

[Op. cit. p. 116:] But he (Hermes, the primordial priest) is as the agrarian intelligence, the eternal bread. He is the oil of joy (as the discoverer of the oil-tree). He is the quickening drink out of the chalice of grace. Whoever takes him up into himself is consecrated; whoever drinks from his cup is refreshed, his longing is stilled; on whoever his lantern shines is in the light; whoever looks into his mirror sees through all nature and creatures. Such a one is the priest, he is Hermes. He reads in the stars, he writes the script of heaven, the hieroglyph, he interprets it into common writing for the people; he advises the people, he helps them in body and spirit. He stands at the side of the king. He is physician, teacher of the law, judge, the one who makes the offering, the one who prays, soothsayer; he is the undertaker of those who have died, and builds the houses for the dead and the temples for the gods. In a word, the priest is through and through Hermes, λόγος.

Already with the early Egyptians astrology had, as it were, a musical side: it was a life in the eternal harmony of the stars, a deep listening to the harmony of the universe. And religious astrology of the future will be concerned again with such life in the harmony of the stars, not on the arbitrary reduction of astrology for egoistical everyday purposes. Moreover, the fatal, fatalistic pull that astrology as pursued today has for many people will then be a thing of the past. In living oneself into the eternal harmonies of the stars, the human being carrying the priestly [role] will come precisely to a new higher stage of the Christened experience of freedom, in the eternal harmonies of the stars he will experience his freedom. In the little book *The Spiritual Guidance of Man and Mankind* [GA 15], Dr Steiner has explained how Christ—that is, Jesus of Nazareth from the moment when in the Jordan-baptism the Christ-being was united with His bodily vehicle—always lived fully in the harmony of the stars. He took every step in full accord with this harmony of the stars and the respective whole constellation of stars. He realized *'in every moment the horoscope'*, that is, the influence of the stars—for normal people only present in the moment of birth—is, as it were, fixed in the human birth-horoscope. The constellation of stars was at work in every moment of the life of Christ, fashioning afresh and creatively; the 'I' was here free in every moment in the midst of cosmic eternity, of the cosmic circle of stars, ⊙ the Son in the Father ('the Father in me and I in him'). Precisely in what Christ lived through, in the conscious placing-oneself into the universal harmony of the stars of the cosmos, not in a subjective arbitrariness, lies the Christened experience of freedom and the ideal of freedom. The human being can only step by step approach the path shown at the beginning, for the way how in Christ, in Christ-Jesus, the Father lived in the Son. This eternal harmony of the stars living in the 'I' was unique in the history of the world. As a concern of humanity all this is a matter of *Spirit-man* that still lies in the future. The human being of today striving towards the spirit stands between:

[i]    the *karma* that he brings from the past and which is exactly expressed in the constellation of stars of his birth-horoscope and

[ii]   that Christ-ideal of freedom of the future, the creative realization of the entire harmony of the stars in every moment, in which the 'horoscope' as such (as something that has become rigidified at the moment of birth) is overcome.

The Resurrected One who appears at the beginning of the Apocalypse [Rev. 1] to the seer of Patmos holds the seven planets, the stars of destiny, in His right hand. Only by holding the scales between both aspects can one find today the correct attitude towards the fact of the birth-horoscope. Each non-Christened, fatalistic stance towards the horoscope is in the same way misleading as is the dilettante, illusionistic wish to brush aside the fact of the birth-horoscope. This is also confirmed in various places by Dr Steiner, to the details of which I shall return.

At the Freiburg Conference, the question was raised: can one as a member of The Christian Community get one's horoscope read? I would say—because I did not myself have to answer this question— as a human being striving towards the spirit one can actually not do such a thing simply without more ado. To allow one's horoscope to be mapped by somebody or other, which one then regards as an astrological diagnosis that in its justification is not understandable, opaque and uncontrollable, is not to be recommended for a human being striving towards the spirit and the Christian [ideal]. One can only do it without harm when one has the possibility to assess and fundamentally understand the details. Anthroposophy gives us the possibility for this. One can say, in the life between death and a new birth, in the transit through the spiritual, planetary spheres, I have worked out the karma of my earlier life in such a way that the planetary situation of the hour of my birth can express the karma I have now woven for myself. If through [pursuing] serious self-knowledge one has beforehand a picture of one's spiritual being, furthermore, if one has a clear imagination of the spiritual meaning of the planets and the signs of the zodiac—through anthroposophy this can be achieved—then without harm, although possibly not without some deep shocks, one will look at the horoscope of one's birth-karma.

For a basic orientation towards the horoscope (details to follow) initially the following is to be said:

The horoscope in Rudolf Steiner's view (see the recent *Anthropos. Mitteilungen*—the 'anthroposophical news-sheet') is the harmony produced by [the Archangel] Michael between karma and the star-script (in this case, that is the starry constellation of the moment of birth). An ideal of clairvoyance—still unattainable today—would be to *view* the birth-horoscope of somebody else without further calculation—and to see in oneself one's own. What is important for us is not the H.K. [horoscope-karma] of the other person but one's own. These things simply lie in the line of karmic self-knowledge. In my new book [*John's Gospel: The Cosmic Rhythm*. p. 156] I wrote:

> All sorts of reasons exist for avoiding such an experience—it is a matter of wanting or not wanting to do it; on the other hand, on this path there is no serious possibility of denying experienced facts. When the will for self-knowledge is present, if the calculation is properly conducted, the result will be correctly understood.

The correct attitude to these things does not lead to fatalism, but to a more correct self-knowledge and a more correct moral activity, consequently also to freedom. The horoscope shows me my karmically acquired *difficulties* (what are called the less useful aspects) that I may overcome them out of the 'I'—and likewise my *possibilities* (what are called the useful aspects), so that through my own efforts I activate them and work with them. The 'I' itself, that originated this whole web of destiny, does *not* appear in the horoscope. Thus it can be that one and the same aspect is found in the horoscope of a criminal and that of a saint. The saint overcomes out of the 'I' and transforms some kind of difficult tension (a horoscopic 'cross'), which still lays low the criminal because his 'I' is too weak to transform. It is said, the criminal may be gifted with conceivably the finest sensitive instrument for cosmic tensions, giving way in nervous sensitivity to any momentary (astral) stream conditioned through the stars, living it out completely without checks from the side of the 'I'. For those who are dedicated to pastoral work of consultation with criminals, a knowledge of these things is of the greatest significance.

A great viewpoint that arises from Rudolf Steiner's lecture-cycle *Human and Cosmic Thought* [Berlin, 1914. GA 151] is this: The human being himself and the individual human life is a thought of the cosmos. The human being is thought by the hierarchies of the cosmos. Planets and signs of the zodiac are as it were the alphabet, the linguistic expression, in which the hierarchies of the cosmos think.

Thereby is also indirectly said what the horoscope is: a rune of the cosmic script that expresses how a human being and a human life is thought by the hierarchies. But, Dr Steiner adds, we are *not only the hierarchies*, but also an 'I'. The human being is not only thought by the hierarchies, but he also thinks the hierarchies. In this lies his being an anthroposophist, his struggle for freedom for the 'I'. The point that does *not* stand in the horoscope, even if it were so small as the tip of a needle, is here precisely the decisive point, the 'I'-point and freedom-point governing the human future, whereas the horoscope-karma expressing his past is his karma. (More on this in my new book, p. 35ff. [*John's Gospel: The Cosmic Rhythm*]: I will cite this passage from time to time. We shall yet come to elaborate on the whole question of the birth-horoscope.)

Concerning what I understand here generally as 'Christened astrology of the future' leading to freedom and the 'I' is discussed at length in Dr Steiner's lecture-cycle *Christ and the Spiritual World* in connection with the Holy Grail as the bringer of the new star-wisdom. This cycle was actually meant for one leading person in the astrological field, who at that time was present and was personally known to Dr Steiner. Yet the later work of this person (still outside the Anthroposophical Society), who calls himself with the pseudonym '[C. Aq.] Libra',[27] did not meet his expectations. And so up to now there has not yet resulted what Dr Steiner intended with the work in the astrological realm and for which he wished. Then came the [Great] War dashing many hopes, initially giving the Anthroposophical Society a different direction. Certainly, the hopes expressed by Dr Steiner in the Berlin lecture-cycle have not yet been fulfilled. For us, this can be another reason to work with all our forces precisely in this realm.

I mentioned before Uranus, standing beyond the 'seven planets' and hitherto rather disregarded from the anthroposophical side. I have some basically important things to say about it in the next *Contribution*, as an important inspirer in the whole realm of star-knowledge. For today I will only mention one thing, that is probably not insignificant since many of our friends come from the Youth Movement, that in the years when Uranus stood in its sign the Waterman (1912-19), as an example, the Youth Movement, too, had its high point. Please take this initially only as an indication, a thorough justification of which will follow.

# II
# Uranus I

Dear Friends,

First of all a correction to the otherwise clearly typed first part. A small mistake[28] right at the beginning distorts the meaning. Not 'nicht *um*' ['not *concerning*'] the birth-horoscope, but 'nicht *nur*' ['not *only*'] the birth-horoscope. For, of course, I am *very* concerned to illuminate in the right way the eminently important fact of the birth-horoscope, as I have already mentioned in that first *Contribution*. It would simply be a contradiction if I would have said that I do not want to present this. I only wanted to say that what I intended to present is not exhausted in those horoscope matters, in the birth-horoscope. I am above all concerned to emphasize and show in astrology the cosmic, religious aspect, useful for priests as it has to do here with a *stage of anthroposophical work* that may not be without meaning. I could also call it extracting the Uranus viewpoint contained in anthroposophy, as a progression from Saturn to Uranus.

Since we are here concerned first of all with the horoscope, I would like to cite the passage in my book on *John's Gospel: The Cosmic Rhythm* (p. 36f.), already mentioned last time. One cannot say these things clearly enough, especially at the beginning of the work, in order that no fatalistic errors may occur which would produce an undesired effect in the soul. With this remark I link to Dr Steiner's indication in his book, *The Spiritual Guidance of Man and Humanity* [GA 15, Chapter 3], where he mentions how the starry constellation at the moment of birth, the heavenly firmament of the hour of birth is impressed into the aura of the infant's brain, in order to stand for the whole earthly life of this human being as the birth-horoscope. My remarks about this are as follows:

> The destiny of an earthly life is to a large extent determined through this constellation at birth. Rightly understood, this does not contradict 'human freedom'. What is expressed in the horoscope is simply what someone has themselves woven in earlier earthly lives as a specific configuration and constellation of 'astral [= stellar]' tensions, harmonies and

disharmonies. To a high degree this manifests things of a destiny-carrying and destiny-demanding nature. What the 'self' does with this 'self-woven' astral weaving of destiny is a matter of freedom—as far as such a matter has already been achieved.

In the horoscope there stands not the self, but only that tapestry woven by the self before birth, much less what the self will then make out of this tapestry. One could say with the Indian Buddhists, the 'householder' does not stand in the birth-horoscope, but only the house that he built. Or, speaking in the technical, astrological sense, the specific constellation of the house and configuration of the house is shown by the birth-firmament. It is evident to everyone that for everything that the earlier builder of the house and present householder in the house takes on, the state, character and arrangement of the house to a great extent is decided. Likewise, that the 'freedom' of the householder to do just what s/he wants is not affected. Only it is quite obvious that this 'freedom' can manifest only within certain limits determined by the situation. There exist rather clumsily built, restricting houses, that make it difficult to take on any intended profession or activity, whereas a well-situated, cleverly built and well-furnished house, well-orientated to all the directions of heaven, benefits the free unfolding of the householder.[29]

It was my intention in these *Contributions* to write methodically about the zodiac, the individual zodiac-signs, and also the individual planets. With the zodiac, the important question would have been to write about 'sign and constellation', about which in general today little clarity exists. With the planets I would also come to the question, or rather questions, about Uranus: how do Uranus and Neptune relate to the seven planets? For here, too, an important question lies, which is somewhat avoided until now in anthroposophical approaches to this question. It can be especially shown how the question of sign and constellation and the question of Uranus are mutually connected. The one problem touches on the other.

As it happens, I have sometimes touched on the Uranus-question in these *Contributions* as well as elsewhere; it is of principal importance to understand the knowledge of the stars, for Uranus ('the starry heaven') counts as the significant thing for astrology. Moreover, [Rudolf] Frieling has now built on the Uranus viewpoint his beautiful and interesting study on the relationship of the Creed to the zodiac. So, to understand the now topical matters, it is actually necessary to say a few things about this Uranus viewpoint. To understand the Creed from this viewpoint, the whole perspective of the problem before us, it is helpful so to characterize the Creed, or the zodiacal key to the Creed, that the Waterman ≈ (governed by Uranus-Saturn) is placed above at the top, followed by the usual series (H ♈ ♉ etc.) to the left below. This differs from the usual characterization, also in my books on the gospels. The Lion appears below, opposite Waterman. Finally, the sign of the Goat (♑) governed by Saturn—in the Creed: 'They may hope …'—closes the circle, that is, leads again to the Saturn-Uranus sign ≈, in which the serpent of eternity bites its own tail. Beginning and end of the Creed here both embrace in both Saturn-signs (the one forming the zenith is at the same time the sign for Uranus). It is also significant that in the lecture-cycle, *Human and Cosmic Thought* [GA 151], of basic importance for our concerns, Dr Steiner ascribes to the viewpoint of *Saturn* the cosmic conceptual mood of *gnosis*.[30]

For clarity in this ordering of the planets to the zodiac, in view of the later detailed *Contributions*, I will briefly give here the principle. Proceeding from the Sun in the Lion and the Moon in the Crab, both have only *one* house in the zodiac. One finds the 'houses' for the other planets—that is, the signs where the planets unfold their influence most purely, directly and unhindered—by ascribing the planets in the sequence known in astronomy, from the one nearest the Sun to the one most distant from the Sun, to the individual zodiacal signs to left and right. From the starting point Crab–Moon, the series runs:

Mercury–Twins,
Venus–Bull
Mars–Ram
Jupiter–Fishes
Saturn–Waterman.

From the starting point Sun-Lion, there results:

Mercury–Virgin
Venus–Scales,
Mars–Scorpion,
Jupiter–Archer,
Saturn–Goat.

If according to this principle one wants to decide on the 'houses' for Uranus and Neptune, one proceeds from the Sun (not from the Moon) and then finds: Uranus–Waterman, and Neptune–Fishes (which is not just something thought up, but can be confirmed in astrological practice, and also in spiritual science. In Waterman, then, alongside the

influence of Saturn a Uranus-influence exists, whereas the Goat is governed alone by Saturn; in the Fishes alongside the influence of Jupiter is
an influence of Neptune. And we would have, as both houses:

    Mercury: Twins and Virgin,
    Venus: Bull and Scales,
    Mars: Ram and Scorpion,
    Jupiter: Fishes and Archer,
    Saturn: Goat and Waterman.

In astrology one of both houses always appears as the 'day house', the
other as the 'night house'. (The Sun has *only* a day-house, the Moon only
a night-house.) What it does, I will explain later. Here only a brief indication that this differentiation does *not* have to do with the division of the
zodiac into a diurnal (♈ ♉ to ♎) and a nocturnal side (the five dark signs
♓ ♒ ♑ ♐ ♍). This corresponds to the 'five loaves' of the 'nocturnal'
Feeding [of the 5000], the 'seven loaves' of Mark 8 belong to the other, the
'daytime Feeding' [of the 4000]. Rather it has to do with the difference of
the kinds of ether (the higher kinds of ether are feminine, the night; the
lower kinds of ether—e.g. light-ether—masculine, the day), which are
also important for the division of the zodiac into four triangles.

***

In 1781, shortly before the French Revolution, the planet Uranus
(the first planet beyond the [orbit of] Saturn) was discovered by the
astronomer Herschel. In 1846 (that is, shortly before the '48 Revolution) Leverrier discovered the second planet beyond Saturn. I hope
that readers are clear about the purely astronomical significance of
these discoveries, which extend the astronomical picture.

For those who are still virginally untouched by astronomy, in short,
the following. Imagine the Sun, the fixed star that shines by itself and
by far exceeds all the planets, in the centre of the planetary system.
(For a good reason I use the Copernican view, although I know how in
the *spiritual* perspective all viewpoints change. One can then no longer
speak of 'distance' and 'size' of the stars in such a way as astronomy
does today from its material viewpoint. And yet it is for certain reasons quite important initially to proceed from this 'earthly thinking',
in order later to reach the 'cosmic' thinking in a sure and solid manner. Even if all imaginations of size, distance, matter, etc. of the stars
changes and ultimately only the spiritual element of the stars remains,
as 'picture' they still retain their meaning.) And so, the astronomical
picture has the Sun in the centre. Between the Sun and the Earth's orbit,

firstly both planets near the Sun, or 'inner planets', circling the Sun, come Mercury and Venus. Mercury, nearest to the Sun, is smaller than the Earth; Venus is roughly the same [size] as the Earth. Then, beyond the Earth's orbit comes Mars as the first in a certain sense already an 'outer planet', more 'distant from the Sun', yet still near to the Earth, in many respects the planet most similar to the Earth. (Later, something to the situation with regard to the 'material' of the planet.) Then there follows the 'asteroid belt' (many quite small planetoids, only visible with a telescope), which according to Dr Steiner is the debris of an extinguished greater planet, the battle field of the 'war in heaven', which in the cosmogonic primordial time was to be found in the sphere between Mars and Jupiter (appearing in ancient sagas and myths of various peoples). Then, only beyond this belt, comes in a very significant distance from the Earth the far planet Jupiter, alongside Venus as the brightest [wandering] star in the starry heavens, in appearance (crudely speaking) as great as Venus (yet this varies very much in its closeness to, or far distance from, the Earth), in reality (i.e. in Copernican reality) a hundred times greater than the Earth and Venus. Here it is similar as with the Sun and the Moon. The Moon is much smaller than the Earth, the Sun a thousand times greater, and yet it shows the harmony of the cosmos (not arbitrarily but resulting out of the consciousness of spiritual beings). In looking at the heavens, the solar disc and the lunar disc for the inhabitant of the Earth appear the same size (i.e. the possible difference as a result of the variations of position is minimal; one recalls the phenomenon of the 'ring form' possible in a solar [annular] eclipse, when the lunar disc does *not quite* cover the solar disc).

On the other side of Jupiter's orbit is Saturn, another outer planet far distant from the Sun, for Copernican thought not quite as big as Jupiter. Seen in the starry heaven, because of its greater distance, however, much more indistinct, it appears as a dusky star of second magnitude, the last and furthest distant of the planets known to antiquity. Then follows Uranus, only discovered in 1781, much more distant from the Sun, twice as distant as Saturn, as a star of sixth magnitude hardly visible to the naked eye. And over three times as distant than Saturn, Neptune was discovered in 1846, only visible with a telescope. (Interestingly, it was discovered by mathematical computation from certain irregularities in the orbits of the other planets.) Uranus and Neptune, about the same size as each other, are both (viewed in the Copernican manner) very great planets, much bigger than all the planets near the Earth, yet smaller than Jupiter and Saturn.

In this way, purely astronomically and still apart from all astrology, we would arrive at three categories of planets:

(i)    the inner planets Mercury and Venus,

(ii)   the outer planets, or those more distant from the Sun, Mars, Jupiter and Saturn (whereby Mars is closer to the Earth, Jupiter and Saturn further distant from the Earth),

(iii)  planets most distant from the Sun *beyond Saturn*, Uranus and Neptune.

One can differentiate: Mercury, Venus and Mars as close to the Earth; Jupiter and Saturn and the other two are those more distant from the Earth. (Forgive this diversion as an insertion for those somewhat ignorant of astronomy. Human experience has confirmed, unfortunately repeatedly confirmed, how necessary such 'inserts' are.)

I intended to write about *Uranus* and will now proceed to do so. Uranus and Neptune, as arises from what has been said, are invisible to the naked eye, hidden from the outer (unassisted) view, and consequently in this purely outer sense are *occult planets* (as they also are in the spiritual sense for astrology). They were unknown *as individual star-individualities*, that is throughout antiquity up to modern times. Antiquity always reckoned with the *seven planets*, whereby in astrology the pre-Copernican (Ptolemaic) astronomy was understood, apart from the five planets known then, Mercury, Venus, Mars, Jupiter, Saturn, also the Sun and the Moon. The Earth itself for this geocentric viewpoint was not included. (For the Copernican heliocentric view, the Earth itself is a planet, a satellite of the Sun; the Moon is not a 'planet' (= satellite of the Sun), but a satellite of the Earth.

Dr Steiner always emphasized that Uranus and Neptune originally did not belong to our solar system, *they joined it only later* [GA136, lecture 6]. (One would have to imagine that it concerns a cosmic event lying in the far primordial past, when the cosmos was still super-physical, in an etheric-astral condition.) Even this is admitted in a certain way by outer astronomy, for here it is shown that the moons of Uranus and Neptune revolve in the opposite direction to that of the moons of the other planets.[31] This already shows that Uranus and Neptune originally belonged to another system. In this case, as otherwise, too, the outer facts have to be correctly taken into account, not contradicting spiritual knowledge, but actually confirming it. Consequently, for all striving for knowledge it is important not to neglect the *facts* of what is called 'outer science'—different from offering (often wrong) *theories*.

The words of the spiritual researcher are then rightly understood when one is sure that through the existence of Uranus and Neptune, the concept 'seven planets' (including the Sun and the Moon) is not made redundant. Rather, *Uranus and Neptune*, originally belonging to another system, *stand beyond the seven planets*. However, it would not be true and *not* correspond to what Dr Steiner always meant, undoubtedly, when as sometimes appears—also sometimes found in Dr Kaiser's[32] work—that Uranus and Neptune do not exist, or are without spiritual meaning, because the writer thinks that Dr Steiner would have said that these planets do not signify anything important. Here it should be clear that the stars in general are spiritual beings with influences. It is no different with Uranus and Neptune; either they are, or they aren't. As Lic. Emil Bock once explained with complete justice in a [similar] critical situation, 'I am indeed simply here', so too these two cosmic wanderers far distant from the Sun can also say with complete justice: 'We too are also simply here.'

What Dr Steiner intended was this, that when with Saturn the concept of seven planets was established (geocentrically conceived, not the Copernican, heliocentric viewpoint), one does not simply proceed purely outwardly and just add more planets. One should recognize *with Saturn a quite specific, spiritually significant boundary is reached*. What outwardly lies beyond this boundary is something completely different from what lies within it. What is the reason for this boundary?

If we look in *Occult Science*, we find how all the planets (including the Sun and Moon) from the Earth, or rather from Mercury-Venus, are mutually connected as far as Saturn. They belong together, are siblings of *one* family, that is, siblings of the Earth, parts of the Earth; all together they form the *Earth* in its cosmogenic primordial form. 'Ancient Saturn' (which contains the later Sun and all later planets) is simply the Earth in its earliest incarnation ([Ancient] Saturn, [Ancient] Sun, [Ancient] Moon and the Earth follow, as is known, the sequence of the four stages of incarnation of planet Earth—of course, over immeasurable periods of time). That which ends with *Saturn*, having its first, true boundary is consequently the Earth (in its great, cosmic primordial sense). Saturn (the orbit of Saturn) is the border of the great cosmic-planetary system, which the *Earth* once was—and in a certain sense *still is* today, as is shown especially with the destiny-reality of birth-astrology. Consequently, especially from Saturn, at least on the one side, earthly influences proceed of earthly weight/ gravity, the *forces of lead*. Saturn is the great cosmic guardian of the border, the *guardian of the threshold*. On its *one* side there lies everything that is Earth, that belongs to the Earth, that contains earthly forces in itself. On its other side there lies—*the heaven [of fixed stars]* (Gk. *Uranos*).

If we take into account various other things, we now know initially who Uranus is. It was mentioned above that Uranus and Neptune, as certain spiritual star-individualities not yet known in antiquity, were only discovered in 1781 and 1846. We have to emphasize the words *'as certain spiritual star-individualities'*, for—and what follows is very important—as spiritual spheres they, or Uranus-Uranos, the one who interests us now in the first instance, were well known. In the Egyptian Mysteries (which we find with Creuzer, ibid., Vol. II, 49) *eight Cabiri spheres* were distinguished. These were the known seven planetary spheres up to Saturn, *including the starry heaven* (Gk. *Uranos*) as the eighth one. This was taken over to the Greek Mysteries. We are indebted to the Greeks for the great Uranos-myth, so important as a spiritual key for many things, to which I shall soon return.

What then is Uranos? The upper starry heaven, the *world beyond Saturn* as the actual *heaven*, whereas Saturn in the cosmos is the border of the earthly element, that is in this sense, is still *Earth*. *Uranos*-Uranus and *Saturn* behave like Heaven and Earth. (In the light of this fact, one may look once again at the first sentence of the Creed, in Frieling's explanation.) From this it becomes clear how the name Uranus makes deep sense for the planet newly discovered by Herschel in 1781. For what do we recognize now as this 'planet Uranus'? Of course, it is not *the starry heaven* [itself], the *Uranos* from which it received its name? But like a first boundary stone, marking a border of this *Uranos*, of the heavens in the higher sense, this planet stands as Uranus in the cosmos, facing Saturn standing as representative of the earthy element, of the Earth in the cosmos. Saturn astrologically signifies the *earthly element*; Uranus signifies the starry element lying beyond it. Consequently, as I have already indicated, it becomes a significator for astrology.

With this we stand in particular at the beginning of an account of the very interesting and important question of Uranus. But because this *Contribution* has already grown to such an extent and your digestive capacity is not unlimited, I will save further explanations of the question of Uranus for the next *Newsletter*.

# III
# Uranus II

What we always call the *seven planets* here plays a role in early as well as modern times as *different models*. Antiquity lists the seven planets: Sun, Moon (the 'two great lights' [Gen. 1:16]), Mercury, Venus, Mars, Jupiter and Saturn. More recent astronomy lists Mercury, Venus, Mars, Jupiter, Saturn, Uranus and Neptune. The geocentric viewpoint of early astronomy (Ptolemaic system) also allows the Sun and Moon to appear as planets, whereas the Earth, taken as the centre, is not included. For the heliocentric viewpoint of modern astronomy (Copernican system) neither includes the Sun, taken as standing in the centre, nor the Moon, only regarded as a satellite of the Earth. The Earth, earlier thought of as the centre, itself becomes a 'planet'. With the planets Uranus and Neptune discovered later, and including the Earth, we arrive at eight, which with Pluto, newly discovered in the spring [1930] (if its planetary status[33] survives), we arrive at nine planets. But here it has to be considered that for a *spiritual* consideration of the influence of the stars, that is for everything astrological, the heliocentric standpoint of the more recent astronomy[34] can never be considered.

The question always arises: 'How does any aspect of a planet concern the Earth?' For this questioning, the Earth as the place of the 'I' always stands in the centre. Everything is then 'planet' which, different from the immobile fixed stars, the 'stars at rest'—at least, from the viewpoint of one short earthly life—draws its path on the ecliptic as a 'wandering star', even if it only involves a view as seen from the Earth. In this way, the Sun and Moon, the 'two great lights', also become planets. This is valid for modern as well as early astrology. And the Earth itself, as the spiritual centre and place of the 'I', is excluded from the list of planets. For all astrology, for all talk about the spiritual influence of the stars, only the geocentric standpoint exists. In this—quite apart from the fact that ultimately *all* standpoints, not excluding the Copernican view, are always only *relative*—there lies no non-knowledge, or non-scientific attitude. For a spiritual, astrological observation this geocentric standpoint is the natural and given one; for an astronomical-mathematical observation the heliocentric standpoint of Copernicus is the most natural, simple and most obvious.

*Astrologically*, we retain the early view of seven planets: Sun, Moon, Mercury, Venus, Mars, Jupiter and Saturn, whereby Sun and Moon as the 'two great lights' are after all something special. In modern astronomy,[35] if we disregard this special nature of these lights, the seven planets: Mercury, Venus, Mars, Jupiter, Saturn, Uranus and Neptune become nine with the addition of both great lights. Later I will have to present how in fact a spiritual relationship of Uranus to the Sun and of Neptune to the Moon appears to exist for a spiritual observation (astrology).

Now it can, indeed has to be felt as a problem, why and on what grounds does spiritual science (and anthroposophy in general) still speak of 'seven planets' with Saturn marking the boundary, when meanwhile Uranus and Neptune have been added as more recently discovered planets? Are these two treated (to adapt Christian Morgenstern)[36] simply in the sense of 'non-existent'—in this sense probably not a 'bourgeois', but a cosmic 'convention'? This can obviously not be, as I tried to show in the previous *Contribution*. And yet my *Contributions* would be completely misunderstood, if it is assumed that I wanted somehow to violate the 'seven planets' as taught in spiritual science. This too cannot be. On the contrary, I took the trouble to show what meaning the discussion of the seven planets actually has in spiritual science, even in what sense it rightly exists faced with the revealed reality of Uranus and Neptune. And I pointed to what Rudolf Steiner always emphasized: the movement of the moons of Uranus and Neptune move in the opposite direction[37] from those of the seven planets. It shows they originally belonged to another system. They arrived from without, from distant cosmic spaces, to our solar system, or planetary system.

Precisely the spiritual observation (which on this point fully confirms the 'astrological empiricism' favoured today) shows that with *Saturn* really something like a *cosmic boundary stone* is reached. The whole great system in the primordial beginning was once *Earth* (see *Occult Science*). Here it had its boundary. Astrological practice shows how from Saturn earthly influences of earthly gravity, or weight, proceed. The heavy lead is the Saturn-metal. If something similar is sought for Uranus, one would arrive at 'radium',[38] the radiating element of emanation of modern natural science. The discovery of this higher element indeed relates to the arrival of the influence of Uranus into the life of the Earth. (On this there is much of interest between the lines of the last lecture [1 April 1913] of the Berlin cycle: *The Life between Death and a new Birth in Relation to the Cosmic Facts*. GA 141.) Some time ago I read an interesting newspaper article discussing the clearly interesting discovery of the transformation of radium into lead. If proved correct, this would correspond to the cosmic transition from the sphere of Uranus to that of Saturn.

*Saturn* is the cosmic boundary stone of the *earthly [context]*; *Uranus* is the cosmic boundary stone of the *starry [context]*. In a certain cosmic sense, the *earthly realm* reaches right to *Saturn*. With *Uranus* the actual *realm of the stars* begins, this zone of the upper starry heaven from which, as we have just heard, Uranus has only been added later—although still in a cosmic primordial time—like a messenger of these upper realms. On Earth a border stone signifies the boundary between two realms, likewise between *Saturn* and *Uranus* the two realms, the *earthly* and the *starry*, are cosmically distinguished. As Saturn spiritually signifies the earthly context, the Earth, Uranus signifies the starry context, *the starry world in the higher sense*. Consequently, as I have already mentioned, in the horoscope it is the significator for astrology. How far one understands these *Contributions*—or anything astrological generally—does not only depend on the qualities of the reader's general understanding (that would be Mercury in the horoscope), but also of his/her Uranus placement. Only when I discovered from various horoscopes known to me, how many interesting, indeed splendid Uranus-positions we have in our circle, did I gain the courage to write these general *Contributions*—and in particular concerning Uranus.

It is important to understand that we do not at all take *Uranus* everywhere only largely and one-sidedly as *the individual planet*, but as the *significator of the starry world as such*, of the trans-Saturnian, higher starry world. In a certain sense (and with a certain right) one could compare Saturn = Earth, Uranus = the stars, or 'the heaven'. In the previous *Contribution*, I have mentioned that already in the early Mysteries, long before the planet was discovered by Herschel, in this sense the Uranus-sphere, the *Uranos*, was known as the eighth sphere of the higher starry heaven beyond the seven planets, as the trans-Saturnian world, the world beyond Saturn—Dr Steiner always used this expression. The spiritual Moon-sphere comprehends everything between the Earth and the Moon (the Moon's orbit), the spiritual sphere of Venus everything between the Earth and Venus, the spiritual sphere of Jupiter and Saturn everything between Earth and Jupiter-Saturn. So too,

*Uranus* in the spiritual sense is everything lying beyond, the 'upper starry world'. Certainly, we have once again to differentiate this comprehensive Uranus-concept, this concept of *uranos* as the spiritual Uranus-sphere, from the confined concept of Herschel's planet Uranus. The planet Uranus is like a cosmic border stone but presents this *Uranos* for our spiritual eye. However much this Uranus planet actually does spiritually relate to this *uranos* sphere, apart from all astrological empiricism and practice, it is shown once again by pure outer astronomy. Its indications we have increasingly to learn to regard as the picture and parable, or symbol, for spiritual reality. We face certain attempts cropping up in our circles simply to avoid modern astronomy with its calculations and numbers as unspiritual. Dr Steiner himself, as the astronomy lecture-course[39] clearly shows, stood completely above these attempts; indeed, he warned about it as a possible danger. We should much rather learn to perceive what is revealed as a parable, as spiritual connections, in these numerical revelations—without making the mistake to project purely earthly concepts and calculations of distance in kilometres [or miles] into the cosmos. This calculating in kilometres, which for earthly conditions is relatively correct and practically useful, the more it is projected into space leads to something impenetrably incorrect, indeed ultimately nonsensical. Nevertheless, the relative element of the planetary distances from the Sun calculated by astronomy, the relative element of these relating numbers, can also be something spiritually thoroughly significant.

When we look at the *orbital times* of the planets calculated through astronomical observations, of *Uranus* in particular, a highly significant fact exists. This period of revolution, already shown through an approximate evaluation of the values, between themselves [appear] quite irrational, that is, they cannot be brought into a simple mutual mathematical relationship. Dr Steiner did speak about it, how especially the stability of the cosmos and of the planetary system rests on this fact. Thus for the rotation of the Earth (seen geocentrically, the revolution around the Sun) is the well-known $365 \frac{1}{4}$ days; for the rotation of the Moon around the Earth $27 \frac{1}{3}$ days (synodically, that is, taking into consideration the movement of the Earth for the phases of the Moon, resulting in $29 \frac{1}{2}$ days); Mercury 88 days; Venus 235 days; Mars 1 year and 322 days (almost double that of the Earth's rotation), but in such a way that the exact relationship of 1:2 does not exist, for 40 days are still missing for this proportion to arise); Jupiter 11 years and 315 days (that is *almost* 12 years, so that Jupiter *almost* remains one year in each sign of the zodiac, though again not exactly, yet in such a way that approximately 50 days are missing to make this proportion 1:2); Saturn 29 years and 167 days (here 30 years would be the exact measure, 12 x 2½ , but there are c. 200 days missing from this exactitude).

Now comes the special and interesting thing: *the orbital time* of *Uranus is 85 earthly years and 5 days.* That is, the irrational element, which in the cosmos can and may *never be quite absent*, consists here only of 5 earthly days, in relation to the extremely long revolution of this planet of 85 years. Here a remarkable fact exists that, disregarding this minimal remainder, the time of the revolution of Uranus in relation to the Earth (or the Sun) stands exactly 84:1. But 84, already with the Indian Buddhists a sacred number, is 7 x 12; 7, the number of time, multiplied by 12, the number of space (Rudolf Steiner speaks of this in his lecture 'The Children of Lucifer'[40]). The mystery of this number is clearly revealed. Uranus, standing beyond the seven planets, *summarizes in itself this planetary septenary and its relationship to the zodiacal duodecad*, by tarrying exactly (the difference doesn't even amount to half an earthly day) *seven years in each of the twelve signs of the zodiac.* Marking the border of the more confined planetary system, facing the higher starry world, Uranus in itself summarizes on the one side the starry worlds, and on the other side the whole planetary system. *With Uranus we no longer stand with the individual planet, but in the comprehensive [situation] of the cosmos, of the upper starry world, of* Uranos.

And thus Rudolf Steiner, in his lecture-cycle *Human and Cosmic Thought*, Berlin 1914, so important for us, speaks of the twelve main world-conceptions (arranged to the 12 zodiac-signs) and the 7 worldview-moods (arranged to the planets, once again the seven planets bordered by Saturn). Thus (regardless of a mentioned further differentiation, less important here) 7 x 12 = 84 possible worldviews and spiritual viewpoints result. All these viewpoints (that allow a precise spiritual position of a specific planet in a specific zodiac sign) are certainly possible and important, yet narrow and one-sided. From what viewpoint does the lecturer speak who gives us this gift of an utterly significant consideration of the various viewpoints of world-conceptions; from what standpoint does the anthroposophist Rudolf Steiner speak? He speaks from the higher standpoint outside the 7 x 12, summarizing in itself the 7 x 12, like Uranus standing outside the planetary septenary summarizes this planetary septenary with the zodiacal

Twelve (the upper starry worlds) in the open secret of the number of its revolution 7 x 12 = 84. Rudolf Steiner—or we could also say, anthroposophy—does not speak of this or that planetary, narrowly limited viewpoint, but he (it) speaks from the comprehensive, cosmic, *Uranus viewpoint*. Only for this reason does anthroposophy consider Uranus not as a single planet in the series with the others, only for this reason it does not simply add Uranus to the list up to Saturn, because it regards Uranus as the summarizing and all-embracing [planet], standing over the planetary septenary, summarizing the duodecad of the starry cosmos. Anthroposophy has the Uranus viewpoint, because through and through it is nothing but the Uranus viewpoint. (From the astrologer's viewpoint the interesting fact might be mentioned that Rudolf Steiner himself had Uranus at the peak of the eighth, of the esoteric house.)[41]

For sacramental understanding this Uranus viewpoint is of decisive significance. To what fine results his attention to the Creed leads, [Rudolf] Frieling shows in *Contribution* [Introduction] how the first sentence the Saturn-Uranus sign of the Waterman sounds together with the Father-motif of 'Heaven and Earth' (Uranus-Saturn). Here I would like to mention the application, the significance of this viewpoint for the seven sacraments themselves in their relationship to the Burial Service, standing outside the sacramental septenary, which Frieling in his booklet *Die sieben Sakramente* calls the 'octave' of the Baptism. How the seven sacraments are somehow arranged to the seven planets can certainly be shown in detail. That which standing beyond the seven sacraments, yet as a continuation of the same, appears *beyond* the earthly situation, would then stand in connection to *Uranus* as the trans-Saturnian sphere. In a passage in Frieling's little book,[42] quoted below, is the remarkable comparison with the rainbow:

> Seven[43] colours are visible to us, but there are still the 'ultra-violet rays'. And so all the liturgical deeds relating to the earthly human being join to form a sevenfold sacramental rainbow; to the service for the one who has died belongs the ultra-violet realm. The Burial Service is the 'octave' of the Baptism ...

In astrology, too, Uranus is often regarded as the octave of the Sun or of the planets Mercury-Venus nearest the Sun (more details later). Its relationship to the Burial Service, that is, where the earthly (Saturn) is beginning to pass over into the heavenly (Uranos), is obvious. The name *Uranus* itself has to do with this, for it contains an indication of the German word *Urne* ('urn'). Compare the linguistically interesting book by Rudolf Falb, *Das Land der Inca*, Leipzig: [Weber 1883; Fournier 1989; Nabu Press 2010], p. 15, where the connection of the Latin *urna* with the Germ. *Born, Brunnen* ('fountain, spring'; in Eng. place-names: '–born', and '–bourne', etc.—*Tr. addition*) and the Gk. *Uranos* 'heaven' is indicated, and the Indian Varuna (godhead of the nocturnal heaven, the night sky, and of the waters, one of the Vedic primordial divinities) finds its place. This helps us:

[i]    on the one side to think of the two water urns of the Waterman (cf. the pictorial representation in my book on *Mark's Gospel*), which indeed is the Uranus sign (concerning this, see the chapter on the Marriage in Cana in the book on *John's Gospel*) and

[ii]   on the other side of the burial urn.

Indeed, I would almost like to add: the cremation, the reducing to ashes, receives a new and deep meaning for someone who has assimilated the Uranus viewpoint. To all this one can place the saying of Novalis from his *Fragmente/Fragments*: '*Alle Asche its Blütenstaub, der Kelch ist der Himmel*'—'All ash is pollen (literally: 'flower-dust'), the [flower-] chalice is heaven.' One experiences something wonderful about it, how the mystery of the urn of ashes, of the chalice of ashes touches that of the heavenly urn, of the chalice of the heavenly origins and of heavenly renewal (Uranos = source). This mystery of our heavenly origin and source is nowhere more beautifully and more revealingly expressed than in the Greek myth of Uranos, to which, as a further primal motif of humanity, I will discuss in more detail in a subsequent *Contribution*.

# IV
# [Why write about Uranus?]

Our studies have led us also to the mystery of the name Uranus (Gk. Uranos, 'heaven'). We recognized the connection of this word with the Germ. *Urne*, Lat. *urna*, and recalled the burial urn and the two water-urns of the Waterman, which as the zodiac sign is the house of Uranus. In Indian the name of the god Varuna was mentioned, the god of heaven, or the sky, and of water (Rudolf Falb, opus cit., p. 164, *'Wasser-Himmel'* and *'Himmel-Wasser'*—'water of heaven' and 'heavenly water'), in particular of the initial dark night-sky, in the Vedas connected with the mystery of death, illness and misfortune (karma, visitation of destiny) (R. Falb, p. 163, *'Urn des Todes'*, 'urn of death'), something like an Indian aspect of the Father-God (to Whom also the 'primordial water' points; cf. the connection likewise mentioned of *urna*, 'urn', with the Germ. *Born*, 'fountain').

Concerning the name 'Uranus' for the planet discovered in 1781 by Herschel, this name could possibly also be meaningless, it could be coincidental. For we no longer live in a time when name-giving generally springs from a higher clairvoyant gift. But already the previous studies, moreover astrological empiricism and practice also increasingly show how much this name for the planet standing like a border stone of Uranos (in a higher sense), of the upper starry heaven, is indeed a thoroughly meaningful name corresponding to the facts. (Rudolf Steiner, too, has somewhere pointed out that the naming of this planet was still governed by some sense.) *The name 'Uranus' can be felt as inspired by the spirit of the age.* (In a certain sense, this, as will be shown, is also the case with Neptune, which is at home in the 'Fishes'.) Such inspirations do exist from the spirit of the age for the right names when the clairvoyant strength for giving names is running dry. In connection with the question of Uranus, a side glance to chemistry may perhaps be suggested here on the naming of the element *uranium*. As is known, radium is produced out of the uranium mineral, especially the uranium pitchblende, which we mentioned in the previous *Contribution*. The relationship of radium: lead = Uranus: Saturn does suggest something significant. It seems to me especially important that natural science suspects that traces of radium are contained everywhere in the solid earthly crust, and that the content of radium increases towards the interior of the Earth.[44] Connected to the question of Uranus, the question here of Christ and the Earth appears to us to begin to light up.

Why do I write so much on Uranus, about which I am not through by a long way? Now:

- firstly, because I believe that it interests my readers;
- secondly, because, as I say, Uranus is the *significator* of the whole area that we want to discuss;
- thirdly, because hitherto anthroposophic work on this question is by far inadequate. (For example, Dr Kaiser [Dr Wilhelm Kaiser, 1895-1983], the interesting and deserving anthroposophic astronomer, did not venture to use the name 'Uranus'; he believed he did the right thing by Dr Steiner with a complete deathly silence concerning Uranus. For me it is always the case that when I see that someone somewhere comes off badly with his fellow human beings, I have to assume his part all the more. This is connected with the Scales in my ascendant, which is a *significator* for correct balance;
- fourthly, because in actual fact the whole advance of astrology and the development of anthroposophy—in the sense of what Dr Steiner has given us—leads in an eminent way to the question of Uranus and the viewpoint of Uranus;
- fifthly, because certain predispositions mentioned earlier to these questions are present in the circle of priests (connected with the highpoint of the Youth Movement at that time under its ruling sign Waterman, I mentioned at the end of the first *Contribution*). Finally,
- sixthly, because precisely in this winter special reasons are present for a prolonged occupation with Uranus. This concerns the following:

Regarding all planetary influences, including Saturn—and with Saturn really significantly—basically we always have to do with earthly effects. The super-earthly begins in the realm of Uranus. In the last lecture of the Berlin cycle 1912/13 on *The Life between Death and a new Birth in Relation to the cosmic Facts* [GA 141], Rudolf Steiner shows how out of this trans-Saturnian sphere the new cultural impulses and cultural initiatives enter earthly life. Between death and a new birth, the human soul (as shown in the lecture-cycle) proceeds with more or less consciousness through the individual planetary spheres (which then are experienced as the pure

spiritual spheres). The Saturn-sphere is seldom lived through in full consciousness by people today. Only few manage to keep conscious through
the Saturn-sphere. But even if it were not always the case, human culture
could never advance. For out of the trans-Saturnian, that is, the sphere of
Uranus, it receives all new impulses. (How this fact is connected to the
Impulse from Golgotha, the Christ-Sun-Impulse, Rudolf Steiner shows
in the above-mentioned lecture-course.) Moreover, recent astrology does
point to this significance of the sphere of Uranus for the advance of culture and cultural impulses. Our new natural-scientific and technological
discoveries and inventions, radium, electricity, and all kinds of higher,
imperceptible rays, aeronautics and other technological developments,
are all connected with the influence of Uranus.

Much, too, belongs here of what the Ahrimanic beings seek to possess. Revolutions in human thinking and feeling, too, in the realm of
art, in fashion and worldview and changes in life-styles belong to the
influence of Uranus, to the entrance of the cosmic outer realm. These
influences are in no way always a blessing. The Ahrimanic nature seeks
to get hold of these things. It is worthy of human beings to master
all these technical discoveries, radium, X-rays, aeronautics, and so on.
Yet in all these discoveries beings govern who do not want to allow
this mastery, seeking to reverse the spear-point and to enslave human
consciousness. Everything negative in our culture is connected with
this. One should not only pay attention to the acidic critics of culture,
but feel part of human nature which, taken up in tremendous cultural
movements—for our natural science and technology draws on a tremendous cultural stimulus—is in danger from these beings that for
their part need to be overcome in all these realms that should be mastered. And these beings seek to overcome and rend human thinking
and imagination. They are the dragon that is to be overcome through
the power of Michael, of the powerful Christened 'I'-impulse.

Moreover, the date when such a planet as Uranus is discovered—
similar later with Neptune, and today perhaps with Pluto—is not
something arbitrary. The spirit of the age adds the discovery of
such a new (that is, not new, but hitherto unknown) cosmic body,
when its rays for the human being and human consciousness begin
to gain in significance. This is far from claiming that this influence
at the same time is a conscious one. On the contrary, for a long
period it will be unconscious. For it is double-edged; its effect is
chaotic. This applies to a special degree to Uranus and, as we shall
see later, also to Neptune.

The assimilated influence of Uranus signifies an intensification in consciousness. This conscious linking-oneself with the rays of Uranus in the light of the Christ-Michael-Impulse, signifies an enhancement of human nature, the blessed opening up of new doors to life and paths of life. The non-conscious assimilation of the influence of Uranus brings all sorts of ruination, upheavals, revolutions and overwhelming, sudden catastrophes. Uranus is the great cosmic builder, but also destroyer of what is established on Earth. It has often to effect destruction, in order that it can proceed to re-build, in the cosmic sense of the great world-plan. Expressed differently, the cosmic influence, unmediated and without the corresponding preparation of the consciousness, meeting the earthly situation, frequently effects upheaval, revolution, destruction and catastrophe. (With me, for example, for in my birth-horoscope I have the highest planets in the house of profession, Uranus thrice disrupted my whole outer life,[45] until now I begin to align myself somewhat more consciously with its rays.)

Uranus is also the star of sudden catastrophes, bringing the effect of cosmic dynamite and explosions. Today humanity is experiencing initially much more of this its catastrophic side, than its other side preparing blessing in the lap of the future. For this reason, it is absolutely necessary, precisely as a priest, spiritually to come to terms with the question of Uranus. And the reason why it is to be done now, that is in these present weeks and months, is that these present weeks and months stand under particularly difficult starry constellations, in particular Uranus-constellations. Later I shall speak in more detail of the nature of harmonic and discordant aspects of the stars. Here in anticipation only this short report, that all harmonic influences rest on the triangle (that is, trigon = 120°, sextile = 60°, etc.), all discordant influences of everything heavy with Earth on the *cross* (opposition 180°, square 90° is the most acute, most critical of all aspects).

At the moment we stand at a time of difficult cosmic squares. Already in 1929 we had a heavy square of the two planets Uranus and Saturn, which move very slowly. (When I was asked in Nuremberg from acquaintances concerning a catastrophic explosion that had occurred, I found at this time the meeting of these Saturn-Uranus squares with various other squares.) Because of the retrograde motion of the one and then of the other planet, the square of Uranus and Saturn, which had dissolved several times, had re-formed; for the last time it was exactly at the beginning of April this year 1930, and on 12 December we will experience again the exact square of Uranus and Saturn (Uranus 11° 28′ Ram, Saturn 11° 28′ Goat). When this square (which then was not quite exact) coincided with a solar eclipse [Oct 21, 1930], we experienced the disaster of a heavy explosion in Aachen,[46] soon followed by a similar one in the Saarland.[47] But here this Saturn-Uranus square is not the only one by a long way. Jupiter, which also moves slowly (it stands approximately one year in each zodiac sign) is found standing in the Crab, also already for a long time in a square position with Uranus, in opposition to Saturn. Through a longer period, this position was heightened through a conjunction with Mars in the Crab (which since the end of October has moved into the Lion). Moreover, the recently discovered Pluto, if it exists—which [to date—*Tr.*] is not finalized—stands in Cancer and enhances all these effects of squares and oppositions. (Perhaps this is connected to the earthquake we experienced recently.)[48] There is, then, just now a real cross spanning the heavens above humanity:

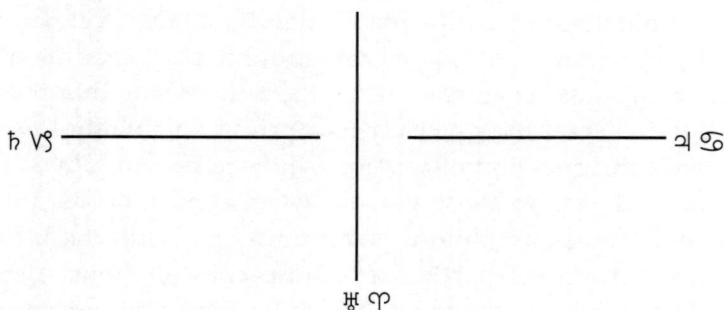

Children, born at this time, will sense this in their life and destiny. (I say this here not, for instance, that the priest who is to conduct a baptism belonging to his pastoral work is anxious concerning these things, but that he/she receive it [this dramatic cross—*Tr.*] sympathetically into his/her own consciousness.)

We all have this cross hanging over us (in which the Uranus-Saturn square plays a main role), felt as a dull pressure of destiny. Not least we as priests; for *Jupiter*, involved with this cross and with this Uranus square, is indeed the priestly planet. With myself, it is like this, that I not only sense this pressure of destiny, but at the same time when— for example, in writing these *Contributions*—I direct my consciousness to these questions, there is something liberating about it. Becoming conscious in working out the influence of the stars counters the effects. Later in discussing the horoscope I will have to show how also the squares, if people exercise with them their forces of consciousness and of overcoming, can become a source of strength and blessing.

In any case, we have also in the Movement some heavy matters to expect this winter. Here it would be good, when we work out these things, to try to make clear for ourselves what a state of affairs Uranus and the Uranus-influence brings! This—I have had to reach out somewhat longer—is the sixth reason why I speak on Uranus precisely in the Introduction to these *Newsletter Contributions* in the present moment and in such detail.

Later with the presentation of the horoscope I will have to show how a horoscope was quite differently experienced at various times and in the various stages of consciousness and development of humanity and the individual, how different stars at different times and for different people had a quite different significance. Characteristic for the 'old' astrology, limited to the 'seven planets' (including Saturn) was actually that it still had nothing to do with the actual stars. It was an 'astrology without stars'. For the planets up to Saturn are—in the cosmic sense—only 'Earth'. The zodiac-signs, too, meant in astrology are not the starry constellations of the fixed-star heaven, but their earthly reflection. (Further details on this important question later.) The specific position of a planet was decided by one of the 'signs' and remained thereby still in the earthly situation. The actual 'stars' are only the fixed stars, and they appear here to play no role at all. A fixed-star wisdom in the Egyptian Mysteries that existed during primordial times already became lost in antiquity. In the future, not yet today, it will be there again through the Christ-impulse. Rudolf Steiner speaks significantly (*The Spiritual Guidance of Man and Humanity* [GA 15]) how with the birth the whole fixed-star heaven is imprinted on the aura of the infant's brain, how only *in this* is the true essence of the horoscope completed. This is not understood in concrete terms by astrologers today. It is still a purely future question. Humanity has first to grow into the actual starry world of its cosmic origins (from which it was alienated through the Fall of man), into the upper starry heaven, the Uranos, there to find again its 'eternal name' (cf. Chapter 1, 7 on the starry mystery of the eternal name in my book on *John's Gospel*, p. 127; I also spoke about it at the synod in Ulm). Today humanity is but on the way. Yet of greatest significance for this fact is the discovery of the new planets Uranus and Neptune, which already standing beyond the more confined planetary system begin to speak as mediators of the actual starry world to human beings in this age. We can feel this like a greeting out of cosmic distances, from the starry homeland. Connected with this, as astrological observation and experience show, precisely Uranus (as the actual mediator and opener of the true, the upper starry world in the horoscope of the spiritually developed human being), will be increasingly decisive, more important, whereas other planets step back.

How in a wonderful manner the Greek myth of Uranos already points to this great question of humanity's development, on this, then, in the next *Contribution*. (On pp. 60 & 81 of my book on *John's Gospel* the Uranos myth is cited as an important motif for gospel research.)

# V
# Uranus and Neptune. The Uranos Myth. The Venus-Mercury question. To conclude, *Der Vogel Gryff*, by Fr. Doldinger

I regret, in the interest of those willing to read who had then to read everything at once, that in the previous *Newsletter* three *Contributions* appeared simultaneously. The *Contributions* were written at different times (which can also be recognized through their style). *Contribution* No. II was written in October, No. III somewhat later. I intended to offer the friends some cosmic entertainment during the heavy weeks of November. The intention was good, but fate unfavourable. Also, over the *Newsletter* there hang the heavy square (♅ □ ♄ + ♅ □ ♃, that is, Uranus square Saturn, Uranus square Jupiter), which I sketched in the previous *Contribution*, which lies over this whole heavy winter. It works in this case like a cosmic 'stop' signal, so that the *Newsletter*, for a long time ready for dispatching, could not leave Urachstrasse. The 'stop' signal could change to 'go' only during the days when the Sun passed from the sign ♏ Scorpio into the sign ♐ Archer (which always creates relieving possibilities of life, effecting favourable progress). The comparison is fitting to what in astrology is meant on the one hand by a square and on the other by a triangle; the earthly-technical signal, about which Herr Strakosch[49] once held a lecture in Dornach, basically coincides with astrology, with the spiritual meaning of the cosmic-astral angle-placements.

90° astrological square, disharmonious aspect, 'stop' signal;
120° astrological triangle, harmonious aspect, 'go' signal.

Consequently, let us be happy that the *Newsletter* with its convoluted *Contributions* now receives the signal to 'go'.

Meanwhile—still before the publication of the previous *Newsletter*—another large *Contribution* by Frieling has appeared that illuminates to the brightest degree the whole of the Act of Consecration of Man from the cosmic viewpoint (zodiac and planets) presented by me in my *John's Gospel: The Cosmic Rhythm*. It is published along with this *Contribution* (and a short special *Contribution* from me at the same time). I am very happy about this kind of collaboration.

To understand all these *Contributions*, it is important to establish the need to distinguish Uranos (the trans-Saturnian—or super-earthly—heavenly sphere itself) from Uranus (the planet discovered by Herschel in 1781). Neptune, discovered by Leverrier in 1846 (already mentioned on occasion), also belongs to Uranus in the extended sense. The question: how do Uranus and Neptune mutually relate? has certainly quite often been silently posed. To gain an understanding concerning Neptune is not unimportant, because for some time it has a great, although not always favourable, importance and effect in our Piscean age, the age of the Fishes. We live astronomically since the year 0 CE, or rather 33 CE, in the age of the Fishes (the beginning of which in anthroposophy is dated 1413 CE, a moment in which the spring-point had already passed through the middle of the zodiac constellation by a long way). Already in the first Contribution, I wrote that the astronomical transition, too (as the event of Golgotha clearly shows), spiritually means something (see on this, p. 34f. of my book on *John's Gospel*). Now the Fishes as the 'house of Jupiter' is at the same time the house of Neptune (see *Contribution* No. II for the arrangement of houses). Uranus governs alongside Saturn in the Waterman; Neptune alongside Jupiter governs in the Fishes. With that which enters in the Jordan-Baptism as an influence of Jupiter from the 'Ancient Sun' (in the sense of *Occult Science* [GA 13])—[present-day] Jupiter is the boundary stone of 'Ancient Sun', as Mars that of 'Ancient Moon', and Saturn that of 'Ancient Saturn'—an influence of Neptune is linked like an 'echo from the cosmic distances'. This phrase used on p. 73 of my book on *John's Gospel* corresponds well to the essence of Neptune. Uranus belongs to the light-ether triangle (≈ ♊ ♎, see the Figure in the Appendix to my books on *Mark* and *John*, which is basic for all these observations) and Neptune to the sound-etheric triangle (♓ ♋ ♏), also termed the Johannine triangle. Like the Moon which is close to the Earth, Neptune, in the farthest distances from the Earth, is a planet of cosmic music (e.g. my own relationship to music—the whole work on the gospel as well as the astrological work originally came to me out of my impulse to orientate the musical keys according to the zodiac; the musical element for me was also the point of departure for the astrology—it is linked with a close conjunction of Moon-Neptune, whereby Neptune with me, moreover, is found in the musical sign of the Bull. I believe that such occasional personal remarks to an orientation to the whole subject is not out of place. One has to speak of one's own stars, because it would be most indiscreet to mention those of some [contemporary] person).

The musical significance of Neptune is especially clear in the horoscope of Richard Wagner, likewise in that of his royal friend Ludwig II of Bayern. Wagner had the favourable Neptune influence, Ludwig II the unfavourable, in particular a very catastrophic Neptune-Saturn-Mars conjunction (these are the three planets of death) in the Waterman! For this reason, the tragic destiny of his death in Lake Starnberg [13 June 1886].[50] At the same time, Wagner's relationship to Ludwig II through Neptune is explained. Neptune is a very occult planet whose influence easily becomes oppressive. (In my horoscope the Neptune-conjunction is protected through a favourable Mars-triangle, which at the same time creates possibilities—for Mars is the activator for the earthly realm—to introduce occult matters into normal earthly activities.)

Whereas the influence of Uranus, in this context, steps back to an increasing extent, in our age the activity of Neptune plays a really great role, precisely because it is the age of the Fishes (and thereby at the same time a Neptune age). This influence is present since the turning point of time, intensified since 1413. For this reason, already in the Middle Ages we notice the extensive occult endeavours. Today we still do not know *how* rich the Middle Ages was in this relationship. In particular alchymy[51] touches especially on the influence of Neptune-Mercury. It is consequently initially withdrawing, whereas the astrology oriented to *Uranus* has its actual future *before* it. Nothing is more incorrect than to seek astrology only one-sidedly in the past; it is in the most eminent sense an opportunity of the future.

Just here lies the critical point of the influence of Neptune, that for a long time it plays such a great role actually *before* the influence of Uranus. This influence of Uranus will only be there in the Waterman-Uranus age beginning after 2000 CE; today it only casts its shadow ahead. (In this sense these contemplations would like to be taken.) Uranus is the real boundary stone of Uranos. Between Saturn and Uranus there lies cosmically the *spiritual threshold*, which at the same time is like a threshold between Heaven and Earth. Saturn is the cosmic Guardian of the Threshold. Only when we have passed it, do we come properly to Uranus. This is already possible today for the individual, for humanity as a whole only in about 150 years [written 1930]. With Neptune it is different; already today in this whole age of the Fishes, humanity in a certain sense has arrived at Neptune, which not only in the horoscopes of highly developed personalities, but also with very less developed personalities, indeed frequently plays an outstanding role in the horoscopes of criminals (also mediums, somnambulists, psychopaths of all kinds). And one senses Neptune today with the people; Uranus one senses very little, only with some individuals. But what does this mean?

Neptune enters strongly, even before humanity actually is over the threshold, which lies between Saturn and Uranus-Uranos! This effect has somehow to be premature, untimely. Only when one arrives at Uranus will the Neptune-influence be a favourable and beneficial one. Then the human being will be consciously able to unite in the right sense also with these influences out of distant worlds. Here everything depends on *consciousness*. One intuits, or rather sees, how important in this realm that we enter here, the *Christ-impulse* is, the conscious 'I'-impulse. Not without world-historical significance did the Neptune-influence enter precisely into the age, and only into the age that was the first Christ-era, with the Jordan-Baptism. But we know precisely out of anthroposophy how little in this first Christ-era the real Christ-'I'-impulse was received into the soul. All usual Christianity still lies under the niveau of this Impulse. For this reason, the very significant Neptune-influence in this [our] age is at the same time so very double-sided, frequently oppressive. Where the Christ-impulse, the conscious 'I'-impulse, is still lacking, Neptune still works chaotically, dreamily, mediumistic. Everything occult, which is not penetrated in the consciousness, appearing mystically nebulous, proceeds as a damping down of consciousness. Today this has a lot to do with the influence of Neptune. Uranus, when no conscious relationship is produced for its rays, manifests as more catastrophic, sudden, heated, explosive, like cosmic dynamite. Neptune manifests as more chaotic, dreamy, sleepy, mediumistic, somnambulistic and narcotic, like cosmic morphine. Occult deceivers and charlatans, imposters and the like, criminals generally, have a lot to do with Neptune. (This should not be taken too one-sidedly; we may not forget that in the cosmic realm actually everything is good, that only in the earthly realm can it become evil, or bad, that there also exists a good, a Johannine influence of Neptune, that Neptune indeed precisely in the Johannine triangle is at home, as Uranus is in the Matthean triangle—one recalls the 'Star of Bethlehem'.)

With many people Neptune proves itself especially critical in the Twins (but, of course, nobody should for this reason worry. But as Uranus stands for 7 years and Neptune almost 14 years in one sign that always embraces grand (*stattliche*) years, that, of course, [may] include 'such and such' [= all sorts]). Through the Christ-'I'-impulse, especially if the Christ-Sun-impulse unites with the Christ-Uranus-impulse, every Neptune influence can be salutary. (It is interesting that, for example, Neptune—and indeed a really difficult Neptune square aspect [♆ □ ♂ ]—is present in the horoscope of Therese Neumann of Konnersreuth [1898-1962, a German Catholic mystic and stigmatic].)[52] Uranus and Neptune are in an eminent sense the two 'occult planets'; but unless the Neptune-influence is supported through the influence of Uranus—or through a beneficial influence in another manner—it often leads to unsound occultism and nebulous mysticism, to that kind of occultism which in anthroposophy and The Christian Community we rightly always seek to free ourselves.

Here, however, we reach the point concerning 'anthroposophy', something very important. Observation, that is, comparison of the facts has resulted that a specific Neptune-aspect, precisely in the birth-constellation of personalities whose path in life has led them to anthroposophy, has played an important role. That is the conjunction of Neptune and Mercury, of the planets farthest and closest to the Sun in the horoscope, for which Mercury has to do with the understanding, with earthly thinking, whereas the occult Neptune is the significator of the distant cosmic realm. Earthly thinking, then, developing towards cosmic thinking ('Anthroposophy is a path of knowledge, which seeks to lead the spiritual in the human being to the spiritual in the universe' [R. Steiner, *Leading Thoughts*, No. 1], which one can well imagine as the meaning of this constellation, appears confirmed by experience. Forces of Neptune are received by a solid earthly thinking.

In actual fact such a conjunction is to be found in Rudolf Steiner's horoscope, which has Mercury 27 1/2° ♓, Neptune 28° ♓. This is a very close conjunction, moreover, in the Neptune-sign of the Fishes. Frau Dr Steiner has this conjunction, likewise very close, but in the sign of the Ram: ☿ 10° ♈, ♆ 11 ½° ♈. And the examples can be followed with numerous closer and more distant anthroposophical acquaintances, indeed multiplied *en masse*, only in this whole realm very necessary discretion does not allow detailed description; moreover, as a rule I do not write about details that I meet from time to time, and do not record them in my memory. Urachhaus is already full of examples for the anthroposophical Neptune-Mercury conjunction. One example I may include: my own horoscope. Here, as already stated, Neptune on the one side, has the close Moon-conjunction, towards the other side, something further removed, Mercury. One person born on the same day as myself, even in the same year, a prominent member of the Anthroposophical Society (that is, an interesting case of a horoscope double), because he came into the world a few hours before me, has Mercury even nearer to Neptune than I do.[53] For this reason he also came to anthroposophy a few years earlier (as far as I know). Apart from both quick-moving planets Moon and Mercury (already with Mercury the difference is quite noticeable), both of us have the same stars, that is, all the planets are in the same zodiac sign, even almost the same position, apart from the Moon and Mercury. Nevertheless, our destinies are quite different, for one thing because the Moon, the star of the personality, through its different position makes things quite different, and through the different hours of birth a completely different 'division of the houses' comes about. What it concerns here, I can only explain later.

Now, it would again be a trap of Ahriman—there are many in this realm—to say, so, my becoming an anthroposophist is simply determined by my birth constellation, depending on a kind of world-necessity. This, of course, would be wrong. That which ultimately makes an anthroposophist is the will in the 'I'. And this in particular does not stand in the horoscope. But the hindrances that are overcome by destiny in order to reach anthroposophy are quite different in different cases. Some people bring with them the prerequisites for the greater part, others have to work painstakingly for their anthroposophical existence. Moreover, it also does not depend *only* on such a Neptune—Mercury position in one's destiny, but experience does show how the stars here in many cases alleviate the path to anthroposophy.

Several times I have indicated a relationship of Neptune to the Moon. As in the first instance the Moon, so too in a somewhat different way the occult Neptune, relates to the personal, human soul-and-feeling element—whereas Uranus and the Sun are eminently *spiritual* stars that have to do with the human essence. In Uranus the human being experiences the depths of his own origin, the heights of his own spiritual reality (about this, more details later.). Thereby the frequently adverse effect of Neptune too strongly pressing and oppressing the soul. If here a 'relationship of Neptune to the Moon' is mentioned, one has again to be clear that this, of course, cannot be meant in the Copernican, astronomical sense. A relationship to the Sun does exist, you could also say to the little Earth (for in the Copernican view Neptune is the bigger and more mighty planet), but how should the distant Neptune be concerned about the insignificant moon of the Earth? For indeed, like Uranus, Saturn and Jupiter, and so on, it has in the first instance its own moons that concern it. This objection is quite useful, because it helps clearly to distinguish the astronomical from the astrological viewpoint, which is our concern. Of course, Neptune will not be concerned overmuch about the Earth's moon, which is not being maintained.

In astrology it has to do with something quite different. There Neptune is not the planetary ball calculated by astronomers with a diameter of 54,979 kilometres, 4,494½ million km. distant from the Sun, but the spiritual sphere of influence between Neptune's being and the Earth-star as the place of the 'I'. In the same way, Moon means the spiritual sphere of influence between the Earth and the Moon. The way the rays of the Moon (the rays of our earthly Moon) meet the Earth, or as it meets *us*, can indeed have much to do with the way the rays of Neptune meet us. Only in this case, because it is much nearer the Moon is also much the mightier; compared to this the effect of the distance of occult Neptune, beyond the visibility to the naked eye, retreats, only noticeable in modern times. But as occult influence it is likewise present, and the facts of empirical observation do show that between this occult effect and that of the Moon nevertheless all kinds of relationships come about. The Moon is also, even in the first rank, the planet of occultism—if not the occult planet. In his lecture-cycle *Human and cosmic Thought* [GA 151, 4 lectures, Berlin 20-23 Jan. 1914], so important for this whole question, Rudolf Steiner has even related the world-conception of 'occultism' with the Moon (and empiricism with the Sun, voluntarism with Mars, transcendentalism with Mercury, and so on).

We can also say astrologically, Neptune (the influence of Neptune) is a higher octave of the Moon (the influence of the Moon), as Uranus is a higher octave than the Sun (on this, further details soon). Moreover, there is a relationship of Neptune to Mercury, of Uranus to Venus, which astrologically is *very* important (on this, too, further details soon).

The relationship of Uranus to the Sun, and of Neptune to the Moon (in the astrological sense meant here, not in the astronomical sense) is widely known in astrology and has always particularly impressed me in my astrological researches and observations. Now, everything astrological is really rooted in the cosmogony of *Occult Science*. And so, the question for me was always, if Uranus and Neptune did not originally belong to the [solar] system, if they only came later, as Dr Steiner says *'hinzugeflogen*—flew in',[54] when did these events take place?

Researching this question there resulted for me—this is not a solution but a viewpoint—always a relationship of Uranus to Ancient Sun and Neptune to Ancient Moon. This does not answer the question, for after Ancient Sun there was initially a *pralaya*, likewise after Ancient Moon. In the Earth evolution there follow three [shorter] *pralayas* (cosmic dissolutions of the world) before in the Polarian age (followed by the Hyperborean, then the Lemurian ages) the fourth earthly round [properly] begins in which we still live today. So not yet in its present form but in some condition, Uranus must have been present during Ancient Sun, and Neptune during Ancient Moon, then again in the second and third round, and the definite arrival of Uranus would then be placed in the Hyperborean and Neptune in the early Lemurian age (when everything was not yet as today in the physical condition, but more in the supersensory-etheric condition). This should initially only be a hypothesis. I do not know if in reality it is like this. What at the moment is for me important is not the hypothesis, but only the fact that Uranus must have a relationship to Ancient Sun, and Neptune to Ancient Moon. This, of course, only concerns Uranus; Uranos (in the sense always intended here) is something definitely pre-Saturnian and beyond Saturn; it also existed during the time of Saturn (before Saturn, there was Uranos).

And now the important thing, where these things can now also be found in Dr Steiner (instead of applying the working method favoured today simply to disregard Uranus—whereby anthroposophy would not be served, one would only discredit it in the eyes of the world; I find it important to show how one can find these things in Dr Steiner's work if one only looks properly). Uranus and Neptune are mentioned for the first time in the Düsseldorf lecture-cycle *The Spiritual Hierarchies and their Reflection in the Physical World* [GA 110], lecture 6, and then once more in lecture 10. What is mentioned there finds an important addition in the Munich lecture-cycle, *Wonders of the World, Ordeals of the Soul and Revelations of the Spirit* [GA 129], lecture 8, where the important Greek Uranos myth is mentioned. In the first-mentioned cycle (lecture 6) the more known astronomical aspect, the counter movement of the moons of Uranus[55] and so on is pointed out in order to show that Uranus and Neptune belong originally to another system. The other decisive important observation comes in lecture 10, where the relationship of Uranus to the Sun and Neptune to the Moon is pointed out, which astrology always presumes quite independently of Dr Steiner and *Occult Science*. From there I, too, derived these things quite independently—as I wrote in my last *Newsletter Contribution*—and I was as if struck down, but with a joyful feeling, when some days ago I found these things again in one of the earlier lecture-cycles, which I had not read for decades and had completely escaped my memory. Dr Steiner says there that beings who during the time of Saturn still had something to do with us withdrew and formed dwelling places outside [the solar system]. When Saturn progressed to Jupiter (that means, to Ancient Sun, for which Jupiter today is the boundary stone), then that which in Saturnian primordial evolution had withdrawn returned in a certain way, that means, in the Sun(Jupiter)-development as *Uranus*; during the Moon-development—or, as Dr Steiner says,[56] during the 'Mars-evolution', for Mars today is the border marking the 'Old Moon'—*Neptune* joined from the same sphere (Uranos sphere). The text from Rudolf Steiner at this place runs:

> Just in the same way as Jupiter has been condensed, pushed together, so something was pushed together through beings who have withdrawn, something that has nothing to do with our development, but with those withdrawing beings has become at first *Uranus* and during the Mars-development has become *Neptune*.

(As has been shown here and is shown elsewhere in Dr Steiner and in many things that follow, the phrase 'has nothing to do with our development' is to be understood *cum grano salis* [with a grain of salt], for of course the later coming-back-in has indeed something to do with the meaning of the world and human development.) What is important is what Dr Steiner says, that those beings from whom later a part, like messengers, have come back to us as Uranus and Neptune, had something to do with us on Saturn. About this, more in the Munich lecture-cycle, where in lecture 8 the Greek Uranos-myth is so meaningfully cited.[57] This myth, which forms the central motif of my book on *John's Gospel* (pp. 60, 81) runs as follows:

> The father of Jupiter-Zeus, of the father and ruler of the gods and man, was Saturn-Kronos (the word Chronos also in Greek means 'time'). Jupiter-Zeus was a son of Saturn-Kronos; Saturn was a descendant of Uranos (Uranos: 'heaven'). Uranos is violated by Saturn-Kronos and castrated. The power of propagation of Uranos falls into the cosmic ocean. Out of the semen of the stars of Uranos that has become the foam of the sea Venus-Aphrodite arises, the one 'born out of the waves'.[58]

This beautiful myth contains all the profundities of the universe and of the human being; all the mysteries of astrology and alchemy are contained in it. That they are, nevertheless, not so easy to recognize is connected to the Fall of man, with the further destinies of Venus, which can be gleaned from the Uranos-myth itself or can easily be connected with it. But at present [not pursuing] these destinies of Venus, the Mercury-Venus question and the Venus-Mars question, we shall remain with Uranus-Uranos and Dr Steiner, who himself relates to this Uranos-myth in the Munich lecture-cycle.

On Saturn, Rudolf Steiner says,[59] Uranos (that which later returns to us as Uranus and Neptune) still had something to do with our development. Where and when on Saturn? The answer is given, in connection with *Occult Science*, clearly and explicitly in the Greek myth. Kronos also means 'time'. There occurs that primordial division, primordial separation, where in *Ancient Saturn* time comes about (tr. Creeger p. 149; Monges, p. 131; Adams, p. 126), that is, in the middle, fourth of the seven periods of Saturn. Here the 'warmth', the warmth-ether, the primordial fire arises, in which the Archai arise as the birth of the sacrifice (of the Thrones to the Cherubim), who are the 'human beings' on Saturn, who go through their human stage [beings who awaken to self-consciousness—*Tr. note*]. (The human being of today on Saturn is still at the lowest elementary stage.) The three previous periods where the Thrones, the Spirits of Wisdom and the Spirits of Movement reveal themselves, are not yet in time; they belong to the realm of 'duration', of eternity. There, in eternity, Uranos is still connected with the primordial Saturn. Saturn-Kronos is the son of Uranos, not in the sense of a divine *succession*, but Uranos is the Father beyond time, the Father in eternity. There is the true origin the true homeland of man. For nothing would be more incorrect than to understand Dr Steiner and *Occult Science*, that one would say that the origin of man lies in Saturn. For from whence did man come to Saturn? What were these sublime Beings who emanate the members of their being into primordial Saturn (cf. the words of the Offertory of the Act of Consecration of Man)? The Beings of the environment of Saturn, the Seraphim, Cherubim, Thrones, and so on? They, especially the Seraphim and Cherubim indeed spiritually seen, are Uranos. As the Thrones belong to Saturn, so Cherubim and Seraphim belong to Uranos. There in this region, in Uranos, with the Father in heaven, is the cosmic origin of the human being. The sign of the zodiac, the Uranus-sign of the Waterman, not without meaning and reason in the sense of *Occult Science*, is connected with the human being and to human origins. The Uranus-triangle in the zodiac (≈ Ⅱ ♎), the Matthew triangle, is also the triangle of the human being. The true home of the human being is the radiant Uranos.

This homeland lies beyond time, in eternity. The sombre Saturn is but the origin of what in the human being is temporal and transient, the point of the first separation, of the first division, of the parting of Heaven and Earth, the beginning of time. Our human consciousness today can be shocked when one says: the actual starry heaven, the heaven of fixed stars, Uranos (whose planetary messenger and mediator is Uranus), is not of space and time, is something which actually cannot be laid hold by human thought. (Rudolf Steiner says almost the same during the astronomical lecture-course [*Third Scientific Lecture-Course: Astronomy*, Stuttgart, 1-18 Jan. 1921, GA 323]: 'We cannot grasp the starry heaven; astronomy is something that does not fit into one's head.') Instead of complaining immediately about all the modern natural-scientific and astronomical things and to reject them prematurely with a certain pride, one may think of the famous 'light years' of astronomy with which they measure the distance of the stars (the time that light-beam requires to reach from one star to another). I know all that is raised as objections here; I am clear that all these concepts have to be translated into different, spiritual concepts, that ultimately nothing is spatial about the starry heavens, but I find it important to hold on to the results of scientific research today as a starting point. What then do the light years tell us? The star which we see is not 'now', but was years ago, or decades, centuries or millennia ago, in short everything in time is in chaotic flux, everything spatial in the starry heaven is already dissolved for the scientific observation of today, which is accused of being materialistic, into a time-chaos in which time itself crumbles apart, all earthly concepts of space and time become a shambles. Indeed, Uranos is beyond time, and also no longer spatial in the earthly sense; it belongs to eternity. There, in eternity, is the true origin of the human being. Not in vain does our Creed begin, according to Frieling's faultless explanation, in the Uranus-sign of the Waterman (see below, pp. 360-61).

Uranus, then, which is still connected to primordial Saturn, separates from it with the progress in time of Saturn (in the middle period of Ancient Saturn), which at the same time is the primordial stage of the cosmic primal Fall (which nevertheless was necessary for all development, for everything fair and good). In grand pictures of the

Greek Uranos-myth, of 'the castration of Uranos by Kronos, time', this is revealingly expressed (how the mystery of love, Venus-Aphrodite stands in connection to all this we already divine; more on this later). Rudolf Steiner's *Occult Science* is through this brought into a tremendous perspective.

In the relevant passage in the Düsseldorf lecture-cycle [GA 110], lecture 10, Rudolf Steiner uses a wonderful phrase for Uranos, calling it the 'crystal heaven', and speaks of the primordial Being of the World, that which was prior to the Saturn evolution—that means Uranos—called the 'crystal heaven'. This is the region out of which later Uranus and Neptune have arrived, about which Rudolf Steiner says in what follows that Uranus can be connected to the evolution of Ancient Sun (of 'Jupiter') and Neptune with the evolution of Ancient Moon (of 'Mars'). In the Munich lecture-cycle Steiner speaks of where 'Ancient Saturn or Kronos, begins to crystallize', something which is secretly entered into this Kronos goes against the universal evolution. A part of the beings remains with the Saturn-Sun-Moon evolution; another part tends to go upwards, back to Uranos. From thence, from the Uranus-side comes our conscious being (into which Lucifer and the Fall of man have entered), from the other the Saturn-side, our unconscious being (which has remained pure from the Fall)—Byron deals with his theme magnificently in his mystery-drama *Cain*. But from the other side, towards which Lucifer leans, there still comes another Being that has remained in the advancing stream of world-evolution, the Being Who in the Baptism in the Jordan connects with the earthly element, the Christ (*Wonders of the World...*, lecture 8). He brings with this the Mystery of Ancient Sun and with it the Mystery of Uranos-Uranus into the earthly realm. Here the Christ-Sun impulse connects with the Christ-Uranus impulse. In a grandiose manner Rudolf Steiner explains cosmogonically the relationship of Uranus to the Sun, which astrology today has come to quite independently from Rudolf Steiner. But Rudolf Steiner speaks here of *Ancient Sun*, but whose being nevertheless is pictorially represented by the Sun today, 'There arises out of the cosmic space in which previously only the Imaginations of other gods had lived, such a divine thought, which is real' (he means Christ in His relationship to Uranus and Ancient Sun). I regret that none of our known 'cycle experts' have discovered these things, but it can't be helped. Even 'cycle expertise' has its finesse and its merits!

Not quite as Uranus today, Uranos-Uranus is revealed on Ancient Sun, where the whole cosmos was still different, much more etheric than today—and on Ancient Moon, when Neptune in its primal form joined the earthly planetary system, also according Dr Steiner. Only much later did the whole cosmos, and with it Uranus and Neptune, take on its form of today. The Neptune-revelation is still connected with the Christ-Uranus-Sun revelation; it is wonderfully meaningful how the Christ-event of the Baptism in the Jordan stands precisely in the sign of the Fishes, where with Jupiter-Christ Neptune is the co-ruler: with the Christ-Sun event of the Jordan Baptism (Jupiter = Ancient Sun), mysteriously connected here is the 'sound from cosmic distances' [Mark 1:11—*Tr. note*], in Neptune as was mentioned at the beginning (cf. my book on *John's Gospel*, p. 73f.). Already from then on for the Christ-era, the existence of an occult influence of Neptune is characteristic. Connected to this stands the occult blossoming of Christian mysticism in the Middle Ages, with its Rosicrucianism and alchymy and with it, as we have seen, also anthroposophy of today. The actual Christ-Uranus influence will enter later; it belongs to the age of Waterman-Uranus, still lying before us [written in 1930], from about 2000 CE.

John's Gospel, however, contains a wonderful indication of the future Mysteries in the Marriage in Cana. This lies in the zodiac axis ≈≈—♌ (Waterman—Lion). The Lion is the Sun-sign; the Waterman is the Uranus-sign. Through Christ one day Uranos will become the higher Sun in the heart.

> One day the stars, down dripping,
> Shall flow in golden wine:
> We, of that nectar sipping,
> As living stars will shine.
> [Novalis, from *Hymns to the Night*, V. Tr. George MacDonald]

It is wonderful, how the Russian poet Dostoyevsky in the chapter 'Cana of Galilee' of his *The Brothers Karamazov*, in feeling anticipates this Uranus-Sun-Mystery of the future. One could at least read the chapter on Cana in my new book on *John's Gospel* (pp. 212-14), for it is completely immersed in this Uranus-Sun-Mystery. And through the Russian Dostoyevsky this speaks to human hearts today, that which otherwise remains a Mystery of the coming Waterman-Uranus epoch. How full of content the one sentence of the Dostoyevsky [tr. Constance Garnett] (p. 213 of my book): 'The silence of earth seemed to melt into the silence of the heavens. *The Mystery of earth was one with the mystery of the stars ....*' Moreover, in the Lazarus story and the Mystery of

Golgotha, with the entombment, the whole constellation resonates again, the Uranus-Sun-Mysteries. (This, too, is intuited by Dostoyevsky.) The words from Goethe's poem [*Symbolum*]: '*Stille ruhn oben die Sterne/ Und unten die Gräber*' receive a wonderfully profound meaning.

> Interrogate them, as we will,
> The stars on high are silent still;
> Silent the graves, nor make reply
> The dearest lips therein that lie.
> [Tr. Arthur John Lockhart]

Everything earlier regarding Uranus and urns, burial urns, and things said at burials receive a new and deep meaning. In a unique manner the two Water-urns of the Waterman-Uranus-sign standing over the marriage in Cana flow together with the Mystery of the burial urn (with Dostoyevsky the whole story takes place at the coffin of a dear one).

To disregard Uranus in anthroposophy (as many attempt to do nowadays) would mean to disregard the richness of the Christ-impulse in it. For with the Christ-Sun impulse, a Christ-Uranus impulse is connected; this is especially mentioned also in the last lecture of the Berlin cycle 1912/13 on *The Life between Death and a new Birth in Relation to the cosmic Facts* [GA 141]. There Dr Steiner explains how (in the sense of the above-mentioned) all the impulses towards progress are brought in from the regions beyond the sphere of Saturn (that means, out of the Uranus-region); all outer earthly progress in the individual cultural epochs is to be looked for beyond the Saturn region. Moreover, the planetary system of today, the seven planets, derive only from Ancient Moon, but the Christ-Impulse from Ancient Sun:

> For this reason, the soul contains in itself, besides what it was before the Mystery of Golgotha, that which is more than everything that is contained within the planetary sphere which is deeply founded in the universe, that which *initially* descends from the Sun to the Earth, but in the spirit belongs to much deeper regions than those which we have before us in the (seven) planetary spheres.

This means, with the Christ-Sun impulse, a Christ-Uranus impulse is connected. And it is true, according to Dr Steiner elsewhere, everything that is brought down from the starry worlds (Uranos) for the culture of the Earth is to be regarded as a kind of *earthly body*, which then is ensouled through the Christ-Sun impulse. Expressed differently: Uranos, the starry heaven, becomes through Christ a higher Sun in the heart; 'One day the stars, down dripping/ Shall flow in golden wine'. And Dr Steiner also says in that lecture:

> Only through the fact that one can practise self-knowledge, is one able to enter those regions which then go beyond the region of Saturn, and consequently with it beyond our solar system into the cosmic life of the universe, from where souls have to bring what really effects earthly progress.

Between Saturn and Uranus lies, cosmically seen, the *threshold of the spiritual world*. Saturn is the great 'Guardian of the Threshold', this side of the threshold lies the earthly realm in space and time; on the other side is the heavenly realm beyond space and time. In order safely to enter the region of Uranus one has to cross the threshold, otherwise the effect of Uranus is catastrophic and brings disaster. One recalls how natural science in its own way brings down 'fire from heaven' (πῦρ ποιῇ ἐκ τοῦ οὐρανοῦ, Rev. 13:13; one of the most interesting of the numerous Johannine Uranus-passages). The Uranus-fire, brought down in such a way (q.v. radium, X-rays, electricity, and so on, easily lead into the sub-sensory realm, into the power of the two-horned beast, mentioned in this passage from the Apocalypse). First, Christ has to connect Uranus with the Sun within the heart. The Waterman—Leo (Uranus—Sun) constellation of the Wedding in Cana points towards this. Perhaps I was inspired to write all these Uranus-Contributions, because I myself have Uranus in the Lion, in the Sun-sign of the heart, where Dr Rittelmeyer also has it (he in the esoteric 8th house, I in the 10th, in the house of profession, close to the *medium coeli*.[60] That Uranus, with regard to our [solar] system 'has nothing to do', is only so far true as we do not possess the link to it through Christ. These planets have 'flown in' for nothing, unless they ultimately *do* intend something with us. The impulse of anthroposophy itself is thereby made possible, that Uranus and Neptune have united with the life of the Earth and are taken up by the influence of Christ. I express this insight initially confidentially to the priests, because I know that in certain groups today it could not be tolerated.

Let us now return again to the Uranos-myth. Time, division, death, evil, the whole estrangement of the earthly from the heavenly, of the human being from his homeland (see the story of the Prodigal Son) is prepared in Saturn, even if it first comes to manifest on the Earth in the manner of today.

But heaven does not neglect its own without comfort. Out of the starry semen of Uranos which had fallen into the earthly ocean, castrated by Kronos-Saturn, by *time*, Venus-Aphrodite rose, Venus-Urania, the one born out of the foam of the wave. The starry element of Uranos, which was lost for humanity through the deed of Kronos-Saturn has nevertheless come to Earth in Venus-Aphrodite, in love, which in its origin is divine. 'Yes, love indeed is light from heaven', as Byron ['The Giaour', l. 1131] says.

With this we already touch the wondrous Venus-mysteries, which are so closely linked with the Uranus-mystery. The Venus-Uranus question (or Venus-Mercury-Uranus question) is the actual esoteric [content] of astrology, in the same way as Venus in its true being (which today through the Fall is so deeply veiled) is the *esoteric [content] as such.* A mystery of divine love in general is connected with the mystery of the star that once fell out of the crown of the Lord of Light as he fell[61] and today shines as the heavenly Grail so comfortingly over everything earthly, of the star which through Christ has become sacred again (Rev. 22: 16: 'I am the root and offspring of David, the brightly shining Morning Star.')

Observe Venus purely in the sky and compare her to the other planets visible to the naked eye. We know the starry element only begins with Uranus; cosmically speaking the earthly element, the Earth, reaches up to Saturn. Consequently, all the known seven planets are actually not 'stars' (these, in the actual sense of the word, are only the fixed stars), but only 'Earth', siblings of the Earth. (With this I did not want—as one of the friends says—to suggest priority to the earthly planet, but only want to point to the mutual relationship of siblings of these various planetary fragments originating from the primordial planet Saturn.) So, there is actually no starry element in the planets. This is also confirmed, if one intimately observes the outward appearance. The obscure, leaden Saturn is certainly not 'starry', just as little is the obscure, red Mars. Jupiter, too, if one looks at it exactly, is rather more sun-like than in the actual sense 'starry'. But there is one exception; one of the planets we always felt in our heart as a proper 'star', the same one which the spirit of language experiences as such when one speaks of the 'Morning Star' and 'Evening Star'—our lovely star Venus. (You [my colleagues], may allow that I address in such a way the ruler of my horoscope with a certain natural respect.)

Some of the friends have in their horoscope the beautiful Venus-Uranus trigon [triangle] (it is also found with me), the one of which speaks of the Venus-Uranus relationships that are indicated in the Greek myth and possibly gives many things a certain inclination of destiny towards the content of this myth. But such a trigon should also not be over-evaluated; in reality one has first to work from the 'I' on its spiritual content. This is an important basic rule of the new astrology. Only if I myself have consciously, inwardly worked on such a trigon, even if it exists in my horoscope, only then do I truly own it. Venus, then, as I think, is the really starry one amongst the earthly planets. It nevertheless carries in itself something heavenly, something of Uranus, the representative of the starry world. So profound is the Greek Uranos-myth! Whoever begins really to lay hold of it will notice that it belongs to the most blessed, the most beautiful gifts of heaven that are given us for this earthly life. It then becomes revealed to us that all true astrology is a work and gift of Christ.

These are things which Rudolf Steiner describes and establishes in his Leipzig lecture-cycle *Christ and the Spiritual World* [GA 149]. There he shows how already in primordial pre-Christian times this influence of Christ through the being of the Nathan-Jesus—who was present then, tarrying in the spiritual world—how this being, watched over by Christ, an 'ensouled being' at that time on its cosmic circuit through all seven planets, 'en-Christ-ened' these planets. The planetary beings, known to us in Greek mythology as Jupiter-Zeus, Venus-Aphrodite and so on, as Rudolf Steiner shows in the Leipzig lecture-cycle, are based on Greek mythology. All of a sudden, we are aware of the wonderful depths of Greek mythology which are gloriously revealed in astrology and its practice. In astrology one sees really clearly how Mars, Venus, Jupiter, and so on, are not mythological inventions, and actually not astronomical objects that one observes through telescopes, but living beings who move in our midst, who are livingly revealed in every human being, in one a more Mars [mood], in another more Venus, in a third more Jupiter or Saturn, and so on, individually though also Uranus and Neptune.

From the Leipzig lecture-course, lecture 3, I cite a sentence:

> When the Greek looked up to his heaven of the gods, he perceived the shadings and mirror-images of the influences of Christ-Jesus on the individual planets and many other things, as I described earlier.

The wonderful Christ-significance of astrology illuminated for us out of the Leipzig lecture-course also throws light for us on how the true astrology is a gift of Christ for cosmic development, the actual heavenly Grail, over which certainly today Satan-Ahriman and Michael engage in struggle.

I still have many things to say on the Venus-Mercury question in connection with Uranus, that can be discussed in the next *Contribution*. To end with, after what has just been said about the Christened astrology, a few things concerning horoscopes. Rudolf Steiner speaks in the Leipzig lecture-cycle [GA 149] about the new astrology, the new Christened wisdom of the stars, as the heavenly Grail. He says much about Kepler, who said that he had taken away the sacred temple vessels from early Egypt.[62] Elsewhere (*Mysteries of the East and of Christianity* [Berlin, 3-7 Feb. 1913. GA 144]) he shows how in the Holy Grail the starry wisdom, the astrology of the early Egyptians came to life again. The third post-Atlantean epoch, the Egyptian-Chaldean age with its 'astrology' is repeated in our age today, in the fifth post-Atlantean epoch, now penetrated by the Christ-'I'-impulse (although, as Dr Steiner says, the early astrology was a deed of Christ, especially the Egyptian one). In the gospel itself, the lines of connection between Egypt and Christianity are indicated. The Leipzig lecture-course shows how Christ works as the inspirer of the starry harmony through the whole history of humanity. The musical element of the early Egyptian starry culture receives new life in the Christian-Johannine [stream], which likewise is throughout inspired by the cosmic musical element. The Johannine triangle in the zodiac (♓ ♋ ♏) is at the same time the sound-ether triangle. In my book on *John's Gospel*—also in my book on *Mark's Gospel*—I have pointed out in detail these points of view and their meaning for research on the gospels.

With the mention of the musical viewpoint for astrology, already mentioned in my first *Contribution*, I touch once more on something important for the horoscope, which came to me quite strongly recently during a lecture on [Mozart's] *The Magic Flute*. In the first of the Dornach 'red booklets', *Umwandlungsimpulse für die künstlerische Evolution der Menschheit*,[63] Rudolf Steiner strongly emphasizes the musical element of the astral body (p. 17): 'We ourselves are an instrument.' 'The cosmos with the help of the astral body plays our own being.' 'Humanity knows nothing concerning the [fact that the] human being is a musical instrument in relation to his/her astral body.' Rudolf Steiner also pointed towards [the disciple] John in this connection, and how he 'heard the music of the heavenly Jerusalem'. Indeed, the human astral body is the cosmic musical instrument. Through this fact, it becomes immediately clear, as through nothing else, what the horoscope is in reality. With cosmic exactitude it inscribes all the musical sounds of the planets, as they are arranged on this cosmic instrument, showing the condition of the instrument as, according to our karma, we bring it over from an earlier life into this earthly life. How, furthermore, we keep it tuned, or gradually learn to tune it better, and above all *how we play on it, how the 'I' plays on it* is our own concern. This depends on the 'I'. The 'I' is the player and the astral body, which is exactly delineated in the horoscope, is the instrument. (Of course, because the approximate knowledge of the hour of birth, and for other reasons, the horoscope calculation is seldom *totally* exact.) Only the instrument is written in the horoscope, not the player.

It became suddenly clear to me what *The Magic Flute* is. Especially when I remembered Doldinger's[64] *Vogel Gryff,*[65] at the well-known scene where the Männli presents to Hans the little whistle with the planetary notes, where all the seven planets are so beautifully characterized in their being by Doldinger. Such a cosmic musical instrument of such a high order becomes the astral body (the horoscope) in the hand of an awakened, self-conscious 'I'. With the unawakened human being of everyday conscious, it is often comparable to a wind-chime, which is moved in this or that way by each cosmic breath of wind (by each momentary starry constellation). Everything comes still more from without. With the spiritual human being this is different. Here the impulses come from within, out of freedom. There the 'I' is already at work. Then the astral body expressed in the horoscope is no longer a wind-chime; here we already have the flute, or the little whistle, which is played by competent player (by an awakened 'I'). *How* the 'I' plays is his concern. Papageno's little bells, which one simply 'allows to sound' do not require great art to be played, is something between, more similar to the wind chime than an actual musical instrument. With this, it is quite exactly explained what the horoscope is and how it stands towards freedom and the Christ-impulse. The whole richness of the Christ-impulse will one day still be necessary in order to evoke the musical sounds from the cosmic musical instrument of the horoscope; the Christ-impulse alone can evoke these musical sounds. In future it will increasingly depend on the *player*, not merely on the instrument. But anybody can only play *his/her* instrument. This is the true sense of the new, the Christened astrology. About this, more later. In the next *Contribution*, first more concerning Uranus, and the Venus-Mercury question.

# VI
# The Myth of Uranos and the
# Venus-Mercury-Mars Question

## A Christmas & Epiphany Contemplation

[*Tr. note*: Professor Beckh uses the word *Geheimwissenschaft* 'occult science', or 'esoteric science', which is both a subject and the title of the
main textbook by Rudolf Steiner on the subject (GA 13, 1910), particularly Chapter 4 on cosmic evolution, subsequently supplemented by
him in major lecture-courses. Later it is clear that the book is meant and
passages are even quoted, so the decision was mostly to use italics, as for
a book-title. In this *Contribution*, however, Beckh is also reading between
the lines on the basis of the lecture-courses.]

The Uranos-myth we are studying I want now to take as known in
what follows. In order to gain the right spiritual-scientific starting
point for moving on, let us look once more at the connection of the
individual planetary spheres with the [heavenly] hierarchies, as it was
first developed by Rudolf Steiner in the Düsseldorf lecture-cycle [GA
110]. We have:

(i)   in the *Moon-sphere*—this is neither the Moon disc visible in the
      sky, nor the globe of the Moon (the Moon-ellipsoid) of the astron-
      omers, but everything that weaves and works in an etheric and
      astral sense between the Earth and the Moon—the sphere of the
      *angels* (Angeloi).

(ii)  In the Venus-sphere, the 'occult Mercury' (about this old and often
      confusing exchange [of names], which also makes the reading of the
      Düsseldorf-cycle difficult to read in many places—further details in
      this Contribution) the *archangels* (Archangeloi). That is, the archan-
      gels belong to the astronomical Venus, to the occult Mercury.

(iii) To the astronomical Mercury, the occult Venus, belong the Archai
      (Primal Powers, Spirits of Time, Spirits of Personality).

(iv)  To the Sun, that is everything between the Earth and the Sun, to the
      'planetary element of the Sun', we could call it, belong the Spirits of
      Form (Exusiai), Powers. (That Sun-like [quality] in the higher sense

which belongs to the Sun as a fixed star are the Spirits of Wisdom, Kyriotetes.)

(v)   The Spirits of Movement (Dynamis), Forces, belong to Mars, which is also the border stone of 'Ancient Moon'.

(vi)  The Spirits of Wisdom (Kyriotetes), Rulers, belong to Jupiter (that means: everything which exists between Jupiter an Earth-Sun)—this is, then, a huge, extensive realm of rulership. We recall how Jupiter is the border stone of the 'Ancient Sun' in the sense of occult science and consequently understand the relationship of the mentioned hierarchy to the Sun-like quality.

(vii) In this sense the Thrones belong to Saturn. Out of the sacrifice of the Thrones to the Cherubim there arose on Ancient Saturn (for which the Saturn today is the boundary stone) in the primal-cosmic sacrificial fire, the Archai, who then lived through their 'human' stage (the human being himself was a humble elemental being).

It would be easy and obvious to write about, and schematically to present, the relationships: Uranus (Cherubim), Neptune (Seraphim)—but I never said this, and it would not correspond to occult science. Cherubim and Seraphim actually belong to the starry worlds (which in Uranus find their boundary stone towards the upper starry heaven, towards Uranos—to the fixed-star heaven in astronomical terms, to the 'crystal heaven', in occult, esoteric terms. In a certain sense these hierarchies appear to be only something like a *maya*-realm in the mentioned maya-planets (for this is what Uranus and Neptune are). With this occult science agrees with what is said of the relationship of Uranus to Ancient Sun and Neptune to Ancient Moon, whereby the following come into consideration:

According to *Occult/Esoteric Science*, during the development of [Ancient] Saturn, [Ancient] Sun and [Ancient] Moon, *all* the hierarchies are involved, nevertheless the main role in each of these developments is always given to a specific hierarchy.

(i)   The decisive thing in the first instance, according to the lecture-cycles (here the Berlin lecture-cycle 1911, *Inner Realities of Evolution* [GA 132]) on Ancient Saturn lies with the Thrones (the ones who made the sacrifice [of themselves]) and the Archai (who were the result of the sacrifice and then lived through their human stage; the Thrones themselves were at the stage of the 'Spirits of Form', were Spirits of Form on Ancient Saturn).

(ii)   On Ancient Sun the ones sacrificing—the ones 'bestowing gifts', as Rudolf Steiner says in this case—are the Spirits of Wisdom (Kyriotetes). Through their sacrifice arise the Archangels, which then again fly towards the Cherubim and live their human stage on Ancient Sun. The Cherubim no longer belong directly to the realm of forces of Ancient Sun (as they still belonged to the pre-historic, primordial Saturn), but work from without, overseeing the Spirits of Wisdom. This working-in from outside of the Cherubim on Ancient Sun at the same time does explain the working from without of Uranus on Ancient Sun, as it is presented by Dr Steiner himself in the Düsseldorf lecture-cycle. That is, with this there is a relationship of the Cherubim to Uranus, which does not exhaust the nature of this hierarchy. With the [Ancient] Sun-evolution, the main hierarchies are the Archangels, the Spirits of Wisdom (Spirits of Light), and Cherubim (Spirits of Harmony).

(iii)  With Ancient Moon, Moon-evolution, the Seraphim (Spirits of Movement), Dynameis, and the Angels (Angeloi), who live through their human stage on [Ancient] Moon. With the Seraphim working in from without, the working-in from outside of Neptune during the evolution of Ancient Moon (according to Dr Steiner) will somehow be connected. One connection of the Seraphim to Neptune would exist, as well as the Cherubim to Uranus, but which would not in the least exhaust the nature of these hierarchies. One also recalls what has been said earlier in the astrological sense on the relationship of Uranus to the Sun and Neptune to the Moon.

Now comes something very important. So far, we have only spoken about the heavenly hierarchies, but not of the Holy Trinity governing above and in them. This, of course, is the pinnacle of the heavenly ladder, that which ultimately is at work in the realm of the stars. How is God Himself, how is the divine Trinity involved in the becoming of Saturn-Sun-Moon-Earth? In Ancient Saturn, the *Father* is revealed above and in the Thrones (Dr Steiner has also spoken about this), and on Ancient Sun above and in the Cherubim the *Son* (as the highest Christ-aspect, besides which still others exist; on the Sun itself the archangel-aspect of the Christ-being, as well as the aspect of the Sun-spirit of the Christ-being. All three main hierarchies on Ancient Sun contain a revelation of Christ). On the Ancient Moon there is revealed above in the Cherubim, the Spirits of Movement and the Angels, the Holy Spirit (if one prefers, the feminine, maternal quality in the world). For, 'Father, Son and Holy Spirit' is only the exoteric aspect of the Trinity, the esoteric is 'Father, Mother, Son', that is, Archetypal Masculine, Archetypal Feminine and a Third that is neither male nor female but both together—the Hermaphrodite. This relationship of the Holy Spirit to the Moon is something deeply significant. It is already expressed in language, for *manas* 'Spirit-self' always relates to the element of the Moon (as *buddhi* 'Life-spirit' does to the Primordial Sun and *atman* 'Spirit-man' to the Primordial Saturn), [Skr.] *man* 'to think' is connected to *mr̠* 'to measure' (*mās* 'moon', the one that measures the phases of time) and with the word for Moon itself (Lat. *mensis* = month, and the Germ. '*Mond*' [Moon] etc.). The connection of spirit (*manas*)-Moon-man [human being] is already given in the primal languages, also the connection of the Moon with the feminine and water (the etheric primal waters, 'the waters of birth'). (On Ancient Moon, the human being comes into being in the Uranus-sign of the Waterman.) One may also think here of the picture of the Madonna in the Christmas mood and its artistic presentation connected to the moon-sickle. All this allows us to look into the depths of occult science and reveals a Mystery of the Holy spirit, which in a special sense is a Moon-mystery.

If with all this we recall how on Ancient Saturn the primordial bases of the physical body, on the Ancient Sun those of etheric body, and on Ancient Moon of the astral body were laid, then we have:

for Ancient Saturn the series: Father—Thrones—Archai—human being = physical body.

for Ancient Sun: Son—Cherubim—Spirits of Wisdom—Archangels—human being = ether-body

for Ancient Moon: Holy Spirit—Seraphim—Spirits of Movement—Angels—human being = astral body.

In the primordial Earth evolution, the highest hierarchies have withdrawn even more; there the main event lies directly between the Spirits of Form (Exusiai, Elohim) and the human being, who through the beings mentioned enters here his 'I'-stage. Instead of this the Spirits of Form (Elohim) are here as it were overshadowed by the whole divine Trinity (Father, Son, and Spirit). This reveals deep Mysteries of the biblical story of creation and for the development of the Earth. We would have the sequence:

Divine Trinity—Spirits of Form (Elohim)—human being = 'I'.

This means, in the 'I' the hierarchy 'human being' is completed (which in its further development, as we know, for the time being suffered misfortune). It belongs to the development of the 'hierarchy human being' that it (or rather the Earth) at a certain stage is left free, that Earth and man are left alone (*cum grano salis*, with a pinch of salt, for somehow everything is always connected with the divine). Only human 'I'-development demands a certain stepping-back of the hierarchies. Consequently, the connection of the human being with the realm of the stars of the hierarchies, which comes about, or is retained through Michael through the birth-horoscope at the moment of birth, is something astonishing and deeply important.

Now, in order to understand everything astrological, it is important to follow exactly with the help of *Esoteric/ Occult Science*, how with the development of the Earth, the development of the planetary system takes place, which in its primordial beginning first takes place on 'Ancient Moon' (only the Saturn-Sun division really occurs on 'Ancient Sun', in the same way as the beginnings of Uranus go back to Ancient Sun). What then during the Ancient Moon evolution comes about as the planetary system goes firstly once more into *pralaya*, into cosmic dissolution, in order then slowly to develop to its present condition in the 'Earth evolution' (firstly in the third decisive round, then in the fourth, the present round). This means, with Earth-evolution, it concerns not only the often mentioned 'separation of the Sun' and 'separation of the Moon', but, with these two separations, the separation of the other planets also takes place (the expressions need not appear strange to us, for 'outer science' imagines similar things in the 'primal nebula' theory of Kant-Laplace, only more mechanically dead and un-ensouled, a primal nebula, out of which through rotation slowly the small nebular globes are separated which later condense.) This is similar to the experiment, so often mentioned and criticized by Dr Steiner, of the drop of oil, which only succeeds when the teacher is standing alongside and activates the revolutions. This means that such theories of nebulae are nonsense unless at the same time one keeps in mind the spiritual powers that spiritually move the whole thing, the hierarchies as the actual, real beings of the starry worlds. Consequently, with the explanation of *Esoteric/ Occult Science* of the birth of worlds and of the planets nothing exaggerated or strange to the world is demanded. The material elements are already given through natural scientific experiments; occult science merely adds the spirit.[66]

Here it is also important in studying *Esoteric/ Occult Science* how still *before* the separation of the Sun, that is, before the separation of the Sun and the Earth (which then still contained the Moon and the other planets), there followed the split of the Saturn of today from the Sun close in time to the Sun-Earth separation itself then the separation of Jupiter (beings who do not remain on the Sun but also do not continue with the Earth form the Jupiter-colony). Somewhat more towards the separation of the Moon (if I rightly understand, somewhat before it) the separation of Mars occurs. Thus, after the separation of Saturn, Jupiter, Mars (of the 'outer' planets, distant from the Sun, as we recall), we have now facing the Earth the Sun and the Moon, whereby the Sun still initially contains Venus and Mercury. Dr Steiner describes all this in such a way that the outer cosmic planetary [realm] exactly meets with the inner processes of the beings involved in this whole develop-ment; the important connection between inner world and outer world clearly appears for all spiritual observation, for all anthroposophy.

\*\*\*

This whole broad introduction was necessary in order to say what I intended for this Christmas Contribution. We have reached the point where towards the outside we have the outer, farther planets, Mars, Jupiter and Saturn (Uranus and Neptune remain at first unmentioned). This is as it were the *head* of the system. From Steiner's agriculture lec-ture-course[67] we know, for example, how these planets (Saturn, Jupiter and Mars) also govern the head, that is, the roots of the plants. In the heart of the system we have Sun, Moon and Earth, and, what is import-ant, Venus and Mercury still connected with the Sun. These inner plan-ets, as we know from the agriculture-course and other indications, are connected with the digestion, the flowery, blossoming nature of the plant. (This in the first place involves Venus.) The actual 'heart' is the Sun, which we have so far regarded as a planet (Spirits of Form), but can also be regarded as a fixed star (Spirits of Wisdom and the Cheru-bim); then the Sun in a certain way belongs to Uranos (that is, not for the geocentric Earth-consciousness, but for the consciousness of a[n order of] being, the Seraphim, who, like modern astronomy, overviews *many* fixed stars and planets—only astronomers do it mathematically and the Seraphim spiritually.

The relationship of the Sun to Uranos is eminently important, espe-cially for the spiritual [viewpoint], for all Christian astrology (one may always bear in mind, how especially according to Dr Steiner, Uranus is connected to Ancient Sun). Here the point is now reached where we have to recall the primordial Saturn and beyond it Uranos. For what follows, the Uranos myth now becomes important. (Those who do not have it in their head—it should be their hearts—can look it up on p. 53 [*Contribution* No. 5]. See also pp. 60 & 81f. of my book on *John's Gospel*.)

The castration of Uranos through his successor Kronos-Saturn in the sense of the Uranos-myth, coincides with that which in the sense of *Occult Science* is the coming into being of time of Ancient Saturn. (It is important for all that follows, to regard occult science, or anthroposophy, together with the myth of Uranos.) Ancient Saturn, like all developments, has seven main stages: only during the middle one does *time* come about, and indeed as *beings*, in the Spirits of Time, the Archai, which are the result of the sacrifice of the Thrones to the Cherubim and which lead their existence in the cosmic warmth (warmth-ether, primordial fire), as the sacrificial fire of this great cosmic sacrifice. The primordial Saturn (the three first stages of which) is not yet temporal; it is still beyond time in the eternal, in 'duration'. Here—and this is already clearly derived from the lecture-cycles yet can be read between the lines of *Esoteric/ Occult Science*—the primordial Saturn and Uranos are still connected. Only with the becoming of time on Saturn does the separation occur, the event to which the Greek Uranos myth points.

Here I have to add something short concerning the zodiac, which later should be discussed in more detail. Dr Steiner in the Düsseldorf lecture-cycle places:

- the Earth's primordial beginnings in Taurus,
- the primordial beginnings of the [Ancient] Moon in Aquarius,
- those of the [Ancient] Sun in the Eagle (Scorpion), and
- primordial Saturn in the Lion.

This means the cosmic heart begins to beat on [Ancient] Saturn in the Lion and there also ceases to beat. The life of the [Ancient] Sun begins in the Eagle and receives in the Scorpion the sting of death (more on this, see my book on *John's Gospel*, p. 173ff.). The relationship of Saturn to the Lion has probably to do with the becoming of time on [Ancient] Saturn, the evolving of the Archai (Spirits of Time), which are the 'human beings' on [Ancient] Saturn. The heartbeat of the world and through it time—time is the heartbeat of the world (see my article 'The Riddle of Time')[68]—begins in the Lion, which is indeed the sign of the heart.

But that which precedes time, primordial Saturn, Uranos, the actual point of the 'eternal Father' in the universe, as the first starting-point beyond time of all cosmic evolution—this is the Uranus-sign of the

*Waterman* (on this, see Frieling's explanation of the first sentence of the Creed: 'An Almighty Divine-Being, spiritual-physical', etc, see below, p. 360f.). As we are with Waterman-Uranos, and the Lion is indeed its counter-sign, here Saturn, *with its fall into time* (which is the primordial prototype of the earthly Fall of man) falls into the opposition, which is the Lion. *Waterman-Lion* is the primordial axis of cosmic events, it is the important constellation in which the Christ-Earth-future Mysteries, the Uranus-Sun Mysteries, are shown us in the Marriage in Cana (see my book on *John's Gospel*, p. 199). The Uranus-sign of the Waterman is a point of departure in cosmic evolution, not first on Ancient Moon, but already in primordial Saturn. The Waterman is the actual primordial sign and esoteric centre of the whole zodiac.

On Uranos, before [Ancient] Saturn, the divine Trinity governed above the Cherubim and Seraphim;

in [Ancient] Saturn the Father was revealed above the Thrones. This part of development then, via the Spirits of Wisdom (Ancient Sun) and the Spirits of Movement (Ancient Moon) passed further to the Earth (Spirits of Form), whereby on Ancient Sun once again the Cherubim (connected to Uranus) were revealed, and on Ancient Moon the Seraphim (connected to Neptune). Over the primal beginning of the Earth itself once again the Trinity [govern]. *A Trinitarian primordial revelation of Uranos is repeated once again on the Earth and in the planetary [cosmic evolution] of the Earthly.* Here *Esoteric/ Occult Science* tells us once again the Uranos myth in such a grandiose manner. In what way?

We recall the esoteric aspect of the Trinity, which is as easy and humanly understandable as the exoteric theological explanation—an eternal crux—is difficult to understand. I mean the esoteric aspect: Father, Mother and Son. The Father as the primordial, creative, masculine element of Will. The Mother (the 'Holy Spirit'), as the cosmic-virginal, primordial lap, the Feminine element. And the Son, is not simply masculine but Masculine-Feminine, Hermaphrodite, the spiritual human being [Adam-Kadmon of Cabbalistic tradition—*Tr. note*] of the primordial beginning (Gen. 1:27), the creative result of the Elohim, the 'Son of the Godhead'. This Trinitarian primordial aspect, which exists beyond the temporal, earthly [situation], beyond the threshold of Saturn, lies with Uranos in eternity. It is revealed in the temporal earthly [situation] of planet Earth [itself] *on this side of the threshold of Saturn*, in what we have latterly found with the planetary development, in the Trinity *Sun, Moon, Venus-Mercury.*

After they separated from the Sun—after the separation of the Earth—Venus and Mercury were united for a period. This original unity of Mercury and Venus is a cosmogonic primal fact of the highest importance. In this and in no way only in intention to make the matter difficult and confusing, lies the cause of various exchanges and confusion of Mercury and Venus in occult descriptions. Already the usual symbols ♀ and ☿ express their mutual relationship. (This original unity of Venus and Mercury initially within and then outside the Sun is, of course, not more difficult to imagine than all the other things in planetary development. There is precisely only the one primal solar system, which gradually becomes ever more differentiated, dividing into individual spheres. Naturally, the planets in their present condition today cannot split apart, but the split must have taken place in a primordial time, when everything was much more in the supersensory, etheric condition.)

Consequently, the triune primordial Trinity, Father, Mother, Son (Hermaphrodite) is now presented, as it were beyond the threshold of Saturn in Uranus,[69] and on this side of the threshold of Saturn in the planetary trinity Sun, Moon and Venus-Mercury (or, Mercury-Venus). But Mercury-Venus is 'hermaphrodite', for Mercury = Hermes, Venus = (is like) Aphrodite, Mercury-Venus = Hermes-Aphrodite, the Hermaphrodite.

This is, as already said, a primordial fact of humanity of the most important kind. Only in passing I want to insert here that these astrological matters also have drawbacks in alchymy (on this I am working much at the moment; a book [Eng. tr. *Alchymy: The Mystery of the Material World*] will shortly appear in the new year). Here the hermaphrodite was always called the 'philosophers' stone—stone of the wise' of which it was said the Sun is its father and the Moon its mother. (Cf. the old baptism-verse, which I have given in a German translation in *Ursprung im Lichte*, Note 16, p. 75;[70] which admittedly only few have read, yet is nevertheless interesting with all the connections to our baptism liturgy, water, salt and ash, and so on.) In alchymy, too, with the Trinitarian aspect of Sun (Father), Moon (Mother), Venus-Mercury (the Son, the 'Hermaphrodite'), we stand on a central point of cosmic Mystery.

The Trinitarian aspect, which here I always call the esoteric one, the picture of *Father, Mother, and Son*, contains in itself simply the primordial fact of divine love. As eternal love it was and is present beyond space and time, beyond the threshold of Saturn, in Uranos. The event of cosmic evolution takes place, which in occult science is called the becoming of time during Saturn—Saturn splits from the super-Saturnian realm. In the Greek myth this is the violation or castration of Uranos by Kronos-Saturn (Gk. *chronos*, 'time'), the separation of the eternal divine realm from the temporal earthly realm, the separation of Heaven and Earth, of Uranos and Saturn (who contained in himself Sun, Moon, Earth and the lower planets). The human being is pulled down from his Uranian, starry, archetypal homeland where he had his true, starry origin, into the dark temporal, earthly realm. Here he commences his long, long path of incarnations through the progression of the aeons of [Ancient] Saturn, [Ancient] Sun, [Ancient] Moon and the Earth. The 'Son of the godhead' in the sense of Genesis 1:27 has now become the 'lost, prodigal son' [Luke 15].

But here too eternal love, the love of the Father, of Uranos, does not leave the 'lost son' alone, the human being, at the great separation, during his great Fall into the earthly realm, during the long, dark, painful wandering through the realms of time. He does not leave him without heavenly comfort. Consequently, he gives him as the gift of light and a gift from the stars, a spark of the Uranean heavenly fire, *love*, into the earthly realm—out of the starry semen of Uranos that had fallen into the cosmic ocean, Venus-Aphrodite emerges, born of the foam of the waves, the 'star of the sea', Venus-Urania. The divine primordial Mystery of love is hidden in the myth of Uranos.

The divine Mystery of the love of the Son is again present in the Hermaphrodite, in Venus-Mercury. And the Greek myth, when you look exactly behind it, shows this unity of Venus-Mercury when you come in particular to the alchymical depths of the picture. For we have here Venus, born of the sea, rising from the waves (one recalls the beautiful painting of the goddess Venus Anadyomene [from the Gk. 'rising from the sea'] in the seashell by Botticelli [in the Uffizi Gallery, Florence, Italy]), and the sea—Rudolf Steiner once spoke about it—in occultism is the cosmic drop of Mercury, the cosmic drop of quicksilver (we can also think of the trinity of water, salt and ash in our baptism service that corresponds to the alchymical trinity of Mercury, Salt and Sulphur). This alchymical trinity lies in the Uranos myth, for the Mercury drops of the sea carry in themselves the bitterness of salt (from here the connection of Lat. *mare*, '*Meer*' ['sea']; *amarus* 'bitter'; '*Maris*', '*Meerstern*' ['Star of the sea'] and the Heb. names Mariam and Miriam), and Venus-Aphrodite herself is the bearer of everything to do with the starry, floral, blossoming in the earthly element; her actual element is this blossom, the flower chalice, the sulphuric element. (*'Alle Asche ist Blütenstaub, der Kelch ist der Himmel'*—'All ash is pollen [literally, 'flower-dust'], the [flower-]chalice is heaven' [Novalis]—this we have discussed in an earlier *Contribution* [No. 3], concerning the question of Uranos and funeral urns.) The symbol for Venus is ♀, for the sulphur signum we have:

♁

In the fairytale told by Klingsor (in Novalis' *Heinrich von Ofterdingen*) the being referred to here is called with its Teutonic name Freia and portrayed enthroned on a *sulphur* crystal. So, in actual fact the trinity Mercury—Salt—Sulphur is contained pictorially in the Greek myth of Uranos in the picture of Aphrodite born of the sea.

However, it is not alchymy we want to discuss, but astrology—yet it is a fact that astrology and alchymy are intimately united; they mutually depend on each other. First of all the unity of Venus and Mercury is important, as it is expressed in the myth, which, translated back into astrology, is in fact the two planets. As we said, an important primordial fact of humanity is expressed in this union. It corresponds to the condition of humanity before the Fall of man, when he was still male-female (Gen. 1:27), the 'herm-aphrodite' (Hermes-Mercury, Aphrodite-Venus). This union of Venus and Mercury is the cosmic counterpart to the hermaphrodite condition of the human being in the Hyperborean age (the second of the great earthly periods; followed by the Lemurian and the Atlantean age, then the post-Atlantean age in which we are at present). The decisive separation of Venus and Mercury would have taken place in the early Lemurian, or the end of the Hyperborean age. And this event is connected to another, with the Fall of Lucifer (preceded by the story of the Temptation [Gen. 3]). On Ancient Sun, Lucifer was still amongst the progressing hierarchies, the brother of Christ. On Ancient Moon the Fall of Lucifer took place. These events, however, have somehow to be reflected within Earth-evolution. In union with the Sun and in union with Mercury, Venus at one time originally revealed the divine element, whereas the Venus-Mercury separation is somehow connected with the decisive later event. Venus did not remain as the star of Lucifer, which it originally was, but it is the heavenly precious stone, the heavenly Grail, which in the Fall [of Lucifer] fell out of the crown of the Lord of Light. Every earthly longing—Rudolf Steiner spoke of this in his lecture-cycle *Wonders of the World*... [GA 129]—is connected with the longing of Lucifer for his lost star.

There comes an important fact concerning the zodiac. We have to regard the sign of the Virgin as that region governed by Venus-Mercury. Venus sinks towards the Earth, which at the same time is a sinking towards Mars. Then she is placed by the progressing beings between Mercury (in the Virgin) and Mars (in the Scorpion) in the Scales, in the zodiac sign of the Scales, whose spiritual origin itself is connected with the cosmic situation of the Fall of man. *Sometimes* at least (this is certainly only *one* viewpoint, for from other viewpoints the unity of twelve is something fundamental) the matter is so presented that there were originally only ten zodiacal signs; the Archer directly followed after the Virgin. The deadly arrow of the Archer—this would be the reflection of the human Fall—wounds the Virgin. Thus, the sign Scorpion first came about ($\nearrow$ Archer + ♍ Virgin = ♏ Scorpion)—which, according to another way of reading, was earlier the Eagle. One can understand these things purely astronomically, when one is clear how these three zodiac pictures really interpenetrate. For example, the sting of the Scorpion extends into the Archer, again one of the stars of the Scales is within the Scorpion; one can really regard the whole area of the heavens as a great constellation, and also the customary signs $\nearrow$ Archer, ♏ Scorpion and ♍ Virgin express the original relationship. So that the deadly sting of the Scorpion does not continue to wound the Virgin, to attack the still existing Virgin-region (here one recalls the story of the 'Tree of Life' [Gen. 3]), the Scales were placed between Scorpion and Virgin. (Here one is not to imagine merely astronomical happenings, but the cosmic reflection of earthly-human events into the heavenly script.)

There comes, moreover, to this zodiacal fact of the splitting up of the Scorpion, Scales and Virgin, the above-mentioned planetary fact of the split of Venus and Mercury, whereby Mercury remained in the Virgin, Venus was placed in the Scales where she is protected from Mars. Everything sexual, as we said earlier, has nothing to do with Venus. Particular daemonic and aggressive sexual inclinations belong to Mars, whereas the higher rhythmical, and in a certain sense feminine aspect of sexuality belongs to the Moon. Venus in her actual nature is the austere, maidenly planet, having initially nothing to do with sexuality (even in physiology her sphere is not sexual—that is the Moon here—but another). Only in human beings is she entangled in sexuality, that is, in the region of Mars.

A well-known passage in Homer [*Odyssey*, Book 8, 265-366] expresses this entanglement that has entered human nature through the Fall of man. On this point there appears on the scene in particular the impossible, suppressing, dark nature of all popular astrology.

One can simply no longer properly distinguish Venus and Mars; one carries darkness into the matter through the manner *how* one introduces the things. Basically, with Venus one reaches the point where one can no longer present the matter in words. For Venus, love, is the esoteric element pure and simple; to her Mystery one only has esoteric access, found through earnest inner work. This work consists in releasing the original virginal being of Venus out of her entanglement in Mars within human nature, to that point again where she stands before us in the Uranos myth as the one born out of the sea, out of the ether. For this reason, one can basically never reduce astrology, and likewise alchymy, to a mere academic knowledge. Only through Intuition[71] are both understood, and everything that one writes or publishes can only make sense in stimulating inner work gradually to give rise to Intuition, which is what it is about.

The beautiful Uranos myth remains closed to people, though it actually contains the key to all cosmic riddles; only through meditative inner work and Intuition are we gradually able to open up its profundities. Thus altogether one does not want to imagine true astrology as some kind of sensational reading that is brought home.

Consequently, we have first inwardly to strive again for that Venus which in the Uranos myth stands before us in the original nature united with Mercury in order really to understand the Uranos myth. We have to release Venus out of the Mars entanglement, in order to lead her back to her maidenly union with Mercury. That is what is meant here by 'esoteric path'.

If we look now once again at the Uranos myth, which contains the Uranos Mystery and the Isis-Venus Mystery, they can become at the same time a doorway to the Mysteries of Christ. How significant the waves of the sea are in the Uranos-Venus myth, is fully told us in the gospel story of the storm on the Lake with Christ walking on the water (Mark 6, John 6). This event we always place with the sacrament of marriage, and, what is significant for our fifth post-Atlantean cultural epoch of today (that is, this picture waited in a quite particular sense to be understood by people *today*). This picture from the gospel stands in the gospel rhythm in the *Scales*. And the Scales is the sign of Venus, one of the two regions governed by Venus where she is the releasing love that leads back to the heavenly source, Venus-Urania. The planetary aspect of Venus-Urania supplements the zodiac sign of the Scales (see the two chapters on the planets in my book *John's Gospel*).

We feel how all this leads us back directly to the Uranos myth, or supplements it from the Christian side, to the door opening from this comprehensive picture to the Christian Mystery. In my books on the gospel I have always pointed to the connection of the Scales, waves and billowing (*Waage, Woge, wogen*). The sign of the Scales is really the picture of Venus born of the sea, as in the gospel it always is that sign belonging to the 'I-am' of Christ (Mark 6 and John 6, 'I-AM, fear not'). I cannot now demonstrate this here in detail; I have to point to the two books that contain the detailed demonstration [not to forget Beckh's illustrations and comments in the later *The Language of Tonality* and the linguistic details in *The Mystery of Musical Creativity: Man and Music*, as well as *The Source of Speech—Tr. addition*].

In the Scales, where Venus is revealed as Venus-Urania, heavenly resolving love, we have also the connection with the picture of the sea of the Uranos myth. Only through this will the full depths of the name Venus-Urania be revealed. Now we know what the spark of the star and the star-semen of Uranos is and how it lights up in the I-AM of Christ. All connections of Isis-Venus and Mary, the 'Star of the sea', appear thereby all at once in the soul. The whole esotericism of Mary in the Middle Ages (*Ave maris stella* [Hail, Star of the Sea...]) sounds in harmony here and reveals its wonderful depths. Everything becomes deeper and more significant when we recall how Venus-Mercury, the Hermaphrodite, is indeed originally 'the Son' (☉ Father, ☽ Mother, ☿ Son). Dr Steiner invariably related David of the Old Testament to the Mercury Mysteries and brought the Psalms as the revelation of Mercury. The expression 'Root of David' would then have a hidden meaning in the light of the Venus-Mercury Mystery—apart from the immediately following historical meaning. And what depths are contained for us in the parting words of Christ in the Book of Revelation of the New Testament, of the whole Bible, where the Risen Christ Himself links His I-AM with the essence of the star of heavenly love shining over the Scales [Rev. 22:16]: 'I am the root and offspring of David, the bright Morning Star' (☿).

# VII
# The Seven Planets, especially Saturn, Jupiter and Mars, in the Light of *Occult Science*—and touching on the little book on Saturn and the *Wolkendurchleuchter* ['He who illumines the clouds'] by Dr Friedrich Doldinger

### *Present-day situation*

Already in the previous *Contribution*, I indicated how the cosmogony of *Occult Science*, and what was said there concerning the separation of [Ancient] Saturn—Sun—Moon—Earth, also about the separation of all the remaining planets during the course of earthly development, can lead us, pointing out our path, in order also to understand what astrology has to say of the spiritual beings of the planets in the light of cosmic facts. Many things that the astrology of today says in its way about these things—I think now particularly of the really somewhat dim astrological literature (the English counterpart has a somewhat higher niveau)—is not in the actual sense of the word 'wrong', but rather through the way it is put incredibly depressing and obscure. It is a sin against the spirit—out of which everything astrological should alone be understood.

Thus, one reads, for example, in one of the now popular and not even uninteresting astrological calendars, on one of the first pages on general information, about the beings of the planets:

Sun = head of the country, rulership, power, existence;
Moon = the people, femininity, the nature of the sea, democracy; ...
Jupiter = calm, peace, success, law, religion, prophecy, wealth, banks;
Venus = enjoyment, feasts, the arts, theatre, feminine youth.

I wonder why the writer of the calendar with Venus did not add 'flower shops, flower shop-assistants'. This he could have done with a certain appearance of doing the right thing. Venus indeed is the star-power and consequently the flowery part in human life—and hence also 'female youth' as 'bloom of humanity's spring'. I mean, one could undoubtedly really establish some kind of characteristic Venus-influence in the horoscope of a flower-shop assistant who is working not by chance, but as a representative of her profession.

All these things are not 'wrong', they are just impossible through the whole way they are expressed here and there. And everything in this realm depends on the *how*. Through a certain way matters today are brought to humanity, they are simply profaned—apart also from the really wrong or 'half-correct', and consequently only really misleading, mixing in with what in a certain sense is correct. Astrology, which should always be felt as something sacred, as a Christ-opportunity, becomes something profane, dragging the soul down into dark abysses. There is a great difference whether, for example, as in the previous *Contribution* one seeks to understand the cosmic backgrounds, the connections of the Sun and of Uranus, whether one points, as happened here, to the earnestness of the Venus-Mercury question and of the Venus-Mars question in the light of the cosmic fact of the 'Fall of man'—or whether one expresses quite peripheral things, without regard to the centre, that in their manner they agree with everything of the lower human nature caught in the Fall of man (♂ in ♏). Everything to do with Venus, as I already mentioned, forms here a critical point in popular astrology; Venus is confounded with Mars, she is exchanged for that which she has become through entanglement with Mars.

How the matter rests with the Sun, Jupiter, and so on, we shall soon try to establish. One only feels quite clearly with regard to that calendar: it's no good like *this*, the things can't be expressed like *this*, certainly not before the spiritual bases have been laid, upon which in the end those things can be understood that in some horoscope or other as purely personal relationships of life are to be taken one way or another. I believe, precisely with this example, I have clearly shown what it actually means to create a new 'Christianized astrology', and wherein lies the task of this new astrology. It can only comprise that one really consults the spiritual, cosmogonic backgrounds of *Occult Science*, really seeking to link the astrological facts to this cosmic background. I am now increasingly aware of the significance of a saying of Dr Steiner in the Leipzig lecture-course *Christ and the Spiritual World* [GA 149]—I have already said, he regarded it is as the basis for a new, Christened astrology. It contains a whole programme for this astrology. The lecture-course he held in the first instance for a gentleman,[72] who in the end failed to fulfil the task in the way Dr Steiner proposed—as is usual, or at least as it frequently transpired. As a participant during those beautiful Christmas days of the Leipzig lecture-cycle 1913/14, I number this as one of the most beautiful, unforgettable experiences of my life. When I asked him what one has to study in order to engage in this realm, Dr Steiner replied emphatically, 'Only theosophy.' At that time he said 'theosophy', not 'anthroposophy', although the Anthroposophical Society had already been founded for almost a year (I add this simply to be quite correct in reporting the facts). So, 'only theosophy', or as we would say today, 'only anthroposophy'. I have always kept to this advice.

When I wrote my book on *Mark's Gospel*, and as it was being printed, I knew *nothing* of popular astrology. Only somewhat later was I placed by destiny and quite without my doing before the 'existence of astrology'. This was through someone,[73] who meanwhile has joined the group of co-workers for the journal *Die Christengemeinschaft* with a fine article on Kepler.[74] I was led through the most difficult karmic shocks and crises—it was precisely shortly before the death of my sister, whose destiny I had to learn likewise to understand out of the starry script. For me the things were not 'anthroposophical', presented on the background of spiritual science. In the face of these new and confusing, indeed shocking facts, I had to find my way alone, out of my 'I'. For half a year I wrestled intensely for an inner equilibrium. It is obvious that in such cases this equilibrium can only be found through anthroposophy. Consequently, my path was given. Only it was not a very easy path, on which even Frl. Vreede's astrological *Newsletters*[75] were not decisively helpful. I recognize and did recognize, of course, the many positive and valuable things contained in these *Newsletters*. Particularly from the viewpoint of astrology I discovered that, besides the positive and valuable things contained in these *Newsletters*, 'many other things are also facts' that are not written in those *Newsletters*. And I had especially to deal with this serious realm of facts, for me shocking, until finally in *Occult Science* and in Rudolf Steiner's lecture-cycles, in the first instance the Leipzig cycle (to whose programme Frl. Vreede, as she told me, had paid very little attention), I did find the decisive connecting points. Consequently, many things from astrology have entered into my book on *John's Gospel* coming from anthroposophy.

Already in the Introduction, for many people the difficult question concerning 'sign and constellation' was clearly explained (about which I shall have to write here, too), that problem about which in anthroposophy so much hopeless lack of clarity exists (Frl. Vreede also expressed to me her agreement). Indeed, it was cleared up in full agreement with Rudolf Steiner's lecture-cycles, especially with one important place in the Leipzig-cycle, the importance of which had hitherto hardly been noticed, also not by that astrologer who was present at the Leipzig lecture-cycle.

This personal insert may possibly more closely justify the task taken up in this *Newsletter*, also from its 'karmic' side, and it shows my intention here to attempt to connect astrology with anthroposophy, with the cosmogony of *Occult Science*.

## *The Concept 'Evil-Doer'*

Something particularly characteristic for the 'old', normal astrology in general, is the manner certain planets are spoken of as '*Übeltäter— evil-doers*'. You find it even in the most modern astrological calendars. What is usually meant with this phrase is the two planets to do with critical destinies, Saturn and Mars, including (I found this in the above-mentioned calendar) our good friend Uranus, about which I hope that I have succeeded to awaken in my readers another picture, where (check the earlier *Contributions*) I have not been silent about the factual situation. Concerning this, I could imagine that it has led the one or another astrologer to make this qualification.

After writing much on Venus and Neptune, let us remain with the 'seven planets', in so far as 'evil-doer' comes into question for certain stars of destiny, with Saturn and Mars. If we are serious about searching for a 'Christened' astrology, we feel immediately that the designation 'evil-doer' has to be a straightforward impossibility, that we simply forbid such an expression. Not as though we did not know or did not recall that all the planetary beings in the cosmos are connected to the fact that somehow beings have remained behind the primordial divine Being, not able to keep up with the advancing development. In these Contributions I myself have developed how the proximity of Venus to the Earth (which when it is closer to the Earth leads to an observable glorious revelation) is connected with the fall of Lucifer, as it comes out of the earlier connection with Mercury into proximity to the Earth—and with this into the proximity of Mars. Not as if Venus simply would be the 'star of Lucifer', as is sometimes said. It is precisely the star *lost* by Lucifer during his fall. And we have heard, too, how Venus, especially Venus in the Scales—the Scales is the sign of the Christ-I-AM—as Venus-Urania has become again the Christ-star;

Christ takes up the essence of this star and leads it again into the divine. The Book of Revelation, and therewith the Bible itself, ends with the words where the Risen Christ unites His I-AM again with the essence of this star [Rev. 22:16]. And as He raises Venus again into the divine, so likewise the essence of all the other planets.

Here one especially recalls our *Earth*. What is the Mystery of Golgotha other than that the divine, that Christ takes up the ruined earthly star of the cosmos—having become estranged from its actual starry essence—into the whole divine starry context again, so that the Earth, seen from the cosmos, can be seen again as a star shining amongst other stars? That Christ so takes up the Earth into the divine starry context, is only the final conclusion. It is preceded by other events—so beautifully developed by Dr Steiner in the Leipzig lecture-course [GA 149, lecture 3, 30 Dec. 1913]. The being of the Nathan-Jesus at that time tarrying in the higher worlds, Christ took again right through all the other planets to the Divine. As will be described in more detail, the being who later became the Nathan-Jesus, the cosmic Christmas-child, overseen by Christ, entered its cosmic circuit through the individual planetary spheres. Thereby it gathered again these planetary spheres themselves into the Divine, also rectifying several things in human nature corresponding to them. Dr Steiner emphasized how the significant things of Greek mythology—in actual fact built upon these planetary beings—rest on their connection to this planetary deed of Christ. (Only out of astrology is one convinced of the eminent significance of this Greek mythology of the gods, without which no really practical psychology is possible. One does not arrive at human psychology with some kind of abstract notions, but only with a feeling for the real beings Mars, Jupiter, Venus, and so on, just as they are revealed in the human being.)

## *The Primordial Fall*

The fact that, cosmically regarded, in all the planets a Fall, or at least a 'regression of beings' is revealed, should not obscure our vision for the divine element in the planets—revealed precisely through and in Christ—in all starry connections in general. It gives us no right to speak of the individual planets, like Saturn and Mars, as 'evil-doers'—for this phrase would apply to *all* the planets. But from the beginning there can be no talk like this. And precisely with Saturn and Mars, with the destiny-star of both these planets, which in a certain sense are also 'planets of death', we shall very strongly recognize the influence of the advanced divine powers. Here too, where one speaks of planetary beings—and this applies to all the planets—of 'fallen' or 'retarded' beings, this never applies to the whole complex of beings of a planet. It always applies only to certain beings who in their development play a role. It is precisely always those who, as expressed in *Occult Science*, live through their 'human stage' on that planet, or in that planetary condition. On Ancient Saturn it was the Archai, on Ancient Sun the Archangels, on Ancient Moon the Angels. One sees *the 'being human' is always something critical, associated with crisis, bound to the danger of falling.* Not only is the human being today injured,[76] has 'slipped down', but other beings preceded him in this 'plunge' during earlier planetary incarnations and pulled him along in their Fall. And yet all this is only a splendid cosmic drama, from one point of view or another ultimately also God-willed. Out of the plunge the intention is to draw a still higher, more free ascent. The world as a whole is still divine, even if it is important to see how in this grandiose cosmic drama certain roles are bequeathed even to the adversary of the divine. Such references help us better to understand everything astrological than certain all-too-human and sentimental categories of notions, such as 'evil-doer' used for some planets like Saturn and Mars, in their influences admittedly indeed sometimes uncomfortable.

And if all the beings who on a planetary incarnation already go through their 'human stage' thereby go through a certain 'crisis', when they are the 'questionable' beings of the respective planet (as we human beings are today the 'questionable' earthly inhabitant, at the 'critical' stage, who always have something 'not quite in order'), then we should not overlook that with each of these planetary spheres and stages also very high divine beings are connected. With Saturn not only are the questionable Archai connected (who pass through their human, critical stage there), but also the sublime Thrones; with Ancient Sun the Spirits of Wisdom, who then also belong to Jupiter, which in the planetary system is now the boundary stone of Ancient Sun. The Spirits of Movement belong to Mars as the boundary stone of Ancient Moon; to Venus the Archangels (now truly in the sense of the advancing divine beings); to the Moon belong the Angels. This means divine beings are spread out everywhere before us in the planetary spheres, and if we look uninhibitedly into the starry realms, the unerring element, that 'all this is revelation of the divine', then we cannot speak of single planets, appearing to us astrologically uncomfortable and personally not suiting us, as 'evil-doers'. We would have to feel this as a sin against the divine and sacred [powers].

Not in order somehow to justify that designation which rightly goes against the grain, but only to understand what is meant by it, we would like to look now somewhat closer at the planetary beings of Saturn and Mars. If all the planetary existences are originally based on some kind of falling away of certain beings, what do we actually experience on [Ancient] Saturn—especially if we draw the lines of communication from today's Saturn, for this is essential with an astrology based on an anthroposophical cosmogony? Nothing other than the primordial falling away, the primordial separation of the anti-divine—that later becomes material substance—from the divinity as the spiritual element. In the face of this primordial cosmic fact it is not necessary immediately to crucify oneself, but rather seek to understand how it is the necessary absolute starting point for all cosmic becoming and cosmic events, as it is the divine primordial love that is revealed in this sublime cosmic sacrifice.

The whole Ancient Saturn, as Dr Steiner elaborates in *Occult Science*, is reflected being. In the primordial cosmic sacrifice, the divine Beings have rejected the anti-divine beings, the negative element of the primordial divine-positive element. Later this negative element becomes matter. This now mirrors back the divine life. In this 'mirrored existence'—which only on Ancient Sun progresses to a living existence—all creation is originally revealed. Now, the mirror, mirror-existence, the mirror revelation has always something strange, uncomfortable about it (cf. *Spiegelmensch* by [Franz] Werfel[77]). And from this one can understand how everything *Saturnian* contains this uncomfortable element, this uncanny mirroring. (In *Spiegelmensch*, one experiences something of the 'Guardian of the Threshold', and Saturn, as we have already touched on, is the cosmic 'Guardian of the Threshold'.)

Not without reason and deep meaning, our friend and *Lenker* Friedrich Doldinger has drawn on the cover of his new book, *Alter, Krankheit, Trennung, Tod*[78] ['Old age, sickness, separation, death'] an image of Saturn. For all these life-situations, enumerated in the Buddhist 'truths of suffering', are connected to the material element, to the entering of the spirit into material existence. But this takes place on Ancient Saturn, on primordial Saturn, of which the Saturn of today is the planetary mirror. Of course, all earthly suffering, or everything that we initially feel as suffering in our earthly life, derives from that great cosmic, primal separation that took place on Ancient Saturn. For the first time the great [polar] contrast of eternity and time, of spirit and matter, was manifested. This, of course, is extremely serious and critical, and yet necessary for many things in which later the divine Love could again be revealed.

## The Myth of Uranos and Saturn

We stand once more before the Greek myth of Uranos that in another connection has been extensively discussed, how the 'birth of time' of Saturn, the origin of time on Ancient Saturn, in the sense of *Occult Science*, is connected to what in the Greek myth is called the violation, the castration of Uranos through Saturn-Kronos (*chronos* in Gk. means 'time'). Of course, age and death are conditioned by time, illness as well is caused by material existence in time, including separation and all kinds of earthly suffering and care. All this already belongs, as we now see, to Saturn, and consequently some people called him the 'miscreant'. But one can immediately feel—only read Doldinger's little book—how with regard to Christ this is not acceptable. Christ teaches us to look otherwise on old age, sickness, death and suffering, differently from Buddha. Opening Doldinger's book, I find on page 37 the beautiful passage from Dr Steiner:

> And the deeply veiled, yet incredibly revealing Saturn-Mysteries, these Mysteries which ... as it were hide the deepest things of the cosmos, the Saturn-Mysteries, are revealed if one looks back to that which occurs between the age of 56 to 63.[79]

Certainly, Saturn—as we saw earlier—carries in itself the earthly element, the forces of earthly heaviness, of lead. The forces of lead emanate from it (astrologically-alchemically, lead belongs to Saturn as gold belongs to the Sun). We can well understand how everything connected to the element of Earth and the heaviness of the Earth is initially experienced as the element of suffering in the earthly realm. Yet this is precisely only *one* side. Seen from this one side, Saturn is the cosmic representative of the earthly [realm] and the suffering connected to it. With this one side it beholds the Earth and itself is cosmic Earth. *But with the other side it beholds the heavens, beholds Uranos*, from which in the primordial beginning it separated itself, before whose boundary realm and threshold it now stands in the cosmos as the 'Guardian of the Threshold'. Saturn—we have frequently seen and said—is the cosmic 'Guardian of the Threshold', the cosmic reflection of all the mirror-experiences and threshold-experiences that the human being on the esoteric path experiences in soul and spirit. Saturn, as Rudolf Steiner discusses elsewhere, is the Preserver of the cosmic primordial memories. In Saturn the primordial world-events begin, here it is spiritually preserved as a great cosmic primordial memory. In [Rudolf Steiner's] verse, 'The Ephesian Mysteries', recalling New Testament language (Rev. 5:12), with [Gk.] *plutos* 'riches' is meant the 'riches of cosmic primordial memories' as the planetary virtue of Saturn. This belongs to Saturn as other 'virtues' or qualities belong to the other planets. (The 'Ephesian Mysteries verse' is also important for understanding the Johannine Revelation, for John's Gospel was inspired in the region of the Mystery centre of Ephesus.)

As the 'Guardian of the Threshold' Saturn governs and reveals the most sublime cosmic Mysteries, since it not only draws us down into the earthly element, bringing us earthly suffering, sickness, separation and death (one recalls 'Saturn's scythe'), but he, Saturn, is there when we pass him as the 'Guardian of the Threshold', also the one who *opens for us the heavenly door to Uranus*, helps us find the further ways to Uranus and into the heavenly realm of the stars (Uranos).[80] This is the other side of Saturn. For this reason, it is not only unchristian, but at the same time arch-trivial and Philistine to speak of him simply as the 'evil-doer'. For he is the Ruler and Guardian of the highest spiritual revelations and Guide into the spiritual supersensory realm. Amongst the 'seven moods of world-conceptions' (Steiner's lecture-cycle *Human and Cosmic Thought* [GA 151, 4 lectures, Berlin 20-23 Jan. 1914]) Gnosis belongs to Saturn.

For the person standing on the everyday viewpoint this side of the threshold, in the un-spiritual, earthly element, Saturn may in particular be the bringer of earthly suffering, of sickness and death, the 'evil-doer' in this sense. For human beings who have developed the spiritual viewpoint, it is completely different. For them Saturn has for a long time no longer been the 'evil-doer', but all things being equal (of course, it always depends on the influencing rays) the strongest, most effective Promoter. Even unfavourable influences from Saturn can be transformed by spiritually-minded people into a real source of strength, as Rudolf Steiner describes. Indeed, one can say, for the spiritual person Saturn is more or less generally the most important of all the planets—as Uranus, for a time still lying today in the future, will be the most important planet of the spiritually-minded. The influence and importance of a planet are not the same at all times. This, too, changes in the course of development, with the change of the 'I'-consciousness. In earlier ages one saw Jupiter as the strongest and most effective of the planets. Today he is still mighty, but perceptibly receding. For spiritually striving people, Saturn already today is more decisive than Jupiter. In no way is Saturn only the 'evil-doer' but can become the Benefactor in the highest sense of all. Today, one can also say, humanity as a whole has arrived at the 'Guardian of the Threshold', which cosmically is *Saturn*.

Saturn has two 'houses', or main spheres of influence, in the zodiac (concerning which I shall soon have to speak in more detail. See p. 287f). These are the signs Goat and Waterman. At the time of writing we stand in the Goat, or rather the Sun stands, until 21 January (I mean the sign Goat, not the constellation [in the sky]), then it moves into the Waterman. There Uranus is co-ruler with Saturn, whereas in the Goat it is alone 'at home' by itself. Consequently, the Goat is the earthly, dark Saturn sign, and Waterman the Uranian tinged, brighter sign, more easy of the earthly element. Saturn in the Waterman counts as especially favourable in astrology (in the sense indicated). Amongst the organs of the human body Saturn corresponds to the spleen,[81] amongst the metals the heavy lead (which is easily understandable from what we have said about the earthly element and 'earthly weight', or 'gravity'). In Mark's Gospel we experience the appearance of John the Baptist, the 'Elijah-John being', in the two Saturn-signs Goat and Waterman (to the latter belongs the 'baptism by water' and meeting the etheric Uranian element that takes place in it).

On Ancient Saturn, when in the separation of Uranus *time* is born, the Archai—they come into being as the result of the cosmic sacrifice of the Thrones to the Cherubim—experience their *human stage*. At the same time they are the bearers of the Saturn element of warmth, the fire of cosmic sacrifice and the warmth of cosmic offering. As always and everywhere, as the beings who experience the critical *human stage*, they are the questionable beings on Saturn, amongst whose ranks we also find the fallen beings, the representatives of the Saturnian primordial evil. The Archai, who as Spirits of Time are at the same time 'Spirits of Personality', are also called Asuras. There exist 'black and white' Asuras.[82] The black ones, the embodiment of evil on Saturn, oppose the gods as the 'personal' element. Dr Steiner spoke little and only as indications concerning the evil Asuras. They stand above the Ahrimanic beings (who originate on 'Ancient Sun', and the Luciferic beings on 'Ancient Moon'). Between Ahriman and Lucifer, Christ holds the balance. We human beings in earthly life are everywhere placed between the opposite forces of Ahriman and Lucifer, having to reckon with them on a practical level. The Asurian evil is different; it does not place itself alongside Christ but excludes Him. Here it is not 'Christ between...' but 'Christ *or*...'

It has been suggested that *Saturn* is connected with *Satan*, or 'Satan' with Saturn (I cannot now demonstrate the linguistic correctness, but I find it almost believable). This should not be misunderstood, that one immediately torments oneself and takes everything Saturnian as it if were Satanic—this is already sufficiently refuted through Dr Steiner's words, quoted above—nevertheless, the Satanic element has something to do with Saturn and originates there. (Moreover, the coming about of the primordial evil, the primordial Fall of spiritual beings, lies in the cosmic plan of divine Love). Now the word Satan—I have to say something again about the linguistic use—also in anthroposophy, is frequently taken as meaning the same as Ahriman. (This would be the evil of Ancient Sun, not the Saturnian evil being. Moreover, in the story of the Temptation in the gospels the word *Satanas* stands, according to Dr Steiner, in the sense of Ahriman (*Diabolos* for Lucifer). I myself would rather speak here only of 'Ahriman', and reserve the word 'Satan' for the Saturnian evil being, the Asurian evil being. (One finds samples of this 'Asurian evil being' in the final pictures of Doldinger's *Wolkendurchleuchter*.[83] Soradt[84] appears to me to be not only an Ahrimanic, but a being touching the Asurian [rank], who in an Asurian-Saturnian manner projects into 'Ancient Sun'.)

Now I briefly note what that writer of the calendar believes he has to say concerning Saturn:

> Saturn = catastrophe, cares, suffering, crimes, need, misery, poverty, illness and destruction, retardation, hindrances, resistances, misfortune ('evil-doer')',

only to give a sample of 'un-christianised astrology' and to show how impossible such statements are, which are held much too vaguely and generally, even if they are not actually 'wrong'. In looking to the spiritual-cosmogonic primal foundations, things change their names: that which appears to the non-spiritual person, still far from the threshold, as something that (seemingly) brings suffering (for in reality this 'suffering' is also a furthering and testing sent by the good gods); for the spiritual teacher, the one who comes close to the threshold, it will become an advancement, a blessing, a good fortune, an inner enrichment. Compare the words of Benedictus to Capesius in Rudolf Steiner's mystery-drama *The Soul's Probation* [GA 14], Sc. 1:

*Gewöhnet euch, zu wandeln mancher Worte Sinn,*
*Wenn wir uns ganz verstehen sollen.*
*Und wundert euch dann nicht,*
*Wenn euer Schmerz in meiner Sprache*
*Den Namen ändern muß*

*Ich finde euch im Glücke.*

Prepare to change the sense of many words,
that we can fully understand each other,
and do not marvel
if in my way of speaking
your suffering must change its name.

I find you in good fortune.[85]

Such a planet of good fortune can Saturn become for the spiritual seeker. It can open for him the gate to Uranus; it can reveal to him cosmic Mysteries. The terminology 'evil-doer' collapses here. There are no 'evil-doers' as such in the heavens. In the human being alone is hidden, as the consequence of the Fall, the evil-doer (or: the two evil-doers on the cross, Ahriman and Lucifer). Through them the human being has estranged himself from his starry being and from his starry origins. And yet—as we read in the now newly published Michael letters, Rudolf Steiner's *Michael Mystery* [GA 26]—especially through the good, progressive beings (that is, through Michael) the connection of the human being with the starry worlds of his origin, *at least in the moment of birth* is nevertheless retained. *This* (already touched on several times) *is the Mystery of the birth-horoscope.*

But from here we can also understand how this connection with the starry worlds—yet still brought about in such a manner—of the (actually already) star-alienated human nature has to carry within itself something double-edged. The god-alienated human nature in many respects has to be shown as 'suffering', that which in its truth precisely is the purity of the divine being, until the human being on the path of spiritual knowledge has passed through the trials and purifications of this path to make himself receptive for the purity of the divine being. The eschatology of the Avesta (the 'Bible of Zarathustra') relates how in the hour of judgment the spiritual ether-stream, with which every soul comes into contact, will be for the one a higher life-element, a 'refreshing stream of milk', [but] for the other a consuming fire (see my little-discovered book *Zarathustra*,[86] p. 105).

It is the 'pure ethereal spheres, which alone can bear the guiltless on the glancing waves of spirit ...' We increasingly recognize how behind this superficial, trivial terminology 'evil-doer' stand earnest threshold questions.

The decisive thing to understand the Saturn-nature revealed itself to us out of the cosmogony of occult science by looking into the primordial cosmic separation which took place on Ancient Saturn, the separation of eternity and time, Heaven and Earth, spirit and matter. We could name this separation anthroposophically exactly as the Saturn-Uranus-separation. We know that it took place not at the beginning of Saturn-evolution, but only in its middle (in the fourth of the 'seven cycles') in the evolution of Saturn, at that moment which also the Greek Uranos myth captured in its own manner. This is not yet a 'planetary separation'; it still lies in the super-planetary realm. Basically Uranus does not lie in the planetary, but in the super-planetary realm. Only as a kind of planetary *maya* does it stand today amongst the 'planets'. Later we shall return to it; here, however, let us turn our attention to the 'seven planets', starting from Saturn.

### The Seven Planets: (i) Saturn

Saturn itself, which in the 'Ancient Saturn' evolution is still all in all, the whole planetary, or solar system, appears as a separate planetary being first on 'Ancient Sun'. This brings the progress from the mirror-like, dead mineral, dead mechanical, corpse-like existence of Ancient Saturn (not in vain is Saturn in astrology a 'dead planet') towards the etheric, living, as it were cosmic plant-like existence (the human being itself appears here as a kind of primordial plant). The heavenly being (Uranos) that already radiated into Saturn, but could only awaken there a mirrored life, has now brought forth real life. Not from primordial Saturn, but from its divine surroundings, from Uranos, comes this primal life. This 'Ancient Sun' likewise still contains in itself all the elements of Saturn, but later expels it as something that goes against the etheric, living element (*Occult Science,* 1925 edition, p. 143).[87] This means, beings remaining on the Saturn stage now create for themselves a place to live corresponding to their nature on Ancient Saturn.

If I am right—through my illness during the Christmas Conference I lost touch a little with the latest literature and beg for possible correction—this 'expelled Saturn' surrounds Ancient Sun as a kind of Saturn-ring (see Doldinger's little book). This separation is repeated on Ancient Moon, and once more (actually three more times) during the earthly evolution (in its second, third and fourth cycles), the final result of this [repeated] separation is the Saturn of today. (I have already pointed out how in looking at the Kant-Laplace nebular theory, which one only has to lift from mechanical into the spiritual thought, as a contemporary person one can well imagine this creation of the planets.)

The separation of Saturn, the existence of Saturn as a special planetary being, already belongs to 'Ancient Sun' (whereas the Saturn-Uranus separation goes back to Ancient Saturn); on Ancient Sun we saw that Uranus joins the system from outside.

On Ancient Moon, when the separation of Saturn was repeated, something new was added, initially the important separation of Sun and Moon (after the separation of Saturn), but apart from this—as Dr Steiner in *Occult Science* expressly states—still further planetary separations. The actual genesis of the planetary system, he says elsewhere, originates on 'Ancient Moon'. And at that time (even if in another form than today, more in the etheric, supersensory realm—beyond Saturn) its Jupiter and Mars came into being, but, for reasons still to be discussed, not yet Mercury and Venus that can only belong to [the later, fourth stage,] 'Earth-evolution'.

This 'Earth-evolution' will mainly interest us when we keep in mind the cosmic origin of the planets and want to evaluate their astrological nature. When reading *Occult Science*, it always depends on our discovering how a planetary, cosmic drama is at the same time always the outer picture expressing in soul and spirit an inner drama of mankind, retrospectively experienced within. To understand this interpenetrating drama of mankind and the cosmic drama, is what the study of *Occult Science* entails.

In Earth-evolution, then, we have initially again the separation of Saturn, and are clear about what separates off in this planet Saturn. That is, the elements of the primordial material, of earthly weight/

gravity, the dead mineral nature that produces the pressure of matter and of sickness in earthly life. And yet without this separation of Saturn a normal becoming of the Earth would never have taken place. Then, of course, there followed—after long pauses—the separation of the Sun and the Earth, first in the 'third cycle', then in the 'Hyperborean age' of the 'fourth cycle', in which we today still stand (I mean the 'fourth cycle' and not the 'Hyperborean age', long expired in prehistoric times). With the Sun the Christ-being also withdrew out of the general substance and remained with the Sun, in order from there to radiate living forces to the Earth from without (one thinks of the process with plants which also receive sunlight from without).

## *(ii) Jupiter*

Now we have, apart from this separation of Sun and Earth, and in connection with it, still the important *separation of Jupiter*. I will allow Dr Steiner's words[88] to describe the event:

> There were souls who found no place on Earth already at the time when the Sun separated from the Earth. They were removed to another planet to develop further. Under the guidance of cosmic beings, this planet detached itself from the general mass of the cosmos that was still united with the Earth at the beginning of its physical evolution. (The Sun had already disconnected itself.) This planet is the one whose physical expression is known to outer science as Jupiter. (The names of celestial bodies and planets are used there in exactly the same sense that a more ancient science spoke of them. The intended meaning becomes clear from the context. Just as the physical Earth is only the physical expression of an organism of spirit and soul, this is also the case with every other celestial body. And just as observers of the supersensible do not use the name 'Earth' to mean merely the physical planet or the name 'Sun' to mean merely the physical fixed star, they also have broad spiritual contexts in mind when they speak of 'Jupiter', 'Mars', and so on. Of course, the shapes and functions of the celestial bodies have changed since the times described here. In a certain respect, even their locations in space have changed. We can only recognize the connection between our present-day planets and their ancestors if we are able to trace their evolution back into the far-distant past by means of supersensible cognition.)

We immediately understand—returning now straight away to astrology—how this Jupiter-being has to be basically totally different from the Saturn-being, because in contrast to the dead mineral nature of Saturn, it carries in it the living etheric of the Sun. I have already pointed out from the earthly view, Saturn has something obscure and lead-like, Jupiter on the other hand something of the 'Sun nature' (actually they are both not 'star-like', as I mentioned earlier; amongst the planets only Venus is 'star-like'). As we saw, a gigantic chasm lies in the separation of Saturn (eternity and time, spirit and matter, Heaven and Earth). With the separation of Jupiter there is no such chasm at all. The actual chasm lies between Sun and Earth, only so that certain beings, who in no way pass over to the Earth, who nevertheless neither wish to nor can remain directly in the life of the Sun, pass over to Jupiter. Jupiter, as we saw, is the boundary stone of Ancient Sun and also thereby somewhat related to the life of the Sun (astronomers, too, establish that Jupiter emits a certain amount of light of its own,[89] and is thus like the Sun). And we know that also a very elevated hierarchy is connected to this Jupiter-sphere (like that of Ancient Sun), the Spirits of Wisdom, revealed in all the wisdom-filled life of plants, the etheric life in general in all the wise lawfulness of nature. These 'Spirits of Wisdom', the bearers of the actual qualities of the Sun, are also termed Kyriotetes, 'Dominions', Lat. *dominationes*. We can immediately understand how in astrology Jupiter is the bearer of everything full of wisdom, exerting a dominating, lording influence. It has to do with that might and lordship a human being can thereby exercise over others, because he incorporates wisdom-filled benevolence. He knows, carries and feels this 'law' that is also livingly present in everything. The primordial wisdom of the Sun becomes in Jupiter earthly, as it were exoteric, but it remains wisdom. Mercury has to do with everything intellectual, of the understanding, whereas Jupiter has 'wisdom' as its virtue.

### (iii) Mars

There is still much to say about Jupiter, but we shall forego this. After what was said about Saturn, we have now especially to interest ourselves with the other 'evil-doer', *Mars* (I have already delivered a criticism of the ghastly expression '*Übeltäter*, evil-doer', above). We could understand the critical aspect of Saturn directly out of the cosmology of *Occult Science*, likewise the wisdom-filled, benevolent, lordly aspects of Jupiter—astrology calls him, like Venus and the Sun, 'benefactor'— thus once again the critical aspect of Mars. We have seen how and when the separation of Saturn, how and when the separation of Jupiter took place, how with Saturn a contrast to the Sun-being governs, and with Jupiter the opposite situation, something of the Sun-nature. How is the situation in this respect with Mars? How, where and when did the separation of Mars take place?

*Occult Science* again answers us (p. 203).[90] The separation of Jupiter lies near to the separation of the Sun and the Earth; the separation of Mars near the separation of the Earth and the Moon. This can be understood as follows: the Earth, branching away from the Sun, enters into its planetary sundered situation, still bearing in itself its hardening Moon-forces. After the Sun had distanced itself with its enlivening elements, Earth-evolution, Dr Steiner shows, would have been hardened and become wooden, had not now the other, polar opposite, hardening, mineralizing Moon-element also moved away. Now the tremendously important cosmic moment—the trinity 'Sun, Moon and Earth' came about. The Earth kept a balance between Sun and Moon. Here, however, it is interesting to see how this Earth-Moon separation cannot take place without at the same time—or somehow near in time, inasmuch as one can speak of proximity in time with these immense cosmic processes—as also with the Sun, a parallel situation takes place, the separation of Mars. Like the Sun, thus we see this separation of Mars still has something Moon-like in it, striving into the material element, in a certain way an Ahrimanic element, which departs with 'Mars'. And we feel, furthermore, how this Mars relates to the Moon (to the Earth-Moon), as is confirmed by astrology. And we know from *Occult Science*, or the Düsseldorf lecture-cycle,[91] how Mars is the boundary stone of 'Ancient Moon'—as Jupiter is of 'Ancient Sun' and Saturn of 'Ancient Saturn'.

Out of all these facts it is clear that in Mars we do not find the Sun-like amity of Jupiter, but much rather once again the contrast to the Sun, that is the critical, adverse forces related to the earthly element and related to matter. And if we do not allow the questionable manner of expression, do not join in its use, yet we can understand how Mars is reckoned by the astrologers once again amongst the 'evil-doers'. Like Saturn, it is also a planet of death (nevertheless without thereby exhaustively summarizing the being of both [planets]), taking indeed into consideration how Mars is apparently related to the Latin *mors* (= death).

The 'Spirits of Wisdom' (Dominions) belong to Jupiter, in the same way as the 'Spirits of Movement', which also play a decisive role on 'Ancient Moon' (they are also called Dynameis, Virtutes, 'World-Powers') belong to Mars (see the Christmas liturgy [Inserted Prayer]). Of these Spirits of Movement, we know how they also govern and conduct the movement of the blood. We recall how iron, the metal iron, belongs to Mars (like the trace that has been left in the Earth of the planetary being Mars, from the one-time connection with the Sun, for Mars did not immediately separate from the Earth). We also recall how iron in the blood plays a known role, how it is an important constituent in the blood and also gives blood its red colour, which in observing the heavens we can also see again in Mars, [the red planet]. If we regard these connections and with it the 'Spirits of Movement' as the spirits of the movement of the blood, we feel we are not looking at an adverse being, but at something sublime, divine (the chemist may recall how iron works as a de-poisoner, taking away cyanide, taking away from cyanide most of its terrible poisonous effect, for ferro-cyanide is almost non-poisonous). And we sense a sublime connection between the Mystery of the blood on Golgotha and the Mystery of Mars.

Indeed, the Mystery of Golgotha would not have been effective without the power of Mars—which in Christianity in general plays a decisive role—and the daemonic powers of Mars, too, are thereby not without importance (cf. the Scorpion-chapter, 'Judas, Peter and Pilate', in my book on *Mark's Gospel*, p. 359ff.).[92] This 'daemonic side of Mars' belongs to the *Scorpion*, as one of the two governing realms, 'houses', of Mars. This is its so-called 'night house', because the Scorpion belongs to the element of water and the sound-ether, that is, the feminine, and for this reason in the sense of astrology the 'nocturnal' element. Its other, its 'day house' is the Ram, which is a 'fire sign', that is, it belongs to the 'masculine' warmth-ether. (Concerning the important 'four triangles' in the zodiac, also touched on in a decisive manner by Frieling, I shall shortly be discussing this in detail, meanwhile, please peruse my book on *John's Gospel*. Concerning the 'houses of the planets', and the thoroughly natural, logical manner one can establish them, I have written in one of the previous *Contributions* [No. 2, above].)

Mars simply belongs tremendously strongly to the earthly forces, as the cosmogonic facts of *Occult Science* show. Mars in the Ram is nothing other than earthly influence, a strong entry into earthly activity. In the Ram, Mars unfolds its good, active forces (without this force of Mars there would be no earthly activity, no earthly results), whereas in the Scorpion more its daemonic, passionate side is expressed. Here is revealed the 'contesting of the elements', in which Mars, fiery by nature, stands in the water-sign of the Scorpion (whereas the likewise fiery Ram lies very well with it). How far Mars in the Scorpion has to do with the 'Fall of man', I have already discussed earlier in discussing the Venus-Mercury question.

Venus, originally in her union with Mercury, at home in the Virgin, approaches the Earth in the Fall of Lucifer and therewith comes also into the vicinity of Mars; between Mercury in the Virgin and Mars in the Scorpion she is placed by the good gods in the *Scales* and governs as the heavenly-redeeming Venus-Urania. And so, with *Mars in the Scorpion* the zodiac without doubt has a certain 'critical corner' in which critical facts of human evolution are cosmically reflected.

But, moreover, with the Mars-being and the Mars-activity there is nothing merely daemonic in it. In what we have termed the 'daemonic side of Mars' (Mars in the Scorpion) something, too, is included by the good gods in a wise world-plan. All revelation of Venus, of love, is first made possible. Only thereby is the revelation of Venus, love of individual to individual, possible in the workings of the world, which earlier had produced the division of individualities (as far as separation through hostility!). And the power that effected this division of individualities is precisely Mars. We think here of the saying of Heraclitus, that Strife is 'the father of everything'. An important side of Mars' being is indicated here (our Lörrach friend Ernst Moll[93] shed an interesting light on this not long ago). This is not to be understood as if Mars were *only* war and militarism. Certainly, all military action has to do with Mars, but the field of activity of Mars is very much wider than the military realm. For example, an especially favourable and strong Mars, indeed as one assumes, the most favourable of all Mars positions is Mars in the Goat. Here, however, he is completely un-militarist; here he becomes purely spiritually militant, as the spiritual Mars. Here he can with greatest determination engage for the realization of spiritual aims. Here he can be the spiritual worker, altogether a first-class helper and fosterer of those who want to establish spiritual [principles] also in the earthly realm, a 'benefactor' in the most eminent sense.

Concerning Mars in Scorpion (this, again, is the 'daemonic Mars'), I have earlier already said how sexuality belongs to his realm (in no way belonging to Venus, who is only love). In particular male sexuality and aggressive sexuality belong here, that is, the daemonic side of this realm, whereas the higher, more divine side of this realm, the higher rhythm, the feminine side of sexuality, one can also say, belongs to the Moon.

## *(iv) Venus and Mercury*

There are, of course, many other things to say concerning Mars, and Jupiter, too, which will be pursued here with further opportunity. First of all, I have here to round off the fundamental survey of the planetary beings in the cosmogony of *Occult Science*. And so, apart from Sun and Moon, who present a central Mystery, there are some things to say concerning Venus and Mercury, about which I have spoken in another connection. We recall how the first separation of Saturn is traced back to Ancient Sun. It is later repeated a few times. Most of the other planetary separations appear first on Ancient Moon, in order then to be repeated during the Earth-evolution (of which the Ancient Moon, and so on, are an earlier incarnation). Apart from the Sun and Moon separations, this involves only Saturn, Jupiter and Mars (the present outer planets, far distant from the Sun), not yet the inner planets, closer to the Sun, Mercury and Venus. They indeed also separate from the Earth and the Moon, but not on Ancient Moon, but first during Earth-evolution.

So, the closer, astrological planets Venus, Mercury and the [present] Moon—we know that the Moon astronomically is not a planet, but it is astrologically—appear as independent entities only during Earth-evolution. Of these three planets, the Moon originates out of the Earth, it carries in itself the earthly element, the opposite of the Sun (on the other hand, it is a wonderful 'Sun reflector'), indeed, its element is much more hardened than the Earth itself; it is 'over-dense'.[94] It is otherwise with the planets Mercury and Venus, who right into Earth-evolution remain united with the Sun (until, as I suppose, the Hyperborean age). Venus and Mercury—this is a very significant cosmic fact—are the planets united with the Sun the longest, and they remained united with the Sun precisely during the time the anti-Sun-like Saturn had long ago taken itself off, but when Mars, who likewise bears in itself a counter-element, and likewise the Earth itself (plus the Moon), had already left the Sun.

There was, then, a period during cosmic evolution, when the Sun, so to speak, was most itself, was most purely Sun. She[95] no longer had anything Saturn-like, Earth-like, Moon-like, and Mars-like. Even the mighty Jupiter stood apart from her, where in herself she is through and through the most loving, purest, most amicable Sun-being. At that period, she still had within her the two planetary beings Mercury and Venus. And we know from earlier considerations these two planets still at the separation were mutually united ('Hermaphrodite'), how later they separated, and in what manner the earlier union and the later separation stands with regard to the destiny of mankind.

Already through simply presenting these cosmogonic facts Venus and Mercury are actually already characterized in a far-reaching manner in their individual astrological being. There also comes into consideration the following. The Sun, as we saw, stands not only as the central star in our planetary context, but she carries in herself the fixed-star, Uranian realm; she belongs by standing in the fixed-star context of the cosmos to Uranos, for he is the fixed-star heaven, whereby Uranus is but the planetary representative of Uranos. For us Earth-dwellers the fixed-star Sun is 'the Sun'; for the consciousness of a Seraphic being who overviews the many fixed stars, the many solar systems, it is only *a* sun. (Astronomers of today, we already said earlier, see as matter, what the Seraphic beings overview spiritually.)

Now let us think now what all this means for Venus and Mercury. The Sun at that time had expelled the Saturn-element, the Earth-element, the Mars-element striving against the Uranian influence. This was when she had still contained Mercury and Venus, still purest Uranian being. Then she still contained everything starry in herself. This she then expels in Venus and Mercury (we feel how later also the transition of the Christ-being from the Sun to the Earth is connected with this). Now we may understand afresh, that means altogether from the facts of the Greek myth of Uranos, whereby Venus-Aphrodite brings the starry semen of Uranos into earthly development. Does the fact not wonderfully fit, how, also for the outer view, she is the most starry planet, amongst the planets the only really starry one?

And what about Mercury, was he not still with her and still today stands close to her astronomically? With Mercury, as we know, it is because of his nearness to the Sun (the closest planet to the Sun) that one can equally glimpse him with the naked eye or not at all. He is occasionally to be seen by a sharp eye when he stands relatively far from the Sun. Like Uranus and Neptune, he belongs to the occult planets, also spiritually in a certain sense; Uranus and Neptune are occult through their distance from the Sun, Mercury through his exceeding proximity to the Sun. Mercury, as it were, has not yet freed himself out of the Sun's rays, lives still in the radiant being of the Sun (in astrology an especially close conjunction of the Sun and Mercury as it appears in birth-horoscopes is not infrequently called, a 'burnt Mercury'). Because of this nearness to the Sun, Mercury has not quite achieved a visible revelation.

*Venus* on the other hand has developed this visible revelation all the more. She is on the one hand larger and more important, and then also through her cosmic destinies frequently mentioned, has come into a greater proximity to the Earth. In her there comes to the fullest and most radiant revelation of what we called above the Uranian element of her one-time Sun-being. Venus is the visible revelation of δόξα (doxa, 'glory') of this Uranian starry element in the solar system. Consequently, in Rudolf Steiner's Ephesian Mystery verse and Rev. 5:12, δόξα is the planetary revelation of Venus. In Venus is revealed in the planetary realm the Uranian starry splendour, δόξα of the Sun.

# VIII
# The Seven Planets, especially Venus, Mercury and Mars

## *The Glory of Light*

*Doxa*[96] is always translated by Luther as '*Herrlichkeit*' [Eng. 'glory, splendour']. This is not, as is maintained here and there, 'wrong'. Much rather, Dr Steiner explains in a passage in a lecture-cycle,[97] how the self-revealing streams of sunlight in which the Archangels on Ancient Sun float towards the Cherubim equally bear sunlight out into the widths of space. In ancient esotericism this is called 'glory of light'. Consequently, it is this 'glory of light', the Sun-like 'revelation of the light', and this word 'revelation', which today is more understandable, is always given by Rudolf Steiner as the proper translation of the Greek *doxa*. An intimate revelation of the Mysteries lying between *Sun* and *Venus*, furthermore, is seen by us when we recognize in the light of the Johannine Mysteries, how *doxa*, the 'revealing beauty'—in the Ephesian Mystery verse it is called '*liebetragende Schönheit*—love-carrying beauty' [Adams renders as 'grace-bestowing loveliness']—is the planetary virtue of Venus. This Ephesian Mystery verse,[98] given by Rudolf Steiner at the Christmas Conference—published in GA 40 & GA 233a and as a motto in my book on *John's Gospel*, pp. 55 and 69—touches in a significant way with the verse in Apoc./ Rev. 5: 12, which in [the KJV/AV, the equivalent of] Luther's somewhat nondescript, general, tautological translation runs: 'Worthy is the Lamb—having been slain to receive the power and riches and wisdom and strength and honour and glory and blessing'.

In the original Greek text the seven mentioned predicates are: *dynamis, plutos, sophia, is-chys* [sic], *timé, doxa* and *eulogia*. The relationship to the seven planetary virtues of the Ephesian Mystery verse can obviously be well understood when one thinks that John's Gospel—which also carries in itself the seed for the Johannine Apocalypse—is inspired by the Mystery plays of Ephesus. Ephesian planetary wisdom has directly flown into John's Gospel and the Apocalypse/ the Book of Revelation. In the Ephesian planetary verse:

- *is-chys* appears as power of the Sun ('firm framéd by the Sun') and

- *dynamis* 'with Luna's might';
- *plutos* 'riches', the virtue of Saturn, as 'Saturn's ancient memoried inwardness' (in these *Contributions*, I spoke of the relationship of Saturn, of the 'richness of the cosmic primordial memories', this corresponds to what Rudolf Steiner meant);
- *sophia* 'wisdom' is the virtue of Jupiter, in the Ephesian verse 'Jupiter's all-wisdom';
- *eulogia* (Luther/AV translate meaninglessly with *Lob*/ 'praise') is the virtue of Mars and literally means 'the gift to speak beautifully'. As I have explained in these *Contributions*, Mars as the planet of the word gives in this realm 'the push towards the outside', the power of the word that manifests and is convincing. This Martian virtue of beautiful speech appears as 'life-stirring song', whereas
- Venus is more the inwardness of the word, the power of love active in the word; Heb. *amor*, 'to speak with', Lat. *amor* 'love' are related in their speech-sounds. Venus, as it were, is the *healing living in the word* in the Ephesian Mystery verse.

Mercury, at home in the Twins (think also of the two snakes on the staff of Mercury, the black and the white, as also of the 'heavenly Twins', the one nocturnally dark, the other bright as day), holds the balance of both wings that he bears, or both pans of the scales which he holds in his hand, weighing, judging (weight, number and measure is in the primordial Mystery-impulse of Hermes-Mercury). For this reason:

- *timé* literally 'judgment, balanced judgment', the virtue of Mercury, in the Ephesian Mystery verse is 'swift-wing'd Mercury's motion in thy limbs'.

There remains the planetary virtue of Venus, which in the verse of Rev. 5: 12 is *doxa*, and:

- *δόξα* 'glory, revealing beauty, revelation' as the planetary virtue of Venus is that which in the Ephesian Mystery verse is called 'love-carrying beauty', or [in G. Adam's translation] 'grace-bestowing Venus' loveliness'.

*Doxa*, the 'Sun-splendour', the revealing radiant beauty, is at the same time the *planetary virtue of Venus*. Herein lies not only something to do with the feelings, but something to do with deep cognition. The starry, Uranian element, the Uranian heavenly fire, also lives in the Sun, is revealed in the Sun. The Sun, in discharging from itself during the course of cosmogonic development Saturn, Mars, the Earth (with the Moon), it reveals ever more purely this Sun-like, Uranian heavenly fire, out of which it is itself a part (in the consciousness of the Seraphim). One recalls in *Occult Science* at the beginning of that development—of which astronomers today would speak as the 'whole solar system in the condition of a primeval nebula'—Dr Steiner does not call it 'Sun' or solar system, but Earth. The Sun *is* not yet there but *will be*; only through the extrusion of the saturnian, earthly, lunar and martian elements does it *develop* to its actual *Sun-existence*. The *Uranian-element* in it has overcome the *earthly, planetary element* and pulled back. 'Ancient Sun' was already a pushing on of the Uranian element, as opposed to 'Ancient Saturn', which was a pulling back and negating of the Uranian element, a dividing-off of the earthly planet from the Uranian planet. On the 'Ancient Moon' we see this earthly-planetary, anti-Uranian element advancing, whereas earthly evolution, through very many crises in the end achieves the balance.

So, at the moment when the Sun has expelled Earth, Mars, Saturn, and so on, yet still retains Venus and Mercury, it, as it were, achieves the climax of its being as Sun, then it is the purest revelation of the Uranian heavenly fire. Today it is already strongly declining, yet for the inhabitants of the Earth it is still 'the Sun'. But precisely in this earthly Sun-being lies a certain erasure of the Uranian element: since for us the Sun is the star of day, it erases the starry heaven, Uranos. The earthly, starry element in the Sun—for the consciousness of the Seraphim still present—we cannot see with earthly eyes in earthly daylight. That Venus—with Mercury—split off from her, the Uranian starry element, as described earlier, is revealed in Venus, and only in it, not in the visibility of Mercury, obscured by the Sun's rays. Venus reveals (*doxa*) the Uranian element of the Sun, the earthly representative of the starry Uranian element. For this reason, it is the only starry planet (we have always differentiated the planetary from the actual starry element). So, in recognizing Venus as the revelation, *doxa*, of the Uranian element of the Sun, we recognize always more deeply *doxa*, the revealing radiant beauty, as the planetary virtue of Venus.

The matter advances a step in anthroposophical knowledge when we recall from the lecture-cycles how the tangible, significant process with the 'Sun splendour', *doxa*, the 'splendour of the light' in the ancient revelation of the Sun, is that which the Archangels carry out into the cosmic spaces, weaving towards the Cherubim. Who then are the Archangels? They are the beings of the Venus-sphere. Who are the Cherubim? The beings of Uranos, of the Uranian sphere. The relationship of the Sun-element and at the same time of the Venus-element cannot be expressed more grandly than in this sublime picture of the Archangels weaving towards the Cherubim, as Rudolf Steiner describes in the lecture-cycle. Here we learn to understand ever more deeply of the relationship of the Sun, but also of Venus, to Uranos-Uranus (Uranus is the planetary representative of Uranos, which in astrology is very significant). The Uranos-myth repeatedly and ever afresh will become a key to the deepest cosmic mysteries.

Consequently, Venus is the starry revelation, *doxa*, of the Uranian element in the Sun, the representative of the Sun-splendour (*doxa*) in this sense. In the Ephesian Mystery verse, this *doxa* as the planetary virtue of Venus is translated [literally] as the 'love-bearing beauty'. So far, we only heard of the 'radiant beauty', 'revelation of beauty'. But what is all the Sun-splendour, all this sunlight, all the Uranian element in its innermost being? What are the rays of the Sun that now [at the time of writing] again in spring magic forth all the green, burgeoning life out of the Earth? Nothing else but 'love that awakens', the same power through which Christ-Jesus, the revelation of the Sun-logos, released Lazarus out of the slumber of the grave. With the revelation of the light, there is connected in the Sun, seen as a Being, the revelation of love, and in this again the Uranian primal mystery is enclosed (more on this in my little book on *Alchymy: The Mystery of the Material World*, which until the appearance of this *Newsletter* will have long ago[99] been published). Uranos, the *Father*, has given the starry gift of love, the spark of the Uranian heavenly fire, during the great separation (Saturn-Uranos) to the 'lost/ prodigal son', to man, during his wandering throughout aeons throughout the regions of time of the earthly planet. This is the relationship of Venus as the revelation of love (*doxa*), as 'love-bearing beauty', to Uranos, to the Uranian heavenly fire, also to the Uranian element in the Sun. In the astrology of birth, Uranos in all these connections is represented through the planet Uranus.

In that which connects the revelation of love of Venus, especially of Venus-Urania (the often-mentioned picture of the ocean with Venus in the Scales and its relationship to John 6)[100] with that revelation of Uranos-Uranus, the love of the Father in the primordial beginning, lies the esoteric element of the two planets Venus and Uranus. The Mystery of Love is the esoteric element as such (the Mystery of which Novalis says, that it was revealed on Golgotha and yet remains forever unfathomable).[101] Venus and Uranus consequently represent the esoteric element in astrology, in the same way as Uranus and Neptune are the two occult planets. This is also Mercury in a certain sense, which originally was still connected to Venus also after the separation from the Sun (earlier I mentioned this one-sided connection of Venus and Mercury and its later separation, [and] the connection of this separation with the Fall of Lucifer, and so on). Venus and Mercury in their union carried the Uranian element originally in themselves and with it the occult, esoteric element of the Sun, the Mystery of the Hermaphrodite (Hermes = Mercury, Aphrodite = Venus). This is deeply significant, right into the subject of alchemy (more concerning this in my little book on *Alchymy* [in Chap. 4]) and corresponds to a lost condition of human consciousness. Through the Fall of Lucifer, Venus approaches closer to the Earth and to Mars (the reflection of the human Fall) and is placed by the gods as Venus-Urania into the Scales (the sign of Christ's I-AM).

## *Hermes-Mercury*

Thus Hermes-Mercury originally took part in everything to do with the esoteric element, the height of esoteric origins in human development. This is still clearly expressed in the Egyptian Mysteries, the Egyptian religion and mythology. There Hermes-Mercury (Egyptian: Thoth) is the esoteric primal teacher and inspirer of the Mysteries. As such he is also originally closely connected to Isis-Venus, the ruler of the Egyptian Mysteries during the period of its primal flowering. This period lasted during the epoch when the spring equinox of the Sun lay in the Venus-sign of the Bull. (This time was a Venus-epoch, in the same way as the later Ram-age, the Graeco-Latin time, was a Mars-epoch, because Mars rules in the Ram). Venus still united with Mercury stood originally above Ancient Egypt.

Also important for the astrological understanding of Mercury is the fact that in Egypt Hermes-Mercury, the esoteric primal teacher, inspires in particular that which then also becomes pure *exoteric spirituality*. Hermes-Mercury, the bearer of all hidden insight (one recalls the expression 'Hermetic seal'), the 'Hermetically sealed' primordial wisdom, the sublime high-priest and primordial initiator, it is he who assisted humanity in primordial times to that which today lives as thoughts, language and writing in the exoteric, daily manner. Out of the sacred writing of the priests, the hieroglyphs, the normal writing of daily use came about, out of the living primal thinking came abstract thinking, out of the sacred primal word the daily language. Moreover, the impulse of measure, number and weight were traced back to Hermes-Mercury. Out of the eternal, heavenly measures incorporated in the pyramids originate the earthly, everyday measures, out of the primordial mysticism of number earthly mathematics and so on was born. Today everything in this realm brought down into the exoteric marketplace and the schools originates in the esoteric primal impulses of Hermes-Mercury.

Thus today the primordial spiritual nature of the Sun in Hermes-Mercury—as on the other hand also in Jupiter—has, as it were, become exoteric. With Jupiter it still appears as 'wisdom', with Mercury it has simply become earthly understanding, intellect, abstract thinking. Here an important significance of Mercury in the birth-horoscope (not the only one) is indicated. And yet it is important to note that precisely this apparently only exoteric, intellectual, abstract element of the understanding goes back to sublime, esoteric primal impulses. Only in looking at this duality of esoteric and exoteric originally inherent in Hermes-Mercury does one properly understand the essence of Mercury also in the astrological sense.

One of the two signs of Mercury's rulership clearly points to this duality, the sign of the Twins (Ⅱ). Not for nothing does it appear like the Roman number ['two'] II. Here amongst the world-conceptions (lecture-cycle by Rudolf Steiner, *Human and Cosmic Thought* [GA 151, 4 lectures, Berlin 20-23 Jan. 1914]) belongs mathematics, mathematical thinking and the study of the mystery of number of the world (the initiate Pythagoras brought this Hermetic mathematics from Egypt to Greece). Everything to do with polarity, the impulse of duality and the twin-impulses in human existence is connected to Mercury. His other governing sign, the Virgin, also carries this twin-nature in itself in the way the highest ether is here united with the lowest element, as star-mystery with the mystery of matter—for this reason the Virgin is the priestly and the alchymical sign as well. (More details on this in the *Contributions* soon to appear on the zodiac, following the conclusion of these on the planets.) This works right into the gospel, where precisely in one of the passages standing in the sign of Mercury, it narrates the double manner of His [Christ's] teaching: an exoteric form through parables for the outer world, and an esoteric in the special explanations for the disciples (the Parable of the Sower and the Seed [Mark 4: 1-20]; see my book on *Mark's Gospel*).

Thus, in Hermes-Mercury something very sublime is originally united with something apparently humble. And so, Mercury (next to the Moon) is the planet to move the quickest through the zodiac-signs. Despite his two 'houses' especially allotted to him, he can actually feel everywhere 'at home', the most accommodating of all the planets, also the planet of commerce and marketing, of the marketplace and merchants, indeed (with corresponding unfavourable influence) of thieves. All these observations of ancient mythology are true, right into astrology, but just require to be understood out of the cosmic backgrounds. And here it is important to see how precisely with Mercury everything apparently humble and exoteric is but the diversion of something higher and esoteric. The whole essence of intellectual thinking, which in the first instance has to do with Mercury, can only be rightly understood from this viewpoint. Astrology properly understood is at the same time an understanding of the world, true understanding of the world. This is precisely the hidden, the 'occult' nature of Mercury (which even for the naked eye is the most elusive planet), that it completely hides its originally esoteric nature, only turning its exoteric side to us.

## *Venus-Mercury*

As the esoteric primal teacher and primal priest—the Virgin, one of the two houses of Mercury, is eminently the priestly sign, especially, too the sign of our own Movement—Hermes-Mercury was still united with Isis-Venus. In Mercury the spiritual essence of light lives; in Venus lives and lived the spiritual essence of love, of the Sun. In the division of Venus, Hermes-Mercury, as it were, gave over the esoteric element to Venus, love, and kept back for itself the exoteric element, the understanding that has become earthly. And the actual primordial Mystery of humanity even today still lies in the union of Venus and Mercury, in the hermaphrodite. (In his occult novel *The Golem* and other of his writings, [Gustav] Meyrink[102] wrestles, even though in an obscure manner, with this Mystery.) And the reason why this esoteric element today is hidden for humanity, why the mystery of love, although revealed in Christ, nevertheless remains unfathomable, lies in the near proximity of Mars and the entanglement into which Venus in human nature has fallen. It has been frequently mentioned and has to be repeated, how for its part the daemonic element in the sexual realm, sexuality in general, has nothing to do with Venus but with Mars. The entanglement lies only in human nature. Here lies a main reason for the lack of clarity and entanglement also in the usual astrological literature. A book which one could almost recommend, such as the one by Oskar Schmitz, *Vom Geiste der Astrologie*,[103] shows in this point certain personal restrictions and obscurities; this can be precisely studied with him. Certain uncomfortable experiences in his life with aged virgins and mothers-in-law[104] have also flowed into his judgment of the sign of the Virgin.

This sign of the Virgin was in a certain way the house of Venus who was still united with Mercury. The house remained near to the Sun, for Mercury and Venus were placed by the gods in the Scales— the whole spiritual existence of Venus is the cosmic counter-picture to certain processes in the human being. There she is Venus-Urania, in the now more frequently discussed sense, the heavenly redeeming one, and comforting one in the darkness and sea-storms of the earthly existence, Venus leading back to the archetypal spring of existence— in the Creed (see Frieling's *Contributions*) the following words belong to her: 'He will unite with those who, through their bearing, He can wrest from the death of matter.' The other house of Venus is the Bull, her 'night house', as one says, because the Bull is an earth-sign and life-ether sign; this is consequently a 'female' ether. which means for astrology 'nocturnal'. The Scales, on the other hand, stand in the light-ether triangle, which is also the Uranus triangle; this is a 'masculine' ether, in astrology possessing the character of day, consequently the Scales is the 'day house' of Venus. One should never confuse this point of view with what is otherwise said about the day-side and night-side of the zodiac.

### Venus in the Bull

So, the Bull is the 'night house' of Venus. There she is the 'earthly Venus'. This with today's concepts and context of consciousness, in view of Venus' described entanglement with Mars in the human being, directly resolves certain errors and misunderstandings. The word 'bull' has something to contribute here, too, which is indeed confusing if one thinks that the 'Bull' is a female element, a sign belonging to the female ether! ('Cow', or at least the neutral 'ox', would in many ways be more correct, but would lead to even more misunderstandings and annoyance. The relationship of the Egyptian Isis to the cow and the cow's horns is well-known.) Venus in the Scales is the heavenly one and heavenly redeeming one, the Venus which leads back to the primordial source of existence; Venus in the Bull points to the earthly element as the 'love in the primordial beginning of existence'—a painting by Segantini[105] is described like this—'love in the primal beginning' (*il primo amore*),[106] the maternal element leading into existence, as such also the 'healing power of love'. In the gospel she is the planetary element of the power of love that heals in Christ's word; all the healing deeds of Christ belong to this sign (Venus in the Bull).[107]

The connection becomes immediately clear when we recall Raphael's *Sistine Madonna* (already in the name 'Raphael' lies this healing element). Dr Steiner has spoken of the health-giving, healing forces of this painting, which reveals to us so beautifully the divine side of the feminine, maternal nature; he points out its connection with the Egyptian presentations of Isis with the child Horus and the role this picture plays in the Egyptian temple-Mysteries during the 'temple sleep'.[108] Those who were sick, who because of the 'sickness of sin' were physically sick, were placed before the healing forces of this picture. Nothing can correct our confused concepts of the sign of the Bull and of the planetary element of Venus better than when we make clear to ourselves, how especially Raphael's *Sistine Madonna* is the revelation of 'Venus in the Bull' portraying to us what Venus in the Bull signifies. In the Creed, the following sentence relates to this: 'The birth of Jesus on Earth is a working of the Holy Spirit, who spiritually to heal the sickness of sin on the bodily nature of mankind, prepared the Son of Mary to be the vehicle of the Christ.' In this connection Frieling beautifully and revealingly points to the 'Queen of the May' (as Mary is called in Catholic contexts)—and the Bull is indeed the sign of May, the sign of the full bloom of the year. And we could also point to the name of Queen Maya, the mother of Buddha, or more correctly of the Bodhisattva, as the Indian-Buddhist name of Mary.

## The Venus-Mars Mystery and the Esoteric Nature of Astrology

Indeed, the two pictures of the *Sistine Madonna* and *The Birth of Venus* (the beautiful painting by Botticelli [in the Uffizi Gallery, Florence] is well-known) relates to Venus in the Bull and Venus in the Scales, as the earthly and the heavenly Venus, however uncomfortable this remark may also appear to certain pre-conceived, unimportant notions. Here is the point where we are tested for adequate and moral thinking. Here is revealed the deep moral nature and at the same time the esoteric nature of astrology. Here is shown that one cannot study, and why one cannot simply study it out of books. As I discuss in a passage of my little book on *Alchymy*, recently published, this is indeed the actual Mystery, the esoteric nature of astrology as of alchymy, that one cannot gather book-knowledge out of it, but that it places us before this test of the 'I'. And it consists in nothing else but solely the esoteric path leading to the Venus-Mercury Mystery; in our own inner exertion and Christian meditation we seek to release Venus out of her entanglement with Mars in human nature, seeking to raise into purity the whole relationship of Venus and Mars in human nature. Everyone has to do it themselves; all liturgical, sacramental life can be a way towards it. No lecturer or writer of books can spare us the effort. The nature of all esoteric life consists in having to face it ourselves and experience it ourselves. And Venus, with Uranus, is the esoteric planet *par excellence*.

This, however, can once again lead to new errors and misunderstandings. One might perhaps think one's thoughts concerning Venus have been cleared up and imagine all the more to view *Mars* as the 'guilty partner'. But the Mercury-Mars problem, as one likes to say, 'is a tricky one'. It is the actual obstacle and the actual touchstone of all astrology. Certainly, Mars has this daemonic and passionate nature in its qualities, certainly it plays a decisive role in the human Fall into sin. At the same time, we also recognized the positive side of Mars. Indeed, we saw how decisive, too, its other side in world-events is, recalling the saying of Heraclitus that 'Strife is the father of everything'. Here once again we have to differentiate certain effects of Mars in human nature (♂ in ♏) from that which Mars is in its divine nature. The following thought can perhaps lead us furthest: We observe a red rose, enjoy the red of the rose. Now, no rose can be red, bring pleasure through its redness, without the power of Mars. The rose is the divine revelation of Mars *par excellence*. Here the forces of Mars have regained the divine forces of innocence—read [Albert] Steffen's beautiful poem 'Die Rose'.[109] Or think on what we said concerning the Mars-forces in the red of the blood. Moreover, the Grail chalice cannot shine divinely carmine red without these forces of Mars. Without them even the Mystery of Golgotha could not have taken place. To Mars belongs the whole Mystery of iron, touching on the Sun-Mystery of Michael (Sun and Mars are related as are the ash and the oak: the Sun-tree and the Mars-tree). We have already mentioned iron in the blood, of the poisoning—in the cosmic and earthly spheres.

In this connection, we recall Dr Steiner's words on Michael that refer to the Mystery of iron: '*O Mensch, du bildest es zu deinem Dienste,*

*du offenbarest es in seinem Stoffeswert in vielen deiner Werke. Es wird dir*
*Heil jedoch erst sein, wenn dir sich offenbart seines Geistes Hochgewalt.'*[110]
['O man, you bring it into your service, you reveal its material value in
many of your works. However, it will only assist in your redemption,
when it reveals to you its high spiritual might.'] With these words the
Mystery of Mars is clearly characterized. And these words can help
us to a correct moral thinking in astrological contexts. We see ever
more clearly that we cannot simply shift some fault or other, or sin of
mankind, on to the planets, without at the same time touching on the
divine. In human nature, in our own being itself, we have to seek for
all the fault and sin, for the 'evil-doer', Lucifer and Ahriman. Only
then are we able to release Venus out of her entanglement with Mars
and once again in human nature unite her with Hermes-Mercury, the
Lord of initiation and of the higher priesthood. Then Venus-Urania
extends to us the key to all the starry mysteries (astrology) and the
mysteries of matter (alchymy). This was named above as the 'esoteric
path' for which no book-knowledge can be a substitute. This long path
for mankind still lies before us.

In the divine perspective things appear completely differently
from what we imagine from our human perspective and its thinking.
Here Mars, too, is not stamped as the evil-doer at Venus' cost, but
here Venus loves Mars; she conducts a cosmic dialogue with him—as
Dr Steiner so eloquently explains in the lecture on the planets held in
Dornach.[111] (When 'love of Venus for Mars' is mentioned, of course,
straightaway there arise certain earthly notions and comparisons.
These have simply to be put aside if we want to understand what is
meant.) Precisely in the separation of individuals, Mars prepares the
ground for the later work of Venus to re-unite what is separated in
love and harmony. Consequently, Venus loves Mars in a divine, not
in a human manner. She is the love that endures everything, who calculates or demands nothing, who never achieves her ideals through
severity or force, but simply through that which she rays out revealing
in beauty (*doxa*), gaining and harmoniously uniting hearts. Ahrimanic
cynicism may smile about the 'love of Venus for Mars'; the *rose* once
again reveals the divine truth. Is not Venus the goddess of flowers,
the being who bestows all the flowers, also those of beauty and art,
into earthly existence? As we said earlier, like everything of a starry
nature in earthly existence, all flowers and blossoms belong to Venus.
Star and flower belong together. Venus is the goddess of flowers. But
as the Queen of Flowers she has chosen the red rose, which, in so far

as it is precisely a rose, belongs to Venus, but in so far as it bears red rose sap, it belongs to Mars. In a purely divine manner, the red rose reveals the Mystery of the love of Venus to Mars. In the rosy-cross, in the cross with the red roses (as Goethe places before us in his poem 'Die Geheimnisse') the Mars quality in the Mystery of Golgotha is led over to the Venus-quality.

Nothing leads so much to a moral contemplation of the world—in the highest sense of the word—and a moral trial of the 'I' than astrology, rightly understood. But nothing, too, can bear so little of a *certain* manner of moral contemplation, I mean, a certain moralizing, an astringent moralizing that one finds here and there. In thinking through the whole context of the Mercury-Venus-Mars problem, this difference of the true moral discussion from that of a narrow moralizing, becomes clearly evident.

## The Ether-body and the Planets

As an addition to what has been said about Mercury, Venus, Mars and the planets in general, I wanted to add how seven ways of working, or 'movements' in the ether-body are ordered to the planets, as given by Dr Steiner.[112]

- To Mercury belongs the 'movement of breathing',
- to Venus the 'movement of the glands',
- to Mars belongs the 'movement of speech' (we always spoke here of the connection of Mars with the strength of the word),
- to Saturn the 'movement of coming into uprightness',
- to Jupiter the 'movement of thinking',
- to the Sun (in order to anticipate), the 'movement of the blood' (what was said of Mars is related to the forces of iron in the red colour of the blood, not to the 'movement of the blood' meant here),
- to the Moon the 'movement of reproduction' (as discussed earlier, the sexual function from the viewpoint of its higher rhythm, the divine side of this realm, whereas the more daemonic side belongs to Mars).

The viewpoint is also important, given in the Hannover lecture-course (*The World of the Senses and the World of the Spirit*, GA 134), lecture 6, in connection with what is said in the Prague lecture-cycle (*An Occult Physiology*, GA 128) on the organs belonging to the individual planets:

Saturn—spleen,
Jupiter—liver,

Mars–gall,
Sun–heart,
Mercury–lungs,
Venus–kidneys,
Moon–the sexual element.

This is also important for medical astrology and the medical judgment of the birth–horoscope.

To this there comes in the Hannover lecture–course the relationship of the human being to plants:

root–brain,
leaves–lungs,
blossoms–kidneys,
seeds–heart,
fruit–blood system.

So, the blossoms belong to the kidneys, and the kidneys once again belong to Venus, about which we have heard how she is the goddess of flowers and blossoms, how all the flowers and blossoms belong to Venus. 'Leaves–lungs' would then mean Mercury, the lord of all breathing movement and the lungs. This leads again to all possible 'Hermetic' connections, for the breathing contains an esoteric, a Yoga-Mystery, a 'Mystery of the philosopher's stone', as Dr Steiner has said here and there.[113]

That Venus in the human organism belongs to the 'sphere of blossoms' of the kidneys, has a deeper meaning when we recall how the kidneys are the ordering, harmonizing influence in the whole organism. The ordering, rhythmizing, harmonizing element, however, is completely the sphere of the activity of Venus.

Amongst the 'moods of the world-conceptions' Mercury belongs to transcendentalism, and Venus to mysticism, the most inward of the [twelve] views (*Human and Cosmic Thought*, GA 151, 4 lectures, Berlin 20-23 Jan. 1914).

# IX
# The Seven Planets (Conclusion): Sun and Moon

## (An Easter Contemplation)

In the attempt to present the essence of the individual planets the Sun, too, was always implicit. We recall in particular how we found the Mysteries of Mercury and Venus bound with the Sun-Mystery. The whole method of our observations was that we proceeded from the cosmogony of *Occult Science*, that we kept in mind how out of the entire system—which Dr Steiner in its original embodiment called 'Ancient Saturn', in its later, its fourth embodiment continuing today, called 'Earth'—the individual planetary spheres divided off and were differentiated. We sought to form a picture in this fact of the individual essence of the planets. These 'planetary spheres' are initially something very different from the present condition of the planets. Only through long periods of time did the solar and planetary system develop out of a more supersensory-etheric condition towards their condition today.

We also discussed how the astronomer today and the contemporary person generally thinks of the whole process more in a material-mechanical manner and how such notions have led to the Kant-Laplace theory of a cosmic nebula. This hypothesis itself and its criticism through Dr Steiner is well-known. Whoever can view this more mechanical-material picture of the birth of the planets in the style of Kant, Copernicus and Laplace *together* with the spiritual-cosmogony of *Occult Science*, whoever can glimpse and recognize in the outer apparently material processes everywhere the revelation of spiritual beings who ultimately have been at work in fashioning human destiny, such a person will gain many things from viewing together both ways of observation that will become a key with which to understand everything astrological. The cosmogony of *Occult Science* itself will make it more easily understandable for many people today that they can *view both in the right manner together,* with certain other ways of conceiving that include the hypotheses of cosmic creation that have arisen more out of the spirit of our 'materialistic' manner of observation anchored in the physical body and in the first instance bound to it.

What I say here is *not* against Rudolf Steiner and the spirit of anthroposophy. Did not Rudolf Steiner repeatedly emphasize (see, for example, an important place in the lectures about the karmic connections of the Anthroposophical Society),[114] that materialism is so difficult to counteract *because it is right*, because it is the naturally-given view of the human being stuck in the physical [existence]? It is one of the twelve possible world-conceptions, the one belonging to the zodiac sign of the Crab.[115] This understanding of its relative correctness consequently belongs to materialism, in order to deal with it in the right way. Many errors and misunderstandings arise because, especially in anthroposophical circles, one believes one has dealt with it without actually having done so. Similarly, with the thinking of Kant. Especially in the realm of anthroposophical-astronomical work, this attitude—it has to be said—does not always play a happy role. One behaves as though Copernicus and Kepler—who are also referred to by Rudolf Steiner everywhere in the astronomical lecture-course[116]—are no longer relevant, whereas they have given us the great possibilities of calculating and predicting the planetary courses, although these predictions initially arose out of being stuck in the physical body. So, one is not properly placed into life today if one simply undervalues these things, as is increasingly becoming the case amongst anthroposophists.

In his lecture yesterday,[117] [Emil] Bock pointed out how recent research shows that in Ancient Egypt, that is, a country with a high spirituality, a knowledge of Kepler's laws already existed. The essence of these things was essentially already known then. Kepler himself, to whom Dr Steiner always referred in this sense, especially in the Leipzig lecture-course *Christ and the Spiritual World* [GA 149], is a shining example of how one can connect these techniques of modern astronomical methods of calculation with a deep spiritual insight into the spiritual starry contexts, indeed with a prophetic view for the new Christened astrology of a human future. Moreover, in addition to all this, in the realm of traditional astrology, too, one should know the subject in the right way.

The method I employ in these *Contributions*, by referring ever again to Kepler, Copernicus, Laplace and so on that helps provide the most immediate notions for astronomical matters closest to the imagination of the contemporary person, is indeed in no way contrary to the mind of Rudolf Steiner. It is not one of the 'non-methods' so favoured today, but corresponds to what Rudolf Steiner wanted, concerning which in the recently published *The Michael Mystery* [GA 26] he clearly spoke. There he writes [Chapter 6: Mankind's Future and the Work of Michael]:

> Today one has to be able to speak about nature in such a way as the stage of development demands of the consciousness-soul. One has to be able to assimilate the purely natural-scientific way of thinking. But one must also learn to speak—which means, to *feel*—about the world of nature, too, in a manner befitting the Christ. Not only about redemption from Nature, not only about the soul and things divine, but about the cosmos, we must learn the Christ-language …
>
> Anthroposophy sets due value upon all that the naturalistic form of scientific thought has learnt to say about the world during the last four to five hundred years. But anthroposophy has another language to speak besides this one, about man's being, his evolution, and the becoming of the cosmos. Anthroposophy would speak the Christ-Michael language. For if both languages are spoken, then the continuity will remain unbroken and evolution will not pass over to Ahriman before the finding again of its primordial, divine, spiritual origin.

In the cosmogony of *Occult Science* Rudolf Steiner speaks the Michaelic language for which he has the full right—though in linguistic expressions here and there with a certain leaning towards modern ways of expression. *Our* task has to be, precisely in the sense of which Dr Steiner spoke, that we attempt to show how this spiritual cosmogony is to be seen with the outer cosmic picture. We attempt to lead from the Ahrimanic language of outer astronomy to the Michaelic language of a Christened astrology. *Occult Science* is not a book that one can simply quote but that sets specific tasks. Every sentence is actually a task for knowledge, for recognition, which has first to be worked on. It is just the same with the lecture-cycle *Christ and the Spiritual World*, which contains the basic outline, the programme of a Christened astrology of the future. Only this pro-active manner of reading is too little in favour today. People find it more comfortable 'to read lecture-cycles' and simply to make dogmas of the words. Like this one will never attain the world, never find it.

An important and difficult problem for knowledge lies in particular in the manner Dr Steiner speaks in *Occult Science* of the *Sun* and the *Earth*. Here 'Sun' is not at all as we contemporary people imagine it as almost obvious, to take it as primary and the 'Earth' as secondary, but the reverse. That cosmic whole, for the astronomer today precisely the 'solar system', or what still as undeveloped primordial nebula is carried in it leading to this solar system, Dr Steiner calls 'Ancient Saturn'. This Ancient Saturn is nothing other than the *Earth* in the primal stages of its embodiment. It is as we emphasized in our first *Contribution*: Ancient Saturn (and following it, Saturn today) is astrologically actually the *Earth*, is through and through nothing other than the Earth. In the contrast of Uranus-Saturn, we discover the contrast of 'Heaven and Earth'.

The next embodiment this cosmic-planetary whole, which for the astronomer would be the 'solar system' or 'primordial nebula of the solar system', Dr Steiner nevertheless called 'Ancient Sun'. But this Ancient Sun, too, is the *Earth* on a specific stage of its embodiment, or incarnation. Likewise, the 'Ancient Moon', the third stage of the incarnation of the Earth, which at a specific stage of *its* evolution expels the solar element as the Sun.

Finally, the fourth stage of the Earth's embodiment, in which the entirety arises again out of the cosmic night, the *'pralaya'*, is called by Dr Steiner in a still special sense 'Earth'. This is the Earth on the fourth stage of its embodiment, the actual earthly stage. In this earthly evolution, in its middle 'fourth round' [of seven]—moreover [sub-divided] during its fourth race[118] and [during that race's] fifth cultural epoch, we stand today. Also at the beginning of this 'Earth evolution'—this is important to keep in mind — we have indeed the great, general 'primordial nebula' once again (I need to use this materialistic expression, although I know that the reality standing behind this 'primordial nebula' is an undulating, active weaving, *ein Wogen u. Wirken u. Weben*, of spiritual beings.)

For the astronomer this primal whole at the beginning of Earth-evolution would be precisely the *solar system* in its primal nebulous condition. And what comes about would primarily be the Sun, and secondarily the planets. And least of all could such an astronomer go along with Dr Steiner, who explains how *the Sun separates from the Earth*, how spiritual beings—amongst whom the Christ—withdraw the Sun out of the Earth and there on the Sun make their homeland. For this astronomer it would be likewise obvious that previously Mars, Jupiter and Saturn separated *from the Sun*, whereas Dr Steiner describes these planets separating from the *Earth*, because he calls that which governs everything the *Earth*.

I cannot really be content that, like certain anthroposophists working in astronomy (I do not mean Frl. Vreede here, whom I do not want to implicate in this *Newsletter*) who simply say, this astronomer is simply a materialist, a simpleton, completely incompetent, and from now on we should have nothing more to do with him. I cannot join in such a thing, holding it to be erroneous in the worst sense. It would be a sure method that would hinder anthroposophy from fulfilling its earthly task. For me, however, it's like this: the problem exists *why* did Dr Steiner name what for the astronomer is simply 'Sun' or 'solar system', entirely '*Earth*'? *Why* did he say the Sun divided from the Earth, and not the Earth from the Sun? Whoever does not feel this as a *question, a task of knowledge*, or *recognition*, as a problem one has first to struggle with, is far removed from really understanding *Occult Science*, or anthroposophy in general. He is a dogmatist, about whom I should not concern myself further, feeling I have the right not to bother about him.

## The Place of the Earth

The viewpoint of the *primacy of the Sun*, from which the astronomer of today starts in a thoroughly justified contemporary manner, is obvious. The spiritual viewpoint, out of which the cosmogony of *Occult Science* is written, just as obviously leads to the primacy of the Earth. Indeed, the viewpoint of Dr Steiner here is a karmic viewpoint, one of world-*karma*. I will explain more clearly what I mean. Our primal equation that was the starting point with these *Contributions*: Uranus:[119] Saturn = Heaven: Earth will once more help us.

An Indian expression, too, can help here. In Indian the Earth is called, *karmabhumi*, which means, *karma* = Earth, 'the place of *karma*'. The Indians mean, the Earth is the place for *karma*; the great cosmic-karmic experimental laboratory and spiritual seed-bed. This is correct and remains correct, indeed, becomes increasingly correct for Christian *karma*-contemplations and star-contemplations. For only in the Christian-[stage], in the light of the Christ-event, does one fully and completely understand what 'Earth' is. John 8, the well-known episode where Christ writes into the Earth the obligations of the adulteress, the *karma* of the adulteress, is of central significance.[120]

What does begin on Ancient Saturn? The primordial cosmic *karma* as the spiritual process of separation and division of certain beings from the primordial substance of divine being. This primordial substance of divine being is what we here always call Uranos, in accord with an ancient esotericism as well as John's Gospel (The name of the planet

Uranus derives from Uranos, because it joined the solar system of planets, not from the planetary, or earthly side, but from the heavenly side, that of Uranos.) The primordial world-*karma* begins on Ancient Saturn, that cosmic primordial fact to which the here often-mentioned primordial Greek myth of Uranos contains the poetic, revelatory indication (Christ's parable of the Prodigal Son [Luke 15] stands instructively close to it).

What begins on Ancient Saturn in gigantic, cosmic dimensions comes finally to effect on the tiny Earth, the 'speck of dust in the universe' (even Dr Steiner uses this expression).[121] Already on Ancient Saturn the event of the Earth is laid as a seed. What began there comes here to the last—or provisional last—result (for the Jupiter, Venus and Vulcan stages of the entire development of the Earth are still to follow). What takes place regarding the cosmic drama and crisis between [Ancient] Saturn and the Earth cannot be expressed here in detail, for it contains the whole drama of cosmic events extending for aeons. But when, for example, Christ writes the obligations of the adulteress into the Earth, then one has to understand how this really relates to connections that took their beginnings on Ancient Saturn and now on this Earth through Christ are balanced out. Christ is the Lord of world-*karma*, or earthly *karma*. And so, He writes the *karma* of the woman into the Earth. The Earth is the carrier and the substance of all *karma*, because it is that into which the primordial connections of Saturn have finally crystallized and condensed. Our Earth unites in itself the quintessence of all *karma*, which took place through the extensive aeons of world-connections of Saturn, Sun, Moon and so on (since the Uranus separation).

The seed contained in the fruit is small in comparison to the whole being of the plant. So, too, the Earth today is small in comparison to the primordial planetary context out of which it arose. It is the 'speck of dust in the universe', about which, however, Rudolf Steiner showed ever and again how it is future-carrying and decisive for the future. It carries the seed of a new world in itself. The Earth, on which the Christ incarnated, which He Himself took as His body, is the balancing-out of the whole planetary *karma* and the seed of the future resurrection. Concerning this viewpoint of *karma* in *Occult Science*, the *Earth* appears as the primary [fact] of the planetary [development]; from this viewpoint Ancient Saturn is already seen as *Earth*. The scene in John 8, where Christ writes in the Earth the *karma* of the adulteress, is a main key to understand the whole of astrology, or those cosmic contexts out of which alone an understanding of astrology is possible.

## The Sun

In the light of the viewpoints in these considerations, what, furthermore, is the *Sun*? Earth, earthly being, earthly nature has to do with the *karma* of the planet. The Sun's nature has to do with that being from which everything karmic of the planet has separated and divided, that is, with that which is beyond the planetary, karmic, Saturnian element, which is the *Uranian*, the divine primordial substance and primordial being (one thinks of the sign of Uranus standing at the beginning of the Creed). The relationship of the Sun to the Uranian realm—and thereby to Uranus, too—has repeatedly cropped up in these studies. Lastly and most clearly it appeared in the Venus-Mercury study, for Venus and Mercury are the only planets that, also in the sense of *Occult Science*, separated from the *Sun* and not from the Earth. Uranos, as we mean here, is also not the astronomical fixed-star heaven, but the heavenly primordial fire and primordial light in which the Being of the Father is revealed— that is, what is meant here is not the dark, primordial fire of Saturn, the 'black fire' of the Rosicrucians.[122] The astronomical fixed-star heaven is after all only *maya* offering itself to the physical eye.

Ancient Saturn where in the primordial separation world-karma arises, is consequently, if we proceed from the pure spiritual imagination of the separating beings to what is externally visible, to be perceived like a dark smoke, in the face of the bright heavenly fire, but now illuminated by it, receiving its influence and so completing its own development. And so there finally came about the 'coloured light of Saturn' out of light and darkness, the glimmering described in *Occult Science* (in particular, when the Angels and Archangels begin to work in the Saturn-sphere).[123] But the Saturn-fire, in which the Archai are revealed, is a dark fire. Throughout Saturn a dark entity predominates, the earthly, planetary [being], even though the Uranian heavenly fire always rays in and plays in.

On 'Ancient Sun', that takes on the *karma* of Saturn, it is different. Here it comes to a penetration and overcoming of the heavenly fire, the Uranian element. Thereby is already said what Sun-existence is in contrast to earthly existence: the revelation of the Uranian element in the planetary [existence]. Certainly 'Ancient Sun' is also *Earth* on a certain stage of its embodiment, but still an earthly condition in which the heavenly fire, the Uranian element, overcomes the dark earthly element, especially after this Ancient Sun has expelled the dark Saturn (this is the only planetary event of 'Ancient Sun', after which it still carries Jupiter, Mars, the later Earth with its earthly Moon).

Then follows, as the third embodiment, 'Ancient Moon', which, after the expulsion of the Sun, and the planets (Saturn, Jupiter and Mars), still contains the earthly element in connection with the lunar element (the later Earth-Moon). At this stage, the Sun-nature experiences a refining; the earthly nature but in the Moon-condition become more crude and hard. Here, then, at least in so far as the Earth, the 'Ancient Moon' itself comes into consideration, the earthly planetary element, the 'Saturn element', as we could also say, comes again to the fore. (In astrology, too, the relationship of Moon and Saturn is significant, as the strongest emphasis on the earthly element.)

Finally, the Earth in the narrow sense, as the fourth embodiment of planet Earth; of all these karmic events it is finally the balance. Here, in the Christ-event, the Uranian heavenly fire once again penetrates the earthly planetary existence; Christ unites with the Earth, 'that it too will one day become a Sun'.[124] In the Christ-event lies that which the whole planetary evolution, to which these astrological *Contributions* are dedicated, signifies. It contains the key to the whole of astrology. Astrology is a concern of Christ.

## The Christ-event and its Three Precursors

Out of these astrological and cosmogonic contexts the Christ-event itself will be best understood. The whole cosmic evolution—Saturn, Sun, Moon and Earth—is geared towards the event of Golgotha, carrying it as a seed from the beginning onwards. No true astrology exists without regarding this event, which itself carries the key to all astrology. In the Leipzig lecture-course [GA 149] Rudolf Steiner shows how this earthly deed of Christ on Golgotha, the revelation of the Christ-'I' in the physical world, was preceded by three other Christ-events. They took place in the Lemurian and Atlantean ages, when the Christ-revelation still remained in the etheric and astral element and in the cosmic, planetary sphere. The Christ-being that is 'ensouled' in the Nathan-Jesus connects with the whole series of planets, thereby bringing various things in the human sensory system and soul-organism into order, which through the Fall of man had fallen into disarray. This helps us in a wonderful way to recognize how the influence of Christ, which only in the Mystery of Golgotha as a revelation of the 'I' finally reaches the earthly and physical world, was already previously present. Previously only in the higher cosmic regions, it penetrated through the whole earthly evolution. And we sense, moreover, how this Christ-influence did not take its very first beginning in the Lemurian age—although there, as a result of the 'Fall of man' that took place at this time, a new occasion for a concrete penetration was given. But we sense how it rises further, ever higher, until a Christ-sacrifice is located in the primordial Saturn-evolution, which then on Ancient Sun and Ancient Moon is renewed to an ever-higher degree. It accompanies the whole cosmic event, the whole cosmic evolution, carrying it in itself, in order finally to find its conclusion in the Mystery of Golgotha in the physical, earthly [depths].

Not, though, in the sense that now the influence of Christ is concluded. For only now has the Earth become the body of Christ, in order gradually and increasingly to penetrate it with Uranian heavenly fire, in order to raise it to Sun-existence; in order to raise it up with the total evolution, which on Golgotha reached its deepest, most profound depths, in order to raise it again to the Uranian 'origin in the light'. I already indicated that all this is sublimely expressed in Christ's parable of the Prodigal Son, linked to the Greek myth of Uranos. Christ brings back the 'son of the lost human being' to the origins, that is, the direct offspring of the Uranian origins in the light now lost to humanity, for the human being as the lost son (who has forgotten and lost his origin and homeland). The whole cosmic development is a sublime cosmic sacrifice of Christ that only has its ending in Golgotha, which there brings about the turning point of its evolution. The seed of cosmic sacrifice lies now in the Earth and in the human being. Now the human being has to respond to the offering and raise it to an Act of Consecration of Man that becomes a cosmic Act of Consecration (Apocalypse). The Apocalypse [of John] contains the indication of the true conclusion of the Christ's cosmic deed of offering (the New Jerusalem, in [the terminology of] *Occult Science*, is Jupiter, Venus and Vulcan …).

Only out of astrology and the cosmogonic studies do we understand all these contexts and thereby the full meaning of the deed of Christ. This deed as none other shows us how the totality of earthly deeds and human deeds is the parallel of the heavenly Deed. To have penetrated into the meaning and essence of this parallel situation means to stand at the beginning of a spiritual understanding of astrology. And the whole book *Occult Science* is written that we increasingly live into the 'cosmogony', into this parallel situation, learning to conceive cosmic becoming at the same time as human becoming.

## *Venus and Love that Renews*

In looking into this context, we have also the most significant of all *proofs* for the deed of Christ, that, despite all 'religious renewal' and anthroposophical communities, still so easily remains for people mere 'belief' or dogma. Whoever begins to sense the meaning of what I am always relating here about the line of development leading from Uranos via Saturn-Earth and to the Sun, is thereby also on the way to assimilate *in cognition* the deed of Christ out of its deepest cosmic backgrounds. One arrives at the point where one has to ask: well, if the whole story of Christ in the Holy Land does not rest on truth—and also the authentic seeker for truth who from the start simply 'believes' nothing has also to reckon with this possibility—where, then, are the human events to be sought in which the descent of the Sun-logos, which lies in the whole cosmic line of development, as the bringer of the Uranian heavenly fire (see Christian Morgenstern) has its earthly correspondence? And search wherever we may, we will finally come neither to the Buddha, nor Socrates, nor Plato, nor Jesu ben Pandira, nor Apollonius of Tyana, nor Mani, but precisely only to that Figure, Who stands at the centre of our gospel narratives and to the events which are recorded there. We touch here on that which is always called the 'results of the spiritual research of Rudolf Steiner', and begin perhaps from afar to sense something of the ways of this research, I mean: of that which we are not able ourselves to do, at least to entertain a distant idea. For without these results of spiritual research of Rudolf Steiner not a single sentence of these astrological contributions could have been written.

The examples I have chosen (Buddha, and so on) are not arbitrarily chosen, but I take here a number of personalities from whom one feels that they have something or other to do with the approach, or the already achieved entry (thus with Apollonius and Mani), of the deed of Christ. Already 500 years before Christ, Rudolf Steiner reports, the Sun-aura of Christ began to approach the Earth. This leads to the time of the Buddha, whose influence, even if he is not the Christ, has a very significant connection with the Christ-event.

That cosmic being who oversaw him, the Buddha, is that of Venus-Mercury (*budha* in Sanskrit means Mercury). Dr Steiner explains that this is the 'occult Mercury', that is, above all the Venus-being. In this presentation we have heard how closely the Mystery of Venus-Mercury is united to the Sun-Mysteries. The Venus-Mercury revelation lies already in the Sun-revelation and cosmically precedes it. Likewise, the Buddha-event precedes Christ's deed and already lies in its rays. Buddha leads humanity to the purity of the inner zero-point; the filling-out with the 'I' lies then in the Christ-impulse. In Buddhism itself this is mirrored always in the manner how there one speaks of the radiant revelation of the Morning Star (Venus), which shines before the sunrise. Not for nothing with the Buddha does precisely Venus appear, who is revealed in her Sun-like splendour, the highest of all earthly revelations of the divine; so it is named in the Pali text Itivuttaka that 'as at the end of the night, with the break of day, the Morning Star shines and sparkles and rays forth, also love, the release of the heart, shines and sparkles and rays forth.'[125] Thus Buddha already acknowledges Venus as the star of love, as the special revelation of the Sun-Mystery of love.

Please excuse this small excursion at a place that has to do with showing how the right view on the cosmic, astrological processes does connect to those Christ-events narrated in the gospel, with the Mystery of Golgotha. For this reason, too, there are significant indications to astrology right at the beginning of the gospel, in the story of the star of Bethlehem at the beginning of Matthew's Gospel, which before any other gospel has the 'Uranus viewpoint'. This was shown in my book on *John's Gospel* out of purely astrological assumptions, to which Frieling in his beautiful *Contributions* has now added the theological evidence. The time will come when the connection of the gospels and the Christ-event with astrology will be understood afresh. In our next incarnation in the Waterman-Uranus age ... (See on this Steiner's important lectures on the karmic contexts of the Anthroposophical Society, what are called the Chartres-lectures.)[126]

## *Christ and the Sun-Mysteries*

And so we stand before the whole drama of cosmic evolution as a concern of Christ. The Uranian primordial being becomes turbid in Saturn, darkness separates from the light; the light, however, shines in the darkness: 'The darknesses live shining from the light, but the light streams into the darkness...' and so on. The division (Uranus-Saturn separation) had to happen, so that a world-drama, a world-event, a world-history can happen at all, which ultimately concentrates into a short earthly history. All *evolution*, however, is only thereby possible because the *darkness*, that at the same time *in itself is inactive* (these two concepts also include that which is also used in astrology, with the division of the zodiac, the much used Indian word *tamas*), receives the influence of the light, so that in the Saturnian element the Uranian once again rays in. Uranos is the original periphery of Ancient Saturn, before Uranus from there enters into the planetary realm on Ancient Sun. Then on Ancient Sun the Uranian being of light comes again to the fore, to which there also comes the planetary addition of Uranus. The relationship between the Sun and Uranus has been frequently mentioned here.

Uranos (not Uranus, which is only its planetary representative) is the pure, primordial divine being and essence of light, resting in itself. So, too, the Sun (not only the astronomical Sun, but also everything Sun-like in the pure spiritual sense) is the revelation of the Uranian element in the planetary realm and in the earthly, human realm (which indeed always is the astrological and cosmogonic parallel of the planetary realm). Uranos itself (of whose existence the Uranus planet should in the future increasingly remind us) is for us basically unreachable (also in thought), is the 'inconceivable, eternal light' (*lux perpetua*), 'light in the primordial light', about which it is said in *Light on the Path*:[127] 'You will enter the light, but you will never touch the flame' (p. 4). The sublimity of the nocturnal fixed-star heaven is only its *maya*-expression. The child's remark, once related by Dr Rittelmeyer: 'Father, if the unimportant side of the heavens is already beautiful, how beautiful must the proper side be!' closely meets the fact of the spiritual relationship. Only a being out of the hierarchy of the Seraphim would be able in beholding to recognize this earthly concept of the inconceivable Father-being of Uranos, beyond space and time; for such a being the earthly Sun, despite Wilhelm Kaiser,[128] would be only a spark of light in the great cosmic ocean of light of Uranos.

But for us Earth-dwellers the *Sun* is the earthly representative of Uranos, the divine unity and Father-being, the 'Father in the heavens'. That which *in the occult sense* (in the inconceivable and ineffable) is Uranus, and is represented as a planet and in astrology through Uranus, is in *the earthly revelation the Sun*. Uranus in the horoscope has to do with the highest occult individuality and essence of the human being; the Sun has to do with the revelation of this individuality in the earthly world. The Sun is in the earthly *maya*, the daytime representative of the Father in the heavens; the nocturnal fixed-star heaven is His night-time representative. The early Indians already had this differentiation very beautifully in the Rig Veda, where Mitra is the divine day-revelation of the Sun, Varuna the night-revelation of the divine. I have already shown[129] how this word *Varuna* purely linguistically is connected with Uranos and also with 'Waterman', with the Mysteries of water and the ocean, also of the heavenly ocean. Mitra has become in Persian Mithra, consequently the Mithras-Mysteries. The two sides of Christ's being basically lie in the Indian duality Mitra-Varuna, the earthly Sun-like and the cosmic-Uranian [sides], Christ-Sun-impulse and Christ-Uranus-impulse. These two exist, and they unite in the Mystery of the Marriage in Cana, as they do in the Mystery of Bethany and in the Mystery of Golgotha:

> One day the stars, down dripping,
> Shall flow in golden wine...[130]

Uranus becomes the Christ-Sun in the heart. The constellation standing above the wedding in Cana connects the Uranus-sign Waterman with the Sun-sign of the Lion.

As the earthly expression and representative of the divine, the universal life the Sun also carries all the planetary [life], everything revealed as separated in the individual planets. This can be found beautifully expressed in the book by Oskar A.H. Schmitz, *Der Geist der Astrologie*,[131] p. 219:

> The Sun is the visible symbol of infinity, of the creative [impulse], of the divine, which is presented in it in radiant, fiery unity (i.e., still as Uranian fire. [H. B.]), before its power divides into the variety of the active creative influences. Consequently:
>
> - the Sun is the spontaneous primal power, but not yet like Mars stained in the earthly realm;
> - it is beauty, but not yet as Venus bound to matter;
> - it is primal wisdom and goodness, but not yet as in Jupiter embodied for the gods and men;
> - it is the reproducing primordial lap, but not as the Moon made fruitful for the giving birth of creatures;
> - it is the spirit, but not yet like the intellect adjusted for the battle for existence (Mercury);
> - it contains in her fire even the destructive principle, but not yet as Saturn, by which outwardly the *fatum* [fact, deed, accomplishment] of matter, even binding to the gods, rigidifies.

This central meaning that includes all the planets, the Sun possesses also in the human horoscope, where it individualizes itself again according to the twelve zodiac-signs, but also in other ways. Here the forth-coming zodiac studies will contain what has to be said about the Sun. If one points towards the position of the Sun in the horoscope, one speaks always in a certain sense of the whole human being, which then individualizes only through the single planets and zodiac-signs. The human ether-body, *life* as such, is the Sun. Amongst the human organs, it is the heart, amongst the metals, gold. Most of the known connec-tions of astrology and alchymy light up for us.

In my little book on alchymy,[132] I quote a very revealing passage from one of Rudolf Steiner's[133] lectures in Dornach:

> For gold, the representative of the Sun-like qualities within the Earth's crust itself, gold is indeed something that does in fact enshrine an import-ant secret. Gold stands materially in the same relationship to other sub-stances as in the realm of thinking the concept of God does indeed to other concepts. The only question is what is made of this mystery.

And in one of the lectures on colour,[134] we find quoted:

> They [the early Mystery teachers] said: the human heart is a product of gold that lives everywhere in light; that which streams in from the universe actu-ally forms the human heart... Everywhere in the light there is gold. Gold weaves and lives in light. When the human being stands in life ....

Gold is the remains of light that has become earthly and physical, from the time of the union of the Earth with the Sun, something that the Christ has left behind in the Earth when it increasingly fell to the Ahrimanic, hardening forces. In this sense the statue of Christ in Dornach shows how Ahriman is bound to the Earth with chains of golden light—or rather, he binds himself. The Mysteries lying between the Sun and the Earth light up in the gold. And these Mysteries are the Mysteries of Christ.

The *Sun-Mystery* experiences the greatest revelation through the *Moon-Mystery*, about which I will say something to conclude [the matter] in these *Contributions*, which should, or are intended, to appear before Eas-ter, because between Sun and Moon there lies an Easter-Mystery *par excel-lence*. And it has a deep meaning that the evangelist John in his triangle (Frieling's *Contribution* on this will appear at the same time) that has espe-cially the Moon-sign of the Crab, not as one would think the Sun-sign that has been left to Mark. The Sun is 'at home' in the Lion, in the Ram it has its 'exaltation', there it is the enlivening one, the spring-Sun in which it is revealed particularly during Eastertide—Easter is the sign 'Ram' (which is not identical [today] with the constellation of the Ram). In particular John, whose initiation is completed in the Crab (on this, see my book on *Mark's Gospel*)[135] reveals through *the Moon-Mystery*, through the Mystery of Easter the actual depths of the Sun-Mystery. We are reminded of the famous Grail-picture: the image of the Sun in the Moon-disc, which at Eastertide stands in the heavens in quite a special sense.

## *The Moon-Mysteries*

Rudolf Steiner spoke in the deepest and most revealing manner on the Sun-Moon Mystery in a passage of *Occult Science* [tr. Creeger, pp. 180-86; tr. Monges, pp. 161-67; tr. Adams, pp. 149-54], during the evolution of Ancient Moon, when the mutual play of Moon and Sun appears for the first time, when Sun and Moon separate. (Earth itself was then Moon-like.) How many of us have read this and are still able to remember it? For not in vain does Rudolf Steiner say at one juncture, occult science takes its name because it appears to people, even when read, as occult = 'hidden'. Even solid-read 'cyclo-phages'[136] don't like to go into these things ...

But the place which I have just now cited belongs to the most beautiful, most revealing, of all that Rudolf Steiner has given us and left with us. The whole meaning of *Occult Science* and its cosmogony was revealed to me for the first time through this passage. It became a key for me to everything else, to Saturn, Sun, Moon and Earth as such. Rudolf Steiner speaks here of the alternation of the two conditions during Ancient Moon, the one time when the Moon, the [condition] of the Earth, is turned towards the Sun and receives the Sun-influence, giving itself to the life of the Sun; the other time is when the Moon turns away from the Sun, but then is given to the Universe. Corresponding to this are the different conditions of the human being and human consciousness. During the Sun-period the physical body and the etheric body grew and flourished; during the Moon-period the activity of the astral body grew, thereby the physical body became hardened. During the Sun-period (I mean now always the Sun-period of Ancient Moon) human consciousness is duller, but more selfless, more cosmic, given over to the Mysteries of the Universe (throughout the Sun-life) as to a sublime music of the spheres:

> He felt as if the causative forces of the cosmos were streaming into him and pulsating through him. He felt as if intoxicated with the cosmic

harmonies in which he took part. During these times, the astral body was as though freed from the physical body; a part of the life-body also withdrew from it. This formation consisting of astral body and life-body was like a marvellous, delicate musical instrument, and the Mysteries of the Universe resounded from its strings. The elements of the physical-etheric part of the human being that was less influenced by consciousness were shaped according to the harmonies of the universe, because the Sun-beings were at work in these harmonies. In this way, that part of the human being was shaped by the spiritual tones/ musical sounds of the cosmos [tr. based on Creeger, p. 184; cf. Monges, p. 164f.; Adams, p. 151f.].

In today's earthly life the two conditions described on Ancient Moon have their parallel in the alternation of sleep and waking, and then in that of living and dying. To the wakefulness of day and its life there corresponded that which turned away from the Sun-life, and to the falling asleep and dying that condition of the Ancient Moon which was given towards the life of the Sun. But much more than today the two conditions merged into each other at that time—I mean now, sleeping and dying on the one hand and waking and entering life on the other hand. The Sun-condition corresponding to dying was much rather like an enhanced reviving and an expanding into the universe (*Aufleben und All-leben*); it united the characteristics of a deep-sleep consciousness given to the spheric harmonies and a consciousness living into spiritual worlds after passing through the portal of death. Dying was closer to sleeping, nearer to the cosmic [condition]. At the end of *Tristan and Isolde* [culminating in the *Liebestod*, the 'death for love'], Wagner had sensed something of the Mysteries of these conditions of consciousness.[137] And nothing in the communications of the spiritual researcher is so revealing concerning the Mystery of death, than this description of the Ancient-Moon condition of consciousness, which was a synthesis of sleep and death, preceding today's earthly consciousness.

It is important for astrology, how *both these sides of Ancient Moon* described in *Occult Science* (the Earth-Moon as it was then) are reflected even today in the astrological double nature of the [present] Moon. And this astrological double-nature of the Moon once again has its purely astronomical reflection in the fact that the Moon always turns only the *one* side to us, that it also has another, as it were occult ['hidden'] side, completely open to the universe, of which we Earth-dwellers know nothing.[138] The Mystery of the Moon is how it combines the tendencies completely geared towards the earthly and earthly-hardening with the completely occult, profound, cosmic tendencies. For this reason, amongst the moods of the [twelve] world-conceptions (see the lecture-cycle, Rudolf Steiner, *Human and Cosmic Thought* [GA 151, 4 lectures, Berlin 20-23 Jan. 1914) the Moon corresponds to *occultism*, which is then at home in the Crab, in *materialism*. (Matter is the most occult of all spiritual phenomena.)

The descriptions in *Occult Science* between the contrast of the Sun-like and the Moon-like are splendidly presented. What Sun-existence, Sun-life, what the spiritual situation of the Sun really is, is nowhere so artistically and poetically expressed, in such a cosmic-musical manner, as there. And the Moon is indeed also deeply intertwined with the Mysteries of the sound-ether (which points again to John [the Evangelist and Apocalyptist]); it is a deeply musical planet. (Here also partly lie its astrological relationships to Neptune.) With all this the Easter picture of the Grail, the Sun-spirit in the Moon-dish, appears again before the soul.

At another place in *Occult Science* (tr. Creeger, p. 173) Dr Steiner relates that after the separation of the Sun and the Moon during Ancient Moon, the Moon-body related to the Sun-body as, at one time, the Saturn-body did to the whole surrounding cosmic development (that is, to Uranos). [Ancient] Sun related to Uranos, as the [Ancient] Moon did to Saturn. Thereby we behold that side of the Moon-being and the Saturn-being which is the earthly, hardened part.

Saturn was a mirror of the universe, or, if you like, of Uranos (even before the planet Uranus was a neighbouring colleague). The Moon [today] is a mirror of the Sun. This is deeply significant also for all astrology. Much earlier on [*Contribution* No. 2], I pointed to the significant fact that Moon and Sun appear optically the same size (both are the same size, experiencing only slight variation, as, for example, shown in the rare phenomenon of a ring-form during a solar [annular] eclipse [when the Moon disc appears slightly smaller]). The significance of this fact does not suffer the least harm when, to the spiritual-scientific study, one adds the purely astronomical, Copernican viewpoint, as Dr Steiner himself wished in the 'Michael Letters',[139] to combine the language of Michael with the other. Precisely when one says (the Copernican view): the Sun is so gigantic, thousands of times larger than the Earth; the Moon is much smaller than the Earth, and only because the Sun is so much farther distant they *appear* the same size to us, though they are not so in reality—precisely then one has to admire the 'pre-established harmony' of the universe (that is, to leave the Leibniz-like manner and take up the anthroposophical way of expression: the wonderfully conscious and harmonious collaboration of spiritual beings, who bring about everything in the universe in such a way that it corresponds precisely to the earthly conditions and human conditions), the harmony that now precisely for the earthly conditions artfully balances out these two discs, so that the Moon really does appear as the mirror of the Sun. (For me the equality of both discs was always one of the strongest proofs for the rational governing of spiritual beings in the cosmos.)

Like [Ancient] Saturn, also the Moon is a being that *mirrors*; like Saturn, it too carries in itself the earthly and earthly-hardening forces. The physical [element], which on [Ancient] Saturn was still always in etheric form, only becomes disposed to the earthly, physical stage on the Earth through the forces of the Moon. If in the development of the Earth the Moon had remained in the Earth, then the Earth through these Moon-forces would have become hardened in itself and died. But through the withdrawal of the Moon out of the Earth (after the Earth and the Sun had previously divided), it became the benefactor of the Earth. Then the balance entered, in which the Earth stands between Moon and Sun. Concerning the spiritual significance of the trinity Sun, Moon, and Earth, Rudolf Steiner spoke frequently (e.g. *Human and Cosmic Thought* [GA 151], Berlin; and in the Leipzig lecture-cycle, *Christ and the Spiritual World* [GA 149], on the relationship of 'thinking, the feelings, and doing').

The Moon, the clinker in the cosmos, stands in relationship to its physical nature still below the earthly condition. The forces of the earthly and physical proceed from it. The (spiritual) sphere of the Moon, the sphere between the Earth and the Moon, which is also the sphere of the Angeloi [angels] and the one the human being before his/her re-entering into earthly incarnation lives through as the last sphere. Only there is this earthly incarnation first determined in its physical details, in particular the gender. (The sphere of gender belongs to the Moon, in the same way as to Venus belong the kidneys, to Mercury the lungs, to Mars the gall, to the Sun the heart, to Jupiter the liver, to Saturn the spleen. With the Moon, the following points in the same direction: Moon, movement of reproduction; Venus, movement of the glands; Mercury, movement of the breathing; Sun, movement of the blood; Saturn, movement of achieving uprightness; Jupiter, movement of thinking; Mars, movement of speech.) In passing through the Moon-sphere, what develops within the womb is determined. Thus, the Moon is the planet of the feminine nature and motherhood. It shows the sexual element, especially from its high, rhythmic, divine side. It regulates the rhythm of the sexual life.

Mars, as I always say, is the other side of this realm. Mars today, we saw earlier on, is the border-mark of Ancient Moon, and the Mars separation from the Sun (or from the Earth, in the sense of *Occult Science*) stands according to *Occult Science* in some kind of relationship to the separation of the Moon from the Earth. Both, Moon and Mars, are related to the sound-ether, consequently also to the Johannine [element].[140] So, the relationship of the Moon to the sexual sphere is related partly to the physical as such, only this is not to be valued as something low. On the contrary, the lowest, darkest of all realms also carries in itself the highest secrets of life. The Scorpion carries in itself the Sun-Eagle (this is precisely the Johannine element in this realm). The sexual element is only the lower aspect of esoteric, cosmic Mysteries. It is *one* side turned towards earthly consciousness, in the same way as the Moon also turns only the *one* side towards us, the other side, turned towards the universe is hidden for us. This is its cosmic, its *occult* side.

Consequently, the Moon is a planet of occultism, at home in materialism (the Crab), but matter itself carries again the highest secrets within itself. In alchymy one spoke of the white tincture that is to transform the ignoble metal into silver, as the tincture of the Moon: of the red, gold-producing one as the tincture of the Sun. Gold belongs to the Sun, silver belongs to the Moon. Jahve [Yahveh], Rudolf Steiner explains in the lecture-cycles, is the reflection of Christ.

The Moon, then, despite its relationship to what is the most earthly [element], is at the same time a completely occult planet, a being that is most deeply connected to the occult element in the cosmos, and so also to 'occultism'. Indeed, to very high and also to very low occultism (the *'bleiche Hekate'*—'pale Hecate'). Consequently, also the early Indian culture was related to the Moon: in the primordial Indian age the Sun had its spring equinox in the Moon-sign of the Crab. The early Indian astrology (which has only come to us in a decadent, gipsy-like form) was a lunar astrology. Rudolf Steiner speaks of the seven Rishis, the carriers of the early Indian primordial culture, as those who have withdrawn into the spiritual sphere of the Moon, into the 'stronghold of the Moon'.[141] There they worked inspiringly for the souls between death and a new birth. All this had its counter-picture, also in outer astronomy, where the Moon has a visible, Earth-side and an invisible, cosmic side.

The Moon in its astrological meaning in a mysterious manner also combines all these contrasts: here, too, it is as reflection and mirror of the Sun the planet of the personal element, of the earthly manifestation of the most earthly part of the human being. The Sun is the higher spiritual being of man; the Moon is the earthly persona, the earthly element. Somehow everyone carries his/her Moon 'at the tip of his nose'. It is a shame that discretion simply forbids characterizing the individuals of our circle simply according to their Moon-position! In human intercourse people are mostly judged by other people—unfortunately, one would like to say—simply according to their Moon. One sees the surface; what is important in the background is often not seen. In particular the people who do not understand anything of astrology and do not know the stars of the other person, are those who, without wanting to know, judge the other in the most unbridled manner, only according to the other's stars, often only according to their Moon. What I am striving for in these astrological observations lies in the opposite, the anthroposophical direction. Later on, I will have to communicate more about the meaning and effect of individual Moon constellations. The realm of the Moon in particular is indeed immeasurably important, many-sided and complicated.

The Moon in astrology, for reasons that now can be well understood, is the planet of the female element. Moon in the 12th house (this is the 'house of the difficult destinies', more on this later) can show catastrophic influences from the female side of existence; Moon in the 11th house (the 'house of friends') can relate to many friendships and helpers from this side. The Sun in the horoscope is often related to the father (not only to the heavenly Father but also to the earthly father), the Moon in relationship to the mother. Here, too, the viewpoints also cross over. That which in the physical world is masculine, becomes in the etheric feminine and vice versa. But the relationship of the Moon to the physical, feminine element is initially decisive in the horoscope. In the horoscope of a man the Moon means (besides what else it might still mean) the woman; in the horoscope of the woman it means her own femininity. In alchymy it is said about the hermaphrodite, of the philosopher's stone, that the Sun is its father, the Moon its mother (in the 'hermaphrodite' itself the 'son' is contained, the Venus-Mercury question). In so far as in Sun + Moon + Venus-Mercury there lies a trinitarian aspect, this is a very esoteric aspect which I have discussed earlier. Here with the Moon, one can also not speak about the Mysteries of the feminine without coming immediately into very esoteric realms. Uranus and Neptune, outer planets far distant from the Sun, are occult planets; so, too, (although within limits) are Mercury and the Moon as inner planets close to the Sun and the Earth. (We see the astronomical Mercury virtually not at all with the naked eye, and only half of the Moon.) According to Rudolf Steiner, 'occultism' belongs to the Moon, 'transcendentalism' belongs to Mercury.[142]

We have already talked about the side of the Moon of the sound-ether and cosmic music. From this viewpoint (already mentioned here) it relates to Neptune, likewise a planet very much to do with cosmic music and with music on the Earth. And so we arrive—here, too, lies something occultly significant—to the Moon, the nearest planet to the Earth as Neptune is the farthest (I do not include the debatable Pluto just now). A 'musical sound out of cosmic distances' connects Neptune with the lunar element, a conjunction Moon-Neptune in this regard can be something expressive. This is something humanly completely personal in a person's relationship to cosmic music, 'the musical sound out of cosmic distances', whereas the conjunction Moon-Saturn is something heavy with Earth. Neptune, too, is related indeed to the personal element (only in the occult sense, as the Moon is in the solely earthly aspect) and in so far to the Moon, whereas the Sun relates to the Uranian [influence], to Uranus. (That our earthly Moon, purely astronomically, is not concerned with Neptune does not prove anything to the contrary.) In astrology 'Moon' means the sum of the spiritual and astral relationships that exist between myself and the Moon; 'Neptune' means: the sum of the relationships between myself and the sphere of Neptune. Both factors can most certainly be compared and even relate to each other.

In its relationship to the sound-ether, the Moon leads us also to the musical feeling, as it were, of the Sun-life; here it becomes the cosmic-musical revealer of the Sun-element. Here we arrive again at that section of *Occult Science* [quoted above]. One would like to wish that many friends read it, precisely at Easter. For at Eastertide the Moon and the Sun enter a cosmic relationship they do not have throughout the whole year. In these relationships live all the rhythms of the cosmos, and with this the rhythmic element of the human being. All the Christ-Sun Mysteries live and shine in the Moon-Mystery. There the Moon becomes in quite a special sense the Grail-vessel, which reveals the 'connection of the Lord of the world with the lunar Mother', that of which the connection of the disciple John with the Mother under the cross in John's Gospel is again a picture. The Easter Moon-experience becomes a Grail-experience. And I conclude with the wish that this *Newsletter Contribution* (which because of delays unfortunately appears as a double number) may become an Easter study, also the *Contribution* on Venus-Mercury. For the Easter Grail-picture in the sky is only then complete as a trinity, when—as sometimes beautifully experienced in the sky—in the chalice of the Moon (the Moon-sickle) carrying the 'Sun host', the spiritual element of the Sun (the reflection of the sunlight from the Earth), there also appears the Star of Venus, when the spiritual element of the Sun then also unites with Venus.

# X
# Zodiac 1: Sign and Constellation

As with the planets, when we ask about the actual reality ultimately (or 'at first'), we come with the zodiac, too, to the *spiritual essence*. The spiritual essence of the zodiac and of the individual zodiac-signs is revealed as *above* in the *cosmic spatial realm*, as well as *below* in *the earthly-temporal realm*.

- The revelation in the cosmic spatial realm, or rather its pictorial expression in the heavenly script, we call the *starry constellation*;
- the revelation in the temporal, earthly realm, in the rhythm of the year, we call the *sign*.

Now the essence of each 'clock' consists in measuring the course of an event in time with a spatial movement. And when today we want spatially to orientate the earthly, temporal [aspect] of the sign to the great cosmic, celestial clock of the zodiac and its starry constellations—then we know it for an astronomical fact that the signs can no longer be determined without more ado according to the constellation (the position of the Sun to a particular constellation [in the sky]). The sign (that means, its spatial orientation in the celestial clock) and the constellation are not the same today. They differ by the approximate extent of one constellation, because of the precession (more correctly, the retrogression) of the vernal equinox, the spring point [where the Sun rises on the first day of spring]. This distance will progressively increase till c. 26,000 years (Steiner gives the number 25,920) when the circle is complete; then sign and constellation will coincide once more.

This consequently means [for example]:

(i) the earthly Scales, the 'sign Scales' (the autumnal equalizing, coming into balance of days and nights, the autumnal equinox) is orientated spatially no longer according to the heavenly Scales today. The Sun then does not yet rise in the zodiacal Scales, but in the Virgin.

(ii) If we look at the celestial clock, towards the celestial Ram, the earthly Ram (the 'sign of the Ram'), the earthly Eastertide and the beginning of spring, is no longer orientated today to the zodiac-sign of the Ram. The Sun still [visibly] stands in the sign of the Fishes. The 'Easter lamb' derives from the time when the earthly Ram, the earthly Eastertide, still took place in accordance with to the heavenly Ram.

Nevertheless, as I try to show in these *Contributions*, this divergence exists only outwardly. The spiritual essence revealed above in the cosmic region of the Ram is ultimately the same, governing below the Easter section of the annual rhythm, the earthly Ram, even though this section of the annual rhythm is no longer determined according to the position of the Sun in this constellation. As long as we look at the 'spiritual being of the Ram' we do have again the unity. Consequently, the justified equality of the names, despite the characterized outer difference.

Against this situation we may not object that it is too complicated, that we would rather have it simpler. This derives from the accusation (I no longer recall by which king)[143] against the Creator, that He should have constructed the universe more simply. Any kind of advance in astrology is completely out of the question without a clear focus on the difference between sign and constellation. Precisely from the Christian viewpoint this whole difference in astrology is important. This will soon become more clear.

With this whole series of studies, I would like to take some things from astronomy as known. In particular, that the zodiac, or the ecliptic, is the approximate region in which Sun, Moon and planets complete their courses—not all on the same line. Here a certain difference exists, also significant for astrology. And hopefully everyone is clear that it concerns a specific view of the heavenly constellations from the earthly viewpoint. For earthly notions the tremendously distant planets, to be found in the cosmic widths, still have measurable distances, whereas the fixed stars through which we determine the zodiac-pictures are to be found in the immeasurable realm. This basically can no longer be regarded as earthly and spatial.

In reality the planets have always to do with the Earth, never with the fixed stars, even if one says the planets stand in this or that sign. All in all, there is nothing that leads astray so much from any agreement concerning zodiac questions than if one thinks with the zodiac-signs always immediately of the astronomical element of the fixed stars. This actually is a terrible materialism. The zodiac has nothing at all to do with the astronomical element of the fixed stars. But in order truly to imagine the zodiac one has to be able to raise oneself *to imagine the essence of space*, and how this essence of space is connected with the essence of time. In order to reach this essence of space and time, one may not remain stuck with the fixed-star imagination of outer astronomy [on this see also the quotations from Steiner and Novalis in my book on *Alchymy*, Eng. ed. p. 18ff.].[144] Here, too, true astrology is a test for spiritual thinking. One must not confuse the *picture of the heavenly script* with the essence of the zodiac itself.

## Gyroscopic Motion

The precession, or retrogression, of the vernal equinox, upon which rests the discrepancy of the sign and constellation (of the earthly zodiac and the starry zodiac), has to do, viewed astronomically, with a specific gyroscopic movement of the Earth's axis. This once again is explained mathematically out of a specific position of this earthly axis to the ecliptic in union with certain [gravitational] attractions of the Sun and Moon. Gravity wants to achieve the per-pendicular position for the Earth's axis, upright to the ecliptic. The rotation of the Earth—so the astronomers say—hinders the Earth's axis from achieving this position; the axis inclines at an angle to the ecliptic. The result of the various play of forces is the gyroscopic movements of the Earth's axis, in which it describes a spherical sur-face around the axis of the ecliptic. The Earth makes its movements in space not as a train on a track, but she dances, does eurythmy. This gyroscopic motion of the earthly poles causes the apparent circular movement of the celestial poles (for this reason in differ-ent ages there was always a different star as pole star; the change of the vernal equinox is accompanied, of course, by corresponding changes of all the other points of the ecliptic).

This means, the zodiac, and with it the whole starry heaven, lies always differently over the horizon in different periods of the Earth's history. Today, where the constellation of the Fishes is the spring sign, as it were the rising sign, it forms the ascendant of the Earth-time horoscope. At the zenith the heavenly Twins occupy the heights, the zenith of the zodiac. That can always be observed on winter nights towards the spring. The highest, bright part of the zodiac arches over the star-picture Sirius-Orion, the 'sacred mount of the heavens'. Then the two stars of the Twins, Castor and Pollux, which, in the middle of the great constellation of the Twins, embracing many stars, pre-senting in the narrow sense the 'heavenly Twins', really form the tip of this 'sacred mountain' (similarly, as in the gospel the 'two sons of Zebedee', James and John, abide with Christ on the mountain). Before the turning point of time, that time when sign and constellation met and coincided, the Ram was the rising constellation, the Crab in the zenith. Today the 'sign of the Ram' lies in the constellation of the Fishes (i.e. it orientates essentially according to this constellation); the sign of the Crab lies in the constellation of the Twins.

One can view this by choosing the place of Jupiter this year and the past winter. With an Ephemeris,[145] one finds Jupiter in the Crab. From astrology we know that this, the 'ascension' of Jupiter works more strongly (i.e. in that sign next to its actual governing signs or 'houses' Fishes and Archer). One saw, or one sees in the sky during this whole time, Jupiter shining with the heavenly Twins. For Jupiter it does not depend on the fixed stars of this constellation, but on the fact that the zenith-sign as such is rising. Jupiter, the dominating planet, rises in the celestial zenith, in the 'sign of the Crab', orientated today to the constellation of the Twins. Particularly with this example the difference between sign and constellation becomes very clear.

It is of great significance that as a consequence of this gyroscopic motion, or dancing, of the Earth's axis, it allows the Earth always to look out to changing views, to fashion ever and again other constellations as rising ones or occupying the zenith, and so on. The whole change of the destiny of the times, the whole advance of humanity's developing consciousness is connected to this—when we are clear in general with the celestial picture and the earthly event, upon which all astrology rests. Here again is a point that becomes especially visible, rather as we discussed earlier with the apparent same-sized discs of the Sun and Moon. That which astronomy explains purely mechanically through mathematics—that is, quite outwardly and superficially out of certain laws of attraction, rotation and angle-inclinations—is yet connected to the essential things of the world and the spiritual facts in the course of world-history.

Of course, the subject does not involve the astronomy of the fixed stars, but the essentials of the cosmic spatial regions. The Earth becomes always different in the various periods, beheld by the countenances of spiritual beings. Always different beings determine the spring, the summer, the autumn and the winter. This quaternity relates to what is called in astrology (more on this later with the horoscope) the four (highly important) 'corner houses' (I, IV, VII, X). And one can understand that for the evolution of the world it is not indifferent in what sequence the regents of the four great, cosmic corner-houses are arranged.

From here one can once again approach the question of 'sign and constellation' more closely. For also in the birth-astrology the 1st house (the ascendant, i.e. the sign beginning to rise at the birth, is always the 'individual Ram' whether this sign falls in the Ram, or in the Scales, or in the Scorpion, or wherever—here somehow are mixed the qualities of the Scales, the Scorpion, etc. with the qualities of the Ram. Likewise, with the great horoscope of the Earth, the 1st house, the 'sign of the Ram' falls today essentially in the constellation of the Fishes. In a not-too-distant future it will fall in the constellation of the Waterman. In the age of Christ's earthly ministry sign and constellation coincided, earthly Ram and celestial Ram (and correspondingly, every other sign and constellation). This is in so far as such a coinciding is possible, for constellations are irregular in size and not so clearly outlined, many overlap, whereas the signs, mathematically precise, present equal sections (all are 1/12 of the whole circle, that is 30°). The dissimilarity of sign and constellation—though from the cosmic, spatial side of the constellation, influences reach the earthly and temporal aspect of the signs—is a decisive factor in the cultural progression of mankind.

The celestial picture just presented is most clearly and beautifully actually beheld in practice, if one chooses the hours before midnight (about 10 o'clock at night) on a February night. February, the Waterman-Uranus month, in our latitudes is also the month of the most beautiful revelation of the starry heaven. The central star-picture Sirius-Orion shines still at its most bright (at the time of writing, the beginning of April, it takes its leave from us, inclining in the evening sky to set early, in order to appear again towards Christmas in the evening sky—already in the morning sky during August. Sirius, not a constellation but only a star, is yet by far the greatest and brightest fixed star in the entire starry heaven. The constellation to which it belongs is called the 'the great dog', the guardian of the celestial herd (for this reason Sirius is also the 'dog star'). One can, though, also feel Sirius with Orion as *one* constellation, for the Egyptians the celestial picture of Isis (Sirius, Egyptian 'Satit', 'Sothis') and Osiris (Orion, the primal human being in the sky). Together they form the 'sacred celestial mountain',[146] around which in winter still arch the starry constellations of the upper zodiac. They are called the 'summer' constellations, since they are the ones through which the Sun passes during the summer of the year, or 'winter' constellations since they are visible in the winter sky (cf. on this the Introduction to my book on *Mark's Gospel*, p. 36ff.). The summer signs are seen during the winter, because they are concealed by the Sun during the summer, and vice versa. During the summer the zodiac rises more horizontally over the horizon (a fact known to everyone, that on winter nights the Moon rises much higher than on summer nights, so, vice versa, during the day the Sun rises higher than in the winter).

## All the Constellations

In order to receive an impression of the zodiac-pictures, one has patiently to observe the starry sky throughout the whole year. But in February there will be a climax in observing the night sky (of the brighter, upper zodiac); during August (when the starry heaven that has become pale during early summer begins to shine once again) a climax comes for observation of the summer sky, that is, for of the lower, dark part of the zodiac, the winter constellations. On a February night one will see over the peak of the 'sacred mountain' Sirius-Orion high in the zenith, the two characteristic stars of the great sign of the Twins, Castor and Pollux, the 'heavenly Twins', and receive such an impression that is unforgettable. It belongs to that which we should know of the starry heaven. On the western slope of the 'sacred mountain' one will see the Bull below the Twins, the great shining, starry picture, with the smaller constellation of the Pleiades, the seven stars often mentioned in the Bible, and the Hyades, reminding one of an upturned triangle or circle, the brightest star being Aldebaran.[147] A smaller, less shining and less characteristic starry constellation amongst them is the Ram; only two stars, the 'horns of the Ram', come to the fore. The constellation of the Fishes, with few stars (also in this, two stars are characteristic) is then already setting in the West. This certainly very dark constellation is replaced today by the bright sign of the Ram (Ram, Bull, Twins, Crab, Leo, Virgin and Scales are the 'seven bright, upper' constellations); Scorpion, Archer, Goat, Waterman and Fishes are the 'five dark, lower' ones—in particular one thinks of the two Feedings in Mark's Gospel. I have discussed this at length in my two books on the gospel; it would be difficult to bring it in here once again).

## The Crab–Virgin with Sirius

On the Eastern slope of the 'sacred mountain' the bright Twins are initially followed by the pale, insignificant Crab, along with the Scales the smallest of the constellations, with the two well-known 'donkey stars', important for gospel research (see my book on *Mark's Gospel*, p. 309). But then deeper below in the East follows the majestic Lion with its four brightest stars ordered into a beautiful trapezium, the biggest amongst them the regal star Regulus. Then finally from February onwards one will see rising further down in the East the great constellation of the Virgin (the zodiac sign of our Movement), with the beautiful radiant star Spica shining in strangely white, calm light; known to us all, it has made its impression. It is by far not as bright as, for example, Sirius, but to a more intimate observation one of the most beautiful stars (reminding one of Venus). For the Egyptians this, like Sirius, like the planet Venus, was a star of Isis. For us it is the star of the Last Supper. It helps us to experience the essence of the 'heavenly provisions for the way' as no other star in the sky. (Spica means 'sheaf of grain', heavenly bread.) The Scales still lower down in the East one will only clearly recognize towards spring and in the summer. This small constellation with its three essential stars one will imagine like a [pair of old-fashioned] scales with its crossbeam held from above downwards.

## Scales–Scorpion/Eagle

The part of the zodiac observable on a summer night begins with the Scales—also the Virgin which rises in the early spring can be seen during the first months of summer. Already from May this especially characteristic zodiac constellation—the Scorpion—is well visible (it is seen, of course, much earlier in late summer when the nights draw in). From the viewpoint of the position of the Sun it would be called a 'winter star-sign'. For as the November constellation it introduces the winter half of the year (for this reason in the gospel it relates to the 'flight in winter' to the Scorpion and its sting of death, see my *Mark's Gospel*, p. 370f. & 374). However, the main time to observe this 'winter' constellation is, of course, during the summer months. Somewhat threatening, like a dragon's tail, appears to lie in this beautiful, perhaps most striking of all the constellations, which with a more amicable imagination has also been called 'flowering twig'. The spirituality of the Scorpion is actually like this: it combines the highest heights with the deepest abysses. It is the Sun-Eagle, which through the Fall of man carries the sting of death. Thus, precisely the Scorpion is the mystical Johannine sign. With the Crab and the Fishes, it forms the 'Johannine triangle', about which, in the meantime, one may be informed through Frieling's *Contributions*.

One can really find all this in beholding the Scorpion constellation in the heavenly script. *The spirituality of the Scorpion is really expressed in the constellation of the Scorpion*, even if the period of time when this spirituality of the Scorpion governs the earthly rhythm (c. 24 October to 23 November, the 'sign of the Scorpion'), is not when the Sun clearly stands in the constellation of the Scorpion. (The Sun still stands at the beginning in the Virgin, later in the Scales, which is a very small constellation, only from approximately the middle of November in the Scorpion.) (The signs always change around the 21st day of the month—for this reason this is the true beginning of the month (as it lies spiritually as the basis of our Breviary); with the constellations it changes according to their size and in general cannot be more exactly fixed.

From the 'dragon's tail' (or 'flowering twig')[148] sweeping in front of the Scales—from which then the three characteristic stars standing one above the other spread out like a sparkling sheaf—is the bright star Antares in the Scorpion. Amongst the fixed stars, it is somewhat similar to Mars amongst the planets. (A conjunction Mars-Antares would sharpen the character of Mars in a horoscope. Only when it stands in close conjunction to a planet, does one assume the influence of a fixed star into a horoscope.) The actual curved 'Scorpion's sting' lies towards the other side and already projects into the Archer. In Germany it can only be seen in the south, and then in countries further south. This entering of the one constellation into another is important. One has to answer those who want to reckon the constellations as is done with the signs, in degrees. It cannot be done. The signs alone can be precisely reckoned; the constellations lie in the imaginative and flowing realm, not to be worked out with the precision belonging to physical reckoning.

### The Archer

The Archer, with many bright stars, rises out of the mist of the Milky Way. In the summer nights it is already visible where the Milky Way rises over the southern horizon. In the gospel the Archer is the sign of Golgotha, and in my gospel studies, when mentioning the Milky Way—the Indians call it the 'heavenly Ganges'—I always pointed to the stream of life springing from the event of Golgotha, the 'new Paradisal stream'. In the rhythm of the earthly year the spirituality of the Archer is at work in the period when the Sun initially still stands in the sign of the Scorpion (today the 'sign of the Archer' lies in the constellation of the Scorpion). In the horoscope, the Archer in the ascendant signifies (always the 'sign') a gentle unfolding of life (right into the bodily aspect); Jupiter, too, in the Archer (where he is 'at home', as one of the two signs he governs) is in this direction somewhat favourable. In the Creed, it is known as the sign of the developing Church: 'Communities, whose members', etc.; see what Frieling in his *Contribution* (appearing in this issue) says concerning the connection of Church *kyriaké* with *kyrios*—i.e. belonging to the Lord'—the *'kyrios Christus'* is connected to Jupiter [see below, p. 228]. All this can be read in the celestial script of the sign of the Archer, and yet one knows at the same time that it is revealed on Earth when the Sun stands in another constellation.

## The Goat–Waterman–Fishes

The Goat is a strange dark region in the sky, in which nevertheless two stars standing mostly aslant, the one under the other—the 'horns' of the mountain Goat—are very striking and can easily be found. The celestial picture helps us to feel the Saturnian element of this region—which is the dark Saturn-sign—whereas the large constellation Waterman, rich in stars but in its form not very striking (the Saturn-Uranus sign), has more a starry quality. The constellation of the Fishes (with the 'two fishes'), with its few stars, has already been discussed. In that time-period, when the Earth's yearly rhythm stands today in the *sign* Waterman, we find the Sun essentially still in the Goat; in the time of the Fishes it stood in the constellation Waterman; in the Ram [the original] Eastertide ('the sign of the Ram') it stood in the constellation of the Fishes.

I have not written this whole section concerning the heavenly picture of the zodiac in order to divert attention from the question of 'sign and constellation', but on the contrary in order to lead attention in the right way towards it. Clarity must reign with regard to all these constellations which only involve a *picture of the heavenly script*, and that furthermore the *spiritual element of the beings of the zodiac*, for which these groups of stars are a *picture*, is revealed everywhere,

- as above in the cosmic space,
- so below in the earthly and temporal,

and, moreover, in many other contexts:

- in the human gestalt and in its twelve members,
- in the twelve senses, in the spiritual human being as such,

- in the twelve main world-conceptions (see *Human and Cosmic Thought* [GA 151, 4 lectures, Berlin 20-23 Jan. 1914]),
- in music in the circle of the twelve keys (see my little book *The Essence of Tonality*) [Leominster: Anastasi 2008; and the more expanded *The Language of Tonality*, Leominster: Anastasi 2015] and so on.

For the revelation in the earthly, temporal element of the yearly rhythm the 'sign' corresponds to the spiritual element of the being of the zodiac carrying that name. But it no longer directly relates to the 'picture of the heavenly script'. That means, the revelation can be related to the position of the Sun in the respective constellation, but through the precession of the vernal equinox a divergence has occurred which in future will increase.

## A Misunderstanding

A lack of clarity has now arisen, because certain remarks by Dr Steiner are understood by some as if he said one should only look at the constellation and not at the sign. With this, any astrology would become impossible. This is contradicted especially through the fact that Dr Steiner himself, like any practical astrologer, has calculated according to the *sign and not the constellation*, in particular when he looked at the horoscope which was the most important thing for him, that is, at the horoscope of the First Goetheanum, at the laying of the foundation stone (20 September 1913): 'Because Mercury as an evening star stood in the Scales'[149]—for Mercury stood in the *sign* of the Scales, in the constellation of Virgo. Moreover, certain periods of time important for the Priests' Breviary have been given, as already mentioned, according to the calculation of the sign, not of the constellation. One would only bring Dr Steiner in conflict with the facts if everything he said were to be taken as a one-sided acknowledgement of calculations according to the constellations.

The main place to which attention is drawn is found in Rudolf Steiner's lecture-course *Agriculture* [Koberwitz 7-16 June 1924. GA 327]. There the extermination of certain animal pests is mentioned, which would be the most effective during the period when a certain planet was in a certain constellation. But here:

[i]   firstly, it concerns not astrology but agriculture, and that the animals still have a direct relationship to the cosmic regions of the zodiac (from which it derives its name in the German language, *Tierkreis* 'animal circle') can be well imagined, and

[ii]    secondly, one could have expressed the same meaning reckoning from the signs, instead of 'constellation Scorpion', it would be 'sign Archer', and the result would be the same. But Dr Steiner had certain reasons here to proceed from the constellation.

## The Two Zodiacs once again

In all these studies we 'look' basically as little one-sidedly to the sign, as we do to the constellation. But *we look primarily to the spirituality of the zodiac being*, which in the 'constellation' has only its reflection in the celestial script. It is revealed in the most varied cosmic and earthly, and human relationships on Earth. And the revelation in the earthly time of the rhythm of the year, the 'sign' (which today is no longer to be orientated according to the constellation) is only *one* of these revelations, but one that is particularly important for astrology. Basically we have in the 'twelve signs' of astrology, which are not identical with the twelve starry constellations in the sky, an earthly picture of the heavenly zodiac, but it is indeed a reflection of the rhythms of time, whereas when we look from there to the celestial clock we meet once more the divergence caused by the precession of the vernal equinox. Here we have an *earthly zodiac*, which it is true is a picture of the *starry zodiac*, but no longer relates spatially to it. The difference, so important for astrology, between 'earthly zodiac' and 'starry zodiac' then lights up for us.

It is not that we should neglect the starry zodiac because of the earthly zodiac. On the contrary, the question: what is the relationship of the earthly to the starry zodiac; what does the starry zodiac behind the earthly zodiac mean? This will concern us everywhere.

We have already recognized and sufficiently discussed the significance of the starry zodiac for the Earth and earthly history itself, for the change of the cultural periods and their connection with the precession of the vernal equinox. On the other hand, astrology shows with the birth-horoscope—and with the horoscope of the Goetheanum Dr Steiner proceeded in the same way—the primary significance of the sign, that is, of the earthly zodiac. Even if it says, such and such planet stands in such and such a sign—for example: Mars would stand in the Scorpion—then it is not meant that he would stand with the stars of the starry constellation in question, but a 'Mars in the Scorpion' will have to be looked for in the sky with the stars of the Scales or (earlier in the month) in the constellation of the Virgin. (The last degrees of the sign of the Scorpion can already be found in the constellation of the Scorpion.) Through making a birth-horoscope a *relationship to the Earth*, not a relationship to the fixed stars, is expressed, the planet *x* is found in the sign *y*.

Not for nothing did Christ write the guilt of the adulteress, the karma of the adulteress, into the Earth (cf. H. B. *John's Gospel*, 148f., 294ff.) Here it is asked how a planet—in this case, for example, 'Mars in the Scorpion', in an unfavourable influence with Venus—stands to the *Earth*, not how he stands to the fixed stars. The whole separation caused by the Fall of man, of the Earth as a planet, from the cosmic, starry, Uranian realm, comes here to our consciousness. It suddenly becomes clear concerning what it ultimately has to do with—the whole differentiation of *earthly zodiac* and *starry zodiac*. The differentiation of the earthly, planetary realm from the cosmic, Uranian realm—well known to us from all our planetary studies—stands once again before us.

## The Mystery of the Starry Zodiac

What, then, ultimately (or 'at first') is the *zodiac of stars*, whose reflection enters into the earthly temporal sphere? Nothing other than the super-planetary, super-Saturnian being whom we here always call *Uranos*. We have differentiated this from the planet Uranus that receives its name because only later did it join the solar system, arriving from the celestial side, the side of Uranos. The planet Uranus marks the Uranian, celestial realm, as Saturn does the earthly planetary realm. The visible, astronomical sky of fixed stars is to this Uranos-being only *maya* ['illusion']. (In the same way as the planet Uranus could be called here for once the 'planetary *maya*'.) Uranos itself is the unfathomable Being of Light of the Father, or the [Holy] Trinity. This is what in the Grimms' fairytale of '*Marienkind*' [No. 3, 'Our Lady's Child', or 'A Child of St Mary'] the young girl glimpses behind the hidden thirteenth door, the Mystery of the 3 in 1 hidden behind it—here, too, with the twelve other doors the Mystery of the zodiac is sounding. Earlier [*Contribution* No. 6], we discussed the revelation of the Trinitarian Mystery of Uranos in the solar system.

Of the beings of the higher hierarchies, the Cherubim and Seraphim belong to the realm of Uranos, whereas the Thrones—Saturn—are the first hierarchy to sacrifice themselves into the planetary realm. We have to think of the Seraphim as those beings who have the purest view of the Father, or the Trinity, whereas the Cherubim are those who already look down and work in the planetary realm, the mediators between the Uranian and the planetary realms. And that realm where the Uranian element works into the planetary realm, where it enters into relations with the planetary realm, is indeed the *zodiac*. It embraces, indeed also for the outer view, not the whole starry circle, but that starry belt in which (appearing to earthly eyes)—in addition to the Sun and the Moon—the planets move. But, of course, this zodiac extends over the whole of the starry heaven—compare what is said above concerning the relationship of the 'sacred mountain' Sirius-Orion to the zodiac. Here one cannot see the boundary so clearly. Moreover, with Dr Steiner there are passages where the word '*Tierkreis*', zodiac, somehow stands for the heaven of fixed stars in general. The starry zodiac is above all the Cherubinic aspect of Uranos. The planet Uranus itself, if the sphere of influence is limited in Saturn, must already lie in the sphere of the Cherubim. And in exactly the same way the starry zodiac is a Cherubinic revelation. The essential thing of this starry zodiac, this cosmic, spatial side of the zodiac, are the Cherubim.

Where, above all, do they reveal themselves, and with them the starry zodiac? Let us look once again at the cosmogony of *Occult Science* (what I mean here is expressly stated in the Düsseldorf lecture-cycle on the hierarchies [GA 110]). There the great cosmic regions are mentioned, out of which in the primordial beginning the planetary system, or rather the four stages of its sequential evolution descend. Dr Steiner sketches the twelve positions of the zodiac, within which once again the four main regions forming the cosmic cross, the four great corners of the world, out of which in [Ancient] Saturn, Sun, Moon and Earth the influence of the Cherubim shine down. It is the great cross (in my gospel studies, presented as the 'Cross of the Holy Spirit'), which lies on the two axes Waterman–Lion and Bull–Eagle (Scorpion). This is the well-known cross of the four creatures, to which the four evangelists are arranged:

Matthew Waterman, etheric primordial man,
Mark Lion,
Luke Bull,
John Eagle.

Out of these four great cosmic corners in the primordial beginning (or the four great stages of world-becoming) the Cherubinic influence comes down. Dr Steiner relates Saturn to the Lion, Sun to the Eagle, Moon to the Waterman, Earth to the Bull. On [Ancient] Saturn the heart of the world begins to beat and there ceases to beat. In the Eagle the Sun-life begins on the Ancient Sun and receives in the Scorpion the sting of death, and so on. We will rightly understand what Dr Steiner gives here, when, of the named four regions, we regard the Waterman as the actual primordial region, the Uranus-Uranos region. We then recall how Saturn in its first, anterior stage (before time) was still united with the starry periphery, with Uranos (I only found this expressed again in the recently published *Karmic Relationships*[150] by Dr Steiner). *This* situation, the point, where the spatial and temporal mutually meet with the super-spatial and super-temporal, corresponds entirely with the Uranus-region of the Waterman. Furthermore, Frieling's *Contributions* on the Creed revealingly show how there the 'Ground of Existence of the Heavens and of the Earth', lies in the Uranian primordial region of the Father (see below, pp. 350 and 360f.).

Saturn–Lion will be so understood that *in the Fall into time*, into the coming-into-existence of time of Saturn, it is to be regarded as a Fall into the opposition, for the Lion is in opposition to the Waterman. (In reading these *Contributions* to make all these relationships clear it would be helpful to consult the diagram of the zodiac—see the figs. in my books on the gospels and those included below pp. 338-44.) The sign of the Lion, which is also the sign of the heart, belongs not to the Uranian primordial Saturn, but to time's becoming during [Ancient] Saturn—but this is the often-mentioned Saturn-Uranus separation. In my article on *time*,[151] I attempted to explain how *time* (cf. the English 'tide', Germ. *Gezeiten*, the ebb and flow) is the pulse-beat, or heartbeat of eternity. Where in the temporal realm the heartbeat of eternity begins, we are in the sign of the heart, of the Lion. This is the relationship meant by Dr Steiner of Ancient Saturn to the Lion. And the fire-sign of the Lion, the warmth of Saturn, is enkindled. But the Saturn-Uranus region, from which we proceed everywhere here, is the Waterman. The primordial temporal event on Ancient Saturn stands in opposition; on the [Ancient] Moon—where the primordial expression of life according to Dr Steiner begins in the Waterman—in conjunction; in Ancient Sun and in the primordial beginning on the Earth we stand in the square (Scorpion and Bull are in both squares of the Waterman, that is, astrologically, they stand to it at an angle of 90°).

Wherever we have to do with a cosmic primordial revelation, the primal emergence of everything planetary out of the Uranian realm, it has to do, of course, with the starry zodiac, or rather with the Cherubim element that today is revealed in the starry zodiac. For at that time the starry zodiac, the starry heavens, was in no way like today, and in particular there was no human consciousness to behold it, in the way that people today look at the stars. In the *Leading Thoughts* Dr Steiner distinguishes four great stages of development of the starry world: Being—Revelation—Activity—the Work [Leading Thought, No. 6]. Today we experience the 'work'. This is the macrocosm that has died, the starry heaven that can be astronomically calculated. This [stage] is preceded by the living activity and the [stage of] revelation, and still prior to all the revelation of the stars in the outer side of the heavens, there was the stage when *only* the Beings were present, working. This means, when Dr Steiner speaks of the region of the zodiac, one cannot at all think about the astronomical starry zodiac of today. With all zodiac observations, to look at the astronomical element of the fixed stars is actually always only confusing. Dr Steiner never meant this astronomical element of the fixed stars, but of the fixed-star heavens he gives a completely different spiritual Imagination. All its details cannot be discussed here, but it is the same when I always speak here of Uranos. All discussion of the 'starry zodiac' has to be removed as far as possible from the astronomical concept of the fixed stars. It has to be raised towards the Imagination of the essence of space itself, as we find it in the *Fragments* of Novalis (see the beginning of my book on *Alchymy*) [Fragment 1719, ed. Kamnitz; Wood, English translation, 1095. See end of the present *Contribution*].

## The Earthly Zodiac

When, then, the essential reality of the starry zodiac lies in the Cherubinic beings, how is it with the earthly zodiac, with the earthly zodiac of the signs, which we have to see as the spiritual mirror of the starry zodiac? We did say, ultimately (or to begin with), it is would be the same Being, Who is revealed in the cosmic space (the starry zodiac) as well as in the earthly temporal, planetary realm (in the earthly zodiac of the signs). This is important, but one can also take it on to an anthroposophical, more exact expression. We recall how in the earthly zodiac how the sign is simply experienced in the yearly rhythm, in the twelve sub-sections of that period of time which, through the seeming annual movement of the Sun, or seen in the Copernican manner is given through the revolution of the Earth around the Sun. Such things, too, astronomy today from its outer viewpoint explains in an understandable manner, though only mathematically, mechanically (one thinks of the famous laws of Kepler of the movements of the planets, of the relationship of the time of the rotation and distance from the Sun. Do not forget with this that Kepler possessed a very spiritual head, was a great astrologer).

One will have to ask: Which beings are active in these rhythms of planetary rotation? We find this in the Helsinki lecture-cycle[152] as the 'Spirits of the Rotation of Time'. There certain 'descendants' of the 3rd Hierarchy (Angels, Archangels, Archai) are the nature-spirits; descendants of the 2nd Hierarchy are the group-souls; descendants of the 1st Hierarchy (Thrones, Cherubim, Seraphim) the above-mentioned 'Spirits of the Rotation of Time'. This point is important. For we see how in the cosmic spatial realm, in the starry zodiac, the 1st Hierarchy (Cherubim) is directly revealed; they are revealed in the earthy, planetary reflection of the zodiac in the yearly revolution and rhythm of the year, in the earthly zodiac of the signs, *through their descendants*, the 'Spirits of the Rotation of Time'.

In the starry zodiac, that is, the effects of the 1st Hierarchy work *directly*, in the earthly zodiac *indirectly*. Cf. Goethe: *Faust*, Part One. Faust's study (I) 447-453:

*Wie alles sich zum Ganzen webt,*
*Eins in dem andern wirkt und lebt!*
*Wie Himmelskräfte auf und nieder steigen*
*Und sich die goldnen Eimer reichen!*
*Mit segenduftenden Schwingen*
*Vom Himmel durch die Erde dringen,*
*Harmonisch all das All durchklingen!*
To build the Whole how each part weaves,
One in the other works and lives!
How heavenly powers are rising and descending,
The golden vessels to each other lending!
Their pinions redolent with blessing,
Down through the earth from heaven pressing,
Harmonious all the All embracing!
        [Tr. W.H. van der Smissen; see endnote 250]

'As above, so below'. Our sentence, that One and the same spiritual Being reveals Him/Herself as above so below, in the starry zodiac as in the earthly zodiac of signs, may *cum grano salis* [with a grain of salt] remain.

## Summative Discussion: Zodiac Beings and Signs, the Horoscope and Karma

It is quite good to gain clarity for oneself concerning the *beings* of the zodiac (starry zodiac as well as earthly zodiac). The Hierarchies are always the actual, real beings at work in astrology. However, many people pursuing astrology today act as if this question were completely insignificant for them, the pure empiricists in this realm, who on principle do not enter into the question of the spiritual backgrounds of astrology. For many people the signs today are merely a method of reckoning, a means of dividing the whole, the full circle of 360° into single sections (each 'sign' the same 1/12 of the whole measures 30°). You can find Ephemerides in which the names of the zodiac-signs are left out completely. They begin with 0° (which one otherwise calls '0° Ram'); for the beginning of the Bull 30° is written, the Twins 60°, for the beginning of the Archer 240°, of the Waterman 300°, and so on. Many follow suit, because they think the 'signs' would, after all, not be real, would only be a form of reckoning; only the constellations are the reality, and now the signs don't account for anything.

I seek, on the contrary, to show with my entire *Contributions*, how despite the sign and constellation no longer coinciding, nevertheless also in the sign that being is revealed who gives the constellation its name. For example, in the earthly Ram that being 'Ram' really is at work, although the Sun stands somewhere else [in the sky]. And I would really hold it for a materialistic error if one completely got rid of the naming of the signs and replace it with a mere mathematical calculation of the degrees (if, for example, instead of 25° the Virgin, one would say 175° from the zero point). An essential element would be lost for astrology if one no longer had the consciousness that in the sign—even if it no longer corresponds to the position of the Sun in the constellation of the same name—there is still revealed the same spiritual being that also rules in the corresponding cosmically spatial region, the 'constellation'.

For astrology in the narrower sense, I mean for birth-horoscopes, it is important to establish that not only when the position of the Sun is discussed, but the position of some planet or other, here everywhere the *sign*, not the constellation, is meant. A horoscope is simply made, reckoning according to the sign, not according to the constellation, only for this reason, because (as we have already seen) only the sign can be exactly reckoned—which could be convenient for the reckoning, yet for the subject-matter wrong—but also for objective reasons. Dr Steiner, too, as we recall, in the one instance, where for him the horoscope computation was decisively important, reckoned according to the sign, not according to the constellation.

When we initially look at the human birth-horoscope, after everything given above, can we not discover a quite strong, enlightened reason for this reckoning according to the sign and not according to the [present-day] constellation? The starry zodiac, as we saw, is ultimately the Uranos, the super-planetary realm, and therewith (as we saw earlier [*Contribution* No. 4]) also the super-karmic region. Cosmic karma is connected with the birth of the planetary solar system in Ancient Saturn, or expressed differently, with the separation of Saturn and Uranos in the birth of time with Ancient Saturn. The Earth is after all only the testing place and seedbed of cosmic karma. Here ultimately only that cosmic karma and earthly karma begun in Ancient Saturn is condensed into the 'speck of dust', the Earth, which itself once again is called to become the seed of a new [planet]. In the event of John 8, how Christ writes the karma of the adulteress into the Earth, lies this whole planetary, karmic context, right back to Ancient Saturn and the cosmic division.

We saw on the one hand how all karma, earthly destiny and the destiny of humanity, rests on these planetary contexts, going right back to the Saturn-Uranos separation. And on the other hand we know the relationship of the starry zodiac to Uranos (seen as beings, to the Cherubim, to the 1st Hierarchy), how the signs for the earthly, planetary side of the zodiac that begins in Saturn, are completed on the Earth; and to the Earth's being (to those beings, who as 'Spirits of the Rotation of Time' are precisely descendants of the 1st Hierarchy). Because Uranos lies beyond cosmic karma growing into earthly karma that begins in Ancient Saturn, for this reason also the starry zodiac (that is indeed only an aspect of Uranos) lies beyond that karmic context of destiny, which is initially shown in the birth-horoscope. In the primordial cosmic separation, in that which lies *this side* of Saturn, originate all the connections of destiny expressed in the human birth-horoscope. For this reason, such a horoscope is reckoned according to the earthly planetary aspect, according to the sign, not according to the Uranian aspect, the constellation.

Such a reckoning according to the signs actually expresses how the planets stand to the Earth, not as they stand to the heavens, to the fixed stars. As the constellation belongs to Uranos, the *signs* belong to the earthly planetary aspect, which in the horoscope shows the workings of destiny, the karma of the earthly human being. The signs are the earthly, planetary reflection of the starry zodiac.

The Christ-being during the three years of His earthly sojourn in the Holy Land stood outside and above earthly *karma*. He had no human *karma*, as Rudolf Steiner shows in his important book *The Spiritual Guidance of Man and Mankind* [GA 15, in Chapter 3]. For this reason, this Being had no birth-horoscope in the human sense. In every moment of His earthly life, as Rudolf Steiner says, He manifested the horoscope. He stood in every moment of His earthly life in full, living connection with the whole universe, with the Father in the heavens, the Uranos, whereas human beings only have *this* connection in the hour of their birth. Then the firmament of the hour of birth, or of the moment of birth, is impressed, as it were, into the brain-aura. This recorded impression from the hour of birth—the birth-horoscope—the human being carries with him his whole life.

In this horoscope, the positioning in the brain of the firmament at birth, is exactly expressed in the [individual] karma, that is, what the human being in his destiny has made of himself in a previous life. What he furthermore does in this life is a matter of the 'I' and his freedom—so far such as an 'I' and such a freedom has been achieved. The fact of the 'I' and of freedom is never infringed in the slightest through the fact of the horoscope. The 'I', that created all this, is the one reality; the other is karma, what has been created (*karma* in Sanskrit means 'deed', 'what one has caused'). The one reality is the testing for the other. The horoscope as expression of karma is in this sense always the past, whereas the 'I' is the future-fashioning factor. *Both* factors are to be considered of that which is involved in taking the step from illusion into reality.

## *Harmonizing the Primordial Separation*

The human being through the Fall of man actually broke away *completely* from the starry world. This starry world—to the astronomical, mathematical view the 'work' (in the sense of Steiner's *Leading Thoughts* No. 38)—had to dry up. Nevertheless, the relationship at the moment of birth does exist, corresponding to the [original] living relationship. And that it exists is the deed of Michael, who—as Dr Steiner expresses it in the Michaelic letters, *The Michael Mystery* [GA 26]—has to achieve this, for human beings inconceivable, harmony of the karma of a human individuality with the firmament of the hour of his birth, to the satisfaction of his [Michael's] Sun-like will for life. Astrology is a concern of the Christ and the work of Michael.

Here it depends above all to show how the horoscope is connected to human *karma*, and so also with the primordial separation, the primordial Fall of man. It has to be shown how this connection to karma also touches on the fact that astrological experience simply results and ever and again freshly confirms that for working out the horoscope the signs, not the constellations, is the primary measure. For myself it has happened that working on my own horoscope as on those of other people this fact has led to the most marked proofs. Only for reasons of discretion, and also not to become too complicated, I have to refrain from describing individual cases.

That Dr Steiner did not contradict what really is meant here, is found not only in the fact of the already mentioned case where he himself clearly reckoned with the signs, but above all in the clearly recognizable manner he spoke in the Leipzig lecture-course, even if only understood by the few, concerning the question of sign and constellation. He spoke directly on the matter for an astrologer who was present at the time—I could name him[153]—and who had the task to develop an astrology from the aspect of a Christian consciousness, but who then failed to fulfil this task for Dr Steiner. In these lectures, so significant for the new, Christened astrology—also in the question 'sign and constellation' discussed in the Introduction to my book on *John's Gospel*, which should be read in connection with these *Contributions*, I mention these things—Dr Steiner three times mentions a saying of the astronomer Kepler (from *Harmonices mundi* [most notably in *Christ and the Spiritual World*, Lect. 6] and strongly emphasizes it:

> A certain picture of the zodiac and of the whole firmament is imprinted by God into the soul of the Earth, *into the aura of the Earth* [as Dr Steiner adds].

With these words (the Kepler quotation, as it appears, is not quite word for word, but Dr Steiner gives it in these words, which I cite exactly) nothing else is given than the precise differentiation of constellation and sign; it is said as exactly as possible what the difference is between sign and constellation, and in what the relationship consists between sign and constellation. *The sign is the impression of the cosmic constellation in the earthly aura, in the etheric-astral periphery of the Earth.* And we have only to imagine how this impression in the earthly aura is, as it were, held fast, how it is bound as it were to the rhythmical sections of the circuit of the seasons of the year; whereas the constellation—that is, the position of the Sun orientated according to the constellation in the rhythmically recurring period of time in question—with the precession of the vernal equinox itself undergoing a continuous precession (the precession of precisely 1° takes place every 72 years, the span of a human life; Dr Steiner frequently points to the connection between pulse beat, breathing rhythm, course of the day, course of the year, the duration of a life-time and the cosmic year; it takes 25,920 years to complete the whole precession). In this way the sign and constellation fall increasingly out of their shared alignment.

The relationship becomes more clear when we ask: *When* was it that sign and constellation came together as completely as possible, when, that is, did this impressing take place to which Dr Steiner refers, this impressing of the celestial zodiac-pictures into the aura of the Earth? We already know that was the turning point of time, the moment of time of the Mystery of Golgotha or the Jordan Baptism. At that time the vernal equinox that took place during the whole Greco-Roman age in the constellation of the Ram, arrived at 0° in this constellation, in order to proceed to 30° Fishes (the movement of the vernal equinox is retrograde; thus 0° forms here the end, not the beginning of a period). So roughly around the turning point of time (the reckoning with the constellation is never as absolutely precise as with the sign) 0° Ram (constellation) came together with 0° Ram (sign). Here the agreement of sign and constellation was as its most complete. *During the time of the His earthly ministry Christ impressed the celestial picture into the earthly aura.* At that time the heavenly script corresponded most completely with the rhythm of the Earth. This is a most significant fact concerning Christ. And now we recognize that the difference between sign and constellation and the primary preference for the sign with the karmic reckoning of the horoscope should be far removed from contradicting the basic principle of a 'Christened astrology', much rather precisely *in this fact in the most eminent sense a fact of Christ, a fact of the Mystery of Golgotha* is expressed.

Not for nothing in this connection is the fact of the birth-horoscope and Rudolf Steiner's explanation indicated. In the moment of birth—Steiner tells us—the whole starry firmament is imprinted into the aura of the brain of the human being passing through the portal of birth into earthly existence. So, too, in the moment of birth of the 'I' of the Earth—this, however, is the event of Golgotha—the whole starry firmament with the celestial zodiac is impressed into the earthly aura, into the astral-etheric periphery of the Earth. The constellation gives the 'sign' its imprint, and it appears then justified that this 'sign', as it were, recorded in the earthly aura, from now on keeps its name received from the constellation, even when through the precession of the vernal equinox a shift takes place in the orientation of the signs according to the constellation itself.

At this juncture many questions could arise: how was it with the vernal equinox before Golgotha, for instance, in the Egyptian age? It lay at that time in the constellation of the Bull, in which the sign of Venus corresponding to the cult of the Isis-Mysteries (the Bull was at that time the 'earthly Ram'), and must have been in some primordial time or other—26,000 years past—previously coincided with the Ram. Was there also a Christ-event at that time? The Leipzig lecture-course [GA 149] gives the possibility perhaps also to answer this question, since Steiner speaks indeed of earlier Christ-events that took place in the Lemurian and the Atlantean age, and not yet on the physical plane. I mentioned this earlier [*Contributions* Nos. 5 and 10], and because this *Contribution* has again become extensive, it cannot be followed up in detail. There are many problems, but Dr Steiner has also given us the possibilities to answer them. Precisely the Leipzig lecture-cycle helps us to feel to what extent the *whole of astrology* is a Christ-question. For now, the fact remains significant that out of these connections to Christ, this naming of the signs is the decisive and remaining fact that results out of its coinciding with the constellation in the earthly life of Christ.

It would be of great significance to say more on the astrological significance of the *constellations*. Yet space has been exceeded. More can be found in my book on *John's Gospel*, in the final chapter of Part 1, 'The Star-Mystery of the Eternal Name: the Book of Life and the Book of Destiny' [Chapter 7, p. 127-68]. This 'Book of Destiny' or karma is that which, as we have seen, is expressed in the horoscope. There, for reasons with which we have become acquainted, the *sign* is taken as the lower earthly, planetary part of the zodiac, which corresponds with the karma. But, in the end, as we have seen, this Earth-sign-zodiac is only the imprint of the starry realm in the Earth.

There, in Uranos, is the human being's true primordial home from which he only separated himself in the Fall of man; it is the *world of the Eternal Names*, where also his spiritual name as a primordial musical sound is heard in the eternal harmony of the stars. That name man has only forgotten, and through this in a certain sense has lost. Our name stands in the Book of Life as long as it is not erased through sin. It stands freshly inscribed, when the inner connection with Christ exists in consciousness. In karma, in the Book of Destiny, it is reckoned with the sign; in the other one, the Book of Life, it is reckoned with the actual reality of the stars, with Uranos. With the strengthening of the Christ-impulse in human consciousness, the Uranian connections of the starry element increasingly gain in significance beyond the karmic, planetary [connections] of the mere earthly signs. Consequently, Dr Steiner speaks how at the moment of birth the whole starry firmament is imprinted in the aura of the brain of the infant. This is the heavenly script of the eternal name. The concrete interpretation of these Mysteries touched on here by Rudolf Steiner lies in the future of astrology. No astrologer of today has fully grasped this. It is not possible to bring into abstract concepts; it has to be a living, pictorial beholding. Each horoscope can and has increasingly to become for us such a living pictorial beholding.

In any case, we do already touch the sphere that *lies beyond karma*, the eternal human essence, the name in the Book of Life. But in order to find the way to this *world of the eternal name* we have initially to deal with the world of our karma, with the entries in the Book of Destiny. And these entries in the large account book of our karma—but this, as far as it comes over to us from an earlier life, is the horoscope—are initially written in reckoning with the signs. This we have first to understand. But behind the signs themselves there always stands the constellation, as these observations have shown. This still leads to very many questions, which I can no longer deal with today. Perhaps I can point once more to the two chapters of my book on *John's Gospel*, the Introduction ('Sign and Constellation') and Chapter 7 on the 'Star-Mystery of the Eternal Name'. There it is shown how much all these questions are especially Johannine questions.

## Added Excerpt

Hermann Beckh, *Alchymy: The Mystery of the Material World*, from Chapter 1:

> This viewpoint, ahead of a whole future development of human thinking, is once again expressed in words by Novalis (*Fragment* 1719, ed.

Kamnitz; Wood* 1095), the profound cosmic sense of which human thinking today can hardly grasp:

The opinion concerning the negativity of Christianity is excellent. Christianity thereby becomes elevated to the level of a foundation—the projecting forces for a new edifice of the world and humanity—to a genuine heavenly firmament—to a living moral space.

This wonderfully relates to my ideas regarding the hitherto misunderstood nature of *space* and *time*, whose personality and archetypal force have now become indescribably illuminating to me. The activity of *space* and *time* is the force of creation, and their relations are the hinges of the world.

Absolute abstraction—annihilation of the present,—apotheosis of the future, of this veritable better world: all belong to the inner core of Christianity—and thereby unite it with the religion of the ancient world, with the divinity of the ancients with the restoration of antiquity, as its second principal wing.—And like the body of an angel, both hold the universe in eternal suspense—in an everlasting enjoyment of *space* and *time*.

Already at this point in the discussion we can sense how the 'chymical' future perspective on Christianity given here by Novalis meets the Johannine apocalyptic vision of the 'New Jerusalem', of the chymically transformed Earth of the future and its revelation of the Mystery of space enclosed in its symbol of a cube (Rev. 21:16). Something like the inner progress from the abstract imagination of space, in Kant's view, to the living revelation of space in the anthroposophical view, becomes visible here. Rudolf Steiner leads us nearer to understand all these connections, first pointed out by Novalis, when discussing the apocalyptic seals and pictures (Berlin 1907. *Bilder Okkulter Siegel und Säulen. Der Münchner Kongress Pfingsten 1907 und seine Auswirkungen*. GA 284, p. 94. See also the lecture, Stuttgart, 16 Sept. 1907. *Occult Signs and Symbols*. GA 101).

(* Novalis: *Notes for a Romantic Encyclopaedia*, tr., ed., and with an Introduction by David, W. Wood. Albany: State University of New York. 2007. P. 182.)

# XI
# Zodiac 2. Sign and Constellation

## *Is the Constellation overlooked?*

My last *Contribution* would not be understood if one were to think that in it, because of the earthly reality of the sign, the heavenly reality of the constellation—or the spiritual reality standing behind the constellation—would be overlooked, as if the stars behind the earthly manifestation are pushed very much into the background. This is not the case. *One* spiritual reality, as we saw, is revealed above as well as below, in the cosmic spatial and starry realms, as well as the earthly rhythm of time (we saw that the sign actually leads towards the latter). In order rightly to understand the 'sign', one has to leave spatial thinking completely and enter a time-thinking, a rhythmic thinking. I was able to point out, for example, our Breviary[154] is built up on this reality of the rhythm of time, that means, of the *sign*, which always changes around the 24th of the month (with certain calendar shifts, from the 20th-24th), where always around this moment in time a new monthly verse begins.

The four main corner-points of the yearly rhythm, the spring and autumn equinox, and the summer and winter solstice, clearly point to the reality of the sign. And for the two signs between [each section]—the eight remaining signs—the corresponding moments result. The 'Ram' as a sign is always the earthly Eastertide; the Crab as sign always the time after the summer solstice (when the Sun, which first goes further northwards has reached its highest point then turns southwards, entering its 'crab walk'); the Scales as sign is always the time of the equalizing of day and night at the autumn equinox, and so on. Even out of astronomical reasons that have been extensively discussed, the position of the Sun in the corresponding periods of time no longer orientates according to the constellation bearing the same name.

Hereby the significance of the constellation as such is in no way overlooked. It initially lies already in the fact that the constellation has given its name to the sign. When did this happen? During that time when sign and constellation came together, that means, when the earthly Ram was orientated to the celestial Ram, the earthly Scales to the celestial Scales, and so on. When was this? It was in the fourth, or especially towards the end of the fourth cultural epoch, the time of Christ, of the Mystery of Golgotha. And we recall the saying of Kepler, quoted with emphasis by Dr Steiner during the Leipzig lecture-course [GA 149 (1987), p. 112], how an impression of the heavenly zodiac has been impressed into the soul of the Earth, the aura of the Earth, as the earthly zodiac. And when we ask when this impressing took place, we are led to the time of the Mystery of Golgotha. Then the heavenly entered the earthly, united with the Earth. There heavenly script and earthly rhythm were mutually in tune.

## *Both Sign and Constellation*

In a wonderful way there stands behind the whole relationship of sign and constellation the Mystery of the Christ's deed. The whole shift of sign and constellation is connected with the changes of earthly cultures, with the whole movement of development. The coinciding of sign and constellation is connected with that which as Christ's deed stands at the centre of all earthly changes and development. In the Christ-era, in the three years of His earthly ministry, as we can also see this, the heavenly picture, the heavenly script, was imprinted into the Earth. It corresponds especially in a wonderful way to a *Christened* astrology, to look at this difference and yet at the same time at the inner relationship of sign and constellation. Both are something essential and real. It is not so that only the constellation is real and the signs only something like an unimportant use of language. No, both are real; both are heavenly realities on the one side, and earthly realities on the other side. The sharing of the names is justified despite the divergence, because one and the same spiritual reality, or being, is revealed—above as below, in the cosmic-spatial, as well as the temporal, earthly realms—even if this temporal, earthly element no longer directly orientates to the cosmic-spatial moment.

We have also enquired concerning the beings who reveal themselves above and below, and we found:

[i]    in the one case the Uranian beings of the 1st Hierarchy, the Cherubim (the starry zodiac leads into the Cherubinic sphere, the Uranos), and

[ii]    in the other case, with the 'sign', in the earthly rhythm of time those beings who are called the 'descendants' of the 1st Hierarchy (Helsinki lecture-course, GA 136), the 'Spirits of Rotation of Time', who govern all the planetary courses.

(The Earth's rhythm of the year is connected, of course, with the rotation of the Earth around the Sun.) Precisely this relationship of the Cherubim of the 1st Hierarchy to their descendants, the 'Spirits of the Rotation of Time', wonderfully illuminates the whole relationship of constellation and sign, helping us to understand why it is the constellation rightly gave the name.

And so, behind the reality of the sign stands the other, higher reality of the constellation. This is the one thing, the first viewpoint, helping us clearly to see how we take into account the constellation behind and above the sign.

## The Constellations

We also have to look at the constellations as the cosmogonic primordial region for that time when an Earth and an earthly rhythm were not yet there, when in the primordial beginning [Ancient] Saturn, Sun, Moon and the Earth were to emerge out of the womb of worlds. This cosmic, spatial situation governed the temporal and earthly situation.

We have seen what significance the round of celestial pictures in the shift of the vernal equinox has for the whole development of earthly cultures, that it is spiritually not indifferent that over each of the earthly cultural periods a different vernal equinox stood:

- over the primordial Indian culture, the constellation of the Crab,
- over the primordial Persian, the Zarathustra culture, the constellation of the Twins,
- over the Egyptian-Chaldean the constellation of the Bull (actually the Cow),
- over the fourth, the Greco-Latin culture, the constellation of the Ram.

- The Ram is a Mars-sign,
- the Bull a Venus-sign,
- the Twins a Mercury-sign,
- the Crab a Moon-sign.

- The Indian culture was really a Moon-culture. Rudolf Steiner speaks of it, how the ancient Indian primordial teachers passed over into the spiritual sphere of the Moon.
- The Zarathustra-sign (actually constellation) of the Twins is a Hermes-Mercury sign;
- the Bull is a Venus-sign, indicating the Egyptian Isis-Venus culture (Isis was the planetary [manifestation] of Venus).

## Birth-horoscope

Whatever the meaning might be, which initially the 'sign' also has as a karmic fact for the human birth-horoscope, the way we are looking in a certain way not at the short-term human life, but at the long earthly life, to the great historical evolutionary course of the whole Earth, on the *horoscope of the Earth*, we are led immediately to the great celestial script of the constellations. In *these* great connections we are only concerned with the *constellation*, no longer with the sign. Here it is immediately revealed that we do full justice to the constellation. And astrology is truly more than merely birth-horoscopes; it is also concerned with the great facts of the historical evolution of the Earth.

With the human birth-horoscope, behind the earthly reality of the sign, there stands the celestial reality of the constellation. We have to be clear how the human being through the karmic connections—and their exact reflection we do find in the birth-horoscope—that people have fallen out of the celestial connections of their starry origins. We have freed ourselves from the starry origins, have sunken ever more into the earthly situation. This earthly condition itself has become increasingly estranged from the starry context from which it originated. We have pointed to the significance that Christ-Jesus in John 8 writes the karmic account of debts into the *Earth*. This corresponds very exactly to certain facts of the birth-horoscope, which simply shows us experientially how for everything which a birth-horoscope points to of karmic facts and connections, the sign and not the constellation is the measure.

One cannot say, one may only change the connections, to say for the Ram one would have the Fishes, for the Bull would have the Ram, that is, one would have certain observed characteristics of the Ram attributed precisely to the Fishes (as the constellation essentially corresponding today to the Ram-sign). Whoever looks for the *spiritual side* of the Ram, the Fishes, and so on, will find that it really is the spiritual qualities of the Ram that are revealed in someone born under the sign Ram (that is, under the constellation Fishes [in the sky]), and initially not the qualities of the Fishes that are totally different, unlike those of the Ram, as the feet are different from the human head.

The Fishes is concerned with devotion, self-abnegation, washing of the feet, and so on. For example, Venus in the Fishes is *serving love*, whereas the head-sign of the Ram points to high-flying Idealism (also in the Berlin lecture-cycle *Human and Cosmic Thought* [GA 151, 4 lectures, Berlin 20-23 Jan. 1914], Rudolf Steiner takes Idealism with the Ram). Venus in the Ram is here something completely different, a love with high-flying Idealism, which on the Earth is difficult to satisfy. Someone who has Venus in the Ram, with some self-knowledge, will be able to distinguish this from Venus in the Fishes. And yet for someone who in this sense has Venus in the Ram (that is, in the sign of the Ram), actually has Venus from his/her birth in the constellation of the Fishes. I have observed many cases, and striking ones. They show quite clearly, for one who wants to see, that with the karmic reality of the birth-horoscope the sign and not the constellation is that with which it is primarily concerned. These are facts which one cannot simply brush aside. And they find precisely in the light of anthroposophy their significant explanation.

Through his/her earthly *karma* the human being has fallen away from his/her heavenly connections and is entangled in the earthly contexts. It is this entanglement that is expressed through the sign that is distinguished from the constellation and increasingly falls away from it. Frl. Vreede once said this in a similar way in one of her *Newsletters* [First Series, 11th letter, July 1928], that above and behind the sign stands the above-described higher reality of the constellation, giving the sequence of earthly cultural periods their changing stamp. This is connected to the fact that at different times on the Earth, as well as in human consciousness, truly all things are different. Spiritual differences also exist. The sign of the Ram is always the sign Ram, and reveals spiritual qualities of the Ram, even if the constellation of the Fishes today stands behind it. And yet it is revealed in different ways during different times on Earth. When the constellation Ram stood behind the sign Ram, the effect was different from today when the sign Fishes stands behind it. In a certain way, qualities of the Fishes then modify those of the Ram. How this is the case has still to be researched in detail; here important future tasks lie for an astrology built up in the light of anthroposophy.

Whoever has Venus in the Ram might discover how here the spiritual qualities of the Ram are connected more with his past, how that in his destiny belonging more to the future, points more to the Fishes. I mention this in this way here only tentatively and as a hypothesis. Here lie fine and complicated future questions we do not want to pass by unnoticed.

## Future Work

It is certainly the case that the higher reality of the constellation will become increasingly more significant for the human being in future, that as much as *karma* is superseded and worked off, the 'sign' increasingly retreats. Relating to this tremendous question lying here, I have pointed to the extensive Chapter 7 of my book on *John's Gospel*, 'The Star-Mystery of the Eternal Name: the Book of Life and the Book of Destiny'. What I call here biblically the 'Book of Destiny'—one recalls again John 8, Christ and the woman taken in adultery, in connection with certain passages in the Apocalypse—that is, the karmic reality that is also expressed in the birth-horoscope, for which (as we have seen) the sign as distinct from the constellation primarily gives the measure. In the 'Book of Destiny' what is reflected in the birth-horoscope (so we may also say) is reckoned according to the earthly sign, not according to the constellation.

But beyond this 'Book of Destiny' there stands the other, the 'Book of Life', in which our eternal names are written. That they are written in the starry script is told us in the beautiful saying from Luke, more than once quoted in my book [Luke 10:20]: 'Nevertheless do not rejoice in this that the spirits are subject to you; but rejoice that your names are written in heaven.' In the starry realm of Uranos lies the eternal origin of human beings and their eternal homeland. Here the eternal names are written, which human beings through their entanglement have forgotten and in a certain sense have lost. They have fallen away from the world of their heavenly origin, their heavenly homeland, as this is expressed in meaningful pictures in many fairy tales and sagas of the world. Difficult earthly *karma* has made the name in the Book of Life to appear as erased. This *karma* lies completely between the Earth and the stars of destiny, that is, between the starry sign (not the constellation) and the planets.

Here one thinks of the significant sayings in the Apocalypse (listed in my book on *John's Gospel*, p. 130f.), Apoc. 13:8 and 17:8: 'whose names have not been written in the book of life belonging to the Lamb that was slain from the creation of the world.' 20:12, 'And I saw the dead, great and small, standing before the throne, and books were opened [that is the Book of Destiny]. Another book was opened, which is the book of life.' Beyond the reality of the Book of Destiny there stands radiantly that of the Book of Life in which the eternal names are written in the starry realm that begins to shine again when the dark entry in the Book of Destiny is erased through Christ (one recalls again John 8). This Book of Life lies in the starry realm of Uranos, of the realm of the Father, in humanity's eternal homeland. As the Book of Destiny (which is written in the astrological 'stellar script') records everything to do with karma, inadequacies and limitations, so the Book of Life belongs to the realm of eternal freedom. That the human being, the 'I', stands written in the Book of Life as the eternal name. This astrologically is the world of the eternal 'I', of the eternal name and freedom of the actual starry world, the heaven of fixed stars (the world of the 'resting stars'). Not for nothing, in his book *The Spiritual Guidance of Man and Mankind* [GA 15], does Rudolf Steiner point out that the whole firmament at the moment of birth is imprinted on the aura of the brain. A higher astrology of the future will once again discover in this birth-firmament and written in all its fixed stars the eternal name, the 'I' of the human being.

Every human being has his own special star. Seventy-two years, that is, a human lifespan, is the time during which he covers[155] this star, if we take its extent of raying as 1 degree. For in the shift of the vernal equinox the Sun circumnavigates the 360 degrees of the zodiac in 25,920 years; 72 years occupies *one* degree, the span of a human life. In the *karma*-lectures [GA 235-40] and elsewhere, Rudolf Steiner points to the significance of this fact, which is to show how in the depths of his nature the human being is connected to the actual starry world. Here we find his higher 'I', his eternal name, which is only fallen from his consciousness through his earthly *karma*. This earthly *karma*, however—and here we touch on the important thing for astrology—as that which is rejected from the higher world is then precisely not written into the *upper* starry world. The earthly karma is written in those starry realms which already belong to the Earth and its cosmic destinies, that is in the planets, actually siblings of the Earth, which are the actual stars of destiny, in particular with regard to their positions relative to the Earth. That it is not written in the fixed stars is the decisive element and its karmic statement for the horoscope. This position of the planets to the Earth leads again towards the sign, in so far as it is distinguished from the constellation. The free and [eternal] 'I' is written in the upper stars, but that which created in that free 'I', the earthly limitation, is written in that which lies between.

The more we not only ask the karmic question concerning the human being, but look towards that in him which begins in him to overcome *karma*—and with each genuine anthroposophical development such a process does take place—the more the whole meaning of the horoscope shifts, the more the fateful planets with the houses and signs in which they stand recede in significance, the more the actual starry heavens—and with it the constellation—gain in significance, although today we cannot bring this significance into concise astrological Imaginations. This whole question still lies very much in the future. Only on the path of Imagination, Inspiration and Intuition can it be solved. We could also say: man will evermore grow out of the realm of the fateful planets and increasingly grow into the actual starry realms, in which his actual name is written.

Here, however, we arrive at a point which is important for astrology today. Did we not at the beginning speak a good deal about that planet, which originally did not belong at all to the solar system? It only arrived later from the other, the celestial side, standing as a mediator between the actual world of the planets and the higher starry sphere. It is Uranus, whose name derives from the actual starry sphere, Uranos. In the horoscope it is the *significator*[156] for everything to do with the stars, for astrology itself. Only in recent times has he been recognized, only in recent times did he appear to gain ever more in significance, which will grow even more in future. An increasing number of people today and in the future will be receptive to the influence of this planet that takes its name from the starry heavens. Should this not be connected to the fact that the human being is beginning in his essence really to grow more into this realm of the stars of Uranos? Does something lie in this star, even if the astrologer today views it as a planet, something that leads beyond the earthly, planetary sphere into the super-planetary stellar sphere, into the realm where no longer the 'sign', but the constellation is decisive?

It is the question which today we are initially only able gently to approach. Yet one can already see out of the indications how we do not remain with the more narrow planetary sphere and the earthly sign, but look beyond this to the higher starry realm of Uranos, and sense how from there the whole question of 'sign and constellation' can experience a new orientation, even if today the precise expression for it is missing. But not for nothing do we speak incessantly of an astrology of the future, penetrated by Christ-impulses, opening to the seeking human soul ever new viewpoints.

## *The Starry Heavens*

Apart from the role which the constellation, the actual starry heavens, already play in the birth-astrology, there comes especially into question the significance of this starry heavens, the actual fixed-star heaven, has for the world of animals, plants, the stones and crystals. With human beings it actually has to do with the fact that he is the most estranged from his Uranian original homeland. With him most strongly the earthly planetary and earthly zodiacal aspect (I mean by this the earthly sign in contrast to the constellation) come between him and the starry heavens. Already with the animals it appears to be somewhat different. Not for nothing one speaks [in German] of the *Tierkreis*, 'animal-circle' [in English, 'zodiac']. Animals do not have a *karma* like human beings. The human being separates his *karma* from the higher starry world, limiting him in the connections of the earthly planets and the earthly signs. With the animals the original starry element is much more effective. For this reason, it happened certainly for a good reason that Dr Steiner in the agriculture lecture-course,[157] where he deals with the extermination of certain animal pests, reckons with the starry zodiac, whereas with the more important making of a horoscope he proceeds from the sign.

A still important viewpoint on this, how in the future the real starry heavens, the actual stars beyond the mere planets with which astrology today almost exclusively reckons, will achieve increasingly more significance, is inferred out of anthroposophy when one looks at certain connections of Ancient Egyptian Mysteries and the way Rudolf Steiner spoke about the development, or rather the decline of consciousness, in these Egyptian Mysteries. For this question of the Egyptian Mysteries, what are called the Sothis (Sirius)-periods are important. They initially arose out of a characteristic in the Egyptian way of plotting the calendar and are periods lasting 1,460 years. The calendar originally reckoned the beginning of the year with the rising of the star Sirius in the morning sky in the middle of July. This was the beginning of the Nile flood, upon which depended the harvest, the time of the great hope of the year. In a cultic festive ceremony—more details to be found in Creuzer, *Symbolik und Mythologie der alten Völker* (1812, Vol. II, p. 104ff.)—the Egyptian priests observed this rising of Sirius and according to it made the yearly horoscope.

The Egyptian year was reckoned with 360 days + 5 intercalary days (that were sacred to the gods); the actual duration of the year is $365\frac{1}{4}$ [days], a quarter of a day remained over. From year to year the first day of the new year shifted, in order then after 4 times 365 = 1,460 years to return to its original point of departure, which is connected with the rising of Sirius. Thus came about the Sirius-periods or Sothis-periods of 1,460 years, about which Rudolf Steiner tells us that they also had an historical significance regarding consciousness, especially for the Mysteries.

In 1,322 BCE such a Sothis period had again been completed. According to Rudolf Steiner it was the year in which Moses led the Hebrews out of Egypt. He took with him spiritual Temple treasures, spiritual wisdom. At that time a specific stage of Egyptian Mystery knowledge dropped. What sank was the old 'wisdom of the elements', the clairvoyant beholding into the connections of the etheric realm of life, the realm of the 'elemental' nature of the Earth. What remained was the sensory knowledge of today. Old clairvoyance sank into the grave of the earthly-physical realm. Before this epoch of elemental wisdom there existed in the Egyptian Mysteries another age (also linked to the Sothis periods), the age of wisdom of the planets. It was preceded by yet another older period reaching back to the primordial time, the period of fixed-star wisdom, the actual higher wisdom of the stars. We have, then, the following list of Sothis periods:

5702 BCE until 4242 BCE a wisdom of the fixed stars
4242 BCE until 2782 BCE a wisdom of the planets
2782 BCE until 1322 BCE a wisdom of the elements
1322 BCE until 138 CE a knowledge of the senses.

In this list, one sees how the age of the primordial star-wisdom, the fixed-star wisdom, reaches far beyond the third post-Atlantean cultural period into the second, into the age of Zarathustra. The star Sirius, decisive for this whole reckoning of time of the Egyptians, is indeed the Star of Zarathustra (linked precisely with the Mystery of the Christmas-star, the star of Epiphany). And Zarathustra is the actual inspirer of the primordial star-wisdom in the Mysteries. Beyond all star-wisdom stand the Mysteries of the star Sirius, which according to the Ancient Egyptians was a second, higher Sun, a central Sun, that star which is connected with the great cosmic new year of Zarathustra, which was 6,000 BCE, which will be renewed 6,000 CE. Rudolf Steiner discussed this in a significant Dornach lecture, New Year 1915.[158] 6, 000 BCE, during the time of the great Zarathustra, we are told, the soul in its consciousness was one with the astral body. It was one with all the star-mysteries of the universe (astral means 'starry'); 6,000 years after the turning point of time it will renew this. Then the human being will once again enter a new consciousness of the cosmic stars. That which in the pre-Christian Mysteries was a fall in consciousness, will then in the Christian age be ascent in consciousness. Everything lost in this drop in human consciousness, even the sunken glory of the Ancient Mysteries, will be there once again on a higher 'I'-stage in the light of Christ. All the ancient fixed-star wisdom, which can be traced back to the primordial age of Zarathustra and the primordial Zarathustra's new year, will be there again on a higher level of consciousness in the coming 'cosmic new year'. That is a good 4,000 years away; that still lies an endlessly long time hence. One can understand how all the ancient starry wisdom and astrology initially has the character of a merely planetary wisdom.

## *Future Union of Planetary and Stellar Astrology*

From this we can perhaps understand how in astrology today one still beholds in the first place that which lies between the planets and the earthly realm, the 'sign', whereas by bringing in the connections of the fixed stars—and to this belongs the 'starry consciousness'— only in the future as something to an ever higher degree will be seen as justified. The human being himself, at first, will have to grow into the actual starry contexts, until it is possible to have again in a justified manner a new Christened fixed-star wisdom. Then he will be able to unite the planetary astrology predominant today with a still higher fixed-star astrology. And such a fixed-star astrology belongs to all true reckoning with constellations, as planetary astrology belongs to all reckoning with the signs. So, only in a still quite distant future will it become clearer what has to be said in astrology of the constellations beyond the signs.

In what follows I turn to the important presentation of the three crosses and the four triangles in the zodiac. For everything astrological and anthroposophical these two viewpoints are of the greatest significance. With this whole series it will not depend so very much on the difference between sign and constellation. We shall simply proceed from the spirituality of the zodiac and look at all the different revelations of this spirituality, to which sign and constellation (revelation in the earthly rhythm and revelation in the heavenly picture) only belong to the specific single case.

# Addition: Reckoning the Cultural Epochs according to the Vernal Equinox

It is known and often mentioned here that the cultural epochs in anthroposophy are reckoned according to the vernal equinox, according to the movement of the vernal equinox in the great cosmic year (29,920 years), which renders for one period 2,160 years (a twelfth of the whole, corresponding to a section of the zodiac). There are still a few difficulties, if, for example, it is said, already in the turning point of time, in the year 0 would astronomically be when the vernal equinox entered the zodiac-sign of the Fishes; the fifth post-Atlantean epoch, however, as the 'epoch of the Fishes' is only reckoned from 1413 CE, that is, from a date when astronomically the vernal equinox had already reached the third of the constellation, indeed not a little.

## *Two Rhythms: one faster, the other much slower (and retrograde)*

The matter, however, is quite simple when one imagines everything tangibly. We have to recall that the movement of the vernal equinox is actually retrograde, i.e. in the great cosmic year the signs follow the opposite order then the usual course of the year; after the Bull (Egyptian era) follows that of the Ram (Greco-Latin era), then after the Ram the Fishes (our era today), and so on. As I have shown in my [recent] book, this is the rhythm that governs John's Gospel (at least at the beginning), whereas Mark's Gospel follows the usual rhythm of the year.

The matter is like this: the purely astronomical beginning of the age of the Ram lies at the beginning of the second century before Christ (reckoned as the cultural epoch from 747 BCE), this proceeds, because of the retrograde movement, from 0° Bull to 30° Ram, and in the turning point of time 0° Ram was reached, proceeding to 30° Fishes. (For the sake of simplicity, I now reckon the constellations that in reality are of different extent, all at 30°, like the signs.) The movement is retrograde, that is, begins at 30° of a sign and then in approximately 2000 (2160) years backwards to 0°, beginning in the next sign at 30°.

So, around the turning point of time the transition of the vernal equinox from 0° Ram to 30° Fishes took place; today it lies already in the last, or rather first, degrees of the Fishes, in a not-so-distant future it will reach 0° Fishes and then continue in the Waterman.

What does it mean, quite concretely, that the vernal equinox lies in 30° Fishes? (This would be the constellation of the turning point of time.) This means: On 21 March the Sun stands in 30° Fishes. Then it stands on 22 March already 0° Ram, on 23 March 1° Ram, on 24 March 2° Ram, on 25 March 3° Ram; towards 21 April it reaches 30° in order then to continue in the Bull. One sees that we are still standing in the time of the almost complete coincidence of sign and constellation, also when the vernal equinox itself already stands in the Fishes (30°), the whole of the rest of the month of Easter still continues in the Ram. This changes only very slowly and gradually, for only after 72 years has the spring equinox shifted further by 1°. 300 years after Golgotha it is still only shifted to 4° Ram, i.e. here the Sun stands the first four days of the Easter month in the Fishes, all the rest of this month still in the constellation of the Ram. Only after approximately 1,100 years is the half-way point of the Fishes-constellation reached. Then, too, the whole second half of the Easter-month lies in the constellation of the Ram. And one can well understand, that only when half of the constellation is passed, when, that is, already the greater half of the this month belongs to this constellation, only then are we really in the cultural epoch belonging to this constellation, only then does the whole age carry the predominant impression of the new starry constellation.

The year 1413, which Dr Steiner gives as the beginning of the age of the Fishes, falls during a time when the constellation of the Fishes, facing the constellation of the Ram as the sign of the spring, was already to be felt on the increase, when already the greater part of the Easter month (21 March to 21 April) about $\frac{2}{3}$ already fell in the constellation of the Fishes and only the last ten days (11 April to about 20 April) saw the Sun rise in the constellation of the Ram. Imagining all these things concretely (to do such a thing is a good exercise)—when already at the turning point of time the Sun had reached in the vernal equinox the constellation of the Fishes, yet the actual era determined by this constellation begins much later—then one will well understand why this date 1413 will then no longer be felt in contradiction with the astronomical facts.

# XII
## Questions of the Time.
## Horoscope of the Movement etc.,
## Zodiac 3: The three crosses in the Zodiac,
## the Cross of the Father,
## the Cross of the Son,
## the Cross of the Spirit

### *Introduction: Questions of the Time*

With the appearance of the previous *Contribution* I omitted to mention the square that was formed between Saturn and Uranus, in the same way as I have pointed out the square that had appeared last December (12 & 13 Dec.). At that time, besides many other things, the crisis in the Anthroposophical Society (also the World War 1914 was preceded in 1913 by the great Theosophical-Anthroposophical crisis that then led to the founding of the Anthroposophical Society). For the case in December, I had extensively pointed out in a *Newsletter Contribution* the significance of such a constellation. I also pointed out then the significance of the July-square in many private conversations before its occurrence (21 July 1931). This coincided quite exactly, which is certainly remarkable, with the great financial crisis.[159] Weeks and months before one felt a heaviness in the air. In our meeting in Eisenach we clearly talked about the meaning of the events especially *for us*, what is waiting for us in the future. We pointed to the connection of the outer catastrophes with the coming Christ-events which are approaching. And the 'signs in the stars' of which our Advent reading speaks (Luke 21) receives a new meaning in the light of astrology.

The Saturn-Uranus square was and is not the only example of these signs, the only one of these constellations, nevertheless it stood in the centre. Through frequent repetition—connected to the sometimes (seeming) retrograde motion of the planets (once of Saturn, and again of Uranus)—this constellation was and is decisive for the whole year 1931 (as already for 1930. Our crisis, too, already in the previous year had to do with the above-mentioned constellation). The essence of a square between Saturn and Uranus in particular is that as it corresponds to the essential contrast of these planets (Uranus: Saturn is like heaven: earth), heavenly forces work into the earthly element, judging and toppling, evoking catastrophes. What is morose and brittle in the earthly realm is brought through this celestial influence to fall and dissolve; what has dried up in the earthly realm, what is no longer fit to live and carry the future is burnt up in the Uranian fire (Matt. 3:10-12).

The divine love—for in its actual being heaven, Uranos, is of course always divine love—is revealed as divine wrath. This as such is always *maya*, that is, the outward manifestation of divine love. Out of a Christian thinking, it is already possible to find an attitude towards such a Saturn-Uranus square. We will increasingly recognize that especially this viewpoint from which we approach astrology in these *Contributions*, will also lead us ever more deeply towards an understanding of the Christian viewpoint.

Already now I would like to point out that the square between Saturn and Uranus had become exact in July, was still not the last one, that it will renew itself because of the temporary (apparent) retrograde motion of the planets that I have mentioned. This will happen on 16 and 17 October. This is then the fifth (and as far as I am informed) for the time being the last square within the period of two years. But because of other constellations which are involved, it will be an especially serious square (above all since the Sun and also Mercury will almost form a square with Saturn, like an opposition to Uranus. Then Mars and Venus both stand in the Scorpion, the former forming a square with Jupiter). Certainly, this, too, one will feel sometime before, the pressure which at this time never quite leaves us will become ever stronger, although in this moment a certain alleviation can be felt. And when the moment has arrived, we will experience what the question of the constellation means in the events of the world, what kind of catastrophes they bring about. For our Community a certain comfort exists that at least the priestly Jupiter at this moment will have a favourable constellation, that means, a harmonic triangle with Uranus.

## Our Movement

With this I touch on an area concerning which we could speak in our meeting in Eisenach, I mean the firmament (horoscope) of our Movement and our Community. Concerning the destiny of the latter—here

Bock is completely right—above all the details at Breitbrunn relate. The details in Dornach relate to the actual destiny of our Movement, The Christian Community as such. What I could relate at Eisenach was only a first necessary beginning of the calculations. I only had the dates just before starting the journey, and these too were only the most necessary. Because of the detailed calculations I have specially to beg your patience. For this is needed in this region, as in others. And above all I would be grateful if I could obtain reliable times, to a quarter of an hour, for the Dornach details (the first address of Dr Steiner), the first completion of the transformation in the first Act of Consecration celebrated by Dr Rittelmeyer. Whoever could establish this exactly please contact me.

It would certainly be highly interesting, particularly regarding the reigning crises, also in such a manner to compute the stars of the Anthroposophical Movement. Although I myself was present at all the events under consideration, apart from the first laying of the Foundation Stone, I do not have the exact information, that is, exactly to the minute, or quarter of an hour. This would be the exact details of that brilliant address of Dr Steiner in the Architects' House, Berlin, on that Sunday morning in January 1913, when Dr Steiner broke the relationship hitherto existing to the Theosophical Society; then the exact details for the laying of the Foundation Stone of the First Goetheanum (it was an evening hour on the 20 September 1913 'when Mercury as the Evening Star stood in the Scales'—I have already pointed to how Dr Steiner at that time purposely made the horoscope according to the sign and not according to the constellation (in this case that would have been with Mercury in the Virgin)—and finally, the exact details of the beginning of the Christmas Conference 1923/24, and those of the completed, new (spiritual) laying of the Foundation Stone.

Such computations perhaps show most clearly what topical importance the astrological side can be for our endeavours and tasks. Of course, it depends very much on the 'how'. Dr Steiner, too, undoubtedly and openly took account of the starry constellations with all significant projects, probably, too, with organizing conferences. It is really a pity that it is still so difficult today within the Anthroposophical Society and Movement itself to introduce the astrological side in a tactful and anthroposophically oriented manner. There is simply too much fear present in this area, even when much that is incorrect, which is also present in the world, explains the fear.

However, for this reason, it appears consequently also necessary, once really to attempt in a solid manner to build up astrology on the basis of anthroposophy. The cosmogony of *Occult Science* and many other things given us by our great spiritual helper for its closer understanding, has consequently also in these contemplations to be and remain our point of departure. And the impatience of those who always want to steer by the account and interpretation of horoscopes, will have to take on themselves a certain restraint. I have already conveyed some basic and important things to do with regarding and evaluating the birth-horoscope. But before I can proceed on a closer explanation of the horoscope, after speaking initially on the planets, these contributions on the zodiac have to be brought to some conclusion. Zodiac and planets, as the foundations also of all horoscope matters, have to stand in clear pictures before the spirit of anyone who wants to approach in a redemptive manner the facts of the horoscope. And everything that we will later need as building stones for our contemplations on the horoscope must draw from the spiritual goods of anthroposophy according to trusted methods.

I shall now have to present the zodiac from the viewpoint of the 'three crosses'[160] and above all the 'four triangles'. If this presentation reaches a certain conclusion, after the previous discussion of the twelve zodiac-signs we shall be able to turn to the question of the *twelve houses*, which are so decisively important for every horoscope (also, as shown in Eisenach, for those of our Community) and are indeed in no way identical to the twelve zodiac-signs. Already sign and constellation, as we saw, are not the same, and the 'houses'—or 'fields'—are really something quite different, even if they relate to the signs, similar as these do to the constellations. When these zodiac contributions are finished, I will turn to consider the horoscope intensively. I will go into how a horoscope is worked out, how it is recorded, and so on. But I ask those who are only intent on working out horoscopes, *rather in good time to cancel their copy of these Contributions,* so that during this time of financial crisis a useless stream of paper does not flow into the sea of superfluous written ballast influencing our living space and soul-space.

## The Spiritual Zodiac

If I now turn in what follows to the central, important presentation of the three crosses and the four triangles in the zodiac—important for all astrology, gospel studies and explanations of the liturgy—and first of all the three crosses, we have to establish one thing. Basically, we initially mean neither the zodiac of signs nor the starry zodiac, but simply that *we will proceed from a spirit-zodiac, from* the *spirit-zodiac*. To arrive at a notion of such a spirit-zodiac, if we really are to enter an understanding of astrology, will become ever more important. However important astronomy is for everything astrological, experience repeatedly teaches how all gluing ourselves on to astronomical concepts—which mostly is based on unacknowledged materialism—obstructs the real entrance to the spiritual knowledge of the stars (astrology).

To attain a concept of the spirit-zodiac, from which we proceed, one is best helped by the important Berlin lecture-cycle of Dr Rudolf Steiner, *Human and Cosmic Thought* [GA 151, 4 lectures, Berlin 20-23 Jan. 1914], to which the other basic cycles to build up a new astrology chronologically join in a significant way, *Christ and the Spiritual World* [GA 149], Leipzig 1913-14; Berlin 1913 *The Life between Death and a new Birth in Relation to the Cosmic Facts* [GA 141]. The lecture-cycle meant here [GA 151] is the one where the spiritual world-conceptions—twelve directions of world-conceptions, seven world-conception moods, etc. all combine the variety of possible different world-conceptions. These relate to the zodiacal twelve, also to the seven planets, as something initially to be laid hold of purely spiritually. The celestial pictures are but reflected; they have their outer revelation. But not the only one. We have indeed already seen hitherto in the contemplations how the spiritual zodiac-signs are revealed in the earthly zodiac and the earthly rhythm of the year, and in the heavenly zodiac-pictures. To this comes the purely spiritual revelation in thinking that Rudolf Steiner developed in the cosmic element of the world-conceptions, then especially also what I show in my monograph *The Essence of Tonality*, the musical revelation in the twelve key-centres.

For me personally, if I may say this here, this musical subject of the keys was the starting point of all my zodiac and star research. From this I came much later to my gospel research—the cosmic rhythm in Mark's and John's Gospel—and from there to everything that one understands in the narrower sense as 'astrology' (birth-horoscopes, etc.). And for all deeper understanding of astrology, the musical element is of very great significance. The early Egyptians knew this, with whom the musical element in astrology played a significant role—more details on this in Creuzer.[161] They still had a musical, spiritual astrology; the outer astronomical element in astrology arrived first with the Chaldeans. In the musical element of the spheric harmony originates the deeper mystery of astrology. When in the harmony of the planets the individual primal musical sound of a certain soul begins to sound, when through its earthly *karma* it comes to a certain moment, then the soul feels called to appear in existence, and its birth-horoscope, tuned according to the individual planets and individualized, is that which expresses the music of the spheres.

From this spirituality of the zodiac our presentation—crosses and triangles in the zodiac—takes its starting point and is now to follow. Each zodiac sign shall exactly and tangibly form the focus from all the various viewpoints that exist here:

- from the earthly viewpoint and rhythmical viewpoint (sign)—here the rhythm of the day, not only of the rhythm of the year, plays a role;
- from the celestial viewpoint and starry viewpoint (constellation),
- from the musical viewpoint (key),
- from the thinking viewpoint (worldview),
- from the viewpoint of the human gestalt (the twelve members),
- from the viewpoint of the twelve senses,
- from the viewpoint of the human supersensible members (these too are cosmically and cosmogonically arranged to the zodiac-signs).

And many other viewpoints exist, for example, that of the twelve precious stones, which I point to in my monograph on *Alchymy*.[162] Then above all the Hierarchies and their cyclical engagement in world-becoming. Then the viewpoint of the gospel events and the gospel rhythm—also elsewhere the zodiac rhythm governs, for example, in the poetic work [Wolfram von Eschenbach's] *Parzifal*, then the twelve disciples, the twelve tribes of Israel, and so on. In the twelve deeds of Hercules/Heracles the zodiac rhythm is revealed, in the twelve main events in the life of the Buddha, in the twelve members of the Buddhist series of causes,[163] and so on. With each one the twelve zodiac-signs, it has furthermore to be considered how it stands to the seven planets once again, as they are revealed in [the kingdoms of] nature and in the human being.

To all this, moreover, there come the viewpoints, so beautifully and exactly worked out by Rudolf Frieling, which also reveal the spirit-zodiac (in which the planets are inherent) in the liturgy, in the rhythms of the Act of Consecration of Man, pre-eminently in the twelve sentences of the Creed. Concerning these twelve sentences, Frieling initially wrote a concise *Contribution* in RB 116, *The Cosmic Rhythm in the Creed*, upon which in his later *Contributions* he presented the whole in full detail from the viewpoint of the four trigons (triangles) in the zodiac to which the four evangelists are aligned. More than everything else, Frieling's *Contributions* show how very much this whole question of the zodiac, how very much all astrological questions, also touch the realm of our liturgy, how all these cosmic rhythms also explain the more profound contexts of the liturgical realm; indeed, I would like to say, in what appears precisely as individual heavenly signs— and with them the respective planets—in the liturgy, above all in the Creed. Here they reveal to us their highest, their most spiritual meaning; here we arrive the closest to the actual primordial meaning, the archetypal Christ-meaning of these heavenly signs. Here the cosmic Christ is revealed to us, the creative Logos itself, from stage to stage, bearing the cosmic sacrifice right through all the heavenly spheres. In connection with the gospel-meaning of the twelve heavenly signs, as I attempted to unlock through my work, these signs reveal their liturgical and Credo-meaning, the highest of all viewpoints, out of which we are able to behold the zodiac-signs and the planets. And many things in the Mystery-nature of humanity thereby become clear, in the astrological details, right into the horoscope. I would like to appeal to whoever is seeking to penetrate more deeply into these astrological contemplations that they should take to heart above all the most exact and repeated working through of Frieling's *Contributions*. In my observations, I shall have to present the matter in all sorts of ways from below, whereas Frieling in his *Contributions*, so to speak, supplies the highest and ultimate viewpoint.

## Zodiac 3: The Three Crosses in the Zodiac, the Cross of the Father, of the Son and of the Spirit

First of all, and foremost the twelve zodiac-signs are ordered and grouped in *three crosses*. Following this and connecting to it, we shall become acquainted with the even more important viewpoint of the *four triangles*. The three crosses come about of themselves, when we proceed as is usual in astrology from the cardinal axes, the zodiac axis Ram-Scales.

[i]   In my observations on the musical keys, in regarding C-major with the Ram, I have also taken this axis of the cross Ram, Scales, Crab and Goat. Then

[ii]   that cross that for me was always the 'Cross of the Middle' and the 'Christ-Cross', the cardinal cross for the gospel studies

(see the figures at the end of the books on *Mark* and *John*; as a help-ful basis for all that is to follow in these studies, I would like to take this opportunity with emphasis to mention). The cross Fishes, Virgin, Twins and Archer, with its axis Fishes-Virgin, the 'Last Supper con-stellation' is in particular also the *cross of our Movement*.

[iii]    Lastly, that cross that again from another, the cosmogonic viewpoint, we can call the 'Cardinal Cross', the cross Waterman, Lion, Bull and Scorpion. This is the actual primary cross of cosmic evolution, whose four corners, however, in another sequence correspond to the four-fold Saturn, Sun, Moon and Earth and also the four evangelists, cor-responding to the well-known 'four beasts'.

A simple glance at these *three crosses*—the expression immediately recalls the 'three crosses on Golgotha'—shows always two signs fac-ing each other, as opposites[164] they stand 'in opposition', as one says in astrology, e.g. with the first cross listed above, the signs Ram and Scales. Then the signs Crab and Goat (it is advisable to have the image of the zodiac livingly before one, so that at any moment one knows exactly *which* signs stand opposite). Worked out mathematically, that is related on the circle, this contrast, or opposition, means an angle of 180°. In the one half of this circumference of 180° lies one sign that to the two lying in opposition [in elongation] it is always at an angle of 90°, forming [a right-angle, or] a *square*, as one says in astrology. (At the beginning of our observations, we spoke of a significant square for this year, a Saturn-Uranus square. In our explanations, we approach ever closer to these concepts.) If I proceed not from the sign to its opposite (that is, from Ram to Scales, from Crab to Goat), but each time go from one sign to the one adjacent on the cross (that is, from Ram to Crab or Goat, from Crab to Scales, from Scales to Goat), then these signs, so seen, between themselves form a number of squares. It will be clear how making such squares are always the half of an opposition. The essential quality of a cross is that it is formed out of such oppositions and squares.

Here we immediately touch on what is important for astrology in the character of this cross, these oppositions and squares. They signify for astrology the same as what one means in normal life when one uses the expression 'standing crosswise'. When two people stand 'crosswise' to each other, one means that they can-not get on well together, that they have to bear mutually opposite characteristics. In astrology, I mean in the narrower sense, in the birth-horoscope, it is not for instance the opposition, but the square that is the strongest and sharpest of all aspects. Earlier astrology spoke of favourable and unfavourable aspects. In the first instance this had to do with what are called squares. So, when two planets form together an angle of 90°, or almost 90°, they stand in a square, and only secondarily in opposition. The square, then, is the unfavourable, the 'worst' of all aspects, the opposition is the second unfavourable aspect. Everything else, which otherwise still 'lies on the cross', is taken as an unfavourable aspect, that is, next after the opposition, the half-square or 'semi-square', that is a planetary aspect in which an angle of 45° or approaching 45° is formed.

We have, however, already discussed the 'evil-doers' amongst the planets (Mars and Saturn), how here the concepts of the old and conventional astrology change in the new, Christened astrology. Mars and Saturn are in no way simply only the unfavourable planets, but in the higher sense favourable planets. They can be decisive cherishers of all higher development. And so it is also with what are called unfavourable aspects, the oppositions and squares. They only announce in the horoscope where difficulties and constrictions lie in individual *karma*, those points where through overcoming actually existing tensions the decisive, aimed for advances can be made. In any case, taking the horoscope no longer simply as a fatalistic occasion, as something *static,* as it were, but as a possibility, as a task, as something dynamic, as the aim and direction of a development, then all these aspects become something quite different. They then show precisely the tasks and possibilities, and the way that leads to realizing these possibilities.

In spite of everything, it cannot be otherwise than that such a square, and similar things, even in the slightest degree, an opposition, is *initially* experienced as something painful, as a source often of difficult conflicts, will perhaps also be experienced as difficult, threatening illnesses of body and soul. Whoever in particular has a square, will certainly feel the 'sharp corners' in the destiny of their life. An opposition is much less sharp; it frequently means only an important struggle, an important balance that is to be achieved. Concerning the feared Saturn-Sun opposition (the Saturn-Sun square would be stronger still), Rudolf Steiner (who himself had this aspect in his horoscope) showed how important precisely this opposition is for the gaining of powers of concentration, to concentrate and meditate. When the decisive stars of two people (especially the Mars each has) stand to each other in the square—we touch here the important

and interesting question of the mutual relationship of different horoscopes with people who are friends, or enemies, married, related, or
in-laws, or in any other way in life have to do with each other. Then
they will have to wrestle their significant difficulties with each other
in life, and perhaps at some moments heftily clash. Of course, such
an aspect is never an excuse for such clashes, on the contrary, if one
knows something of the horoscope, or astrology, then such an aspect
has simply to be felt and realized as an invitation to overcome the
existing difficulties through self-direction, the 'I'.

Nevertheless, the danger is great with such a mutual constellation with two people. Much more harmless in this case (I mean the
mutual relationship of two people) is the opposition. This does not
always need to be in an opposition that carries in it a conflict, but
frequently means only that kind of opposite, which can become the
source of productive contrasts and mutual complementing. Consequently, it is not at all bad when the stars of spouses [partners] are
partly in mutual opposition: the marriage is then in much less danger of becoming boring than in the other case, although at times
it can come to tensions or argument. It can even be an attraction
between people, when some of their stars stand in opposition. That
is especially the case for the ascendant (the sign which at the moment
of birth is rising). One looks at it, as it were, as favourable, when
the ascendants of two people stand in mutual opposition. For what
does it mean: opposition of two ascendants? It means as the one has
his ascendant, his '"I"-field', the other has his/her descendant, his
'you-field', where the one has his 'you-field', there the other has his
'"I"-field'. 'I' and you are most beautifully complemented. If both
had the same ascendant, then they would be in important relationships possibly too similar to each other, then the one would be indifferent or boring because she/he has nothing important to learn from
the other.

Thus far already with the horoscope (about which I have said here a
few things, because many people like particularly to hear about this).
Moreover, when we move over to other realms, such as gospel studies
or observations about culture, we will find with the opposition not
only the viewpoint of sharp contrasts, but also the aspect of productive arguments. Contrast does play a role. Think, for example, of the
arguments between Christ and the Pharisees, the word of love and the
rigid word of the law, a contrast which we always meet in the opposition Bull-Scorpion. This in general is a strong opposition; for example,

in the Last-Supper axis Pisces-Virgin, the aspect of balance and supplementing govern much more.

In spite of everything: within the cross, with opposition and square, it initially always involves some kind of opposition, as we shall see later even more clearly, with the triangles it has to do with highest harmony, about purest sounding together, that means, to do with the same or similar [matters]. This one can become aware of especially beautifully and clearly with music—which is why I put special value in astrology on music, the aspect of the keys. Let us remain with the first of the above-mentioned 'crosses'.

With the cross Ram, Scales, Crab and Goat, when we translate this into the musical realm (see my monograph, *The Essence of Tonality*) [Leominster: Anastasi 2008 and *The Language of Tonality*, Anastasi 2015], then we will easily hear with the Ram scales the opposite quality of C-major to F#-major, a sharper contrast one cannot find in music than the one of the opposite keys whose fundamentals stand in tritone—augmented fourth. In music *this* contrast, that is, opposition, decisively still stronger than the square: C-major to A-major, A-major to F#-major, and so on. Here it is somewhat different than with the horoscope (you see that here the starting point are but facts, nothing is 'constructed'). Nevertheless, keys like C-major and A-major, A-major and F#-major, E♭-major and C-major also do not stand especially close to each other. The keys standing to each other in a triangle are much closer to each other: C-major and E-major, E-major and A♭-major, A♭-major and C-major. To each other, although they stand in the circle of fifths far apart, they give the most beautiful and most colourful harmonic connections.

The cross, from which we initially began here, also in music (this cross would be C-major, F#-major, A-major and E♭-major, or also C-minor, F#-minor, A-minor and E♭-minor), that is, the cross of Ram, Scales, Crab and Goat, I have called in my book on *Mark's Gospel* the '*Cross of the Father*'. For clearly the three crosses in the zodiac relate to the Trinity of Father, Son and Spirit, or if one will, also to the Trinity, Ahriman, Christ and Lucifer (for specific reasons, I have to put Christ in the middle), to the 'three crosses on Golgotha'. The Fishes-cross would then be the '*Cross of the Son*', the Waterman-cross the '*Cross of the Spirit*'. For observations on the gospels, which concerned me at that time, this viewpoint is of decisive importance. In the old astrology there were other names. The Ram-cross, from which we, too, begin, the cardinal cross (some people, like Schmitz,[165] also call it the 'mobile cross', under which we mostly understand our 'Son-cross', the

Fishes-cross. This, our Son-cross, the usual astrology calls the mutable or mobile cross (sometimes also the 'doubled' [cross], where really nothing proper can be laid hold of), our Spirit-cross (the Waterman-cross) it called the 'firm cross'.

Indian expressions are preferred today, with astrology that is mingled with Anglo-Indian theosophy:

- the cardinal-cross, our Father-cross, is then called the *rajas*-cross,
- the Son-cross *sattva*-cross,
- the Spirit-cross *tamas*-cross.

*Sattva*, *rajas* and *tamas* are the three principles of the Indian Sankhya-philosophy that play a similar role as the three principles light, dusky, and darkness do in Goethe's *Theory of Colours*.[166] *Rajas* 'dusky' or 'the colour red' also expresses passion and movement, *tamas* 'darkness' also the rigid, immobile, *sattva* 'light' also keeping the spiritual middle in the mutable, changeable region.

I was very pleased to find in Creuzer that for the Indians themselves a relationship exists between these three principles and their divine trinity, and indeed *raja* corresponds to Brahma (Father), *sattva* to Vishnu (Son), *tamas* to Shiva (the Indian 'Holy Spirit'). With astrologers today, their favourite Indian-theosophical viewpoint coincides exactly with what I independently found there. We can speak of the Father-cross, the Son-cross and the Spirit-cross without falling into contradiction with some ancient astrology or other. And these studies will go on to show how important especially this trinitarian viewpoint (Father-cross, Son-cross, Spirit-cross) is for astrology and for the spiritual understanding of the zodiac.

And what concerns the astrology governing today it seems everywhere important to draw it away from Anglo-Indian theosophy still controlling it today and to place it on the healthy ground of Rudolf Steiner's anthroposophy. This is the actual main reason and essential content of this whole study: to build astrology afresh on the Christian foundations of anthroposophy and for the great cosmic aspects which in astrology we have to gain in general for the revelation of the cosmic cross in the stars. For the centring of the entire astrology in the Mystery of Golgotha it is of decisive importance to perceive the three crosses in the zodiac as the crosses of the Father, the Son and the Spirit.

- The cross of the Father, that is, the Ram-cross, from which we began (Ram, Scales, Crab and Goat) we can also name the *physical cross* or cross of the earthly element.

- The Cross of the Son (Fishes, Virgin, Twins and Archer) we also name the cross of the etheric element.
- The Cross of the Spirit (Waterman, Lion, Bull and Scorpion) we also name the cross of the astral element.

Why and with what right has still to be developed in detail in the following observations. What has been said hitherto contains initially *statements* the proof of which is still to be produced.

We are clear, though, about this, that in the four corners of each of the three crosses opposites are incorporated, that these four corners contain rather disharmonious points then harmonious points (whereas the three corners of each of the four triangles are thoroughly in harmony between themselves). But precisely contrasts in their combination express the characteristic qualities of the respective cross. In a certain relationship these four points also share something between themselves. This common element was delineated as a specific 'dynamic', that is peculiar to each of the crosses. For the nature of this dynamic, reference was sought to the Indian expressions *sattva, rajas* and *tamas*, which we would now replace with other, Christian expressions. Concerning all these viewpoints, concerning the three crosses in the zodiac as a whole as in the details, and more things, we address in the next *Contribution*.

# XIII
# Report on the Astrology Congress in Wiesbaden (8–12 November 1931) Preliminary observations

The invitation to this Congress came from the *Astrologische Zentralstelle*, President Dr H. Korsch,[167] Düsseldorf. Members and friends had become aware of my work on the gospels (of Mark and John) and, as a student from Berlin had written to me, found in it valuable viewpoints, right into horoscope interpretation. Certain questions that were for some time the focus of interest, had hitherto been obscure, or rather the earlier attempts to solve them had remained unsatisfactory (Drews, etc.),[168] may now be guided from quite new viewpoints towards what seems to be a satisfactory solution—this is the gist of the letters I received. People were immediately prepared to discuss the books in astrological journals and this also took place.

This focussed interest in academic work stood in favourable contrast to many things that one frequently experiences in our, I mean anthroposophical, circles in this direction. Here works that touch on cognition are often left unnoticed or are even felt as uncomfortable disturbances. Furthermore, the way those circles of that Astrological Society regard the anthroposophical approach at least without preconceived judgment and without blind opposition, gives one hope. In the journal *Zenit*[169] of the Society in question, I found in the July/ August issue of this year a reference in one of the articles to Dr Wachsmuth's book *The Etheric Formative Forces* as well as to Dr Steiner himself, quoted in recognition and agreement. I decided to accept the invitation to the Congress because the programme appeared to me without exception highly interesting and showed themes with which I felt deeply concerned. And amongst the lecturers were astrologers partly known to me by name. (The Congress ticket I had received as a compensation for a review copy of my work on the gospels. In any case, I combined the Congress journey with three other lectures that I gave in The Christian Community in Wiesbaden and Mainz.)

My expectations, however, were not too high, for according to earlier experiences (especially with the Congress of the Schopenhauer

Society in Dresden some years ago where I had to speak)[170] such 'exotic' events affect one who comes with anthroposophical presuppositions as mostly very disappointing. Especially the aesthetic element, the aesthetic one-sidedness of the Schopenhauer Congress, was difficult to stomach. But this time the impressions were completely different. One realized immediately that astrology according to its whole nature can never be dealt with in such a way that is only aesthetically one-sided. Rather through its whole inherent being, whatever direction in it one follows with it, whether more spiritually or more with the material, technical matters, it leads with inner necessity into the deepest moral questions and trials.

## Extending Scientific Pursuit

Concerning this to be sure, no doubt should exist that generally today in astrological groups, especially in groups that are scientifically serious (and only those groups were present in Wiesbaden, the decadent gipsy-astrology played no part there but was completely excluded) the spiritual aspect of astrology is very much pushed into the background. People strive in many places—and this striving has at present a certain majority—to pull astrology as a statistically empirical science as far as possible to the level of our academic sciences researching with material, empirical methods. Many people find this a high aim to which one should aspire. In Wiesbaden, too, most of the participants—including the President, who was shown to be an excellent, impartial and exact Chairman of the event—might have stood for the view of the empirically calculated astrology. These things one should not simply sweep away completely, but one has to find it interesting that a realm like astrology, which in its primal foundation is so spiritual, is, in such a way, open to calculation, to the mathematical realm. Hereby one can receive an inkling of the spiritual backgrounds, especially, too, those of mathematics. Perhaps one can also smile that Ahriman with his empirical, statistical, calculating method starts already today to be interested in astrology, to include it into the circle of his own Ahrimanic interests and to wrest it from his brother Lucifer, who until now was the lone lord in this realm. If Ahriman follows Lucifer in this, then there is only *one* step missing in order to bring the subject into the direction on which the future of humanity depends.

Consequently, most of the people in Wiesbaden may have been of the opinion just characterized. The main thing, the deep impression with the whole subject was for me that especially the most splendid representatives of the subject, those who were also the leading speakers, saw through the one-sidedness of the viewpoint and strongly emphasized the spiritual side of astrology. In the first instance there was a young man from Switzerland, Karl Ernst Krafft,[171] from Zürich, a statistician by profession. He has gone through astrology itself to the bitter end with statistical methods. He represented in the strongest fashion the view that one cannot reach the aim by these methods, that one has to see and seek the spiritual element of astrology. It was a pleasure, indeed a deep human experience to listen to this young man. For he is still a young man, hardly passed through the middle of his life, and yet he appeared much more mature than the older people whom one had already heard in the Congress. He possessed that inner maturity that otherwise is only gained through a long life and many painful life-experiences, which were clearly not missing in his own life. That element which impresses itself into the features and the voice of a human being through the suffering he had to endure under the dullness of comprehension, self-opinionated arrogance, under the narrowness, the blinkers and prejudices born out of people's fears—all this lay in the features and voice of this young man. He was not only a great, a deep scholar with all the technical abilities at his fingertips, but was also a profoundly spiritual human being who truly deserves the name *anthropos*, human being. Even if outwardly he has not yet found the connection, he simply belongs with us, to anthroposophy. Some things in the way he spoke and came across reminded me of Englert-Faye.[172] He strongly emphasized that originally, astrology was not at all empirical, but essentially 'irrational'. He said: 'Everything of the far past points towards the future, and everything of the future is [already] contained in the past. Only the present is always confusing.' He spoke rather like Novalis in his *Fragments* of the essential profundity of space and time, which I quoted in my book on *Alchymy* (p. 18f.). What he said pointed very much in the direction of a saying of Dr Steiner in *Karmic Relationships*,[173] that astrology in its true original being had been an intercourse with the living intelligences of the cosmos (as alchymy has been with the spirits of nature). All in all it was often the case in this Congress that one perceived certain directions given by Dr Steiner for astrology, even though the words of the Doctor were not actually spoken.

People spoke—Krafft was not the only one; other speakers did, too—especially seriously concerning the qualification, including the moral qualification, to be an astrologer, or one who interprets horoscopes. They spoke about it so that one could see there is hardly anyone who in a quite serious sense really has the ability to interpret a horoscope. There came to me ever again the saying of Dr Steiner, also reported in the accompanying 'Personal Observation regarding Astrology' accompanying this *Newsletter* (I warmly ask the friends to read this text). He said: 'Only the greatest initiate at the end of his life should interpret for another person his/her horoscope.'[174] Of course, anyone can be interested in astrology, but when interpreting horoscopes one is warned to take care.

K.E. Krafft, furthermore, emphasized that astrology could never be a *science in the sense of today*; all striving towards this would do it an injustice. With regards to a critique of science today, the following saying of Krafft was a credible statement: in this science one pays too much attention in the 'use of the right method' and does not ask enough about the *right results*. Another sentence: '*Die Allgemeinheit ist die Summe der Gemeinheit Aller.*' ['The general is the sum of all baseness.'] In his lecture, Krafft strongly emphasized what we always say, external living space today is saturated; the decisive things will soon no longer be received from without but only from within. The outer world is saturated, but the inner world has to be made ever more productive. Moreover, many quite concrete directions were given about the zodiac and the planets, which I cannot reproduce here in detail.

Besides Krafft, Dr Rolf Reißmann[175] from Berlin was one of the most excellent speakers; he also had to hold the one public lecture at the Congress. Though not actually spiritual, with his intellect he always touched the spiritual realm. (From one of our newly ordained friends, I heard recently that, as a critic for *Der Tag*,[176] Reißmann discusses spiritual and occult lectures; in this capacity has already discussed Bock's lectures in a warmly positive manner, though still keeping a distance from anthroposophy.) Earlier I compared Krafft with Englert-Faye; Reißmann could be distantly compared, all things being equal, with W.J. Stein.[177] The same penetrating intelligence and brilliant use of language, in addition a certain similarity in the sound of his voice, indeed in the shape of his head. This only by the way. He spoke interestingly about the question of destiny, about freedom and necessity, so that I now feel stimulated to work through *The Philosophy of Freedom* again from new viewpoints. What is presented in our Breviary as the opposites of what is preordained with the laws of nature, became clear to me in a new and deeper sense, in the tangible sense of astrology. Perhaps I can give more details later in a study on the Breviary, as suggested in Eisenach.

There was also much talk about Einstein and modern natural science, of the breaking through of the law of cause and effect that natural science believes already to have found in the atomic world. Even if one could not follow in all the details (a certain determinism was alarming for many people) and many things seemed to be too materialistic, one did feel stimulated to a new far-reaching questioning. This was generally the case in Wiesbaden. One saw new perspectives everywhere ....

### The Realm beyond Saturn

Already with the first Congress lecture, which was held by Dr Heinz Artur Strauß (Munich),[178] a serious zodiac researcher, there appeared how people find particularly the zodiac a serious, difficult and in many ways an obscure problem today. This especially relates to the two zodiacs, the earthly zodiac as well as the fixed-star zodiac, about which I have written several times now in my *Contributions*. In the Introduction to my book on *John's Gospel*, too, this question is dealt with from new Christian viewpoints. In our anthroposophical circles, one often takes this problem in a far too light and facile manner. One often acts as though one knows everything, without a sense of into what dilettantism one falls. In Wiesbaden it was different. Here, too, one certainly didn't hear the final word that can be proclaimed in this realm, not yet the actual spiritual side. Instead, however, one might have the first thing about the zodiac, the earthly side, which with us is sometimes bypassed. Humanly and scientifically, Dr Strauß (I know from some of his writings that he is the writer of a valuable book on Kepler)[179] made a very sympathetic impression. His wife[180] did, too, who commendably assists him in his researches; she was active in organizing the Congress and also spoke. Zodiac research, the question of the relationship of both zodiacs, is her special subject. In personal conversation it was established that I had already met her on the Zugspitze [the highest peak in Germany]. It was during my Breitbrunn time.[181] At that time she was unmarried; two of her sisters were in a country boarding-school with Herr Uz (known to many of us). I first met her on this tour of the Zugspitze on the ascent to Knorrhütte.

The deepest impression of the whole Congress made on me was of a Dutchman who spoke right at the end, who was very apologetic for his impossible German. He is called Theodor J.J. Ram,[182] and is in outer life a school master in Amersfort near the Zuiderzee. Inwardly, he is something completely different, a human being of mystical leanings, with strong occult eyes, extremely warm and friendly in sheer humanity. He spoke about the world beyond Saturn, the mystical planets, and touched thereby directly on the well-known special realm of Uranus research, I mean the various things about which I have written in the first few of my *Newsletter Contributions*, and also later. He connected—and this is doubtless correct—these occult or mystical planets (Uranus, Neptune, Pluto and those still to be discovered) with those future forces, which as new forces (in an occult manner) are to appear in humanity. Such forces can appear initially unmastered, and after that mastered. The unmastered forces already play a role today (e.g. in Spiritualism, in all kinds of psychic and pathological phenomena); the mastered for the greater part still belong to humanity's future, to higher development. But everything proceeds in a certain harmony with these mystical planets, indeed one can say—this viewpoint I add here—that the spirit of the age introduces the discovery of such a new mystical planet when those forces connected with it begin to play a greater role in the consciousness of humanity.

## Uranus

First of all the Dutchman spoke about *Uranus* as the greatest power, the highest power, that re-arranges and transforms. The forces of electricity have for a long time been ascribed to Uranus, likewise certain mysteries of warmth (Uranus is known as the 'torrid planet'). Then he pointed out how through warmth conditions can be changed, how solidity can be changed through warmth into liquid and liquid into gaseous conditions. Similarly, he added, *Uranus produces in the spiritual realm*, in the soul it produces *the transition from one condition of consciousness into another, higher consciousness*. This is a very important, an eminently essential viewpoint!

If I may add something here, it would be a saying of Novalis. One also recalls what was said of the connection of Uranus with electricity. Now, one finds in the *Fragments* of Novalis (No. 611, ed. Kamnitzer) the saying: 'Like an electric spark, we spring into the world yonder.' He means in particular the transition of consciousness in meditation, the springing over of the spiritual spark into higher worlds, comparing it to the natural phenomenon of the electric spark. The Uranus viewpoint with all this is clear and obvious. The whole thing is a colossal bringer of light, wonderfully illuminating the spiritual side and leading into the spiritual side. It was with the whole lecture in general of the Dutchman in question, that one no longer heard the spoken word at all, but by speaking, a whole panorama unrolled before the spiritual eye, that one inwardly felt all sorts of things springing up, that a new door, ever new glimpses of the spiritual worlds appeared to open. One felt stimulated to active inner collaboration to work at fine things.

## *Neptune*

With what he then said about the next mystical planet, *Neptune*, I had to think of many things we discussed in Eisenach. With Uranus, [Ram mentioned] the transporting of consciousness to higher levels, with *Neptune*, in a word, *recollection*. He came to that which Rudolf Steiner calls the 'akasha chronicle', the occult record of the past in the cosmic ether. (The term he [Ram] did not use, but other, more modern pictures, in order to meet the consciousness of today.) A Neptune mastered, he said, means that one has everything to hand in one's recollection. That an *unbridled* Neptune can bring much that is harmful, I have extensively emphasized in my first *Contributions*; this has to do with dulling the consciousness, with narcotics, morphine, etc. With a mastered Neptune — this became abundantly clear to me through Ram's lecture — it has particularly to do with what one can call the *Christening of recollection*, in the sense of what Dr Steiner says about it, and what is found expressed in certain meditations.

This Christening of recollection is one of the important matters of our age, the age of the return of the etheric Christ for humanity to work on 'occult powers'. Not for nothing does *Neptune* stand in the sign of the Fishes, with co-governor Jupiter (the actual planet or our Movement, the Christ-planet, *Kyrios* [the Lord]), which in the age of humanity is part of the axis Fishes-Virgin (this axis, what is called the Last-Supper constellation, is at the same time the axis of our Movement, as I have often emphasized). Neptune, the lord of the cosmic distances, sends 'sounds out of the cosmic distances' already in the Jordan-Baptism, as I mentioned in my book on *John's Gospel*.[183] These are wonderful Christian perspectives! The Wiesbaden Congress, even if not everything that was spoken was Christian, yet for me nevertheless was an eminently Christian experience, an experience of humanity in the highest degree. I felt this most strongly in the lecture of the Dutchman Theodor Ram.

## *Pluto*

From Neptune, we proceeded to the newly discovered *Pluto*, whose planetary existence and planetary status in the cosmos can be taken now as astronomically secured. The Dutchman called it Pluto-Osiris (like Pluto, Osiris is indeed in Egyptian mythology the Lord of the Underworld). Neptune has to do with the past and recollection; Pluto-Osiris has to do with the future and the will, introducing certain will-forces lying in the future, the forces of a new will. These forces one can call in the anthroposophical sense—again, an addition from me—Asurian powers, of a double-edged character; they have a bright and a dark side.

Immediately I am drawn to a passage from Rudolf Steiner's [fourth] mystery-drama *The Soul's Awakening*, Sc. 4, where Benedictus speaks to Strader of such powers:[184]

> I saw you joined with special kinds of beings
> who would work evil if already now
> they would take hold of human spheres of action.
> Yet now they live as germs in certain souls
> to ripen for the earth in future times.
> I saw such germs alive within your soul.
> that they're unknown to you is for your good.
> They will first recognize themselves through you.
> But as of now the road is barred for them
> which leads them into realms of earthly matter.

This would be the sense of this lecture in Wiesbaden concerning Pluto-Osiris. Neptune has to do with the past and recollection; Pluto has to do with the future and the will, and so another planet still to be discovered has to do with the synthesis of both, of past and future. This planet—Isis—is truly linked to the being that can say of itself: 'I am everything that was, that is, that will be.' All higher harmony and synthesis, also in the artistic realm, belongs to this planet Isis.

- Uranus in the Saturn-sign of Waterman is a colleague of Saturn;
- Neptune in the Jupiter-sign of the Fishes is a colleague of Jupiter;

- Pluto in the Mars sign of the Ram is a colleague or a higher octave of Mars.
- Isis, simply following inner planetary and zodiacal knowledge, in the Venus-sign of the Bull would be the higher octave and colleague of Venus. As already in the Egyptian Mysteries, Isis and Venus also belong together as planets in the cosmos.

Theodor Ram then spoke about two other future planets. (Whether there really are two more, not only one, that with 7 (up to Saturn) + 5 (from Uranus) there would then be twelve, is still questionable to me; on the other hand the thirteenth, although the lecturer did not directly say it, would then be the Christ-planet.) These two planets he called:

- Hermes (colleague with Mercury in the Mercury-sign Twins) and
- Horus (in the Moon-sign of the Crab, the cosmic reflection of the Sun-forces.

If the first has to do with manifesting (exteriorizing) the etheric and astral [nature], the higher human members, then the latter, the Christ-planet (this title he did not use) *Horus* has to do with *incorporating these forces right into the physical world*, or, expressed differently, with the *resurrection forces of Christ*. Since already beforehand through exchanges with the Dutchman, I had to support him in the exact pronunciation of Indian names (with which he works a lot) and some Sanskrit words, I could also here easily interject, 'Here you are simply with the Christian resurrection!'

It was really a wonderful Christ-perspective in which for me the lecture of the Dutchman, and thereby the whole Congress, came to a conclusion. I already mentioned that for me this Congress was a human experience of the first degree. Not only the scientific but also the human niveau of the Congress was very significant. Quite by itself people sought to make my acquaintance, although I was not a speaker, simply because they knew of me and my work and because at the Congress it was simply that people were humanly interested in each other, that here one could experience, where the focus really was on great questions of spiritual knowledge, how one awoke to people. Rudolf Steiner's saying (unsure where it is exactly, so I cannot extract the exact words), that sometimes it is not in anthroposophical groups and connections where anthroposophical concerns such as we are doing are pursued, came to me often and set me thinking.

## Conclusion

What did one especially good at the Wiesbaden Astrological Congress was the whole atmosphere of academic earnestness and at the same time academic humility, purely from the aspect of knowledge, of the mental attitude of the Congress participants. An atmosphere existed in which nothing narrow or dogmatic could enter, also the empirical dogmatism that today in astrological circles certainly appears was not entertained by the most excellent speakers, as I mentioned. I must quite openly say that it was an atmosphere in which I felt spiritually good, in which I felt spiritually free and unhindered to breathe, whereas everything only of a distant pastoral or dogmatic nature that easily leads to arrogance always oppresses me. Certainly, true and genuine anthroposophy lies far remote from everything dogmatic, because according to its nature it concerns knowledge, is a path to knowledge. The tragedy is only this, that many of its followers do not understand that tendencies ever and again enter to dogmatize anthroposophy. Thereby one makes it impossible in the world. And thereby arises the narrowness and oppressive character which one sometimes feels in anthroposophical and related contexts.

What I mostly missed in the Astrological Congress also with the best speakers was an open mind for the knowledge of karma and reincarnation, or better said, the recognition of the serious significance of this whole question especially for astrology. For with this question, with the recognition of repeated earthly lives, stands and falls the whole possibility of a really spiritual and Christened understanding of astrology as such. What should I think of astrology if I cannot say that the birth-horoscope is precisely the expression of karma, the past woven by the human 'I'? Every other understanding of astrology has to become a danger for Christianity and Christian recognition, has to coerce the soul into a hopeless determinism. This danger was in particular clearly perceptible with Reißmann's otherwise spirited presentations.

With this Astrology Conference it was clearly recognizable why it is so necessary today to bring the knowledge of karma and repeated earthly lives to humanity. Once again, the one-sided objection against astrology may not be raised, that up to now it omits or at least appears to omit this important knowledge (for also the best speakers do not yet speak of this subject, although they might be considering it for themselves). Yet a part of the objection applies to us, applies to the appearance of dogmatism, which, as I already said, is sometimes awoken by the representatives of anthroposophy. The world today is not served with some sort of dogma; it wants knowledge. And many people are discouraged from the search on the anthroposophical path of knowledge today through some things offered by the Movement. That's why it can be especially important and commendable also from the viewpoint of astrology, when now Dr Rittelmeyer[185] has brought out a book on repeated earthly lives. Let us hope this publication may prepare the way far and wide for an understanding of this important fact.

For me, too, the way is clearly signposted that I have to go with the attempt to participate in the attempt at astrological knowledge present in the world today. Already before the Congress, I was asked for an article for the astrological journal *Zenit*. I will try to write the article, by showing in the most exact manner a grounding in a theory of knowledge, where today the points lie that are important for a spiritual deepening of astrological insight with regard to anthroposophy. Earlier in astrology (e.g. Alan Leo [1860-1917, sometimes termed the 'father of modern astrology'—*Tr. note*]) a certain link to the Anglo-Indian Theosophy was sought; today the attempt is to throw overboard everything theosophical. But this only leads further when one replaces it in the right way with anthroposophy as the contemporary form for spiritual endeavour. In the whole Astrology Conference in Wiesbaden one actually saw oneself inwardly shown the way to pursue Rudolf Steiner's astrology, and I believe to introduce anthroposophy at an important place in the spiritual struggle of our time may not be shunned.

# Supplement

## *Anthroposophy: Epistemological Basis for Astrology*[186]

Astrology of today that has to be taken seriously clearly emphasizes that it does not intend to be a 'warmed up ancient superstition', but that it owes its results and experiences to a critical view and works with rich empirical, statistical and factual material. It works with the same methods as science recognizes today. Nevertheless, in the scientific community it still has to wrestle for recognition; it is still not taken seriously as a science of today and is probably still put down on many sides as 'old superstition'. If one enquires concerning the reason for this rejection, which as a representative of scientific astrology one may regret, then one may receive the answer of the common thinking of today concerning the starry world. As long as one does not think differently about the stars, in the way as is the case in science today, or in humanity generally today, as long as one looks at the stars mainly as a heap of material, earthly-spatial material, as long as one does not wrestle through to a knowledge of spiritual starry wisdom, then so long any talk of spiritual starry influence basically has always to be felt as nonsense and superstition. Everything that astronomy has worked out *mathematically* one can fully admire—in calculation, mathematics, science has reached a high level. Scientific *thinking* still moves, as it were, in earth-bound concepts with which one cannot reach the starry worlds. Especially on the foundation of astronomy this appears more than with any other science; here every materialism in thinking reaches much further in its general cultural consequences than in any other realm. With the progress of science today, in pure factual research as in calculation, it is easily overlooked that the progress in thinking has not kept up the same level.

If it is true that from the thinking of today one cannot reach a recognition of spiritual, starry influence, and when nevertheless an astrological direction of research of today, which is to be taken seriously as science, bases its results and experiences on the application of the empirical, statistical methods common in science today, then this fact should be taken as a stimulus to overcome the materialistic one-sided thinking that is still preferred today in science. Instead of the materialism predominating today, one works on a thinking with which one can again lay hold of the spiritual starry wisdom and recognize the spiritual starry influence.

This prerequisite is fulfilled through anthroposophical spiritual science founded by Dr Rudolf Steiner. It creates the adequate epistemological foundation in thinking for a new contemporary astrology. Not only in a vague and uncertain manner—this one could find today elsewhere—anthroposophy speaks of spiritual, starry wisdom and spiritual starry influences. However, it shows in a scientifically exact way the path that leads out of a materialistic one-sidedness and bondage to the earth of the thinking of today. The thinking about the stars, too, is led into a higher thinking conforming with the physical starry being itself, into a higher way of knowledge adequate for the spirit. This also enables the one-sided statistical methods in the astrological realm to be overcome, which alone can assist us to a deeper knowledge of the stars.

Because anthroposophy in this sense has to demand a *transformation of the thinking common today*, a 're-thinking', it is at first *uncomfortable* for that thinking. Consequently, many people *dislike* it. Yet it should be understood that without such inner progress and overcoming, without a corresponding exertion and inner strengthening of thinking, a scientific exploration in higher realms of knowledge is not possible. In astrology that has become contemporary again, a realm of knowledge of the highest kind is knocking at the portal of human knowledge. Especially the rejecting stance of science today based on today's common thinking and mental picturing, and towards the empirical results of astrology today, could and should be seen as a warning to revise thinking.

Facing abstract thinking, that is, the way of thinking today that is abstracted from the objective world-events—this especially affects Kant's theory of knowledge that places thinking as facing the world but does not place it into it—anthroposophy emphasizes that our thinking itself is an integrating part of world-events. Novalis already expressed that our thinking is an effective factor of the universe. In this universe the originally free 'I' finds itself. Today it faces the events of the world and of nature, which in themselves compulsively carry the causal necessities. The astronomical starry lawfulness of today, too, is a part of this objective world-lawfulness. It also carries in itself the original free deed of creative beings. In the way that anthroposophy enables the right demarcation of freedom and necessity in world-events, it allows the 'I' wrestling towards its freedom also to find the right stance towards the fact of its birth-horoscope. The anthroposophical concept of *karma* in particular shows how the original freedom later becomes the necessity of destiny, the destiny of a later life, and how this destiny is slowly worked through and overcome by the strengthened 'I'. The whole way that all human life is carried by a higher starry life, from the viewpoint of anthroposophical spiritual research, appears especially meaningful and significant when it is recognized how the free 'I', or the 'I' wrestling towards its freedom, finds in itself the centre. At the same time, this is the centre of the whole starry life, this whole starry harmony. In this sense anthroposophical spiritual science arrives at the recognition of the cosmic Christ, where the connection of cosmic mystery and human mystery, human riddle and star-riddle, begins to find a solution. The question of the birth-horoscope, too, is removed from the realm of the completely opaque into the realm of surveyable knowledge that at the same time makes possible a moral worldview.

## *Uranus and the Planets beyond Saturn*

In a meaningful manner, the more recent astrological practice also includes in its calculation the distant trans-Saturnian planets Uranus and Neptune, and more recently also Pluto, discovered a few years ago [1930]. With these planets special connections are found with the supersensible, esoteric realms of the higher soul-forces and facts of consciousness, with Uranus in particular the creative genial and inventive powers, with that which brings new influences into the cultural and spiritual life, also with that which reforms in a revolutionary manner, upsetting general human life. Hereby astrological practice will not be inclined basically to differentiate between these planets and the others. It will simply arrange each discovered planet adding them according to the astronomical series. It will consider the seven planets that in the ancient world reached to Saturn—in which the Sun and the Moon are counted as astrological planets, but the Earth is not. This septenary will be seen as surpassed and overcome by the new astrological discoveries —Uranus was discovered in 1781 and Neptune in 1846.

Without excluding the fact of the planetary existence of Uranus, Neptune, Pluto and perhaps further planets yet to be discovered,[187] the anthroposophical attitude nevertheless takes as important the viewpoint of the earlier astronomical and astrological tradition on these 'seven planets'. It points to the well-known astronomical fact that the movement of the moons of Uranus and Neptune is the opposite of those of the other planets (up to Saturn; see *Contribution* 10 above). It recognizes in this fact a connection with the results of spiritual research that finds in Saturn the original boundary of the planetary system. 'Ancient Saturn' is the name given to the creatively woven primordial condition or 'primal fog' forming the spiritual entity that only gradually split into the later planets. Uranus, Neptune and so on would not yet have been woven into this primordial system, but only later joined the system out of the higher realm of stars. For this higher world of the starry circumference of 'Ancient Saturn', whose astronomical manifestation today is the heaven of fixed stars, the early Greeks had the word *Uranos*. It is worth noting that in the early Egyptian and Greek Mysteries (see Creuzer, *Symbolik und Mythologie der alten Völker*) people spoke of eight planetary spheres (kabiri spheres). Beyond the sphere of Saturn as the seventh sphere, lies the eighth sphere of the higher starry heaven, the actual starry world called *Uranos*. When in recent times the planet Uranus was discovered, it was given the name of this higher starry sphere from whence it originally came. Such a name could, of course, be coincidental. But also Dr Rudolf Steiner points out how in this case with the name-giving a meaningful inspiration of the time-spirit held sway.

As the Saturn of today marks the boundary of 'Ancient Saturn', that is, of the primordial planetary system, consequently it is also understandably the carrier of earthly-planetary limitation, individualization, and of the limitation of the temporal sphere—for the pre-Saturnian conditions were not yet temporal in the sense we know today. The Greek myth also begins with Saturn-Kronos, with the 'fall into time'. The forces of earthly weight, of lead, of the binding of age, illness and death given by the earthly condition are connected with Saturn. In contrast to this [earlier incarnation of the] 'earth-planet' Saturn, the boundary marker of the earthly-planetary realm in the narrower sense would be *Uranus*, 'the starry planet' in the higher sense. This is the boundary marker of the actual starry realm, with the heavenly, super-earthly, starry qualities of *Uranos*. In this sense we distinguish it from the earthly-planetary situation.

Anthroposophy also emphasizes that all new and higher impulses of the cultural life come from the upper, trans-Saturnian, starry world, the higher realm of the stars. What recent astrology through its way of research finds concerning the characteristics of the influence of

Uranus, would then again be reviewed through anthroposophical spiritual observation in the surveyable field of knowledge. The name of the chemical element (uranium), out of whose mineralized ore radium is extracted—in which one is inclined today in the first instance to glimpse the influence of Uranus—would then be a meaningful choice. Through the results of certain recent scientific experiments, of the transitions and transformation of radium into lead, this would all gain in importance. The transition of the Saturn-sphere into the Uranus-sphere would, at the same time, be the transition of the earthly sphere into the higher sphere of the stars and vice versa. A spiritual, stellar view of the boundary region between the earthly-planetary and the cosmic-starry realm, the 'spiritual threshold', is found with Saturn. Saturn becomes the cosmic 'Guardian of the Threshold', a viewpoint that it already represented in earlier astrology.

From here, it becomes particularly understandable how Uranus is involved in everything to do with raising consciousness, awakening a higher consciousness in the human being. Anthroposophy especially emphasizes how this side of the influence of Uranus, with what is taken today too one-sidedly as revealed in the realm of nature (electricity, radium, and so on; anthroposophy speaks here of 'sub-nature'), should be supplemented. This development of higher forces, this higher Uranus-influence, should be sought out of the 'I'. For *both* these sides of the influence of Uranus appear to be uniquely illuminated by a saying in the *Fragments* of Novalis—in which Uranus is not directly mentioned: 'Like an electric spark, we spring into the world yonder' (No. 611 ed. Kamnitzer).

Anthroposophical observation will emphasize that the discovery of new planets is not something coincidental, but results when the fine and distant rays begin to gain an enhanced significance for human consciousness and human culture. This viewpoint appears fruitful precisely in turning to the planet Uranus. Uranus, Neptune, and so on can be felt today as mediating between the earthy and a higher starry region, in which lies our human origin and human future. Uranus, which is also seen by astrologers as the 'octave' of the planets close to the Sun (Mercury-Venus), would at the same time be seen as the planetary representative of the higher starry heaven, the higher planet, the planet of the higher-'I', that is also regarded by anthroposophy as the 'octave' of the normal earthly 'I'.

# XIV
# Zodiac 4:  (Introduction, then:
# The Cross of the Father)

## *Introduction*

After a pause, in which the debate on the theme 'astrology in the light of anthroposophy' that lies at the basis of all these *Contributions* here, which we are trying to carry out hitherto in the peaceful, contemplative world of the thinking spirit, there took place in the battling sphere of outer life a kind of drama of destiny:[188] I now return to my *Contributions* in the hope that the stance and attitude of the circle of friends makes this continuation possible for me. Consequently, I have to renew my urgent plea made before because of a tangible occurrence *to allow nothing of these contributions under any circumstance*[189] *to be shared with others outside this circle*, for otherwise confusions would occur that would certainly lead to the early end of these *Contributions*. Certainly, there can be an occasion for a serious reason to point someone towards these *Contributions*, but then I would like to ask in such cases to turn to me and take 'no answer' as a negative reply. But it would be better we do not make such exceptions, for later in a more worked through form that I have to find, I intend in any case to publish the content of this work on star-knowledge. Of course, I have no objection—this, too, is good to emphasize once—to these *Contributions* being read by and with Priests' wives if they are interested in the subject. *So* exactly one does *not* need to draw the line of separation. I do not see why the wives of Priests should not participate in these purely cognitional observations. For this, it is not seldom that the woman has a great, indeed greater understanding.

To the question of 'sign and constellation' I wanted to add that simply as a human being one can quite directly feel and experience the *independent reality of the signs*. Always around the 20th of the month, or a few days later (you simply recall only the time of the solstice and equinox), as is well known, there is the respective transition into a new sign (completely independent of the constellation, from the position which the Sun occupies in the starry heavens. Recently the transition from the Scales took place into the Scorpion on 24th October, from the Virgin into the Scales on 21st September, and so on (the *Ephemeris* shows us here, too, the exact moment in time). One can always feel how at this moment always something changes in the quality of the air, in the whole mood of nature. With the transition into the Scorpion it was especially characteristic this year. Until then (until 24th October) we had in the beautiful, late-autumnal sunny days, the typical mood of the Scales (which, like the mood of May, is a revelation of Venus, but now in the reversed direction, pointing upwards—Venus-Urania; the most beautiful were those October days when Venus was in the Scales at the same time as the Sun; then Venus still during the Sun-Scales time, entered the Scorpion (the sign, not the constellation), where it remained until 1st November. Now it stands in the [sign] Archer, that is, the constellation Scorpion. On the day of the transition of the Sun into the Scorpion the whole mood of nature changed this year especially perceptibly. The beauty of Venus-Scales was no longer there. Instead of which, all of a sudden there was a feeling of dying, characteristic of the Scorpion governed by Mars ([cf.] Mars, Lat. *mors* 'death'), the mood of dying of nature.

It is not seldom that the transition of the sign is revealed in the outwardly perceptible change in the weather (whereby, of course, I do not mean that only with the change of signs the weather changes, for there are many other reasons). Whoever observes exactly will actually be amazed how frequently it is the case. Even when in the individual case it does not come out so clearly, the somewhat sensitive human being is always able to feel the transition in the mood of nature, even his own mood, in one's own blood one would like to say, in the mood of one's nerves. To attend to such nuances is important. For, firstly, such attention belongs generally to train a higher, spiritual life (in the sense of Rudolf Steiner's *Knowledge of the Higher Worlds: How is it attained?*), and furthermore through such finer experiences one will be directed to the *earthly reality* of the signs, a reality initially completely independent of the stars. The signs—Ram, Bull, Twins, and so on,—which here are always the subject of discussion, then cease to be abstract concepts. They will then become something tangible, something directly present in life.

And, my dear friends, so very much depends on this. There is a great difference, whether, for example, one receives these *Contributions* in unfocussed, conceptual (to avoid saying 'paper') abstraction, or in a living actuality. Then all sorts of things can be enlivened in a wonderful manner. For example, from one of the friends,[190] I have heard how he has been stimulated by my contributions on the stars to write music.[191] This can enter right into the work of the Priest, in celebrating the Act of Consecration of Man. In this respect I am most grateful to our friend, Rudolf Frieling. We have, for example, the starry rhythm he sketched from the Creed. I choose the Creed because the matter is most clear and at its simplest, and consequently most easily assimilated—not simply intellectually, abstractly understood, but really intimately assimilated right into the forces of the heart, so that it flows through one's whole being and is also perceptible in celebrating the Act of Consecration of Man.

## *The Cross of the Father*

In continuing our *Contributions*, we stand with the 'three crosses' in the zodiac—which we always primarily regard as the 'spiritual zodiac'; the starry zodiac and the earthly zodiac are only two different revelations, they mutually relate as the 'upper' and the 'lower'. All sorts of different terms often confuse the understanding. In traditional astrology these three crosses are:

- the Cardinal Cross,
- the Mobile or Mutable Cross, and
- the Fixed Cross.

Or instead of these, also with Indian terms

- the *rajas*-cross,
- the *sattva*-cross and
- the *tamas*-cross. In the last *Newsletter* but one, attention was drawn to the connection established in Indian thought with the Indian trinity Brahma, Vishnu and Shiva.

So far, the three crosses were named in my work on the gospels as:

- the Cross of the Father,
- the Cross of the Son, and
- the Cross of the Spirit.

The more I work on these things, I feel that these terms have proved themselves, that they are useful and suitable to lead to the Christian depths and backgrounds of astrology. For only out of the Christian depths can astrology in a health-bringing way really be understood.

All other astrology that is pursued is so conformed as to lead the soul into the abyss, to rob it of its consciousness of freedom, its 'I'-impulse, its Christianity. Such a viewpoint—as with the naming of the 'three crosses of the zodiac—one has to test in a tangible manner with the gospel-rhythm, or the rhythms in the liturgy now shown by Frieling, in order to recognize to what degree it brings light.

The cross, then, that for traditional astrology was always called the 'Cardinal Cross', we called the Cross of the Father. We could also call it the 'Cross of the Physical Element', or the 'Earthly Cross'. What concerns the expression 'Cardinal Cross' appears something quite relative. For everything to do with the horoscope, the details of which will be discussed later, the Father-Cross does appear in fact as the cardinal, the main cross. Everything about horoscopes has very much to do with connections with the Father, spiritual inheritance, with karma and destiny. On the other hand, with my gospel-work I have always found that there the Cross of the Son (that is, the 'Mutable Cross' of traditional astrology), as the Christ-cross and 'Cross of the Middle' is the main cross, the cardinal cross. The figures in the books on *Mark's Gospel* and *John's Gospel* are correspondingly drawn [see below, p. 334-44].

Finally, I have pointed out earlier in my *Contributions*, that when one focusses on the world's becoming in the sense of the cosmogony of *Occult Science*, here precisely the third of the three crosses—the 'Fixed Cross' of traditional astrology—our 'Cross of the Spirit', that is, the cross Waterman–Lion–Bull–Scorpion, is the main cross, the cardinal cross, for in this the four great cosmic corners are designated, out of which the cosmic events ([Ancient] Saturn–Sun–Moon–Earth) take their point of departure. The relationship of the zodiac to the First Hierarchy, especially the Cherubim, came in particular to our consciousness. With Dr Steiner in the Düsseldorf lecture–cycle *The Spiritual Hierarchies and their Reflection in the Physical World* [GA 110], lecture 7, one finds further indications, also in the introductory chapter of Part 2 of my book on *John's Gospel* ('In the beginning was the word …').

But let us remain for now with the Cross of the Father, which is also the 'Cross of the Physical element', the 'Cross of the Earth'. The signs belonging to it are Ram–Scales–Crab–Goat. If one orientates this cross to the parts of the human body, head and hips, chest and knee, one will clearly feel how securely the human being is placed here into the earthly forces. The Mars-sign of the Ram—in the Ram the active, positive Mars is at home—opens the yearly rhythm indeed as the spring-Easter sign: here the Sun is exalted,[192] the Sun as the quicken-ing power, leading up again the greening and sprouting life of nature.

One should distinguish the 'exaltation' of the planets from their 'houses'; thus:

- the *Sun* is at home in Leo, but in the Ram it becomes prominent, it unfolds its forces especially strongly and well.
- *Mars* is at home in the Ram and the Scorpion, but in the Goat it comes into prominence, where he influences as 'spiritual Mars', as spiritual activity of the highest order.
- *Venus*, at home in the Bull and the Scales, is prominent in Pisces, the sign of serving love. Moreover, in the rhythm of the gospels (see my book on *Mark's Gospel*), the sign of the Ram always belongs to the beginning of the earthly activity of Christ. On the other hand, it is revealed, as with the healing of the possessed boy, as the sign of becoming upright and standing up (Mark 9:27. Cf. the beginning of Frieling's *Contribution*, RB Nov. 1931). In the Ram and the Scales (spiritually viewed: thinking and inner balance) the human being places himself properly and normally into the earthly world. And these earth-forces at the same time are the forces of the Father, which are revealed in the 'resting head'.

## *The Ram*

In music, the Ram belongs to C-major, the key of 'Let there be light!' in Haydn's oratorio *The Creation*.[193] Here the transition takes place from the lower, dark keys of the circle of keys [circle of fifths] to the upper, brighter keys. Compare the C-major with Brünnhilde's awakening in Wagner's *Siegfried*. C-major is the key of awakening, the sober key of the clear understanding, as the Ram of the sign of awakening, of the forces of consciousness of the awake understanding.

The rhythm of the signs is present both in the course of the year and in the course of the day. In the course of the year, the sign of the Ram is allocated to the becoming of spring, to the 'lightening up of the year', the equalizing of day and night in the spring, to Eastertide; just as in the course of the day [it is allocated] to the sunrise, the hour in which we rise and begin the day's work. Every revelation of the Ram's being during the course of the year is what we have called the 'sign of the Ram'. We know that in the sky this 'sign of the Ram' cor-responds (essentially) to the position of the Sun in the constellation of the Fishes. This is likewise correct as the other allocation, that the spirituality of the Ram in the heavens, in the heavenly constellation, is in reality revealed in the constellation of the Ram. To this constellation people have always compared the Ram lying in the meadow (thus it was pictured by the early Egyptians, cf. the zodiac from Dendera).[194] One is reminded of the 'resting head'.[195]

The zodiac-signs can also be arranged to the supersensory human members. The Ram corresponds to the physical, earthly body. This coincides once again with the viewpoint of the Cross of the Father.

With respect to the arrangement of the zodiac-signs with the 'twelve senses', there are various, but essentially two viewpoints. Both can be traced back to Rudolf Steiner. In my work on the gospels I rely on the lecture on the twelve senses in the cycle *Cosmic Being and Egohood* [also pub. as *Towards Imagination*, lecture 3, Berlin, 20 June 1916. GA 169], in connection with the Appendix to the book *Von Seelenrätseln*, Eng. title *The Case for Anthroposophy* [GA 21] and find there with the Ram the sense of the ego (considering also the significance of the 'two-petalled lotus-flower' between the eyebrows). Here [Dr] Kolisko[196] places the sense of speech (which I put to the Twins, for remarkably enough *both* put the sense of thought to the Bull, both the sense of smell to the Scorpion; otherwise it is so that always with each two signs the allocation is reversed. For example, with the Lion I find the sense of warmth and with the Waterman the sense of life; Kolisko finds the reverse: with Lion and the sense of life, with the Waterman the sense of warmth.

Amongst the world-conception configurations (given in the Berlin lecture-cycle *Human and Cosmic Thought* [GA 151, 4 lectures, Berlin 20-23 Jan. 1914] that is so important in laying hold of the beings of the spiritual zodiac), according to Dr Steiner's indications to the Ram is allocated *Idealism*. Cf. to this, also the expressive illustrations in the *Anthroposophical Soul-Calendar* drawn by Fr. von Eckardstein[197] according to Dr Steiner's indications. (These pictures, to which I shall return later [see *Contribution* XXIV], are of eminent importance generally in relation to the zodiac, to human development during the course of cosmic development). The rhythm begins in this case with the Fishes, moving in the Johannine direction of the great cosmic [Platonic] year— concerning this, see my book on *John's Gospel*, that is, in the direction Waterman–Goat–Archer and so on, until it finally ends in the Ram. Here the Ram presents the highest completion of the human being in beholding Spirit-man, or the higher human being. This is revealed in the picture in the *Soul Calendar*).

In the 'great cosmic year', which I just mentioned, one can likewise find a Ram-viewpoint. The age of the Ram, the 'fourth post-Atlantean cultural epoch', the Greco-Latin age, in which there also falls the earthly embodiment of Christ, the Mystery of Golgotha. Notice how this warlike age at the same time was a Mars-age (Mars in at home in the Ram), whereas in our age of the Fishes today, which is a Jupiter-age (notice how Jupiter amongst other things is also the planet of our Movement), outer wars have become something completely out of place, worn through, purely Ahrimanic (one thinks of the Great War). In the earlier Mars-age, wars still had something to do with 'progressive development'; today they have become human catastrophes. Today everything that involves the cherishing of Christianity on the Earth (also in the liturgical sense) belongs to the age. The coming age (Sun in the Waterman) will be a Uranus-age (about which I have written earlier); Christianity then will have taken on a marked Johannine character (the Marriage in Cana, and so on).

Amongst the 'twelve world-conception tendencies' (in the sense of the Berlin lecture-course), as we said, the Ram corresponds to Idealism. It is repeatedly shown how these indications made by Dr Steiner, apparently from a viewpoint outside the horoscope, are time and again valuable for horoscope interpretation. Thus, for example, Venus in the Ram (I pointed this out earlier), a Venus that in many respects wants to reach beyond the earthly element, a Venus not really satisfied in the earthly element, the most extreme denial of a homemade ideal of marriage. The dreamed-of ideal of love arising out of the imagination of the head, is a dream difficult to realize on the Earth.

## The Scales

When the Ram is, as it were, the ascendant (the rising sign) of the Father-Cross, then the Scales lying opposite is its descendant. The Ram is a Mars-sign, the Scales a Venus-sign—regarding the allocation of the planets to the zodiac-signs, it is clearly obvious, indeed already out of the purely astronomical facts; I have to refer the reader to what was said earlier. The sign Ram in the course of the year is the April-Sun, the sign Scales the October-Sun, as we have experienced so beautifully this year. Golden autumn days rightly correspond to this Venus-sign of the Scales. For in the Scales Venus is the spiritual, the heavenly Venus, Venus-Urania, whereas in the Bull it is the earthly, Venus manifested in the becoming of the Earth. We [in the Northern Hemisphere] experience in the month of May allotted to the Bull, that Venus is the 'Queen of the May'. This season of growing and blossoming is past in

October, the Michaelmas season. The splendour and revelation of the earthly world wants to leave us again, turn away from us. But also the year 'dies in beauty', nature is revealed in its whole beauty, in the rich splendid colours of autumn; this time precedes the actual death-time of the Scorpion, attributed to the present time of writing—that is, November. This is the one beauty that at the same time we feel more serious than the beauty and time of abundant blossoms of May, because at the same time it speaks to us of the coming spiritualization, of the earnestness of the great passing over. In this sense Venus-Urania is the governess in the Scales, at the same time somewhat serious, very different from the 'Queen of the May'. This year (1931) her revelation was especially expressive; they were the most beautiful days of revelation when, alongside the Sun in the Scales, Venus itself also stood in the Scales (I was permitted to experience these days in actual fact in Oberstdorf).[198]

When we rightly consider all this, we will understand how with the Greeks, in the Greek Mysteries (Creuzer[199] reports on this) something of an Aphrodite-Nemesis, a Venus of world-judgment, could exist. One increasingly notices how little the conventional ideas of Venus correspond to the reality. It has to be repeatedly emphasized how Venus in the higher, esoteric sense is not how it is taken by people. It is precisely that planet whose reality—although it is so deeply united with man's being and man's becoming—is the most difficult for people to get hold of, because it is the one who is mostly darkened through the Fall of man; in the same way as the human being himself is basically the most difficult to lay hold of by the contemporary person. Consequently, we need a 'higher knowledge of the human being', an anthroposophy [= wisdom of the human being]. We might also recall the lecture Rudolf Steiner once held for us in the Priests circle about the Mystery of the human being. We should work on this lecture ever afresh.

We recall how the Scales, in which Venus as Venus-Urania, as the Michaelic Venus is the governess, indeed at the same time is the sign of Justice, the sign of earthly justice as well as cosmic Justice. In my book on *John's Gospel* (pp. 265-322) I have discussed this viewpoint at length. It has to do with the second section of John's Gospel, Chapters 6-10 (Chapters 1-5 are 'Mystery Chapters'), where the Christ, after previously moving in certain Mystery-spheres, for the first time appeared openly amongst humanity (this was prepared already at the end of Chapter 5). There the meeting of Christ with humanity leads to the adverse powers governing in humanity, to the great conflict, to the division of spirits, to the crisis (as it is always called in the Greek original text), which can be felt as a reflection of the great cosmic assizes in the earthly realm. Also in this crisis, brought about through the entry of the Christ into humanity, Divine Love is revealed, Venus-Urania, as it is later revealed on Golgotha. Particularly what happens in Gethsemane stands significantly in this sign of the Scales, the Venus-Urania.

I have pointed to how in one of the chapters of crisis coming under consideration here, in John 7 (where the crisis for the first time breaks out as open, confused conflict), also the specific time given in the gospel ('Feast of Tabernacles') pointing to the time of year coming into consideration here, is the time of the Scales (today's Michaelmas). This, however (as I always emphasize), is not for instance a viewpoint under which one could understand the whole gospel rhythm—that would already not be right for Mark's Gospel, and for John's Gospel, which does not at all follow the course of the year, but at least in the early chapters follows that of the cosmic ['Platonic'] year, it really cannot be right. Only in separate cases does one find this coinciding of the gospel rhythm with the rhythm of time of the zodiac-signs. Such a case is given in John 7. We are placed into the sign of the Scales, also into the time of year of the Scales, into the Michaelmas of today. In my presentation I indicate how all possible motives, for example, also the earthly jurisdiction, play in as 'motifs of the Scales'.

We can also so understand all the chapters of John's Gospel standing in the Scales (Chapters 6–10) that here the picture of the Christ in the sense of 'the Group' [the carved wooden statue] in the Goetheanum, CH-Dornach, passes before the soul. 'The Representative of Man' holds the balance between the two adversaries, one to the right and the other to the left. (In my book on *John's Gospel*, p. 278f. and again on p. 293, I have pointed to this Imagination). It is—and this was shown—in these chapters it is in actual fact so that they do not simply stand in the Scales, but that with it one experiences the Scales, the sign of balance and of the 'I'. A struggle always takes place with both neighbouring signs (the bright sign of the Virgin and the dark sign of the Scorpion), that the Scales is not simply as it were at rest but oscillates upwards and downwards between the two other signs.

In the Scales, the sign of outer and inner balance, there is significantly revealed everywhere in the gospel (already in Mark) the I-AM of Christ. The 'I-AM the Light of the World', as above all already in the 'I-AM, do not be afraid!' stands in a Scales-passage. The storm on the sea in the gospel—this I already showed in the book on *Mark's Gospel*—belongs to the zodiac-sign of the Scales. We recall in this tremendous picture of the storm on the sea the struggle of the disciples for inner balance. It is the storm on the sea and the storm in the soul, the storm in the astral element, which is only stilled by achieving the 'I', that Christ reveals Himself as the One walking on the waves, the bearer of the great 'I', and calling to the alarmed human soul the 'I-AM, fear not'. This all plays in the gospel, in Mark as in John, in the sign of the Scales.

One thinks with the linguistic connections of *Waage* and *Woge*, *wagen* and *wogen*, *Woge* and *wiegen*, *wägen*, and so on.[200] And perhaps on the picture in Homer, how Leukothea, the 'white goddess', throws the saving veil to the shipwrecked Odysseus,[201] wrestling with the salty billows of the sea, and with this picture we have again reached Venus-Urania as the being of divine love, the Christ-love and the 'love in the 'I'', which as a planet governs the sections in the gospel to do with the storm on the sea and the Scales. In my book on *Alchymy*, I pointed out how from this point onwards, we can feel all the connections with Mary, the Star of the Sea (cf. the early church hymn, '*Christ Kyrie, komm zu uns auf der See*'[202]—'Christ the Lord, come to us on the water'). It is one of the most profound pictures that exists, which Botticelli has given to us in his *The Birth of Venus* [Uffizi Gallery, Florence]. All the Mysteries of Venus-Urania, who embraces all the Mysteries of the stars and the Mysteries of matter in herself, connecting astrology with alchemy, can be found in the picture, although it affects numerous people merely erotically. (This effect, too, which is a Mars-effect and not a Venus-effect, Botticelli in his revealing picture has brought to meaningful expression in the powers of the wind that blows briskly towards the goddess, who in virginal purity rises from the salty billows of the sea, so that she quickly takes the warmly enveloping, covering garments extended to her by feminine beings who approach her on the other side.)

All these things ultimately are revelations of Christ in the sign of the Scales. With this example I wanted to show clearly how the meaning of the twelve zodiac-signs from the most varying viewpoints, as we seek to show here in our presentation of the three crosses in the zodiac, can also be recognized in the rhythm of the gospel. Here precisely the original divine-spiritual meaning of the twelve zodiac-signs, the divine primordial meaning of the zodiac and plan-etary beings are revealed. Moreover, the mutual relationship, the characteristic opposites of Ram and Scales clearly appear in the gos-pel, especially in Mark's Gospel—especially in the relationship of the two episodes on the sea in connection with the two Feedings. For the gospel-narration, it is characteristic how after the story of the sacramental Feedings (Last-Supper constellation Fishes–Virgin) the sea-episode (Ram–Scales) follows. With one of these episodes, corresponding to the sign of the Ram, comes the sentence 'And crossing over onto the land …' [Mark 6:53, literal meaning of the Greek], that is, to the firm land, which here, in contrast to the surg-ing sea, at the same time is the picture of waking-up, of passing over into day-consciousness. The character of the 'earthly cross' appears here in the plain light of day.

In the horoscope the 'opposition' Ram–Scales is not so sharp as that for instance of the Bull and the Scorpion. Already earlier I emphasized that opposition and opposition in astrology are two different things; it can mean not only sharp opposition but also the productive struggle. Thus we have with the Scales (whose revela-tion in the heavens is the constellation that really looks like a weigh-ing scales, a balance with two sides, or a cross-beam), in the course of the year the Michaelmas season, on the human figure the hips (in which the human being physically keeps balance), in the gospel the 'struggle to keep the balance' in the picture of the storm on the sea and the 'verdict', the 'judgment', which is what the appearance of the Christ amongst humanity signifies for the latter (the 'division of spirits', as also in the zodiac the Scales divides between above and below, bright and dark, Virgin and Scorpion). Earlier, that is, in the primordial beginning, the two were indeed one, at that time when the human being was not yet properly developed, the becom-ing of man not yet advanced as far as the actual human figure, as I frequently discuss in my works. For this only happens in the Scales (during that cosmological progress of the event which in reverse zodiacal order begins with Pisces and ends in the Ram. Venus-Ura-nia there is the being that also gives the human being the harmony of the actual human figure. Consequently, the Scales, the sign of I-AM of Christ, is rightly also the *sign of the human being*. Here I would like to add that astrology sees in the Scales also the *exaltation of Saturn*,[203] of the Lord of the powers of the Earth: through these Saturn-Earth forces it happened that the Virgin and Scorpion separated, properly parting (the Scorpion cosmically arose, as the arrow of death of the Archer wanted to wound the Virgin, his previous neighbouring sign), so that between the forces above and below the human figure can develop in its beauty and harmony.

Thus the Scales, the sign of Venus, is also the sign of harmony, beauty, the artistic element, of right proportion in everything—the sense of balance, which one certainly wants to find in the Scales, belongs to it, seen from the one system of ordering; seen from the other the sense of taste (which is not completely without meaning) if one thinks not only of physical taste, but also, for example, of artistic taste, that is, when one thinks something eminently Venusian. The sense of balance would then belong to the Archer, to which sign the two thighs belong.

In the order of the directions of the twelve world-conceptions given in the Berlin lecture-cycle [GA 151], to the Scales belongs Realism, and to the opposite sign of the Ram Idealism; in the course of the day the sunset, and to the Ram the sunrise (we discussed above something of the correspondence of autumn—spring). In music, where C-major is the Ram-key, then the key lying opposite would be F#-major/Gb-minor, the key of the Ram. F#-major and Gb-major in exact tuning are not the same; they appear together in the 'tempered tonal system', the meeting of keys with sharps arriving from above, with those with flats coming from below; keys with sharps and keys with flats meet in F#-major and Gb-major, as it were, in the Scales. C-major leads from the darkness up into the light of day; F#-major/Gb-major leads from the light into the darkness, from the day-world to the spiritual world. Consequently, with Richard Wagner's work I can always clearly show in quite tangible examples such a thing as the key of the great crossing of the threshold, the *threshold to the spiritual world*.

In the Scales the human being and humanity experience the meeting with the Greater Guardian of the Threshold. For this reason, the chapters of crisis of John's Gospel are expressively aligned to this sign, which already for the Greeks was the sign of Venus-Urania, of Aphrodite-Nemesis. The spiritual being speaking to us here intends lovingly to lead us out of the earthly meadows into the regions of the spiritual world. This is also expressively revealed in that the sentence of our Creed 'He will in time unite...' (see Frieling's work) is arranged to the Scales and Venus-Urania. In these words, the Christian meaning of the Scales and Venus-Urania is most sublimely expressed. In the Ram, the sign of the active Mars, we found the sentence: 'In Jesus the Christ entered as man into the earthly world.' Whoever meditates deeply enough *finds in our Creed* the whole of astrology.

In the next *Contribution* more of the pair Crab and Goat, forming the longitudinal axis of the Father-Cross, before we then go on to the 'Son-Cross'.

# XV
# The Cross of the Father

Of the 'three crosses of the zodiac' we have already begun to present the first, the 'Cross of the Father', or 'Cross of the Physical Element' ('Cross of the Earth'), the 'Cardinal Cross' of horoscope-making. In the previous *Contribution* [No. 14] the constellation Ram–Scales standing above the 'horizontal axis' of this cross was discussed. Today, observations on the horizontal axis, Crab–Goat, now follow.

In the Ram we find the active Mars-sign, in the Scales the sign of Venus-Urania ('He will in time unite …' [The Creed]), in the Ram a fire-sign, in the Scales an air-sign (and with it at the same time the light-ether sign). The Crab, seen in relation to the planets, is the Moon-sign (house of the Moon), the Goat a Saturn-sign, moreover, the 'dark Saturn-sign'—why? On the one hand, because the Goat is the 'dark Earth-sign', the darkest of all the signs, in the same way as the part of the yearly rhythm corresponding to it, the 'sign Goat' (into which we enter 23 December) is the darkest section of the cycle of the year, although precisely into the greatest darkness of the Earth there falls the light of grace of Christmas. This aspect, Christmas, belongs to the Goat, which amongst the triangles in the zodiac, belongs to the 'Luke-triangle' (Bull–Virgin–Goat), the triangle of Luke's Gospel, which indeed in the first instance is the 'Christmas Gospel'. The Bull–Virgin–Goat (as we will get to know more closely later with the observations on the triangle in the zodiac), the signs of the triangle of the Earth, are the three Earth-signs.

Of these three signs:

- the Bull stands in the astral (Spirit-Cross),
- the Virgin in the etheric (Son-Cross),
- the Goat, however, in the physical (Father-Cross), in the Son-Cross.

For here the Earth-Cross meets the Earth-triangle (whereas the three other points of the Earth-Cross belong to the other three triangles). For this reason the Goat is the most earthly of all the signs of the zodiac, the 'dark Earth-sign', and as such the one house of Saturn, the lord of the earthly forces, the 'dark Saturn-sign', whereas the other Saturn-house, the Waterman, belongs to the air-triangle (and light-ether triangle), and for this reason is the lighter and brighter Saturn-sign. Here, as it were, it is not the earthly side but the heavenly side of Saturn, where the heavenly Uranus is co-regent, whereas in the 'dark Saturn-sign' the Goat alone governs, as it were revealing its earthly side.

It is thoroughly characteristic for Saturn that it has these two sides (spiritually meant):

- the one where it looks towards the upper heavens, the Uranus-side, and
- the other where it looks towards the Earth, revealing itself as the primordial Earth and lord of the forces of the Earth, the earthly side.

For this reason, it is indeed the great boundary in the cosmos, the great Guardian of the Threshold. (From earlier presentations we recall how Saturn can be seen as marking the cosmic boundary of the earthly realm, and Uranus as the cosmic boundary of the heavenly realm. The relationship of the Saturn-sign Goat to the earthly element thereby sheds light on its significance in the 'Earthly Cross' (Father-Cross).

Likewise, however, for the other sign on the longitudinal axis of this cross, the Moon-sign of the Crab. Also we have seen of the Moon how it has two sides, an earthly side and a cosmic, heavenly side. With the Moon this is expressed already in the outer, astronomical fact that it always turns the one side to the Earth, the other (not visible to earthly inhabitants) away from the Earth towards the cosmos. On the one side the Moon reflects the heavens, on the other side it reflects the Earth. Already in this a most significant relationship of the Moon to Saturn is given. Primordial Saturn as well (on this, see *Occult Science*) was a heavenly mirror, a mirror of the Uranian element, of the life and weaving of the upper hierarchies. In such mirroring processes the whole primordial development of the Earth has been introduced. This primordial Saturn, Dr Steiner relates, was a 'constriction', a pushing back of the Uranian, heavenly element. In it, the earthly planetary element is contrasted to the Uranian element. Then, in the later phase of development, in 'Ancient Sun' (as we recall from earlier *Contributions*), the Uranian element again comes forth. 'Ancient Sun' was intensive life, the primordial enlivening of the whole system out of the heavenly forces. Then, during the lunar phase of evolution, 'Ancient Moon', a new constriction, was brought forth, a new pushing-back of the Uranian element, a new advance of the materializing process, of the planetary element, of earthly hardening. In this, out of *Occult Science*, it becomes quite clear that in this consists the relationship between [the present] Saturn and Moon, which from completely different starting points is also accepted in the conventional, horoscope-astrology. For example, the conjunction between Moon and Saturn means something especially heavy, earthly and hardening. In medical astrology, under special preconditions—it always depends on the grouping of the houses and other influences—it appears as a cause of the hardening of tissue, cancer, and so on. Nevertheless, nobody who has this conjunction in his horoscope, should become alarmed by this fact alone, for many things work together.

This indication towards the relationship between the Moon and Saturn was made here in order to clarify the relationship of the two zodiac-signs, the Crab and the Goat forming the horizontal axis of the Father-Cross. In other relationships many-sided contrasts exist once more.

The Goat is the 'dark' Earth-sign; the Crab by contrast is a very bright sign. If on the one hand we orientate the Goat according to the musical element we come [firstly] to the key of Eb-major, which can also be felt as the key of the 'Sun at midnight' (end of Mozart's *The Magic Flute*) and the key of Christmas (especially with Bach), and [secondly] above all to the dark C-minor. With the Crab, on the other hand, we come to A-major, the most light-filled of all the keys, the actual zenith of the musical keys (the Grail-key in Wagner's *Lohengrin*).

As in the Moon itself, the greatest contrasts combine in its 'house', in the Crab. On the one side, the Moon—and this also applies to its 'house', the sign of the Crab—carries the hardening forces that lead into the hardening of the Earth, into the material element, the crude material element. For this reason, in the Creed (see Frieling's *Contemplations* [below]) the Moon-sign of the Crab combines with Christ's 'Descent into Hell', His descent to the souls who had died ('in death He became the Helper...'). At this place we can feel the whole pull of the Earth's gravity and of earthly matter. Amongst the 'twelve world-conceptions' of *Human and Cosmic Thought* [GA 151, 4 lectures, Berlin 20-23 Jan. 1914], to the Crab belongs 'materialism'. In the same lecture-cycle the 'seven moods of the world-views' are also developed in connection with the planets. Here to the Moon belongs 'occultism', that is, the most sublime of all the possible world-conceptions. This should not be felt as a contradiction, but an understanding has to be sought. I still recall what impression it made on me; long ago before the [Great] War when these things were first spoken about in anthroposophy, Dr Steiner replied to my question where occultism was at home (hitherto the 'homes' of other 'isms' were discussed); he answered: 'In materialism.'

### *Penetrating Materialism*

Materialism, too, like the Moon and the Crab itself, has a double side, a double countenance. On the one side there really is a crude, lower materialism, leaving its signature on life today in so many respects. This, too, has to do with the Crab and with the forces of the Moon. On the other side, as Dr Steiner also emphasized to me once, what is called matter is the most complicated and mysterious of all evolutionary phenomena of the spirit. (It might interest the student of nature that the metal silver associated with the Moon shows the most complicated of all formations, the most grotesque branchings and ramifications. Amongst all the 'occult figures'—with Agrippa von Nettesheim we find similar things pictured [*Three Books of Occult Philosophy*, Book 2, Ch. 22]—the figures for the Moon are the most complicated, with many formations.)

Even if one does not take literally, word for word, the atomic theories of today and the electron theories of natural science, yet they do show us beyond all conceiving how complicated and wonderful is the structure of 'matter', how unfathomably deep the Mystery of the material world is. Dr Steiner purely from the theory of knowledge has many objections against the theory of atoms and electrons. On the other hand, he did emphasize how contemporary natural science, to observe these things in its way, actually completely and utterly leaves the ground of the sensory, visible world. It completely penetrates into the invisible, super-sensory, 'occult' realm, where, without intending or admitting it, in its manner it actually pursues the purest, most extreme, most exaggerated occultism. Natural science today, Dr Steiner once remarked, is occultism through and through. And, of course, this is but a viewpoint that allows us to find in today's materialism the occult element.

If we really want to establish the Mystery of matter, we will be led far beyond natural science. We arrive at alchymy, concerning which we have to say to ourselves that its true being can only be understood out of the highest spirituality and the highest spiritual approach to knowledge. In order really to get hold of the Mystery of matter the highest most spiritual occultism is demanded, not only that of today's natural science. We heard from Dr Steiner once that material is actually the nothingness, the emptiness in cosmic space, the actual void. On another occasion matter's being is compared to light's shadow, spiritual reality is compared to the light. We do have to understand how in illusion, which we today take as 'solid matter', Ahriman is at work. On another occasion, how it is sublime beings of the First Hierarchy, the Thrones, who have hardened for us the solid ground under our feet. Cf. Goethe's well-known words:

*Da steh ich nun, ich armer Tor,*
*und bin so klug als wie zuvor.*

And here, poor fool! with all my lore
I stand, no wiser than before:
[*Faust* I, 358-9. Night. Faust's study. Tr. Bayard Taylor]

[Cf. also Goethe 'Über den Granit—Concerning Granite',[204] sitting on a naked mountain crag: '*Hier auf dem ältesten, ewigen Altare, der unmittelbar auf die Tiefe der Schöpfung gebaut ist, bring ich dem Wesen aller Wesen ein Opfer*—Here on the oldest, eternal altar, which is built directly on the depths of creation, to the Being of all Being I bring my offering.'] Only then can we understand how in today's experience of matter the highest Hierarchies govern and, together with Ahriman's influence, we approach the Mystery of matter. Or we recall Dr Steiner's explanations in the Hanover lecture-cycle [*The World of the Senses and the World of the Spirit*. 27 Dec. 1911–1st Jan. 1912. GA 134, lect. 4]:

- mineral matter is the form into which the virginal condition bursts;
- vegetable matter the bursting through into etheric form;
- animal material the bursting through into astral form.

I mention all these passages here, not in order to say the last thing about the Mystery of matter, but only in order to indicate how deeply hidden this Mystery of matter lies in occultism. All these in a certain sense are Mysteries of the Moon and with it Mysteries of the sign of the Crab. One should not separate planets and zodiac so much, as is widely done, but should understand that it is, so to speak, *one* spiritual reality that appears to us in its planetary aspect as 'Moon' and in its zodiacal aspect as 'sign of the Crab'. The Moon with its phases is the changeable planet; the Crab is the changeable sign, where the Sun after it has reached the heights of its yearly cycle turns [momentarily] retrograde. It is also in a higher sense (which we have yet to discuss) the 'sign of change'.

Consequently, the lower, sensual, crude materialism may belong to the Crab and the Moon, revealing the lower side of these beings, but in order to understand more deeply the Mystery of matter or even to approach it, the highest, most spiritual, most sublime occultism is necessary. Then we will better understand why the Moon, the star of occultism, is at home in the Crab, in the sign of materialism. In my book on *Mark's Gospel*, p. 246, I have expressed that there also exists a higher, spiritual, Johannine materialism. Here we understand the penetration of the Mystery of matter with the world of the Johannine initiation. For where is the actual Mystery of matter, right into its last depths, really being penetrated? Only on Golgotha, in the Passion of Christ-Jesus.

One may read from this viewpoint the most moving book of world-literature, the visions of Anna Katharina Emmerich,[205] *The Dolorous Passion of our Lord Jesus Christ* [reprint of the 1928-translation, pub. by Tan Books, Rockfort 1983, later translation *The Lowly Life and Bitter Passion of our Lord Jesus Christ*] recorded by Clemens Brentano. When one has, one cannot say 'read through', but 'suffered through', one understands more deeply than before what significance Dr Steiner actually placed on the Christ-event for human history and world-evolution. Anthroposophy will then make sense in a yet much brighter light. I believe that it belongs to the meaning of this incarnation that we do not allow ourselves to pass by this book. Altogether, anyone who intends to enter into astrological things should get to know it. Here in this connection I mention this book because the things narrated in it stand in an exact connection with the Mysteries of the alchymical process (further details in my books on *John's Gospel* and on *Alchymy*).

The Mysteries of matter were fought for on Golgotha. They were *recognized* by that disciple who stood under the cross, and for this reason he is also called in the alchymical tradition 'John the alchymist'. (The Apocalypse is also full of alchymical Mysteries.) For this reason, it is not the Indian-Buddhist initiation, but precisely the Christian-Johannine initiation that leads to the full penetration of the Mysteries of matter. But all this belongs to the Moon-sign of the Crab; the Johannine initiation is completed, reaches its climax in the Moon-sign of the Crab—which we find again alongside the Scorpion and the Fishes in the 'Johannine triangle' (see the work on the Gospels). Now it might perhaps be a degree clearer why the key of the Crab, A-major, is the Grail-key in *Lohengrin*, the key of the distant Holy Grail shimmering in sublime light.[206]

The penetration of the Mysteries of matter meant here also includes in itself the 'transformation of matter', the Mystery of metamorphosis, of transubstantiation. This Mystery also stands in the zodiac with the Crab. It is really the highest heights and the deepest depths that are linked in the Mysteries of the Moon. For this reason, the Moon is also the shining, heavenly Grail-vessel that carries in itself the mysterious host of the Sun. In this Moon Grail-vessel, as Rudolf Steiner describes in his lecture-course *Christ and the Spiritual World* [GA 149, Leipzig, 28 Dec. 1913–2 Jan. 1914; see lecture 6], shining in the letters of the heavenly script the name 'Parzival' stands written in the heavens.

The word *matter*, whose Mysteries we always link here with those of the Moon and of the sign of the Crab, is connected with the word 'mother'. Matter is actually nothing at all in the sense of material, as we imagine it today, but it is the maternal side of the feminine revelation, the revelation of the divine in nature (the Indian Sankhya philosophy differentiates the primordial duality purusha, the spirit, the masculine principle, and prakriti—actually 'the productive force' of nature—the feminine principle). This 'maternal' principle is also aligned in astrology to the Crab, which indeed is a 'feminine sign' belonging to the (feminine) element of water that is ordered to the feminine chemical ether, or sound-ether. (The Moon, too, like Venus, is regarded as the 'feminine planet'.) On the human form the Crab is allocated to the chest with the ribs, the ribcage, then in a special sense of the female-maternal also the mother's breast. (The picture of the Crab-sign ♋ with the two ribs or spirals is known.)

At this place I would like also to point out the story of the creation of Eve, or the female principle becoming independent, from Adam's rib. This event means an important turning point in world-events. A cycle of development, a higher level of Paradisal life (where man was still hermaphrodite, masculine-feminine) comes to its end here. A new descent begins (the beginning of the separation of the sexes.) In the Johannine initiation the opposite takes place. There the double gender in a certain sense is overcome, the hermaphrodite condition is regained on a higher spiritual level, consequently the connection of the disciple with the mother under the cross through the Crucified. In the gospel, too (see my books) this lies on the axis Crab–Goat: the physical event at the cross takes place in the Goat, the spiritual process in the Crab. The Lazarus-events also stand in the Goat, the corresponding experiences of John in the Crab.

In my book on *Mark's Gospel* I have explained how also in the gospel story the meeting of two cycles of development takes place in the Crab: the old body dies, the new body appears in the resurrection seed; the old Temple made of stone and earthly matter falls into decay, the foundation stone of the new temple, of the resurrection body is laid; an old consciousness (remains of decadent clairvoyance) sinks down (the story of the Cursing of the Fig Tree relates to this), a new consciousness arises (new clairvoyance). All these viewpoints meet in the Mysteries of the sign of the Crab, finding expression in the pictorial language of the gospel in the two donkeys, on which (according to Matthew) Christ-Jesus enters into Jerusalem. The one relates to the old body, the ancient Adam, the bodily nature inherited from Adam (the 'old donkey'), that means, the past, the other, the young donkey is the embodiment of what comes and what will become, of the 'youth' and the impulse of youth, of the resurrection future, the new body. It has also been pointed out that in the zodiac-picture of the Crab, two stars are found that carry the name 'donkey stars' [known today as $\gamma$ and $\delta$ Cancri] (more about this in my book on *Mark's Gospel*, p. 307f.).

The winter solstice takes place in the Goat; the summer solstice in the Crab. It becomes especially clear here what the sign is, compared to the constellation. The essence of the earthly zodiac-sign of the Crab in the rhythm of time is revealed in that the Sun, which has moved towards the summer solstice ever further north, now turns again towards the south. It starts to move backwards, in a crab walk. In the Christ era, in the middle of time, the Sun also stood in the constellation of the Crab. In the meantime, sign and constellation have diverged—ever widening their distance as time moves on; when the rhythm of the year stands in the sign of the Crab, the Sun today still finds itself in the constellation of the Twins. (When people pointed to the two 'donkey stars' in the constellation of the Crab, the sign and constellation of the Crab were still one.)

On the human form, the ribcage belongs to the Crab; the knees belong to the Goat. John the disciple and Christian initiation belong to the Crab in the same way as John the Baptist and the early pre-Christian initiation, for example, that of the Buddha, belong to the Goat. Early Mysteries carried incorrectly into later ages can turn into black magic. Consequently, we find, for example, in the gospel in the Saturn-sign of the Goat (the relationship of Saturn and Satan was pointed out earlier) the dark, black magic of Herod and Herodias, in the era of the earlier Herod, also the murder of the children in Bethlehem. The black magic of the murder of the children connects with the cosmic blessing of the Christmas event in the sign of the Goat. These two viewpoints also connect in the experience of the respective (the present) time of year; beside the blessing of grace of Christmas one experiences in this section of the year something especially dark (consequently also the virtue 'courage' suggested for meditation by Dr Steiner for January; 23 Dec. to 23 Jan.—brings experiences that have to be met with courage in the soul). One may also think of the experiences of the Christmas midnight.

On the human figure, the knees (and the elbows belong to this) relating to the zodiac-sign of the Goat possess this double meaning. On the one hand they have to do with the rigid, stubborn, self-willed and insistent quality (think of the meaning of 'elbow-room') expressing the selfish tendency to self-affirmation; on the other side bent in prayer they point towards the reverence before the divine, the 'change your thinking'. In this sense the sermon of John 'repent, change your thinking' stands in the sign of the Goat. Goat and Waterman, the two Saturn-signs, in Mark's Gospel are always the sign of John the Baptist, and as such they form the prelude to the rhythm of the gospel. The sign Waterman is placed to the baptism by water and its etheric experiences; the sign of the Goat is placed to John's sermon to 'change your thinking'. The world-conception 'materialism' (in the lower and higher sense) belongs to the Crab; to its opposite the Goat, according to the Berlin lecture-cycle [GA 151], the opposite world-conception, 'spiritualism' (the Goat is a very spiritual sign, in the same way as Saturn is the planet of 'gnosis'), whereas to the other Saturn-sign, Waterman, belongs the related 'pneumatism'. With this one looks more towards the undifferentiated spiritual element, with spiritualism one looks at the differentiation of the hierarchies, of the 'spiritual beings'.

So much for today. Next time I will have to say some things summarizing the Father-Cross and then we can move on to the other crosses in the zodiac, to the Cross of the Sun (of the etheric element), and the Cross of the Spirit.

# XVI
# The Cross of the Son

To the 'Cross of the Father' (Ram–Scales–Crab–Goat) discussed in the previous *Contribution*, known in conventional astrology as the 'Cardinal Cross', we can also add the name the 'Cross of the Physical Element'. The Father-forces are revealed in the physical world. In the 'rhythm of the signs' we notice the four corner-points of the rhythm of the year, the spring and autumn equinoxes, the summer and winter solstices. The 'rhythm of the signs' revealing the earthly viewpoint finds its four corner-points in the cross of the physical world in the earthly cross. At the time of the Mystery of Golgotha, when the earthly rhythm and the heavenly rhythm coincided, this was also the viewpoint of the starry constellations.

In our era today the four corners of the rhythm of the year, oriented towards the heavenly starry constellations, lie in the Cross of the Son:

- Easter (sign of the Ram) in the Fishes,
- Michaelmas (sign of the Scales) in the Virgin,
- St. John's-tide (sign of the Crab) in the Twins,
- Christmas (sign of the Goat) in the Archer.

This is not insignificant for the whole stamp of the age, because the heavenly always makes its mark on the earthly. The earthly Ram remains the earthly Ram (that is, the beginning of the life of the year). And yet it is not a matter of indifference for the experience of the time of the Ram whether the Sun stands in the Ram or in the Fishes.

The great constellation of the Fishes with its few stars, two of which are horizontally placed and quite characteristic stars, one can best see in the autumn. The best time to see the Virgin is now (written beginning of March). This is a very large constellation whose grouping one can clearly see at its best according to the star-map. Its pride is the bright star Spica (sheaf) with its mild, white light, one of the most beautiful stars of the whole starry heavens, currently on good view in the east in early spring already before midnight. Already in the early Mysteries the constellation of the 'Virgin with the sheaf', or the 'Virgin with the child', played a great role. The 'Twins' in our age today (age of the Fishes) are the actual zenith of the heavens, the seat of the upper, bright zodiac, which from the viewpoint of the Sun's course one can name the summer zodiac, and from the viewpoint of the visibility in the night sky the winter zodiac. Most impressive is the picture in the hours before midnight about February. Then the Twins, or its two bright stars Castor and Pollux, form the 'heavenly Twins' in the narrower sense (for the constellation of the Twins is much larger), the 'peak of the Sacred Mount', that is, the zodiacal arch extending high over the central constellation of Sirius-Orion (in summer the zodiac lies more level nearer the horizon). In my gospel work I have pointed out how this sign always relates to the 'Sacred Mount' upon which Christ gathered the disciples and gave them the impulse to initiation. Already with Zarathustra, whose cultural impulse falls in the age of the Twins (the spring equinox in the Twins), we find the 'Sacred Mount of initiation', which has its sign in the heavenly script precisely in the constellation of the Twins. The two stars ε and ζ constitute a second pair for the observer of the Twins motif, though most characteristically with the stars Castor and Pollux.

The constellation of the Archer one sees most beautifully in the night of high summer, when it rises over the horizon with its many bright stars out of the river of the Milky Way.[207] In my gospel work I point out how, as the sign of the Mystery of Golgotha, it relates to the great River of Life.

In the following contemplations, we intend to proceed everywhere from the spirituality of the zodiac, whereby the 'constellations' are precisely but 'pictures of the heavenly script'.

The 'Cross of the Father' (Ram–Scales–Crab–Goat) is the 'Cross of the Physical Element' (Earthly Cross); our age today is governed in a special sense by the Cross of the Son (Fishes–Virgin–Twins–Archer): the 'Cross of the Etheric Element'. In the gospels it appears as the Christ-cross simply as the cardinal cross (whereas the horoscope astrology always regards the Father-Cross as the cardinal cross). For the revelation of Christ in our age (prepared during the age of the turning point of time) it contains the decisive signs. The constellation Fishes-Virgin, that is, the transverse axis of the Sun-cross, which in the gospel governs the two 'Feedings' as also Christ's Last Supper itself, I have always called the 'Last-Supper constellation'. It is at the same time the constellation of our Movement. Not only for this reason, because when the priest-circle in the making gathered in Breitbrunn and Dornach the Sun stood in the Virgin (in the sign of the Virgin), but out of more inner reasons Dr Steiner has pointed out how today all normal Christ-events lie on the axis Fishes-Virgin, whereas in the axis Twins-Archer certain abnormal impulses come to effect. All this applies to our age today. We are all moving towards an age that will be completed in the sixth post-Atlantean cultural epoch, when the decisive Christ-event will take place on the axis Waterman-Lion. In John's Gospel the Marriage in Cana lying in this constellation points with its great mystical impulses of transformation to this [future] age (as Dr Steiner says in the lecture-course on John's Gospel [lect. 5. Hamburg 1908. GA 103]). The sign Twins relates to everything coming to effect 'like twins' in polarity, whereas the axis Fishes-Virgin today points to the correct Christ-middle.

In each cross each corner belongs to another triangle, and thereby another element, another kind of ether. Thus of the Cross of the Son:

- the Fishes belongs to the Johannine triangle, the water-element and the sound-ether;
- the Virgin (Luke-triangle) to the earthly element and the life-ether;
- the Twins (Matthew) to the air-element and the light-ether;
- the Archer (Mark) to the fire-element and the warmth-ether.

The four points of this cross are so ordered to the planets that Fishes and Archer are Jupiter-signs, presenting both houses of Jupiter. Likewise, Twins and Virgin are both Mercury-houses. With the Father-Cross we had four different planets, whereas with the Son-Cross—this is characteristic—we have only two that have to do with *thinking*. For Jupiter is the higher, wisdom-filled thinking, Mercury the more earthly thinking of the understanding. (Harmonious aspects between Jupiter and Mercury are something favourable in horoscopes.) This agrees very well, that the etheric Son-Cross results as the 'Cross of Thinking', from a completely different viewpoint independent of the planets. For in thinking—anthroposophy shows us ever again—we meet the essence of the etheric; in living thinking we lay hold of our etheric nature. The physical, the Father-Cross is at the same time the Cross of the *Will* (will-activity is already indicated by the Mars-sign of the Ram), and if the Son-Cross, the etheric cross, is the 'Cross of Thinking', then the third, the astral cross (Spirit-Cross) would be the 'Cross of the Feelings'. From the musical viewpoint this is understandable, when one considers all the keys belonging to it. Furthermore, to the viewpoint of Intuition, Imagination and Inspiration[208]—I give this order on purpose—one will be able to find in the three crosses.

From the planetary viewpoint it should be added that the Fishes is the house of Jupiter [and] the 'exaltation of Venus' (that is, a sign in which Venus comes to more significant, 'exalted' influence). This results precisely in this case in a beautiful, Christian meaning. For Venus, love, in this devotional sign of the Fishes, inclining deeply to the Earth (consider that on the human figure the Fishes correspond to the feet) becomes 'serving love', to that which is revealed as Johannine in Christ's washing the [disciples'] feet (John 13). The Fishes is indeed also the point where the Son-Cross meets the Johannine triangle. All this helps us to see the deeply Christian meaning of the sign of the Fishes (note that, for example, Dr Steiner was born in the month of the Fishes), to which in the gospels is allocated also the Baptism in the Jordan, the Transfiguration, and one of the two Feedings.

Apart from the fact that the Fishes is the one house of Jupiter and the exaltation of Venus, we find here, if we want to extend the allocation of houses to the trans-Saturnine, the mystical planets, the house of Neptune. Many observable facts speak for the correctness of this allocation. The distant cosmic element, the 'sound out of cosmic distances' (we are indeed in the 'sound-ether triangle' and the relationships of Neptune to cosmic music was mentioned earlier) is linked here with the rulership of the *Kyrios*-planet Jupiter (the Jupiter-sphere is that of the Kyriotetes, the Spirits of Wisdom) with the Christ-sphere of the Jordan-Baptism and the Washing of the Feet. In this is specially expressed the cosmic influence, which in the Christ-impulse intends to enter Earth-development. Neptune, too, in its highest aspect is the planet of cosmic, universal love, and which beautifully unites itself already here with the 'exaltation of Venus' as 'serving love' in the Christian sense.

Thereby it should not be overlooked that with this sublime aspect of Neptune still other less favourable ones are connected. As 'the planet of cosmic distances' Neptune governs the distant cosmic element, the occult or esoteric realm, especially that realm which is not penetrated by consciousness. The esoteric, cosmic realm gains a special significance in our age, which indeed is an age of the Fishes (the spring equinox of the Sun in the constellation of the Fishes). Already at the Jordan-Baptism the spring equinox began to move towards the Fishes. With Christ also the cosmic, occult ['hidden'] realm intends to enter into humanity's evolution. This is the connection of Jupiter and Neptune in the sign of the Fishes. But it is to be noted that it wants to enter *with Christ*. Wherever the Christ-impulse, as the Impulse of the Christ-filled

'I'-consciousness, is not taken up, the Neptune-influence is naturally a very double-edged, critically dangerous influence. Then it appears as something nebulous, consciousness-dulling, as something that is not penetrated by the consciousness, as obscure occultism, as a pathological pursuit. And today this plays a great role because we do stand in the Fishes-Neptune age. The Uranus-influence belongs more to a later epoch of humanity, to the age of Aquarius (that is, to the sixth post-Atlantean cultural epoch) and consequently for most people it is still a matter of the future, for only in the future does it come to its full height, whereas the Neptune-influence already often plays a devastating role today. For its balance it needs the Christ-impulse, then it can be favourable, then the age of the Fishes is rightly experienced.

I would like here to add something about the position of Neptune in the Twins (which also belongs to the Cross of the Sun), because for many in our circle it is of topical concern. As is known, Neptune remains for a long time (13-14 years) in one [zodiac] sign, consequently making its mark on a whole period of time, over half a generation. For people growing up in a certain period, consequently, certain positions of this planet are simply characteristic. And amongst those of a certain age who gathered in Breitbrunn [second half of August 1922], Neptune in the Twins plays a special role (whereas our younger members have gradually advanced towards Neptune in the Crab). One could say that Neptune in the Twins is a critical stage, for it stands there in a square with its house, the Fishes, and we remind ourselves of Dr Steiner's indication that on the axis Fishes–Virgin the right occultism, but on the axis Twins–Archer often the wrong occult element enters. That means, the occult Neptune-effect in the Twins *in this connection* would be something unfavourable. On the other hand it has to be said that the Twins are the Mercury-sign, that means, when Neptune stands in the Twins, a connection exists of the Neptune-influence with the Mercury-influence.

But what is this connection of the Neptune-influence with the Mercury-influence, of cosmic thinking with earthly thinking? Nothing other than the anthroposophical impulse. In this sense, as touched on earlier, one has always pointed out how Dr Steiner in his horoscope has the characteristic close conjunction of Neptune and Mercury in the Fishes. And other prominent personalities in anthroposophy who were close to him, and indeed many anthroposophists including our circle have a similar constellation. But now it is not the same yet something similar, where Neptune does not have the Mercury conjunction but stands in a Mercury-sign, as is the sign of the Twins. Here too there exists astrologically, in a certain way, a connection of the Neptune-influence with the Mercury-influence, of course only in such a way that, if rightly understood, it has to be taken now as a *challenge* to bring out the anthroposophical influence and develop it, for which in such cases with such a constellation, certainly a good basis exists. Then the Neptune-position will have a favourable effect, whereas in the other case the described critical danger exists, a danger which, as the history of the past shows (Berka)[209] the priest-circle could not always avoid.

In general one would like to say: priesthood as such means to be anchored in the impulses of the axis Fishes–Virgo, that in contrast to this the Neptune-Twins constellations may not make an actual counter-effect. It should only be felt as a challenge to confirm the anthroposophical impulses. 'This is in general *all* rightly understood astrology of the future['][210] this impulse can give my work a *rightly understood constellation.*

To the meaning of the crosses and triangles in the zodiac and to astrological things in general, one best orientates oneself as a priest with the Creed,[211] which includes both zodiac and planetary matters. We initially meet the Johannine Christ-sign of the Fishes in the sentence which is the only one to mention the name of Christ ('Christ, through Whom ...'), where the re-enlivening of the dying Earth-existence is stated. In this re-enlivening precisely the activity of the etheric element, is revealed to which the Son-Cross is aligned, the Christ-influence. (Even the word 'Son' is found precisely in this sentence of the Creed aligned to the Son-Cross.) In Fishes–Virgin we have the higher ethers (sound-ether and life-ether), representing the ether of the Tree of Life, whereas Twins–Archer [relate to] the lower ethers (light-ether and warmth-ether). The enlivening influence of the ether is that of the upper ethers. Moreover, the meaning of the sign Virgin standing opposite the Fishes is explained through nothing better than the Creed '... the Lord of the heavenly forces upon Earth'. The Virgin represents in the etheric cross the earthly element, to which triangle it belongs. It is an earth-sign, thereby, however, at the same time a sign of the highest ether, the life-ether. For the highest ether corresponds to the lowest element. Here the highest contrasts meet, heavenly forces and earthly activity. And all this stands there in the moving, etheric cross, in the Christ-cross. Here above all we have that which is the magical [lasting] influence of Christ, in the alchymical sense, as also the liturgical working of the Eucharist. The alchymical significance of the planet Mercury also plays a role here; the Mercury-sign of the Virgin is the alchymical sign of the chemical Mystery of the Earth.

On the human being the Virgin corresponds to that which lies under the heart, the solar plexus, as the organ of a mystical visionary ability in the sub-conscious. The forces of the Virgin are at the same time forces of the unconscious, the subconscious realm. Here, as is said in astrology, Mercury has its 'night house', in the Twins its 'day house'. This form of expression derives from the fact that:

- the two lower elements (earth and water), as the two upper kinds of ether related to them (life-ether and sound-ether, also called chymical-ether) are regarded as the feminine, nocturnal element.
- The two upper elements (air, fire) and the two lower kinds of ether that correspond (light-ether and warmth-ether) are felt as the day-bright, masculine element (in this sense the Archer would be the day-house, the Fishes the night-house of Jupiter).

Something concerning the Twins and its relationship to everything of a twin-nature, in the striving of polar opposites, has already been discussed. In the Creed, the corresponding sentence runs: 'The Christ-Jesus suffered under Pontius Pilate ...' If I rightly recall, Frieling has already pointed to a Twins-motif contained in the name Pontius Pilate (which indicates certain Mysteries of initiation).[212] We behold the two forces of the Adversary between which the Christ is here crucified. On a specific stage of cosmic development, the primordial cosmic polarity is revealed as Lucifer and Ahriman. The mount of initiation becomes the mount of Golgotha. Zarathustra, from whom the impulse of initiation of the Sacred Mount originally proceeded, was the first great proclaimer of the cosmic opposites, light and darkness, good and evil. Ormuzd (Ahuramazdao) and Ahriman (Angromainyush). Amongst the world-conceptions we find mathematism with the Twins (*Human and Cosmic Thought*, GA 151). Not for nothing does the sign of the Twins look like a Roman number two: II. It is the point where we really begin to count two, where out of unity there arises duality, and with it the archetypal principle of mathematics.

The world-conception aligned by Dr Steiner to the Fishes is psychism, with the Virgin phenomenalism (one thinks of the 'mystical organ of sight'; I find under the 'twelve senses' with the Virgin also the sense of sight, though this allocation is debated).

With the Archer we find in the Creed the sentence: 'Communities, whose members ...', that is, briefly, the fact of the Church.

(The word *Kirche* 'church', Scottish 'kirk', derives from *kyriaké*;[213] one recalls *Kyrios* Jupiter as the lord of the sign of the Archer). That here, as the sign of Golgotha, the great, the new river of life springs forth, has already been mentioned. In John's Gospel, Chapter 4 (Jesus and the woman from Samaria) the alignment to this constellation is explained out of the above-mentioned viewpoint. In my book on *John's Gospel* I have indicated it, how one finds the Christ-motif 'I thirst' significantly not only in the chapter with the Samaritan woman, but also in the chapter on Golgotha, in the Archer.

The Archer as the ascendant, as the astrologers say, supplies uncomplicated possibilities of life, right into the bodily nature, into sports—the old picture of the Archer is a bowman mounted on a horse, a picture that derives from the centaurs, as the original picture of the ancient forces of humanity. In the Archer the diminishing old and the freshly springing new source of life meet (as in the gospel Christ with the Samaritan woman); for this reason, here too the newly springing, uncomplicated possibility of life. And so we find here, too, the source of the new church: 'Communities whose members feel the Christ within them ...'

And we recognize how important precisely the Christ-Son-Cross in the zodiac discussed in this *Contribution* is for we priests of The Christian Community. In the axis Fishes–Virgin we recognize the entry of Christ into the earthly world, the basic Lord's Supper, Eucharist impulse. With the Archer [we recognize] the Church (not only the visible, but also the invisible Church) as the stream carrying the life of humanity, which takes its origin in the Mystery of Golgotha. And finally, in the Twins that impulse which rightly understood leads people to anthroposophy, whose importance for our priesthood is very clearly revealed through the position precisely in this cross.

# XVII
# The Spirit-Cross (Cross of the Holy Spirit)

We have discussed two of the three crosses, in which for our spiritual contemplation the twelve signs (or spiritual constellations) of the zodiac are distributed, the Father-Cross (Ram–Scales–Crab–Goat) and the Sun-Cross (Fishes–Virgin–Twins–Archer) with the 'Last-Supper Constellation', so important for us. Now we turn to the third of the three crosses (Waterman–Lion–Bull–Scorpion), the cross of the Holy Spirit. In conventional astrology it is usually termed the 'fixed cross', frequently, too, with an Indian name '*Tamas*-cross'. (*Sattva, rajas,* and *tamas* in Indian Sankhya philosophy are the three constituents of natural existence, the three archetypal principles of world-development in Indian, the three *gunas*.

In an earlier essay that grew out of the Dornach Schooling Course,[214] I attempted to show how a relationship exists between these three Indian *gunas sattva, rajas* and *tamas* and the three principles of Goethe's *Theory of Colours*, light, duskiness and darkness. I have always held this description '*Tamas*-Cross' as misleading, for *tamas* means darkness, dullness and similar things. One will be surprised how such a bright sign as the Bull and such a fiery sign as the Lion have found their way into the 'Cross of Darkness'. Now, in contrast to the active, fundamental cross (Father-Cross) and the Son-Cross, which is seen by traditional astrology as the mutable cross, the third cross is seen as the 'Tranquil Cross', and tranquillity suits the spirit.

I myself at least cannot do much with these traditional names, especially the introduction of Indian terminology into starry wisdom I do not find advantageous. I call the third of the three crosses with the Trinitarian viewpoint as the 'Spirit-Cross', a name which with further discussion and practice is justifiable. The Indians themselves brought their *tamas*-principle together with Shiva, the Holy Spirit of the Indian trinity, as they connected Brahma, the creator, together with *rajas* (the principle of activity, which, for example, as '*Trübe*— duskiness' enchants colour out of light and darkness) and Vishnu (the 'son', the god in the Earth's evolution) they connected with *sattva*. Consequently, let us remain with our Christian Trinitarian naming. With this the cross Waterman–Lion–Bull–Scorpion is the 'Spirit-Cross', the cross of the Holy Spirit.

That astrology today, which calls this 'Spirit-Cross' the 'Fixed Cross', calls what we call the 'Father-Cross' (Ram, etc.) the basic cross, the Cardinal Cross. This viewpoint suits horoscope-making and many other things. Already in earlier *Contributions* I pointed out that from various different viewpoints one can see *each* of the three crosses in the zodiac as the 'cardinal cross'. Thus for all studies in the gospel, for certain topical viewpoints of our age and for our movement, The Christian Community itself, the middle one, the Cross of the Son, is the cardinal cross (also the Spirit-Cross, from another viewpoint, is called the 'middle' one), carrying the 'Last-Supper constellation' (Fishes— Virgo), stands in close connection to our age of the Fishes today. But also the Spirit-Cross, from another viewpoint, and perhaps in a still more archetypal sense, is the cardinal cross.

Let us look once again simply at the twelve signs of the zodiac as they are revealed in the rhythm of the year, in the Earth-rhythm as earthly signs. Here they simply correspond to the passage of time of the twelve months, only if one looks exactly, the transition from one month into the next does not fall on the first day of the calendar month, but it takes place around the 20th (until 24th; it changes with the individual months). When I say for short 'April, May, etc.' I mean the period from 21 March to 20 April, from 20 April to 20 May, and so on.

The April-sign, the Ram, the spring-sign and Easter-sign, simply the beginning of the year's activities, belongs as the cardinal sign to one of the four great corner-points of the yearly rhythm, to the spring equalizing of day and night. (In his lectures on the archangels,[215] Dr Steiner shows how these four corner-points of the yearly rhythm are connected with the activities of the four archangels Raphael, Uriel, Michael and Gabriel, who 'The golden vessels to each other lend' [Goethe, *Faust* I. Act I, Sc. 1]. This whole viewpoint, as we shall see more clearly later, is especially revealing to understand the earthly zodiac.) The other corner-point (summer solstice) is then the Crab, the third (autumn equinox, Michael) the Scales (which always belongs to Michael), the fourth (winter solstice, Christmas) the Goat.

One can, however, view the matter differently, enquiring not about these corner-points (the beginning of spring, summer, autumn and winter), but form the question: when actually does the life of the year in spring, summer, and so on, reach its climax? Then one comes, for example, in spring not to the Ram (from 21 March to

20 April), but to the Bull, the month of May; for the summer to the Lion (July-August), for the winter to the time of the Waterman (21 Jan.-19 Feb.). For a number of years, almost for decades, it is noticeable how the winter has as its peak the time of frost with snow-crystals at the beginning of February, in the Waterman phase. Each of the four seasons begins with a prelude with the first month in the Father-Cross, always followed by a middle month (Spirit-Cross) as the time when the season comes to its climax, most fully unfolds its nature, whereas the closing third month (June, September, December, March) already presents a transition from spring into the summer, of the summer into the autumn, of the autumn into the winter, of the winter into the spring, that is, a sounding-away of the character of the season. If we understand the cardinal sign as signs of climax then there results as such the signs for spring, summer, autumn and winter the signs Bull, Lion, Scorpion and Waterman, our 'Spirit-Cross' then appears purely with the earthly seasons as the *Cardinal Cross*.

There is also another viewpoint, more distant from the Earth, from the cosmic (this too I have indicated earlier). In the Düsseldorf lecture-cycle [GA 110] and elsewhere Dr Steiner orientates the four main stages of world-evolution [Ancient] Saturn, Sun, Moon and Earth (in the sense of *Occult Science*) according to the four heavenly signs Lion, Eagle/Scorpion, Waterman, Bull. He shows, for example, how:

- The primordial Saturn life, that is, in this case the rhythm of time begins in the Lion and in the Lion ceases.
- The Sun-life, life on Ancient Sun (only here is it actually etheric life) begins—not now in the Scorpion, but—in the Eagle, in the Sun-Eagle, which, when life ceases, only becomes the Scorpion by receiving 'the sting of death'. (This relationship of the Eagle to the Scorpion has frequently been discussed, presented from various viewpoints in my books on the gospels.)
- The Moon-life, the Moon-revelation of the etheric primal human being begins in the Waterman, the 'sign of the human being'.
- The sign of the Earth's primordial beginning is the Bull, which once again is so significantly united to the Eagle. For this reason, these signs also stand over the beginning of John's Gospel.

Wonderful things are to be found in Dr Steiner's *Karmic Relationships*, Vol. 2 [GA 236] ('Forms of the Mysteries').[216] Eagle and Bull are linked in the Earth's primordial beginning; Lion with Waterman in the beginning of Saturn (Bull–Scorpion and Waterman–Lion each form an axis of the Spirit-Cross). The Lion, the heartbeat, relates only with the becoming of time on Saturn, in the middle of the seven periods of Saturn (where through the sacrifice of the Thrones to the Cherubim the Archai, the Spirits of primordial fire, come into being in the primordial element of warmth), whereas the actual primordial Saturn still lies in duration, in the eternal realm (in union with Uranos-Uranus). The fire-sign Lion relates to this primordial fire during the time of primordial Saturn, the primordial beginning of the world is the Waterman, which we already know as the sign of Saturn–Uranus.

On this point, with contemplations on the zodiac we see more clearly than elsewhere how the planetary side lies. Here we have to return to the spiritual beings of the zodiac, that is, the Cherubim. In the Düsseldorf cycle [Lect. 4], Dr Steiner draws the figure how in the world's becoming, especially the coming into being of 'Ancient Sun' (which repeats the primordial events of Saturn on a higher stage) the Cherubim approach the archangels, the bearers and proclaimers of the light. This they do from four sides, out of the spiritual region of the Bull, of the Lion, of the Eagle, and of the human being (alias Waterman, that is, the etheric human being. These we recognize as the well-known 'four beasts', the four signs of the 'Spirit-Cross'). Under the twelve Cherubic beings of the spiritual zodiac, the named four, corresponding to our 'Spirit-Cross', are in a certain way the main, cardinal ones.

One can divide the zodiac into four quadrants—more on this important viewpoint later, but first after something on the 'four triangles'. In each of the four regions, or 'quadrants' ['quarters'] are these beings, that are each time the middle ones, and thus far, the decisive ones. In this cosmogonic sense our Spirit-Cross is the cardinal cross, and one may recall the fact that also the very well-known, ecclesiastical viewpoint dividing the four evangelists (John Eagle, Luke Bull [Mark Lion and Matthew Angel-Man]) is based on this cross (more details in my books on the gospels and especially in Frieling's liturgical star-*Contributions*).

Much more than today this cross will be recognized as the 'cardinal cross', when we will have entered into the following, sixth post-Atlantean culture-epoch, and thereby the actual Waterman-age, whereas today we are still in the age of the Fishes. (I have often explained, how the spring equinox here is the measure.) In anthroposophy the beginning of a cultural epoch is reckoned when the spring equinox has already past the mid-point of the respective constellation. Thus, in the year 1413, in the beginning of the age of the Fishes, the spring equinox was already about two thirds through, if the turning point of time is reckoned with the first entrance into the constellation of the Fishes. That also this entrance, this first beginning of a sign is really of great spiritual significance, is shown simply by looking at the turning point of time, at the Mystery of Golgotha. And thus many astrologers today would like to place the beginning of the age of the Waterman, the Waterman-Uranus-age as something to happen already quite soon (for various things on this, see the very first of my *Contributions*). It is a characteristic of our time, that wherever astrology is pursued today, people look towards Uranus (that is allocated to the Waterman). Indeed, today already much mischief is perpetrated. These things are dragged into the political parties where it is attempted to place a certain leader of a party as the one chosen by Uranus.[217]

Dr Steiner, too, has shown in the last lecture of the Berlin cycle on 'the spiritual life between death and a new birth, with reference to the cosmic facts', how the new cultural impulse changing earthly life comes from the trans-Saturnine realm, that is, the Uranus-Uranos-realm (he does not directly name Uranus). It is certain that today in a special sense heaven seeks the Earth; the earthly should and does intend to extend, to expand into the cosmos. The step from the physical into the etheric, into the cosmos is increasingly sought and is achieved. Human consciousness itself should and does intend to extend and expand into the etheric, into the cosmos. Not for nothing do we speak of the revelation of the Christ in the etheric, expected in these years at whose beginning we stand. Surely the time has come today when it may be indicated that in the gospel itself this viewpoint of a cosmic consciousness is contained, especially initially with Mark as the representative of the etheric element.

In the gospel itself cosmic thinking can be found, within which human consciousness today wants to raise itself, can raise itself. If one speaks about it, one mostly meets people today for whom all this is too difficult, much too far-fetched, that 'everything is only thought out'. They shy away from the toil of changing their thinking, the inner effort that belongs to it in order *really to think* these things, even when one tries ever so hard to make these things easily understandable.

But where it does not concern the gospel but has to do with things of a completely lower niveau, economic matters and promoting the party-line, here whole newspapers so teem with the zodiac and Uranus viewpoints. These things are misused in the most shameless manner and are dragged down into the earthly realm. Certainly one can rightly be concerned about this nonsense, and yet one should recognize that in it something is expressed which should appear in another form and, because it is not accepted by people in a form as it should and will come, as a higher cosmic consciousness, it seeks now these other dingy channels, where it is brought to people in an all-too-earthly distorted form, in economic matters and politics, or all sorts of gipsy superstition. The person of today still finds it quite difficult to raise himself out of the narrowness of the earthly and physical realm into the widths of the cosmic and etheric realm.

And yet the cosmic, heavenly, etheric element seeks today more than ever the human being and the Earth. Consequently, man seeks to pull down on to his level the heavenly, Uranian element, to which he cannot yet raise himself, cannot yet find the courage to raise himself. All our natural-scientific, technological discoveries and inventions are basically nothing else. The whole one-sided use of electric power (which should find its complement in a spiritual force that belongs to it) belongs to this. Not without meaning and justification, one has always connected this electrical power with the power of Uranus. As prophetically indicated in Rev. 13:13, man today pulls down heavenly power from above, where it becomes destructive, a force which brings destruction (the astrologers also complain of the destructive Uranus effects), instead of man learning to kindle the heavenly power in himself. See on this Rudolf Steiner's words from *Anthroposophy*:[218]

> Could I but kindle everyone
> With the Spirit of the Cosmos,
> That he might be a flame
> And unfold his being's essence as a flame.
>
> Others would take water from the cosmos
> To quench that flame
> And make all being
> Dull and watery within.
>
> O Joy!
> To see the human flame
> Burning brightly
> Even when at rest.

O bitterness!
To see man
like a thing bound,
when he would be free.

This would be the *right* Uranus influence, the right anthroposophical path of knowledge.

One can easily understand why many astrologers today want to place the Waterman–Uranus age already as something quite imminent. For the things really do cast their shadows before, as the Christ-age of the Fishes was already announced in the previous centuries of the early Greek development of consciousness. But the influence of Uranus, about which one speaks so much today is only the Uranus-daemon, not the sublime Uranus-power. The whole of astrology, as it is pursued today, is much too one-sided following the daemon, oriented towards the earthly-daemonic (important things on this earthly-daemonic aspect in the recently published third volume of esoteric contemplations by Dr Rudolf Steiner).[219] Not for nothing did Goethe write over the first, strongly astrological verse of his 'Orphic Verses' with *'Daimon'* (daemon).[220] (More on this in my recent essay on 'Goethe and Star-Wisdom'.)[221] People want to drag down the Uranus-influence; they also seek if possible to make the age of Waterman–Uranus imminent, that certainly today casts its shadow before, but precisely especially daemonic shadows. Even until its astronomical beginning, it will certainly take a few centuries—many people want to put its beginning at 2000 CE. One cannot just say so exactly, because the borders of the *constellation* (in this case it has to do with it) are mobile (only the division of the 'sign' is mathematically precise). And the actual, real age of the Waterman is indeed not until the sixth post-Atlantean cultural epoch, which then first begins when the spring equinox takes place after the third of the Waterman-constellation has been passed. But this will be the case only in the fourth millennium CE.

In my chapter on the miracle of the Marriage at Cana (*John's Gospel*, p. 199ff.), I have pointed out how already at the beginning of John 2, this prophetic indication of the age of the Waterman is contained. This indication derives from Rudolf Steiner himself (*The Gospel of St John*, Hamburg 1908. GA 103, end of lectures 4 and 10, quoted in my book on p. 201f.). The whole first chapters (Mystery-chapters) of John's Gospel (1–5, or certainly 1–4) are based upon such a prophecy of the future. And the cosmic rhythm in John's Gospel (discussed in my book) concludes with inner logic, how John 2 (Marriage of Cana) lies in the zodiac axis Waterman–Lion (as John 1 in the axis Fishes–Virgin, and John 3 in Goat–Crab, John 4, the Samaritan woman, in Twins–Archer, and John 5, the Invalid at Bethesda, in the axis Scorpion–Bull).

## Central Key

This leads us to a tremendously significant question, which leads far beyond that which the astrologers today can tell us of the Waterman and Uranus. I would like to say, it has to do here with the central question out of which the whole of astrology becomes understandable in its sublime, Christened sense. It concerns that central key to which the often-mentioned Greek myth of Uranos points in such a grandiose manner. That is also the reason why at the beginning of my *Contributions* I presented the Uranos-Uranus in some detail, because therein lies a central key to all astrology. Only recently did I come to realize that also the difficult fairy tale of Klingsor by Novalis in *Heinrich von Ofterdingen* is opened up with this key. It presents the whole pathway of humanity from Uranos (the crystal heaven) to Uranus, how the whole Venus–Uranus motif, the whole dramatic destiny of love in human nature and human becoming flows into it. And especially the Christ-Impulse, the Christ-Event, becomes understandable from here in its whole cosmically comprehensive significance, as I attempted to show earlier.

This leads then again to the motif of the Marriage in Cana, which with Novalis is expressed in the words:

One day the stars, down dripping,
Shall flow in golden wine:
We, of that nectar sipping,
As living stars will shine.
[Novalis, from *Hymns to the Night*, V. Tr. George MacDonald]

The starry realm, which is indeed the Uranos, the crystal heaven (also expressed by Dr Steiner in his notebook entries, long ago published in the News-sheet [and more recently issued as *Notizbücher von Rudolf Steiner*, ed. E. Watari, R. St. Verlag, Dornach, 2001]):

*Der Mensch einerseits Fixsternwesen—anderseits Sonnenwesen. Des Menschen Seele zu den Fixsternen hin* (Dr Steiner's actual words).

'The human being on the one hand fixed-star being—on the other hand Sun-being. The human soul towards the fixed stars.'

Of course, with all this it has to do not only with the planet Uranus, but with the spirituality of the starry heavens, the trans-Saturnine realm as such, whose boundary-marker, however, is precisely the planet Uranus. (As clear the difference between Uranos and Uranus is on the one side, so insignificant it is on the other side, for what come from Uranos has to pass Uranus, the sphere of Uranus; it is as when a train arrives in the main station in Dresden, two people start arguing. The one says, 'It comes from Frankfurt', and the other, 'No, it comes from Kötschenbroda' (for the train arriving from Frankfurt, or let it be Paris, has to pass through Kötschenbroda and Radebeul, in order to reach Dresden).

The actual question of the human 'I' lies between Uranos-Uranus and the Sun, the Christ-Sun in the heart: 'One day the stars, down dripping, ...' Rudolf Steiner shows, in the cited Berlin lecture-cycle[222] and elsewhere, how this problem is understandable from *Ancient Sun*. One increasing concludes how with the Christ-Sun-Impulse a Christ-Uranus-Impulse is connected. I have recently been following up this important question out of the lecture-cycles and books by Rudolf Steiner; a fat exercise book resulted. You can really find a huge sum of material when you look between and behind the lines and rightly connect the matters (which is not yet a generally recognized 'method' in anthroposophy, but all the more one that carries the future). These things could be presented here in much more detail, but it would lead too far from our theme of zodiac and spiritual cross. I did not intend to discuss Uranus as such here (much has been covered already, and we shall return to it), but Waterman and Lion. But the Mysteries of the zodiac-axis Waterman–Lion are indeed precisely with the planets that of Uranus and the Sun, and so we arrive at the whole problem. Here I would only like to recall from my earlier accounts once more how the word Uranus Uranos itself is linked with Waterman. For it is linked, as I showed earlier [Nos. 3 & 4], with *Urne*; not only the Mysteries of water-urns, or jars—in the constellation the 'Waterman' is pictured with two water-urns—but also those of burial-urns play in (liturgically, see Frieling's *Contributions*—the Mysteries of the burial ritual). In Indian the word [for] Uranos appears in the form Váruna, and Varune (emphasis on the first syllable) is at the same time the divinity of the night-sky and of the dark blue ocean, of the water (*var, vari, das Wasser*, 'water'). Here too the relationship Uranus-Waterman is clear.

And the Uranus–Sun–Mystery appears again in the Indian Rig Veda as the Mystery of Mitra and Varuna, Mitra, the bright Sun-being, the bright day-sky, appears then in Persian as Mithra, the divinity of the Mithras-Mysteries. Important above all, as also in our Creed the first sentence relates to the Father, the Fatherly Ground of the World, which stands in the sign of Uranus–Waterman (Frieling).

That the Uranus-sign Waterman is also a Saturn-sign has often been mentioned. But because indeed the earthly dense Saturn in this sign is linked with the heavenly Uranus, for this reason the Waterman is the lighter, the earthly lighter Saturn-sign (it belongs also to the air-tri-angle, to the light-ether-triangle, is an air-sign and light-sign, con-sequently easy of earthly weight). On the other hand, the Goat, the other Saturn-sign, where Saturn alone governs without Uranus as a colleague, is the earthly-dense, the dark Saturn-sign. Waterman, then, the sign of light and air—light and bright; the Goat—dark and dense. The relationship of the Sun to the fire-sign Lion has already been dis-cussed a lot, so I pass it by for the moment.

We noticed how with the three zodiac-crosses the one axis always belongs to the lower, masculine, the other to the upper, feminine ether. Thus, the axis Waterman–Lion stands in the air-element and fire-el-ement, in the light-ether and warmth-ether, that is, the lower, mas-culine side (more details on this with the presentation of the 'four triangles' in the zodiac). The axis still to be discussed Bull–Scorpion stands in the earth-element (Bull) and water-element (Scorpion), or, in the life-ether and in the chemical ether (sound-ether), the feminine, the upper ether. With Waterman–Lion we had as planets the Saturn—Uranus–sign and the Sun–sign. With Bull–Scorpion a Venus-sign and a Mars-sign; Venus in opposition to Mars; this is a sharp antipathetic contrast. It is like the contrast of life and death: Venus in the Bull as the life-force (the life-ether corresponds to the element of earth) and healing force of love (with this sign I always recall Raphael's *Sistine Madonna*), Mars in the Scorpion as the passionate Mars of death (Mars in the Ram is the good, active Mars), the death-sting and poisonous sting, the death-bringing aspect to sexuality (which in the higher side of its being is presented through the Moon).

In my work on the gospels I have pointed out how especially in the gospel-rhythm, how this contrast comes clearly to the light of day. In the Venus-sign of the Bull we always experience the healing influ-ence of love, especially Christ's healing of the sick; in Scorpio the dark Pharisaism which turns against this influence of the love of Christ,

[only] in this seeing damage to the sacred Sabbath. One recalls that the Bull (on the human being the larynx, the speech organ) is also the sign of the word (Venus is the inwardness of the word; this is frequently also mentioned by Dr Steiner).[223] Here in the gospel the healing power of love in the word of Christ is opposed by the 'dead law of Jewishness'; the Pharisees cling onto the dead letter of the law, as the dark element of the Scorpion. Amongst the disciples, Judas in particular is connected to the essence of the Scorpion. The same applies to the Romanism of Pilate (not for nothing did the Roman legionaries wear the Scorpion on their uniform),[224] also the darkening of Peter's consciousness and the denial that is connected with it is caused through the power of death of the Scorpion (to which Christ Himself points with a clear Greek word that clearly is like the word 'scorpion' at the end of John 16 (similarly in John 10).[225] The connection of Bull and Scorpion is also seen purely physiologically, of speech organ and sexuality—one thinks of the breaking of the voice in puberty. For the theme 'spirit-cross' it appears important that the forces of the Scorpion-forces transformed through Christ in the Creed appear as the Holy Spirit = the Healing Spirit: 'Through Him can the Healing Spirit work.' Moreover, with the opposite, the Bull (Venus, healing forces of life) it says: '… is a working of the Holy Spirit' (again the Spirit-Cross).

Of course, many viewpoints could be mentioned about these four signs of the Spirit-Cross. But in order that this *Contribution* does not become too extensive and because the things have to be presented once again from the viewpoint of the 'four triangles', I will finish for now. Next time, concerning these triangles, firstly the ones concerning the warmth-ether and light-ether (that is, the lower element).

For the Spirit-Cross, I would like only briefly to mention the aspect of the musical keys. One may observe how G-major, the key of the Bull also with Wagner in *Tristan and Isolde* is always used of the healing life-force of Isolde, Db-major (Scorpion) in *Tannhäuser* for the dark forces for the lap of the Earth. It becomes beautifully clear with Wagner that Bb-major (Waterman) is really the Uranus key, the key of the stars: in Act 3 of *Tannhäuser* the musically extraordinary eloquent light of Venus is carried out really characteristically in the key of Bb-major, which in the following passage, where Wolfram characterizing the being of Venus-Urania so beautifully, goes over into the serious relative minor, G-minor.

# XVIII
# The Four Triangles in the Zodiac

After discussing the 'three crosses' in the zodiac, we turn now to the 'four triangles', which are especially important for all astrology. We see in the concept of twelve in the zodiac how that of three and of four— by addition rendering the concept of seven—play a special role. The zodiacal twelve are arranged into three times four (which would be the viewpoint of the three crosses) and then into four times three (this would be the viewpoint of the four triangles). This at the same time is a contribution to the qualities of number developed in Bindel's book on the Pyramids.[226] Both 3 x 4 and 4 x 3 as merely abstract quantities = 12, but qualitatively 3 x 4, nevertheless, is not the same as 4 x 3. The three crosses (or squares, as they can also be presented) are somewhat different from four triangles.

We have seen with the crosses how their four corners are all united through a shared dynamic viewpoint but in themselves present more or less sharp contrasts. The points standing opposite each other really do form a cross together. As we have seen, for astrology it is a very decisive viewpoint. First of all we have the opposite signs. They form what is called in astrology the 'opposition'. This is not always hostile contrast. It can also be productive argument (for example, when married couples have an opposition in one of their signs). No aspect in the sense of a progressive astrology is simply *bad*; when overcome, transformed, rightly evaluated, it leads to a strengthened blessing. Even the notorious square, the hostile, most astringent of all aspects, can become something beneficial; it proves itself then especially as the strongest of all aspects, still more strong than the harmonious triangle. But initially squares, like oppositions, express conflict, something contrary, and the square above all is the 'sharp corner' *par excellence*. And in each of the crosses the signs are then united, which between themselves stand in opposition (180°) or in a square (angle of 90°). Moreover, connected to this is what in earthly life one calls a 'cross', which in a Christian meaning taken up and carried, can form the point of departure for a Christian education.

Thus in the Father-Cross, the Ram-Cross, the 'Cross of the Physical Existence', the two signs lying mutually opposite, the Ram and the Scales, form an opposition (one recalls, how also the two planets governing them, Mars and Venus, present such a contrast, similar to that of the masculine and feminine principles). It is similar with Goat and Crab. On the other hand, Ram and Crab, Ram and Goat, Scales and Crab, Scales and Goat form a square. These are contrasts. It can be viewed musically, with the musical keys. We have Ram C-major, Scales F#-major/Gb-major, as the sharpest contrast of all that exists between the keys. Futhermore, C-major Eb-major (Goat), C-major A-major (Crab) do not go very well together (I have already discussed that in music the opposition is stronger than the square, that is, opposite from what it is with the stars).

With the 'four triangles' the matter is the opposite. The signs are united to a triangle; between themselves they stand in the greatest harmony. The cross (the opposition, the square) expresses the hostile (or often hostile) contrast, of disharmony; the triangle (the trigon) expresses highest harmony. Furthermore, the remaining and 'harmonious' aspects of astrology are based on this: in particular the 'sextile' (60°) is half a trigon (120°). The highest of all cosmic trigons, or triangles, is the one which in the Christian sense, or also the Indian sense, we call the divine, or Holy Trinity; Brahma, Vishnu and Shiva. And we know how the threefold human soul, how all trinities that can be found in the human being and in nature, as root, leaf and blossom, etc., picture the archetypal trinity. In my book on *Alchymy* I point out these connections. The alchymists spoke of an archetypal trinity *sal* (salt), mercury and sulphur, which then the Rosicrucians (see Dr Steiner's[227] lectures concerning Christian Rosenkreuz) linked to the human soul-forces, with thinking, feeling and will. And the equilateral triangle viewed in a Pythagorean manner is the symbolic expression for all these contexts. To keep all this in one's mind will lead to an easier and better understanding of the question of the four triangles in the zodiac.

Here, too, music—important for the Pythagoreans—can help us to perceive the facts. We have seen how C-major and F#-major, C-major and A-major, C-major and Eb-major (the keys linked in this cross) stand more or less mutually opposed. Bring to mind or play how the keys belonging to the trigon facing each other harmonically interpenetrate, how the transition of the triads C-major, E-major, Ab-major and C-major present a beautifully coloured, harmonious transition, indeed how these keys or triads still much more 'lie in each other' than those following sequentially in the circle of fifths. In music theory, as I always find, this is too little observed. One can come to quite a different, a more starry theory of harmony if one wanted to become somewhat more emancipated from the boring circle of fifths.[228] In astrology no person would think of looking at the zodiac-signs lying side by side as closely related, on the contrary, and in music one could do this similarly. Instead of the favoured jump into atonality today, an interesting and fruitful transition out of tonal music into the more atonal music[229] would come about. A musician should arise who uses a truly star-related thinking applied to music theory. Today we already have compositions in which this starry element lives at least already as an idea. But there are beginnings. And what I mean is that the starry thinking—regarding which I attempt to show, how, for example, it governs the gospel—should find entry into conscious musical thinking. In my next incarnation I will certainly take up these things.

Through a looking at the gospel, the whole viewpoint of the four triangles in the zodiac, which has to be discussed, becomes immediately more familiar and accessible. For we then find, or rather have already known for a long time that these triangles, which in traditional astrology were named according to the elements as:

- the fire-triangle (Lion, Archer and Ram),
- the air-triangle (Waterman, Twins, Scales),
- the water triangle (Scorpion, Fishes, Crab),
- the earth-triangle (Bull, Virgin, Goat),

at the same time they correspond to the four gospels, or evangelists, when we consider how in John the Scorpion becomes again the Eagle, the Sun-Eagle, which it originally was. It is simply the well-known four beasts that behold us from the four triangles of the zodiac, the one of the Bull, Lion, Scorpion/Eagle and Waterman. The cosmogonic, primordial Mystery of the human being contained in this picture beholds us out of the four triangles of the zodiac. We become aware on ever-new paths how the primordial human being and the primordial starry being are united, how this primordial cosmic context is revealed in the four evangelists:

- Mark Lion,
- John Eagle,
- Luke Bull,
- Matthew the Human Being.

The Saturn–Uranus sign Waterman (Waterman, etheric-spiritual primordial human being) is what is most closely connected to the Mystery of our human origin.

Before we proceed to present the details, we should tarry a little with the expression 'triangles of the four elements'. For it belongs to the many things one usually simply takes from an old tradition without asking what it actually signifies, what meaning to attach to it, how this meaning is established, and the whole manner of its connections that allows it to be justified. For instance, when one looks up to certain regions of constellations, or let's say regions of the earthly zodiac (which is a reflection of the starry zodiac), that is, in any case towards specific spatial regions, it can't obviously be meant that in some kind of conceivable sense one would hit on the four groups of beings of the elements. Even the imagination that somehow the four groups of elemental beings, undines, salamanders, sylphs and gnomes according to such viewpoints would be grouped in space, would obviously be nonsense. But what then does the whole story signify? One always takes it up so easily, often asking so little of what one is reasonably to think.

Before I undertake to attempt to answer this somewhat delicate question, I would like beforehand to emphasize that this differentiation of four triangles in the zodiac according to the viewpoints of the four elements in no way has to do with only taking up 'the old astrology'. Precisely this basically important, indeed perhaps most important viewpoint of the entire traditional astrology has found in anthroposophy its full justification. This is not at all obvious without more ado. We know sufficiently how a certain traditional astrology at every step meets contradictions in anthroposophy. These two spiritual directions—I mean the one of a traditional astrology, which is beginning to spread afresh,[230] and anthroposophy—are actually at war with each other. Because certain foundations of all anthroposophy, because all spiritual methods of the anthroposophical path of knowledge are brushed aside and disregarded in astrology today, and are replaced through an abstract, Ahrimanic empire, anthroposophy cannot follow such an 'empire making'—and vice versa, most astrologers see anthroposophists of today as arrogant, ignorant dogmatists. The contrast is the sharpest and most hostile.

On the other hand, towards astrological theory Dr Steiner has always emphasized what is valuable today in the ancient tradition, which indeed derives from the primordial wisdom. Dr Steiner did say where it is simply built on the primordial wisdom, astrology would be correct, only when the astrologer begins to think in his own way does the matter becomes false. I have to preface these remarks because in these *Contributions*, as we all know, undertakes for the first time truly to lead astrology on to anthroposophical bases; it may consequently achieve little success but, in any case, the attempt is well meant.

In particular, with the teaching of the four triangles in the zodiac and its differentiations into the four elements, it is true that this teaching is confirmed through anthroposophy. We find this confirmation in Wachsmuth's book[231] about the etheric formative forces, Vol. 2, p. 15 (Wachsmuth has these things, of course, from Dr Steiner). Only through anthroposophy a very essential viewpoint is added to one of the elements, as this has become traditional in astrology for ages: the viewpoint of the four kinds of ether. The four triangles in the zodiac appear there at the same time as those of the four etheric formative forces, corresponding to the elements:

- to the lowest element, earth, corresponds the highest ether, the life-ether, of the four elements the highest one, closest to the spiritual realm;
- to the highest, nearest to the spirit of the four elements, to the fire corresponds the lowest ether, the warmth-ether (that means, fire in the sense meant here and warmth-ether are the same; in fire the elemental touches the etheric).
- to the element of air there corresponds the light-ether,
- to the element of water, the chymical-ether, which is also the sound-ether.

A meditative penetration into all these relationships will be made easier through the verses on the four elements in the Egyptian temple-scene from *The Soul's Awakening* [Rudolf Steiner's fourth Mystery Drama, Scene 8]. In these verses which are of outstanding meditative meaning Dr Steiner has given at the same time something highly important for the knowledge of the elements and kinds of ether and their mutual relationship. It is known and quite often mentioned in these *Contributions* that the higher kinds of ether, the life-ether and sound-ether, are the feminine ones. The lower kinds, the light-ether and warmth-ether are the masculine ones. In the etheric realm the feminine (the Eternal Feminine) is the higher life-element. With the elements, or rather in the physical realm, it is the reverse. There the earthly dense elements earth and water are the feminine ones; air and fire are masculine.

For astrology all this is of the greatest importance. From the viewpoint of the gospels one might be reminded that Luke's Gospel belongs to the life-ether and the element of earth, in the most eminent sense it has the viewpoints of the feminine, the maternal side; Matthew's Gospel corresponds through its kind of ether to the paternal side.

Through this viewpoint of the four kinds of ethers, what is taught in the astrological tradition about the triangles of the four elements is supplemented in a most important manner from the side of anthroposophy. This is most important, right into the subject of horoscope-making. Consequently, if experience teaches that the Virgin is an earth-sign, is an especially sensitive etheric sign, it becomes much more understandable if one becomes clear that earth, the lowest, firmest element, corresponds to the most etheric ether, the life-ether. Already with Alan Leo, who principally regards the element, not the kinds of ether, one finds the sign Virgo characterized in this way. (Alan Leo, the most distinguished representative of English astrology, no longer alive [d. 1917, aged 57], is the one astrologer to whom Dr Steiner also gave his birth dates[232] as well as his photo with a friendly dedication. With this he certainly did not sanction Leo's astrology; but he would not have done it if he had thought Alan Leo to be a mere vile person who was destroying cultural development.) From this case one can well understand the result of the astrological experience when one is aware that the Virgin is not only an earthly sign but also the sign of the life-ether, moreover, part of the Son-Cross, in the etheric cross (each triangle belongs with its three corners to the three different crosses, that means, that two aspects of the etheric coincide with the Virgin, helping it to be felt in a heightened sense as an etheric-sensitive sign. One sees in this case, how through a rightly applied anthroposophy, astrological indications can also find their confirmation and how important it is with the zodiac to complement the aspect of the four elements with the four kinds of ether.

The question is still unanswered, how one should actually imagine the various distributions of the elements and kinds of ethers to the individual zodiac-signs. Shall we perhaps imagine now the various ether-kinds distributed over the various spatial realms, or even the fixed-star spheres (as Wachsmuth in his book presents the matter)? In order to understand Wachsmuth rightly, one would have to raise oneself from the astronomical imagination of the sphere of the fixed stars towards the incredibly extremely differentiated, spiritual Imagination that Rudolf Steiner gives. This is not so easy, demanding comprehensive knowledge, special studies and also a complete re-thinking of all the ideas about today's science concerning the starry cosmos (see Rudolf Steiner *Third Scientific Lecture-Course: Astronomy*, Stuttgart, 1–18 Jan., 1921, GA 323, and Frl. Vreede's *Newsletters* [see footnote 69]). For me it is the most obvious to say here that it does not concern some groupings in space with the kinds of ether. Here we rather have to penetrate, as everywhere else, to the purely spiritual aspect of the zodiac, towards the spiritual zodiac (it also seems to me that Rudolf Steiner's indications have to do with this). From this spiritual zodiacal being is directed the starry zodiac as well as the earthly zodiac, which is its mirror and in the first instance comes into question with all astrological calculation.

The fiery element, heat, which relates to the warmth-ether, is inherent in the *spiritual* essence of Leo; the light, bright, airy element that relates to the element of air and the light-ether belongs to the spiritual essence of the Waterman, and so on. I cannot imagine the relationship to the elements and the kinds of ether directly in terms of space, but can only find it on a detour through the purely spiritual realm, in the same way as an astrological influence of Jupiter or Mars does not mean that something rays down spatially from Jupiter or Mars, but how the whole Jupiter sphere or the Mars sphere (enclosed by the orbit of Jupiter or Mars) raised in spiritual Imagination is consequently what is the effective thing, and *yet* the spatial position of the visible Jupiter or Mars in the sky at the same time has a symbolic meaning. Thus, too, it will be with the zodiacal signs: the purely spiritual perspective, right into the grouping of the elements and kinds of ether, will be the determining factor; and yet spatial relationship stands there like a *picture* for the essence of these relationships.

After prefacing these general aspects, we will now turn to the individual triangles in the zodiac.

# XIX
# The Fire-Trigon

## *(Triangle of the Warmth-ether)*

Ram, Lion and Archer are arranged with the same distance of 120°—
this is the angle which in astrology is called the 'trigon'; half of this
would be a 'sextile'—together they form the fire-triangle, the trigon of
the warmth-ether. It is consequently called the 'fire-sign'. We can well
imagine the fiery element with all three signs.

- First of all, with the impulsive, advancing Ram that opens the yearly
  rhythm, the impulse for the events of the entire year; it gives the
  enlivening, warming power of the Sun. It is the house of the active
  Mars, and we recognize how through this planetary viewpoint the
  zodiacal nature is meaningfully supplemented. The active sign of
  Mars, the fiery Mars, stands at the beginning of the events of the
  earthly year.
- Then comes the fiery Lion, in which the hot, warming power of the Sun
  progresses to its height and for this reason is called the 'house of the
  Sun', as the Ram is the 'exaltation of the Sun' (the spring Sun as the
  'enlivening Sun'; this enlivening element is no longer part of the hot
  August Sun).
- Thirdly, the Jupiter-sign of the Archer, the most spiritual of the three
  signs, from which proceeds the strong spiritual and etheric life-im-
  pulse. All three signs of the fire-triangle strongly indicate these
  impulses.

If we initially proceeded from the experience of the yearly rhythm,
we have to be clear that it concerns the 'earthly zodiac'. The warming,
enlivening spring Sun, which in its governing, active, fiery impulse
of Mars and the Ram is not manifest today when the Sun stands in
the constellation of the Ram, for it still stands at this time in the constellation of the Fishes. Nevertheless, the constellation of the Ram,
not the constellation of the Fishes, symbolizes that which this section
of the yearly rhythm, this spring, Eastertide signifies for the events
of the whole earthly year. The connections of Lion and Archer lie
accordingly. If the question of constellation is asked concerning the
Lion, one has to remember that the constellations are unequal in size.
The Crab is particularly small, the Lion especially large. A part of the

Lion-rhythm will fall on to the constellation of the Crab; with another part following, however, the constellation of the Lion will correspond to the sign of the Lion. I regret that these things continue to be somewhat complicated. If at the creation of the world I had been asked for advice, then like the Spanish king [mentioned in *Contribution* 10] I would certainly have arranged many things more simply; however, we have to take things as they are if a description is to be given of cosmic matters.

## *The Decanates*

In this connection, is might be the place here to go into the definition used in astrology of the *three decanates* of a zodiac-sign. Earlier I mentioned it has nothing to do with ecclesiastical Deans. The word comes from the Gk. *deka* (ten); what is meant is that the 30 degrees of a sign (each sign mathematically takes up 30° [of a circle], whereas the constellations are unequal in size, also basically not mathematically bounded and for this reason not at all to be mathematically calculated) are divided into three subsections, each measuring 10°. Every zodiac-sign falls into three decanates. Astrologically each has its meaning. It is not indifferent whether someone is born in the first, second or third decanate of a rising sign, or in which of the three decanates some planet or other stands in the birth-horoscope. Each of the three decanates has its own 'decanate ruler, or governor/ governess'.

To communicate this is *quite easy*, and the key one uses lies simply in the arrangement of the triangle, in the trigonal division of the zodiac, concerning which we are discussing at the moment; this is the reason why in this connection I introduce the decanates into the story. If we seek the decanates, for example of the Ram and the three decanate rulers, this results in the following: The fire-sign Ram is governed by the planet Mars, by the fiery, active Mars.

- To it the first decanate belongs; Mars is the ruler of the first Ram decanate. The two other decanates are simply determined through the two other corners of the Ram triangle. After the Mars-sign of the Ram comes first the Lion, in which the Sun is at home. That is,
- the Sun (which in the Ram in any case has its exaltation) governs the second Ram-decanate.
- The third corner of the Ram trigon is formed by the Jupiter-sign of the Archer. Jupiter, then, is the ruler of the third decanate of the Ram.

- (One does *not* need to find *these* things complicated, for they are *quite* simple.)
- With the Lion the first decanate would belong to the Sun, the second to Jupiter, the third to Mars.
- With the Archer, the first would belong to Jupiter, the second to Mars, and the third the Sun.

With all three signs of a triangle, it is the three planets with each sign that also divide into three decanates. We see through the whole arrangement of a trigon the question of the three decanates with the three single signs is implicitly completed. For astrology this whole viewpoint is thoroughly important.

One can make the essence of the single zodiac trigons clear for oneself by throwing light on their signs from the most varied viewpoints. That is, alongside the already-mentioned viewpoint of the yearly rhythm (that of the earthly zodiac) the *musical* one, which with the triangle Ram–Lion–Archer leads to the already-mentioned keys C-major, E-major and Ab-major, which amongst themselves make the beautiful, richly colourful transition (Wagner uses this [mediant] transition in *The Mastersingers* as the '*Morgentraum-Deutweise*—morning-dream music'. We feel how C-major corresponds to the Ram. The Ram signifies the victory of the light over the darkness in the course of the year, the rising of the bright summery half of the year over the dark wintery half. And C-major signifies the same in music, the rising of the bright keys with sharps over the dark keys with flats, the 'Let there be light' (of Haydn's oratorio *Creation*), the day-bright, active quality presenting itself in the clear light of consciousness and, in so far, also sober, plain. The Ram is the fiery, active Mars-sign; C-major is also the key of fiery military marches. The active will-filled element lives in the C-major fanfare of the sword-motif in Wagner's *Ring*. We feel the connection everywhere.

And the key aligned to the warmth of the Lion, E-major, we can feel as the warmest key. Finally, the dark Ab-major carries in itself the Mystery of the blood of the Holy Grail (Wagner's *Parsifal*); here we see a mystical fire in the blood shining out of the darkness. In the Archer, which is also the sign of Golgotha (see my books on the gospel), we experience the fire of the warmth-trigon especially as the Christ-fire, as the fire in the blood—here, too, Mars carrying the Mystery of the blood is the decanate ruler).

- Or, if we go to the aspect of the human figure, we recognize:
- the Ram as the head,

- the Lion as the heart,
- the Archer as the thigh (also the upper arm), that is, that body-part, the seat of the motoric strength for all earthly activity.

Wherever I walk, or stretch my hand, however I allow earthly activity to flow through my hands or feet, it takes place through the motoric power of this sign (which as ascendant in the birth-horoscope gives light movement, dexterity in bodily movement, sports and the like). Imagine a marching body of troops, who perhaps are singing the song 'I have given with heart and with hand', who really is enthused by the forces of this song; here we have visible all three points of this fire-trigon like a picture before us:

- the heart (Sun, Lion),
- the head, in which the active decision (Mars) lives,
- the hands and feet, which bring it to manifestation,

revealing the ruling power of Jupiter. Forces of Mars, the Sun and Jupiter flow together visibly in the effect of the fire-trigon. And the picture can make clear to us how we find ourselves here in the masculine sign, how the fire-trigon belongs to the masculine aspect, the warmth-ether.

With the evangelists this appears as the Mark-triangle, the Lion carrying in itself the fire-trigon. Mark, the Lion-evangelist, is aligned to the triangle of the warmth-ether. In my book on *Mark's Gospel* I have pointed out how for the rhythm of Mark's Gospel it is characteristic that precisely here the Lion is not expressly presented [with separate sections of the gospel] like the other eleven zodiac-signs. There the Lion is so to speak the carrying sign of the whole [gospel], standing as such in the middle, at the core, managed by the evangelist in a certain way esoterically, as I say in my book. (Gospel expositors like Drews have been offended by this fact they do not rightly understand.) The powerful, striking characteristic of Mark's Gospel agrees with the masculine element of the fire-trigon. Amongst the temperaments we would align the choleric to Mark, which likewise corresponds to the essence of fire and of the warmth-ether. The terse brevity in the style of Mark's Gospel is connected to this.

The Ram characterizes in Mark's Gospel the entrance of Christ into His earthly ministry. The healings of the possessed belong to this sign. The words, '…took him by the hand, and lifted him up; and he arose' (Mark 9:27 AV/KJV) directly speak of the meaning of this sign. We can find such phrases for all twelve signs of the zodiac. In the rhythm of the day the Ram rules the morning hour, the hour of getting up.

To conclude, we pause awhile that from the three corners of the fire-trigon:

- the Ram belongs to the Father-Cross, the physical,
- the Archer (to which in the gospel belongs the entry into the Mystery of Golgotha) is aligned to the Son-Cross, to the etheric;
- the Lion belongs to the Spirit-Cross.

# XX
# The Triangle of the Element of Air and the Light-Ether

## (Waterman–Twins–Scales)

The triangle of the element of air and the light-ether, now to be discussed, is of special significance in the zodiac. In the sense of the well-known arrangement of the four gospels in the zodiac, it appears as the *triangle of the human being*. (Mark–Lion, Luke–Bull, John–Eagle, Matthew–Human Being.) The *Waterman*, the main determining point of this triangle, is indeed the watercarrier, the water-man, that is, the human being of the etheric primordial waters, the etheric primordial human being, as he still was at the time of evolution of Ancient Moon. Consequently, in *Occult Science* and in the Düsseldorf lecture-cycle [GA 110] it was oriented towards this Waterman-corner. This corner, as we have seen in an earlier *Contribution*, in a certain sense is the starting point of all the becoming of the world and of the human being; it belongs to that primordial condition of Ancient Saturn, when Ancient Saturn was not yet in time, but was still in the Uranian element, having as its periphery Uranos (the encompassing starry being, of which the later planet Uranus received its name). In the planetary arrangement, the Waterman consequently appears as the sign of Uranus. We also know it as the house of Saturn. The Goat, where Saturn governs alone, is the earthly dense and dark Saturn-sign, whereas the Waterman, where the heavenly Uranos is co-ruler, is the light-filled Saturn-sign, easy of earthly weight.

We know from Frieling's liturgical work how this Saturn-Uranos sign significantly connects with the first sentence of the Creed,[233] in which the expressions 'divine being, spiritual-physical' and 'ground of existence of the Heavens and the Earth' point towards the connection of Saturn and Uranus. In the sign of the Waterman we have the primordial connection and relationship of Heaven and Earth, of the Uranian and the Saturnine element. And in this primordial relationship of the heavenly and earthly we also look at the deepest cosmic origins and primordial grounds of the human being himself, to that which the profound Greek mythology expresses as the primordial connection, the cosmic primordial marriage of Uranos and Gäa, the heavenly divinity and earthly goddess. In an important and interesting lecture,[234] Dr Steiner connects this Uranos being with human primordial consciousness, which we have to imagine still standing on the level of Intuition. Then during a later, still far distant time this was taken over by a consciousness of Inspiration, which was a Saturnine consciousness flowing with time—our consciousness of today is purely spatial, which basically cannot lay hold of time. Still later this consciousness was taken over through an Imaginative Jupiter-Zeus consciousness. This remained as a higher consciousness with the gods, whereas human beings fell into the outer material consciousness of the senses.

In all this, besides the connections with the often-mentioned Uranos myth, we clearly have the astrological progression of Uranus–Saturn–Jupiter, corresponding to the line of development of *Occult Science*, Primordial Saturn [duration], Saturn in time, and Ancient Sun. (In the Düsseldorf lecture-cycle, Lect. 8, the becoming of time of Saturn is allocated to the Lion, standing opposite the Waterman. In these *Contributions*, the importance of the axis Waterman–Lion has frequently been mentioned. It becomes the axis of the coming age, the sixth post-Atlantean cultural epoch. The 'Marriage of Cana' of John's Gospel [John 2] contains a prophetic indication of this.[235]

Thus, in the zodiac the Uranus-triangle Waterman–Twins–Scales, the triangle of the light-ether and of the air-element is linked in a special way with the Mystery of the human being and of human origins. The depths of the Uranos-myth are illuminated for us precisely with this triangle (which also contains the sign of the sea, the Scales, containing Venus-Urania). It seems to me helpful that, with the zodiac figure given in my books on the gospels, precisely this triangle has its apex above. The human being, [Gk.] '*anthropos*' (meaning, 'the one getting up, making for the heights'), stands before us in this picture. The upper point appearing in this figure is formed by the Twins, the actual zenith-sign and 'sign of the Sacred Mount'. In a still deeper esoteric sense one could also draw the figure so that the Waterman, as the sign of the origin of the world and of the human being, occupies the upper point. This so to speak would be the point of view of the Creed, as Frieling has emphasized in his *Contributions* [see pp. 350, 355, 360-61 below]. This presentation of the Zodiac one sometimes meets.

In astrology we find the viewpoint representing that the trans-Saturnine, occult planets Uranus and Neptune, should not be arranged exclusively to *one* sign, but that in a certain sense each relates to a whole triangle, that is:

- Uranus to the light-ether triangle (astrological tradition says: air triangle),
- Neptune to the sound-ether triangle (that means, Uranus to the masculine, Neptune to the feminine ether).

This is also significant for the decanate relationship (concerning the principle of which I have already mentioned what is necessary). This means especially with the light-ether triangle, the planetary governors of its three corners are the following:

- with the Waterman Saturn–Uranus (that is, Saturn with Uranus as co-governor);
- with the Twins Mercury;
- with the Scales Venus (that is, Venus-Urania).

Then, with the sign Waterman:

- Saturn–Uranus is the governor of the whole sign, also of the first decanate;
- Mercury the governor of the second decanate;
- Venus the governess of the third decanate.

With the Mercury-sign of the Twins:

- the first decanate belongs to Mercury,
- the second decanate belongs to Venus,
- the third—now, we should say belongs to Saturn—Uranus, not simply say (as is often the case) to Saturn alone. Saturn as the *sole* ruler of the decanates in the Twins (with the third decanate), and the Scales (with the second decanate; the first decanate belongs to Venus, the third to Mercury) would *not* correspond to the bright, easy-of-earth, airy character of this trigon.

The case is completely different for the earth-triangle (life-ether triangle) Bull–Virgin–Goat; here, too, we have:

- Venus in the decanates, the governess of the sign of the Bull,
- Mercury, the ruler of the sign of the Virgin, and beside them
- Saturn as the ruler, and that means sole-ruler, of the sign of the Goat.

The dark, earthly-dense Saturn also belongs absolutely to this earthly triangle. But here one has to feel the difference between this earth-triangle and the completely different bright and light-filled air-triangle.

Moreover, no case exists of a complete coinciding of a zodiac-triangle in relation to its decanate governor. The fire-triangle and the water-triangle coincide with respect to the involvement of Jupiter and Mars, but nevertheless are differentiated through the abiding, still-remaining decanate in the one case through the Sun, in the other through the Moon. And similarly, the difference lying between earth-triangle and air-triangle, whereby the first simply has Saturn as the governor of the decanate, and the second on the other hand Saturn–Uranus, with a preponderance of Uranus. Indeed, although Saturn remains the co-ruler of the Waterman-sign, I feel, consequently as right and corresponding to this triangle if one does not speak of the Saturn-decanate of the Twins and the Scales, but only of the Uranus-decanate. I know horoscope formulas where the formula is different; I do not find this way of presentation quite corresponds to the facts. For the air-triangle we would have the following division:

- *Waterman*, I Saturn-Uranus, II Mercury, III Venus;
- *Twins*, I Mercury, II Venus, III Uranus;
- *the Scales*, I Venus, II Uranus, III Mercury.

In this whole trigon we see in an interesting way how the Uranus-question is connected to the Venus–Mercury question. These three planets are the esoteric planets—Alan Leo also points towards this,[236] but this also comes about independently of Alan Leo, out of all our earlier observations. Uranus, Venus and Mercury have a special esoteric significance that already stems from the Greek myth of Uranos, which I have frequently mentioned (see my book on *Alchymy*, Chapter IV; where especially the esoteric side of the Venus-Mercury question in connection with Uranus is discussed). In astrology Uranus is often mentioned as 'the higher octave' to Mercury, or also to Venus (correct for both), as it is from another point of view the octave of the Sun (Neptune is the octave of the Moon, in a certain relationship also of Mercury). In Venus (or Venus–Mercury) the Uranian starry being is revealed, in the earthly Sun-like [quality] and in proximity to the Sun. And all this is expressed from one viewpoint or another *in all three signs of the light-ether*, of the Uranus-trigon. We can also call this trigon a Venus–Mercury-trigon—but this would also apply to the earth-triangle, which still more tangibly we could also call the alchymical Venus–Mercury-trigon. Above all we could also call this, the Uranus–light-ether triangle, 'the triangle of Venus-Urania'–Venus, involved in the earth-triangle, is the earthly Venus, the governess in the Bull.

In a strange way this whole trigon is linked to the Mysteries of human becoming. In the Waterman we have the primordial cosmic human origin, we behold there the spiritual primordial human being in the still pre-Saturnine world. In the Scales—various things can be found in Steiner's lecture-cycles—the actual human form in the evolution of the Earth is raised to its actual harmony and beauty; here we glimpse the influence of Venus-Urania. Previously the human form was sub-human, on the stage of the Scorpion it had arrived at its deepest, lowest point. And at the stage of the Twins—more details can be found in an esoteric observation of Dr Steiner to which I shall return—development will have proceeded so far that the human being reaches the stage of the new, higher childhood, in which the contrast of gender is overcome, the hermaphrodite is achieved, corresponding to the essence of this Mercury-Venus sign. From the original *Anthroposophical Soul-Calendar* [1912] we recall how here two strange babies appear (one male and the other female, as we may surmise) as the Imagination of this sign [the drawing which represents later June in the calendar, p. 337]. I shall return to these things later.

In this connection a viewpoint has still to be mentioned, to which Frieling already points in his *Contributions*: how in some sense each of the three signs of this trigon has something of the nature of twins. So, firstly, with the Waterman we have the contrast so beautifully expressed in the Creed of the spiritual and the physical, of heaven and Earth, astrologically corresponding to the uniting of Saturn and Uranus in this sign. As the Saturn-Uranus-sign (whereas the Archer is merely a Saturn-sign) the sign of the Waterman from the first has something of the Twins nature, double-edged. Then above come the Twins, which have indeed taken their name from the Twins' nature. Horoscope astrology in this sign really has the character of the Twins, double-edged. There is a higher, esoteric influence of the sign, [one] tending towards the childlike and childlike innocence, and another that can lead to all sorts of ambiguities in the [respective] being, the educator, for example, makes a certain conscientiousness in this direction into a duty. Thus, for example, Neptune in the Twins is a critical matter. Out of what is not comprehended or mastered (Neptune) all sorts of difficulties can flow in the forming of a character. On the other hand, again this constellation has something very positive. Since the Twins is a Mercury sign, something lies in its connection with Neptune which contains an indication towards the 'anthroposophical constellation', the Mercury-Neptune connection (connection of earthly thinking and cosmic thinking). Therein lies a quite good, active signpost how one has a particular constellation to live through, if favourable things are to result.

The heavenly script also very clearly expresses this Twins-nature in the Twins constellation. In this very large constellation, we find the two Twin-stars Castor and Pollux, the actual 'heavenly Twins', who, when one has got to know them and kept an eye on them, are the most inevitable incorporation of duality appearing in the starry heavens. And not quite so marked, but similar, the same Twins-motif returns a couple of times in the same constellation. One clearly sees here that it really does concern the Twins-constellation, that it is no mere coincidence and experienced at the same time, that the revelation of this Twins-being does not happen in the earthly context when the Sun or a planet stands in this heavenly sign, but when they stand in the constellation of the Bull (according to which the sign Twins in the earthly rhythm is essentially oriented).

The 'heavenly Twins' Castor and Pollux (in early times the light twin-brother was differentiated from the dark twin-brother) are only a part, but the most characteristic part, of the constellation of the Twins. They emphasize above all the Twins-character of this sign in the heavenly script. In addition to the sign of the Twins, which is also the 'sign of the Sacred Mount', one can out of the gospel add to the Twins the Temptation of Christ, or rather how that temptation where the two tempters Lucifer and Ahriman on the pinnacle of the Temple approach Christ, relates to the Twins. The one wants to lift Him up, the other to throw Him down. Something of the airy mountain peak (or Temple pinnacle) with its danger of falling is part of Twins-aspect of this sign with which the character of the element of air is the most evident. (How far one can place this in quite an exact manner will become clearer later, when we add to the aspect of the four triangles in the zodiac the aspect of the 'four square': then the offensiveness for some people of the fact, indisputable in astrology, that 'Waterman' is not a water-sign but an air-sign, will be removed. We shall return to this later.)

Amongst all the zodiac-signs, the Twins-sign is the one in which one has the least firm ground under one's feet. The effect of this sign ('the Icarus[237] sign') with regards to aeronautics in horoscopes should be researched and has certainly already been done. In these things I have too little practice. Amongst the world-conceptions, the Twins according to Rudolf Steiner belongs to *mathematism* (as *pneumatism* belongs to the Waterman, the looking towards undifferentiated spirit). Not for nothing does the sign for the Twins have the character of the Roman numeral for two, II. Here is the origin of the primal Mystery of duality, all departure from the primordial unity into number. Out of the one the two emerges, that is the actual primordial Mystery. Once you have duality, you have the principle of the many, of number in general. These things are correct right into the horoscope: mathematical talent in connection with a specific influence of the sign Twins.

So we have the Twins-quality in the Waterman, as established with the Twins itself. How does it stand in this relationship with the Scales, the third sign of the air-trigon? In this sign the Twins-character of the whole trigon is brought *into balance*, in this equalizing, harmonizing, the influence of Venus-Urania is expressed, the governess of this sign. In the picture of the Scales itself is included that of the two weighing pans, which are brought mutually into balance. We have already pointed to the Twins-aspect with the traditional sign for the Scales ♎. Moreover, this Twins-character is contained in the two lines of water of the Waterman-sign ♒, and in the sign of the Twins we found the number two itself.

## *Music*

We can take this aspect further, for example, by bringing in music. With Waterman we would have the key of B♭-major, with the Twins D-major, that is, in the first case the key with two flats, in the other the case with two sharps. Of course, this *could* be a coincidence. But it is at least a nice one, it speaks for the genial, originality of our notation that in this case fits objectively. And with the Scales we have especially this Twins-character, which appears here that in F#-major (six sharps) and G♭-major (six flats) the two groups of keys; keys with sharps (the upper, brighter keys) and the keys with flats (lower, darker keys) comes into balance, which here enters into balance, enters the Scales, that here in the tempered system the balance is being created making possible of the closing the circle of keys into a concept of twelve (non-tempered, so-called pure tuning, would lead to an unlimited number of keys that in practice could never be realized; in particular the tempered system that appears to contradict reality is in fact the one corresponding to earthly reality. With each earthly musical system, it will have to do with such an adapting of the cosmic musical element into the earthly conditions. One would like to point out here that musicians will have to achieve the ability one day to use a tangible starry thinking in relationship to music on the Earth).

In the Scales, where in music F#-major and G♭-major coincide, 'meet in the Scales', the upper and the lower part of the zodiac meet, the sensory world and the spiritual world. C-major (Ram) rises from the dark to the bright, from the spiritual world to the sensory world, and with the Scales lying opposite the way down again into the darkness, from the sensory world to the spiritual world. Here, with this sign of Venus-Urania, and musically also with this key (F#-major, G♭-major), is the threshold to the spiritual world, the crossing of the threshold. We experience this with Wagner particularly clearly and tangibly. A well-known G♭-major piece is in *Tannhäuser*, the 'Prayer of Elisabeth' in Act III[: 'Almighty Virgin, I implore you show mercy, grant my prayer…']. This is no mere 'prayer', but a real crossing over the threshold: sacrificing herself for the loved one, Elisabeth overcomes human existence; she crosses the threshold to the spiritual world, becomes a saint. This is clearly expressed by all the words and the notes of this 'prayer', moreover, with a meditative, impersonal quality of the woodwind instrumentation.

'Elisabeth's prayer' stands completely in the sign of the Scales of Venus-Urania, thus how the entry of Elisabeth at the beginning of Act II 'Great hall of song, I give thee greeting…' is likewise expressively placed in G-major, the other Venus-key (the Venus in the Venusberg is only the unreal, daemonic counter-picture, whose key is characteristically D♭-major, the Scorpion-key and key of the dark lap of the Earth). In connection with which, it may be noted how, in that in Act III of *Tannhäuser* the shining of the Evening Star follows the prayer of Elisabeth, the key changes from G♭-major to B♭-major, the key of the Waterman-Uranus. In that everything depicted before now passes over into the real star-experience, this allows Wagner characteristically to bring the Waterman-Uranus key of B♭-major to be heard as the actual starry key. There is of course much in the musical repertoire that is not in this way characteristically starry, but that it is precisely what marks out Wagner, that he, without somehow pondering theoretically over the things, introduces purely intuitively this objective, tangible starry depiction into his music. One may like today to create a musical style that is contemporary, yet on this objective, starry quality one could learn from Wagner, could have learnt from him; one should not pass over it.

Otherwise, Wagner also uses the key of the Scales F#-major / Gb-major, especially Gb-major as the key of the threshold. It appears thus in *The Rhinegold* with the Rainbow Bridge, over which the gods enter Valhalla. In *Parsifal*, with Titurel's consecrated Christmas-night experience of the spiritual Hierarchies; in the Quintet in *The Mastersingers* as the threshold over which entrance is found into the land of art and higher poesie, and so on. The character of Venus-Urania, who is the governess of the sign of the Scales, is borne most clearly in the Prayer of Elisabeth. One can also find in general, especially in the music of *Tannhäuser*, which in many regards is an early work, the starry element is especially expressed.

In music not by Wagner we find Gb-major as the key of the Scales and the key of Venus-Urania characteristically used in Verdi's *Aida*. The shared death of the two lovers becomes here, too, a passing over the threshold to an entering into the light-filled fields of eternity. ('May Isis open for you the Gate of Heaven' are the parting words of Amneris, which point exactly towards Venus-Urania and is here, too, correct right into the musical key.)

## The Ethers

Through emphasizing Uranus and Venus-Urania this light-ether triangle possesses something light-filled, starry, something that is especially related to astrology. We recall how in Matthew's Gospel, which belongs to this triangle, the early astrology enters straight away at the beginning in the story of the Wise Men from the East and the Star of Bethlehem. Through the Sermon on the Mount [Matt. 5-7] this gospel is especially related to 'the Sacred Mount', which is allocated to the sign of the Twins. In this of lightness and brightness, the light-ether aspect meets the element of air. It may be recalled how, with the verses of the four elements in *The Souls' Awakening* [Rudolf Steiner's fourth Mystery Drama, Scene viii (GA 14, Germ. ed. p. 491)], this changing relationship of the light and airy nature comes out beautifully:

Der Vertreter des Luftelementes:
*Dem Schwergewicht des Erdenseins entflieh,*
*es tötet deines Selbstes Sein im Sinken,*

*erteile ihm mit Lüfteleichtigkeit.*
In Weltenweiten such' das Sein im Leuchten,
*verbinde, was du findest, deinem Schein;*
*im Fluge wird es dir das Sein gewähren.*

*Representative of the Air Element*:
Free from the heavy weight of earth existence.
It kills the being of thyself in sinking.
Escape it with the lightness of the air—
*seek for true being in the radiance*
*of world immensities*, and there unite
what thou hast found with thine own semblance.
It will secure thy being in its flight.
[Tr. Adam Bittleston, p. 458, emphases added.][238]

In the expression of light's expanses we find this connection of the concept of the airy space with the shining element. In the German language, the alliteration of the words *Licht* and *Luft* ('light' and 'air') already shows a mutual relationship.

It has frequently been emphasized how the two 'lower' kinds of ether, warmth-ether and light-ether, were also delineated as the 'masculine' ether, as the masculine element of existence, and the two 'upper ethers', sound-ether (also called 'chymical-ether') and life-ether as the feminine element of existence. Thereby a fineness, a differentiation reigns within the light-ether. In our presentation we found the masculine element with the warmth-ether trigon with its Sun-sign, Jupiter-sign and Mars-sign more one-sidedly marked than with the light-ether triangle with its signs of a Twins-character, where already:

- the Waterman encloses the contrasts of 'heaven and Earth',
- the Twins strongly oriented towards the hermaphrodite and childlike qualities, the union of both genders in the childlike [condition], and
- the Scales as the sign of Venus-Urania.

This 'trigon of the human being' is oriented more according to the pure human and comprehensively human [picture] than according to the one-sided masculine [division]. Out of Wachsmuth's presentation of the etheric formative forces we know how within the light-ether a split occurs, between the 'warmth-light' belonging to the lower element, and the 'pure light', the 'cold flame', that is associated with the upper element.

Chemically the warmth-light relates to common oxygen, $O_2$, the cold light to ozone, $O_3$ where the pure light, the cold flame, is revealed, for example, on the Earth in all manifestations of phosphorus. Wachsmuth points out in his book, Vol. 1,[239] how the differentiation of the warm and the cold light already exists in ancient religious texts. In early Egypt people spoke of Isis as the 'feminine light' (Creuzer, *Symbolik und Mythologie der alten Völker*, Vol. 3, 403). Thus we divine the 'cold flame' of the higher worlds, the 'cold flame of the cosmic fields of ice' that is mentioned in Steiner's Mystery Dramas, is the feminine light of Isis the feminine one, that side of the light-ether that is turned towards the higher 'Eternal Feminine'. In the same way as the one earthly part of the light-ether is turned towards the masculine warmth-ether, so is the other turned towards the life-ether as the element of the Eternal Feminine.

In my book *From the Mysteries*, in the essay 'The Tree of Life' (Germ. ed. p. 202), I attempted to show how this relationship of cold light and life-ether in the regions of the cosmic-feminine is connected with the Mysteries of the ice-maiden, which in the Hibernian Mysteries is still reflected in the names related to Isis, the names Isot, Isolde = Ishild, Eishilde, Eisholde.[240] The 'higher life-element' that in the Mysteries played a well-known role, is basically not limited to the life-ether and sound-ether, but carries in itself still an element of the 'cold light', the 'light of Isis'.

Thus we have the lower masculine element of existence in the warmth-ether and warmth-light, the higher feminine element of existence in the sound-ether, life-ether, the cold light. And we would then also allocate in the zodiac the 'triangle of the light-ether' not, as that of the 'warmth-ether', quite one-sidedly to the masculine element, but would find, that which indeed also thoroughly corresponds to the 'Twins-character' of this triangle, that here an Isis-element of the higher Feminine, an element of Venus-Urania, plays into that of the 'masculine ethers'. The light-ether triangle in a certain sense already presents a connection with the 'feminine ether'. Right into the zodiac-Mysteries we find a certain preponderance of the feminine element within the higher regions.

If now in what follows we move on to the actual triangles of the feminine ethers and feminine elements, to the earth-triangle and the water-triangle (life-ether and sound-ether, or chymical-ether), so according to the outer sequence we would come first of all to the sound-ether (the water-element), followed by the life-ether (the earth-element). But here, too, it is once again so that we will find the feminine element most developed with one of the two triangles, with the life-ether. This, with the gospels, is connected to Luke's Gospel, whereas with John more the union of the feminine with the masculine is emphasized.

A special relationship also exists through the element of the cold, feminine light precisely between the light-ether and the life-ether. In the zodiac this relationship is expressed in particular through the fact that in the decanates we have a similar division. As in the light-ether triangle of the Saturn–Uranus–sign of the Waterman, we have in the life-ether triangle of the Saturn-sign the Archer, and the two other decanates fall in both triangles in the same way to the planets Venus and Mercury. We have for this reason already emphasized how essential it is to differentiate both triangles in respect of the third decanate (the one Saturn, the other more Uranus). In any case, the mutual relationship is clear. We should keep in mind with the following observations in the first place the trigon of the life-ether, the 'earth triangle'.

# XXI
# The Triangle of the Earth-element and the Life-ether

### (Bull, Virgin and Goat)

From the lower, 'masculine' kinds of ether (warmth-ether and light-ether), we turn now to the higher, the 'feminine' kinds of ether (life-ether and sound-ether, also called chymical-ether), to which we already recognized in the light-ether an element of relationship and connection. The triangle of the life-ether, which we discuss in what follows, is called in astrology the *earth trigon*, a designation which is likewise correct, because the highest of the kinds of ether, the life-ether, corresponds to the lowest element, the element of earth.

The relationship of the rulership of the decanates between light-ether and life-ether was also discussed. As there, so here, we have:

- a Venus-sign, the Bull;
- a Mercury-sign, the Virgin;
- a Saturn-sign, the Goat.

However, whereas the Saturn-sign in the light-ether triangle was the Waterman-sign, easy of earth, where alongside Saturn Uranus is co-ruler, we were also able to find that for the corresponding decanate of the Twins-sign and the Scales actually not Saturn but rather Uranus comes into question. We have in the earth-trigon (life-ether trigon) the other, the dark, earthly dense, the completely earthly Saturn, which with the Bull and the Virgin, and in its pure earthly Saturn-quality, is involved as the decanate ruler. This also absolutely corresponds to the nature of this trigon that as earth-trigon is strongly aligned to the Mysteries of the element of earth. And to these Mysteries of the earthly element there also belongs those of the life-ether, out of whose change, consolidation and enchantment the earthly element came into being.

Earth is enchanted life-ether. 'The human being transforms the life-ether into earth-spirits,' says Dr Steiner in *Christ and the Human soul*, in the same way as the animal transforms the chymical ether into water-spirit, and the plant the life-ether into air-spirits.' I would like to point out one more thing, which I find nowhere *directly* in this lecture-cycle of *Occult Science*, but which I nevertheless believe it is based on some truth. As the chymical-ether is also the sound-ether, the 'sounding element', so, it appears to me, the life-ether is also the 'element of scent'. Such a thing cannot be proved in the conventional sense, but it can be experienced as such.

Also, using the method of quoting, one can especially point out how in *Occult Science*, with the development of the Earth, Dr Steiner says how here for the first time the element of earth is added to evolution (for with Ancient Saturn only the element of warmth was reached, with Ancient Sun the element of air, and with Ancient Moon the watery element). This element, though, is not added immediately as the coarse earthly matter of today, but like a very fine element of dust, a kind of essence of scent. The element of earth meets there completely with the being of the life-ether, which somehow still has to be related to the element of scent. (Wagner has an intuitive divining of this at the end of *Tristan and Isolde*.)[241] The [early] Indians, too, knew this, in the way they saw the relationship between the elements and the senses. There:

- the sense of seeing corresponds to fire,
- to the sense of taste to the water,
- to the air, the sense of touch,
- to the earth the sense of smell;
- the sense of hearing corresponds with the Indian to the ether, *akasha*, as the fifth element,
- and we may assume the sound-ether for them was the ether *par excellence*.

Dr Steiner said somewhere that the Indians with their elements do not mean the element, but the corresponding kinds of ether. The Indian 'element of earth' *(prathivi)* without further ado would be the life-ether, and we would then have even more the relationship of the element of scent = the life-ether. How much the earth is connected to this element of scent we experience especially strongly in a garden after a thunderstorm when the earth breathe out its whole fragrance and in this life-etheric element of scent would be, if we return to *Occult Science,* a hidden Saturn-Mystery that inwardly relates to the zodiac-signs contained in the triangle of the life-ether.

That the light-ether is the most easy of earth of all the elements, Rudolf Steiner brings to eloquent expression in the Mystery-verse [from the fourth Mystery Drama, *The Soul's Awakening*, Scene viii]:

[Representative of the Air Element:]
Escape from heavy weight of earth existence
which kills the being of thy self in sinking.
Take flight from it with lightness of the air.
In cosmic space search for reality of brightness . . .

All this has more to do with Uranus than Saturn. But with the life-ether triangle, the earth-triangle, the Saturn-element is the more pronounced. One notices, for example, how the Saturnine life-etheric element of scent also aligns well with the Bull, where Venus is the governess of the flowers, of the burgeoning blossoming and flowering in the earthly realm.

## *The Virgin*

We found emphasized with the Uranus light-ether triangle, the astrological, starry element; with the life-ether-triangle, if we will, we find an alchemical emphasis. In particular (as I show in my book on *Alchymy*) the Virgin is the sign of alchemy, that sign in which starry Mysteries and earthly Mysteries most directly meet. It is consequently also the sign of transubstantiation, the Last-Supper-sign. In the gospels, especially Mark's Gospel, this her role comes everywhere to the fore. Here we have with Mark in the sign of the Virgin first the Parable of the Sower, the story of the grain of wheat, the whole symbolism of the seed is woven with the Mystery of the sign of the Virgin. In the higher rounds, or octaves [of the gospel], we find in this sign first the Last-Supper Mystery of the Feeding [of the 5000] and finally the Last Supper of Christ itself. The Last Supper is the liturgical expression of the alchymical Mystery of metamorphosis, of transubstantiation, and Communion.

Mercury is the ruler in the Virgin, here particularly the alchymistic one, the medical Mercury, whereas the Mercury, more easy of earthly weight in the Twins, is the more purely spiritual Mercury, the lord of the forces of thinking.

The Mystery of the Earth in the Virgin becomes the Virgin-Earth Mystery, which is praised in many respects by alchymists and mystics such as Jakob Boehme and Angelus Silesius as the *prima materia* of the chymical process. To this alchymistic essence of the Virgin-Mercury and to the sign of Mercury in general, there corresponds the collaboration of Saturn, who in the Virgin is the ruler of the second decanate. The third decanate belongs to Venus as governess of the sign of the Bull. That means, we also find in the sign of the Virgin the alchemistic 'hermaphrodite' (Hermes = Mercury, Aphrodite = Venus). The connection of Venus and Mercury is especially significant, for from what has been said earlier about the planets, we recall that Mercury and Venus originally formed a unity; after their separation from the Sun they remained connected. This is linked to certain higher Mysteries of the original nature of the human being. The union of Venus and Mercury, the 'hermaphrodite' is the starry reflection of that which in the human being, in the division of the genders and the Fall of man in the spiritual-etheric realm, was primordial nature in the pure condition of innocence. And in this their union Mercury and Venus both belonged to the Virgin (we clearly feel how Venus, the aloof, maidenly planet, has somehow to be related to the sign of the Virgin), only with its split, reflected in the Fall of man, did it become so, that Mercury remained with the Virgin, whereas Venus, in order not to succumb to the Scorpion, was placed in the Scales by the gods, where she now is Venus-Urania. Originally the Archer followed the Virgin. That the Scorpion and the Scales became particularly significant zodiac-signs is connected with this Mystery of Venus-Mercury, as discussed earlier [*Contribution* 6].

Thus as ever we recognize a certain inner relationship of the planet Venus to the zodiac-sign of the Virgin (where with Saturn it is the ruler), whereas in the traditional astrology it is frequently so presented as if Venus and the Virgin do not bear one another very well. (Since the Fishes is the 'exaltation' of Venus, the Virgin lying opposite is called the fall of Venus; but ever again it is shown that one should not take these conceptual categories too schematically.) Schmitz in particular, in his much-read book but one not particularly to be recommended, has taken certain liberties. In reality it is like this, that the actual aloof and maidenly character of Venus—of which Dr Steiner speaks in the well-known Dornach lecture on the planets ('it rejects any cosmic dancing', Dr Steiner says)[242]—is expressed especially strongly in the sign of the Virgin. This I have learned in a number of actual cases.

Concerning this, it has to be said that in all the signs of this trigon, Venus alongside Saturn stands as the governess, or governess of the decanate. An all-too-close conjunction of Venus with Saturn in horoscopes, is taken as not so favourable. But this does not mean to say that these two planets cannot suffer each other. Already the facts of this trigon prove the opposite. Venus, who is in general the being of harmony, of a pleasing and easy adjusting, has an especially favourable relationship to Saturn, to the lord of earthly matter. For it is her task to express and bring right into matter precisely the reveal-ing beauty and harmony in the material realm, to carry it right into matter. For this she needs Saturn. And not without deep meaning, in harmony with ancient tradition as with contemporary experience, Saturn has its 'exaltation', that is, the position in which she actually works in the best, most favourable manner, in the Scales, in the sign of Venus-Urania. We have seen how, during the course of the Earth's development, in this sign the Venus-forces have given the human form in particular its harmonious balance. Spiritual form and earthly materiality receive, through the forces of Venus, their beautiful, har-monious balance. The highest, most beautiful, most perfect [creation], the human form, has been wrested from earthly materiality. This was a deed of Venus, in which at the same time Saturn, the lord of earthly matter, has come to his highest effectiveness, to his true 'exaltation'. Thus, in one's own contemplation, with the concepts and imagination from astrological tradition, one can often connect quite a good, excel-lent meaning.

## The Bull

With the Venus-sign of the Bull we have the main corner of the earth-tri-gon, of the life-ether trigon (as of the fire-trigon with the Lion, and of the air-trigon with the Waterman). As with the Lion of Mark's Gospel, with the Waterman of Matthew's Gospel, we have with the Bull, Luke's Gospel, with its inclination to the Mysteries of the feminine, of the vir-ginal and maternal element. Mary, Elisabeth, the childhood stories and some more intimate aspects of this gospel (which Bock has pointed out in his *Newsletter Contributions*) predominantly correspond to the essence of this trigon with its sign of the Virgin, its Venus-sign of the Bull and Christmas-sign of the Goat. What concerns the Bull, as I have frequently emphasized, is that this name does not quite suit, for we stand here in a female sign, a Venus-sign; the sign of the fire-trigon and air-trigon are masculine, that of the water-trigon and earth-trigon pres-ent female zodiac-signs, as indeed also warmth-ether and light-ether present the masculine, sound-ether and life-ether the feminine element of existence. So, instead of the Bull and the red rag, one should think with this zodiac-sign more of the Isis-cow.[243]

With the Indians there is *one* word that means both cow and earth ('*go*', related in sound with *Kuh*, 'cow'). The Indian would name our zodiac-sign simply '*go*'. It is the sign about which we know that it is aligned in the human figure to the larynx, bearing the speech-impulse. This corresponds to the essence of Venus, the governess of this sign. Mars is the power of the persuasive word working outwards (the 'outward flourish'); Venus is the inwardness of the word, the quality of loving in the word (note the Hebrew *amor* = to speak, sounding like [Lat.] *amor*, love). In language tremendous powers of love govern; note the physical power of love and the power of speech (the opposition of Bull and Scorpion). This, too, we have frequently emphasized, that the opposition of Venus in the Bull and Venus in the Scales is not, for instance, that here in the Scales we would have the higher revelation of love and in the Bull a lower one. The revelation of Venus in the Bull is of a divine kind, of Marian quality. This divine quality of Mary is felt by people today more with the picture that relates to this sign, Raphael's *Sistine Madonna*, than with Botticelli's *The Birth of Venus*, which relates to the sublime impulse of the Scales; she is Venus-Urania. Venus in this Bull-sign is aligned to the fullness of blossoming of May, the May-Queen, is healing power of love (in the Ram, Bull and Twins, there lie especially healing Raphael-forces, as we shall discuss later). Venus in the Bull is the Queen of the May and Queen of Flowers, the governess of what blossoms and flowers in life. Flowers belong to her, as she is aligned in the zodiac to the sign of the Bull. The femininity of Venus is more evident with the Bull than with the (masculine) sign of the Scales (Moon and Venus are the two 'feminine planets'); we recall how the Bull is also taken as the 'exaltation' of the Moon. We mentioned the relationship of the scent of flowers to the life-ether.

As ruler in the Bull, Venus also rules the first decanate; the second belongs to Mercury, the third to Saturn. In its allocation to Venus and the Moon the Bull, the Isis-cow, is a strong sign of the Isis-quality. We also know that the blossoming of the Egyptian Mystery-culture fell in that time when the spring equinox was in the Bull. The burgeoning, enlivening forces of the Sun in spring are most strong in this sign, the earthly blossoms are then at their height. This helps us to understand the relationship to the life-ether and to the element of earth.

## The Goat

If we turn from this spring-sign to the third sign of the earth-triangle, to the Goat, we have in it the dark, the earthly dense Saturn-sign, in which Saturn alone governs, that is, does not have Uranus as co-ruler. The second decanate belongs to Venus, the third to Mercury. The relationship to Luke's Gospel will be best understood when we remember that the Goat in the course of the year is the sign of Christmas. In the circle of musical keys, belonging to it are Eb-major and C-minor. Especially the dark C-minor corresponds very much to the dark earthly character of this sign. With no key do we feel so completely deeply below and so firmly standing on the Earth. For here we stand at the deepest point on the circle of keys, as A-major is at the highest point (this Wagner has expressed especially effectively, where he uses in *Twilight of the Gods* during Siegried's death the transition from A-major to C-minor).

It comes into consideration that whereas the major-keys contain a driving, rising element, with the minor-keys the opposite is the case. Here there is a feeling of something falling down, as from a kind of precipitation. Here at the deepest place of the circle of keys with Eb-major = C-minor (C-minor is the relative of Eb-major [sharing the same key-signature and place on the circle of keys], giving the strongest feeling of the oppression of earth. At the same time at this point in Eb-major [the movement around the circle] proceeds to rise again, as also in the course of the year it is the point of the first rising to meet the light. For this reason there also lies in Eb-major and C-minor something heroic, or tragic-heroic, militant. This, too, finds its correspondence in astrology. As the Venus-sign of the Bull is the 'exaltation' of the feminine Moon, the Goat is the exaltation of Mars. Mars here is not the military, but the spiritually militant Mars, in a certain relationship to the strongest Mars (as also favourable Mars-Saturn-aspects in the horoscope are something very strong, giving gravity to the personality and to destiny).

With the earthly quality there is very strongly united in the Goat the spiritual, one could say, spiritual in the Christian sense. Amongst the world-conceptions, according to the scheme of the lecture-cycle on *Human and Cosmic Thought* [GA 151, 4 lectures, Berlin 20-23 Jan. 1914. See endnote 30], spiritualism belongs, whereas we have with the other Saturn-sign, the Waterman (that is, with the bright, 'airy' Saturn-sign), we have pneumatism. What is the difference here? Certainly, spiritualism and pneumatism stand very close to each other, as both indeed are also Saturn-signs. Greek *pneuma*, actually the 'blowing of the wind', 'breath', is essentially the same as the Latin *spiritus*. (The word *pneuma* is found in the well-known passage in John 3, where Luther and the AV/KJV translates at one time with '*Geist*—spirit' and then with '*wind*—wind' [v. 8]: 'The wind bloweth where it listeth …'.) Only with *pneuma* the thinking is more on the consistent, egalitarian, all-encompassing nature of the spirit, whereby the air-element once again stands there as a picture (in the air there is no exertion, no individualizing; even Christ's undivided garment at the crucifixion is related to this by Rudolf Steiner in his lectures on John's Gospel). On the other hand, with spiritualism we think of the different, individualized, tangible beings of the spiritual Hierarchies. This individualizing results precisely when one looks from the earthly towards the spiritual; in the earthly element itself lies the individualizing. And the Goat is precisely the earth-sign. Perhaps one can point precisely here to the Christmas celebration, with its invocation of the different Hierarchies [the Inserted Prayer].

The Goat to an especially strong degree is an earth-sign, indeed, probably the strongest, most bound to the Earth of all the earth-signs. For it belongs not only to the earth-triangle, but at the same time to the first of the three crosses, that is to the Cross of the Father and of the physical element, the earthly cross. Earthly cross and earthly triangle meet at this Saturn–Goat-corner. (The Virgin in the earthly triangle belongs to the Son-Cross, the etheric cross, the Bull to the astral cross, to the spirit-cross; through the rulership of Venus and the exaltation of the Moon, this Bull-corner has very strongly the character of the 'Spirit-self' (Dr Steiner uses this expression),[244] of the *manas*-quality. It corresponds to the being of the dark and earthly Saturn, that at this Goat-corner all viewpoints of the earthly element meet. Precisely for this reason the Goat can also be the sign of Christmas (as it is, simply as a fact, in the rhythm of the year), because at the time of the deepest earthly darkness and earthly hardening the Christmas-event took place (to which Luke's Gospel, corresponding to our triangle, takes a special orientation).

It is no contradiction, but once again corresponds to the facts, that to this Saturn darkness of the year the dark adversary also belongs. In connection with the Christmas story, [King] Herod's Massacre of the Innocents stands. The dark results of black magic, too, belong to the nature of the Goat–Saturn-sign; the Goat here plays a role as a picture. Observations concerning the probable connection of [the words]

Satan and Saturn were made earlier [*Contribution* No. 7]—whereby, however, in no way should everything to do with Saturn be stamped as Satanic.

In a sense that no longer has to do with black magic, the Goat is also the sign of Lucifer, at the same time also of the Holy Spirit, which is the overcoming of Lucifer (as the 'Father' is the overcoming of Ahriman). Thus we find Buddha's enlightenment in the Goat.[245] To this the aspects of the twelve main events in Buddha's life leads (often mentioned by me [for example, *Contribution*, No. 12]), which are especially expressively aligned to the 12 zodiac-signs when we proceed from the first to the sixth then to the eleventh, then to the fourth, and so on.[246] One will observe that this ordering of the zodiac-signs remains the usual one, that thereby one always remains in the corresponding triangle. The usual progression is Ram, Bull, Twins, Crab; here Ram, Virgin, Waterman, Crab, but:

- the Virgin belongs like the Bull to the earth-triangle, the sign of the etheric body,
- the Waterman like the Twins to the air-triangle.

Only:

- the Virgin, the sign of the etheric body, at the same time stands in the etheric cross (which is not the case with the Bull)
- the Waterman, the sign of the astral body, at the same time stands in the astral cross (which is not the case with the Twins).

That is, this progression in a cycle stepping five places is inwardly demonstrated and meaningful. We have:

- with the Ram the physical body,
- with the Virgin the etheric body,
- with the Waterman the astral body,
- with the Crab the sentient soul,
- with the Archer the mind-soul,
- with the Bull the consciousness [or spiritual] soul,
- with the Scales the Spirit-self,
- with the Christ-sign of the Fishes the Life-spirit,
- with the Lion the Spirit-man;

the three remaining signs lead even deeper to the Trinity:

- with the Goat would be the Holy Spirit (the overcoming of Lucifer through Christ in the first Temptation),
- with the Twins the Son (overcoming of both tempters through Christ),

- with the Scorpion the Father (overcoming of Ahriman, the power of death, through Christ).

If we apply this scheme to the twelve main events of Buddha's life (see my *Buddha's Life and Teaching*, Part 1), we have with:

- the Ram the descent to the Earth,
- the Virgin the entry into his mother's womb,
- the Waterman the birth (with the story of the two streams of water, which the gods Indra and Brahma here give forth),
- with the Crab (sentient soul) certain childhood experiences (the first breakthrough of inwardness in the child),
- with the Archer the bow-shot in the contest for the bride (which is very characteristic),
- with the Bull (consciousness-soul) the renunciation of the world, entry into the spiritual life,
- with the Scales (Spirit-self) devotion to the meditative life (completely corresponding to the character of the Scales),
- with the Fishes the 'entry into the circle of enlightenment' (sitting down under the bodhi tree),
- with the Lion the victory over Mara, the ruler of the powers of death ([recalling the Creed 'Then He overcame death ....'),
- with the Goat finally (from which previously we started) the Enlightenment, the actual attainment of Buddhahood,
- with the Twins the first announcement of the teaching (sermon on the two ways of error and the right path, the middle way),
- with the Scorpion [Buddha's] death, the passing into nirvāṇa.

One sees how deeply the Mysteries of the zodiac in Indian esotericism actually penetrate, which outwardly are developed less towards astrology; here we really have a piece of ancient primordial wisdom (what is given today as 'Indian astrology' is mostly a late and decadent product).

The Goat has a certain character of *manas*, also the Virgin and the Bull (the actual *manas*-sign is the other Venus-sign, the Scales, belonging to another triangle), and we could call the earthly-triangle the triangle of the life-ether, also the *manas*-triangle. With the three corners of this earth-tigon and life-ether-trigon, looking towards the sentences of our Creed, we may recall that we find:

- with the Venus-sign of the Bull, the Queen of the May, the sentence 'The birth of Jesus upon Earth...'

- with the 'Son of Mary', with the alchemical sign 'Virgin', the 'Lord of the heavenly forces upon Earth',
- with the Goat, the overcoming of Lucifer, the 'overcoming of the sickness of sin' is mentioned.

If one thinks the twelve sentences of the Creed ordered in a circle, at the end the Saturn-sign Goat ('They may hope …') joins up again with the other Saturn-sign Waterman, which as the Saturn–Uranus-sign ('An almighty divine Being, spiritual-physical…') forms the beginning. That is, the Goat-Saturn joins at the end together with the Uranus–Saturn, with the aspect of eternity, of Uranus '… the preservation of their life, destined for eternity'. Frieling has already pointed to these aspects in his *Contributions*.

# XXII
# The Triangle of the Water-element, of the Chemical-ether or Sound-ether

Of the four kinds of ether, there still remains one, the chemical-ether or sound-ether, which presents the life-ether together with the higher feminine-ether and is allocated to the water-element (as the life-ether is to the earth-element). In the normal order of stages—warmth-ether, light-ether, sound-ether and life-ether—it is not the highest ether but precedes this life-ether. And yet, we discuss it last because in a certain relationship it is the most significant and active ether, as the gospel to which it corresponds, John's Gospel, is the highest gospel. Luke's Gospel relates correspondingly to what in itself is the highest ether, the life-ether, often forming the intimate supplements (more details in my book on *John's Gospel*, where I attempt to show how John is the highest and Luke's, in a certain sense, the most intimate gospel). Just as the chemical-ether is the sound-ether, especially in connection with the life-ether, so is the chymical, the alchymical, the magical ether. As sound-ether it also carries in itself the Mysteries of cosmic music, of the cosmic symphonic element and of the word. We know, and have often discussed, how this aspect of the alchemical-magical (transubstantiation and once again of the cosmic symphonic element, of the cosmic word) meet precisely in John's Gospel.

In the Egyptian temple-scene in *The Soul's Awakening*,[247] Rudolf Steiner brings the sound-ether, or the water-element to which it corresponds, as the last. The sequence of elements is there indeed different from the usual way of listing them. Dr Steiner begins here with the earth-element:

Within the weight of earth's existence, lay hold
upon the semblance of thy being fearlessly
that thou mayst sink into the cosmic depths …

Then follows the air-element:

Escape from heavy weight of earth existence …

then the fire element:

> The error of thy sense of self be burned
> in fire, enkindled in this rite for thee.
> Burn thou thyself with substance of thine error …

and finally the water-element.

If we compare this order with the corresponding zodiac-trigons that we already met in an astrological context, we find the interesting thing that earth and air (life-ether and light-ether), which indeed in this series form the first pair, in their zodiac-trigons both have the Mercury-Venus element. Thereby they are differentiated, as the earth-triangle has the dark Saturn (Goat–Saturn), whereas the air-triangle (light-ether) has Uranus-Saturn, so that in this decanate Uranus occupies the first place.

We can, if we want, summarize these two triangles as the Venus-Mercury-triangle, and at the same time *differentiate* them as the Saturn-triangle (earth, life-ether) and the Uranus-triangle (air, light-ether). Likewise, in the order of the Egyptian temple-scene, the following triangle of the fire (warmth-ether) and of the water (chemical-ether or sound-ether) in their decanates have together the Jupiter–Mars element. They are differentiated in that, apart from these two planets, the fire-triangle belongs to the Sun, the water-triangle, now to be discussed, to the Moon. We could, then, summarize these two triangles, fire and water, as Jupiter–Mars-triangles, and at the same time differentiate them as the Sun-triangle and the Moon-triangle. The planets, then, are divided between the four triangles in the zodiac, so that we can speak of two Jupiter–Mars-triangles and of two Venus–Mercury-triangles, and on the other hand of a Sun-triangle, a Moon-triangle, a Saturn-triangle and a Uranus-triangle.

With the light-ether we found the masculine element belonging to this ether differentiated through Venus towards the feminine side and we could thereby point towards the differentiation of the warm (masculine) and cold (feminine) light, which governs in the light-ether realm. Similarly, the sound-ether in itself feminine (water-triangle) carries in itself besides the (feminine) Moon, the (otherwise masculine) planets Jupiter and Mars. Here they appear not in a purely masculine character, as in the fire-triangle. Jupiter in the Fishes (where Venus is exalted), is something other than Jupiter in the Archer. Mars in the Scorpion (which, as we shall see, is overall the most complicated sign) is something other than the masculine, active Mars in the Ram.

Consequently, the sound-ether triangle carries the feminine character not so marked as the life-ether triangle. (This is quite similar with the relationship of John's Gospel to Luke's Gospel.)

The connection of the water-element with the sound-ether—which makes sense of everyday experience, if one experiences how on the water, for example, in a boat, the voice sounds differently, carried by a special acoustic of the water—is beautifully brought out in the verse in Rudolf Steiner's mystery drama, *The Soul's Awakening*:

> Prevent the world of fire's flaming power
> from robbing thee of self-sustaining might.
> Semblance will not arise into existence
> unless the wave-beat of the cosmic ocean
> can penetrate thee with its spheric tone.
> In cosmic ocean seek reality as wave;
> bind to thy semblance that which thou dost find;
> in surging it will grant thee existence.

That the sound-ether is also the chemical-ether makes sense when we remind ourselves of the effect of the musical sound that orders matter, groups matter, for which Rudolf Steiner always mentions the 'Chladni sound-figures'.[248]

As the three corners of the sound-ether trigon we find the Scorpion, the Fishes and the Crab. These are the three 'water-signs', whereas the Waterman, as mentioned, is an 'air-sign'. In all three signs it is shown how far precisely this triangle of the watery element and of the sound-etheric element, of the chemical ether—we know what especially the watery, the liquid condition, means for all chemical reactions—is the magical, occult-esoteric triangle. The essence of what is esoteric is the hidden reality behind that which is graspable with the senses and of the abundant contrasts of what is sense-perceptible. In particular, the hidden side is revealed through this triangle; that which appears contradictory arises into the light of day when it has to do with pointing towards the occult reality hidden behind the outer sensory appearance.

## The Scorpion

Here initially the Scorpion is the main sign after which this triangle is named (whereby we have to remind ourselves at the same time of the Scorpion-Eagle metamorphosis), the occult, occult-esoteric sign, *par excellence*. Here contrast is the most obvious thing connecting the essence of everything occult ['hidden']. Like no other sign in the zodiac, the Scorpion in particular connects the highest heights and the deepest depths, the dark depths of the dragon and the spiritual heights of the Sun-Eagle (to which Jupiter also points, ruling the second decanate of this sign—'Eagle of Zeus'. The Scorpion-Eagle helps us really to look on to the sunny heights of the source of life—with the Eagle, as Dr Steiner explains in the Düsseldorf lecture-cycle [GA 110], life originates on Ancient Sun, which then in the Scorpion receives the sting of death (as today in the yearly rhythm in the Scorpion lies in that time of November in which natural life receives the 'sting of death'.) And in the depths, where the powers of the dragon dwell, we feel again the origin of the mysterious source of life that carries life up again on esoteric paths. The Mystery of life is connected to the being of the Scorpion-sign in a special sense. The contrast of the Sun-Eagle, of life, with the sting of death, the Scorpion power of death in the depths, is the occult Mystery of this sign. The Scorpion ascendant in birth-horoscopes is something unusual. It gives a special stamp to those personalities who have this sign, that is, at whose birth the Scorpion was rising. Heights and depths are here united. And so, the Scorpion plays a role in the horoscopes on the one hand of criminals, and on the other hand the most outstanding personalities like Goethe, Dr Steiner, and others who have this sign as the ascendant.

The ruling planet of the Scorpion, and therewith also its first decanate, is Mars. For in the Scales that precedes it, we had Venus, and now in the next sign Mars follows as the ruler. The planetary sign for Mars ♂ noticeably relates initially to the sign for the Archer ♐; from this the arrow of death or sting of death in the sign of the Scorpion came about ♏. We have often explained that originally there were ten zodiac-signs; the Archer followed the Virgin. So that the Archer's arrow of death would not wound the Virgin—in the Scorpion-sign ♏ this meeting of the Virgin-sign with the death-arrow of the Archer is already expressed—the Scales was placed in the middle between them by the gods, between the Archer, or the Scorpion, and the Virgin. To the Scales Venus, previously connected with Mercury in the Virgin, now places her realm of rulership as Venus-Urania.

Thus Mars in the Scorpion expresses that which by people is so often mixed up with Venus, but has nothing to do with her. Venus, as we have seen, is rather the opposition to Mars, for opposite the Mars-sign of Scorpion stands the Venus-sign of the Bull (one can also think of the relationship of the forces of speech—for the Bull is the organ of speech—to the sexual forces), in the same way Venus in the Scales is in opposition to Mars in the Ram. In the zodiac Mars and Venus always lie opposite each other. The relationship to the Scorpion-sign towards the sexual element is enhanced, because in the third decanate we find the Moon as a ruler (the second decanate belongs to Jupiter, reminding us here of the Eagle of Zeus).

Amongst the worldviews, we find dynamism here, that view that orientates everything towards strength, emphasizing strength and energy. Amongst the seven world-view-moods (cf. on all this, the Berlin lecture-cycle *Human and Cosmic Thought* [GA 151. See endnote 30]) we find voluntarism, whose most famous representative is Schopenhauer with his philosophy of will). Rudolf Steiner has pointed out in the above-mentioned lecture-cycle, how the tragic turn in Nietzsche's life occurred when, during the course of his worldview, he turned towards this sign, that is, voluntarism in dynamism (Mars in the Scorpion).

All this should not be understood in such a way as if now in a birth-horoscope there would be necessarily something 'bad'. If it is such—and at first only in the conventional sense—rather depends on its influence. Mars in Scorpio, because he is the lord in his house, is in any case always a strong, significant Mars. He is there only comparable to Mars in the Ram (the active and enlivening Mars ready for deeds) the more passive, passionate, emotional, sensitive, in short, the critical Mars. Mars in the Scorpion was also necessary in order that the Mystery of Golgotha could take place. The power of the *Imperium Romanum* belongs especially to it. Not for nothing did the Roman legionaries carry on their armour the Scorpion-sign.

In the rhythm of the gospel, the Scorpion-sign is very clearly connected to the Scorpion's power of death. Especially the disputes of the disciples—at the end, the betrayal of Judas and Peter's denial, before that the episode of Caesarea Philippi stand in Mark's Gospel under this sign. In John's Gospel, the severe illness of the invalid of Bethesda, the illness of Lazarus, the humiliation of Christ before Pilate (*ecce homo*), the gospel points most clearly towards the Scorpion as the power of death—in two passage in John's Gospel, in Chapter 10 with the 'Good Shepherd' and the end of chapter 16—where the Greek word *skorpizein*, 'to scatter', which contains the 'scorpio' in it, 'to bring into individual separation, to isolate', is used by Christ himself.

In John 10 the 'wolf' is mentioned who scatters the sheep: in John 16 the flight of the disciples, the scattering of the disciples. With this the effect of the death-power of the Scorpion is graphically shown. This is indicated in still another picture, in Mark 13, with the 'flight in winter' [v. 13]: 'Pray that this will not take place in winter', that is, not to flee under the influence of this sign of death, which brings human beings into isolation and spiritual loneliness. In the yearly rhythm the Scorpion signifies the time [November] where natural life through the increasing winter rigidifying receives the sting of death.

The corresponding sentence in the Creed in the Act of Consecration of Man is completely attuned to Christ's overcoming of the Scorpion's power of death: 'Through Him can the Healing Spirit work', which very much helps us to participate in feeling the countersign of the Scorpion, the Venus-sign of the Bull, in which the healing power of love works.

In music the sign of the Scorpion corresponds to Db-major, which can be felt especially in its dark relative minor Bb-minor as the key of death and of the power of death. Chopin wrote his Funeral March in Bb-minor. Bach's Bb-minor Prelude in the *Well-Tempered Clavier* carries a most earnest character of Christ's Passion and of Golgotha. In Act II of Wagner's *Twilight of the Gods* the dark, black power of the elves, and in Act II of *Parsifal* the dark onslaught of Klingsor stand in Bb-minor. Wagner uses Db-major especially as the Venusberg-key [*Tannhäuser*], as the key of the Earth's lap (in the Venusberg sense). Also the Mystery of the gold in the depths of the Earth stands for Wagner in Db-major, standing in such a way when at the end of *Twilight of the Gods* as through a great alchemical process out of all the surging of darkness, at the conclusion the pure flow of gold, which rings out from the Rhine-daughters at the re-won golden Ring—this ending is in Db-major. Here, too, we perceive sounding in a significant way the occult heights and depths of the Scorpion-sign.

There would be many other things to say concerning this content-filled Scorpion-sign, rich in occult questions and contradictions. In a later *Contribution* [No. 23] on the four quadrants in the zodiac some things will be mentioned. In any case this has to be said, that many recent astrologers suppose an 'exaltation' of Uranus in the Scorpion. To me it is questionable whether with Uranus and Neptune such an 'exaltation' can be assumed at all, as it is with those planets lying within the orbit formed by Saturn, whether here there is not the effect of such an occult planet in one of the zodiac triangles appearing at this point (and with Uranus that would not be the sound-ether, but the light-ether-triangle). In any case, when it has to do with planets discovered in recent times, one can no longer appeal to an early tradition going back to primordial wisdom. Yet it can be admitted that the occult-esoteric, paradoxical character of the sign of the Scorpion, likewise the very occult-esoteric, problematical character of Uranus, correspond in many respects. Prominent personalities of the circle of priests—not the older ones amongst us—have Uranus in the Scorpion.

## *The Fishes*

Let us now proceed from the Mars-sign of the Scorpion to the next of the three signs of the sound-ether trigon, to the next of the three 'water-signs', to the Fishes, whose planetary ruler is Jupiter. Its second decanate belongs to the Moon, the ruler in the Crab, the third to Mars, the ruler in the Scorpion. Here it appears to us above all important that we have the co-rulership of Neptune with Jupiter. For when we proceed with the planetary ordering from the Sun, and then with the Goat find the Saturn-sign, and with the Waterman that is the Uranus-sign (the Saturn-sign is there for the Waterman, where we proceed for the ordering not from the Sun, but from the Moon), we find Neptune with the Fishes (the allocation of the Fishes to Jupiter results when we choose as point of departure not the Sun, but the Moon).

Now, the distant Neptune is, above all, the lord of the cosmic distances. Because the whole triangle is aligned to the sound-ether, and this sound-ether, cosmic music in particular, belongs to the forces of Neptune, I have spoken here, with Neptune in the Fishes, of the 'sound out of cosmic distances' in my books on the gospels [*John*, p. 74f.]. With the Baptism in the Jordan, which is to be conceived under the Fishes, there comes with this Jupiter-Christ influence (Jupiter always the planet of '*Kyrios Christus*' ['Christ the Lord']) there also enters this influence of Neptune, this 'sound out of cosmic distances'. In that the cosmic Christ, the Being of the cosmic distances, unites Himself with the Earth, we can, as it were, perceive this cosmic spheric sound (Neptune). And thereby at the same time the occult polarity is delineated, which corresponds to the sign of the Fishes (as we found with the Scorpion the contrast of Sun-heights of the Eagle and the dragon depths). It is the contrast that out of our liturgy we know very well as the *worlds afar* and the *Earth near* (cf. the Passion Epistle [of the Act of Consecration of Man]).

No sign is so much a sign of the nearness of the Earth, the direct earthly nature as that of the Fishes. In the gospel we find here above all the Washing of the Feet [John 13], the deepest humbling of Christ to the earthly world. (Most expressive are the words of Christian Morgenstern (1871-1914), from *Wir fanden einen Pfad* (1914, p. 61):

*Faßt ein Herz des Opfers Größe?*
*Misst ein Geist dies Opfer ganz? —*
*Wie ein Gott des Himmels Glanz*
*tauscht um Menschennot und -blöße!*

[*Prose tr.*: Can a heart grasp the greatness of this sacrifice? Can a spirit measure this sacrifice? How a God exchanges the heavenly splendour for human need and [human] dearth!]

From here we also understand best of all why the Fishes, as the 'sign of serving love', is the 'exaltation' of Venus, why above all it corresponds to the Christian sense of the Venus-sign. (This exaltation of Venus, alongside the Moon-decanate, brings the female impact into this sound-ether Fishes-sign with which Dr Steiner—as I want to add straight away—at least in one of the two orders also allocates to the sense of sound, the sense of hearing, with which in the other ordering would fall to the sign of the Crab, likewise belonging to the sound-ether triangle.) In the cosmogony of *Occult Science*, the Fishes signifies the sign in which the supesensory-etheric, primordial human being touched first of all the physical element of the fire-earth. On the human form, this sign corresponds to the feet (cf. the Washing of the Feet), that part with which the human being directly touches the Earth. The scheme given in the previous *Contribution* of the arrangement of the zodiac-signs to the supersensory members of the human being leads here to a very exalted member, namely to the Life-spirit, *buddhi*, to the human etheric body transformed through the power of Christ (the sign of the Fishes is the 'etheric' corner of the sound-ether triangle, the corner of this triangle belonging to the etheric cross, the Cross of the Son, or Christ-cross.)

From here we can also understand why the sign of the Fishes, in a special sense, is a Christ-sign. In the Creed the sentence which aligns with it is the only one beginning with the name [or rather title] 'Christ': 'Christ, through whom men attain the re-enlivening of the dying Earth-existence, is to this divine being as the Son born in eternity.' The word 'Son'—in his *Contributions* Frieling points this out—is also found here as the final word [in the original German] in a characteristic manner, likewise the elevated word 'eternity'. This is relatively seldom used in our liturgy, mostly replaced with another, like 'cycles of time to come' and similar phrases, indicating what lies on the farther side of the Saturn frontier, in the eternal, Uranian realm. This, too, helps us to think how the cosmically distant, trans-Saturnine Neptune is linked here to the *Christus-kyrios*-planet Jupiter.

Like the Scorpion, the Fishes-sign, too, is a strongly esoteric sign. Such signs are in the zodiac the fourth (the Crab), the eighth (the Scorpion), the twelfth (the Fishes). (If one takes the zodiac order, where one advances from the first to the sixth, then to the eleventh, and so on, that is, the key of fifths mentioned a few times, where one, however, always remains within the respective triangle, then the Fishes emerges as the eighth, the Scorpion as the twelfth sign, the Crab remains here too as the fourth stage.)

## *The 'Houses'*

In these *Contributions* I have spoken little of the 'houses' and 'fields' of the birth-horoscope but will do so here as occasion arises. (The details concerning these fields comes later, after the end of the Zodiac studies, that is perhaps next summer, depending on whether we are able to risk giving a special presentation on horoscopes, which will also depend to a large extent on the attitude or view of the circle of priests.) These twelve 'houses' or 'fields' of the horoscope are something essentially different from the twelve zodiac-signs, also the 'houses' of the planets, in so far as one understands with this their preferred realms of rulership (for example, the Lion of the house of the Sun, the Crab the house of the Moon, Fishes and Archer the houses of Jupiter, and so on). When 'houses' of the horoscope are discussed, we may not think why here instead of houses one also speaks of 'fields'. Nevertheless, a relationship of these 'houses' or 'fields' of the horoscope exists to the zodiacal concept of twelve.

These twelve houses or fields come about through the place and time of each birth-horoscope, for each human soul approaching earthly birth in a quite individual manner. The rising sign at birth is consequently the first house or field, the 'ascendant'. As a rule it will not coincide with one of the zodiac-signs [which would be at sunrise], but the point of the ascendant will be in some degree or other of such a zodiac-sign and then the respective first house or field—as a rule, not always—will stretch into the following zodiac-sign, up to a certain degree of this sign (through which this degree-limitation is determined, concerning this later, as far as I am able). In the same way, the second, third, etc. house or field is determined with each birth in quite an individual manner. What meaning is given to the individual fields I will also mention later. For now, only so much, that these twelve houses in a certain way nevertheless correspond to the twelve signs of the zodiac with which they in no way coincide.

The first house or field, if with its point it falls into the Scales, or into the Lion, or into the Fishes, or into the Scorpion, or wherever, is in a certain sense truly always the individual Ram of a birth-horoscope and in this sense truly connects the Ram-quality with the non-erased qualities of the respective zodiac-sign, which in this case is the point of the first house, forming the individual Ram of this birth-horoscope. In the same way, the second house is truly the individual Bull, the third house the individual Twins, the fourth house the individual Crab.

Here I come to the reason why I mention all this here: we spoke of the esoteric character of the three signs of the water-trigon, of the sound-etheric triangle: Crab, Fishes and Scorpion, that is the 4th, 8th and 12th of the twelve zodiac-signs. In the same way, it is assumed in birth-horoscope making, that the 4th, 8th and 12th house or field, that, is those houses, or rather fields, that correspond to the Crab, the Scorpion, the Fishes in the zodiac (but in no way coincide with them) have an especially esoteric, or occult, character: the 4th house, what is called the *imum coeli*, is the depth of the person's being. The 8th house is the 'house of death', but as such at the same time the esoteric field *par excellence*.

### The Fishes

The 12th house finally is seen as the 'house of difficult destinies' and corresponds in this sense to that which the Fishes sign is in the zodiac, as the sign of the Washing of the Feet, as the Christ-sign in a special sense (also the Transfiguration of Christ stands in the sign of the Fishes, as well as the 'Feeding of the Five Thousand', together with the Virgin the sign of the Fishes forms the 'Last-Supper constellation', the horizontal axis of the etheric-cross, the Cross of the Son). Furthermore, certain Mysteries of the birth-horoscope become understandable to us through the presentation of the zodiac triangles concerning the meaning and significance of the zodiac-signs. The *concept of twelve* signs of the zodiac, although in no way identical with the twelve houses or fields in the horoscope, nevertheless carries for these houses and with this for the main questions of the birth-horoscope, the actual key in itself.

In the circle of musical keys there corresponds to the sign of the Fishes the charming, nature-key of F-major, which we feel especially, too, as the key of the flowing wave. We may recall Beethoven's 'Pastoral' Symphony, and also the scene with the Rhine Daughters at the beginning of Act III of *Twilight of the Gods*. It has been said that F is in fact the primal tone of everything musical, that all natural sounds and noises, the murmuring of the spring, sighing of the forest lead towards it, that F somehow lies at the basis of all the weavings of nature. This, if it is correct, would agree very much that the sign of the Fishes, according to the zodiacal ordering of the twelve senses, is also brought into a relationship with the sense of hearing, to the sense of sound (although the fish itself is a mute animal, cf. Chr. Morgenstern's 'Fisches Nachtgesang', 'Fish's night-song').[249]

The inclusion of the 'sounds out of cosmic distances', of Neptune remains for us characteristic of the esoteric and occult nature of the sign of the Fishes. It agrees with the occult nature of the whole sound-etheric triangle that we found the light-ether triangle as the Uranus-triangle, compared to which we can call the sound-ether-triangle the Neptune-triangle. It is, on the other hand, also the Moon-triangle (facing the Sun-triangle as that of the warmth-ether). But precisely between Moon and Neptune the sound-ether, musical relationships rule, which we already thought of earlier in the discussion on the planets.

## The Crab

This leads us to study the last and highest of the three signs of the sound-ether trigon, the Moon-sign of the Crab. This sign of the Crab, too, shows the inner contradictory nature of the concept of occult opposites, [a characteristic] of all the signs of this occult-magical trigon. The Moon itself, the ruler in the Crab, is indeed the lord of the greatest contrasts, and as such also of the actual star of occultism (in Dr Steiner's Berlin lecture-course [GA 151, see footnote 29], of the seven world-conception moods the Moon belongs to occultism, and to the sign of the Crab belonging to it, materialism.) In the sense of the arrangement given by Dr Steiner, the following statement is correct: occultism (Moon), as the most sublime of all the world-conceptions penetrating into the depths, is at home in materialism (the Crab). This is not a conventional contradiction, but indeed a truth that needs to be understood. Here the word 'materialism' signifies not only what we initially understand by it, a remaining attached to the material things of the world, but, in a higher sense, a penetration of the Mysteries of matter. Matter in the sense of occultism is the most complicated of all world-conceptions, the most complicated and full of riddles of all revelations of the spirit. One can compare how silver, the metal belonging to the Moon, shows the most complicated of all principles of form, in its crystal-formations the most subtle branchings that one can find in the mineral collections.

Conventional materialism is precisely insufficient in order really to establish the foundations of matter, but the most sublime occultism is able to do this. Johannine occultism is the most sublime, penetrating into the cosmic-symphonic, cosmic-musical Mysteries, and those of transubstantiation of cosmic alchemy. With this triangle, we find ourselves in the sound-etheric realm of the Johannine trigon. Luke's Gospel belongs to the Bull, Mark's Gospel to the Lion, and John's Gospel belongs to the Eagle, which is the transformation and original form of the Scorpion. Through the Johannine initiation the Scorpion becomes changed into the Sun-Eagle, the power of death is changed into the virginal power of life. That we find the Christ-sign of the Fishes, the sign of serving love (exaltation of Venus) in the Johannine triangle, is without further ado clear and understandable. That the Crab = the Moon belongs to it, however, has a profound meaning.

## The Moon

We find the Sun precisely with the Lion of Mark, in the triangle of the warmth-ether; in the Johannine triangle of the sound-ether we find the Moon, which is the occult reflection of the Sun, containing in itself the Sun-Mysteries once more in an occult form. In my *Contributions* on the planets I have pointed to the pertinent passage in Rudolf Steiner's *Occult Science* (section on the Ancient Moon evolution). But I must say, in all these studies given in the whole presentation on the Mysteries of the stars, no section do I find so unsatisfactory as that of what is said concerning the Moon. With the Moon I always feel that it is and remains a riddle, the greatest of all riddles. In a certain sense this is understandable, for with the Moon it concerns precisely the 'star of occultism'. Of course, in anthroposophy we can find all the explanations in order to penetrate more deeply into the astrology of the Moon. But precisely because the material in this respect is so rich it is also so difficult to encompass. And everywhere one meets contradictions, or apparent contradictions, which are connected to the occult nature of the Moon. On the one hand the Moon is the star of the feminine, maternal nature, and on the other hand there proceeds from it the hardening, male forces of the head, of head activity, the forces ruling in the skeleton. (In this direction also lies the relationship of the Moon-forces to the forces of Saturn, concerning which details can be found in Rudolf Steiner's *Karmic Relationships* and elsewhere. A conjunction Moon-Saturn in the horoscope frequently expresses a hardening in the organism; for this reason, in astrology it is regarded as unfavourable.)

Alongside this relationship of the Moon to the head, to the forces of thinking of the head (abstract thinking), on the other hand we learn in anthroposophy, at the opposite pole to the head, those of the reproductive forces. Of the seven etheric 'movements' in the etheric organism the Moon corresponds to the lowest, the 'movement of reproduction' (Rudolf Steiner, *The Human Being in the Light of Occultism, Theosophy and Philosophy*, Christiania 2-12 June 1912. GA 137). With women the physical body is lunar, the etheric body solar; with men it is the opposite, the physical body is solar and the etheric body lunar. The aspects everywhere mutually cross here.

In this sense already earlier we could point to the double nature of the Moon, that the Moon is the lowest of all, the most earthly, for human beings the reflection and the mask of the personal aspect (as the reflection of the Sun, which presents the being, the higher individuality of the human being). But the Moon is also the most occult of all, the most difficult to grasp, that which is aligned in the human being to the realm of the cosmic-occult and cosmic music. Here in the horoscope to indicate the issues, to recognize where and how far the Moon with a human being is only the usual earthly Moon and what is has to do with personality, and how far it is the 'occult Moon' can be exceptionally difficult. In my earlier *Contributions* I have pointed to this double nature of the Moon that also has a reflection purely astronomically. Concerning this, we know that the Moon has two sides, the one which it always turns to us, and the other that we never see [directly], that is for us, also purely outwardly in the purely astronomical sense there also remains the hidden, 'occult' side. On the one side the Moon reflects the Earth, and the other side reflecting the cosmos; it is the great cosmic, starry observatory, about which Dr Steiner frequently spoke. Here we should recall how according to anthroposophy with the Moon daemonic beings of the lowest order are linked in a spiritual context and, on the other hand, spiritual beings of the highest order. The spiritual being Yahveh is linked with the Moon, precisely with the task, like earthly silver, to correct and balance the Luciferic beings that are connected to the Sun (to which earthly gold belongs). Dr Steiner has frequently spoken how the sublime spiritual teachers of primordial times, the early Indian teachers, now inhabit the spiritual Moon-sphere, have 'withdrawn into the Moon-fastnesses'.

All this is not meant to be taken as dogma but places us before an abundance of riddles. To the last-mentioned fact the other can be placed, that the Moon indeed with the early Indians played a special role, that its whole astrology was a Moon-astrology. They observed differently than we do today the details and differentiations of the Moon's position. The primal Indian cultural epoch is that when the spring equinox was in the Moon-sign of the Crab. Right into the story of the Buddha this preferential position of the Moon in the Crab was highly significant—all significant events in Buddha's life took place when the Moon stood in the Crab.

Everything said here concerning the Moon we could somehow extend to the zodiac-sign of the Crab, where the Moon is lord in the house: the Crab is the zodiacal revelation of those influential forces whose planetary expression is the Moon. As the Moon in its phases is a wandering star, the Crab is the changing sign, where in the summer solstice it changes its course, it enters its retrograde movement, its Crab walk. (It has been said often and clearly enough that here the discussion is not of the sign of the Crab.) Like the Moon, the Crab, related in the human figure to the ribcage, carries in itself the earthly-hardening forces. As the world-conception 'materialism' belongs to it, the Crab has the one, lower, usual side, and the other higher occult, Johannine side. In the Crab the Johannine initiation is completed (more details in the book on *Mark's Gospel*). Both claws of the Crab, which at the same time correspond to 'both ribs' (or sides of the ribcage), there corresponds, too, the two impulses, the impulse of the past, the one at the end, and the Christ-impulse of the future, which is at the beginning; the contrast of the old body inherited from Adam and the new, of the resurrection-body, point in the same direction. Likewise, the picture of the old and of the new temple, which in the gospel plays the well-known role (see the book on *Mark's Gospel*). In the same sense the 'two donkeys' indicate this, which in Matthew's Gospel accompany Christ's Entry into Jerusalem. The other gospels only recognize one, the young donkey; the other coming from the past, the inherited physical body from Adam, is the 'old donkey'.

All this helps us to see how with the Crab and the Moon we stand before strange, characteristic occult Mysteries that bear in themselves apparent contradictions. Like the two other signs of the Johannine triangle, also the Moon-sign of the Crab as well as the Moon itself reveals this occult dual nature; the relationship of the Moon to the occult Neptune rests on this occult, mysterious element.

## The Moon and Neptune

The relationship of the Mood to the occult Neptune, which in these studies we already considered, rests on this occult Mystery. Neptune is indeed, besides Jupiter, the lord in the Fishes, as the Moon is in the Crab. Consequently, we can call the whole triangle the Moon-triangle (in contrast to the Sun-triangle of the warmth-ether), but also the Neptune-triangle (in contrast to the Uranus-triangle of the light-ether). The warmly radiating Sun belongs to the masculine warmth-ether (although its main ether is the life-ether). The coolly radiating Moon belongs to the (feminine) sound-ether. The masculine element is the warm one, the feminine the cool one (Wachsmuth, Vol. 2, Chapter 1, orders Mars and Moon to the chemical-ether, or sound-ether, which corresponds very much to its placement in the sound-ether triangle; moreover, the viewpoints cross here, in as far as the outer planets are determined mostly by the warmth-ether and light-ether, and the inner planets more from the chemical-ether and life-ether.)

In the sound-ether there exists the main relationship of the Moon to Neptune, as both are related to water (one may think of the influence of the Moon on the tides of the sea). The name Neptune, too, is no arbitrary name, but the relationship to water and the element of the sea does indeed exist. With regard to the spirit, Neptune is often more earthly than Uranus, which is nearer to the Earth, although between the earthly Moon and the distant Neptune no actual astronomical relationship exists; if Neptune has nothing to do with the earthly Moon also in this regard, then in astrology the relationship exists between what the Moon means for the Earth and what Neptune means for the Earth (in this way the astrological expression should always be understood). And this lies in the magical, cosmic musical, sound-etheric element. In a conjunction between the Moon and Neptune, especially when it occurs in a musical sign like the Bull or the Crab, this can be expressed in a horoscope. The occult element of the two planets can be very much enhanced through such a conjunction, and the Moon in its occult nature through this is strongly emphasized.

No yet emphasized was that the Moon-sign Crab is also seen as the enhanced Jupiter. This is ancient tradition and corresponds to the existing relationship between the Moon and Jupiter, through which especially the personal aspect in the horoscope is lifted, giving Jupiter recognition, expansion, stature and fullness. It should be recalled that the sign of the Crab lies today in the zodiac of the Twins, that is, in that starry region that we can regard as the actual climax of the zodiac, the summit of the sacred mountain, over the shining Sirius-Orion.

The Moon-Crab musical key is the light-filled A-major which Wagner in *Lohengrin* has expressively chosen as the Grail-key, as the 'key of the far-distant Grail'. This also corresponds to the Johannine character of this sign. In Wagner's *Lohengrin* (Prelude, swan, Grail-narration) we perceive very clearly the Neptunian 'sound from cosmic distances', which relates to this whole zodiac-triangle. Wagner himself has a characteristically emphasized Neptune in his birth-horoscope.

# XXIII
# The Four Quadrants in the Zodiac

After the three crosses as well as the four triangles in the zodiac, the triangles of the four elements and four kinds of ether have been discussed, still not all viewpoints have been mentioned from which the spirituality of the zodiac can be viewed. The things brought in what follows I do not draw from any astrological textbook (from which in general I do not draw at all, although one often has to take a position to what is said in them), and also not from any tradition. It is a viewpoint that has yet nowhere been presented. *It came to me purely out of anthroposophy.* But I have also spoken about this to non-anthroposophical astrologers to whom this point of view immediately made sense. I look forward to developing it, because here we obviously find ourselves more than with all earlier discussions on a purely anthroposophical ground, and certainly this viewpoint immediately connects to what Dr Steiner has given in the well-known lectures on the four archangels (Michael, Gabriel, Raphael and Uriel), important for everything liturgical, then once more summarized in the Dornach lecture of 13 October 1923 [*The Four Seasons and the Archangels*, GA 229], as an Archangel Imagination. There he describes how in spring, at Eastertide, a revelation of Raphael arises, who during St John's-tide passes over to Uriel. During Michaelmas Michael, the archangel of the Sun, follows and during Christmastide Gabriel, the archangel of the Moon. Raphael is the being of Mercury; about the Mystery of Uriel we will have to speak later.

Through the changing revelation of these four beings, the yearly rhythm is divided into four equal sections. These are, since everything is to relate to the zodiac, initially the earthly zodiac behind which the starry zodiac stands, the 'four quadrants', about which I will speak in what follows.

With the whole way they rhythmically mutually alternate, Rudolf Steiner refers to the well-known words of Faust:[250]

*Wie alles sich zum Ganzen webt,*
*Eins in dem andern wirkt und lebt!*

*Wie Himmelskräfte auf und nieder steigen*
*Und sich die goldnen Eimer reichen!*
*Mit segenduftenden Schwingen*
*Vom Himmel durch die Erde dringen,*
*Harmonisch all das All durchklingen!*
To build the Whole how each part weaves,
One in the other works and lives!
How heavenly powers are rising and descending,
The golden vessels to each other lending!
Their pinions redolent with blessing,
Down through the Earth from heaven pressing,
Harmonious all the All embracing!

Rudolf Steiner draws attention in particular to the line: 'Down through the earth from heaven pressing', whereby 'pressing [251] *through* the Earth' can initially be difficult for the understanding, but at least calls up the feeling that Goethe may not have thought much about, or invested much meaning in, this surprising word. But Dr Steiner emphasizes that spiritual-scientific examination reveals the opposite. Here lies an exact occult fact, precisely in this word 'through'. For always, when an archangel is revealed above in the earthly zodiac there will be another one on the opposite side, below the Earth, working with the first one. The streams of activity really go through the Earth. This is to be understood in such a way: when Raphael during the spring, at Eastertide and later, is revealed above in the airy regions, Michael opposite him, is revealed under the Earth, approaching the human soul from the other side (this, of course, is always to be understood applying to one side of the Earth, for if it is summer above, below it is winter, when above is spring, then below is autumn, and vice versa). Consequently, this means when Raphael for the northern hemisphere is above, he is felt by the southern hemisphere below, when Michael for the southern hemisphere is below, he is found above. It is the same for Uriel and Gabriel. Precisely through looking at the whole of the Earth, at the various earthly hemi-spheres and their inversions of the annual seasons, the relationship of the four seasonal archangels, their whole rhythmic play, becomes quite graphic [like a round-dance].

Soon I will show how all this will broaden and complement the aspect of the four triangles in the zodiac, with their relationship to the four elements and kinds of ether. For also with the four archangels and the quadrants of the yearly rhythm relating to them, we will find such a relationship to the elements and the kinds of ether.

## *The Waterman Sign*

In order to make the needs of the whole discussion still more clear, I intend to touch on a critical point over which during the previous discussions perhaps some might already have stumbled. There is the story of the Waterman, of which we claim it is an 'air-sign', belonging to the element of air and the light-ether. This is not tradition, but also in anthroposophy it is not given differently (Wachsmuth, II, p. 15): here the Waterman is related to the light-ether, which according to all anthroposophical indications clearly corresponds to the element of air. This means, there is no doubt about the relationship of the Waterman to the light-ether, air-element; it is unshakable. It is simply incorrect to count the Waterman, simply because he is called Waterman, to what are called the water-signs. (I have to acknowledge that in this connection in the Appendix to the book on *Mark's Gospel* (2014, p. 418) certain errors have crept in, which in the book on *John's Gospel* have been corrected. For when I wrote the book on *Mark's Gospel*, I was a completely empty page as regards astrology. Only when the Mark-book was already printed, did I learn a few things from tradition through astrological acquaintances. In this case, not only tradition speaks, but also anthroposophy speaks clearly *against* setting up a relationship of the Waterman to the water-trigon (even if it is admitted that with drawing in the four temperaments the viewpoints cross once again; more on this in the book on *John's Gospel*).

We may not relate the Waterman, then, to the water-triangle. And yet something in us, in deeper levels of consciousness, does not feel quite happy and satisfied about it. Why the *Water*man, if the water plays no role at all? Is the name Waterman to be a pure coincidence? This could be, but we more frequently experience that the names are somehow meaningful. Should this not be the case with the 'Waterman'?

A similar, only a reversed situation exists when we align the 'Scorpion' to the water-signs. All these designations would be justified with regard to the essence of these signs. Now the Scorpion is absolutely not a water animal, and mainly and essentially neither is the serpent. With the Scorpion, with the poison of the serpent, we think rather of something hot and fiery. How, then, does the Scorpion, the serpent, come under the 'Water-signs'? Here, too, we do not need to doubt that our triangle ordering is correct. I will attempt to show the question of the 'Waterman' is solved from the viewpoint of the four quadrants. This viewpoint will reveal how here, too, the viewpoints cross. How each sign, without damaging its position in one of the triangles of the elements, through the quadrants in which it stands, receives yet another subsidiary emphasis from one of the other elements. Only with every last sign of a quadrant does the aspect of the elements of the quadrant coincide with that of the respective element-triangle. Further details should now be given in what follows.

## The Spring Quadrant

Let us first of all look at the spring quadrant, the Raphael quadrant. It embraces the signs (not constellations) Ram, Bull and Twins. From our presentation we know the Ram as the fire-sign (warmth-ether), the Bull as the earth-sign (life-ether) and the Twins as the air-sign (light-ether). Now, in the Dornach lecture it is shown how in spring the healing forces of Raphael-Mercury in the airy regions of the Earth are revealed. During the spring Raphael-Mercury, 'the great cosmic-physician of mankind', allows his healing streams to flow into the nature-forces. At the same time Michael appears at this time to approach humanity, giving human beings the active, motor impulse. In the autumn Michael becomes the cosmic spirit, and the healing forces of Raphael take hold of people's breathing, the inner air-element of the human being: 'Raphael is the spirit of spring, who circles the Earth, and who during the autumn actually fashions the human breathing system.' In the breathing system, as Dr Steiner always emphasizes, originally all the healing forces reside. (Amongst the organs, Mercury belongs to the lungs.) And the spring allows us to breathe the outer air afresh, to feel the healing, enlivening, harmonizing, rhythm-enlivening [power] that is expressed so beautifully in the Easter Epistle of the Act of Consecration of Man.

From all this we can clarify that the first of the four quadrants is understandable, the spring-quadrant (relating to the zodiac: Ram, Bull and Twins), as the air-quadrant, correspondingly also to that of the light-ether; for the spring is indeed the time of the rising light. This completely agrees, however, only with the last of the signs coming into consideration here, the sign of the Twins, which indeed belongs absolutely to Mercury (Raphael, Hermes), and which is both an air-sign and a light-ether sign. Here the aspect of the quadrants coincides with the aspect of the triangles, whereas Ram and Bull belong to other elements (fire and earth). But here, too, we will feel: although Ram and

Bull are not air-signs, but in the sense of the rising light of the year, are they not in a certain sense light-signs? They were felt by the early peoples as such. With the Egyptians, the character of light of the Bull, and with the Greeks that of the Ram—of which also the 'Golden Fleece' reminds us—plays a great role (cf. in my book on *John's Gospel* [2015, p. 177], it is pointed out how Ram and Bull in the early Mysteries are signs of the primordial revelation of light, how the word for cow and cattle in Indian, in the Vedas, still means the light rays, as it is to be found as in the words 'horns'—ram's horn, bull's horns, as is similar in Indian and Hebrew and the riddle of the ram's horns in the figure of Moses by Michelangelo [cf. Ex. 34: 29].[252]

This means, especially with the Ram and Bull, that apart from their primary relationship to other elements, we feel them very strongly as signs of the rising light. This is explained, although not through their triangles, but nevertheless through the nature of the quadrant in which they stand. And these are the forces of Raphael-Mercury and the air and light ether-forces, which coming in the concluding sign of this quadrant in the Mercury air-sign of the Twins, are also revealed through the Trigon. The *healing* quality of the Raphael-forces is also expressed in the sign of the Bull, where Venus connecting to Mercury—the second decanate belongs to Mercury—is revealed as the healing force of love. When, besides Raphael-Mercury who work from outside during this spring season, Michael the Sun-archangel approaches the human being from within, this is expressed especially in the sign of the Ram. Here besides the influence of Mars, the Sun as the enlivening Sun is in its exaltation, and the individual decanates fall to Mars, the Sun and Jupiter.

## The Quadrant: Summer

We move on to the next, to the summer-quadrant. It embraces the signs Crab, Lion and Virgin. In clear Imaginations, Dr Steiner describes how the earnest gaze of Uriel, revealed in the gold of the Sun penetrates out of the cosmic widths into the earthly depths, comparing the perfection of the crystalline world there with human imperfections and errors; how a raying, silvery radiance from Uriel is transformed into cosmic Sun-gold. (The same silvery raying and golden raying in the subsequent season is Imaginatively revealed in Michael's radiant garment.) Gabriel works into the Earth in the silvery Moon-element; Uriel works in the periphery. During this time—Dr Steiner emphasizes in his lecture on Uriel—the human being is mostly entangled in nature, that is, in the earthly aspect. The revelation of the earthly, of the Earth's interior, shines most strongly in the cosmic light.

We can call this section of the annual rhythm the earth-quadrant, which at the same time has to be the life-ether quadrant; it is the time of the highest springing of life in the earthly sphere. And the earthly sphere here to the greatest degree meets with the highest and purest ether-spheres, as expressed in the Epistle for St John's-tide. The exchange of earthly Moon-silver and the Sun-gold we find here, too, in the respective zodiac-signs, for the Crab is the Moon-sign, the Lion the Sun-sign, and the Virgin, the alchemical Mercury-sign, corresponding to the alchemical character of this season, also emphasized by Dr Steiner. He once uses the expression: 'the earthly silver in a cosmic-alchemical process is changed above into cosmic gold'.

One sees again how Dr Steiner's indications very much agree with the astrological viewpoints. Once again, the final sign of this quadrant, the Virgin as 'earth-sign', once again agrees in the trigon-aspect with that of the quadrant.

Gabriel, the co-ruler of this section, comes again to expression in the first sign, the Moon-sign of the Crab (similar to the previous quadrant of the Michael-Sun in the Sun-exaltation of the Mars-sign of the Ram); Uriel, the main ruler of this season, stands beyond the seven planets. Concerning its relationship to the Sun and Mercury, concerning the whole problem under consideration, I will say a few things at the end.

## The Autumn Quadrant

We next arrive at the autumn quadrant, the Michael quadrant. In Dr Steiner's descriptions [op. cit.], Uriel transforms the healing forces of Raphael into forces of cosmic thinking. Michael transforms these forces into motoric forces, into will-impulses:

> And just as Gabriel passes on to Raphael the nutritive forces, to be transmuted into forces of healing—in other words, he passes on his golden vessel—and just as Raphael passes on his golden vessel to Uriel, whereby the healing forces are made into the forces of thought, so it is Michael who receives from Uriel the thought-forces, and through the power of cosmic iron, out of which his sword is forged, transforms these thought-forces into forces of will, so that in man they become the forces of movement.

And he speaks of the 'the golden vessels of nourishment, of healing, of the forces of thought and of movement'. In the zodiac we find here as the first sign the Ram, as second the Scorpion—questions about this have already been discussed—the third the Archer. Michael has always been attributed holding the Scales, as the 'Scales of Justice' in his hand. In the *Dream Song of Olaf Åsteson*,[253] this is expressed in a manner recalling the early Egyptian tradition. Venus-Urania, the governess of this sign, also appears in the Greek Mysteries as the 'Venus of the world-judgement', 'Aphrodite-Nemesis'. In the Creed the corresponding sentence runs: 'He will in time unite for the advancement of the world with those whom, through their bearing, He can wrest from the death of matter.'

The actual element of Michael and of Michael's fiery sword is precisely the fire-element, the warmth-ether, with which the 'I', the ego-strength belonging to Michael, is kindled. The forces of ripeness and of the seed-forces that are manifested during the autumn are related to this fire-element; in the seed the fire-beings are revealed. With these forces at this time the airy, healing forces of Raphael unite, which now from within, in the breathing, approach the human being. The Mercury-decanate of the Scales-sign points to this (in which Venus and Mercury are closely linked). The fiery Michaelic element is revealed again here in the concluding sign ruled by Jupiter, the fire-sign of the Archer, in whose decanates Jupiter, Mars and the Sun are divided (this is always the Michaelic triad). Here again it is the final, closing sign of the quadrant in which the trigonal aspect and the one of the quadrants coincide:

- the Archer is the fire-sign in the fire-quadrant, as
- the Twins that of the air-sign in the air-quadrant,
- the Virgin that of the earth-sign in the earth-quadrant.

The Archer as the motoric sign in particular suits well the mobile, motor-forces of Michael. As ascendant in horoscopes, too, it is the sign that lends easy mobility to the body. As the sign of the life-stream of Golgotha it is also the sign of the emerging Church ('Communities whose members feel the Christ within them …' [from the Creed]); for us it is above all and in the first line the sign of our Movement, which in connection to the forces of Michael will always stay connected. That part of Michaelic activities proved through the astrology of the three planetary forces—Sun, Mars and Jupiter—is very significant and clear. The Sun participates in Michaelic activities, since Michael is the Archangel of the Sun; Mars participates because Michael utilizes the cosmic iron, because the highest, most noble and most cosmic forces of Mars are at work through him. Jupiter participates because indeed Jupiter-Zeus (the Indian Indra; Teutonic Thor-Donar) controls the Michaelic weapon of cosmic, etheric lightning.

We have still to discuss the middle sign of this quadrant, the Scorpion, in which Mars and Jupiter are likewise involved as the decanate rulers. This sign has raised the question: how does it transpire that this, in some ways a hot sign, actually comes to be a 'water-sign'? Now we have the solution: the Scorpion is certainly a water-sign (chemical-ether, sound-ether), but at the same time it stands in the hot fire-quadrant, and when water and fire meet, it tends to sizzle. This corresponds well to the nature of this sign, as well as the nature of the serpent belonging to it (the dragon of Michael). We know the Scorpion as the sign that unites the greatest contrasts, highest heights and deepest depths. Water and fire amongst the four elements are those which form the sharpest contrast (warmth and light, or fire and air, are accommodating between themselves, likewise earth and water; contrasting are fire and earth; air and earth; water and air. But none of these contrasts is so hostile as that of water and fire. As a meeting in the zodiac we find them only once: with the Scorpion, which is the water-sign in the fire-quadrant (a fire-sign in the water-quadrant does not exist; the fire would be immediately quenched, whereas the water in the fire-quadrant manifests the sizzle).

## The Quadrant: Winter

The remaining quadrant, that of the winter season with its rain and snow, would be the water-quadrant, in which Gabriel rules, the Moon-archangel. The signs of this quadrant are Archer, Waterman and Fishes (with which Gabriel is involved as the ruler of the decanate). Here we finally reach the point which also solves for us the question concerning the Waterman. We have seen and could not shift the fact that the Waterman is an air-sign and light-ether sign. And now at the same time its relationship to the water-element, from which it gets is name, indeed comes out; it stands after all in the water-quadrant, as the air-sign in the water-quadrant. The actual water-sign in the water-quadrant is here, too, the third, concluding sign, the sign of the Fishes, in which the watery Neptune is co-ruler.

Gabriel approaches from without, whereas the testing and judging Uriel is revealed in this season, approaching people from within. This provides the opportunity once again to return to the question of this archangel standing outside the seven planets (whereas the three others coincide with the beings of the Sun, Moon and Mercury, whereby the Mercury-being gains a certain touch of Venus, and the Sun-being a touch of Mars, of Michaelic iron). For this time of the highest abundance of the year and the warmth, one might think of the Sun-archangel, but we know that he, Michael, belongs to another season. For Uriel we are not able, as with the others, to find one of the seven planets. Otherwise, normally the ruler of the season appears in the last, the co-ruler in the first of the three signs of a quadrant:

- in the air-quadrant Raphael-Mercury in the Twins, Mars-Sun in the Ram;
- in the fire-quadrant Mars-Sun in the Archer decanate, Mercury in the Scales-decanate.

In the conclusion of the Uriel-quadrant in the Virgin we have Mercury, Saturn and Venus, and the named three, with the primacy of Saturn, we have in the first sign of the Waterman-quadrant; where is the relationship to Uriel in this?

This being, existing beyond the seven planets, Dr Steiner says in the Uriel (St John's) lecture, whose intelligence basically consists of the weaving together of the planets of our solar system, is supported through the zodiacal influences of the fixed stars. He adds that in his own thinking Uriel actually carries in himself cosmic thoughts. Thereby basically that being is described that, without identifying too narrowly and one-sidedly, we call the planet of the same name, Uranus, as the representative of the trans-Saturnine, starry realm beyond the planets. This viewpoint, furthermore, is strengthened by Dr Steiner through filling-out the picture with a Uriel Imagination, as the picture of the dove arises, in connection with the spirit-Father, material-Mother and Son. The signs of the three decanates that come into consideration (Saturn, Venus and Mercury) become understandable when we consider how Saturn always relates to Uranus (Uranus, the boundary of Ancient Saturn, out of which the planet Uranus joined during Ancient Sun). And Mercury, which in the decanate of the Virgin and of the Archer as it were plays a role as representative of Uriel, is viewed in astrology as the lower octave of Uranus (Uranus as the higher octave of Mercury). A similar relationship also exists with the Sun and Venus.

There appears in the actual Uriel-quadrant firstly the Moon-sign, then the Sun-sign, then the Venus-Mercury sign. In all this there lie indications at the same time about Uranus, of the trans-planetary realm. At the high summertime the earthly [being] mostly streams into the cosmos, into the actual starry regions, which in Uranus have their planetary representative. And the picture of the dove is connected with the Uranus-question, expressing higher cosmic, starry being. In the gospel it appears where Uranus is involved, from where the Christ descended to the Earth. And we have mentioned here one of the most interesting passages, where Dr Steiner, without mentioning the name Uranus, helps us to find an answer to the Uranus-question. It is hidden in a manner that brings light to many astrological matters, behind the name governing the high summertime, *Uriel*.

# XXIV
# The Cosmogonic-Esoteric Viewpoint of the Zodiac

## *According to the Anthroposophical Calendar of the Soul [1912-13]*

To conclude this study of the zodiac, I would like to bring something purely anthroposophical, which after the various aspects that we have already got to know, finally can bring a still most important and most eminent viewpoint of the zodiac lying completely in the esoteric realm. What we have is based on Dr Steiner's notes given to Frl. v. Eckardstein, who made the designs for the *Anthroposophical Calendar of the Soul* [1912-13]. They refer to the cosmogonic and esoteric meaning of these pictures. As is well-known, they are concerned to represent the twelve zodiac-signs. Through a coincidence I came across these notes through Frau Dr Steiner.

The pictures lying at the basis of these remarks are perhaps not known to everyone without more ado [since the first edition was not reissued. But a facsimile edition (2003)[254] is now fortunately available]. *The Anthroposophical Calendar* is a simple annual calendar; it begins with the real spiritual beginning of the year, that is, with the corresponding month of April (the exact beginning would be 21st March) and from there leads through the circle of the year, that is, March forms the ending. We know that the rhythm of the year begins on 21st March with the sign of the Ram—or rather, we name this first section of the year (month) the 'sign of the Ram'. We know, furthermore, that the Sun today for the greater part of this section of the year still stands in the constellation of the Fishes (only in the very first days of the sign of the Ram does it arrive at the constellation of the Ram), that is, the sign Ram today essentially orientates to the constellation of the Fishes. The earthly Ram, we can also say, lies today essentially in the heavenly Fishes. *The Anthroposophical Calendar* is given according to the heavenly, not according to the earthly orientation; it takes into account the starry constellation, not the sign, and the drawings by Frl. v. Eckardstein relate to the heavenly pictures, not to the earthly signs. Thus, at the end of the rhythm of the year in March, we meet once again the constellation of the Fishes.

The middle of March (still lying in the sign of the Fishes) already has the Fishes constellation, for the constellations are unequal in size, whereas the signs are all of equal size, and the Fishes constellation belongs to the larger sign. In the first week of March the Fishes sign corresponds to the constellation of the Waterman.

In the *Anthroposophical Calendar* it is so that the constellation of the Fishes touches the beginning and the end of the rhythm of the year. And the whole *Calendar* relates to this normal rhythm of the year.

With the esoteric explanations given by Dr Steiner of the zodiac-pictures of the *Calendar*, the viewpoint is another. Here it has to do not with the usual course of the year, also not simply with the 'great cosmic year' of 25,920 years (that within the whole of Earth-evolution has already been repeated many times), but with the evolution of the Earth as such and with the manner how within esoteric development it is inwardly imitated and recollected. But here, too, we find the rhythm of the great cosmic year, the recession of the spring equinox through [all] twelve zodiac-signs during long periods of time, established by Dr Steiner. The age of the Fishes (in which we stand today) followed that of the Ram, and the age of the Waterman will follow that of the Fishes. So, too, the greater rhythm to which Rudolf Steiner relates, continues from the Fishes (which forms the beginning) to the Waterman, then to the Goat, to the Archer, and so on. It is the rhythm which he established of John's Gospel, or the beginning of John's Gospel. Thereby we may also say that precisely the constellation in which today, or since the beginning of the Christian era, the spring equinox lies, is that rhythm in which also the great primordial spring equinox had begun, which spiritually corresponds to the actual beginning of the Earth. Here the constellation of the Fishes, which for us today signifies the beginning of the rhythm of the year, is brought together spiritually with the primordial beginning of the Earth. That is, not with Ancient Saturn, but with that which is called the Saturn-repetition within Earth-evolution, the 'first round' (Saturn-round) of Earth-evolution. After each of these rounds there follows once more a 'cosmic night', a *pralaya*; the first *pralaya* follows the Sun-round, the second the Moon-round; only the fourth round is the actual 'Earth-round'.

## The Fishes

All this takes place in unimaginable periods of time, no longer conceivable in concepts of earthly time. Within this fourth Earth-round

Saturn, Sun and Moon are repeated in specific manner, for the primordial beginning time of these rounds, the 'Polarian age' is the 'Earth-Saturn age', the following 'Hyperborean age' is the 'Earth-Sun age', the following 'Lemurian-age' the 'Earth-Moon age'. Here now in the *Calendar* the first picture with the Fishes is to relate to the first round, the Saturn-round, the primordial evolution of the Earth, and Dr Steiner gives as an explanation of this picture [see Fig. 1] the words: '*Die Erdenkeime treten aus dem Weltenschoße hervor, in dunkler Wärme*'—'The earthly germs come forth from the cosmic womb in dark warmth.'

The first germs had an elongated, elliptic form (this form clearly appears in the drawing in the *Calendar*). But through delicate shading the limbs of matter and organs that are to be formed later are inherent. Saturn-repetition in the fiery darkness. (Here, then, is clearly stated that it does not concern the primordial Saturn, but the repetition of Saturn within earthly evolution. As such one can well imagine the constellation of the Fishes with its unique darkness (in which only two equal stars clearly come to the fore; Dr Steiner, too, adds in the sketch two elongated ellipses) as a heavenly picture of that primordial-Earth-darkness.

One experiences the spiritual side of the Fishes as the Mystery of preparation of the germs, with everything inherent, ripening and lying in the darkness. In the yearly rhythm the Fishes is the sign that precedes the actual activity of the events of the year, in the same way as in the daily rhythm in the hour before sunrise (in the Fishes one wakes up, in the Ram one gets up). If one regards the whole thing esoterically as a meditation, then with the darkness of the Fishes one can perceive the spiritual placing of oneself at the zero-point of becoming, in the darkness where the light springs forth.

## The Waterman

We come to the next picture, to the one of the Waterman-sign. This means, in the *Calendar* in the usual yearly rhythm, of course, the Ram follows. But with the viewpoint on which Dr Steiner founds his notes for Frl. v. Eckardstein, the rhythm is another, that of the great cosmic year; here following the Fishes comes the Waterman, then the Goat, and so on.

To this picture of the Waterman [see Fig. 2] Dr Steiner has given the words: '*Sonnen-Wiederholung im Luftförmig-Gasigen*'—'Repetition of the [Ancient] Sun in the airy forms of the gaseous condition.' On

Ancient Sun the evolution of the element of Saturn-warmth advances to the air-element (to the gaseous state), whereby upwards the light-ether is differentiated (we also know this relationship of the airy element to the light-ether from our presentation of the zodiac-triangle). We find the same now in the second round of Earth-evolution, where the Earth goes through the repetition of the Ancient Sun condition (it is never a complete repetition, but always one which adapts to the new context now to be formed on the Earth, above all adapting to the becoming 'I').

In the drawing for the Waterman, as is found in the *Calendar*, we clearly notice this Sun-filled element: out of the dark, swirling formations filling the lower part of the picture, something like a radiant Sun is emerging above. This Sun-quality in the picture presenting the Waterman, its attempted relationship to the Sun-repetition of the Earth, seems significant when we recall from the earlier account the relationship of the Sun-quality to the Uranian, as it is expressed in the Waterman and in the zodiac-axis Waterman–Lion. (The counter-sign of the Waterman, the Lion, is indeed the Sun-sign *par excellence*.) On the Ancient Sun (one finds it expressly in Dr Steiner's Düsseldorf lecture-cycle [GA 110]) the planet Uranus coming indeed out of the Uranian realm, the Uranus-periphery, to the solar system; consequently, the relationship between the Sun and Uranus, known to all astrologers.

From the esoteric aspect, all the contexts become clear in this picture, linking to the Marriage in Cana (more details in my book on *John's Gospel*).

## *The Goat*

Then follows (we have to progress from the latter part towards the beginning of the book) the picture of the Goat, in whose presentation inspired by Dr Steiner, the motif (repeatedly indicated) of the Goat's horns in the dark field clearly comes to the fore [see Fig. 3]. In the heavenly constellation of the Goat there are two very characteristic stars representing these 'horns of the Goat'. In Dr Steiner's Notes we find here the words: '*Mond-Wiederholung, es bildet sich das Wässerige'*—'Repetition of the [Ancient] Moon, the watery element is formed.' Out of *Occult Science*, it is known how, after the air-forms have been fashioned on Ancient Sun, on Ancient Moon the watery (etheric-watery) condition is added, while at the same time upwards the sound-ether is differentiated. After, with the second zodiac-picture, we were with the Waterman, at the repetition of the [Ancient] Sun of earthly evolution, we arrive now to its third stage or 'round', to the Moon-repetition, that relates to the constellation of the Goat. The Waterman, through its countersign the Lion brings the indication of the Sun-quality; the Goat through its countersign the Crab brings the indication of the Moon-quality. The Goat itself we know as the Saturn-sign, the 'dark' Saturn-sign, whereas the bright Waterman is the bright Saturn–Uranus-sign. (With Dr Steiner's sketch this contrast of the bright Waterman and the dark Goat appears very clearly.) Saturn and Moon, like lead and silver, are inwardly related, concerning which we find further details in Dr Steiner's *Karmic Relationships* [Bk. 2, GA 236, 6th lecture, 4 May 1914]. Both are related to that which leads into matter, what hardens into material. In the way Dr Steiner wanted this figure of the Goat drawn, we also find echoes of the well-known sign of the Crab.

## The Archer

After the Goat, we come now to the Archer as the fourth stage in the process of Earth-evolution. After the Saturn-repetition, the Sun-repetition and the Moon-repetition now follows the actual Earth-stage of evolution. Dr Steiner points to this in his indications to the drawing for the Archer: *'Erde, es gliedert sich heraus das Feste'*—'Earth, the solid element is precipitated.' In a certain sense this forming or precipitating of the solid element indeed only takes place in Atlantean times, in the later part of this age. That cannot be meant here, because with the *next* picture the division of the genders is indicated, and this took place already in the Lemurian age. With the picture for the Archer the Earth-round as such must be meant, including its earlier periods. There periods are known as:

1.   the Polarian,
2.   the Hyperborean,
3.   the Lemurian,
4.   the Atlantean,
5.   the Post-Atlantean.

The Polarian, Hyperborean and Lemurian ages still relate to Saturn, Sun and Moon: the ages of earthly Saturn, earthly Sun and earthly Moon.

With the picture for the Archer understanding the details is not quite straightforward. One sees in the heights (I refer to the *Calendar* [Fig. 4]) a somewhat unique countenance, almost more animal than human, then towards the middle a motif which in metaphysical-esoteric presentations of earlier times played a great role, a kind of archetypal motif of generation that I know especially from the old Berlin *Zweigräumen*, meeting rooms of the Society (the time before the [Great] War), which were opened by Dr Steiner himself.[255] Amongst other things this motif appears to me to point to that which in the book *Occult Science* one finds concerning the beginnings of Earth-evolution. The account initially concerns the fiery, warmth-etheric, primordial condition of the globe of the Earth. There we read:[256]

> Within this globe, something we can call 'condensation' then took place. After some time, this resulted in the appearance of a fiery form in the midst of this soul-formation. This form was similar to Saturn in its densest condition and was interwoven with the effects of various beings involved in earthly evolution. It is something like an emerging and diving down again, from and in the Earth's fiery globe, which we observe as an interaction between this being and the celestial body. Thus, the earthly fiery globe was not a uniform substance but resembled an organism imbued with soul and spirit. The beings destined to assume the present-day form of human beings on Earth were not yet in a position to participate much in this process of immersion in the body of fire. They remained almost exclusively in its uncondensed surroundings, in the lap of higher spiritual beings. *At this stage only one spot of their soul-shapes touched the fiery Earth; this caused the warmth to condenses a portion of their astral form.* Through this earthly life was kindled in them...

Especially the sentence, 'At this stage only one spot of their soul-shapes touched the fiery Earth', I believe I recognize in the pictorial motifs the Archer we have in the *Anthroposophical Soul Calendar*, especially in the middle part of the picture. The condensing of the human astral form activated through this process, which is subsequently described in *Occult Science*, agrees with Dr Steiner's Notes for Frl. von Eckardstein for the Archer: '*Erde, es gliedert sich heraus das Feste*'—'Earth, the solid element is precipitated.' The point would be established, where the first gentle, still warmth-etheric beginnings of the later condensation are formed. In *Occult Science* Dr Steiner imaginatively describes the further process. He writes:

> In order to form for ourselves a picture—at once sensory and supersensible—of the human being at this beginning of the physical Earth, we must conceive a soul-form of egg-like shape, contained in the encircling sphere of the Earth, and surrounded at its lower surface in the way an acorn is by a cup; only the substance of this 'cup' consists entirely of warmth or fire.

The sign of the Archer in the *Calendar* reminds me very much of this picture.

If one holds this picture of the Archer once more beside the picture for the Fishes at the beginning of the cycle of development, then the following can result: with the Fishes everything was still germinating, still in preparation. Only here with the fourth picture, the Archer, does the earthly element come forth, as it were, substantially. We still have to establish that the Fishes and the Archer are Christ-signs, that they both belong to the middle of the three crosses, to the Cross of the Son, or Christ (which is also the etheric cross). Above all there exists here still an important relationship to the rhythm of the gospel, as I have presented it in the two books on *Mark's Gospel* and *John's Gospel*. There we find with the Fishes the Christ-event of the Baptism in the Jordan, with the Archer the Crucifixion, the actual entry into the Mystery of Golgotha. Of the latter, Dr Steiner tells us that this is the *birth* of the earthly 'I', whereas the Baptism has to do with the descent of the Christ-being, in order to receive this earthly 'I', that means, the preparation of the later birth.

We can also say, Christ has descended into the dying Earth-existence. Through this He has planted into the Earth the seed of a new becoming, of a new Earth (of the New Jerusalem); the first beginnings of this new becoming take place on Golgotha, in the Resurrection; at the Jordan all this is prepared in seed-form. Consequently, there too, for the new Earth-becoming the preparation takes place in seed-form in the Fishes; the first, still very tender, etheric beginning of a realization in the Archer. And as it is with a new becoming of the Earth, we also find it with the primordial becoming of the Earth, for which the zodiac-pictures should transport us: thereto we find the first seed-like preparation of this primordial Earth-becoming in the Fishes, the first also very etheric-tender beginning of a realization of the actual earthly element in the Archer.

The Archer in general is a sign of *the realization on the Earth*. Consequently, the Archer is related in our Creed to the *Church*, to the beginning of the outer realization of the Christ-connections on the Earth: 'Communities whose members feel the Christ within themselves may feel united in a church to which all belong who are aware of the health-bringing power of the Christ.' In an earlier study we have seen that the Archer, with its three decanates, Jupiter, Sun and Mars, is a strong Michaelic sign, that it consequently forms the ending of the Michael-fire-quadrant. With horoscopes, too, it is the case that people who have the Archer in the ascendant, or a strong constellation, easily realize earthly tasks, that they possess easy mobility on Earth and motor-strength. And this motor-strength stands again related to Michael, who wants to lead us to 'higher divining' of the Mystery of Golgotha, that means, expressed in the sense of the zodiac, to the Mystery of the Archer.

## The Scorpion

Then comes the fifth picture (Fig. 5), the Scorpion, to which Dr Steiner gives the Notes: '*Es trennen sich die Geschlechter*'— 'The sexes divide.' This separation of the sexes took place as an event prior to the Fall, but still strongly connected to it, according to *Occult Science* and *Lucifer Gnosis*[257] during the early Lemurian time. It is the same occurrence to which relates the biblical picture of the creation of Eve out of Adam's rib (Gen. 2:22). The picture drawn by Frl. v. Eckardstein is one of those which artistically can stimulate the most consternation: two somewhat strange faces, a male and a female one, who, like Siamese twins together look in opposite directions, as they cannot quite stand each other; the rest of the body is quite unfinished. Above the two heads there is a spiral indicating development (recalling Gen. 2:2), the whole in an auric form, and around it something like blossoms, radiating (double six-petalled lotus blossom?).

What is meant appears clearly. The latent contrast between the genders begins to appear outwardly. All this takes place, of course, not as a sudden event but in long periods of development, in which we strongly meet the effect of the Fall. The spiritual primordial form of the human being, which at the primordial beginning was like a blossom—or the form of a butterfly (*Geheimwissenschaft* [*Occult Science*], 1st ed. p. 208) becomes the form of a snake, or a dragon. The earthly becoming of the human figure takes place from below upwards, begins with the feet, in the sign of the Fishes (that is why the feet belong to the Fishes, because the still Sun-like human being in this Sun-like sign first touches the Earth. The development proceeds further upwards. The human figure comes down thereby ever more to the animal level. The form of the lizard, the amphibian form, corresponds to the Waterman. And when we have reached the Scorpion, we have reached the lowest, the most sub-human of all human figures that has descended the lowest, now not only the Scorpion but especially the snake, the form of the dragon. This is the lowest lowering, the lowest ignominy of the human being, as Dr Steiner expressed himself with regard to these things in the lecture-cycle on Egypt [GA 106]).

## *The Scales*

The following picture, the picture for the Scales [Fig. 6], is also an artistic expression of a faultless beauty. Dr Steiner gave the following words to it: '*Sonne, Mond, Erde halten sich das Gleichgewicht. Der Mensch trennt einen eigenen Astralleib heraus*'—'Sun, Moon and Earth are held in balance. The human being separates his own astral body.' We will understand this properly when we recall the things in the Leipzig lecture-cycle, *Christ and the Spiritual World* [GA 149], so important for all knowledge of the stars. There the three Christ-events [sacrifices] are mentioned which precede the Mystery of Golgotha as the fourth, and in a sense concluding, Christ-event. The three events in which the Christ-being works through the being of Jesus of Nazareth (the Nathan-Jesus) who was still tarrying in spiritual worlds (as he later, with the Baptism in the Jordan, incorporated in Jesus, he has then— Dr Steiner uses the expression—become ensouled in him. With these Christ-Jesus events, Christ-Jesus deeds, as with Christ-events in general, it has to do with balancing out certain results of the human Fall. With the first of these events, the effects lie in the physical body, in the system of the twelve senses that had become chaotic, vulnerable to the attacks of the adversary. Christ-Jesus, working from the Sun through the twelve signs of the Zodiac, brings this disarray into order. This event falls in the late Lemurian time.

    With the second event, falling in the early Atlantean time, the seven human life-organs, that is, the organs of the etheric body had come into disarray. Christ-Jesus, working from the seven planets, as it were, taking the path through the seven planetary spheres—through which they themselves become harmonized—brings these organs into order.

This event is of the greatest significance for all astrology, for the influence of astrology itself.

The third event falls in the later Atlantean time. Then—in all this I follow what is given in the Leipzig lecture-cycle—the human astral body with its organs of thinking, feeling and doing had come into disorder. Christ-Jesus (the Christ Who works through Jesus, 'ensouling' Himself in Jesus), brings this into balance, from the Sun, Moon and Earth bringing about a balance between Sun, Moon and Earth, harmonizing human thinking, feeling and will, bringing the astral body itself, relatively speaking, into order. This seems to be contained in the words of the Note belonging to the picture for the Scales in the *Calendar*: '*Sun, Moon and Earth are held in balance. The human being separates out his own astral body*' [from disarray].

Now with the Scales we would have arrived in the late Atlantean times, from when we also know that the human form as we know it today became solidified, that the human being then takes on the human form of today, that which we today understand as the human gestalt. That harmonizing of the human astral body is connected with that which ultimately also leads to the harmony of the human form, which gradually leads the human being out of the sub-human, animal form he had hitherto, to the harmony of the human form. Here we have reached exactly that which in a previous study we called the influence of Venus, of Venus-Urania (the Venus who leads us above), who is the ruler in the Scales. From the planetary viewpoint the sign of the Scales is the spiritual effect of Venus-Urania, especially also its influence in matter, in the harmonizing of the human *Gemüt* ['mind, heart, disposition'], and also the human form (what also in the gospel is called *kalōs poiein* 'to make beautiful' [Matt. 12:12] and relates there to the influence of Christ in the sign of Venus). At the same time in the Scales we have the exaltation of Saturn, who is the ruler in the material realm. It is completely illuminating to think that Saturn, the lord of the dark resisting matter, has its illumination where Venus wrestles from these dark forces the revealing beauty and harmony of the human form.

We find this, too, in the *Calendar* drawing: above the radiant Sun, rising from a kind of sea-horizon (the sea belongs indeed to Venus-Urania), below in the dark depths a great black cross in a kind of egg-shape (Moon-form), which together with the cross results in the sign of Saturn (♄) (the Sun above stands in a shining cross with a radiating aura). If one now looks at the Sun-disc with the cross beneath it (the

Saturn-cross) then one has nothing other than the sign of Venus (♀), that is, the sign of that planetary being who rules this zodiac-sign. In that balance of the light-filled Sun-aura above and the dark Saturn-cross below lies pictorially 'the Scales' (one can imagine the whole figure having arisen out of the conventional sign of the Scales ♎). And in this representation of the sign of the Scales one experiences visually the balancing, harmonizing of Venus. The whole picture can be recommended as the subject of meditation to an outstanding degree; it is a genuine Michaelic picture. Taking together everything that has resulted for us concerning the Scales, Saturn, Venus and so on, it not only clarifies a part of cosmogonic development, but at the same time is a component of esoteric development.

## The Virgin

The picture for the *Virgin* follows [Fig. 7]. Her picture in the *Calendar* is something uncomfortable, yet in the occult-esoteric aspect very telling. We see here the mother (standing) with the child in her arms, her cloak in the middle of her body wrapped around the child; at her feet a crescent Moon with a decapitated head (the well-known motif of the Baptist). On her head the Virgin-Mother wears an indented diadem, of which seven peaks are visible (the five others can be imagined lying behind). The head (or the whole figure) is still surrounded with a Sun-raying-aura; the etheric element, of which we have spoken earlier, is predominant in the whole picture. The Virgin belongs to:

1. the etheric cross,
2. the triangle of the highest ether,
3. the quadrant of the highest ether.

She delineates, consequently, that point in the zodiac where the etheric reaches its perfection. The words given by Dr Steiner to this picture: '*Die Jungfrau steht für die ganze Menschheit. Die Menschheit kehrt zurück zum Geistigen durch das Zentralgeschehen des Mysteriums von Golgotha*'—'The Virgin stands for the whole of mankind. Mankind turns back to the spiritual through the central event—the Mystery of Golgotha.' In the development of the Earth we have now reached that point where the Mystery of Golgotha takes place. With the Scales we were reminded of the three preceding Christ-events—or Christ-Jesus events, where it concerns the harmonizing of the physical, the etheric and the astral; this is now followed in the Mystery of Golgotha, the fourth event, and in a certain sense the concluding Christ-event, where the harmonizing takes place in the 'I'. This, as Dr Steiner always said, is the great *'hypomochlion'* (the fulcrum, the point of balance of the Scales) of human development, the human event *par excellence*. Consequently, this sign † is 'for the whole of humanity'. The soul of humanity gives birth to the Christ-child, the Son, which is the bearer of 'life destined for eternity'.

We may observe that the human figure in the zodiac actually appears only twice, with the Twins and the Virgin (the centaur-figure of the Archer is only half-human). Only the Waterman, the sign of the cosmic-etheric human source is often portrayed as a man with two water-jars. (In the *Anthroposophical Calendar*, the Scorpion picture also shows a human countenance.) The picture of the Twins is only shown as two children. The fully complete human figure we only have in the picture of the Virgin.

Here, too, we can easily add to the cosmogonic aspect the esoteric one: it is the point, where the human soul seeks the connection with Christ, with the event of Golgotha. This takes place sacramental-ly-liturgically in the Lord's Supper, the Act of Consecration of Man. One may recall that with the studies on the gospel the Virgin always emerged as the sign for the Last Supper, the constellation Virgin—Fishes as the Last-Supper constellation (see the books on *Mark's Gospel* and *John's Gospel*). It is the same constellation in which we also find the Feedings (the bread belongs to the Virgin with the sheaf, which then has become the Virgin with the Child). The parable of the Sower, the Mystery of the grain of wheat, is also to be found in this sign. That here the Virgin in the *Calendar* points towards the Mystery of Golgotha, does not contradict the fact that in the gospel studies we see the Archer in the narrow sense as the sign of Golgotha, the sign of death and crucifixion.

Beginning with the Baptism in the Jordan, the Christ-event in Palestine, which in the wider sense is the Mystery of Golgotha, is in the gospel narration divided into the twelve, or three times twelve, events, of which the Crucifixion, the Mystery of Golgotha in the narrower sense, corresponds to the Archer. The all-embracing cosmic sense of the Mystery of Golgotha—also expressed by Dr Steiner—lies in the Last Supper, which Christ celebrates with His disciples. To this the sign of the Virgin relates; it is not the Crucifixion in the narrower sense, but the main point where for the whole development of humanity the

Mystery of Golgotha stands. All its spiritual rays, so to speak, gather in the Last Supper, in that which Leonardo da Vinci has captured so impressively in artistic form.[258]

For all this is important that the Virgin also belongs to the middle cross of the three, the actual Christ-cross. The whole arrangement of the zodiac-pictures in the *Anthroposophical Calendar of the Soul* lies on this cross (the Fishes, Virgin, Twin and Archer). For it begins and ends in the Fishes. This arrangement in the Fishes shows the first earthly germs, in the Archer the becoming of the firm element of earth, in the Virgin the centre of the evolution of the Earth and of humanity, and in the Twins as we shall soon see, a climax in the future of humanity and the Earth. All this we can also see as the central Christ-events, Christ-revelations in the Earth and humanity.

## The Lion

With the subsequent picture, with the Lion [Fig. 8] we see into this future development. Besides the cosmogonic viewpoint, the esoteric one increasingly comes to the fore. The words of Dr Steiner are: *'Entwickelung der Herzenslotusblume. Das Blut des niederern Egoismus entströmt'*—'The development of the lotus-flower of the heart. The blood of the lower egoism flows away.' Correspondingly, the picture also shows the twelve-petalled lotus-flower (we actually see 2 x 12 = 24 petals; this also confirms the earlier assumption that the 2 x 6 flower petals with the picture for the Scorpion are related to the six-petalled lotus-flower). Out of the centre of the shining lotus-flower there develops towards the left something like the tail of a lion, clearly fashioned towards the letter L (cf. its Hebrew form [Lamed ל ]).[259] Over the whole, still including the top of this Lion-L, a radiant Sun [is to be seen]. The motifs of heart, Sun, Lion, twelve-petalled lotus-flower are clearly connected in this picture.

## The Crab

The subsequent drawing of the Crab is especially interesting (Fig. 9). The picture of the human skeleton, or ribcage, which in the usual drawing of the Crab-sign is only lightly indicated, comes here clearly to the fore. Here, too, the shining Sun is above (not the Moon as one sometimes assumes, at least not the Moon-sickle, but the Sun which, of course, is also contained in the Moon-sickle and in the light of the Moon). The number of ribs, or spirals, as well as the lotus-petals surrounding is everywhere attuned to the number five (2 x 5 spirals: twenty lotus-petals). Physiologically, too, the Moon-sign of the Crab belongs to the ribcage. The very interesting Note given by Dr Steiner: '*Entwicklung der Lotosblume zu einem leuchtenden Vordergrat, das Rückgrat verschwindet*'—'Development of the lotus-flower towards a shining frontal spine, the spine in the back disappears.'

We recall how in the Munich lecture-cycle, *Secrets of the Threshold* [GA 147. 24-31 Aug. 1913], Dr Steiner says that in the Indian yoga development, the lotus-flowers were grouped around the spinal column, whereas with the Christian Western development they are grouped in front [of the human being]; only there where this development does not take place properly, Lucifer and Ahriman strive—according to Dr Steiner's indications—to wrap the lotus-flowers around the spinal column. Thus an esoteric development, cramped through Lucifer and Ahriman, is distinguished from a development that is released through Christ, in the Christ-sense. For esoteric development, all this is an extraordinarily important picture for the future. With this we can relate everything that we have found in our observations (also in the gospel letters) concerning the Christian-Johannine initiation and its connection with the meaning of the Moon-sign of the Crab. In all the three points of the Johannine-triangle and their decanates we find the Moon. The Mystery of the Moon, or the Moon-Sun Mystery belongs to the Johannine [sphere].

### The Twins

The picture for the Twins [Fig. 10] follows in the *Calendar* drawing, the two strange, somewhat uncomfortable infants in a circumference of dots of light. In the region of the throat[260] of the two babies are strange growths. Dr Steiner's explanation: '*Der Mensch lernt gehen und stehen und sprechen in der grossen Welt. Kindheitskräfte beherrschen sein Wesen*'— 'The human being learns to walk, stand and speak in the outer world. The forces of childhood determine his/her being.' We recall how Dr Steiner, in his small book *The Spiritual Guidance of Man and Mankind* [GA 15]—precisely where he also speaks of the fact and significance of the birth-horoscope—significantly links child-development of the first three years of life with the three years of earthly life of Christ, aligning the child's learning to walk, to speak and to think with Christ's saying, 'I am the Way, the Truth and the Life' [John 14:6]. In the given zodiac-picture at the same time there is revealed here the deeper sense of Christ's saying, 'Except you turn and become as little children...' [Matt. 18:3, cf. John 3]. In esoteric development a higher level of child-hood exists, a higher becoming childlike. The human being wins back the forces of innocence of the child, overcomes in a certain Johannine sense the contrasting genders/sexes (which in the far future of human-ity really will be overcome). The picture of the two infant Twins (of which the one is to be seen as a masculine child, the other feminine) thus stands in a meaningful contrast to the two human faces of the picture for the Scorpion. Amongst all the different aspects of the sign of the Twins, the most significant, the esoteric aspect, is indicated here.

## The Bull

The Bull follows (Fig. 11), to which, in the region of the speech-organs, or the larynx, the sixteen-petalled lotus-flower is allocated. In the *Calendar* picture we only find eight petals. This is understandable without more ado, when we remind ourselves of the passage from *Knowledge of the Higher Worlds: How is it attained?* how eight of these sixteen petals were developed earlier in primordial human times or ancient clairvoy-ance and as it has to do today with developing the eight others through the 'I' (here, too, the 'frontal spine' appears in place of what was there earlier). Dr Steiner's explanation runs: '*Der Kehlkopf wird schöpferisch im Wort*'—'The larynx becomes creative in the word.' After the over-coming of the contrast of the sexes, the larynx will become directly the higher spiritual organ of reproduction (in connection with lungs and heart; the heart is connected to the previous picture of the Lion, the lungs with the picture of the Twins, especially as Mercury, the ruler of the Twins, governs the lungs).

## The Ram

The ending of esoteric development, or the future development of mankind, is then presented by the picture of the Ram [Fig. 12], a human countenance that looks into an abundance of light-rays pour-ing down from above: above the countenance a higher, etheric one is half-indicated, already penetrating completely into the light rays com-ing from above (it appears like the 'higher octave' of the human being, the octave experience, much discussed in Dr Steiner lectures on music. Dr Steiner's words: '*Der Mensch lebt noch im Physischen und zugleich ein geistiges Leben*'—'The human being still lives in the physical realm and at the same time [leads] a spiritual life', supply here the necessary explanation. The human countenance, the head (which does belong to the Ram) is here in its double aspect to reveal Spirit-man. And there is revealed the esoteric sense of the light of the sign of the Ram, as a fire-sign, at the same time presenting the beginning of the light-ether square, as we have seen. In the sign of the Ram there is completed esoterically as the counter-piece of 'our origin in the light' the 'human future in the light'.

*Appendix*: A Challenge (1931)

## Translator's Preface

Now that the personalities involved in the account that follows have passed away, approaching the occasion of the Centenary of the Movement for Religious Renewal seems a good time to review the whole story. Much of the utmost importance is evident. Far from something to be brushed aside, the 'case' of Schult throws into relief several crucial issues. It exhibits:

(i)    Beckh's professionalism and tact,
(ii)   his spiritual leadership,
(iii)  his unswerving policy to stay true to anthroposophy and avoid any concessions. This is not a blind sectarian policy but is a clear example of human integrity that is free from all sectarianism.

Beckh expected of others that which he demanded of himself. That Beckh respected Schult for his erudition and abilities is beyond dispute. Certainly, he was upset to be presented with the horoscopes of himself and Rudolf Steiner—the subject was not his field of research. That he looked for something more from Schult is also clear. The 'case', he insists, is not about a personal difference. *The point is crucial.* And it is also bound up with the generally prevalent, hopelessly erroneous because radically selective—and in a word superficial—view of Hermann Beckh himself ('absent-minded professor', 'neo-Buddhist' and so on).

Beckh's experience with a particular 'professional' in conventional astrology is a situation met frequently by those engaged in taking fresh initiative in any field, while yet upholding original and essential *principles*. Every devoted practitioner sacrifices himself into his work; is it different for the astrologer? In so far, indeed, the devoted window-cleaner, taxi-driver, and nurse are one with the devoted teacher, eurythmist, astrologer and Christian priest. And a 'new star-wisdom' is precisely what the words say.

Beckh's handling of the issue was essential during the early years following the Foundation. A precedent exists in Rudolf Steiner's attitude to 'journalistic misunderstanding' when eurythmy first went public; Steiner appeals to the eurythmists to keep true to their principles. 'Any taste, any trend must emanate out of our endeavour alone' (17 August 1918; see GA 227a, p. 211, Endnote 87). In the present case, Beckh the spiritual leader and pioneer *par excellence* shows he can learn from those who have gone before; he recognizes erudition and abilities in others. But his genius does not deviate from the vision of:

a new future for tonal music,
a new future for linguistic studies,
a new future for gospel research, and (to cap it all)
a new future for human social development that goes hand in hand with a new star-wisdom.

The evidence for all these claims is now available for English-speakers with the publication of the *Collected Works*. All the activities listed above are of a piece because their originator was a remarkably integrated personality, who led a singularly brilliant, indeed apparently unique career. An inter-disciplinary view also supports the claim that Beckh actually derives his impulses from the same central source that he is not shy to name at the appropriate stages of whatever exposition or discussion in which he is engaged—A. S.

# Arthur Schult

Arthur Schult, Beckh's junior by 18 years, published many works. Interested readers may check for themselves whether what Beckh perceived contains truth, and also what developed beyond 1931. The fact of the matter that appears to have caused the commotion, at least as Beckh depicts it, can be put into our own words. A personality of enormous erudition and abilities here confronts a master, that is, one who wears his erudition lightly. The concerns of the latter—Hermann Beckh, and at the same time those of the young Christian Community—are viewed in the perspective stretching from the primordial beginnings to the end of the ages. It is a view from the mountain tops, admittedly, but (as was said of old) it is 'from the hills, whence cometh my/our help'—A. S.

# Arthur Schult (1893-1969)

Wikipedia article [tr. A. S.]:

Arthur Schult attended the Gymnasium in Rheydt and subsequently studied classical philology and philosophy in Münster and Berlin. With his wife Marie († 1947) he founded and was principal of a private educational home in Oberstdorf. He was well-known for his numerous lectures and books on Christian spirituality and esoteric themes.

From 1927-1945 Schult was a member of the Anthroposophical Society. He had many friends who were anthroposophists, in particular Hans-Hasso von Veltheim. His main works can be taken as the book on John's Gospel, the two-volume textbook on classical astrology that looks to found an 'astrosophy' and the posthumous extensive work on Dante's *Divine Comedy*.

b. 4 April 1893 in Odenkirchen; † 9 September 1969 in Oberstdorf.

## *Works*

- *Menschenleben und Johannesevangelium im Lichte der Wandelsterne.* Drei Eichen, München 1958
- *Maria Sophia. Das Ewig-Weibliche in Gott, Mensch und Kosmos.* Turm, Bietigheim 1960, ISBN 3-7999-0122-1
- *Das Damaskuserlebnis des Apostels Paulus und die Gegenwart Christi.* Turm, Bietigheim 1961, ISBN 3-7999-0120-5
- *Denkschrift zur geistigen Situation der evangelischen Kirche in der Gegenwart.* Turm, Bietigheim 1961, ISBN 3-7999-0153-1
- *Pfingstgeist und Christentum.* Turm, Bietigheim 1962, ISBN 3-7999-0123-X
- *Die Weisheit der Veden und Upanishaden im Lichte des West-Ost-Problems.* Turm, Bietigheim 1962, ISBN 3-7999-0125-6
- *Das Johannesevangelium als Offenbarung des kosmischen Christus*. Reichl, Remagen 1965, ISBN 3-87667-017-9
- *Vom übersinnlichen Wesen des Menschen.* Turm, Bietigheim 1966, ISBN 3-7999-0124-8
- *Eros und Agape. Hohes Lied Salomonis und Johanneische Gottesschau.* Turm, Bietigheim 1969, ISBN 3-7999-0121-3
- *Urgeschichte der Menschheit.* Henn, Wuppertal-Elberfeld 1969; Turm, Bietigheim 1989, ISBN 3-7999-0223-6

- *Astrosophie als kosmische Signaturenlehre des Menschenbildes.* 2 Bände. Turm, Bietigheim 1971; 5. A. ebd. 1994, ISBN 3-7999-0206-6
- *Die Weltsendung des Heiligen Gral im Parzival des Wolfram von Eschenbach.* Turm, Bietigheim 1975, ISBN 3-7999-0172-8
- *Weltenwerden und Johannes-Apokalypse.* Turm, Bietigheim 1976, ISBN 3-7999-0173-6
- *Dantes Divina Commedia als Zeugnis der Tempelritter-Esoterik.* Turm, Bietigheim 1979, ISBN 3-7999-0184-1
- *Mysterienweisheit im deutschen Volksmärchen.* Turm, Bietigheim 1980, ISBN 3-7999-0190-6
- *Zeit und Ewigkeit im Jahreskreis. Sonntags-Andachten.* Turm, Bietigheim 1987, ISBN 3-7999-0219-8

# Personal Explanation regarding Astrology

(RB 126, Michaelmas 1931, 8 October 1931)
Hermann Beckh

## I

Herr Artur Schult (Oberstdorf), the writer of an article on Kepler in our Journal,[261] with whom I was recently together, heard in Eisenach from a member of the Priest's circle that, if not actually stated, I had made the impression that his (Herr Schult's) activities were only calculating, not interpreting, horoscopes. Something so untrue has never been said or implied by me, and I must seriously request all friends who feel it concerns them if possible to write to Herr Schult (address given) to put this right, and furthermore to take the trouble to confirm that through careless remarks (including items of gossip) I do not morally discredit those outside, or friends of, The Christian Community (and those who are quite knowledgeable), and through this become robbed of the possibility to offer my *Contributions on Star Knowledge*, that up to now I have selflessly offered to the group of friends, or rather continue to offer them to the friends.

## II

Concerning my acquaintance with Herr Schult and that which I am indebted to him in astrology, I have already reported in the *Newsletter* (*Contribution* No. 7). I related that, when writing the book on *Mark's Gospel*, I still knew nothing of conventional astrology, that only on the basis of my work on the gospel from Herr Schult was presented with the fact of my horoscope and therewith before the fact of [practical] astrology in general. Already with this, and later with many other opportunities, I learnt and appreciated from Herr Schult the exactitude of his computations and the astuteness of his interpretation of the horoscope. It was towards the end of 1928. Already previously Herr Schult became through me [as proposer] a member of the Anthroposophical Society. At that time, I knew nothing of his astrological studies and knowledge.

Apart from him I have met other well-known astrologers, above all Herr Wilhelm Petersen in Darmstadt and Frau Baroness von Bernus in Stuttgart. With the latter I have worked together a lot on astrology. She too possesses a genial gift of interpretation, yet this her gift and her whole attitude to astrology is again completely different from that of Herr Schult. The books of Alan Leo became for me an especially valuable source of knowledge for the astrological tradition, whereas I experienced with Herr Schult and Frau von Bernus the direct living element of an intuitive horoscope interpretation. My astrological *Newsletter Contributions* can show to anybody who really reads them that they are not inspired by any personalities or books, but purely and completely are based on Rudolf Steiner's anthroposophy. I had, have and recognize with spiritual things (including astrology) only *one* teacher, Rudolf Steiner. Only as an aside I want to add here how especially during the Wiesbaden Astrologers Congress, which I had attended not long ago, and about which at that time I wrote a report, this significance of Rudolf Steiner also for astrology has been on the increase.

## III

Nevertheless, it appears, and this is actually based precisely on my *Newsletter Contributions*, or expressed more exactly: on the basis of the merely-glanced-at and not-having-really-read my *Contributions*, the fairytale has arisen that I, too, would be amongst the horoscope-makers. Although I take trouble with my *Contributions* to work against a certain tendency of contemporary people to rush carelessly into the subject of horoscopes, yet I experience ever again that precisely such an attempt is released or strengthened through my *Contributions*. And I try nevertheless ever again to show that astrology can only do the contemporary person good when it is placed on the sure ground of the anthroposophical path of knowledge.

The meaning of my astrological *Newsletter* work, once more briefly put, is on the basis and in the light of anthroposophy to build up astrology in a new contemporary form. This attempt is the first up to now and unique; even Frl. Vreede, whose valuable astronomical *Newsletter* is here in no way infringed or dismissed, neither is Herr Schult involved as a forerunner. What concerns the horoscope-makers and horoscope-interpreters, and serves me, too, first and foremost as the guiding principle, is the statement of our revered teacher Dr Rudolf

Steiner: *only the great initiate at the end of his life should interpret someone else's horoscope for him*. To this the other saying: astrology in its true being is intercourse with the living intelligences of the cosmos.

Now, I see myself (i) obviously not as the greatest initiate, but only at the most as a student of the spirit, (ii) I hope at least that I am not yet at the end of my life, but still want to accomplish a whole lot of work. Already for this reason I am lacking, what in my *Contributions* I attempt to continue to develop, the qualification to interpret horoscopes. In the sense of the strict demands of Rudolf Steiner not one amongst us would have the qualification. That some individual personalities, also in our time, at least have a remarkable disposition to such things, is as it were inherent, is also not denied by Dr Steiner, and the personalities already mentioned here can in this respect serve as examples. Here, too, the ability goes only to a certain point, far from being infallible.

Somehow to measure myself against the personalities mentioned here, to enter with them into some competition as horoscope-maker or a horoscope-interpreter lies completely removed from me. For this I am still too much a beginner, and even if I were not a beginner, Dr Steiner's sayings would restrain me. It is true that in individual cases I have said something to the one or other about some of his aspects. That is in itself still something different from the complete interpretation of a horoscope. And we know how it is in life: one is just so often asked for something and, in the end, has to give in. But this, too, I will in future leave alone, because one sees all too clearly to what unwished for consequences and uncontrollable results it leads, and I ask all friends most earnestly no longer to approach me with such requests. For those interested in the subject I can only repeatedly point the reader to my *Contributions*. With time readers will find in them ever more clearly—for the *Contributions* are by a long way not finished—the way that will enable them to work out a horoscope and confront a horoscope with independent judgment. And everything is so presented—which with conventional astrological literature is not the case—in these *Contributions* that it remains in harmony with anthroposophy, with the bases of a Christian thinking, feelings and will.

## Pressing Supplement to the previous 'Personal Explanation Regarding Astrology'

Herr Schult whose brilliant astrological talent and valued knowledge, which in the last supplementary *Newsletter* I almost overabundantly recognized, has reacted to this in a very unpleasant, indeed threatening manner. Firstly, he sent a telegram demanding in a commanding tone that the explanation which he, without any reason, calls 'completely misleading', be held back. In a letter he repeats this in unheard of, rude expressions, making me the object of attack. Yet it was I who introduced him into our circles and to Frl. Vreede in Dornach. There, during Whitsuntide, it was the case that I used my standing in anthroposophical circles to support him when, with his astrology, he came amiss in Dornach (not completely undeservedly as I myself then believed). He now accuses me, to whom I have brought the greatest sacrifices of friendship, with a deficiency of friendship. He also wishes—which, firstly in general, and secondly strengthened also in this case, appears absolutely impossible—to intrude into the *Newsletter*, which is a confidential matter of the priests' group and should remain so—with a counter-explanation.

The matter is like this, that in Eisenach some individual friends of the group of priests, not named by Schult, in a way that possibly appeared harmless to them, but in a certainly uninformed manner, have talked to Herr Schult about me. Only through this has the very regrettable necessity arisen by allowing someone, hitherto at least a befriended and valued co-worked of our *Newsletter*, to allow him to view the explanation in the previous issue. It was intended to calm things down, but unfortunately had the opposite effect. This has resulted because, especially on this occasion, it has become clear in an impressively shocking way what is *not* yet right with that person and his astrology, because it is not anchored on the foundation of a true anthroposophical-Christian knowledge. Through the events it has now become quite clear to me what lay as legitimate and to be heeded—not only in Dr Steiner's words, which is obvious—but also in Frl. Vreede's somewhat negative stance. *It really does concern the whole endeavour, to keep anthroposophy and also our Movement blameless in the face of every strange influence foreign to it that wants to push its way in at this critical time of great world-events*—precisely during these days (16/17 October 1931), once again that constellation recurs, to which I drew attention in the last *Newsletter* but one. The whole thing is a test of exemplary magnitude and significance. Even if not all members of the priests' group agree with this and act accordingly, our endeavour is threatened.

And so Herr Schult demands from me furthermore the *Newsletter Contribution* No. VII, where I initially said something about my acquaintance with him. *It is not possible to respond to this demand* (the lines that refer to him I will communicate to him, but this, too, can only take place through me), and furthermore it touches on the confidentiality of the priests' *Newsletter*. It would bring about—I would hope, that it has not already happened through some kind of indiscretion—an irreversible damage for our whole endeavour. The fire that basically has already flared up is consequently no longer possible to localize; the fire-catastrophe would then take on dimensions in which The Christian Community would then be damaged or drawn in. So, I express the hope that all the friends are aware of their responsibility and that *nothing, especially not the words of this explanation, be given to Herrn Schult,* that every further attempt of those outside to enter the confidential situation of the priests' *Newsletter* will be hindered.

# Explanation

concerning the astrological *Newsletters* of Hermann Beckh
(RB 127: mid-November 1931)

The astrological *Newsletter Contributions,* already interrupted last time through the report on the Wiesbaden Congress, could also not be continued in this issue. The case of Schult and many other things brought such an abundance of events in my life, connected to which quite a boundless correspondence, so that with all the other work—alongside this a book was being written, whose appearance is postponed—and then uninterrupted journeys, I simply could not get to write this *Contribution.*

In addition, there comes something different, something serious. With my second 'personal explanation', which left the press together with the *Newsletter,* I had so very much requested these things be taken in confidence, and not to let them out, especially to give *Newsletter* explanations to Schult. Nevertheless, I had to learn from a recent letter from Schult, which concerning myself made me most upset, that *my explanation was leaked through members of the priests' circle.* What consequences this has in the future, I cannot overview at the moment. Initially, in the face of such unpleasant events, [we aim] to keep the peace. For this reason, too, I cannot decide at the moment whether under these circumstances it would be possible still to continue to make available to the group of friends my work on star-knowledge (which I obviously want to continue). It depends on the attitude of the priests' group what in future is still possible.

## Once again the 'Case of Schult', 2 November 1931, a few days after the previous report from Prof. H. Beckh, in RB 127, mid-November

The unpleasant case, increasingly threatening to become more critical, has taken a new turn today, on a bright, radiant All Souls' Day such as I have never before experienced, through a letter from Frau Schult to me. Although not all the difficulties are removed, all the differences put aside, far from it, yet it can be hoped that a solution to this case can perhaps be achieved in an anthroposophical and Christian sense. Here, too, from the evil perhaps healing will be wrested. Here I must add an explanation, that with Frau Schult I always enjoyed a good, warm friendship, that she always extended sympathy towards me, even when some difficult or astringent dispute of the married couple—which was frequently the case—threatened to shake the relationship to Oberstdorf. One sees also in this case—and perhaps some in the priests' circle recall similar 'cases'—how through the involvement of the feminine part, critical complications were avoided, brought to an atoning solution, how an understanding that appears hopeless with a man, with the woman is sometimes nevertheless achieved. This also applies especially to anthroposophical contexts. Dr Steiner, in an earlier time, had often spoken about this, how the man, with all his cleverness, in anthroposophical things today finds it many times more difficult. The masculine brain, Dr Steiner said, is too fixed, too hardened, to be able easily to receive anthroposophical things. The brain of the woman that has remained softer is much more suitable for such things. This would be the reason why in theosophical matters (so people said in the Steiner circle) and similar groups, the female element strongly predominated.

And now in this case, in the case of Schult, it has to do precisely with an understanding of anthroposophical matters. Whoever, after what he hitherto has picked up of this 'case', would be of the opinion, it simply has to do here with a 'personal difference', would be in error. Schult is strongly gifted for astrological matters, especially with horoscopes. He also has a strong tendency towards anthroposophy. The anthroposophical attitude of soul—this one really felt also in the summer in Dornach—is still missing with him in many respects. Especially his over-great cleverness and scholarliness becomes a hindrance for him. Many take anthroposophy intellectually; many people wish to make the anthroposophical contents fruitful in their own

thinking, researching, working and doing. To open up completely
to the 'being Anthroposophy', to devote oneself completely, to sacrifice all other wishes of the soul and wishes of the personality, that
is much more difficult. For someone like Schult, who already without anthroposophy and outside anthroposophy, knows so very much
in a quite different area, it is doubly difficult. That in order really
to come completely to anthroposophy, one first has in a certain way
to sacrifice precisely one's favourite study, one's favourite inclinations, one's personal spiritual hobby-horse, at least for a period has
to remove oneself completely—this was expressly said by Dr Steiner
somewhere—an over-intelligent person who lives completely in his
'astrology' cannot once imagine [such a demand] in a month of Sun-
days. That here, too, it means to go 'through a spiritual zero-point',
for this he has initially no concept.

It was like this with [the founding of] our Movement; not all the individuals by a long way could fulfil the task of sacrificing everything of
an individual Protestant character, since the actual future-bearing element vouching for results in the future has to be planted. And astrology with its whole double-edged character, with its various dangers
is here really something critical. This critical element has led to this
situation, to this whole testing, out of which, as I hope, anthroposophy
will emerge in bright, raying splendour, basically has already done so.
Out of Frau Schult's letter it is completely clear that here it really has
to do with such things. Yet she does not yet by a long way see how
these things (I mean everything lying here between anthroposophy
and a certain way of astrology) really stand. Yet of the Oberstdorfer
[couple] she is the more amenable, with more understanding, who is
nearer in her heart to anthroposophy. And I would like to give expression to the hope that with patience and forbearing, it will be possible
to lead Frau Schult—and thereby indirectly Herr Schult—to the point
where a light can be shed for her concerning the points whose non-rec-
ognition and an inability to lay hold of them has led to this whole
'case', this whole crisis.

# FIGURES

1. Twelve designs by Imma von Eckardstein for Rudolf Steiner's *Anthroposophical Soul Calender*

Figs. 1-6

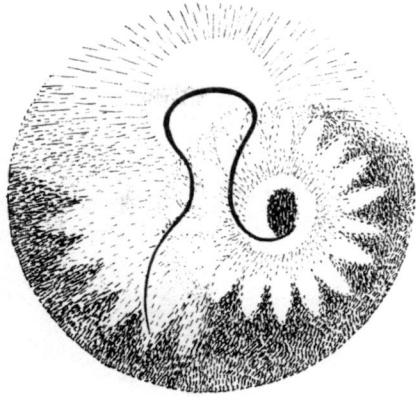

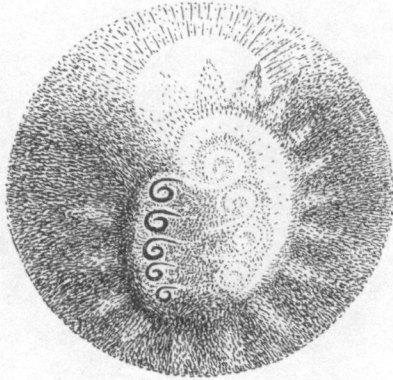

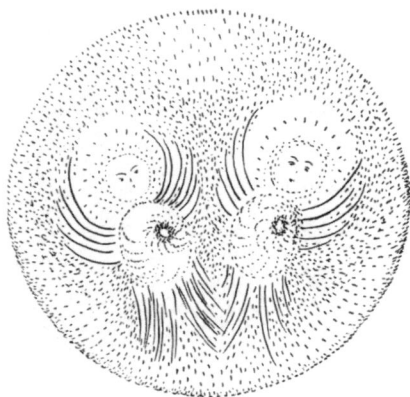

**Figs. 7-12**

## 2. The Four Trigons

The Luke Trigon
Life-ether
Feminine
(Earth Signs)

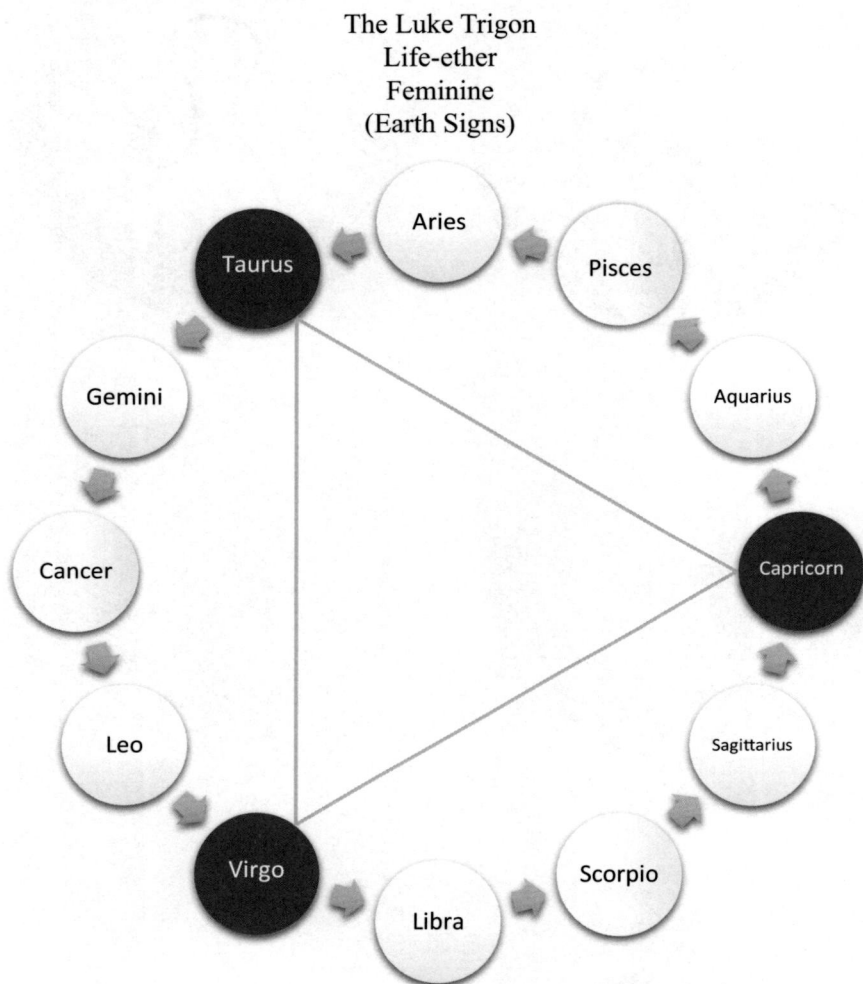

Virgo decanates: 1. (principal ruler) Mercury; 2. The 'Uranus side' of Saturn; 3. Venus.

Taurus decanates: 1. (principal ruler) Venus; 2. Mercury; 3. Saturn.

Capricorn decanates: 1. (principal ruler) 'dark Saturn'; 2. Venus; 3. Mercury.

The John Trigon
Tone-Ether
Feminine
(Water Signs)

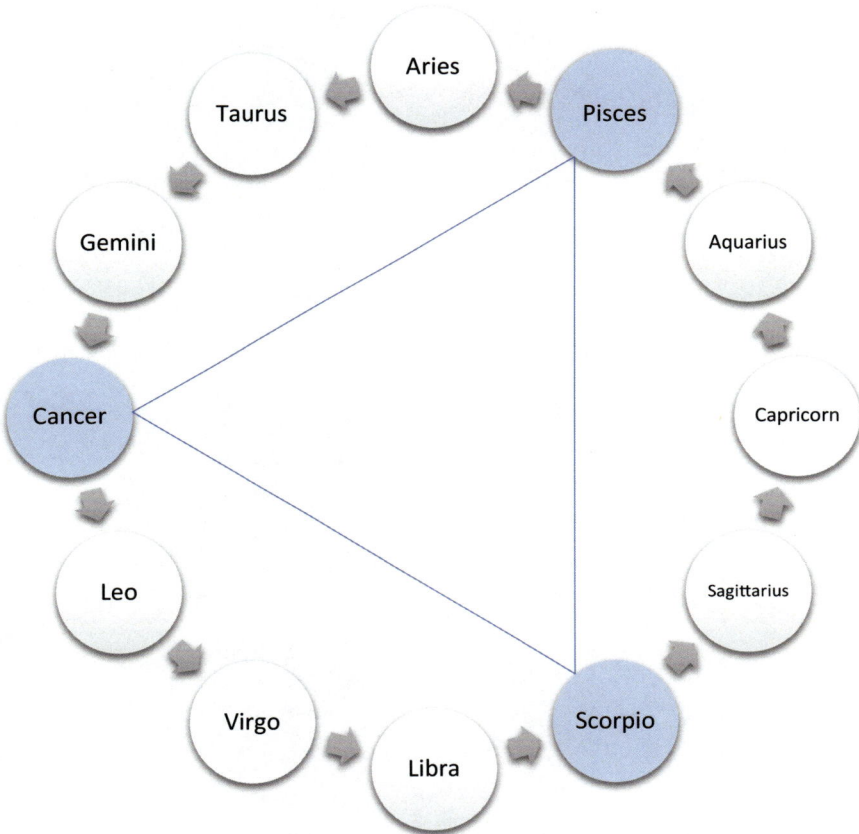

Scorpio decanates: 1. (principal ruler) Mars; 2. Jupiter; 3. Moon.
Pisces decanates: 1. (principal ruler) Jupiter, co-ruler Neptune; 2. Moon; 3. Mars.
Cancer decanates: 1. (principal ruler) Moon; 2. Mars; 3. Jupiter.

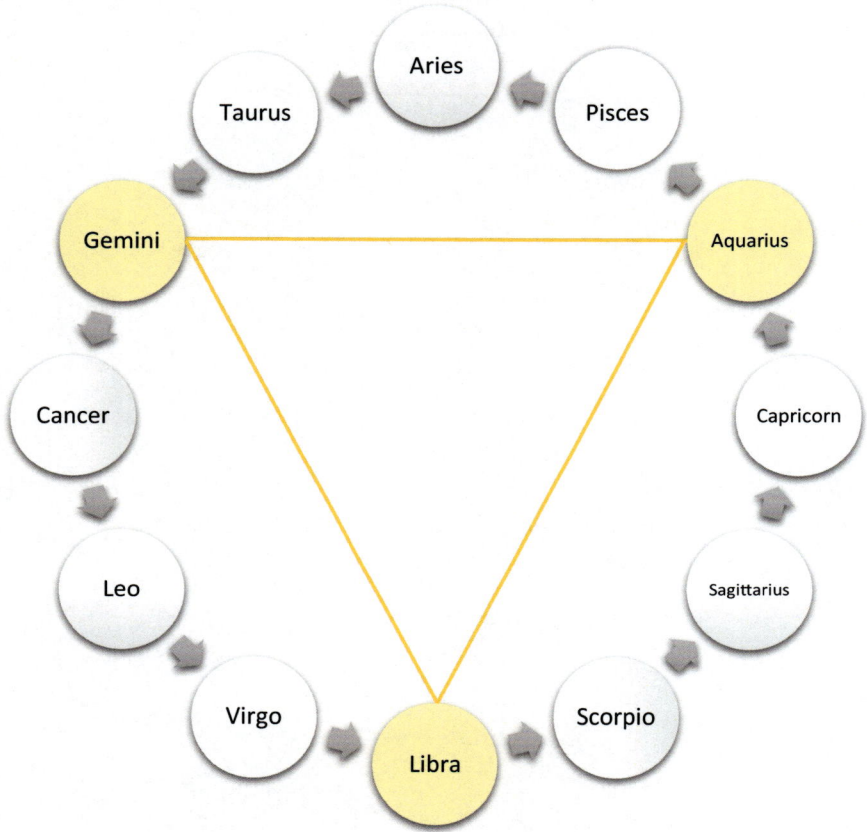

The Matthew Trigon
Light-ether
Masculine
(Air Signs)

Aquarius decanates: 1. (principal ruler) Uranus; co-ruler Saturn; 2. Mercury; 3. Venus.

Gemini decanates: 1. (principal ruler) Mercury; 2. Venus; 3. Saturn-Uranus

Libra decanates: 1. (principal ruler) Venus; 2. Uranus; 3. Mercury.

The Mark Trigon
Masculine
Warmth-ether
(Fire Signs)

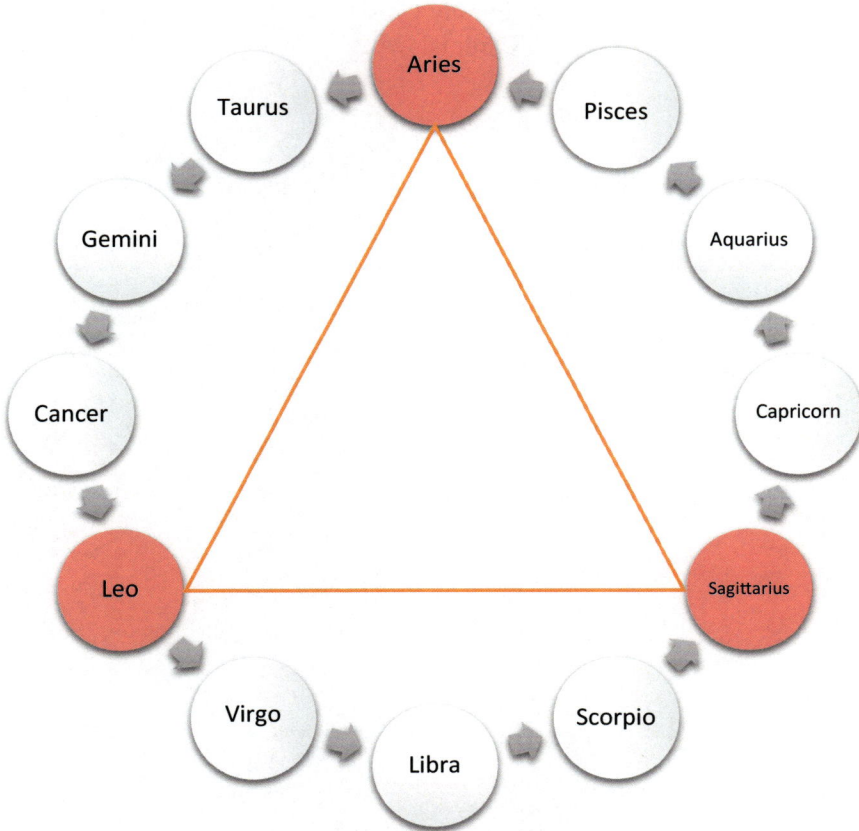

Aries decanates: 1. (principal ruler) Mars; 2. Sun; 3. Jupiter.
Leo decanates: 1. (principal ruler) Sun; 2. Jupiter; 3. Mars.
Sagittarius decanates: 1. (principal ruler) Jupiter; 2. Mars; 3. Sun.

### 3. The Three Zodiacal Crosses

The Father-Cross
'Cross of the Physical Element'
'Earthly Cross'
'Cardinal Cross'

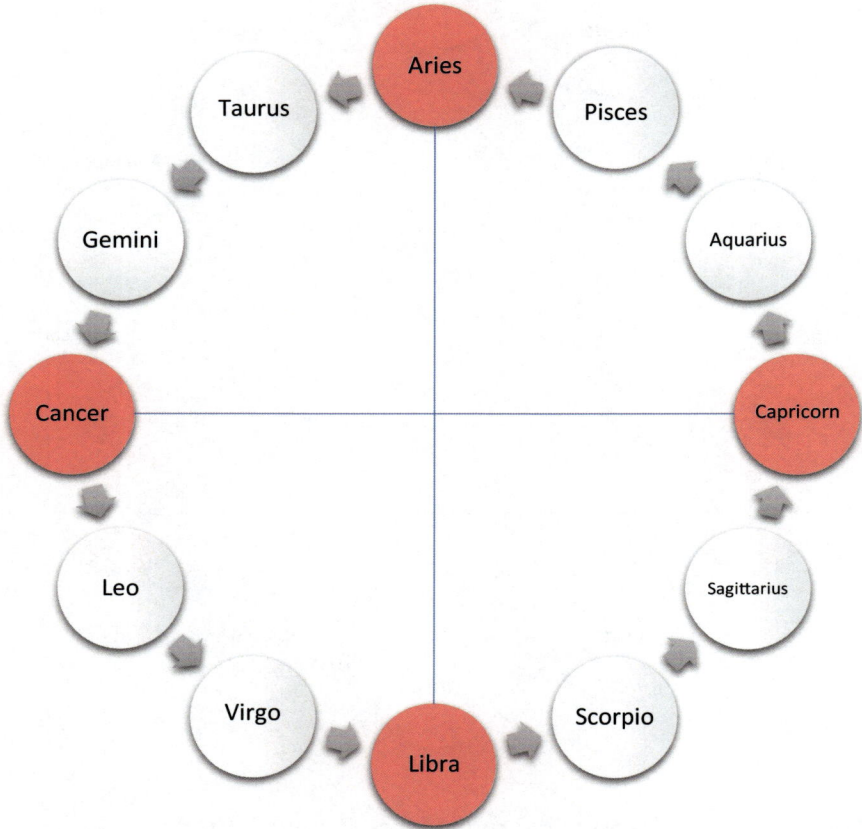

Aries: spring; vernal equinox; sunrise.
Cancer: summer; summer solstice; midday.
Libra: autumn; autumn equinox; dusk.
Capricorn: winter; winter solstice; midnight.

The Son-Cross
'Etheric Cross'
'Mutable Cross'

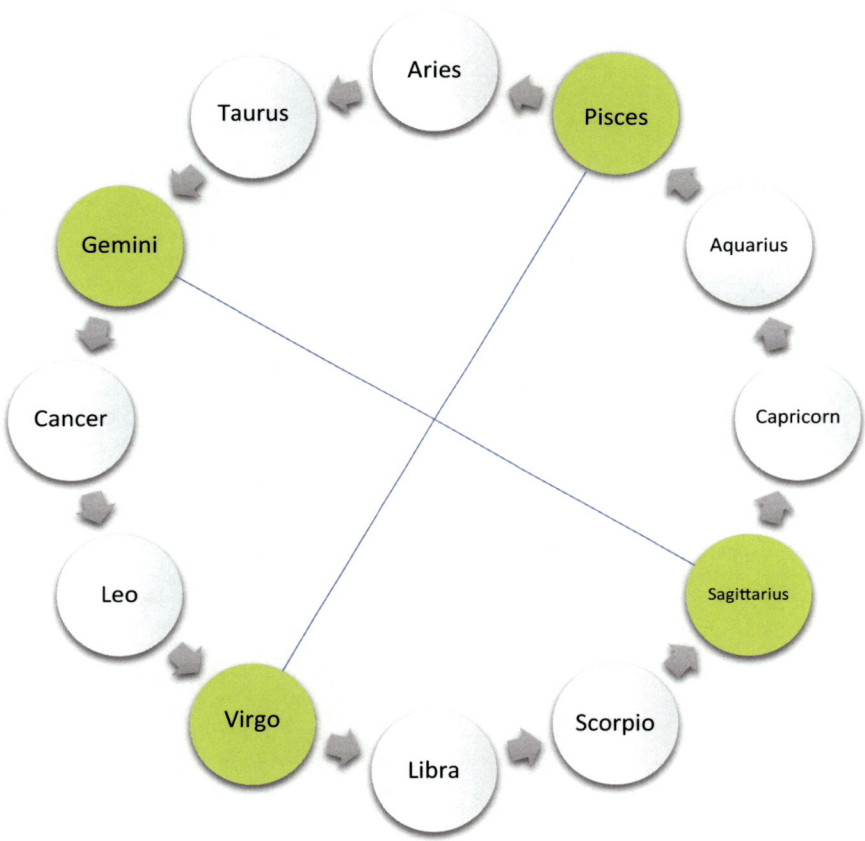

Aries

Taurus

Pisces

Gemini

Aquarius

Cancer

Capricorn

Leo

Sagittarius

Virgo

Scorpio

Libra

Pisces - Easter
Gemini - St. John's Tide
Virgo - Michaelmas
Sagittarius - Christmas

# The Spirit Cross
## 'Cross of The Holy Spirit'
## 'Fixed Cross'

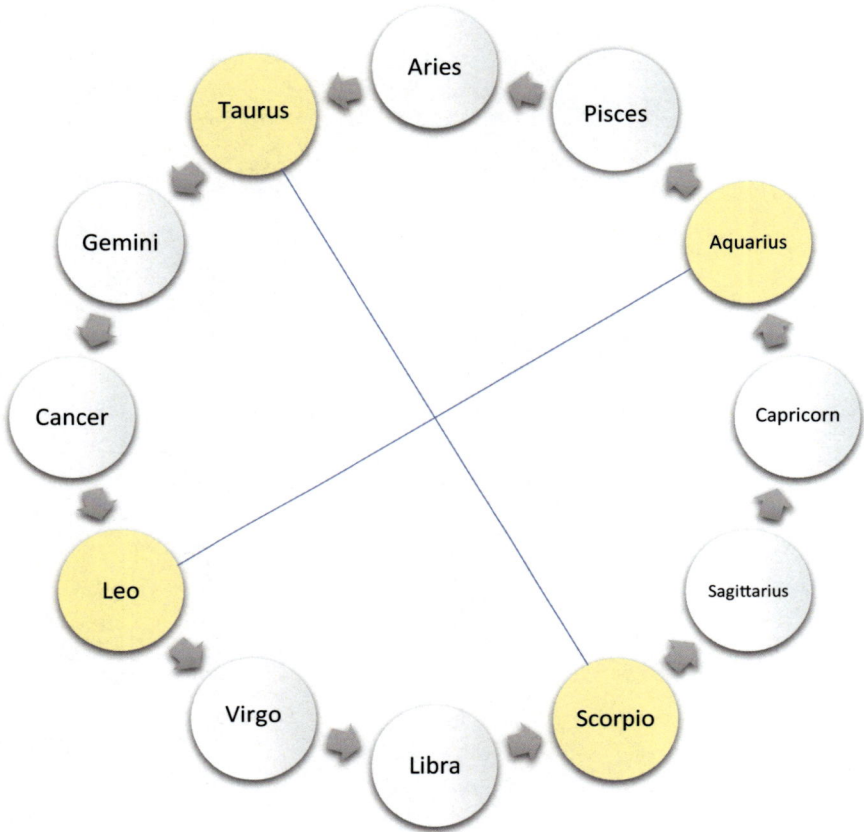

Taurus - Bull - Luke
Leo - Lion - Mark
Aquarius - Human - Matthew
Scorpio - Eagle - John

# RUDOLF FRIELING

# The Cosmic Rhythm in the Creed: for Readers of Beckh's books[262]

# The Creed of The Christian Community

1. An almighty divine being, spiritual-physical, is the Ground of Existence of the heavens and of the Earth Who goes before His creatures like a Father.

2. Christ, through whom men attain the re-enlivening of the dying Earth-existence, is to this divine being as the Son born in eternity.

3. In Jesus the Christ entered as man into the earthly world.

4. The birth of Jesus upon Earth is a working of the Holy Spirit who, to heal spiritually the sickness of sin of the bodily nature of mankind, prepared the son of Mary to be the vehicle of the Christ.

5. The Christ-Jesus suffered under Pontius Pilate the death on the cross and was lowered into the grave of the Earth.

6. In death He became the helper of the souls of the dead who had lost their divine nature.

7. Then He overcame death after three days.

8. Since that time He is the Lord of the heavenly forces upon Earth and lives as the fulfiller of the Fatherly deeds of the Ground of the World.

9. He will in time unite for the advancement of the world with those whom, through their bearing, He can wrest from the death of matter.

10. Through Him can the Healing Spirit work.

11. Communities whose members feel the Christ within themselves may feel united in a Church to which all belong who are aware of the health-bringing power of the Christ.

12. They may hope for the overcoming of the sickness of sin
for the continuance of man's being
and for the preservation of their life destined for eternity.

# [Introduction]

It would certainly be a poor thanks for Beckh's books on *Mark's Gospel* and *John's Gospel* if, as a kind of inflation phenomenon, one suddenly wants to discover the zodiac-signs everywhere, come what may. But if anywhere, then it is most likely allowed to use the key of the cosmic rhythm with the Creed. The meaningful pattern of twelve sentences— we often mention this—invites us to see that in the Creed the starry heavens are at work. Certainly, some people have already thought about it. How then in a tangible form does the relationship of the twelve signs work out? I do not claim for what follows the pretension of a discovery; I only would like to stimulate study by showing that Beckh's key is really useful. When I found the relationships, I did not only experience an intellectual joy, but it was for me a fructification of meditation on the Creed.

Already some years ago Martin Borchart pointed out to me that in the Creed the four cardinal sentences can be related to the evangelists. The seventh sentence was the most evident to me as the Mark-sentence. 'Then he overcame death in three days.' Here one feels without further ado the sign of the overcoming by the Sun-Lion; one also feels the ordered shortness akin to Mark's Gospel. Nearly as clear in the same way was the relationship of the fourth sentence, 'The birth of Jesus ...' to Luke. This sentence contains the tender Mystery of Mary and the Holy Spirit. It speaks of the healing of sickness. One is in the sphere of Luke the physician, in the sign of the Bull. The sign lying opposite is the Scorpion. This corresponds to the tenth sentence: 'Through Him can the Holy Spirit work.' This correspondence becomes plausible, if not at the first glance, then at the second, if one remembers that John transforms the Scorpion into the Eagle. Then the tenth sentence has indeed a Johannine character.

Without reflection on the signs, it can also be meaningful that the two sentences speaking of the Holy Spirit stand opposite each other on the circle of twelves—Nos. 4 and 10.

I was least convinced at the time that the first sentence, 'An almighty divine being' should relate to Matthew and thereby to the Waterman. At least Matthew in particular relates to the Father-element, but the sign of the Waterman did not yet say anything to me at the time.

I remember these four cardinal points of the evangelists in the Creed and took them as a starting point, when, having read Beckh's two books, I looked at the twelve sentences. Thereby I noticed: precisely the characterization given in the two books to the twelve signs is most revealing when applied to the Creed. In particular, too, the aspect of the signs, with the countersigns chiming in, is very important.

1.) In the *Waterman* there initially stands with Mark the Baptism by water of John [the Baptist]. In the following rounds his burial, the one of the Baptist as well as that of Christ Himself. The relationship to the Father-Ground comes about quite organically, 'the Ground of Existence'.

In his book on John, Beckh adds the planetary aspect; this is a beautiful supplement. As planets, Saturn and Uranus are 'at home' in the Waterman. Because here in Vienna I have quite a lot to do with astrologers, I am particularly grateful to Beckh for what he writes on Uranus and Neptune; I have to assume this here as something known. Uranus (whose name is meaningful and beautiful) presents the connection to the fixed-star heavens, leads beyond the actual planetary realm. In the words 'spiritual-physical' as well as 'heaven and Earth', Uranus-Saturn seem to sound together. One may also recall the saying in the gospel: the 'heavenly Father', *pater uranios!* It is remarkable how in Matthew's Gospel, belonging to the Waterman, not only the Saturnine (earthly solid) Father-aspect comes to the fore, but also the 'Uranian' aspect, where in the parallels in Luke we read, for example, 'the kingdom of God (*theou*)', in Matthew we read 'the kingdom of heaven' (*uranou*)'. The Lord's Prayer in Luke only begins with 'Father'; Matthew adds 'Who art in the *uranois*'.

In the phrase 'Ground of Existence' the Saturnine element is more emphasized, the God in the grave, who has 'gone to ground', cf. what Beckh says in the section 'the Grave of Bethany' (JG. 338):

> And so in a special sense we experience with this sign ≈ on the one side the Mystery of the world of the stars the Mystery of Uranus. Something of Goethe's '*Stille/ Ruh'n oben die Sterne,/ Und Unten die Gräber*'—'Tranquil, the stars rest above, and below the graves' ['*Symbolum: Des Maurers Wandeln es gleicht dem Leben*'] speaks to us out of the mystery of this sign ≈.

If we look from here immediately to the counter-sign, we come to the 7th sentence.

7.) The *Lion*. 'Then he overcame …' Of the planets, the Sun is here at home. This should be quite obvious. It is the Easter-Sunday-sentence. It receives still a new nuance if one looks at it as the counter-sign of the first sentence. As planets, 1 and 7, Saturn (although with it Uranus) and Sun, stand facing each other. Easter Saturday (Sabbath) and [Easter] Sunday, lead and gold, the Holy Tomb and the Resurrection.

2.) The 2nd sentence is in a special sense a Christ-sentence. 'Christ, through Whom …' This sentence, carrying on its forehead the name 'Christ' stands in the sign of the Fishes. The higher etheric element, the 're-enlivening', belongs to the Fishes. Beckh points out in his book on Mark, how in the sign of the Fishes at the Baptism in the Jordan and at the Transfiguration, there stands the word of the Son of the Sun: Thou art my beloved Son. 'The Son born in eternity.' Christ as the 'Fish'—there is no need to explain further.

8.) The countersign is the *Virgin*. Beckh calls these two signs the 'Last Supper constellation'; here also stand the Feeding of the 5,000 and of the 4,000, 'Bread and Fishes'. 'He is the Lord of the heavenly forces upon Earth and lives…' During the course of the year Ascension has a special relationship to the sacrifice of the Mass. According to an early [German] folklore, at Ascension 'bread rains down from heaven'. 'He lives in earthly existence, transmuting work of Earth into work of Spirit.' Beckh calls the Virgin, 'the sign of the life-ether and of the Earth, the alchemical sign of the Mysteries of the Earth'. If one looks at the eighth sentence facing the second, there arises a wonderful 'give-and-take', a truly inspiring dialogue between these two signs Fishes—Virgin (I recall an old picture of the Ascension where only the feet of Christ are visible. It is like feeling the mystery of the Fishes chiming into Ascension.)

Jupiter and Neptune belong as planets to the Fishes. According to Dr Steiner, Jupiter has a special relationship to 'Ancient Sun'. 'Out of this realm of 'Ancient Sun', the spiritual primal Sun, the Christ descends to the Earth. He brings it spiritually with Him; the planet Jupiter, which is housed in the Fishes, appears as the boundary stone for this realm' (JG. 73). To Jupiter the Kyriotetes belong (*Kyrios Christos* [Christ the Lord]). Alongside Jupiter in the Fishes stands Neptune, an 'echo from the furthest cosmic distances' (JG. 73).

The Virgin is ruled by the planet Mercury. Cf. Beckh JG. 80, the quotation from Creuzer: '… he [Hermes] as agrarian intelligence is the eternal bread.' His relationship to the Virgin with the sheaf! Hermes mediates between Heaven and Earth.

3.) Following the Fishes comes the *Ram*, who with Mark is clearly evident, characterized as the sign of the placing of oneself on the Earth. 'Landing', getting up, standing on one's feet. 'In Jesus the Christ entered as man into the earthly world.' Regarding planets: the active Mars.

9.) In the countersign of the *Scales* there stands the sentence of the Last Judgement: 'He will in time unite … whom he can wrest from the death of matter'. In this sentence lives the solemn Michaelic decision. The Scales also appear in John's Gospel the sign of the great 'I-AM' (holding the balance between Lucifer and Ahriman). The ninth sentence of the Creed tells how this great 'I-AM' includes the little human 'I's'. 'Through their bearing'—with this union the individual 'I' is not extinguished it has to be pro-active in order to be able to be redeemed by the great I-AM. This call towards responsibility is Michaelic.

Regarding the planets: Venus. See Beckh's beautiful description of Venus in the Scales, concerning heavenly love, the 'love in the "I"'. Venus has the two houses Bull and Scales. In the Bull (May, Mayqueen), Venus is more 'the governess of world-becoming'; in the Scales it is the love 'leading back to the primordial source'. Beckh here quotes Novalis. 'The hand which releases eternal love.' This character of Venus-Urania is heard in the phrase 'He will in time unite'. The gospel-reading for Michaelmas is the Wedding Banquet of the King's Son [Matt. 22].

With 'the advancement of the world' one also could feel the Scales, [as] the holding-oneself upright. The further advance of the great I-AM between Lucifer and Ahriman ([cf.] the wooden statue 'The Group' in Dornach), one could also think of the picture of the One walking on the sea, 'Fear not: I AM' [John 6:20].

The Ram and the Scales stand facing each other. In the Ram: the entering into the earthly world; in the Scales: not to fall into the death of matter but advance (not to 'limp' like Jacob after his meeting with Michael [Genesis 32]).

4.) That the Luke-sentence 'The birth of Jesus' stands in the *Bull* was already mentioned. Christmas–Mary–the Holy Spirit–healing. As has also been mentioned, the planetary ruler of the Bull is Venus. May is the month of the Bull, 'Mary full of grace' is the May Queen, the Christian Venus.

10.) May stands facing November; the Bull stands facing the Scorpion. But in the Creed the *Scorpion* appears in its Johannine transformed form as the Eagle. 'Through him can the Healing Spirit work.'

The essence of the Scorpion as the sign of death sounds at the end of sentence 9, of the Scales. The Scales 'oscillates' between light and darkness, between the Virgin and the Scorpion. This can also be noticed in sentence 9 of the Creed: 'He will in time unite…' still stands in the light of the Virgin, 'the death of matter' is already the Scorpion, which in the Scales casts its shadow ahead. Then comes the sentence of the Healing Spirit, then one does not take this Johannine transformation of the Scorpion into the Eagle as something obvious; through this turning 'He can wrest from the death of matter' one can feel reminded of the grave of Lazarus in Bethany.

Mars appears in the Scorpion in its daemonic form. The transformed Mars-element sounds in the word *'wirken*—work'. 'Through him can the Healing Spirit work.'

5.) The Golgotha sentence would stand in the *Twins*. At first glance this may not be clear but becomes so with Beckh's explanations. At this point the countersign of the Archer one feels quite particularly chiming in. 'The Archer' is the death-sign. Beckh clearly shows that just as Fishes—Virgin is the Last-Supper constellation, Twins—Archer can be called the constellation of Golgotha. In Mark the ascent of the Sacred Mount stands in the Twins. [The motifs are] the high point, the heights of Zarathustra, initiation, the 'great midday' (I have to stick to keywords; the details are to be found in Beckh). Facing this, the Archer is the sign of the deep midnight. The Transfiguration on the Sacred Mount Tabor (Mark 9) stands in the Archer, as the beginning of the dying of Christ into the depths of the Earth, but here, too, the sign of the Twins (Sacred Mount, initiation) chimes in very strongly.

If in the Creed Golgotha stands in the Twins, the viewpoint of the Mount of Sacrifice is thereby important, also that of the 'great midday'. According to John the Crucifixion took place at 12 noon.

The planet involved: Mercury. Hermes the initiator. The cross of Golgotha as the great 'Hermeneutic', the proclamation of the most profound divine Mystery. Cf. the snake raised on the cross [cf. John 3:14], the staff of Mercury. 'Who went through Golgotha for the healing of mankind.'

11.) In the countersign of the *Archer* stands the sentence about the Church. 'Communities … who are aware of the health-bringing power of the Christ'. Here, too, one feels the countersign chiming in especially strongly, that is, the Twins. In Mark the scenes with the twelve Apostles stand for the most part in the Twins. Peter and John, Peter and Andrew, [and] John and James, the two pillars of the visible, and the two pillars of the esoteric Church—all these are motifs of the Twins. The Church is built on the Apostles. But also the sign of the Archer itself comes to expression in the sentence on the Church: 'the health-bringing power of the Christ' is deepened, when one sees the power of healing streaming from the cross as the mystical stream, which feeds the Church, which fulfils its sacrament at the altar 'in reverence for Christ's Deed'. In the starry heavens it appears as though the Milky Way, the great stream of blessing, flows out of the Archer. Out of death streams new life. As with the Scorpion, here too the negative aspect of the sign is already overcome and transformed. Instead of the Scorpion's sting the Holy Spirit, instead of death the new life flowing into humanity, 'the health-bringing power of the Christ'.

Amongst the musical keys A♭-major belongs to the Archer, the mystical key of Wagner's *Parsifal*, of the ruby-red glowing Grail which fashions the new blood community. The planets involved: Jupiter, the representative of 'Ancient Sun'. Looked at regarding the future, the new humanity that feels the stream of the 'health-bringing power', the 'Church', is the seed of the new Earth carrying over development to the 'Jupiter'-existence.

6.) The sign of the heights of the Sacred Mount of initiation is followed by the sign of descent into the lower regions, the *Crab*. Already within the Golgotha-sentence announced its presence: 'and was lowered into the grave of the Earth'. The Crab also relates to the Mother (cf. *Mark's Gospel*) as far as the 'constriction' is emphasized. And so the Christ enters here the lap of 'Mother-Earth'. The laying into the grave is followed by the descent into Hades, the underworld, into the land of the shadows. Here the descent of Christ has reached its deepest point, 'from heights of spirit to depths of Earth'. This deep point is at the same time the 'turning point' (Crab), Christ's Sun-turning-point from the Passion to the new glory of resurrection. At this deep point of the descent there stands: 'In death He became the helper of the souls of the dead who had lost their divine nature.' To the Crab materialism corresponds in the circle of world-conceptions. The hardening Moon, 'reflecting' dead light is at home in the Crab. Through materialism existence after death has become shadow-like; human souls have used up, or exhausted, their heavenly inheritance, have lost the divine glory of their origin, and consequently cannot of themselves illuminate the world after death.

12.) The last sentence corresponds to the one that stands in the *Goat*: 'They may hope ...' Crab and Goat are the two signs of turning, of the solstices. The 6th sentence speaks of the 'those who have died in death' who receive new light; the 12th sentence speaks of 'those who have died in life' who, standing in sensory existence between birth and death, receive the seed of light that is planted. In the Goat stands the Holy Night of 'Christmas'. In the midst of the darkness the Child of Light is born. This final sentence refers to people of today who feel the 'health-bringing power'. They are still caught in the sensory world (as we received the priestly commission in the unenlightened state),[263] but 'they may hope ...'. Sentences 6 and 12 relate to the saying of Isaiah [9:2]: 'The people who walked in darkness have seen a great light.' Those who have died are caught in the spell of the Moon's circuit, those who are alive are caught in Saturn's material realm.

The planet involved: Saturn. The constraint of the sensory world.

['They may hope] for the preservation of their life destined for eternity'—points already to the 1st sentence 'An almighty divine being, spiritual-physical', as being embedded in the carrying substance, in eternal being of the 'heavenly Father'. End and beginning meet; Goat and Waterman are the two Saturn-signs, which in the circle lie mutually adjacent. Only Saturn in the Waterman has Uranus at its side, so that Waterman is brighter than the Goat. In the words 'the preservation of their life destined for eternity' shines in already with starry light of *'pater uranios'* ['Father in heaven'].

Thus the serpent of knowledge bites its own tail, the circle is closed in that both Saturn-signs out of an inner relationship incline to each other.

\*

Dear Friends, may I once again emphasize that all this is no intellectual game concerning relationships, but something really inspiring to lay hold of the Creed. What I have indicated in keywords will lose their apparent arbitrary, ungrounded appearance when one gets to know what Beckh in his two books on the gospel has worked out and developed as evident characteristics of the twelve signs and the planets. The above indications are only possible and understandable against the background of both these books; to thank him is my heartfelt wish.

As a postscript, it should be noted, the Golgotha-sentence governed by the planet Mercury—this becomes clearer when one recalls that for Wednesday (the day of Mercury) the sentence in the Breviary contains the cross. The daemon element of Mars, of Tuesday, is overcome through the cross in the sign of Mercury. Mercury heals the wound caused by Mars.

For Beckh's indication of Jupiter as the representative of 'Ancient Sun', the Thursday verse of the Breviary is cited, where precisely in the sign of Jupiter it speaks of the 'light in the primordial Light', of the early splendour of the Sun. On the description concerning Venus in the Scales, cf. the Friday-verse: union with Christ.

## Contribution from Professor Beckh

To the very interesting and valuable contribution by Frieling on the Creed, which on the basis of my research into John's Gospel is clear to me and appears correct in all its details, I have nothing essential to add. Personally, I would like to say this, that one really rejoices when any work—as in this case my newly published book on *John's Gospel*—is understood, assimilated and evaluated in this active, creative manner. Here with Frieling it has proven to be a direct stimulus also to that realm in which we are placed in the first instance through our profession as priests. Frieling's contribution shows how the cosmic, astrological view of the gospels can be fruitful precisely with the liturgy, right into celebrating the Act of Consecration of Man. For me, too, what I have taken in Frieling's contribution with the Creed comes very much to consciousness in celebrating the Act of Consecration of Man.

That the twelve sentences of the Creed relate to the heavenly Twelve is beyond doubt. Thereby something especially significant emerges for the Creed. Frieling had the intuition to relate the Father-experience of the first sentence with the sign of the Waterman ruled by Saturn-Uranus. In the gospel the Waterman stands for the Baptism through water of John, and the depths of water, the depths of the etheric world and the earthly depths, for the depths of the grave of the earth. Thereby it also appears with the burial of the Baptist (Mark 6:29) and with the burial of Christ (also in John's Gospel). I always point to how one feels in this sign the '*Stille ruhn oben die Sterne und unten die Gräber*'—'Tranquil the stars rest above, and below the graves' of Goethe's Lodge-poem. Thereby the *Uranus viewpoint* enters in which Frieling's explanation of the Creed, the viewpoint is so highly significant for our spiritual future (which will only fully come to the awareness of humanity when the spring equinox will have advanced to the Waterman, the Uranus-sign). Purely linguistically, too, these things are partly expressed in the word 'Uranus'. In my contributions on star-knowledge I shall have many things to say on this Uranus-view-point and on Uranus generally, and I intend, since the questions are directly stimulated by Frieling's contribution, to begin with it already today.

For explaining the sacraments, the Uranus-viewpoint also offers important help. It helps to show how the seven sacraments somehow correspond to the seven planets; the burial service, lying outside the earthly life, completely oriented to the spiritual world—thereby is not reckoned in the narrow sense to the sacraments—it belongs to the eighth, the *Kabiri* sphere, that is, the Uranus-sphere that stands as the eighth beyond the seven planets. The seven planets, in their entirety, [belong] to the *Earth* (corresponding to 'Ancient Saturn'); the trans-Saturnian world, the Uranus-sphere (which in the planet Uranus discovered by Herschel has as it were its memorial stone and boundary stone) corresponds to *heaven* (cf. Heaven and Earth 'spiritual-physical' in the first sentence of the Creed). The burial service is aligned, that is, to the same sign and planets where in the gospel we find the burial, the laying in the Earth. This is again an example that shows how work on the gospel directly touches on the liturgy.

Regarding the suggestion from Martin Borchart[264] concerning the four cardinal points in the Creed, I am very happy that this viewpoint of Borchart exactly fits in with what Frieling has given, in agreement with the results of my work on the gospels. Already with this suggestion the zodiac was basically found and given in the Creed.

It is very beautiful, what Frieling says of the 'May Queen' (Venus in the Bull), with the sentence 'The birth of Jesus upon Earth …' where the discussion concerns 'the Son of Mary'; the placing opposite of ♀ in the ♎ (Venus-Urania) with the sentence 'He will in time unite …' is impressive. In the gospel ♎ is also the sign of the of the judging power of the I-AM and stands in this sense especially over John 6–10.

# The Gospel Trigons in the Creed (I)

In RB 116 ['Introduction' above] the twelve sentences of the Creed were linked to the signs of the zodiac. Especially the relationship with the opposite signs were taken into account. This was presented possibly too aphoristically. Although 'hints' are the language of the gods, I unfortunately lack eurythmical grace, and so an unspiritual sequence of bullet-points resulted. Regarding this, I will now attempt to enter into more detail. The Creed will now be studied, this time from the viewpoint of the trigons. But in using the word 'trigon', I have to divert from my good intentions and already employ a keyword; I can only say briefly, 'read Beckh!' In his two books on the gospel one may read about trigons and study the graphic figures; one can also read in Wachsmuth about the four kinds of ether. I will only shortly remark here, if in the zodiac one relates the four cardinal signs Waterman, Lion, Bull and Scorpion (Eagle) to the evangelists, each of these points is the apex of an equilateral triangle:

Together with the Waterman, the Twins and the Scales form the Matthew-trigon.
To the Lion belong in this sense the Ram and the Archer: the Mark-trigon.
To the Bull belong the Virgin and the Goat: the Luke-trigon.
To the Scorpion belong the Crab and the Fishes: the John-trigon.

Wachsmuth connects the kinds of ether with this.

The light-ether with the Waterman-Matthew trigon,
The warmth-ether with the Lion-Mark trigon,
The life-ether with the Bull-Luke trigon, and
the sound-ether with the Scorpion-John trigon.

This is the sequence at which one would abstractly arrive. Beckh in his book on *John's Gospel* explains it in more detail, how the intimate gospel of Luke relates especially to the life-ether, the musically symphonic John's Gospel to the magical sound-ether.

These trigons can also be discovered in the Creed. Borchart's indication regarding the four cardinal sentences of the evangelists in the Creed can now be extended. Not only these cardinal sentences that are especially prominent, but all twelve relate to the gospels.

Sentences 1, 5 and 9 of the Creed would then form the Matthew-trigon;
Sentences 2, 6 and 10 the John-trigon;
Sentences 3, 7 and 11 the Mark-trigon; and
Sentences 4, 8 and 12 the Luke-trigon.

Now, of course, we can ask: What does it mean for the Creed, if one begins to find the four gospels in it, is it not a playing with analogies? What is the point? The four evangelists, especially because they stand on the four corners, give a comprehensive, all-embracing picture of Christ-Jesus. But in the Act of Consecration of Man, the evangelists can only speak one at a time, and of this evangelist only a small passage can be read on each occasion. Compared to this in the Creed one experiences the all-embracing gesture. The gospel contains the truth especially of the respective day within the Church Year; the Creed each time manifests the whole fulness. The Creed is thus something 'round', a circle of twelve. It contains in the microcosm the whole world of the four gospels. It is inspired in the same way out of the same cosmic regions. This is meant if, for example, one describes a sentence as a 'Matthew-sentence'. One feels this sentence coming out of the same corner of the world as does the gospel of Matthew. The typical 'Matthew quality' belongs to this sentence. It has to do not only with individual content of words and expressions that one finds are analogies, but it is more a kind of 'tasting' of the quality.

This study of the trigons was a great help with the attempt to recognize the precision of the individual expressions in the Creed and their unchangeable nature. It is inherent in all our liturgical texts that in them not the so-called 'language of Canaan' is spoken where it is more or less immaterial how many times 'almighty', 'holy' or 'eternal' appear; this applies to the Creed possibly in an increased measure. Here in a unique way, the Mysteries of Christianity are expressed in a concentrated form. Dr Steiner spoke of the years of studying theology one would need to lay hold of this Creed.

If one asks what one 'gains' from the relationship of the stars to the Creed, then I have to answer for myself: a furthering of a sense for differentiation and nuances.

## The Matthew-Trigon (Waterman, Twins and Scales)

In the Creed this would be the sentences 1, 5 and 9, the sentences of the Father-God, of the death on the cross and of the Last Judgement.

In this, in the sense of our assumptions, one could see the specific Matthean proclamation of the truth. Roman Catholicism gives us a certain confirmation. Matthew is—understood with a grain of salt—the evangelist of the Catholic Church (cf. [E.] Bock and R. Goebel).[265] We find in this Catholicism the exceptional emphasis on the paternal principle: authority, the Pope. Christ is above all the Crucified One (one thinks of the ever-recurring presentation of the Crucifixion, which often errs into tastelessness). The main mood is fear of Hell, Christ as the World-Judge in the sense of Michelangelo's painting. These principles are Matthean, although sometimes distorted into a [fixed] Ahrimanic form. Father, cross, judgment.

### *Sentence 1: Waterman*

is the Matthean cardinal sentence. The planetary aspect *Uranus-Saturn* is certainly described in detail by Beckh: 'Heaven and Earth', 'spiritual-physical'. I may once more recall the strange, frequently occurring word *uranos* in Matthew's Gospel. One can find approximately 60 *uranos*-passages there. We shall return to this.

With the first sentence it is remarkable amongst other things how *'immanence'* and *'transcendence'* are united, if it is permitted to use this somewhat worn-out concept of [theological] discussion. The Father-concept is initially deepened through immanence. The Father is the 'Ground of Existence'. He is present in all existence. Without His presence the world would fall into nothingness. He is 'spiritual-physical'. After immanence has been given its due, the right of the concept of 'transcendence' is expressed in the sentence that also does justice to modern consciousness. This 'distance' between God and man lies in the sentence: 'who *goes before* his creatures like a Father.' The world is seen as a living event—the Church experiences the world-event as a proc-cession, a pro-ceeding; likewise natural science dissolves everything rigid and every object as a pro-cess. The Godhead goes before this procession, this process. When the human being has reached one level of similarity to God, the Godhead in the meanwhile has already moved on. We stand today [in consciousness] where gods once stood, but this difference in time, as Dr Steiner emphasizes, is something real.

The transcendence in the earlier, rigid sense was something antagonistic to development. It pointed the human being back to the limits of his previous condition, opening up an insurmountable chasm. On the one side, indeed the unmoving, rigid existence of God, on the other side the likewise fixed existence of the human being. An attempt to become similar to the gods must appear as a presumption. This way development is blocked. Consequently, Dr Steiner had to combat in his basic (philosophical) writings this early transcendence.

In the first sentence of the Creed transcendence appears in a new form, but now in such a way that it does not check the development, but on the contrary brings the development into flow. In the same way, for example, the truth of reincarnation in anthroposophy receives another key-signature (a plus, in contrast to a Buddhist mood), in this way also the teaching of transcendence receives a new key-signature. Rightly understood, it is revealed as the principle of all progress. The Divinity goes 'ahead', the distance is not rigid but flowing. The going-ahead of the Divinity results in a 'following', the following in a continuous process of becoming similar to the divine. The human being may and should become 'like God',[266] but he never overtakes the Divinity. In this way there is no stagnation, no resting, in the attainment. For example, in his little book on Goethe (*Faust* and the *Fairytale*) Dr Steiner speaks of the horizon opening up ever anew in pursuing the path of knowledge. In the phrase 'goes before... like a Father' there lies the truth of the ever-opening distance, which however, precisely because it opens up in order to be overcome afresh, keeps the world progressing. It is the tension called up in the overcoming itself that furthers life. This kind of 'distance' does not divert people from their task to become god-like. It only raises this task into the unlimited, tremendous sphere.

This truth concerning 'distance' has precisely its organic place in the Matthew-sentence. In the Creed the language of the gospel can be perceived, but in the sense of our present age. The truths of the gospel are assimilated from anthroposophy and taken further. In the first sentence 'Matthew' speaks as he has to today in the twentieth century [and beyond].

## Sentence 5: The Twins

contains the Crucifixion and the entombment. This sentence, too, one can feel without difficulty as inspired out of the Michaelic region.

Matthew is the classical presenter of Christ's 'Passion'. Not by chance has Bach's *Passion According to St Matthew* attained its preeminent position, in which precisely the 'suffering' of the death on the cross is brought to experience, whereas the *Passion According to St John* has quite a different character and ends in radiant major.

In order to find the justification for allocating the 5th sentence to the Twins, one is not only referred to the countersign that chimes in, the death-sign of the Archer. (In both books by Beckh, he shows that the Twins-Archer may in fact be called the Golgotha constellation.) Already in RB 116 ['Intro.'] I pointed out with sentence 5 the Twins-Zarathustra motif of the Sacred Mount and of the great midday. Precisely at midday—'at the sixth hour' [noon]—according to the Synoptic Gospels, the great solar eclipse began, the disappearance of the Sun into the earthly depths. John relates nothing of the eclipse, but he says the Crucifixion took place precisely at midday, 'at the sixth hour'.

## Excursus: The Mount in Matthew

Although not belonging directly to the theme, it belongs to the Matthew-Twins [sentence]. The Mount appears in actual fact especially frequently in the gospel of Matthew that shows the influence of Zarathustra; in its trigon this gospel has the Twins. The viewpoint of the stars here directly promotes an understanding of the gospel.

With the story of the Temptation, Matt. 4:8 emphasizes the Mount much more strongly—'to a *very high* mountain'; whereas the Lucan parallel 4:5 in the original text only has: he led him 'up' (*anagagon*). Then the text [Luther's translation] was adjusted to Matthew, as similarly with the Lord's Prayer, by adding '*auf einem hohen Berg*— on a high mountain'. For Matthew this Temptation on the 'very high mountain' is the most important. He has it as the third and greatest intensification, whereas with Luke it stands in the second place; with Luke the casting down from the pinnacle of the Temple appears as the last Temptation.

- Matthew has the Sermon on the Mount (5:1—8:1), in which is found the parable of the 'city built on a hill' (5:14, only here).
- Matthew has Christ ascend the Mount before the Feeding of the 4000 (15:29), which in the Marcan parallel is missing.
- Matthew has the picture of moving a mountain, which only appears once in Mark and Luke, twice: Matt. 17:20 and 21:21.
- Matthew speaks of the Mount with the appearance of the Risen One in Galilee (28:16).

We clearly feel the quality of the sign of the Twins name that appears only once in the Creed: *the double name—Christ-Jesus*. Through studying the trigons much light is shed on the fine nuances in naming this name in the Creed. One otherwise always finds 'Christ' and 'Jesus' separately (sentences 2, 3, 4, 11). Only 'with Matthew' (if we may abbreviate in this way) is the penetration of God and man especially emphasized. 'True God and true man' formulates the ecclesiastically correct dogma. For this Matthew the 'human being' [Waterman] brings a particular understanding. We can already feel this third sign of humanity, the Scales in the first sentence. The [expression] 'spiritual-physical' has a Twins-Scales echo. The adjacent planets feeling at home in the Waterman, Saturn and Uranus, also have a Twins-character. (The sign of the Waterman, in which stands the sixth post-Atlantean cultural epoch, the Russian epoch, brings the Persian dualism to life afresh.)

In the entire Matthew-trigon one hears the name 'Christ' and 'Jesus' only here in the 5th sentence, and then precisely in this intimate divine-human union: 'the Christ-Jesus'. (To this important motif of naming in the Creed we shall return in the studies on the other three trigons.)

Facing the Twins-like 'Christ Jesus' appears the other double name *'Pontius Pilate'*. Especially when one thinks of the meaning of 'the *getorte* sea',[267] through both pillars that carry the door, the Twins-character also of this name becomes clear. Nowhere else in the Creed are double names mentioned, only here in the 5th sentence they stand alongside each other.

In the opposition of Christ Jesus and Pontius Pilate one can once more glimpse an overarching Twins-motif. The 'God-man' and the Roman-Caesar 'man-god' stand opposite each other like light and darkness. It is no chance that the Roman name, which with its hard sound introduces the historical, factual element into the context, stands precisely in a Matthew-sentence.

The insight that Matthew's Gospel shows an influence of the Twins, is particularly suitable to throw light on a hitherto completely unsolved problem in gospel research, namely the strange *'dualities' in Matthew*. The theological researcher hitherto could only see a remarkable preference, so to speak a 'whim' of this evangelist. It has to do above all with three healings:

- Matt. 8:28-34. Instead of one demoniac, which Mark so graphically portrays, whose daemonic 'Legion' ('Collective') enters into the swine, there are two demoniacs, of which for the rest of the story the same things are reported.

- Matt. 9:27-31 describes the healing of *two blind men*.
- Matt. 20:29-34 speaks of the healing of the blind man of Jericho, also related by Mark. Again, Mark speaks of a clearly recognizable personality, even naming him: Bartimaeus [Mark 12:46]. With Matthew instead of this there are *two blind people*.

Apart from the peculiarity of the repeating duality of these passages, there are sensitive contradictions between the synoptic writers Matthew and Mark. It is difficult to see why Mark who every time presents one characteristic personality should every time have completely overlooked the 'other'.

Here the viewpoint of the stars can supply decisive, helpful knowledge. Matthew has the Twins in his trigon. That becomes here quite tangibly clear. At the same time, one sees in the synoptics how they use their imagination. Matthew has a particular organ for duality (he is the Zarathustra evangelist); he perceives apparently Imaginatively the dualistic nature of those healed. The demoniac is a split personality. Matthew still sees the 'other' as present. Matthew narrates here more imaginatively than Mark (cf. in Beckh, *Mark's Gospel*, with Matthew the 'mother' of the two sons of Zebedee asked about sitting on the right and on the left; with Mark the two sons themselves ask).

With the three above-mentioned especially expressive dualities, mention should be made of the *two asses/donkeys* in Matthew (21:7) in contrast to the one donkey with Mark and John; moreover the 'Persian' sounding second parable in Matthew 13 about the evil fiend who at night sows weeds/tares amongst the wheat (Matt. 13:24), the parable of the two sons (Matt. 21:28-32), in Luke's parable of the Prodigal Son the fact that there are two sons is not primarily emphasized and does not regulate the story as here. The parable of the Wedding Banquet of the King's Son (Matt. 22) carries a duality in itself: to remain outside and go in unclean, whereas the Lucan parallel is built on the number three: the one had bought a field, the other a yoke of oxen, the third has taken a wife. One feels that precisely the Matthew-form has to be our gospel reading [pericope] for Michaelmas. The three different people who want to follow Christ (Luke 9:57-60) correspond to the two in Matthew (8:19-22). The parable standing only in Matthew of The Wise and Foolish Virgins [ten in all] is sharply twofold: 5 and 5. The same is with the division of sheep and goats, the twofold ending, Matt. 25.

I hope this excursus has not led too far from the theme. All the mentioned observations make the sentence tangible for us, that the Twins is a Matthean sign.

It could be added that the word 'to doubt' (*distazo*) in the gospels only appears in Matthew, not for example in the story of 'doubting Thomas' (John 20), but Matt. 14:31. Peter walks on the sea. But he is divided. The 'other Peter' fears, and thus begins to sink. For Matthew, this shows the 'Twins-aspect' of Peter (cf. also Chapter 16). The Christ says to him: 'Why did you doubt?' The other time is with the appearance in Galilee on the mountain (Matt. 28:17): 'But some doubted.'

In the words '*death on the cross*' and '*grave of the Earth*' one senses how the Saturnine Father-element is noticeable in the apex-sign of the Matthew-trigon.

Precisely in the sentences of the Matthew-trigon (sentences 1, 5, 9) are to be found the expressions 'physical', 'death on the cross', 'grave of the Earth' and 'death of matter'.

We come now to speak in the John-trigon of the fine differentiations with which the Creed in the most varying trigons speaks of death.

Matthew on the one side is related to the light-ether trigon (Uranus), and on the other side precisely he has the physical viewpoint (Saturn). The element of dualism is not only represented through the sign of the Twins, it also belongs to the other two signs of the trigon. In the Waterman, the sign of human origins, dualism is already inherent, for human origins means the setting free of time from the eternal realm (Beckh, *Contribution* V and VI). Consequently:

- Uranus, as well as Saturn-Kronos, feel at home in this sign. Such planets in polar opposition would not find their place there if duality were not already present in the Waterman.
- In the sign of the Twins this duality comes openly to the light of day. Here everything twofold has, as it were, its official representative.
- In the sign of the Scales a solution to the question is to be found. In the Scales the Representative of Man expresses his great I-AM striding between Lucifer and Ahriman, between an eternal Earth-escapism and a fettering to the Earth that is estranged from eternity.

In these three signs the drama of humanity is decided: The tearing open of the archetypal polarity

[i] already in the primal beginning (Uranus and Kronos-Saturn)—Waterman,

[ii]   the duality in the Twins (in which Hermes, the messenger of the gods, the mediating Mercury who moves hither and thither, is at home);

[iii]  the solution of the problem [is to be found] in the Scales (in which Venus-Urania governs). On the other hand, the Scales is precisely the sign of the Last Judgement, in so far it has to be shown here whether the human becoming will be attained not.

Whoever has not found the Christ I-AM has missed [the chance] to become [truly] human, which was expressed earlier in the phrase 'eternal damnation'. In the Scales, the true human picture is revealed—because of this also in a shocking way what does not correspond to this picture. The Scales is the sign of the I-AM and human crisis (Beckh, *John's Gospel*). The signs of this trigon lead from the *Ur-'sprung'* (= original 'jump'), our origins (Beckh, *Contribution* 6), to the final balance. From this observation, too, one can see that the death on the cross stands in the Twins-sentence, the healing deed of Mercury that leads from the origin to the balance, from the split of Uranus-Saturn to Venus-Urania.

We spoke of the fact that Matthew on the one side is aligned to the light-ether, and on the other side that he has the physical viewpoint. The degeneration of this tendency is shown in such materialism of the Roman Church, for example, in venerating relics.

## The 'Grave of the Earth'

The *'grave of the earth'* belongs to the specifically Matthean concepts. A small philological observation, which otherwise could sound philistine, is not uninteresting in this connection. For the word 'grave' in all the gospels there stands the word *mnemeion*, meaning 'memory, remembrance. Only with Matthew is it replaced sometimes (not always) by *taphos* (23:27/29; 27:61, 64, 66; 28:1; also 27:7). If one looks at the basic meaning of *taphos* (those who do not speak Greek will recall 'epi-taph'), then one will not be led to the psychological realm, to the soul-processes of recollection, which are expressed in 'my 'I'' (cf. *memoria, memento*), but one comes here to the physical realm; *taphos* means precisely the grave, something dug into the Earth, where one has to take a spade in the hand, where it smells of the earth. In the other gospels this physical aspect is not so important.

With Matthew a special interest of Christ's grave is undeniable, of that which happens especially at the grave, the special events with the Earth. One may read the tremendous passage about the earthquake that stands only in Matthew's account of the Passion (the rending of the veil, or curtain, of the temple, also with Mark 15:38), (Matt. 27:52, 53):

> At that moment the curtain of the temple was torn in two from top to bottom. The earth shook and the rocks split. The tombs broke open and the bodies of many holy people who had died were raised to life. They came out of the tombs, and after Jesus' resurrection they went into the holy city and appeared to many people.

(Incidentally, perhaps the latter part means that through Christ all that was saved and brought into a new light, what the saints, the spiritual carriers before Christ, had begun to work on as the initial beginnings of *atman*. That which was already worked for, already wrested from the physical body, would have been lost, could not be saved for development. But through Christ's death and Resurrection, the pre-Christian gain of *atman* is regained and integrated into the 'holy city', that means, to the heavenly Jerusalem the retrospective connection of Matthew to the past, cf. the two donkeys.)

Only Matthew speaks of the *sealing* and *guarding* of the holy tomb (27:62-66): 'So they went and made the tomb (*taphos*) secure by putting a seal on the stone and posting the guard.'

Only Matthew speaks of the *earthquake* on Easter morning and of that which happens with the tomb. The other evangelists narrate first how the women find the grave open. Only Matthew relates the opening of the grave itself (28:2): 'There was a violent earthquake, for the angel of the Lord came down from heaven and, going to the tomb, rolled back the stone and sat on it.' (Perhaps in this connection of 'grave of the Earth' one can also point out that only Matthew brings the Parable of the 'Hidden Treasure' in the field (13:44) and the narration of the 'Field of Blood' (27:8)).

Particularly with the narration of the holy grave, not only does the Saturnian element but beside it the Uranian element plays in with Matthew in a strange twin-like manner. This direct appearance side-by-side is typical of Matthew.

On Easter morning (28:3): 'His (the angel's) appearance was like lightning, and his clothes were white as snow.' This unearthly, Uranian—the angel 'came down from heaven' (*uranos*) (28:2)—light-ether revelation stands impressively opposite a heavily laden Saturnine element (28:4). 'The guards were so afraid of him that they shook and became as dead men.' The contrast in Grünewald's[268] picture of the Resurrection between the glory of light and the menacing, massive grave-stone and the watch who, in their heavy armour, are lying about 'heavy as lead', is the contrast between Uranus and Saturn as narrated in Matthew.

Fear as a soul-reaction, which comes from Ahriman, belongs to Saturn, to the earthly-material side. Only in Matthew it is said (27:54): 'When the centurion and those with him who were guarding Jesus saw the earthquake and all that had happened, they were terrified (*phobos*) ...' The other evangelists do not include this. The other place has already been mentioned (28:4): 'from fear the watch became like corpses (*nechroi*)'.

With the Easter appearances, too, the element of fear plays a greater role with Matthew than the other evangelists, who nevertheless also— apart from John—speak about fear. But only with Matthew 'joy' and 'fear' stand so characteristically Uranian-Saturnian side by side. With John only joy (John 20:20), with Mark only trembling and bewilderment [Mark 16:8], with Luke transition of initial fear into joy (Luke 24:37, 41), with Matthew alone the things are adjacent (Matt. 28:8): 'So the women hurried away from the tomb, afraid yet filled with joy.'

# *Excursus* on the *light-ether* in Matthew

The Matthew-trigon is the light-ether-trigon; the light-ether since Ancient Sun relates to Uranus.

A detail: only with Matthew does the Easter story begin: '… at dawn on the first day of the week' (28:1), in the original text *epiphosk-ousē*, that is, 'lit up'. *Phos*, light. The angel's garment was as white as 'snow'. Matthew has a preference for *phos*. Luke in the Christmas story describes the tremendous revelation of light of the heavenly hierar-chies, but he speaks of the *doxa*, the Sun-like glory. *Doxa* has perhaps more a golden brightness; *phos* is more like snow, the 'cold light of the cosmic fields of ice', cf. phosphor.

Beckh describes in *Contribution V* why despite its planetary character Venus is a 'star' that has such a mysterious relationship to the Uranian light-ether. It is also called in the New Testament '*phos*-phoros', light-bearer (Lat. *luci-fer*). In II Peter 1:19 (after the 'holy mount'—Tabor—is mentioned, 1:18), '… and the morning star (*phos-phoros*) rises in your hearts'. The passages in the Apocalypse mentioning the morning star (Rev. 2:28, 22:16) use another word.

One should not press this difference between *doxa* and *phos*, but it should gently indicate that *doxa* perhaps lies more in the direction Sun-like; *phos* perhaps more in the direction of the starry quality. Besides, *doxa* is sometimes used for starry light.

With the Transfiguration on Mount Tabor Luke uses the word *doxa* (Luke 9:31 and especially 9:32). But Matthew says: 'his clothes became as white as the light (*phos*)'. (The 'snow' in Mark 9:3 is tex-tually very unsure, perhaps added later, missing in some manu-scripts, so that the one undisputed 'snow' passage in all four evan-gelists would be Matt. 28:3.) This light (*phos*) is different from the light of the Sun that proceeds from the face of Christ. Precisely Matthew has this co-existence (17:2): 'His face shone like the sun, and his clothes became as white as the light.' It is wonderful how the Sun and Uranos are here united (cf. Beckh, Chap. 3), gold and snow. The splendour of the Uranian light-ether Christ takes as a garment around Himself ('He wraps himself in light as with a garment' [Psalm 104:2]), thereby covering his Sunlike Being of love. Only Matthew in the further course of the Transfiguration calls the clouds 'bright', *photeiné*. [Matt. 17:5.] 'While he was still speaking, behold, a bright cloud enveloped them, and behold a voice from the cloud ...'. (On the other hand, all the stronger the Saturnine fear, the horror to be earth-bound before 'the Other'.) Luke says only (9:34) 'they were afraid'; Mark (9:6) 'they were so frightened'; Matthew (17:6, 7): 'When the disciples heard this, they fell down to the ground, terrified. But Jesus came and touched them. "Arise," he says. "Do not be afraid."' The difference in the presentation is clear.

The quoted sentence of Matthew 17:5 shows a further unique aspect of Matthew's Gospel. Something like the strange duality, which the theologians have noticed, but which was only seen as the writer's habitual manner: the word 'behold' that appears so often in Matthew—for example, in the quoted sentence 17:5, appearing directly twice—should not this 'preference' of Matthew also show his relationship to the light-ether? Cf. already Matt. 2:9, 10: 'and lo, the star which they saw ... ; when they saw the star ...'—should it not also have to do with the light-ether, if amongst the three previously-mentioned stories of duality (we mentioned two demoniacs in 'the region of the Gadarenes', two blind people, and two more in Jericho) there are in particular two healings of the *blind*?

The quoted phrase 'you are the light (*phos*) of the world' appears only in Matthew [15:14], in the Sermon on the Mount. In the Sermon on the Mount in particular the word *Uranos* also appears repeatedly. If one wanted to draw the 'holy mount' schematically one would have to draw a triangle. But this at the same time is a symbol for the light-ether, cf. Wachsmuth.[269] It is at the same time the pyramid, which brought together the Uranian light-ether character and the Saturnine quality of the grave. What I wanted to show with the 'holy mount' (in [Robert] Goebel's series of *Contributions*, in the chapter on Noah and Ararat) was the ambivalence of the symbol of the mountain: 'greater nearness of a purer heaven' and a stronger experience of the earthly character of the grave is shown in this double character of the pyramid. Matthew is the evangelist of the holy mount. Only Matthew finds it worth mentioning that the boy Jesus in his tender impressionable childhood experienced the land of the pyramids. Light and the grave (flight into Egypt, Matthew 2).

One thing more: the parable of the light, of the burning lamps of the [Wise] Virgins, is only written in Matthew 25.

It may seem with this light-ether excursion I have moved too far from the theme, but I believe that especially the above-mentioned observations can give us a more intimate relationship to Matthew, to Matthean spirituality out of which the sentences 1, 5 and 9 of the Creed have been uttered. The unifying element, out of which one can feel these sentences 1, 5 and 9 somehow belonging together, can become ever more clear to us.

## The Earthquake

To return from the light-ether *excursus* to the 'grave of the Earth', another 'philological detail' may perhaps be appended. The word for the 'earthquake', *'seismos'* (non-Greek speakers may recall the word 'seismograph') stands only in Matthew (27:51 & 54; 28:2 & 4). When the Saturnine element 'right into its underground fastnesses' is shaken, then *seismos* enters the discussion. It is not completely unimportant that the storm on the sea in Matthew is not explained by the 'great storm of wind / furious squall' [Mark 4:37], but through a *'seismos'*, that is, an earthquake that is conveyed to the water, a 'sea-quake'. It has less to do with the astral element than with the shaking 'solid land' of a physical earthquake. Matthew alone adds the effect of the Entry into Jerusalem as 'seismical', 21:10. AV/KJV: 'all the city was moved'. In the original text *'eses*the'. Right into the details it is shown how fruitful the viewpoint of the stars can be for gospel studies.

To conclude this *excursus*, one more thing. The Waterman embraces the polarity *'oben die Sterne, unten die Gräber'*.

> The stars on high are silent still;
> Silent the graves, nor make reply
> The dearest lips therein that lie.[270]

Precisely, Uranus-Saturn. Now, the Waterman-gospel Matthew contains this polarity in the most literal meaning of the word.

We spoke of *taphos*, the *grave of the earth*, about which only Matthew speaks. But on the other hand, Matthew is also the only one who reports to us the *Star of the Wise Men* from the East (Matt. 2:2, 7:9, 10).

## Sentence 9. The Scales

is the Michaelic sentence of the great decision of humanity, of the Last Judgement. We mentioned above how from the duality already present in the Waterman a path leads over from the Twins to the Scales.

We find a sign of this intimate trigonal understanding of the sentence, a 'continuation' of the concepts, for example, in the word '*Welten-fort*-gang'—'advancement of the world' in the first sentence, '… Who goes before His creatures like a Father'. Precisely when one considers what is said in the first sentence about the 'going before' that includes the living-flowing distance, or interval, between God and man, then one can hear in the name Michael 'Who is like God?' (*Mi-ka-el?*) the great call to follow the Godhead Who goes before and to ever higher levels to become like God. This thought of progression, 'freedom and progress' is Michaelic. The name Michael, that is, contains both: encouragement to become like God, and at the same time the most reverential distance. Both sound into each other. 'Be ye therefore perfect, even as your Father which is in heaven is perfect' (Matt. 5:48 AV/KJV) 'There is none good' (Matt. 19:17 AV/KJV).

An important metamorphosis takes place within the Matthew trigon with the physical world, so important to Matthew. 'Spiritual-physical' (1)—'grave of the earth' (5)—'*death of matter*' (9). In this there lies a whole history. First of all, one recognizes the origin of all material in the Father, our origin in the light.[271] 'Spiritual-physical'—the physical element is not yet separated. It is still the case: nothing is inner, nothing is outer. Everything is still embedded in the divine being. But the split is being prepared. The next stage in the middle sentence of the trigon (5) is the 'grave of the earth'. The physical element has emancipated itself from the spiritual, the earth from the heavens; it has become a grave. But where there are graves, there are resurrections.[272] Here is the great turning point. Through the death on the cross a new connection of the spirit and the physical world, of heaven and earth is prepared. This resolution, however, is not a natural compulsion, but it is allocated to the free will of people. A part of the Earth will become 'heavenly Jerusalem', another part falls as Babylon. Concerning this third stage, from which the Godhead has wrested matter from human sin, the third, final sentence of the Matthew trigon speaks: 'the death of matter'. This is no longer the grave, in which the seed of resurrection is laid, in which the seed rests, but this is the 'other [second] death', the unfruitful, sterile, death alone.

In the first sentence everything rests in the Father. In the fifth sentence Christ fulfils His sacrifice. In the ninth sentence it rests with the attitude of human beings, how far the work of redemption penetrates. In the spiritual-physical, in 'heaven and earth' of the first sentence the death on the cross is prepared (as the consequence of the split);

Golgotha is the preparation for the Last Judgement, where it is shown whether the human aim in free appropriation of Christ's sacrifice is achieved or not. It is deeply grounded in the duality in Matthew's Gospel that in this gospel the 'Last Judgement' plays an especially large role. The tremendous judgement-scene, where the king (like the king in Matt. 22) divides human beings, the one part to the right, the other to the left, stands in Matt. 25:31-46. In Roman Catholicism Michelangelo's *Last Judgement* was painted.[273] Our Creed leads over Matthean thinking of the great division to the modern feeling: Christ does not judge from outside, as it were enjoying his abundant power, but it rests with human beings themselves whether or not He can save them. Limits are posed through the attitudes of human beings to the effect of his universal will to redeem. That the heavenly love that wants to redeem sounding in the motif of the Wedding Banquet of the King's Son 'He will in time unite', that one can especially sense Venus-Urania here at home in the Scales, was already indicated in the previous chapter ['Introduction']. The Matthean Parable of the Wise and Foolish Virgins also ends with entering the room of the Wedding Banquet of the King's Son.

Hopefully, it now no longer sounds arbitrary when one says: sentences 1, 5 and 9 contain the Matthean, the Waterman-Twins-Scales aspect of Christian truth. Father, cross, grave, judgment. A deepening in Matthew's Gospel can help us precisely to speak this sentence of the Creed out of its background.

## More on Matthew: Dualism

Before we turn to the John-trigon, I would like to add a further observation concerning Matthew.

Out of the previous studies it should be clear how the sentences 1, 5 and 9 of the Creed are spoken out of the same spiritual, cosmic region as Matthew's Gospel. We saw how out of the stars Dr Steiner's indication about the relationship of Zarathustra to Matthew's Gospel is confirmed, how *dualism* is a key to Matthew's Gospel. Dualism, which in the light-ether trigon ('Uranus-trigon') is so clearly recognizable: inherent in the Waterman ('Uranus-Kronos') [and] frequently evident in the Twins, [it] is balanced out in the Scales.

In the first Credo-sentence (Waterman) the *'Ur-'Sprung''* (literally, primordial 'jump'), the origin, which runs right through the unity before the beginning (or, the anterior unity), thereby indicates how the first word *'Ein'*, 'An' [in Germ. also 'one'] (*'ein allmächtiges* ... an almighty ...'), then divides into 'spiritual' and 'physical', into 'heaven and earth'. In the first word of the Creed *'Ein'* there lies the whole *sublimity of the anterior eternity of the* Pater Uranios, *Father in heaven.*

To this, there answers, out of the third sentence of the Matthew-trigon, and out of the ninth sentence, which stands in the sign of the Scales, the phrase: *'Er wird* einst *sich vereinen* ... He will in time unite ...' (the subject of uniting is also in the 11th sentence—the Church, but in sentence 9 the word appears for the first time within the Creed; it is here in a certain way inserted as representative).

In sentence 1 the unity *before* the split, and in sentence 9 the unity *after* the branching, in the sign of Venus-Urania. In the middle between both, at the critical point where decisive disagreement threatens, there stands the death on the cross, sentence 5.

# The Gospel-Trigons in the Creed (II)

## Uranos in Matthew

The indication of the approximately 60 special *uranos* passages of Matthew's Gospel will remain as an abstract statistic unless I describe at least a few passages.

The theological experts explain to themselves the noticeable frequent occurrence of *'uranos'* in Matthew, who out of his Jewish devout self-consciousness shunned the divine Name, circumscribing it with 'heaven', which in Judaism is frequently the case. This would in any case 'explain' such passages, where, for example, Luke [a gentile] says: kingdom 'of God', Matthew 'kingdom of heaven'. Yet it would still not explain the marked 'preference' of Matthew for the word *uranos*, which frequently appears in such passages that do not have to do with a circumlocution of the divine Name. One has then to take the word completely literally: *'Umschreibung'*, 'circumlocution'—instead of the 'I' middle point, the circumference, the periphery, is indicated, the heavenly vault.

One finds *'uranos'* especially in connection with the word *'basilein'*, kingdom. That is, what is usually translated as *'kingdom of heaven'*.

The sermon of the Baptist begins (3:2): 'Change your thinking, for the kingdom of heaven (*basileia* tón *uranón*) is near.' The proclamation of Christ Himself after the Baptism in the Jordan sounds exactly the same (4:17). This word has quite a special sound in the first sentence of the Sermon on the Mount that sets the tone, in the first Beatitude. 'Blessed (*makarioi*) are the beggars for the spirit, for theirs is the kingdom of heaven' (in the Lucan parallel, where the mountain is missing, [we read] only (Luke 6:20): 'Blessed are you who are poor, for yours is the kingdom of God (*theou*).') The mountain is the spiritual 'star observatory', where the greater nearness of the heavens can be felt and the stars sparkle more brightly.

When one takes a closer look at the oft-repeated phrase in Matthew *'basileia tōn uranōn'*, one feels a special constellation in placing these two words together. That which is indicated through *'uranos'* of the region of the Waterman (our supersensory origin), requires no more justification. Standing facing the Waterman is the Lion, the kingly

Sun-sign. The word *'basileus'*, *'basileia'* has something of the Sun-splendour of the Lion. *'Basileia tōn uranōn'* lies on the axis *Waterman-Lion*,
concerning which Beckh has written so much of importance. He
describes amongst other things that this is the constellation of the
Marriage in Cana; in this context he quotes the lines of Novalis [from
*Hymns to the Night*, tr. George MacDonald]:

> One day the stars, down dripping,
> Shall flow in golden wine:
> We, of that nectar sipping,
> As living stars will shine.

Beckh says that the starry world of Uranos has to become the higher
Sun in the heart. And indeed significantly at the end of the Cana narration we read [John 2:11] His disciples 'believed/ put their faith', *pistis*
in Him, as the strength of the heart.

In his *Studies in the Gospels*, Bock[274] shows [see Vol. 1, 9] how the
path of seven stages in John's Gospel is also marked in Matthew's
Gospel. He points out something that perhaps at the first glance may
not appear especially evident: the 1st stage—the *Marriage in Cana*—is
to be found in the *Sermon on the Mount*. On this relationship a new
light falls from the stars; from this it is clear that Bock's observation
was no construction. In the Sermon on the Mount we have the first
representative proclamation of the *'basileia tōn uranōn'*. The periphery
of cosmic stars becomes in the 'I'-middle point the *higher Sun in the
heart*. Waterman-Lion: that is the theme.

Prior to the Sermon on the Mount, the words 'kingdom of heaven'
are mentioned in the proclamation of the Baptist (3:2) and Christ (4:17);
it is only the prelude. Here it only means that the kingdom of heaven
'is approaching'. But at the beginning of the Sermon on the Mount
this kingdom of heaven is not only presented as 'near' but is penetrating into the human 'I' ('the ego itself'). The previous proclamation
says only: change your thinking, prepare an inner space for that which
wants to come. The Sermon on the Mount, however, says straightaway
in the first sentence: 'for theirs is the kingdom of heaven'. Dr Steiner
emphasizes the Greek work *'autos'* ('self') that reappears in these Beat-
itudes and lies behind the translations 'theirs' ('theirs is the kingdom
of heaven'). In their self they will have the kingdom of heaven. *'Autos'*
points to the most inner kernel, to the 'I'. There the golden Sun-Lion-
throne is raised, there the kingly power of the Sun-'I' should receive
into itself the starry fullness of the cosmic periphery. 'One day the

stars, down dripping,/ Shall flow in golden wine'—the verse continues—'We, of that nectar sipping,/ As bright (*'lichte'*) stars will shine.' The human 'self' (*autos*) is then no longer dark and darkened, but it begins to shine, it becomes 'blessed'—*makarios*.

The phrase *'basileia tōn uranōn'* may be heard very often in the further course of Matthew's Gospel; at the beginning of the Sermon on the Mount it has something unique, opening up, basic, representative. The Lucan parallel (which by the way is hardly comparable with the Sermon on the Mount) has *'basilein tou theou'*, the kingdom of heaven of the higher 'I'. Luke's formulation refers to the subject, not to the object of this kingdom.

The 'kingdom of heaven' comes a second time in the 8th Beatitude (Matt. 5:10).

The phrase, moreover, plays a very important role in the passage concerning the *law* (5:17-20). Here Christ 'changes the water of the old covenant into the wine of the new'. This passage can be raised into cosmic greatness. Christ says that He did not come to destroy, but to fulfil. As long as 'heaven (*uranos*) and earth' exist, not the smallest letter or jot of the pen ('jot or tittle' AV/KJV) will pass from the law (*nomos*). Law is here not only the Mosaic law, which is only the cultic representative of the deeper cosmic law. In his book on John's Gospel, Beckh shows how the word *'nomos'* in its sounds is already the reverse of *'monos'* (the unique 'I'-point), and how the word expresses its sending strength inwards from the circumference, from the periphery. (Corresponding is *'nomé'*: the 'pasture' of the cosmic round.)[275] The fact of this *'nomos'* keeps the world on its course, ordering it. Order is in a very high sense the 'heavenly' daughter full of blessing.

The 'I' is not to disturb this heavenly order, which 'bears and orders' it. It should become auto-nomous, freely merging with the eternal laws, and itself become a bearer of the world's constructive and preserving forces. Then the existence of the world will no longer be preserved through *nomos* working from outside, from the periphery, but one can say to the higher 'I': 'who bears and orders the life of the world, as you receive it from the Father ...'

'Anyone who breaks one of the least of these commands and teaches others to do the same will be called least in the kingdom of heaven, but whoever practises and teaches these commands will be called great in the kingdom of heaven' (5:19); *megas*, 'great' also means 'magical'. Whoever brings his 'I' into harmony with the ordering of the life of the world, is a greater magician than he who smashes and destroys.

It is expressed in all clarity that these sentences sounding so 'conservative' do not justify the Pharisees and scribes, whom indeed realized an exact keeping of the Mosaic law, for it goes on to say: 'For I tell you that unless your righteousness surpasses that of the Pharisees and the teachers of the law, you will certainly not enter the kingdom of heaven' (5:20). Following the 'conservative' sentences come the 'revolutionary' ones: 'You have heard, that it was said of yore … but I say to you …'

In this sounding into each other of sayings praising the law and the 'I' one feels again the *constellation of transformation Waterman-Lion* (which is indeed the constellation of transubstantiation within the Act of Consecration, where the 'I' 'thanks' the Father for transubstantiating His substance).

It is worth noting how in the basic passage on the law (5:17-20) the phrase *'basileia tōn uranōn'* comes three times. In the chapter of parables, Chapter 13, the phrase *'basileia tōn uranōn'* comes seven times (it is missing in the first parable but is included in 13:11). It appears later, too, though I will keep to the cited passages in the Sermon on the Mount.

Likewise, in Matthew, another noticeable connection with *'Uranus'* is: *the Father in heaven*, or *the heavenly Father (pater uranios)*. This phrase, too, appears for the first time within the Sermon on the Mount and receives here its decisive stamp. And this first representative instance comes in that so genuine Matthean light-ether sentence 5:16 (preceded by 5:14, 'You are the light of the world'): 'Let your light shine before men, that they may see your good deeds and praise your Father in heaven' ('good' deeds is of course not a satisfactory rendering of *'kalos'*, something like: your radiant deeds, beautiful in soul—*kalos* is a seeing-word). What is meant here of 'allowing your own light to shine' is something so selfless that the praise reaches beyond the bearer of the light to the source of all light. The Christians, the *'makarioi'* [the blessed] should bring once more to shine the primordial sacred light of the Uranian Father '… as bright stars will shine'. Earlier 'one praised the Father in the heavens', by beholding the starry firmament. The same should now take place in beholding the *makarioi*. The *human being* as *revelation of the heavens*.

Furthermore, the phrase 'the Father in heaven' appears in the passage about love of enemies, 5:45, 'that you may be sons of your Father in heaven. He causes his sun to rise on the evil and the good and sends rain on the righteous and the unrighteous … Be perfect (*teleios*), therefore, as your heavenly Father is perfect.' Think of the beginning *'Ein...'*, *'An...'*, of the 1st sentence of the Creed. Love of the enemy comes from somewhere far away, out of the primordial region of this still undivided *'Ein'*—One.

*'Sun'* and *'rain'* contain in this sublime connection a cosmically great meaning. The Sun is the mediator of that which streams from the periphery of the cosmos. This it gathers, from starry constellation to starry constellation, and in a certain way 'processes' it, so that it can be received by the earthly world. The rain carries the heavenly Uranian blessing out of the atmosphere down to the Earth. The Sun radiates from the point outwards; the rain comes out of the periphery, out of the girdle of clouds surrounding the Earth. Raindrops do not arrive like the rays of the Sun as it were from a point. Does perhaps this passage of Sun and rain standing only in Matthew reveal something of the constellation Waterman-Lion? Perhaps it is not only a banal allegory when with rain one is in actual fact reminded of the 'Waterman'. The Sun, as mentioned, 'individualises' in itself the cosmic influences and then rays out of an 'I'-point, whereas raindrops come out of the direction of the stars, that is, not out of a point, but out of the periphery. With snow this starry connection is still more clear. The way rain and snow come to us is in a certain way still originally more Uranian than the way the Sun radiates. In them there already lives *'basileia tōn uranōn'*.

One recalls the beautiful children's verse: *'es regnet, Gott segnet'* ('when it rains, God is blessing').

Sun and rain are the conveyers of 'that which is eternally creating and surging around us', they are the revealers of the 'heavenly Father', the Sun already more in an 'I'-manner [with ego-presence].

After this preparation, the *Lord's Prayer* within the Sermon on the Mount 6:9 takes a worthy position. Do not take it amiss when I say once more that only in this Matthean context (not Luke 11) the Lord's Prayer speaks twice of *Uranos*, in the form of address and in the third petition (will).

The two *Uranos*-phrases, 'kingdom of heaven' and 'Father in heaven' unite towards the end of the Sermon on the Mount in 7:21: 'Not everyone who says to me, "Lord, Lord", will enter the kingdom of heaven, but only he who does the will of my Father who is in heaven.'

Those who are interested will find further *uranos*-passages in Matthew's Gospel. I wanted in the first place to limit myself to the most important passages of the Sermon on the Mount, which is precisely a quite special, genuine Matthean revelation of *Uranos* ('greater proximity to a more pure heaven').

I would still like to point to Matthew 18:10, where in following the words about the children we likewise find a genuine Matthean formulation, 'their angels in the heavens see the face of my Father in heaven'.[276]

In the apocalyptic chapter 24 (to which Mark 13 is the parallel), with all the similarities in the parallels with Mark and Luke, the Uranian uniqueness with Matthew can be clearly felt. I refer to the 'cosmic' passage 24:29/30, the only one where the gospels (except Matthew 2) speak of the stars. There it says at first (24:29), in the same way as in Mark and Luke, that the stars fall from heaven and the *dynameis* of *uranos* come into movement. But in 24:30 only Matthew says: 'At that time the *sign of the Son of Man will appear in the sky (Uranos).*' (The following is again 'generally synoptic', only Matthew adds characteristically: 'the Son of Man coming on the clouds' in addition to 'of heaven'. For Matthew the clouds are in a special sense 'clouds of heaven', as he also speaks (6:26) of the 'birds of heaven', whereas there Luke only says 'ravens'.)

The sign of the Son of Man appearing in heaven is the 'speciality' of Matthew, somehow also pointing in the direction of primordial, sacred astrology.[277]

With this the excursi end, and in the next studies keeping strictly to the text of the Creed, the 'discursive' element is to come properly to the fore. If I have still not achieved to be understood by everyone in this regard, please communicate it to me. The RB readership is 'occult' [= hidden], also in so far that I cannot know how far Beckh's books are known. If my contributions are not understandable, becoming a reason to study Beckh's books (for example, to borrow, or helped by well-off members of the Community [written during the Great Depression]) this is not a bad thing. Then, after studying Beckh, one could turn afresh to these RB contributions and be able to understand them, in so far as the latter will not have become lost in the running of the household.

## The Gospels and the kinds of Ether

As preparation for the following studies on the trigons of John, Mark and Luke in the Creed, a few things on the arrangement of the gospels to the supersensible [human] members and kinds of ether can be added.

Confusion might perhaps ensue when one hears that Matthew, who describes from the viewpoint of the physical body, is supposed to relate to the light-ether.

First of all, one has cleanly to differentiate. Initially there is the viewpoint of the supersensory human members.

| | |
|---|---|
| Matthew | physical body |
| Mark | ether-body |
| Luke | astral body |
| John | the 'I' |

Thereby so to speak the special 'spheres of interest' of the individual evangelists are marked.

The viewpoint of the *kinds of ether* is something different. This involves more the soul-forces, with which the individual engages his sphere of interest. A division into 'what' and 'how', however, would be too crude. It is not so simple. Think for instance how Obenauer[278] ascribes to Novalis the sound-ether and to Hölderlin the light-ether. This concerns not only the soul-aspect, the 'how' of their style, but also lays hold of their content. Thus, for example, when Novalis with his flowing, magical style, thoroughly enjoys describing the watery, fluid element.

It is similar with the kinds of ether of the evangelists. We find how 'superficially' we regard the old symbols of Human Being (Waterman), Lion, Bull and Eagle (Scorpion). These are the four cardinal points of the zodiac, at the same time the apexes of the four trigons. In harmony with astrological tradition, Wachsmuth clearly links these four trigons with the kinds of ether. According to him Waterman-Twins-Scales is precisely the light-ether trigon. Already out of this consideration, still remaining in outer things, Matthew's relationship to the light-ether is already given, which is also inwardly evident.

We leave there the viewpoint of the human supersensible members, and align the evangelists to the kinds of ether, initially unconcerned with the old symbols of the evangelists. We have first to keep them separate.

| | | | | | |
|---|---|---|---|---|---|
| Matthew | *physical* | warmth | Mark | physical | *warmth* |
| | etheric | *light* | | *etheric* | light |
| Luke | *astral* | sound | John | astral | *sound* |
| | 'I' | *life* | | 'I' | life |

With this scheme many things can become clear.

# The Evangelist-Trigons in the Creed (III)

## II. The John-Trigon (Fishes, Crab, Scorpion, Eagle)

From the previous studies it has hopefully become clear how far Matthew's Gospel, which is a narration from the viewpoint of the physical body, relates to the light-ether trigon (Waterman-Twins-Scales. See the scheme at the end of the previous chapter).

John's Gospel has the viewpoint of the 'I' ([containing] the I-AM sayings) but his trigon is that of the *watery sound-ether*. In astrology the Fishes-Crab-Scorpion were always called the watery signs, relating individually to the sea, to the flowing and still waters. Wachsmuth recognizes these signs as the sound-ether trigon.

With a certain right one may call the Matthew *light-ether* trigon the *Uranus-trigon*; one may call the John's *sound-ether* trigon the *Neptune-trigon*. Neptune 'rules' in the Fishes, the sign of the sea. Neptune with his trident stirs up the sea, also the sea of musical sounds. Uranus arrived during the Ancient Sun aeon, whereas Neptune points to the Ancient Moon aeon, in which indeed the sound-ether came into being. In this connection, Beckh refers to the sayings of Dr Steiner in the Düsseldorf lecture-cycle [*The Spiritual Hierarchies and their Reflection in the Physical World*. GA 110].

Concerning the *musical* character of *John's Gospel* Beckh speaks frequently in his book on John's Gospel, cf. also Robert Goebel, *Das Evangelium in den vier Evangelien*, pp. 18-21.[279] The world of Novalis can form a bridge to understand this fact. His Johannine character is revealed not alone in his thoughts, but precisely in his characteristic style, in his *Wesensart*, manner of being. Through Novalis one can recognize what sound-ether is. In his book *Hölderlin-Novalis*, pp. 111-16, Obenauer[280] writes on the *'Flüssige'*—the watery element in Novalis (incidentally, with an unobtrusive reference to astrology in a footnote). From Novalis we understand directly why Dr Steiner in the [lecture-course] *True and False Paths of Spiritual Investigation* [GA 243] places precisely the sound-ether as, in a special sense, the *magical* ether. Not by chance does Novalis feel drawn precisely through his manner of being to *magical idealism*. The two basic Johannine elements are heard in this: the conscious [quality] in 'idealism' (in idealistic philosophy the strong element of the 'I' is somehow always present, frequently distorted) the I-am (one may think of Fichte's relationship to John's Gospel), in the 'magical' that mysterious fluid which with the brightest consciousness unites to the wonderful synthesis. The flowing fluidity lies, as has been said, in Novalis in the 'how' and also the 'what'. Just think of the words about the fluid element in *The Apprentices of Sais* or the great vision at the beginning of *Ofterdingen* where the dream-vision of the blue flower appears, in a certain way offered as the key to the magic of the sound-ether. The *blue flower* — perhaps it is no profanation when one thinks of Wachsmuth (*Etheric Formative Forces*, p. 159, Germ. ed.).

The content of *Heinrich von Ofterdingen*—to put it banally—is the development of Heinrich as a poet. Novalis, however, understands 'poet' as master of the sound-ether. A few phrases from Chapter 1 (which as the beginning—[Gk.] *arché*—is of principal significance, where Heinrich's dream is recounted. 'I long to behold the blue flower … Formerly I loved to dance, now I think rather to the music … He approached the basin, which trembled and undulated with ever-varying colours. The sides of the cave were coated with the golden liquid, which … cast from the walls a weak, blue light … thoughts innumerable and full of rapture strove to mingle together within him; … a tall, light-blue flower, which stood nearest the fountain.'

Or from Chapter 6, the dream of being within the 'deep blue stream', where Mathilde 'put a wondrous, secret word into his mouth,' which 'rang through his whole being'.

Klingsor's fairy tale speaks of 'Sophia's blue veil'.

The Sophia who governs John's Gospel, carrying the highest content of consciousness, is protected—speaking in the sense of this picture—in the 'blue veil' of the sound-ether, of the musical element.

The examples from Novalis could of course be augmented.

The 'blue flower' is also the key to knowledge of, or recognition for, the special 'Johannine' sentences of the Creed, which form the 'blue trigon'.

Before we apply this concretely, a brief preview of how the planets relate to the zodiac-pictures. I hope Beckh [in the course of his *Contributions*] will present these things in more detail. I will limit myself to a dry scheme. If Beckh has written on this, it may be recalled.

It is an old experience that a planet to different degrees feels at home in the various signs. It is similar for us when we achieve more in one context, and more proceeds from us than in another where we appear more stupid than usual. In this way the planets are strengthened in the one house, in their element, in another they do not properly achieve their effectiveness. There are grades of influence.

(1)    being at home (regent, 'ruling', or 'governing')
(2)    being exalted (somewhat less [strong] than (1).

Apart from the Sun, Moon, Uranus and Neptune, all the planets are at home in two signs. Sun and Moon each have one: Lion and Crab. Uranus and Neptune each appear in one house as co-regents. With the Sun one can with evidence see that it is at home in the Lion and exalted in the Ram (spring, Easter). First of all, then, simply the scheme: corresponding to the Creed I begin with the Waterman; at the same time it provides an overview of the sentence of the Creed.

| Creed sentence | Zodiac sign | At home | Exalted |
|---|---|---|---|
| 1 | Waterman | Saturn, Uranus | — |
| 2 | Fishes | Jupiter, Neptune | Venus |
| 3 | Ram | Mars | Sun |
| 4 | Bull | Venus | Moon |
| 5 | Twins | Mercury | — |
| 6 | Crab | Moon | Jupiter |
| 7 | Lion | Sun | Neptune |
| 8 | Virgin | Mercury | — |
| 9 | Scales | Venus | Saturn |
| 10 | Scorpion | Mars | Uranus |
| 11 | Goat | Jupiter | — |
| 12 | Archer | Saturn | Mars |

In this context, we take once more the Matthew-trigon. There is only to add, that in the 9th sentence to do with the Last Judgement, alongside Venus-Urania ('He will in time unite …', motif of the Wedding Banquet of the King's Son [Matt. 22]) Saturn is exalted. One could not formulate this phrase better that this: Venus-Urania dominating, Saturn starting to sound solemn. In contrast to the older Credo the accent is placed completely on the positive side of this Judgement: union with Christ. Venus rules the phrase. But alongside the other possibility has to be regarded: death of matter. In the Bull Venus stands alongside the Moon, here exalted, [and] in the Scales alongside Saturn. The one time she reveals herself as the one who leads [souls] into earthly life, the other time as the love leading [them] back to their origin—birth and death.

## The Johannine Sentences of the Creed
### Sentence 2: (The Fishes)

leads from the realm of the Father ([sentence] 1) to the Son.

'Christ, through whom men attain the re-enlivening of the dying Earth-existence, is to this divine being as the Son born in eternity.'

Beckh recalls that, according to Dr Steiner's indications, the *Sun* split from the *Earth* in the sign of the *Fishes*. The Earth was once penetrated by Sun-life. Her necessary evolution, separate from the Sun, brought the Earth near to its death. The Sun and Earth re-unite in the sign of the Fishes for its *'re-enlivening'*. The expression *'re-*enlivening' recalls the primordial time of *union with the Sun*, which now in a new way is to be attained once more. Although culture has only been influenced since the fifteenth century by the Fishes, nevertheless, just at the time of Jesus Christ the Sun entered into this sign.

In the Gospels of Mark and John, the Baptism in the Jordan stands in the sign of the Fishes: re-connection of Sun and Earth.

Especially the three Grail-events: Baptism in the Jordan, the Feeding of the 5,000 and the Transfiguration stand in Mark under the Fishes. 'The re-enlivening of the dying Earth-existence.' The Easter-events, too, stand under the sign of the Fishes. At the beginning of the second sentence, for the first time in the Creed the name of Christ is mentioned. In the Matthew-trigon we found the double-name Christ-Jesus, which appears only there. Through its position in the sentence related to the Twins (5), it has there its significance. Likewise, that the name Christ stands on its own at the beginning of the Fishes-sentence is something special.

The name Jesus can be found in the trigons of Matthew, Mark and Luke, each time once (sentences 5, 3 and 4); only in the John-trigon it is completely missing.

All the trigons contain the name Christ. In 'Mark' even three times, but in the John-sentence (2) it stands in an incomparably significant position, like a planet in its own house is always 'especially strongly placed'. With 'Matthew' (5) the name Christ is drawn towards the name Jesus ('the Christ-Jesus'). There it stands closest to Jesus. With 'John' (2) the name Christ is furthest removed from Jesus. Consequently, it stands there in its greatest proximity to the Logos. Here the Logos-Christ is mentioned in the strongest manner. This is expressed as in a parable through the two planets, Neptune and Jupiter, which are at home especially in this Christ-sign of the Fishes (*buddhi* belongs to Pisces).

Jupiter is the Sun-radiant *kyrios*-planet, *kyrios Christos*. According to the Düsseldorf lecture-cycle [GA 110] Jupiter marks the border of Ancient Sun (cf. the Thursday verse [Breviary], 'Light in the primordial light'). To the bright light of Jupiter there is added like distant starry musical sound, out of the sea of cosmic music: Neptune. Neptune-Jupiter, Logos-Christ. The word 'Christ' standing alone at the beginning of the second sentence [of the Creed] carries here the weight of the double-name Logos-Christ.

Especially John's Gospel is filled with the Mystery of the Name. Beckh points out, how already in the Prologue [this motif is to be heard: 'Those who believing on the name' [1:12, tr. C.C. Torrey]. John has the deepest knowledge of the eternal Star-Name. Think once more of the scheme of supersensible members and kinds of ether. With Matthew the dualistic split of Saturnine physicality and Uranian light-ether; with John *I-am* and *sound-ether*. These two harmoniously are united in the 'Name'. Here the shining I-am unites with the sounding garment of the musical sound, consciousness with magic. Consequently, the Mystery of the 'Name' is so central for John that he speaks about himself only as the 'nameless disciple'. (The 'I, John' in the Apocalypse [Rev. 1:9] is all the more powerful. In order worthily to speak the second sentence of the Creed one would have completely to dive into the nature of the nameless disciple.)

In this connection there appears in the Creed, also for the first time, the word '*Mensch[en]*'—'man/men', standing here in the second sentence in the radiant and resonant aura of the Christ-name, and thus receives a consecration. In John's Gospel the word 'man' is already consecrated in the Prologue, since it sounds after the primordial cosmic word of the first sentences [John 1:6]: 'There was a man sent of God, whose name was John.' Dr Rittelmeyer points out how the word 'man' is ennobled in that it is 'named at all' in this sublime connection.[281] Thus the *ecce homo* of the Passion in John [19:6] is already prepared. It significantly does not say 'through which man attains eternal bliss', but it speaks of the 're-enlivening of the dying Earth-existence'. Here the Johannine spirit is moving—man's interest in the creation, for which he is responsible. It is the spirit of the Washing of the Feet. 'He who is bathed now has need only to wash his feet, to be wholly clean' [John 13:10. . . Torrey]. '*Erlösung dem Erlöser*—Redemption to the Redeemer' [Wagner, *Parsifal*].

This Neptune-sentence also contains that seldom-used word in the liturgy '*Ewigkeit*—eternity'. This word here brings its full star-sound; it indicates the sphere out of which the 'eternal Name' sounds, the sphere also of the Johannine 'remain' [John 21:22].

Like the name Christ, here too the word 'Son' mentioned for the first time in the Creed, ending the 2nd sentence, here in the Fishes has strongest place, it is here particularly 'at home'. Beckh shows, how in Mark's Gospel precisely the two Fishes-passages of the Baptism by John and the Transfiguration are contained in the sentence about the Son, the festive 'expression/utterance' of the Son through the eternal Father Himself. 'You are my beloved Son' (Mark 1:11) and 'This is my beloved Son' (Mark 9:7). In John's Gospel the Fishes-passage John 1:19-51 ends in the sentence: '… the angels of God ascending and descending on the Son of Man.' In general, 'the Son' in John is an important concept.

The 2nd sentence ends [in German] with the word '*Sohn*—son'; here one may really speak of a '*sounding* out'. 'Son' 'sounds' here quite differently in the 4th sentence (son of Mary). Not only because it stands as the final word, but also because of the sounds (O and N in '*geborene Sohn*'—the 'Son born …' here particularly has the character of the something sonorous.)

Earlier we saw with the scheme presenting the zodiac-signs and planets, as in the Fishes not only Neptune and Jupiter are at home, but how here also *Venus* is exalted. Alongside the starry musical sound of Neptune and the shining rays of Jupiter one can feel Venus' element of love like a fine fluidity in this sentence. 'Re-enlivening of the dying Earth-existence.' Venus in the Fishes is the self-abnegating, serving love of the *Washing of the Feet*.

## *Sentence 6: (Crab)*

'In death He became the helper of the souls of the dead who had lost their divine nature.'

Precisely the Johannine initiation (with whom the sign of the Crab plays such an important role, cf. Beckh's *Mark's Gospel*) is connected to the inward, esoteric relationship to death. Lazarus-John remained for 3 1/2 days in death. In John 12, after he is raised, reference to his death is made in the way he is called 'which had been dead' (12:1),[282] cf. Beckh, *John's Gospel*. John got to know the world of death as intimately as only departed souls do.

Here, too, we can think of the world of Novalis; his Johannine being touches on its affinity to death, lending the consecration of the esoteric aspect to his work. Since Sophie's death he had the hidden relationship to the other world. He recognized death as the source of the higher life. 'In death eternal life is made known.' This 'in death' is revelatory for Novalis' being.

*'In death'*—thus the 6th sentence begins. One needs to weigh every word on the goldsmith's scales. Then one will not miss the characteristic nuances already with these first words.

In a finely differentiated way, the different sentences speak of death:

- In the *Matthew*-trigon: 'the death on the cross' (5), 'death of matter' (9).
- In the *Mark*-trigon: 'Then He overcame death…' (7).
- The *Luke-trigon*: Here the word 'death' is entirely missing, instead of which there characteristically stands only here twice the phrase 'sickness of sin' (4 and 12).
- The *John*-trigon: 'In death' (6).

With 'Matthew' death is so to speak seen from outside, experienced from the physical level. Here it is not so much 'death as such' that is the focus, the metaphysical cosmic principle, but it says: 'death on the cross', 'death of matter'.

In the Mark sentence 7 it is different. Here death is something 'in itself', also apart from its relationship to the physical level. There it is the counter-power, which is overcome by the 'Lion'. The 'He overcame death after three days.'

The phrase 'in death' sounds so different in the Johannine-inspired 6th sentence. Here death is no longer viewed from 'outside', but here it is entered into, there is a tarrying awhile in it. The motif of being within, being enclosed, shut in, is bound up in general with the character of the sign of the Crab. The signs are, of course, 'ambiguous', the being-in-it can in the same way take on a nuance of enclosure and imprisonment affecting the breath. This aspect of the Crab is strongly present in the sentence about the descent into Hell. I Peter 3:19 speaks of the 'spirits in prison'. Especially the 6th sentence can be a good example for the ambiguity of the signs. For the souls who have died in 'materialism', the world of death is revealed only as an oppressive 'prison', in the sense of the Johannine initiation entrance into this sphere conveys in particular the 'inwardness' of death.

John had the deepest experience of death, consequently the words *'in* death' inspired from that region [of the experience of death] possesses a certain dignity. (In the seasonal prayer for St John's-tide, belonging to the St John's sign of the Crab: 'life born from death.')

We add now as a further observation that the word *'Sterben'* ['dying'] can only be found in the sentences of the John-trigon.

> Sentence 2: 'the dying Earth-existence' (the Fishes),
> Sentence 6: 'the souls of the dead' (the Crab).

Here, too, the finest differentiations: *'ersterbend'* ['dying'] and *'verstorben'* ['have died']. Sentence 2 speaks of the world that is wilting and decaying, of nature which dies under the curse of man. It is not yet dead. Its inborn, divine-natural fount of life is not so easily exhausted; nature is in the process of dying.

Sentence 6 goes even deeper, recognizing the root of this process of dying: it comes from the *Verstorbenheit*, the state of 'being dead' of the human soul. Here death has become a fact. Because the human soul has lost the inborn, divine splendour, the Earth has to develop sickness, corruption, 'cursed is the ground for thy sake' [Gen. 3:17].

The following heavy, profound words, 'who had lost their divine nature' give us the right to think with 'the souls of the dead' not only of those souls who then precisely in the year 33 CE found themselves in *kamaloka*, but to take this phrase still more 'fundamentally' as a Lazarus-experience of the tremendous fact of human soul-life in general having died.

The 6th sentence, standing between the 5th and the 7th, stands between Golgotha and resurrection. 'Matthew' proclaims the Passion ('suffered the death on the cross'). Mark is the Easter-evangelist.

But 'John' shows the inner side of these two events, the 'esoteric' side of Golgotha and Easter. Because the human nature had died, Christ had to die on the cross, *'der durch Seinen Tod überwunden hat der Menschen Seelentod'*—'Who through his death has overcome man's death of soul' (Burial Service). The 6th sentence gives a deepening to the 5th and 7th sentence. In this Golgotha finishes and is transformed towards resurrection. In this Crab-sentence the great Solstice, the turning point of the Sun, takes place.

The 'divine being' is a special Johannine concept, which we especially know in the form of the great I-AM saying. For Christ saying I-AM is really the highest divine manifestation of the divine being, whereby the 'I' more the 'God', in the 'am' more the 'being' is emphasized. Something of this I-AM one can also feel in the word *'Beistand'* ['standing by', support]. The I-AM is the strong power of the uprightness, of the 'standing'. The 'I' of the souls who have died 'lies lamenting on the ground', lies completely laid low. The nearness of the powerful 'I' of Christ who has passed through Golgotha works as *Beistand*, support, helper.

The word '*Stehen*' ('standing') in the Creed appears only here in the 6th sentence—'*Beistand*', and opposite in the 12th sentence '*Fortbestehen*' [translated as 'continuance'].

One can think especially on the I-am saying of the Lazarus chapter, John 11:25, which also appears in the Burial Service. 'I am the new birth in death, I am the life in dying.' Lazarus-John had already heard this saying from the world of the dead, from 'the other side of the abyss'.

The 'esoteric' element of this 6th sentence is also expressed that here not the merely outer appearing '*Da-sein*'—'existence'—is the focus, but the pure '*Sein*', 'being', in the middle of which one stands only through the I-am experience. The 'being' that is the root of all existence. Sentence 2 of the John-trigon speaks of earthly being; in sentence 6 stands the uncovered, 'merely naked' existence. The world of the dead is the world without the covering of the body, where it has to be shown, how much 'being' the soul has, how strong the 'I' 'is'.

In the Crab the *Moon* is at home, the 'light to rule the night' [Gen. 1:16], to which Novalis had such a deep relationship, going beyond the usual meaning of 'Romantic'. The Moon, according to Wachsmuth, is a sound-ether centre. As indeed also the 'Ancient Moon' was precisely the primordial fluid, sound-etheric world.

The Sun is at home in the Mark-trigon, the Moon in the John-trigon. The (only) house of the Moon is the maternal-sign of the *Crab* ('inwardness'); the Moon is exalted in the Venus-sign of the Bull. (On this, see the study on the Luke-trigon.) In the Crab *Jupiter* stands 'exalted', the *kyrios*-planet; his priestly being one could find in the word '*Beistand*', helper (in tradition, Jupiter has not only the kingly character, but almost more strongly the priestly character).

## *Sentence 10: (Scorpion–Eagle)*

is the cardinal sentence of the John-trigon. It is the Pentecost-sentence standing opposite the sentence of the 'Christmassy' Mystery of Mary (4). Like the cardinal sentence of the Matthew-trigon standing in the actual Matthew-sign Waterman and speaking of the Father-God, the especially Johannine sentence (Scorpion-Eagle) speaks of the proclamation of the *Holy Spirit*. The three Matthean sentences focus on the truth of the Father-Ground; the three Johannine sentences aim for the last sentence on the Spirit.

'Through Him can the Holy Spirit work.'

Through Him—cf. in sentence 2 (the Fishes): 'Christ, through Whom ...' The nuance of this 'through' should not be overlooked; perhaps in this 'through' there lies something of the mediating of Christ in the sense of 'transparency'. [In the ACM] at the end of the Consecration (Transubstantiation) this 'through' is particularly expressive: 'through Christ, through Whom Thou, O Father-God ... through Christ, through Whom Thou, together with ...'

In the opposite Mary-sentence, it says, 'The birth of Jesus upon Earth is a working of the Holy Spirit'. Here in the 10th sentence, 'Through him can the Healing Spirit work.' In the former sentence 'working' is a noun, in the latter a *verb*—'work'. What the Holy Spirit effected on Jesus was in a certain sense something special, historical, and in this sense unique. It was only *'eine Wirkung'*, 'a working' out of the sphere of the Holy Spirit, not yet Its full *Wirksamkeit*, effectiveness, 'entire'.

Sentence 10, belonging to John, proclaims, that the rulership of the Holy Spirit is now 'freed up' for humanity. It has to do something that should happen to everyone. 'You shall be Mary.'[283] The message is not only about a *'working'* but concerns the possibility of a free working of the Spirit created through Christ.

In Luke's Gospel, which stands closest to the Johannine sphere, there is much about the Holy Spirit. Luke reports the Pentecost event in the Acts of the Apostles [Chap. 2]. But if one wants to lay hold of the difference, how the relationship to the Spirit is yet different with John compared to Luke, then one only needs to compare the sentences of the Creed standing mutually opposite in Bull and Scorpion.

It is not by chance that with John the expression is verbal. *In principio erat verbum* [John 1:1]. The planet which is at home in the Scorpion is *Mars*. His destructive daemonic side is transformed with John, who was baptized with fire into the pure glow of the activity in the Spirit. In Lazarus-John Cain is redeemed [see Beckh MG, JG, also *Alchymy*].[284]

In the word *'can'* the potential, future possibilities open up. The 'can' in the previous sentence (9) of the Last Judgement (Scales, Matthew-trigon) has a quite different character. There it is felt as tragic. Christ wants to redeem everyone, but His universal will to redeem is limited through the attitude of people; He 'can only' redeem a part.

With the 'can' of the 10th sentence, one does not feel this tragic 'only'. Here there blows a breath of the future, here the 'can' is full of jubilation, cf. John 7:39, 'By this he meant the Spirit, Whom those who believed in Him were later to receive. Up to that time the Spirit had not been given, since Jesus had not yet been glorified.' Now, after the Transfiguration, after the Son's becoming completely transparent, the Spirit can blow (*wehen*). It says characteristically of the Spirit (Gk. *pneuma*), especially in the sound-etheric John's Gospel: 'Listen to his voice (*phoné*).[285] Something of the '*erschaffendes Klingen*'—'life-stirring song'—of Mars[286] is in this 10th sentence.

Furthermore, in the Scorpion Uranus is exalted. Beckh already mentions how the influence of Uranus is still mostly destructive, 'dynamite'. In horoscopes of criminals it often takes an important place, and, of course, also with innovators and revolutionaries. The Scorpion with Mars and Uranus is something incredibly powerful, but which mostly runs havoc in a daemonic fashion. In the Johannine being there lies in particular the transformation of that strong power.

Consequently, one can feel the 10th sentence of the Creed as an especially powerful sentence radiating energy, completely 'verb'. Especially the terseness of the sentence (it is indeed the shortest in the whole Creed lying opposite the longest, richest in words, the Bull-sentence 4) brings this concentrated energy still more to the awareness.

In order to avoid misunderstandings: it is hopefully clear that the primary purpose with the arrangement of the twelve sentences to the viewpoint of the zodiac, the 'cosmic rhythm', lies on a higher level than the planetary element. The planets add something, bring colour to it. It is indirectly characteristic for a zodiac-sign when the one or the other planet feels at home within it.

In looking back, if one places 2, 6 and 10 side by side: the Christ-sentence (the Fishes), the sentence 'In death' (Crab), the sentence of the working of the Holy Spirit (Scorpion)—if one compares them with the trigon 1, 5 and 9: Father-Ground, cross, judgment—then one will not find it arbitrary when it is said, that we have before us:

- in 1, 5 and 9 the Matthean inspired trigon, and
- in 2, 6 and 10 the Johannine inspired trigon of the Creed.

When priests speak the Creed at the altar, then especially with the sentences 2, 6 and 10 what they have enlivened in themselves from John's Gospel will come to their aid (of course, one cannot take this indication as exclusive and limiting). Two studies follow on the Mark and Luke trigons.

# The Trigons of the Gospels in the Creed (IV)

## III. *The Mark-Trigon*
### (Ram–Lion–Archer)

Mark presents Christ from the viewpoint of the ether-body. On the other hand, his trigon is the 'red' trigon of the warmth-ether (cf. the scheme in the previous *Contribution*, RB 121, p. 341 above).

Mark's Gospel takes the cosmic rhythm as its point of departure. The life of Christ appears here as the triple course of the Sun through the twelve signs. The Incarnation of Christ, His 'taking on the body', means not only a taking on space, but also time. Mark presents the life of Christ as the *time-body* of the three years.

Beckh has made clear that the 'three rounds' in Mark's Gospel should not be related in a 'naturalistic' manner with the three years of Christ's ministry. The 3 x 12 signs do not coincide with the 3 x 12 [calendar] months of that time [30-33 CE], for example, at the Transfiguration 4 signs oversee one single event, which possibly took place in a few seconds, outwardly measured.

But if one now has excluded this misunderstanding that the signs of Mercury would have to be related to the months (if might be the case sometimes, but not always and not as a basic rule), then one may relate the three rounds to the three years. Mark does not bring to the consciousness of the reader the time-body of those three years in a 'naturalistic' diary and chronicle, but in a spiritual-'expressionistic' manner. He leads three times through the twelve moods and conveys in a much deeper manner than in a 'journal' recording the impressions co-experienced during the three years. So far, one can nevertheless say: Mark builds up in those three rounds the time-body of the three years from the viewpoint of the ether body, which indeed is a time-body. But Mark follows these time-sequences with the inner fire and manner of his Lion-nature. Providence took over the presentation of the time-stream of a choleric nature. Thus, the impatient element of urge and urgency comes into Mark's Gospel. Consequently, the frequently occurring word *'euthys'*, immediately, straightway, is typical (concerning this 'immediately' one may read Bock, Beckh and Goebel), the impression of rush lies in it. It is the powerful driving onwards and urging of the great Lion pulse-beat in the heart of the Sun.

Michael Bauer said, 'Time does not urge, but eternity'.[287] Not time as such urges; calm and composed it moves its rounds. But the pulse-beat of the cosmic heart coming out of eternal regions urges. The other two signs of the Lion-trigon are Goat and Archer. To this belong, according to our arrangement in the Creed, sentences 3, 7 and 11: the entry into the earthly world (3), the Resurrection (7), and the Church (11).

## *Sentence 3: (Ram)*

'In Jesus the Christ entered as man into the earthy world.'

In John's trigon we did not find the name *Jesus* as all. In the Matthean 5th sentence (death on the cross) the name Jesus is co-ordinated to the name Christ ('the Christ-Jesus'). In the Lucan 4th sentence 'Jesus' has a greater meaning than 'Christ'; Luke's Gospel in a special sense is a Jesus-gospel (cf. the next section). Mark steps to the side of John, in as far as both are 'Christ-gospels'. Neither have a childhood history. But Mark, of course, stands closer to the two Jesus-gospels than John does.

In the Mark-sentence 3, the name Jesus is mentioned, but (in contrast to the Luke-sentence 4) the interest is turned forthwith to the word *Christ*. The Jesus-sphere is only touched on. The stronger accent lies without a doubt on 'Christ'. Jesus is acknowledged by Mark only in so far as he received in himself the Christ at the Jordan Baptism.

The *Baptism in the [River] Jordan* is the Christmas-story of Mark, John's Christmas story is the proceeding of the Logos, that of Matthew and Luke is the birth of Jesus.

The Ram is the spring sign of the commencement, of the beginning. In our 3rd sentence lives something of the beginning of Mark's Gospel: 'The beginning (*arché*) of the gospel of Jesus Christ' (Mark 1:1). This first sentence is typical for the spirituality of Mark's Gospel.

In the Ram there stands in Mark's Gospel the 'landing'. One meets the firm ground of the Earth, where the divine is to be realized in sacred sobriety. This 'landing' of Christ in the earthly realm is spoken strongly in the Ram-sentence of the Creed: 'entered the earthly world'. Here, too, in the Creed for the first time the ground of the earthly, historical facts is reached. The first two sentences still move in the ocean of the divine supersensory being. With the third sentence the first step on to the earthly plane, the revelation of the Mysteries in a real destiny.

'Logically' seen our 4th sentence of the Creed of 'the birth of Jesus' should actually be the third sentence, 4 and 3 should be swapped: for the birth of Jesus preceded the Jordan-Baptism. Amongst other things one can feel here the aspect of the zodiac. The birth [of Jesus] through the Holy Spirit and Mary stand in the Bull of Luke; they cannot appear in the 3rd sentence in the sign of the Ram. The given sequence Ram—Bull determines amongst other things the sequence of the sentences 3 (Jordan-Baptism) and 4 (birth of Jesus).

*'As man'*—has here in the Ram a special nuance. In Mark's Gospel nearly all the casting out of demons stand in the Ram (only the healing of the demoniac in the region of the Gerasenes stands in the counter-sign of the Scales). The Ram gives the strength of standing upright, of carrying the head high. Through the casting out of the demons, human dignity is restored. Beckh [MG, p. 250] points out how impressively at the end of the casting out of the demons in Mark 9, the words speak about 'lifting to his feet' and 'standing up' (*aufrichten, aufstehen*, 9:27). We recall that from the Epistles of the Act of Consecration of Man, that in particular the basic sacred-sober mood 'conscious of our humanity' belongs to the Ram, as a kind of exorcism of people entering from the demonizing streets of our modern cities, as a becoming upright towards the human dignity of a truly human consciousness. The *Ram* is the *'ascendant' of the Act of Consecration of Man*.

Concerning the planets, *Mars* is at home in the Ram and the Sun exalted. The Martian element is clearly recognizable, in the energetic, strong manner with which Mark's Gospel describes the first appearance of Christ in the synagogue in Capernaum where the tremendous casting out of demons takes place. Entering into the earthly world, 'making it real', is a Martian characteristic. To Ram-Mars, as Beckh explains, the sinister-demonic Scorpion-Mars mood is missing. Here the purely joyful activity of the beginning prevails, the mood of the sunrise and morning.

The *Sun*, which has its house in the Lion, stands in the Ram in its second strongest position. The Ram-Sun is the spring Sun; it carries in itself the strength for the new cycle of the year.

The two houses of the Sun (although actually the Sun only has its house in the Lion and only stands in the Ram as exalted) belongs to the Mark-trigon. The etheric element, which is especially important for Mark, is primordially related to Ancient Sun.

Something of the young force of the spring Easter Sun lies in the already-mentioned opening words of Mark's Gospel. 'The beginning of the gospel of Jesus Christ' (even if the first Mark gospel-reading as a whole relates to the Goat).

Not by chance the Easter gospel-reading is Mark 16. Only Mark speaks expressly of the rising Easter-Sun: 'Very early, as the Sun was rising ...' (Mark 16:2).

One might compare the other evangelists. Matt. 28:1 'when the first day of the week was dawning' (*epi-phoskousē*)—light-ether (*phos*).

Luke only says that it was still early in the morning (Luke 24:1), literally 'deep morning'.

John: 'when it was still dark' (John 20:1). We clearly feel in the 3rd sentence of the Creed something of the youthful forces of a sunrise. Alongside Mars the Ram-Sun. This sentence stands in a triangular relationship to the Easter-sentence, as we shall see below.

'In Jesus the Christ entered as man into the *earthly world.* One really has to weigh up this formulation of the Creed on a gold-smith's scales. One may compare with what differentiation the Earth is mentioned.

In the Matthew-trigon the word 'Earth' appears twice as such. 'Ground of Existence ... of the Earth' [1]. '... grave of the Earth' [5]. Here it has to do especially with the physical aspect of the Earth. In sentence 1, Earth as dark and heavy, the region 'below', in contrast to the light-filled lightness, to the region 'above', to the heavens; in sentence 5, the Earth as grave.

## In John's-Trigon: 'Earth-existence' (2)

In the Luke-trigon there stands noticeably two times 'upon Earth'. The birth of Jesus 'upon Earth' (4), and heavenly forces 'upon Earth' (8).

With 'Matthew' it is the Earth as such. With 'Luke' the 'upon Earth' could possibly be felt in the dynamic alchymical direction (more details in the next *Contribution*). The two formulations 'Earth-existence' (John) and 'earthly world' (Mark) stand particularly facing each other in our connection.

'The re-enlivening of the dying Earth-existence.' '... as man into the earthly world'.

One will initially receive a feeling-impression that one could not exchange this. The special nuance of 'earthly world' dawned on me through Beckh's studies on the zodiac imprinted into the aura of the Earth, the 'earthly zodiac'. In its ascending and descending rhythms of becoming and decaying, we get to know this through the course of the year, which in a certain sense is independent of the actual starry constellations of the spheres of fixed stars. Thus, despite the precession [of the equinoxes], the month of May, for example, carries indelibly the character of the Bull-month. John's Gospel penetrates to the actual sphere of the stars where the eternal Name lives, whereas Mark describes the life of Christ as the triple circuit, not of the starry [Platonic] year (e.g. Bull, Ram, the Fishes, cf. John 1) but of the earthly year, that is, in the sequence of the months, for example, the Fishes, Ram, Bull. The rhythm stamped into the aura of the Earth, which lives in the monthly rhythm in the etheric (time-body) of the Earth, wields throughout Mark's Gospel. In the German word '*Welt*' ('world'), something lies of the rhythmic '*Walten*' ('wielding').

If, consequently, the mere 'Earth' in the Matthew-sentences is the physical grave-like reference, then 'earthly world' in Mark-sentence 3, is the etheric Earth with its rhythmical pulse. At the apex of the Mark-trigon there stands the rhythmically pulsing Sun-Lion heart.

The phrase 'entered into the earthly world' lies at the foundation of Mark's Gospel with its three rounds.

Compared to this, 'Earth-existence' in the Johannine 2nd sentence is completely different; it has a more philosophical nuance. '*Dasein*' (existence) stands in dialogue with '*Sein*' [sentence 6, translated as 'nature', literally 'being'], (cf. the previous *Contribution* on *Dasein* and *Sein* existence and being, in the Johannine sentences 2 and 6). 'Existence' is more the surface, 'being' more the root of things. Being is found in the deep dimension of existence. In this sense 'existence' stands in sentence 2 (to which sentence 6, as explained, reveals the roots in the depths) and also in sentence 1, where the Father's being appears in the deep dimension of the world.

With 'Mark' the interest is present less for the 'deep dimension' than much rather the interest for the 'horizontal' forward advance, from station to station on the course of the Sun-Hero. For this reason, in the Mark-sentence not 'earthly existence', but 'earthly world'.

To test it, one could place 'earthly existence' into sentence 3. Immediately it appears pale, robbing it of its Marcan character.

## *Sentence 7: (Lion)*

'Then He overcame death after three days.'

Mark lives in the element of rhythm, in the element of time that is urged on by eternity (cf. Beckh, The Riddle of Time [in *Collected Articles*, forthcoming], where he speaks of time and 'counter-time', time and tide.) Pulse-beats indeed also mark impulses. (Thus the popular cliché, too, regarding the transference of heat [in mechanical anatomy] does not lack a correct core.) These pulse-beats mark the impulses of the 'urging eternity' towards becoming time, towards becoming flesh. The human heartbeat is truly a urgent knocking of the powers that through our 'I' intend to be realized on Earth; cf. Apoc. 3:20, 'Behold, I stand at the door and knock'. The incarnations of an individuality are the pulse-beats of a great rhythm, where eternity is urging to become time.

According to the Düsseldorf lecture-cycle [GA 110] the heart of the world began to beat on Ancient Sun in the sign of the *Lion*. Beckh wrote how in the Lion, in opposition to the original sign of the Waterman time begins.

Again, we can divine what deep lawfulness and necessity lies in our Creed, when we see how now especially in the Lion-sentence No. 7, that is, in the representative Mark-sentence, the *element of time* plays such an important role. The words *'after three days'* have a special ring. Once more the three Sun-rounds of the three years are mirrored in it.

It is worth checking the Creed right into the syllables. It does not say *'nach drei Tagen'* but *'nach dreien Tagen'*. In this form of 'elevated speech', *'dreien'* the numerical word is led out of the quantitative realm of calculation over into the qualitative, living element. Through this the sentence, moreover, receives something rhythmically swinging which it would not to the same degree without this small syllable.

A note in passing: how is it right, this *'nach dreien Tagen*—after three days'? Clearly, we have to include Maundy Thursday. Thereby the Last Supper is taken much more intimately into the death of Christ. Precisely because He distributed his life-forces to them, the disciples should have supported Him in Gethsemane to keep Him in His body. The Last Supper was no allegory, but entirely serious; it was already the real death of Christ, the death of love.

Apart from 'after three days' there is also the introductory 'Then' of the Lion-sentence, characteristic for Mark's feeling for time. We already mentioned the typical Marcan word *'euthys'* (forthwith, immediately). This *'euthys'* one almost likes to recognize again in 'then' of the seventh sentence. In the *'euthys'* the feeling exists how the narration qualitatively fits with the extent of time, how the urging eternity incarnates with its impulse 'at the right time', how its *'kairos'* exists. A small observation may be added here; the famous sentence 'the time (*kairos*) is at hand', with which Christ proclaims His ministry, can only be found in Mark (1:15). A 'unique property' of Mark is also known, the seed that grows by itself (4:26-29), where the rhythmical, etheric element of the processes of growth come forth in such a strong manner as nowhere else. '...and should sleep and rise night and day, and the seed should sprout and grow, he knows not how. The earth produces of itself, first the blade, then the ear, then the full grain in the ear. But when the grain is ripe, at once (*euthys*, 'then!') he puts in the sickle, because the harvest has come' [Mark 4:27-9].

One would expect that the Easter-sentence could possibly stand in the Ram-Sun. But it is completely filled by the incomparable sublimity of the *Lion*-Sun. To illustrate this, I would like to recall Bruckner's F-minor *Mass*. (Whoever does not know the latter and Beckh's monograph on the musical keys may excuse this illustration.) According to Beckh's arrangement of the musical keys, E-major belongs to the Lion, the key which is the warmest in soul (cf. the E-major fugue in Bach's *Well-tempered Clavier*). In this Lion-key Bruckner composes the *'resurrexit'*. Here I quote E. Schwebsch (p. 224):[288]

> No uprising of Grünewald-like ecstasy as with Beethoven. Bruckner experiences ... the Resurrected One as a cosmic world-event, the enthroned Christ in the sounding realm of the spheres. The octave divided by a fifth, Bruckner's archetypal symbol of swinging, cosmic space, in which the divinity is throned in unceasingly waving pulses through like cosmic swirls of light through the whole vision of the Resurrected One, enthroned on the right side of the Father.

The easterly Ram-Sun throws its 'trigonal-splendour' into our seventh sentence, but more lives in it. It has not only to do with the fact of the Resurrection, but this fact becomes a window into the realm of a comprehensive raying sublimity and majesty.

Our Creed does not say, as the old Creed, 'resurrected on the third day', but it is expressed more 'fundamentally': *overcoming death.* 'Behold, the Lion of Judah has overcome' [Apoc./Rev. 5:5].

During the course of the year the Lion-Sun is the August Sun; it has the most warming power; it has the most 'gold' in itself. On may recall the golden splendour of the ripe crop in the fields during the end of July to August. The name makes sense: August, Augustus! But Augustus means 'the dignified one'. The golden Sun of this time of 'high summer' is revealed as an 'Augustus'. The seventh sentence of the Creed is full of the incomparable splendour and fiery majesty of the August-Sun. Once more: the event of the Resurrection is irradiated by the Sun in the Ram, but the world of the overcoming of death revealed in this event stands in the Lion.

Correspondingly, our Easter Epistle in the Act of Consecration of Man does not emphasize the Resurrection event so very much, but it proclaims in a rhythmically impulsed, hymnal quality the golden, shone-through condition of being resurrected. One 'Suns' oneself in the sphere where death has been overcome. What Schwebsch says here about Bruckner's *'Es resurrexit'* is valid. In RB 117 we allocated the Easter Epistle to the Lion.

## *Sentence 11: (Archer)*

'Communities whose members feel the Christ within themselves may feel united in a church to which all belong who are aware of the health-bringing power of the Christ.'

The death-sign of the Archer forms together with the Twins the Golgotha-constellation. The 11th sentence lies opposite the sentence on the death on the cross (5).

The new life-spring springs forth in the death-sign of the Archer (the 'Milky Way'). Out of the death of Christ there flows forth the life-force of *a new humanity developing towards Jupiter existence.* But this is the *Church.* [The planet] *Jupiter* is at home in the Archer, in the mild light of its radiating wisdom, death is transformed into new life.

The new word '*Church*' stands precisely in a sentence in which the *kyrios-planet Jupiter* is at home. 'Church' comes from '*kyriaké*'. Jupiter, according to ancient tradition, is in the first instance the priests' planet.[289] The Church is a new creation, born out of death, in a special sense the world of the Son. The world of the Father appears here in a new form: it has become human. This becomes absolutely clear in the Creed. Words out of the Father-sentence (1) are heard here again, the '*Macht*—might' has passed over from the Father to the Son. In sentence 1 'an almighty divine being'; here 'the health-bringing power (*Macht*) of the Christ'.

Moreover, the *'ein—an'* and *'All—*Al[mighty]' of the first sentence appears on a new level in this creation beyond the death on the cross. The unity of the Ground of the World, of the Father *uranios* is newly experienced in the symphonic unity of the many individually differentiated human beings sounding together through Christ. John 17: 'That they may all be one'; *'in einer Kirche der Alle angehören, die …—*united in a *Church* to which *all* belong …'.

The Church also overarches individual groups, it is the Community of communities. *'Communities whose members…'*

The archetypal Church was the circle of Twelve apostles. The Twelve apostles were called on the Sacred Mount in the sign of the Twins, Mark 3:13. The renewal of the apostolic commission stands— after the death of John the Baptist—in the solemn counter-sign of the Archer, Mark 6:7. 'Calling the Twelve to him, he began to send them out (*apo-stellein*) two by two.' This beginning of a 'founding of a Church' stands in the death-sign of the Archer,[290] because as its background stands the Baptist's sacrificial death. The definitive founding of the Church has as its background the sacrificial death of Christ Himself. In the 11th sentence of the Creed none of the early, honourable attributes of the Christian Church has been lost—*Una Sancta Catholica Apostolica* [one holy, catholic and apostolic …]. Only it is formulated partly differently, more adjusted to our time.

> *Una*—united in *one* Church.
> *Sancta*—who feel the *health-bringing* power of the Christ.
> *Catholica*—to which *all* belong, who…
> *Apostolica*—whose members … are aware of the health-bringing power of the Christ. This is the internalized apostolic element, 'Christ in us'.

The Lion-sign, which governs and pulses through the whole Mark-trigon, can also be felt in the 11th sentence. One can hear it sounding in the Sun-like sublime saying of 'the health-bringing power of the Christ'. But it is also effective in the remarkably rapidly repeated word *'to feel'*.

'Communities whose members feel the Christ within themselves may feel united …' To feel has here a special nuance in the *fire-trigon* which is pulsed through by the Sun-heart.

In a certain sense it corresponds to the word 'to believe' [*credere*], *credo* [I believe]. Philologically *'credo'* might be exactly connected with *cor, cordis,* Gk. *ker, kardia.* The transpositions of the vowels within the root *c-r-d* is possible. *Cor* (root *cord*) as well as *cardia* means the 'heart'. '... who give Him a dwelling in their hearts' [Children's Service] in this sense the Church is the community of believers and the 'Creed'—understood undogmatically—is its foundation stone. Furthermore, those who only 'feel' the Christ are co-carried by this Church but feeling in this connection is more. It points towards its special relationship of the Christ to the sacred organ of the heart. An important place, only to be found in Mark, about this 'cordial' side of belief is Mark 9:23-24. This feeling can include the whole brightness of consciousness as *'claritas cordis'*.[291] Cf. the Easter Epistle: 'my spirit feels the Vanquisher of death.'

The 'feeling' in the 11 sentence lives in a pendulum swing, in a rhythm: initially it includes the innermost: Christ who lives in the heart of those who 'feel the Christ within themselves'. Out of this comes a new feeling for the world: that one stands within the newly becoming world within the Church, 'Church' according to the use of language is the new humanity as well as the new world, whose new growing point should be, for example, any consecrated space.

The word 'feeling' used twice in succession allows the rhythm of feeling of self and feeling for the world to be felt, both here are spiritualized.

1)    to feel the Christ *within oneself*
2)    to feel *within oneself* the Church.

To conclude, let us consider the *name Christ*, Who—only in this Archer-sentence—noticeably appears twice: 'feel the Christ within themselves' ... 'power of the Christ ...'

In the Matthew-trigon we found the Twins-characteristic 'Christ-Jesus' (5). In the John-trigon 'Christ' only once (2), not Jesus. In the Luke-trigon 'Christ' and 'Jesus' once each (4). In the Mark-trigon 'Jesus' stands once (3), but the name 'Christ' three times (in the Ram-sentence 3 and precisely three times in the Archer-sentence 11). Hereby one will also recall—please do not stop at the empty effect of the outer side of these remarks—that Mark (like John) is a Christ-gospel.

The name 'Christ' takes its strongest position in the Johannine Fishes-sentence 2; its second strongest position in the Mark-Archer-sentence 11, where it is mentioned twice. The Fishes and the Archer are precisely the two *Jupiter-kyrios-signs*. (With the Fishes comes Neptune in addition.)

The mention of the word 'Christ' *twice* in sentence 11 one can, as with the twice employed word 'feeling', likewise feel out of the rhythm of the Lion-heart. (Eventually the other viewpoint would come into consideration, that we here sense in the Archer the chiming in of the countersign Twins, from which all duality proceeds. In the quoted passage Mark 6:7, the sending out of the Apostles in the sign of the Archer, the countersign is shown in the 'two by two' of the sending.)

The Church is a rhythmical, breathing being pulsing with blood. In the daily Mass, in the Festivals of the great 'Church Year' it weaves the time-body of Christ.

In the Introduction to his book on *Mark's Gospel* Beckh observes [p. 45], with regard to the cosmic rhythm: 'The religious rite is splendidly suited to re-awaken feelings' precisely from the viewpoint of the rhythmical-etheric level, helping one to understand why in the Creed the truth of the Church is entrusted to the Mark-trigon. In the catholic sense Matthew is the expressly Church-gospel, but there the Church is built on Peter and the Father-forces, is an authoritative institution.

Our Creed presents the task to feel the Church today more out of the *etheric* element of *Mark*. We are to work for the Church in the world-time of the *etheric* Christ.

# IV. The Luke-Trigon
# (Bull–Virgin–Archer)

The special relationship of Luke to the sacramental element means that this study on the trigons is grown somewhat longer. Here is a short overview:

> The astral-soul element in Luke. The female element. Prayer.
> The life-ether, alchymical aspect of the 'eternal feminine'.
> *Sentence 4*. The *Heiler-Name*, the name Jesus [means] 'Healer' ['Saviour', 'Redeemer']. Mary. *Heiligkeit*: sanctity/ holiness and sin in Luke. *Heilung*, healing, and illness.
> Corporeality. The 'vehicle' ['vessel']. Venus and the Moon in sentence 4.
> 'Humanity' of Paul's pupil, Luke.
> *Sentence 8*. The Transfiguration as the Mystery of the Earth. Meals in Luke.
> > Apparent 'materialism'. The sacramental gospel.
> > 'Jerusalem' and 'peace' from the aspect of the life-ether.
> The alchymical Mercury in sentence 8. '*Dynamis*.'
> The mystical-liturgical 'today'.
> *Sentence 12*. The Lucan meaning of 'hope'. Matters concerning the Trinity.
> > *Resurrectio carnis* [resurrection of the body]. From the 'being of God' to the 'being of man'.

Luke presents the astral-soul aspect. This has often been mentioned in our circles. An entire main theme of Luke's soul-filled nature is contained here when one points out that Luke has written the Mary-gospel. Not only in the childhood stories does the woman play an important role. [E.] Bock and R. Goebel have written several things on this. In any case, however, I would like briefly to mention the main places without pretending to intend anything new.

*Women* in Luke: the Annunciation to Mary; the meeting of Mary and Elisabeth; the hymns 'Benedictus' (1:42) and the 'Magnificat' (1:46). The Christmas story; the prophetess Anna (2:36). The special mentioning of the mother in the story of the 12-year-old Jesus. Then beyond the chapter on the childhood, the widow of Nain (7:12). The great 'sinner'/ the one who lived a profligate life (7:37). The women who follow Christ, amongst them Mary Magdalene (8:1-3). Mary and Martha (10:38). The woman who calls a blessing on the mother of Jesus (11:27). The healing of the crippled woman/ the woman with an infirmity (13:10). The woman who searches for the lost penny (15:8). The reference to Lot's wife (17:32) (which is missing in the gospel parallels). 'You daughters of Jerusalem' (23:27).

Out of this element of the soul-filled devotional nature also the special role of *prayer* is to be understood with Luke. Mary overshadowed by the Holy Spirit—this is the great archetypal picture of the praying soul. Two especially important places are the *Baptism in the Jordan* (3:21) and the *Transfiguration* (9:28), which only with *Luke* are understood in the greatest style as *'prayers involving listening'*. With such 'small things' one sees how finely differentiated the same event is narrated by the synoptics, how, for example, a quite unique Lucan nuance enters when it says, 'As he prayed the heavens opened'. 'He went up the mountain to pray, and when he prayed the appearance of his face changed...' I will briefly mention the well-known passages: the people were praying outside (1:10), the Baptism in the Jordan (3:21). He prayed alone (5:16). He spent the night on the mountain in prayer (6:12). He prayed alone (9:18). The Transfiguration (9:28-29). His praying before the revelation of the Lord's Prayer (11:1). The parable of the Importunate Widow as an invitation to intensive prayer (18:1). The praying of the Pharisee and the tax-collector (18:10). The prayer in Gethsemane (22:44, in Luke much more emphatic). Amongst the three Words on the Cross narrated by Luke, two are in prayer-form (23:34, 46), the other 5 Words [of the 7] from the Cross are not in the same sense 'prayers'.

I would like briefly to point out these connections, which (as mentioned) are well known. It is quite clear: Luke is the evangelist of the astral-soul element, though several other elements that bear Lucan qualities are not yet included in this characterization, for example, that which conventional theology has felt as Luke's special 'materialism', an undeniable interest in the corporeal (3:22: the dove descends in 'corporeal form'; the food of the Resurrected One; His flesh and His 'bones'), furthermore his special interest in the Sacred Meal (we shall come to discuss the details).

Facing these realms, the astral viewpoint (in the sense of the soul-filled nature) proves to be insufficient. We recall the scheme in 'The Gospels and the kinds of Ether', Chapter 2 above [RB 120]: the viewpoint of the supersensory human members—the viewpoint of the kinds of ethers. With Matthew there stands the dualism of the physical body facing the light-ether. Mark shows the etheric with the inner glow of the warmth-ether. With John the viewpoint of the 'I' and the sound-ether are married in the magic-idealistic Mystery of the 'name'.

With Luke: astrality and life-ether. The trigon of Luke is the 'violet' *life-ether*—trigon. Bull-Virgin-Goat are the *Earth-signs*. Thereby there enters into the Gospel according to Luke a particular alchymical note. Some things, of course, touch here on John's Gospel; both stand close to each other as the gospels of the 'feminine' ether-forces. In the sense of [the diagrams in Guenther] Wachsmuth's books,[292] Matthew and Mark are, in short, the 'yellow' and 'red' gospels, Luke and John the 'violet' and 'blue' gospels.

With John the 'I' and sound-ether meet in the 'name'; in Luke such a meeting, where the viewpoints of the astral and of the life-etheric are mysteriously united: the form of *Mary*. The symbol of Mary is in actual fact felt according to these two directions: on the one hand she is '*Maria della anima*',[293] the *soul*; on the other hand she is the 'black Mother of God', the *earthly mother*, whereby one can think of the relationship of the words [Lat.] '*mater*' ['mother'] and '*materia*' ['matter']. Correspondingly, Mary, who is overshadowed by the Holy Spirit, is the archetype of the blessed soul, but then also the archetype of how the Dove of the Spirit hovers over the becoming corporeality. The Dove that hovers over Mary is also the descent of the Spirit into the praying soul, as the indication of the body of Jesus growing in her. 'Blessed are you amongst women and blessed is the fruit of your womb.' In this twofold benediction is expressed the twofold Mystery of Mary.

The Lucan sentences in the Creed are sentence 4 ('The birth of Jesus…'), sentence 8 (Ascension) and sentence 12 ('They may hope…'). The signs are Bull, Virgin and Goat.

## *Sentence 4: (Bull)*

'The birth of Jesus upon Earth is a working of the Holy Spirit Who, to heal spiritually the sickness of sin of the bodily nature of mankind, prepared the son of Mary to be the vehicle of the Christ.'

This—in the Bull—would be the cardinal Lucan sentence. The cardinal sentences have hitherto always shown themselves as especially related to the respective evangelist:

- with Matthew the sentence of the Father-God,
- with John the Holy Spirit,
- with Mark the victory over death.

Here, too, one will have to say that sentence 4 carries in particular the impression of Luke.

This first sentence in the Luke-trigon begins with the name of the Saviour, *Jesus*. The interest in the Mark-sentence 3 passes from the transitional name Jesus to the name Christ, whereas the whole Luke-sentence 4 belongs to the name Jesus, only at the end has the name Christ—in the Luke-trigon only mentioned here—taken a less emphasized position.

Jesus—the one healing through God, the 'spiritual Healer', is in a special sense a 'healing' or 'saviour's' Name. In Mark's Gospel—as Beckh shows—the healings are allotted to the Bull. One also thinks of the fulness of life in the month of May: 'contagious health', excessive vitality, which through sacrifice can benefit those who are sick, instead of being squandered in selfish enjoyment. Luke the Bull-evangelist is the physician. With him the name Jesus is in actual fact in its own house and unfolds here its greatest luminosity in the Creed, brighter than in sentences 3 and 5. (As already frequently discussed: in the John-trigon it is completely absent; with 'Mark' it is less emphasized than 'Christ' (3); with 'Matthew' co-ordinated to the name 'Christ' (5); with 'Luke' almost placed above it in significance (4)).

People have frequently heard in the sound of the name 'Jesus' the Greek word for healer: *iao mai*. (The sound [of the name] Jesus has been compared to [that of] Jason.) With his feeling for Greek this surely was heard by Luke. It is a very interesting observation that precisely this word *iao* (note the three vowels) appears especially often in Luke's Gospel. The other evangelists, firstly, do not have a special interest in the healings, secondly, they almost always use the other word *therapeuo* for them. *Iao* otherwise only stands in John 4:47, 5:13, 12:40; Matt. 8:8, 13:15; Mark 5:29; facing them are ten places in Luke:

Luke 5:17 'The *dynamis* of the Lord was with Jesus to heal the sick (*iasthai*). (7:7 and 8:47 have synoptic parallels.)
9:2 and he sent them out ... to heal (*iasthai*) the sick.
9:11 and healed (*iato*) those who needed healing (*therapeia*).
9:42 healed (*iasato*) the boy.
14:4 he healed (*iasato*) him and sent him on his way.
17:15 One of the ten lepers, when he saw he was healed (*iathe*).
22:51 And he touched the man's ear and healed him (*iasato*).

The above passages are only found in Luke, demonstrating how much the word *iao* is a Lucan term for Jesus as Healer. '*To heal spiritually*'; in this one can recognize in the Creed the name Jesus and the *iao*.

Alongside the name Jesus there stands another name that likewise stands 'in its house' in sentence 4: *Mary*. In his *Contributions*[294] Beckh shows how the Bull is actually a feminine sign; here Venus reigns. In the Bull one is *'in domicilio' Veneris*—'in the house' of Venus—the Egyptian cult of the Bull stood in the sign of the Isis-cult.[295] Concerning this Beckh has spoken in more detail and expressed how Mary is revealed here as the 'Queen of the May'.

How revealing it is that 'Pontius Pilate' stands in the Matthew-trigon, whose planetary ruler (alongside Venus) is the masculine Saturn; 'Mary' on the other hand stands in the Venus-trigon, and actually directly in the Venus-sign of the Bull. Beckh writes about this, too [p. 108 above], how Raphael's Sistine Madonna portrays 'Venus in the Bull'.

*'Jesus-Maria'*—in this something is said concerning the special nature of Luke's Gospel.

The two names are linked in sentence 4 through the *'Holy Spirit'*— this word so sparingly used in our liturgy (otherwise mostly, as already in sentences 4 and 10, circumscribed by the word *'Heiland'*, 'healing') is used, for example, in the Marriage Service: 'holy bond of matrimony'—connected namely with 'Spirit' ([Gk.] *pneuma*) appearing noticeably often in Luke. Precisely the Gospel of the physician Luke repeatedly emphasizes how what endures lies solely in what is holy.

> 1:15 Gabriel prophecies John 'will be filled with the Holy Spirit (*pneuma hagion*) even before he is born'.
>
> 1:35 The angel answered, 'The Holy Spirit will come on you (Mary), … So the holy one to be born will be called the Son of God'.
>
> 1:41 'Elizabeth was filled with the Holy Spirit.'
>
> 1:49 'Holy is his name' (in the Magnificat).
>
> 1:67 'Zacharias was filled with the Holy Spirit.'
>
> 2:25 'the Holy Spirit was on Simeon'.
>
> 2:26 'It had been revealed to him by the Holy Spirit.'
>
> 3:22 the Holy Spirit descended on him 'in bodily form' like a dove. Precisely the synoptic accounts of the Jordan Baptism, sounding apparently the same are, as already mentioned, significantly differentiated.
>
> 4:1 'Jesus, full of the Holy Spirit'.
>
> 10:21 'full of joy through the Holy Spirit'.
>
> 11:2 another early manuscript authority with Luke:[296] 'Thy Holy Spirit come to us and purify us.' Moreover, 11:13 concerning the request for the Holy Spirit.

12:12 'the Holy Spirit will teach you at that time what you should say'. The Matthean parallel (10:20) has characteristically: 'the Spirit of your Father'.

In the Acts of the Apostles, too, written by Luke, we find the characteristic emphasis of the 'Holy Spirit'. Immediately in the story of Pentecost—Mary was with the disciples; the overshadowing of Mary is repeated here. This time Mary is the praying soul of the circle of Apostles, who prepare themselves in prayer and contemplation for receiving the Holy Spirit. I will not now go into the numerous further passages in the Acts.

The special nuance of the Lucan *'holy'* steps more clearly to the fore through the counterword *'sin'*.

Earlier I said that in the Luke-trigon the words 'death' and 'dying' are missing; instead—only here—'sickness of sin' is used (sentences 4 & 12).

In sentence 4 facing 'sickness' there stands the name Jesus and the word 'to heal'. 'Sin' stands facing 'Holy'. Both conceptual polar opposites are genuinely Lucan. With the Bull the Scorpion that always brings sickness chimes in. Behind Luke—as his teacher—stands Paul, who developed the actual teaching of sin and consequently precisely from this aspect was especially significant for the Reformers. Sin— with Luke a particularly important concept.

> 5:8 with the draught of fishes, Peter says 'Depart from me, Lord; I am a sinful man!'
> 7:37 the important Lucan picture of the *magna peccatrix*, the great sinner, where directly in 8:2 the name Mary Magdalene is mentioned.

In the chapter on the Prodigal Son the word 'sin' comes several times, 15:1, 7, 10; 18:21.

> 18:13 the tax-collector says: 'God, have mercy on me, a sinner.'
> 19:7 Zachaeus is 'a sinner'.

Precisely with Luke the feminine [principle] stands facing itself as the holy one, Mary—and the great [female] sinner. This opposition of the pure virgin and the whore not only relates to the astral element. The soul-element purified to *manas* and the un-spiritualized addiction[/s] of the soul, but also of the Mysteries of matter.

[In the Apocalypse] the pure life-ether element of the heavenly Jerusalem is the virginal bride of God; 'fallen' matter is the whore Babylon. *Materia benedicta* and *materia damnata*. Cf. the ending of

Goethe's *Faust*, the Eternal Feminine in the form of the 'Mater gloriosa' (which alongside purified astrality is also 'matter in the light of glory'); the 'fallen' female [principle] in the 'sinner'.

Meanwhile, Beckh's monograph on alchymy[297] has appeared, in which all the important things mentioned here are discussed, and which I would like emphatically to recommend.

Seen from the Mystery of the life-ether, it has a special tone when the Luke-trigon speaks of the 'bodily nature of mankind'. In the Matthew-trigon it was called 'physical' (1) and 'matter' (9). The *bodily nature*—this is more tender and more subtle.

We recall that strange phrase in the Lucan report of the Jordan-baptism, through which Luke was accused of materialistic crudeness: the Holy Spirit descended in 'bodily form' (*somatikō eidei*) (3:22). But here it doesn't concern a coarsening of the tender vision into the miraculous, but it is indicated that the process does not only take place in the Imagination but was strong [enough to penetrate] right into the sphere of the life-ether, right into the bones, that the reception of Christ was an 'Intuitive', an 'embodied' event. We return to this with the Virgin-sentence 8.

The words of sentence 4 '*birth—the bodily nature—vehicle*' all point to the tender Mystery of the 'becoming matter / flesh', which takes place in the body of the mother.

'Birth' stands only here in the Creed. We saw how the word 'born' in the Johannine sentence 2 has a completely different character. The proceeding of the Son from the eternal Father is a process, inconceivable to those bound to the Earth—[with] 'thinking that forms nouns. [John 1:1, Lat.] '*In principio erat verbum*—In the beginning was the word [*verbum* also means 'verb'—*Tr.*].'[298] Only from afar does one sense the Mystery: 'how' 'the Son [is] born in eternity'. This process that can only be expressed as a verb stands, despite its mysterious character, facing the tangibly earthly, even bodily event of the birth of Jesus.

(Concerning the formula 'on Earth', cf. the Virgin-sign, sentence 8.)

Is there a possible relationship in some way between '*Hülle*' ['covering', 'sheath', 'envelope'; translated in the Creed as 'vehicle'] and the Gk. *hyle*? According to the meaning, certainly. In the Greek philosophers *hyle* means as much as primordial substance, matter. But the word is not abstractly philosophical, but pictorially concrete. *Hyle* also means 'wood'. One recalls the fairy tale motif of losing oneself in the wood. The mysterious forest-weaving with its twilight that can intensify to the fear of the generated sinister darkness (Snow White's fear)—these are Imaginations which the soul has when it enters the realm of the becoming of matter.

The Mystery of the forest-weaving in the most sacred sense is reproduced in the wood of Fra Filippo Lippi's Christmas picture in the woods.[299] Here there is not the fear of the soul lost in the enchanted world of matter, but a spiritually blessed entrance into the virginally pure *Stoffeshülle*, envelope of matter. Above the *pater uranios* lovingly opens up his bright starry world, the dove of the Holy Spirit hovers over the woman's Mystery of the becoming of the body. (From this special tuning of the feelings a light may fall associating the wood and the sacred night of Christmas.)

Rudolf Meyer once spoke how in Hansel and Gretel [from the Grimms' collection of fairytales] the white dove leads the way to the house, to birth. The Incarnation is divinely ordained.

In some cults of Asia Minor doves were sacred to Venus, the goddess of mothers. In these cults there is often a very decadent reference to the ancient sacred relationship between the Holy Spirit and the *hyle* that is already heard in Genesis 1:2. [Now the earth was formless and empty, darkness was over the surface of the deep, and the Spirit of God was hovering over the waters.] This subtle realization, distorted into the erotic sphere, entered the realm of the whore Babylon.

The linking of the *dove* and incarnation is wonderfully expressed in the Classical Walpurgisnacht in [Goethe's] *Faust* II, altogether rich in alchymical treasures. Aegean Sea [Act 2, ll. 8339-343]. [Emphases R. F.]:

*Sirenen (auf den Felsen):*
*Welch ein Ring von Wölkchen ründet*
*Um den Mond so reichen Kreis?*
*Tauben sind es, liebentzündet,*
*Fittige wie Licht so weiß.*
*Paphos hat sie hergesendet,*
*Ihre brünstige Vogelschar;*

Sirens (on the rocks):
What a ring, of cloudlets fashioned,
Circles round the moon-orb bright?
*Doves* they are, with love impassioned,
Snowy pinions, pure as *light*.

Hitherward from Paphos wending
Flocks of amorous birds appear.
[Tr. W.H. van der Smissen.]

There was a sanctuary to Venus in Paphos (in the copper island of Cyprus). Here the two feminine planets *Venus* and the *Moon* are magnificently connected: the doves of Venus appear as the halo of the Moon, which with this whole scene stands in the zenith. The Moon (which is at home in Cancer) is in a special sense the planet of mothers.

Now the *Moon* is exalted in the Bull. One could not better indicate the content of the 4th sentence of the Creed than with the two planetary names Venus (which governs in Taurus) and the Moon (exalted).

The 'prepared .... to be the vehicle (*Hülle*)' has an alchemical sound. To 'prepare' is, amongst other things, a term from today's more exoteric realm of the kitchen. A wood-burning stove indicates the 'preparation of the kitchen' by Sarah (Gen. 18:6) as the symbol of the womb.

In Luke's Gospel the Christmas story gently points as the same time the astral and life-etheric Mystery of the '*Hülle*' in the twice-mentioned 'wrapped in cloths/ swaddling bands' (Luke 2:7 and 2:12).

The word '*mankind*' in sentence 4 has a specific Lucan character. With 'Mark' (sentence 3) and 'John' (2) it is simply '*Mensch*' ('men' and 'man'). With Luke on the other hand it is 'mankind' (4) and 'man's being' (12), moreover, in the same sentence where 'sickness of sin' also appears.

For Luke, the pupil of Paul, man-'kind' is no empty abstraction. Paul proclaimed the teaching of Adam, in whom 'all have sinned' [Rom. 5:12 ; 'just as sin entered the world through one man, and death through sin, and in this way death came to all people, because all sinned'] and of the second Adam in whom all will be made alive [1 Cor. 15:22 'For as in Adam all die, so in Christ all will be made alive']. Both [Adam and Christ] did not live an individual destiny, but in both the whole of mankind is involved by com-passion. The Resurrection of Christ concerns the whole of mankind. What took place with the body of Jesus is significant for all bodies (if not *actu*, yet *potentis*); Luke traces the genealogical tree of Jesus not only as Matthew to Abraham, but back to *Adam* (3:38). He thinks in terms of humanity, otherwise shown in the overcoming of national bonds. Paul was the Apostle to the Gentiles, who on his journeys realized the significance of Christ for humanity; Luke writes as theologians have always recognized, especially 'for the gentiles', without especially prioritizing Jewish interests as Matthew does.

The word 'mankind' in our Creed has flowed out of the sphere of Inspiration of Luke and Paul.

Dr Steiner speaks in a Pentecost lecture[300] how the Holy Spirit, Who overshadowed Mary, was not as with other expectant mothers the respective folk-spirit, but the spirit of the whole of mankind, precisely the Holy Spirit. For this reason, Joseph, a 'just man' [Matt. 1:19], that is, deeply rooted in the Jewish folk-spirit, initially strangely touched, since he perceived this universally human spirituality in the aura of the expectant Mary.

Luke is the evangelist who expresses most strongly the universal human feelings of the reader. Still today the exoteric picture of mother and child still mostly calls up in the soul the otherwise expired universally uniting human picture.

## Sentence 8: (The Virgin)

'Since that time He is the Lord of the heavenly forces upon Earth and lives as the fulfiller of the Fatherly deeds of the Ground of the World.'

This Virgin-sentence contains the actual sacramental alchymy. The sign of the Virgin works already trigonally into the Bull-sentence (for example, 'the bodily nature'), but here in sentence 8 the great alchymical motif of 'astra and chaos', of the 'influence of the stars in earthly matter' comes to its full unfolding. One may read Beckh's already-mentioned book on alchymy, rich in content. One recalls how often Beckh has called the Virgin the actual sign of our liturgical, sacramental Movement.

(A note in passing. When our liturgy was initiated in Dornach, the Sun stood in the Virgin, and also during the lecture-course on the Apocalypse.)

### The Ascension and sacramentalism

If I may remind the reader of the observation of the Epistles: here the third Christmas Epistle stands in the Virgin, facing the Ascension in the Fishes. The chiming in of the countersign is especially apparent with Virgin-Fishes. In particular in the third Christmas Epistle, 'facing' *Ascension*, the heavenly *Hierarchies* are invoked. The Creed and the Epistles here differ, in that Ascension with the Epistles stands primarily in the Fishes, with the Creed primarily in the Virgin. The memory of calling on the Hierarchies can chime in, when in the Virgin-sentence of the '*heavenly forces on Earth*' is spoken.

The *Ascension* belongs in the Lucan proclamation of Christianity. Apart from the references John 6:62 and 20:17, it is *only reported by Luke*. Luke 24:50-52 and at the beginning of the Acts of the Apostles 1:9-12. Since our Creed, instead of the traditional 'ascended into heaven' brings the formulation 'Lord of the heavenly forces upon Earth', it prevents that Earth-disdaining, Luciferic misunderstanding of this event and at the same time emphasizes why Luke, the evangelist of the Earth-sign, could bring the *Ascension* as the crowning conclusion of his life-ether gospel. In this case the text of the Creed creates retrospectively an understanding of the gospel.

Why does only Luke write about the Ascension? Because it is the deepest *Mystery of the Earth*. This is also clear in the Lucan text of the Acts of the Apostles. The last words of Christ ascending towards heaven in Acts 1:8-9 are: '... "and you shall be my witnesses in Jerusalem and in all Judea and Samaria and to the end of the earth." And when he had said this, as they were looking on, he was lifted up, and a cloud took him out of their sight.' 'Earth' is here the final word that Christ speaks in Luke's whole narration. Precisely here the Ascension takes on testamentary significance.[301]

'The Lord of the heavenly forces upon Earth'—this is the key to Christian sacramentalism. Also in the short reference to the Ascension, John 6:62, is characteristically presented as the key of recognition for the riddle of the sacred Last Supper. Within the other Johannine indication, 20:17, the Ascension is the prerequisite for the 'tangible laying hold of the resurrection body', i.e. for its experience in the bodily sphere.

The gospel of the Ascension is at the same time the gospel of the Last Supper. (The Lord's Supper/ Eucharist stands with Mark in the sign of the Virgin, as does the Feeding of the 4000; with the 5000 it chimes in as the countersign.)

Perhaps I may remind the reader that in the booklet on the Seven Sacraments[302] I related in particular the Last Supper to the Ascension. This can now be more deeply explained as well as the already-mentioned beautiful folklore saying, that at Ascension 'Bread rains from heaven' (cf. once more John 6:62).

Of all the evangelists, Luke gives the most detailed report of the Last Supper, with the exception of the Letter to the Corinthians by his teacher Paul. Luke 22 is the classic gospel reading of the Christian Church for Maundy Thursday.

## Meals

Theology has noticed what a significant role *mealtimes* play in Luke,[303] even without the Maundy Thursday pericope.

   7:36 The sinful woman comes to Christ at the supper-party of the Pharisee.

   10:7 In the address at the sending out of the disciples only Luke mentions eating and drinking in the houses where the Apostles are invited.

   14:7 The address about the order at table during a meal.

   14:12 When you call a supper-party invite the poor as well.

   14:15 'Blessed is the man who will eat at the feast in the kingdom of God.'

   14:16 Following this the 'Parable of the Great Banquet'.

This is only apparently the same parable of the Wedding Banquet of the King's Son, Matt. 22. With Matthew we have the division so characteristic for him as well as the emphasis at the wedding (Venus-Urania in the Scales); with Luke it is not a wedding meal, also not a regal one, but a great feast, and the last word says, 'Not one of those who were invited will get a taste of my banquet'. (Incidentally, one of the three has bought five yokes of oxen. Oxen and calves only appear in the Bull-gospel of Luke, apart from the one passage in John 2:14; with Luke 13:15, 14:5; 14:19; 15:23; 27:30.)

   15:23 The meal celebrating the return of the Prodigal Son.

   16:21 The table of the rich man.

   17:8 The servant is to prepare the meal.

   22:15-18 in particular detail the preparations for the Last Supper. 'I have eagerly desired to eat this Passover with you before I suffer.'

   22:30 'You may eat and drink at my table in my kingdom and sit on my thrones,' spoken at the Last Supper.

   24:30-35 The meal in Emmaus. They recognize Him at the breaking of bread.

   24: 41-42 The Risen One eats fish and honey. *Only Luke mentions the food the Risen One eats.*

In the Acts Luke continues to emphasize mealtimes. The 'breaking of bread' 2:42, 2:46; 20:7; the Last Supper scene 27:35.

We also find the counter-picture of the sacred meal in Luke. The foolish rich man says to his soul: 'Eat and drink' (12:19).

In the eschatological [view from the future, when the kingdom of God is near] address 21:34 only Luke contains the warning that one should not burden one's heart through 'eating and drinking'.

Already with the Bull-sentence we mentioned *Luke's apparent 'materialism'*. Apart from the 'bodily form' of the dove (3:22) [seen] most clearly in the appearance with the Easter narration, it is not only the eating of fish and honey (concerning this, cf. Bock),[304] but also touching the Risen One (24:39), 'Touch me and see; a ghost does not have flesh and bones, as you see I have'. Moreover, on the further confirmation: 'Do you have anything here to eat?' (24:41). It has to do with the life-ether, 'bodily nature'.

Something more is involved here. The resurrection body is the seed-germ of the heavenly Jerusalem. This appears in the form of a cube (life-ether) and is at the same time the revelation of the Eternal Feminine, the virgin bride of the Lamb. It is noticeable that precisely in the life-ether-gospel according to Luke there is much more mention of Jerusalem than with the other gospels. In our context this apparently co-incidental fact has its meaning and deeper connection. The heavenly Jerusalem is in a special manner aligned to the Luke-sign of the Virgin, the earthly Jerusalem is its prophecy. Christian sacramentalism is building Jerusalem.

Remarkably enough according to ancient astrological tradition the city of Jerusalem is regarded as a virgin-city.[305] Cf. Beckh's book on *Alchymy* on the 'virgin Earth'.

*Jerusalem*
Luke is the Last Supper [or Eucharist] gospel; it is likewise also the *Jerusalem*-gospel.

Firstly, there is the frequent mention of the name Jerusalem in the stories of the childhood (2:22, 25).

2:38 The prophetess Hannah speaks to those who wait for the *redemption of Jerusalem*. This redemption is basically also the redemption of the life-ether enchanted on the Earth. Precisely the concept of the *'lytrosis'*, the redemption, of Jerusalem is linked to a female figure.

In the story of the twelve-year-old we hear the name Jerusalem three times: 2:41, 43, 45.

With the story of the Temptation we read that the devil leads Him to Jerusalem (4:9). The parallel in Matthew does not contain this name; it speaks only (cf. Matt. 27:73) of the holy city. It is well known that the order of the Temptations is different. With Matthew the second

Temptation is in the holy city, the third (for Matthew the culmination) on the very high mountain. We mentioned this with the Matthew trigon (Matthew's interest in the mountain). For Luke who does not have the Twins in his trigon, the mountain is not so important; for Luke the culmination is placed in 'Jerusalem'. He alone mentions this name here. Perhaps from this the solution to the riddle of the different ordering would be found.

9:31 With the Transfiguration only Luke writes that Moses and Elijah 'spoke with him about the exodus which He was to fulfil in Jerusalem'. The Transfiguration on Mount Tabor helps us to divine transubstantiation. The other evangelists refer here to the Resurrection with the descent from the Mount. Instead, Luke in the spiritual discussion at the climax of this experience, allows the sacred name Jerusalem to sound. Mysteries of the life-ether.

9:51 Because His re-entering heaven approached, 'He set his face to go to Jerusalem.'

Especially following the scene on Mount Tabor, there begins the *walk to Jerusalem* so characteristic for *Luke*, for the theologians the Lucan travel report, as the 'framework' for all the following narrations (Chaps. 9-18). Concerning this, cf. Bock, the 'path' to Jerusalem.[306] Already through this it becomes clear that as the goal of an inner path Jerusalem cannot only be the outer city. Only Luke emphasizes the 'path to Jerusalem'.

9:53 'his face' turns towards Jerusalem, furthermore Jerusalem is mentioned in 10:13 and 13:4.

13:22 the theme of the path is taken up again: He walks towards Jerusalem. Following this, the saying of the narrow gate.

13:33 no prophet can die outside Jerusalem.

13:34 The lament 'Jerusalem, Jerusalem ...' that also stands in Matthew.

17:11 on the walk to Jerusalem (18:31 and 19:28 have [synoptic] parallels).

19:11 'He proceeded to tell a parable, because he was near to Jerusalem, and because they supposed that the kingdom of God was to appear immediately.'

19:41 When He saw the city, He wept over it. In the eschatological address, only Luke mentions Jerusalem three times, 21:20, 21:24. 'It will be trampled on by the Gentiles.'

23:28 'You daughters of Jerusalem, .... (Incidentally, the word for 'mother's breast' can only be found in Luke: 11:27, 23:29.)

The story of Emmaus mentions the name Jerusalem three times (24:13, 18, 33).

'Jerusalem' spoken by the Risen One Himself (24:27).

Jerusalem, meaningfully at the end of the gospel, after the Ascension (24:52), 'Then they worshipped him and returned to Jerusalem with great joy.'

All this receives a new aspect when one knows that Luke is the Jerusalem evangelist, and that this, too, is connected in particular with the 'Eternal Feminine'. His gospel ends in Jerusalem (the *first* and *last* scene takes place in the temple of *Jerusalem*: 1:9 and 24:52); the Acts of the Apostles starts from Jerusalem (1:4, 8:12). From Jerusalem the substance of the resurrected bodily nature is to be carried over the whole Earth.

From here the double meaning of the extraordinarily important word 'peace' is being unfurled. In this word, too, there 'meets' the viewpoint of the astral element and the life-ether. On the one hand one can read all the places that have to do with peace, with the 'path of peace' in such a way that they relate to the purification of astrality on the way to *manas*. But the other meaning chimes in. Melchizedek was 'King of Salem'; he sacrificed bread and wine [Gen. 14:18]. Jerusalem is the 'city of peace'; the heavenly Jerusalem has entered the crystallized perfection of eternal peace. [Kurt von] Wistinghausen has written a very fine essay about the snow and peace of its crystals.[307] Cf. also Beckh's 'Heavenly Jerusalem' [in JG, 459-77]. (Then they worshipped him and returned to Jerusalem with great joy.)

In the Act of Consecration of Man, the word 'peace' stands at the beginning of the Communion. This stands in the sign of the Virgin. The words to the one receiving communion are: 'The Peace be with you' related not only to the peace of soul in *manas*, but also has alchymical-'bodily' meaning, which is already shown in the touch. It also means that with the communion a seed towards the heavenly Jerusalem is planted. (It is also no coincidence that especially in the communion under the sign of the *Virgin* the word '*sacrament*' appears, also only here the Lucan word 'medicine' three times: *heilende, ewige, gesundene Arzenei*, medicine everlasting, the healing medicine that makes whole.)

Luke I:79: the path of peace (the path towards Jerusalem).

2:29 Now dismiss your servant in peace (this seemingly meant only on a soul-level, without alchymical undertone).

7:50 towards the great sinner, 'Go in peace', literally: to go right into peace. Go on the path that leads from Babylon to Jerusalem (also 8:48 parallels this).

Only Luke mentions at the address at the sending forth of the disciples 10:5: 'Whatever house you enter, first say, "Peace be to this house!"' (Today, too, the Catholic priest learns that he is to enter his dwelling with *'pax huic domui'*.) And Luke uses here the strange/unique expression: if there is a 'son of peace'. Cf. further 11:21 and 14:32.

19:42 at the weeping over Jerusalem: 'what would bring you peace'.

The places 2:14 and 19:38 should be compared. The song of praise of the angels, 'Peace on Earth'. The song of praise at the entrance into Jerusalem (only with Luke is this said): 'Peace in heaven.' 'Peace on Earth' is the great aim raying out at the beginning. Facing this, what happens on Palm Sunday? The crowd in a last flickering clairvoyance has the vision of the heavenly Jerusalem, of the heavenly City of Peace. Above the earthly Jerusalem, they see hovering this heavenly archetypal picture. The festive element of Jerusalem receiving the Lord on Palm Sunday is once more shone over by its true picture for the last time. Then there follows the great failure; the Holy city has become unholy. To *palmarum*[308] this city was for the last time 'Jeru-salem'; then it became 'spiritually Sodom and Egypt' [Rev. 11:8]. This precisely was the tragedy, that the archetype could not yet descend to the Earth (this is only seen by John on Patmos), but that it says: 'Peace in heaven'—'not yet on the Earth' [Luke 19:38].

24:36 The greeting of the Risen One: 'Peace be with you.' It is not found in Matthew and Mark. It is first found in Luke, and three times in John.

An intimate relationship exists between Luke and John as the gospels of the feminine ether-forces ('violet' and 'blue' trigons in [Wachsmuth's and Beckh's] diagrams). With the exception of John 21, both gospels narrate the main Easter events as taking place in Jerusalem. It is no coincidence that Matthew and Mark do not contain the greeting of peace of the Risen One.

With Mark the Mystery of the heavenly Jerusalem chimes in the mysterious sentence in Mark 9:50: 'Have salt in yourselves and be at peace with each other.' Cf. furthermore in Luke 11:36, the sentence about the 'whole body' being 'full of light, and no part of it dark'.

After these *excursi* intended to point to the sacramental character of the sign of the Virgin, we return to the text of the Creed. *'The Lord of the heavenly forces upon Earth.'*

The planet of sentence 8 is *Mercury*, and here in the Virgin above all the alchymical Mercury. The Mercurial, dynamic-alchymical aspect gives to the 8th sentence its form.

The words that it contains are partly the same as in sentence 1: heaven/ly, Earth, Father, Ground. And yet precisely when one asks oneself how these words in sentence 1 'stand' and how they do in sentence 8, we can recognize the completely different character in the latter. In sentence 1 (Matthew, Waterman) the above-mentioned words are 'tranquil'. They reveal their content as nouns, brought to our consideration. '... is the Ground of Existence of the heavens and of the Earth.' This is really valid: 'Tranquil, the stars rest above, and below the graves' [Goethe, 'Symbolum']. It is quite different in sentence 8. Here instead of the tranquillity there is a flowing lemniscate of the living exchange between both realms. The whole situation is a relationship of forces. The essential thing here is not the presentation of cosmic contrasts heaven—Earth in their factual actuality; the new realization of forces, which through Christ 'since that time' enter into a newly regulated relationship. Mercury rules.

*Since that time* ('time' is in dialogue with word 'eternity' standing in the 2nd sentence (Fishes))—thereby the essential thing of this 8th sentence is said: the newly grounded relationship between the entities revealed in the 1st sentence. In the 'since that time' there sounds the mystical 'today/ this day' of Luke's Gospel. Mark's *feeling for time* lies in the 'straightway/ immediately'; Matthew's 'in those days'. (The Catholic Church uses this Matthean formula *'in illo tempore'* characteristically as the introductory formula with the reading of the gospel in the Mass.[309] The historical point of view. The 'at that time' in Matthew. Cf. Matthew 11:25, 12:1, 14:1, also 3:1, 13:1, 22:23, 18:1). With John it says, 'It will be and is already now'. The apocalyptic feeling of time, which in the present already sees the essence of what is coming.

For Luke, the word 'today' is characteristic. The classic place is:

2:11 'Today in the town of David a Saviour has been born to you.'

3:22 One reading in Luke for the Baptism in the Jordan: 'Today I have begotten Thee.'

4:21 The first proclamation by Christ, His first teachings. 'This day is this scripture fulfilled in your ears/ hearing.'

Cf. also 13:32, 33 and 19:5 & 9.

Finally, the long passage 23:43: 'Today you will be with me in Paradise.' All sacramentalism lives from this mystic 'today': in the sacrament the mystical facts of 'those days' become really present. The sacrament is more than a memorial and a recollection. It re-forms the Matthean 'in those days' to 'today'. Not as though similar phrases ('in those days' and so on) do not also occur in Luke. But with Matthew they have something especially characteristic, as precisely for Luke, as mentioned, the mystic-liturgical '*today*' is characteristic.

Also in 'heavenly forces' we recognize that an especially Lucan nuance *power—dynamis*—is, as theologians have known for a long time, a preferred word. 'Power' is something different from 'might'. The latter in the Matthew trigon 'al-mighty' and the Mark-trigon 'health-bringing power'. 'Might' is somehow more placid, 'power' is more dynamic—flowing, precisely Mercurial.

Some passages in Luke:

1:17 John 'will go before him in the spirit and power (*dynamis*) of Elijah'.
4:14 'Jesus returned in the power of the spirit into Galilee.'
4:36 'With authority and power he commands the unclean spirits' (in the Marcan parallel only *exusia*).
5:17 'and the *dynamis* of the Lord was with him to heal'.
6:19 '*dynamis* came forth from him and healed them all'.
9:1 'He called the twelve together and gave them *exusia* and *dynamis* ([synoptic] parallels only *exusia*).'

Luke's whole gospel *is framed between two* dynamis *sayings:*

1:35 'the power of the Most High will overshadow you' and at the end, as introduction to the Ascension
24:49 'until you are clothed with power from on high'.

The '*on Earth*' we already found in the Bull-sentence. The Matthean-trigon simply says only 'Earth' (1:5), the Mark-trigon has 'earthly world' (3) and the John-trigon 'Earth-existence' (2), whereas the Lucan formula is 'upon Earth'. 'The birth of Jesus upon Earth' (4), 'Lord of the heavenly forces upon Earth' (8). One has to understand it dynamically 'in the alchymical field of forces of the Earth'.

Similarly with the word 'fulfiller'. It does not depend (as in 1) on 'introducing' the concept of the Fatherly Ground of the World into the Creed, and as it were, placing it before the eye of the beholder to contemplate, but the accent lies here in sentence 8, on the 'passing over' from the Father to the Son, that is to the inner-divine *dynamic*. The 'like a Father' in sentence 1 creates distance, in sentence 8 it flows over 'transitively'. The Son has become the right hand of the Father. As one *zu Grunde Gegangener,* who has 'hit rock bottom', He can now work from the *ground* upwards. The Saturnian *Grundgewalten*, basic powers, are united with the powers of life of the Sun: 'and *lives* as the fulfiller'. (How this 'lives' stands facing the 're-enlivening' in sentence 2 was already mentioned).

Here, unlike in sentence 1, the Father is not called the 'Ground of existence', but *'Ground of the world'*. Here it does not concern Being but the dynamic. In *'Welten'*, 'of the world', something of the rhythmic governing is to be heard, cf. the Mark-trigon, sentence 3.

A subtle nuance [in the German] can be found in the opposite *'wie'* (2) *'as* the Son', and *'als'* (8) *'as* the fulfiller'. In the *'wie'* (2) we feel a coy awareness, feeling towards the inner divine Mysteries of Being. The *'als'* (8) precisely describes a competence in a realm of activity, a *function*. Father—Son in (2) concerns the realm of Being, of the fixed stars, tranquillity. The fulfiller of the Father (right hand) in sentence 8 is functional, as planetary movement, Mercurial. In looking at the Virgin-sentence 8 from the sacramental viewpoint the word 'deeds' is not to be overlooked.

### Sentence 12: (Goat)

'They may hope for the overcoming of the sickness of sin
for the continuance of man's being
and for the preservation of their life destined for eternity.'

The Goat as the third Lucan sign is the sign of the Holy Night, the winter solstice. In the contemplation of the Epistles we recalled that the Lucan trigon is the Christmas-trigon. (Christmas Epistle I, 'In earthly night'—Goat; II, 'the Word'—Bull; III, 'earthly body'—the Virgin.) The special relationship of Luke to Buddhism may also have to do with the Goat. Beckh shows that the initiation of the Buddha during the sacred night under the fig tree took place in the sign of the Goat; [p. 276 above] moreover, the Goat gives the tenacity to tread a laborious 'path'.

The Christmas element can be felt in sentence 12. *'They may hope.'* To hope is not a guessing game into the blue unknown, but that something wished for may occur. To hope is something quite concrete, as is shown in the traditional meaningful saying in German, *'guter Hoffnung sein'* (to be in good hope, i.e. in expecting a child).

Luke in particular narrates the wonderfully tender story of the meeting of the two pregnant women, Mary and Elisabeth, who are *in guter Hoffnung*, expecting.

One must be 'able' to hope, there has to be a justification for it: a fructification that has happened. To hope is the soft feeling of burgeoning life. The soul may only then be 'in hope' when it knows that the seed of light is in it. 'Christ in you, the hope of glory' (Col. 1:27).

In the midst of the cold winter the Child of Light is born as a prophecy of a 'Sun-bright' world. Sentence 12 of the Creed speaks of those who in the earthly night and darkness of the senses, in Saturn's realm, may nevertheless be of good hope, whereas [it is implied] those without Christ 'have no hope'.

(Luke's Gospel contains the Mystery of the Holy Night, not only in the Christmas story 2:8, but also in two other insignificant places that nevertheless in the greater context reveal a wonderful profundity, 6:12 'One of those days Jesus went out to a mountainside to pray, and spent the night praying to God'. 21:37 'Each day Jesus was teaching at the temple, and each evening he went out to spend the night on the hill called the Mount of Olives'.)

The content of Christian hope is expressed in a threefold manner. After the Creed has led from the Father via the Son to the Spirit, in this threefold hope one has once more passed through the Mystery of the Trinity, but now in reverse order (as always, when one takes as one's starting point the content of human consciousness, as anthroposophy points out) Spirit–Son–Father.

The *'overcoming of the sickness of sin'*. Here the phrase 'sickness of sin' appears in another passage in the trigon of Luke the physician. Its overcoming is the work of the Holy Spirit. The word 'overcoming' here in the Goat contains the accompanying sound of tireless, unswerving, tenacious perseverance, whereas the 'overcame' of sentence 7 of the Lion has a completely different 'aura'.

'The continuance (*Fortbestehen*) of man's being.' The sphere of the Son. In '*Stehen*' ('to stand') the I-AM is active, cf. '*Bei-stand*', 'the Helper', in the opposite sentence 6. Also 'continuance' here in the Goat has the character of something immoveable, outlasting. Alongside the ruling Saturn that provides seriousness and concentration, the active, masculine Mars is exalted in the Goat.

This 'continuance of man's being' stands at the place in the traditional [Apostles' Creed] *'resurrection carnis'*, the 'resurrection of the body'. This easily materialistically misunderstood expression is avoided in our Creed, but what it actually intends is the bodily understanding of the human being, his further life not merely as a poor soul, but with *atman* as 'Spirit-man'. This closely relates to our formulation 'the continuation of man's being' because for the full human being there belong spirit, soul and body. Consequently, Rudolf Steiner calls *atman* Spirit-man because only in the resurrection-body does the human being becomes really 'human'. Angelius Silesius says: '*Mensch, werde wesentlich!*—O man, get real!'[310] Only the resurrected human being is no longer a non-being, but a cosmically justified being.

The beginning and the end of the Creed meet here: in sentence 1 'divine Being', in sentence 12 '*man's being*'. This 'becoming-like-God', this 'becoming real' of the human being is the deed of the Son. Again, the humanity of Luke's thinking is shown here. In sentence 4: 'mankind', in 12 'man's being', which is still more. In the scholastic sense these are 'realistic' not nominalist concepts.

'*The preservation of their life destined for eternity.*' The preservation in Being is the function of the Father. Here clearly once again the proximity of sentence 1 is to be felt, in which the word 'eternity' there already flickers again the starry light of *pater uranios*. Twice the festive word 'eternity' appears in the Creed: 'the Son born in eternity' (2) and here in sentence 12. The sphere of Christ's origin is the great goal for human beings. Christ comes out of eternity; human beings are to grow into this kingdom.

In the '*destined for …*' there perhaps lies the indication that the 'eternal life' is no self-indulgent enjoyment, but that the human being—the product of the earthly cycle surveyable to our observation—is built into a higher context. Also, the 'their' ('*the preservation of their life destined for eternity*') is not unimportant.

A little excursus on the 'possessive pronouns in the Creed':

Sentence 1: '*His* creatures like a Father'. The intimate connection of the Father with the world. If He took His breath away, everything would fall into nothingness. The world is in a very high sense God's '*Eigen-tum*', 'own-dom', His possession. The word '*sein*', 'His', links Creator and creature. The connection is such, [proceeding] from God.

Sentence 6: 'had lost *their* divine nature.' This is already individualized divine substance. The lost starry part of the human being in the world of the divine Name.

Sentence 9: 'through *their* bearing'. The lesser 'I' within the greater 'I' of God has the possibility and the duty to be active. Christ intends to save but allowing this saving [to happen] is the human being's very own deed. For the first time in the Creed in this Michaelic Scales-sentence human activity plays a role.

Sentence 11: 'feel the Christ *within themselves'*. No longer only God Who carries 'His creatures' in Himself, but for the first time the creature, aware and responsible, may carry God in him/herself.

The crowning of all these passages is in sentence 12: 'for the preservation of *their* life destined for eternity.' It is like a higher synthesis of 'their divine nature', 'their bearing', 'feel the Christ within themselves'. Life in the Higher Self. Individual higher life, held in Being by the Father-ground, is meaningfully incorporated into eternal contexts. It lies facing the Crab-sentence 'who have lost their divine nature' (6–12).

'Their' eternal life—that is the spirit-child in lap of the soul, the fulfilled Mystery of Christmas, the God received by human beings as individuals, who have awoken the 'I'.

Beckh has already pointed out how the Creed ends with the Saturn-sign of the Goat and begins with the Saturn-sign Waterman, as the snake of knowledge biting its own tail, and how Saturn precisely provides the origin of the mood of *gnosis*.

## Summary

To end, the relationship of the trigons in the Creed to the evangelists once more summarized:

*Matthean*-inspired are the sentences about the Father (1), the cross and the grave (5), and the Last Judgement (9).

*Johannine*-inspired the sentences about the eternal Logos (2), the Descent into Hell (6) and the activity of the Holy Spirit (10).

*Marcan*-character is carried by the sentences about entering the earthly world (3), the sting of death (7) and about the Church of those who feel the Christ within themselves, feeling His health-bringing power [11].

*Lucan* are the sentences: Jesus-Maria (4), the Ascension (8), and hope (12).

This provisionally concludes these observations on the Creed. It should be clear that the *12 sentences of the Creed are inspired out of the same cardinal points of the cosmic circle as are the 4 evangelists*. For this reason the Creed and the gospels are mutually illuminating.

Needless to say, that in retrospect the inadequacies of this work are very clear to me. It is difficult to avoid hunting for relationships [for its own sake] and to preserve the right tact. But I hope that the end result is not coloured through a few blunders in detail and that the indications of the cosmic rhythm in the Creed are to an extent established, despite their too aphoristic character at times.

For me at least the impression of the inspiration of our liturgical texts precisely through these considerations is very much deepened and transfigured. The Creed will increasingly become a qualitatively differentiated cosmos. Necessity and exactitude of the sentence-forms becomes ever more clear.

To emphasize once more that without Beckh's books all this would have been impossible or would have hung in the air. My *Contributions* are only the consequences that are drawn out of Beckh's insights for the theological and liturgical realm.

# The Stars in the Act of Consecration of Man

(RB 117. 1930)

## 1. The Seasonal Prayers / Epistles

What follows assumes the studies on the 'cosmic rhythm in the Creed' are known, which for its part assumes Hermann Beckh's books on *Mark's Gospel* and *John's Gospel* are known.

In studying the Creed, it is very fruitful to arrange the sentences in a circle and in this manner bring them into dialogue. Likewise, with the Epistles, finer relationships between them are established when one brings the seasonal prayers into such a circle.

The point of departure for what follows for me was the study of the *three Christmas prayers*, with which the relationship to the 'Luke-trigon' struck me. The trigon of the Christmas-evangelist Luke is the Goat-Bull-Virgin. (As mentioned, I assume Beckh's books are known.)

The *Goat* is the sign of the winter solstice. The Prayer at midnight is related to it. 'In the earthly night, into the senses' darkness ...' (In John's Gospel the nocturnal dialogue with Nicodemus [John 3] takes place in the Goat.) The Goat belongs in the zodiac to the 'Cross of the Father'. The gospel reading of the Midnight Service is taken from Matthew [Chapter 1].

The second Christmas Service, unfortunately the one least attended, is the actual Lucan [celebration]. The gospel reading is the Christmas story of Luke. Here we are in the sign of Luke, the *Bull*. 'Our souls feel the approach of the healing Creator-Word...' The Bull belongs to the 'Cross of the Spirit'.

The third Service shows the greatest proximity to John and stands in the *Virgin*. '... has chosen the earthly body'. To the Virgin belong the Mysteries of Earth-alchymy. In the freeing from 'the senses' unworthy craving' the motif sounds of the pure Mary. The gospel reading, or pericope, is taken from John 21. ('... the light of Thy clear shining power': [the] 'eye' in the hymn to the hierarchies recalls the further aspect of the Virgin: the sense of sight, of the selfless eye is the most Virginal of the senses.) The Virgin belongs to the 'etheric Cross of the

Son'. Taking into account the chiming in of the countersign is also of great importance here.

The Midnight Service in the Goat stands facing the Act of Consecration for St John's-tide in the sign of the *Crab*. One may not expect, of course, that our arrangement is always in harmony with the monthly signs, that indeed, for example, for Christmas already three different prayers are spoken in one day. One is not to expect, for example, in studying the seasonal prayers that the Lion and the month of August coincide, since August belongs to no special seasonal prayer. Yet in three cases they do correspond: Goat–Christmas, Crab–St John's-tide, and thirdly, still to be discussed, Michaelmas–the Scales. To the in-streaming of the light at the midnight hour of the year corresponds the receiving of the light *'in Lichtes-Liebe-Sinn'*, 'light's fullness of love', the walking free-of-the-body in the spirit-land, living in pure ether-spheres. The Crab is a sign of Johannine initiation ('life born out of death').

The second Christmas Service in the Bull would stand facing the *Scorpion*. In the Creed the Scorpion already appears in its metamorphosed form through the Johannine initiation, in the Pentecostal-sentence 'Through Him can the Healing Spirit work', in the Creed lying opposite the Bull-sentence of the Holy Spirit and of Mary. In the sense of this metamorphosis of the Scorpion into the Eagle, one can find in the Pentecost-prayer the sign of the Scorpion, strongly influenced by the countersign of the sacred word of the Bull. (Three times the word 'healing' occurs; the 'World Physician'.) In the words 'weakness', 'infirmity' and 'sickness' the Scorpion can be felt. The relationship between Christmas and Pentecost is always felt. Old pictures portray Mary at Pentecost (according to Acts 1:14 she was 'present') in the circle of disciples, over-seen by the Holy Spirit. Cf. also Bock's article in *Das lichte Jahr* [Stuttgart 1924, pp. 38-43]. Thus, the Bull as countersign chimes into the prayer for Pentecost.

The third Christmas Service in the Virgin is faced in the countersign of the *Fishes* with the *Ascension* Prayer. Here too the signs and countersign sound strongly into each other. Beckh calls the Fishes-Virgin the 'Last Supper constellation' (placed in the etheric Son-cross). In the Fishes the union takes place of the Son born in eternity, of the 'Son of the Sun', with the Earth (Baptism in the Jordan and Transfiguration in Mark's Gospel). The phrase '...Who has chosen the earthly body' standing in the Ascension-text faces the Transfiguration of the earthly element. 'He lives in earthly being, transmuting earthly being with heavenly being'. (In the Creed, cf. sentences 2 and 8, but there respectively the countersign is primarily emphasized, since there Ascension stands in the Virgin.) In the third prayer for Christmas the sign of the Fishes clearly chimes in. As in the 2nd sentence of the Creed, here the festive emphasis of the name Christ is found, 'Christ, the Creator-Spirit revealing the Fatherly Ground of the World'.

That the prayer for Ascension really stands in the Fishes is seen also from the fact that it contains the whole of Christology, similar to the 2nd sentence of the Creed. No other Epistle speaks so comprehensively of the work of Christ, the content of the name of Christ unfolded in such fullness. (That precisely here the name itself is not so obviously cited, we shall discuss later).

We should mention an apparently subsidiary use of a word. Only in those two Seasonal Prayers, to which we have ascribed the etheric Last-Supper Constellation Virgin and Fishes, that is in the prayer for the 3rd Christmas service and for Ascension, do we find the word *'wohnen'*, 'to live, inhabit', '… has chosen the earthly body, in which He chooses to live'. 'He lives with us, in that He lives with Thee.' It is an example of how through the viewpoint of the stars the tangible, occultly precise character of the use of the word can be brought into the right light. 'To live, to inhabit' is clearly an expression 'to do' with the etheric realm. The *Ge-wohn-heiten'*, habits have their seat in the etheric body. In 'living, in-habiting' lies a rhythmical enlivening, coming in and going out. Christ inhabits the body of the Earth in a rhythmic pulsation of the seasons, He inhabits the body of the Earth also in the rhythm of the Act of Consecration, his inhabiting of the human earthly being through the Communion is 'in the rhythms of the world, blessing the souls' [from *The Foundation-Stone* verse by Rudolf Steiner]. This word *'wohnen'*, 'to live, inhabit', thus receives an ever more concrete meaning. The 'inhabitation' through the Communion is a rhythmical life-process in the realm of the higher ethers. In the sentence 'He lives with us in that he lives with Thee' lives this Johannine rhythm of 'Thou in Me and I in them' [John 17].

The three Christmas Services stand thus in the course of the year facing the festivals of St. John's-tide, Pentecost and Ascension that follow each other (in reverse order). In this sequence of festivals, the Johannine trigon is active, also expressed in the pericopes for Pentecost and Ascension, which are indeed taken from John's Gospel. In the prayer for St. John's-tide not only the Baptist lives, but also John the Evangelist (*'in Lichtes-Liebe-Sinn'*, 'light's fullness of love').

- The St. John's-tide prayer in the Crab belongs to the Cross of the Father (which is also recognizable in the text),
- the prayer for Pentecost in the Scorpion-Eagle belongs to the Cross of the Spirit,
- [the prayer for] Ascension belongs to the Cross of the Son.

I would certainly not encumber the *Newsletter* with these studies if it were only an intellectual game of relationships. For me at least it is more, really an inspiring discussion at the round table of the Seasonal Prayers, the Epistles. The trigon of Luke and John mutually converse, as do those of Mark and Matthew.

The *Ram* belongs to the Mark-trigon. The Ram is the sign of beginnings, of the spring equinox that gives the tone. In the Ram one places oneself properly into reality, one steps on to the ground of the facts and experiences the head in this healthy sober, healing consciousness of reality in the related musical key of C-major.

The prayer *'aware of our humanity'* [Trinity] is *the* opening prayer. As John 1 is *the* gospel of the archetypal 'normal' Act of Consecration, which began in Dornach for the first time [in 1922]. In the Ram the active Mars is at home. In the triune-membered prayer one actively places oneself in a sacred soberness on the ground of the Trinitarian facts; one steps on the ground that carries the whole Service. In Mark's Gospel the casting out of demons takes place in the Ram. Those exorcised are returned to the true consciousness of their humanity. Whoever today comes in from the street, out of the demonized and demonizing urges of the modern city, experiences through this opening prayer a kind of exorcism; he contemplates in pro-active, tranquil 'coming to himself' his true humanity, within which it would be an illness not to feel the Father-God. In 'awareness'—in 'experience'—in 'grasping'. It is *the* preparation for the Act of—Consecration—of Man.

The mutually oscillating sign is the Scales. It is found in the 'being weighed' of the Trinitarian sentences. The great I-AM between Lucifer and Ahriman. Our 'humanity' in a special sense. The Trinitarian prayer does not belong to a special festival, it is in a certain sense always present. It is only specialized in the variously coloured festive moods [during the 'in-between' weeks throughout the year]. It is a 'timeless festive prayer', which is always present as an undercurrent and when the special festive thoughts are omitted, appears with an obvious naturalness. In that sense it is not 'timeless', as it has a clear direction towards the time of the rising light. In the Ram lies the experience of the sunrise (cf. Beckh on the musical keys, *The Essence of Tonality*) to C-major. The opening of the Act of Consecration adds to the outer sunrise a second still more meaningful sunrise. The hour of the rising Sun is *the* hour of the Act of Consecration of Man.

The Michaelmas seasonal prayer belongs to the countersign of the Scales. Here we have at the 2 equinoxes, the coinciding of sign and month. In the Michaelmas prayer the actual human element also has its place. In no other seasonal prayer does the word 'man' appear so often. It appears here eight times. In an earlier *Newsletter* I mentioned that the Michaelmas Epistle appears in seven sentences, which stand in their [chiastic] symmetry to each other (1-7, 2-6, 3-5). The middle sentence contains the Scales in a special sense: the 'Under his feet'—against Ahriman. The 'purifying and receiving spirit', the raising up of the earthly element—against Lucifer. In the gospel for Michaelmas, of the Wedding Banquet of the King's Son [Matt. 22], we also find the Scales: the ones who remain 'outside' die the death of matter—Ahriman. The others, impure and unclean, push themselves into the inner sanctuary—Lucifer. The Scales belong to the trigon of the 'Human Being' evangelist Matthew, from where also the 'Wedding Banquet of the King's Son' is taken. In Matthew this Scales-motif of the judgment generally plays a great role. Only in Matthew is there found the Parable of the Wise and Foolish Virgins and the division into sheep and goats. Regarded from the viewpoint of the planets, the sign of the Scales has Venus. Venus in the Scales is the heavenly, the redeeming love. In no other seasonal prayer is the Mystery of Golgotha mentioned in such a way as the great *Liebestod*, death for love ('deed of life and death'). Only here standing in the whole Act of Consecration, only here amongst all the seasonal prayers stands the word 'Golgotha'. (Good Friday is the Venus-day.) Of course, in the Michaelmas text the Ram is also at work with the active Mars as the countersign.

It is not without significance (in order to return to the Trinity prayer 'Conscious of our humanity…') that just this 'normal', 'typical' opening prayer, *the* introduction to the Act of Consecration of Man, carries the Michaelic element in itself (the countersign chimes in). The *Michaelic character of the Act of Consecration of Man* hereby becomes clear.

We find Mark's actual sign of the *Lion* in the *Easter* prayer. 'The Lion has overcome' [Rev./Apoc. 5:5]. In the Creed: 'Then he overcame death.' In the Easter Epistle: 'the conqueror of death.' The word 'heart' stands here three times. The mood of the Lion is quite evident, for example, in the sentences: 'Warmth changes the beat of the heart...', 'The heart is full', and 'My heart praises the Spirit of God.' In the pulsing of the blood and undulating of the breath lives the rhythmic human being, the Lion.

The 'planet' of the Lion is the Sun. The mood of the Sun lives in the great rhythm, in the unfolding of the 'Inserted Prayers', to which Dr Steiner gave the special indication 'to speak with great devotion and warmth'. 'The breath of the Earth lives in the spirit-wakened power of the Sun.' 'Christ has invaded man's rejoicing pulse of life.' In this quite special rhythmically moved hymn the pulsing of the heart of the Sun is present. The character of the Lion of the Easter Act of Consecration speaks to us, too, in the gospel, as the pericope Mark 16.

Facing this lies *Advent* in the *Waterman*. (We shall come to the reciprocal influence of these two signs Lion-Waterman in section II, below.) In the Waterman there stands in Mark the Baptism in the Jordan (immersion into the world of our etheric origin), but then the Entombment, of the Baptist as well as of Christ Himself. In the Creed the 1st sentence (I have to take it that the study on the Creed is known, where the relationship to the Father-evangelist Matthew is discussed) speaks of the spiritual-physical Ground of Existence. The planetary aspect is Uranus and Saturn. *Pater uranios*, the 'heavenly Father'. In the Easter Epistle the resurrection; in the Advent Prayer the germinating tranquillity of the grave, in which the Resurrection is mysteriously prepared. It is the tranquillity of the grain of wheat in the grave.

- '.... *im Weltenschoße verheißend keimt*', '... grows with promise in the womb of worlds';
- '*Die Weltenruhe um uns erfüllt sich mit dem hörbaren Walten*', 'the peaceful world around us is filled with the sound of creation':
- '*Das Walten des Welten-Vater-Grundes*', 'the working of the Father Ground of the World'.

[The German idiomatic saying declares:] 'The Sun will reveal it to the day' at Eastertide. (In the course of the year the 'chiaroscuro' mood lies in the Waterman, the first 'divining of spring' at the end of January to the end of February. In *The Essence of Tonality* [Anastasi, 2008, p. 60] Beckh describes 'a certain basis of hope and trust' in the key of B♭-major. There is nothing of spring to be felt outwardly, but it is prepared in the unrevealed realm.) There is a bluish weaving in the Advent

Epistle, twilight chiaroscuro, Saturnine darkness with a flickering through with Uranian light.

'Our souls deeply musing'—in this is something of the hallowed phlegmatic mood of Matthew, whose main sign is the Waterman. (Moreover, the repeated 'prophetic' is a motif of Matthew, with whom the prophecies of the Old Testament repeatedly appear much more frequently than with the other evangelists.)

There still remains the constellation 'Twins-Archer', and the Epistles for Epiphany and the two for Passion-tide (Lent). I think it is no violation if one takes the latter two as one. This is not out of anxiety before the scheme, so that actually there should not be 13, but 12 Epistles, but it has an organic justification. The three Christmas Epistles cannot be taken as one in this manner; they are clearly to be recognized as pronounced individualities; they are completely different in construction and form. On the other hand, for me the two Passion-tide prayers always appear as 'Twins'; they resemble each other in sentence form and in the words. The Holy Week Epistle is but an intensification, having the same form. Here I do not need to discuss the exact correspondence of the respective five sentences in the detail of every word.

If one may take them as one, then this *Passiontide* Epistle in the death-sign of the *Archer* (the Scorpion is more the origin of death, the Archer is death that has already occurred ('The grave is empty ...'), the counter-sign of the Twins can be noticed in the characteristic of twins—side by side—of two texts of the same form. The fivefold form of the sentences clearly coming to the fore is like an indication towards the dark, nocturnal nature of the underworld. (The absolutely dark and heavy key of F-minor, where light is completely absent, belongs to the Archer.)

If we may feel in the Passion-text, namely Holy Week, the darkest depths, then the *Epiphany* Epistle that stands in the *Twins* leads into the brightest heights. The Star of Grace comes from a still higher region than the light-filled 'ether-widths' of the St John's-tide texts. The Twins are the sign of Zarathustra. They are also the sign of the Sacred Mount (which with Matthew, to whose trigon the Twins belong, plays a special role, e.g. the Sermon on the Mount, Feeding of the 4000 (15:29) and the Easter Mount in Galilee). According to the legend, the Wise Men from the East see the Star of Grace from the Mons Victorialis.[311] The Epiphany Epistle raises us from the light-filled heights of this Mountain of the Wise, from which one sees into the cosmic widths. The Epiphany Epistle in the Zarathustra sign of the Twins is the only place where in the Act of Consecration of Man the *Star* is mentioned, and it is true the word 'Star', including the Inserted Prayer, is heard exactly seven times, [or] including the end prayer [the repeat] twelve times. (Besides the Act of Consecration, the Star appears only in the liturgy of the Burial Service for a Child, where it says, 'enlighten the eye of our soul that it may divine him/her in Thy radiance, in Thy starry spirit-realm'). The word *'ewig'*, 'eternal', sounds special here. Our liturgical texts use this word very sparingly, so that when it does appear, it is something quite special. Only in the Burial Service, which, however, stands outside the seven sacraments, do we find it more frequently.[312] The word *'ewig'* in our texts always has a starry aura. It is found in the Advent Inserted Prayer, 'the Eternal Word'. In the Creed: 'the Son, born in eternity'; '... for the preservation of their life destined for eternity.' The Offertory: 'bury not their eternal being for the sake of their temporal.' Communion: 'medicine everlasting' (*pharmakon athanasius*).[313] Apart from this also in the Ordination Service.

The eternal, that is not to be buried 'for the sake of their temporal' being, is the starry part of the human being.

The phrase for Epiphany 'devoted to the eternal Father-will' becomes still greater and more earnest against this background of the Zarathustra-star. On the Sacred Mount of the Twins this saying has its very own place. (The Creed, in whose twelve sentences it appears twice, likewise stands, as we shall see viewed as a whole, in the Twins.)

The Passion-tide Epistle facing it is thereby characterized, that the eternal is buried in the temporal. The Star has sunk into the depths. The cosmic 'widths of the world' stands facing the narrow, 'cold, spirit-forsaken house of Earth'. Between Twins and Archer exists the greatest divide. It is the polarity between star and grave. That precisely these two Epistles really stand in mutual dialogue shows especially impressively the similar formulation in the following two sentences, wherein the polarity of *star* and *grave* become most movingly clear:

- Epiphany: '... when the spirit-ray of the Star of Grace reaches the eye of the soul.'
- Holy Week: 'from a grave of hope, a ray of grief reaches thy gaze.'

## II. The parts of the Act of Consecration

1.) Amongst the Epistle, we found the Trinity prayer 'Conscious of our humanity...' as *the* archetypal opening prayer, standing in the

*Ram*, whereby the Scales chimes in. The *Ram* is the sign of the *seasonal* prayer. This is no contradiction to what has previously been mentioned that especially was intended to show the variety of the twelve [zodiac]-signs in the various opening texts, the Epistles. It is similar to the spring equinox. The sign of the beginning is once and for all the Ram, disregarding the precession of the spring equinox. One could say that our 'Ram' in the cultural epoch of today is the Fishes; the 'Ram', that is, the beginning sign that gives the tone, which in the sixth epoch will become the Waterman. Thus the 'Ram' in the Easter Service is the Lion.

2.) The *Gospel* [part] stands in the sign of the *Bull*. [The] Word. That is, the healing word livingly penetrated by the 'blessing'.

3.) The *Creed* leads to the Sacred Mount from which one can overview all the widths of the world, where one has the panorama, the view to all sides. Christ gathers the twelve disciples on the mountain height in the sign of the Twins. The Creed with its twelve sentences is truly 'apostolic'. Beckh shows, how in the sign of the Twins the whole concept of twelve shines in Mark's Gospel.[314] In hearing the Creed, one stands with the 'wise of the world' in the 'star observatory'.

4.) The elevated sign of the Twins is followed in the Crab with the descent into depressing lowlands that especially need transforming. After the Creed, with the view towards 'eternal life' has come to a close, there stands the beginning of the *Offertory*, man under the depressive impression of his fallen nature. He would like to give a correspondingly adequate answer to what he has heard, but he is unable to live up to the 'demands' of the gospel. 'Strayings, denials, weaknesses'. One feels the choking narrowness of one's own being (doubly torturous after the descent from the heights of the Mount) and seeks to break through in sacrificing. The triple 'with me …' announces the triple 'pushing through walls'. The Offertory leads to the grave in which the Eternal rests, through the realm of the elements of the liquid (the mixing) and the air (smoke), right to the fire (concerning this I wrote extensively in the *Newsletter* some years ago). The saying standing over the Offertory is, 'He must increase, I must decrease' [John 3:30]. In the sacrifice there takes place the great turning point. The human soul-forces are turning into a new direction upwards instead of downwards. The 'word of flame' of John [the Baptist] is to ignite in the hearts. It is no coincidence the Inserted Prayer at St John's-tide takes its place after the Offertory and belongs to this. The Epistle for St John's-tide stands in the Crab. John is the great sacrificer, the selfless one.

5.) Then there follows the *Transformation* in the sign of overcoming, of the alchymical 'red *lion*'. Crab and Lion as the signs of Johannine transubstantiation are especially mutually connected. Thus, the Offertory and the Transformation flow into each other, whereas the Gospel and the Offertory on the one hand, and the Transformation and Communion on the other hand are more clearly separate from each other. At the end of the sacrifice, in the sentence of the fire we already feel the Lion; at the beginning of the Transformation the sacrifice is once more mentioned. Between Sacrifice and Transformation there is a sphere of contact. In the censing, that especially belongs to the Offertory, the Transformation is also introduced. The Transformation is an Easterly event, the Easter Service as a whole stands in the Sun-Lion.

6.) Above the *Communion* stands the sign of the Virgin, which with Mark is allocated to the Feeding of the 4,000 (which takes place during the day) and the Last Supper, whereas the nocturnal Feeding of the 5,000 chimes in as the countersign. Beckh calls Virgin-Fishes the 'Last-Supper Constellation'. The Maiden Repanse carried the Holy Grail [Eschenbach, *Parzifal* IX, 355].

7.) The Epistle returns; it is the same as at the beginning and yet somewhat different through everything that lies between. At the beginning it stands in the Ram, and the Scales chimes in. At the end the *Scales* is primarily emphasized. This is the starry form of saying this more or less obscure feeling due to its being the same-yet-different experienced while celebrating: the first time Ram-Scales, the second time Scales-Ram. At the beginning it has especially the character of commencing, of a proper introduction. At the end after the deep feelings of the great experiences it should lend the human being the proper balance, so that he can 'take his leave of the sacred event'. One leaves in the sign of the 'great I–AM' that 'strides right through the middle' between Ahriman and Lucifer (see Beckh's book on *John's Gospel*); the departure should in the true sense of the word be an 'exit through the middle'.

In Mark the storm at sea follows the parable of the seed (in the Virgin); in the same way the Feeding of the 5,000 follows the sea-storm. In the Scales the calming takes place, the inner dealing with the spiritual experience, which 'takes presence of mind' (cf. the Michaelmas meditation of the Breviary).

We see the Act of Consecration embraces precisely the *7 Zodiac-signs of the daytime* [seven bright and 5 dark signs are described by Beckh]. Thereby the Act of Consecration has the public character of the 'exoteric' [event]; one does not feel this as inferior, but in the sense that in the liturgical event the esoteric is brought 'to the light of day', manifests it, makes it available to everyone. The Act of Consecration in a sacred, calm manner presents 'Christ's light in our daylight' to the awake, earthly experience of the day. It is celebrated during the rising of the Sun.

The five lower, dark nocturnal signs are in a certain sense the esoteric ones. The John-trigon is the only one in which lie two signs in this dark half [of the circle]. Beckh shows in the new book [*John's Gospel*] how the five dark signs are the world of John's Gospel. The 'esoteric' side of the Act of Consecration is the gospel according to John. The five dark signs, however, clearly chime into the Act of Consecration as countersigns.

In the *Gospel* [part of the Service] the *Scorpion* can be felt. '... pure my heart, pure my word.' It is there like a confession between the lines that we are impure. At the end it is expressed, 'what lives impure in our word'. In the heart, instead of the pure life of Christ, there is the 'sting of evil' (Inserted Prayer, after the Gospel Reading during Passiontide).

If one understands the Scorpion as the Sun-Eagle re-established through John, then this aspect, too, can be recognized in the Gospel. The *'normal'* gospel is the Prologue of John's Gospel, John as the evangelist in a special sense (he is called *Johannnes evangelista*, not only to differentiate him from *baptista*, but also for a positive reason) is deeply related to the 'Gospel', to the angelic message.

The countersign in the *Creed* is the *Archer*. The Creed stands in the 'Golgotha constellation'. Twins–Archer, that means, it encompasses the highest heights and the deepest depths. The Creed is the text within the whole Service that carries in itself the whole extent. It goes through heaven and hell, through the pain as well as the glorious Mysteries. It is something rounded, all-embracing. As far as in the constellation Twins-Archer, the whole circle of twelve appears, the Creed is the most circular part within the Service. All the other texts possess a certain one-sided point of view. The Act of Consecration seen as a whole is still a fragment if it is not experienced within the circle of the year in the various colours [of the altar and the vestments]. But the Creed is always an enclosed whole. Thus, it supplements the respective special gospel reading, which always can only be a section (for example, the Easter gospel, or the Good Friday gospel, through its 'pleroma').

With the *Offertory*, opposite the Crab stands the other turning point, the Goat. The Offertory is the great call to repent, that is, to 'change your thinking', 'turn around'. The sermon of the Baptist. Sacrifice is, as it were, the gesture of 'bending the knees'. To reject the sacrifice, to bury the eternal for the sake of the temporal would mean to fall for the demonic nature of the Goat. The call to repent is followed in Mark by the Baptism in the Jordan, as an immersion into the stream of the original, pure etheric forces. One can notice in celebrating that after fulfilling the Offertory one dives into the 'stream' in which one should stand as celebrant. This immersion into the stream stands in the sign of the *Waterman*, which chimes in at the *Transformation*. Recall what has been mentioned about the first sentence of the Creed, how this sentence of the spiritual-physical Ground of Existence is aligned to the Uranus star-sign Waterman, as it were, the Matthew corner in the Creed. The noticeably frequently recurring phrase with Matthew 'the heavenly Father' was mentioned (*pater uranios*). This first sentence stands facing the Lion-sentence of Easter (transformation). The Transubstantiation stands facing the 'substance' as its prerequisite.

With John, the Wedding in Cana stands in the Waterman-Lion. The freshly drawn water is the 'substance' in the sign 'red lion' there takes place the 'trans-substantiation'. Thus, in the background to the Service are the Father Mysteries (for all sacramentalism has its basis in the 'spiritual-physical' [existence]).

The *Transubstantiation* is an unveiling of the Father. In the 'Gospel' [section] the Father-God does not yet appear. In the Offertory He appears as 'Ground of the World'. So also, at the beginning of the Transubstantiation, but soon replaced through 'Father-God', until finally with the words of institution there appears again the 'simple'—but after such a preparation again surrounded by shudders of Mystery—word 'Father'. '… and looking up to Thee, His Father, thanking Thee', the Transubstantiation is the 'great thanksgiving' which is brought towards the Father, Who bears all substance. The right answer for the gift of the Waterman is found in the sign of the Lion. Through the fact that Christ transforms, he completes the will of the Father. In all festive solemnity this mysterious element of *pater uranios* in the Transformation appears at the end of the transformation: 'Our Father, Who are in heaven …' In the Transformation the request of Phillip is fulfilled,

'Show us the Father.' (Cf. Dr Steiner in the Apocalypse lecture-course concerning showing the Father.)[315]

The Lord's Prayer in the form as it is prayed in the Act of Consecration is taken from the Waterman-evangelist Matthew (Sermon on the Mount [Matt. 6:9-13]). The Lord's Prayer in Luke begins with just 'Father' (without 'our' and without 'in the heavens, *uranios'*, which is so characteristic for Matthew), and, moreover, is not revealed on the Mount (Luke 11:2). The popular Bibles unwarrantedly have adjusted Luke's text to Matthew's; one has to read it in the original text.

The Transubstantiation is framed by the evocation 'O Ground of the World' and the 'Lord's Prayer'. Exactly in the middle, exactly with the Words of Institution there stands the word 'Father', unveiled for the first time.

It will be quite clear that with the *Communion* the Fishes is involved, the countersign of the Virgin. The Virgin is the sign of the ether-body, the Fishes the sign of *buddhi*, that is, life-body and Life-spirit. The second sentence of the Creed. Within our liturgical text the monstrance-like raising of the name Christ seems to be a motif of the Fishes. 'Christ, through Whom man ...'. With the 3rd prayer (Virgo) the countersign of the Fishes strongly chimes at the beginning: 'Christ, the revealing Creator-Spirit of the Father-Ground of the world.' Both times the name Christ is impressively emphasized, like something most sacred which is brought out to be venerated. The following subsidiary sentence in both texts rounds off the Name through the 'comma', so that it is not without more ado included in the continuity of the sentence but left in a certain sublime isolation. In the actual Fishes Epistle, Ascension, the content of the name Christ is so overpoweringly bright and great that here especially (only here in this way) the name is honoured through not being actually mentioned. 'Thou hast sent HIM'. 'He lives in earthly existence.' I do not find this as a contradiction to the sentence that to Pisces the name Christ belongs. Especially out of the Ascension text, the name Christ, which is easily 'used up' can inwardly be freshly built up. One could also say, the Ascension text paraphrases the name Christ, for it includes the whole work of the Redeemer; it is *the* Christological text amongst the Epistles.

Thus in the Communion there repeatedly returns the liturgical solemn address 'O *Christe'* (especially in the second section of the Communion, 'Thou, O Christ, Who did without sickness proceed

...', the character of the Fishes is clear). The 'O' embraces the name, which here appears in its venerable Latin vocative form (outside the Communion [the German text has] 'O Christus'), as an aura of veneration.

A further Fishes-motif in the liturgical texts is the proceeding from the Father.

Creed: 'the Son born in eternity.'

## Christmas III: 'the Revealing Creator-spirit of the Father-Ground of the World'

Ascension: 'Thou has sent HIM.' 'Thou Who without sickness proceeded from the Father-God.'

A further Fishes-motif is the 'life of the world'
Creed: 're-enlivening of the dying Earth-existence.'
Ascension: 'He lives in earthly existence, transmuting ...'
In the Communion: 'Thou Who does bear and order the life of the world ...'

The Fishes is the 'esoteric' aspect of the Last Supper. (Instead of the Last Supper, John narrates the Washing of the Feet in the sign of the Fishes).

In the two magical-alchymical parts of the Act of Consecration, Transformation and Communion, the Waterman and the Fishes chime in as the countersigns, in which also especially the two planets Uranus and Neptune are at home, which point towards the farther distances of the starry cosmos. Neptune in the Communion as 'sound from far-distant worlds' [see above, p. 289].

All these studies—Creed, Epistles, Act of Consecration result for me as a consequence of Beckh's researches, and it would be a wish of mine to have shown through an example the fruitfulness of his viewpoint.

With all this I do not want to say that other arrangements are not possible and justified. Neither do I make any claims; perhaps for many it is nothing new, and perhaps some of the great silent ones in our circle have found much better things. To me in any case these things have come to me with such evidence that I somehow felt obliged to communicate it without fail. Limited time has unfortunately held me back from bringing the way of presentation only marginally on to the heights that would be appropriate to the subject. I beg readers' understanding. Once more, summarized as a scheme:

I. Epistles

| *Luke*-trigon | | and | *John*-trigon |
|---|---|---|---|
| Goat | (Christmas I) | — | Crab (St John's-tide) |
| Bull | (Christmas II) | — | Scorpion (Pentecost) |
| Virgin | (Christmas III) | — | Fishes (Ascension) |

| *Mark*-trigon | | — | *Matthew*-trigon |
|---|---|---|---|
| Ram | ('Conscious of …') | — | Scales (Michaelmas) |
| Lion | (Easter) | — | Waterman (Advent) |
| Archer | (Passion-tide) | — | Twins (Epiphany) |

II. Course of the Act of Consecration

| 1 Epistle | — Ram (Scales) |
|---|---|
| 2 Gospel | — Bull (Scorpion) |
| 3 Creed | — Twins (Archer) |
| 4 Offertory | — Crab (Goat) |
| 5 Transformation | — Lion (Waterman) |
| 6 Communion | — Virgin (Fishes) |
| 7 Epistle | — Scales (Ram) |

## Additions

*To 'Matthew–Waterman–Uranus'*

After the Transformation, in which the Waterman as the countersign of the Lion chimes in, the Lord's Prayer taken from the Sermon on the Mount of Matthew is spoken. In the Lucan form (the German translation conceals it and adjusts it not to upset the simple Bible-reader) 6:2 is missing not only with the address, the 'Who art in heaven' (*uranios*), but significantly [also] the 3rd petition, which only stands in Matthew and possesses a Zarathustrian-magical-male character, 'Thy will be done as in the heavens' (*uranō*), so also on the Earth.' This side-by-side of heaven and Earth, of 'Uranus and Saturn' (cf. the previous RB) can furthermore be found in the magnificent passage in Matthew 28:18, where the Risen One (on the Mount where, according to Matthew, the Lord's Prayer is given), where the Risen One says: 'To me is given all *exusia* on Earth.' Cf. the description of the Resurrection in Matthew 28:2: the angel descends from heaven (*uranos*), rolls away the stone

and sits on it. His appearance is like the lightning, his garment white
as snow. Its uranian light-etheric element ('unearthly' white) and the
grave with its Saturnine heavy stone are here wonderfully contrasted.
(More on this in a subsequent study on the evangelist-trigon in the
Creed, p. 368 above.)

### To the 'Communion–Virgin–Fishes'

I did not express myself very strongly. The motif of 'life', which indeed can
be found in the Communion especially frequently, is, of course, just as well
a motif of 'the Virgin'. The 'Fishes' character can be especially felt where the
etheric [body] is spiritualized towards *buddhi*. The 'further life of human
spirits'. 'Life of the soul'. '… makest it whole through the Spirit.'

### To the 'Gospel–Bull'

Beckh shows in his book on Mark how the section on the Bull is marked
in particular through the frequently occurring word 'word'.

In the *Gospel* (according to our division it stands in the Bull)—as
earlier on H. von Skerst[316] has pointed out—the word 'word' appears
exactly seven times. This is remarkable and significantly frequent,
especially that if appears otherwise only once respectively in each of
the other main parts (towards the end of the Offertory, after the words
of institution, after Communion of the bread, where it is spoken three
times, that is, disregarding the Epistles it appears in the rest of the Act
of Consecration of Man only five times).

Amongst the Epistles the second Christmas prayer possesses the
character of the Bull; it has as its special content the healing Creator-Word. Here in particular one can find several links to the Gospel
chiming in. Only there and in the Gospel does there exist the tangible
reference to the lips (nowhere else). Also the sentences 'Thy blessing
flow living through the Word' and 'His strength flow with blessing to
us' are closely related. The Word as a blessing stream ('*rhema*').

Both times also the connection of the Word with the forces of the
blood, or rather of the heart.

In the *Pentecost* prayer and 'inserted prayer', where the Bull chimes
in as the countersign, it says 'may the Healing Spirit hold sway in the
word of offering'. 'So flame the word of the Act of Consecration', '…
to enkindle its being in the word of praise'.

### To 'Ram–Scales'

If it is correct that the ACM begins with the Ram and finishes in the
Scales, then also the beginning and ending words would stand in these

signs, where solemn phrase 'The Act of Consecration of Man' itself is mentioned.

'Let us …' in the Ram (the active Mars is at home in the Ram).

'… thus it has been' in the Scales. In these words there lie, amongst other things, the calming and ordering gathering of all the feelings that have been brought into movement. For the celebrant it is at the same time the solemn *'scales of judgment'* which he/she experiences with these words that he/she now passes the completed Service to the spiritual world.

*'Addition to RB 117' (from RB 119)*

(1) We found the *3rd Christmas ACM* stands in the sign of the Virgin (Earth-alchymy) [p. 428]. The Ascension ACM, standing in the countersign of the Fishes, has a special relationship to this Christmas ACM. (In the Creed stands the sentence of Ascension primarily in the Virgin.) Here it is significant that especially in the ACM 'lying opposite' [in the year] of Ascension-tide the invocation of all the nine *hierarchies,* of all the heavenly forces, takes place.

(2) We allocated the Advent-prayer to the Waterman [p. 432] and spoke thereby of the first 'tender hope of spring'. This is meant in a similar sense as the 'summer of the soul' at Christmas.

(3) P. 5, in the middle was unclear [p. 434]. The word which in the Twins-Zarathustra prayer at *Epiphany* has a special sound and which then in the Creed (which as a whole belongs to the Twins) appears twice, is the word *'ewig'* (translated 'eternity', sentences 2 & 12). Concerning this, more in the following study on the trigon.

(4) P. 9, in the section Matthew-Waterman-Uranus words are missing concerning what it is about [p. 441]. The Risen One says (Matt. 28:18): 'To me is given all authority *in heaven and on the earth.'*

(5) P. 9 [p. 441], just before the passage just mentioned: the Lucan parallel to the Lord's Prayer in the Sermon on the Mount, Luke 11:2-4. Missing are 'our', 'in the heavens', also the 3rd petition (will) and the 7th (the evil).

# APPENDICES

Arthur Schult

# Christian-Rosicrucian Astrosophy and Arabian Astrology of the Middle Ages: on the 300th death anniversary of Johannes Kepler[317]

## *Life and Works*

Johannes Kepler was one of the great spirits at the turn of the Middle Ages to modern times. He was born 27 Dec. 1571, the Feast of John the Evangelist. At the time of writing [1930], he died 300 years ago in Regensburg 15 Nov. 1630, the 350th [today 440th] death anniversary of Albertus Magnus, the teacher of Thomas Aquinas. During the chaos of the Thirty Years War, Kepler was haunted by financial worries, although he was employed as Imperial Astronomer by Wallenstein.[318] During the *Reichstag*, the Parliament at Regensburg, the 'mathematician to Emperor and Country' was to call on the assistance of the *Reichsfürst*, the Imperial Lord. But a few weeks after arriving in Regensburg, Kepler, already quite weak in body and from constant blows of destiny, finally succumbed to the exhaustion of the long journey. As a follower of Protestant belief he was buried outside the town's churchyard. His grave, which during the later skirmishes around the city was obliterated, fell into oblivion. But unforgotten his spirit and name still shine today, centuries later.

Natural science of the nineteenth century celebrated in the pupil of Tycho Brahe [1546-1601], Johannes Kepler, the founder of the new astronomy. In the struggle for the world-picture of Copernicus, in those days still heretical, he discovered the three basic laws of planetary motion and found essential elements of the law of gravitation (later precisely formulated by Newton); he wrote a classic work on optics, the theory of the lens and the principles of the astronomical telescope, a comprehensive textbook still valid today on knowledge of the heavens [*Astronomiae Pars Optica*]. And he gave the well-known *Rudolphine Tables*, named after Rudolf II [the Holy Roman Emperor],

which for more than a century remained the standard table for astronomical calculations. Mathematicians mention Kepler's name in the
prehistory of infinitesimal calculus; they praise his achievement in
establishing logarithmic tables and besides the development of the
planetary laws, the established Kepler's equation, named after him.

In the twentieth century those writings founding modern natural
science, with their clear knowledge in astronomy, physics and mathematics, are remembered as only part of Kepler's life's work. More
essential to Kepler's way of thinking are those other works, building on
early Mystery knowledge, of which the most important can be named:
*Mysterium cosmographicum* (1596) ('The Sacred Mystery of the Cosmos'), and *Harmonices Mundi* (1619) (*Harmony/ies of the World*).[319] Even
in the scientific community it is increasingly realized that this part of
Kepler's life's work is far more genial than Kepler's laws on which
the new astronomy is based. Kepler's view was not yet limited merely
to the physical side of the world. In him, besides thinking exactly oriented to the physical, sensory plane, live a cosmic perception and ability to think that also includes the supersensory world, ensouled by
deep devotion, daring to reveal the inner side of the microcosmic and
macrocosmic world. Friedrich Doldinger[320] consequently says about
Tycho Brahe and Kepler:

*Ihr lauschtet noch der Erde Sternenchören.*
*Du wußtest noch, daß sie lebendig ist;*
*dir war sie nicht der kalte, tote Ball,*
*nach dürren Regeln geisternd durch das All;*
*die war sie noch der Leib des Heiligen Christ.*

*Du fühltest ihre Seele noch und wie*
*ein Reich von Geistern täglich um sie webt,*
*daß liebend sie zum Sonnenherzen hebt*
*und Schönheit auf ihr schafft und Harmonie.*

[Prose translation:]
You both still hearkened to the starry choruses of the Earth. You still
knew that the Earth is alive; to you it was not a cold, dead sphere, ghostly
moving through the universe according to emaciated rules; to you it was
still the body of the holy Christ. You still felt its soul and how a realm of
spirits daily surround it, which lovingly raise it towards the Sun's heart,
creating upon it beauty and harmony.

With his clear thinking exhibited in his writings, Johannes Kepler, building on early sacred Mystery teaching, carries the Rosicrucian impulse into the future (in the appendix to the *Harmonices Mundi* he describes in detail the ideas of the Rosicrucian Robert Fludd [1574-1647]. Kepler is fully aware that he is to carry the starry wisdom of the ancient Egyptian and Babylonian epoch from the temples of the Orient towards the science of the Christian West. In the Preface to *Harmonices Mundi*[321] [1619] stands the proud claim:

> I am free to taunt mortals with the frank confession that I am stealing the golden vessels of the Egyptians, in order to build of them a temple for my God, far from the territory of Egypt.

To those living in the twentieth century, the questions concerning the meaning of the world and the connections of all things appear again as important, more important than a manner of research—however admirable and conscientious—limited to what is physically perceptible. People found again a certain understanding for the world-wide cosmic consciousness that is alive in Kepler's Faustian works. But many contemporary persons still feel embarrassment when a spiritual-scientific research in natural science takes as completely real Kepler's teaching of the Earth's soul in which there shines a picture of the zodiac, indeed the whole visible starry heavens. Because the thinking of the present day remains easily stuck in mere speculation, people are unable to follow the concrete, living thoughts of the great astronomer on the influences of the stars on the human soul, the lord of the sub-lunar world. They take offence at Kepler's life-long practice of practical astrological activity. In earlier years the attempt was made actively to eliminate practical astrology from Kepler's life by turning the facts into their opposite. It is stated that Kepler himself did not believe his own horoscope; only to make ends meet did he need to make astrological predictions.

Today it is generally recognized that for his whole life Kepler showed a deep inner conviction for a certain part of practical astrology and horoscopes. We now see that also in this field within a practical astrology, Kepler understood how with admirable clarity to distinguish the genuine from the false. He confronted a degenerate Arabian, fatalistic belief in the stars with a Christian wisdom of the stars. Similar to earlier days in the Scholasticism of Albertus Magnus and Thomas Aquinas, he released the binding power of nature into the freedom of the children of God [cf. Rom. 8:21], according to the ancient words, '*Astra inclinant, neque tamen necessitant'*, 'the stars influence but do not determine'.[322] With the strongest weapons he fought an irresponsible interpretation of the stars and of soothsaying, which neither respect human freedom, nor the dignity of an ancient sacred wisdom of the stars. He was totally committed to the correct division of the spirit [cf. Heb. 4:12]. As the great historical example of this example of the spirits, there stands before us the meeting of Kepler with Albrecht Wallenstein.

## Kepler and Wallenstein

Twice in the year 1608 and later 1625, Kepler made a horoscope for Wallenstein. During the last years of his life Kepler was employed directly in Wallenstein's service and Kepler died during parliamentary session in Regensburg where Wallenstein was toppled by the Catholic Dukes. The two birth charts of Wallenstein, with their remarks and a letter from the Commander himself have survived, giving a clear picture of the contrasting manner of thinking of these two significant people, who were profoundly bound in soul and in destiny.

Without knowing Wallenstein personally, and long before the appearance of the Commander in public, already in 1608, on the basis of the horoscope, Kepler wrote, 'Such I may rightly say of this lord in truth, that he has a wakeful, lively, industrious, restless mind, always eager for novelties, who dislikes common human endeavours and quarrels, but who strives for new, untried, or otherwise rare means, keeping much more in his thoughts than what he reveals outwardly.'[323] Furthermore, Kepler characterizes the manner of thinking of the later Commander as 'profound, melancholic and ever awake', his inclination towards alchemy and magic, 'his despising and disregard of human rules and customs, also of all religions'. He points towards a 'great thirst for honour and striving towards the dignity of the occasion and power, through which he would make many damaging public and secret enemies, but most of them he would oblige and prevail [over them]'. He speaks of a possibility of a 'prosperous marriage', of a rise in 'high dignities' and of the danger that he 'one day will be enticed to become the main leader of a malcontent rabble'. Also 'it will seem as if he will entertain some special superstition'. After the general description of his character, there follows a detailed interpretation of the course of his life and destiny.

Furthermore, Kepler turns against Wallenstein's 'particular superstition', who in his research debased astrology into 'astro-romanticism'.

A ponderous critical thinking in Wallenstein blocks his feelings and lames activity; his thinking admits no trust in destiny. Inner uncertainty and weakness of the 'I' was the reason Wallenstein occupied himself with astrology. God did not speak to him in his own breast, consequently he groped in his search for signs and guidelines in the stars. But this path can no longer be travelled. The more uncertain and unsupported Wallenstein found himself in his inner being, the more strongly he felt he needed to know the future. When his stars were unfavourable, under no circumstances could Wallenstein be induced to undergo any action; during favourable conditions he believed he had to use the time in order to achieve success.

During earlier ages, initiates read from the stars the past and the future of their people and of humanity; they regulated the whole cultic-religious and cultural life according to the harmony of the spheres. Only in the Greco-Roman cultural epoch [the fourth post-Atlantean cultural epoch], the time of the mind-soul, were horoscopes made for the first time. At that time the connection of these things with the Christian 'I'-impulse did not take place. Soon after they were made personal horoscopes were placed into the service of the lesser 'I', of the egoistic search for happiness and wellbeing. They consequently tended towards black magic. Moreover, it came about that the Arabs, the Medieval inheritors of the Babylonian traditions, attempted to capture the old wisdom of the stars in a scheme, into an intellectual net of rules and calculations that was spun into an anti-freedom, astral determination of everything that occurs. In a changed form this teaching still lives on today as absolute determinism in the materialistic natural science of our time. As a representative of this astrology that has become decadent, Wallenstein stands before us and with him the Italian, Giov. Batt. Zenno (in Schiller's *Wallenstein*, named Seni).

Kepler, connected deeply to the spirit, rejected this kind of starry wisdom. For him astrology is not narrowed to the limited realm of horoscopes, which only presents the last remnants of a priestly knowledge from pre-historic ages that is much too often darkened through the wishful strivings of petty thinking. In the Preface to the *Rudolphine Tables* (Ulm 1627) we read: 'The science of the stars is twofold. The first is its concern with the movements of the stars (astronomy), the other with the effect of the stars on the sub-lunar world (astrology).' With Kepler the making of horoscopes is embedded in a knowledge of the stars that embraces the history of the universe, earth and humanity.

For the pupil of Tycho Brahe, astrology, as the soul of astronomy, was the mother of all wisdom, the queen of the sciences.

Resting clear and sure in the power of his own 'I', Kepler meets the astro-romantic tendency of Wallenstein, that was born out of an 'I'-weakness. But he is far removed from denying the real spiritual meaning of the firmament at birth. In Book IV of *Hamonices Mundi* he thoroughly welcomed 'that wonderful undertaking of making horoscopes'. In his interpretation of Wallenstein's horoscope, Kepler himself had shown that out of the firmament of a person's birth, the inborn character and the destiny arising from it can be seen with great certainty, clearly outlined. Kepler could speak with Goethe's *Urwort. Orphisch* (Orphic Primordial Word), entitled '*Dämon*':

> *Wie an dem Tag der Dich der Welt verliehen*
> *Die Sonne stand zum Gruße der Planeten,*
> *Bist alsobald und fort und fort gediehen,*
> *Nach dem Gesetz wonach Du angetreten.*
> *So mußt Du sein, Dir kannst Du nicht entfliehen,*
> *So sagten schon Sybillen, so Propheten,*
> *Und keine Zeit und keine Macht zerstückelt*
> *Geprägte Form die lebend sich entwickelt.*

Daimon.

> As on the day you were granted to the world,
> The Sun stood to greet the planets,
> You likewise began to thrive, forth and forth,
> Following the law that governed your accession.
> You must be so, you cannot flee yourself,
> Thus sibyls long ago pronounced, thus prophets,
> And neither time nor any power can dismember
> Characteristic form, living, self-developing.

In his work *Tertius Interveniens* ('Third-party Interventions') (1610), Kepler explains the title:

> This is a warning to many theologians, medics and philosophers, especially D. Philippus Feselius, that they do not throw out the baby with the bath water through a cheap denial of the star-gazing superstition and with this act unknowingly against their professions. To all true enthusiasts of nature's mysteries, as a necessary lesson.

In this apologetic writing on astrology Kepler says,

> Firstly I may boast of this experience with truth, that the human being in the first kindling of his life, when he now lives for himself and can no longer remain in the maternal body, receives a character and an imprint of all the heavenly constellations—or of the pictures of the rays streaming together on the Earth—and retain this character until the grave, which then can be felt in the formation of his face and the other formations of the body, as well as in his human dealings, movements, attitudes and gestures, that is, that also through his bodily figure he finds reciprocal inclinations with other people and sympathy towards his person, and through his actions and what he foregoes he establishes for himself a like happiness, so that the one becomes brave, lively, happy and daring, the other sleepy, sluggish, negligent, light shunning, forgetful, hesitant and what other general characteristics exist.

Furthermore, Kepler knows from his own experience that not only through the stars at the moment of birth is the character and destiny of a person revealed but also through the heavenly movements of the days following the birth. Hereby each day that the newborn lives in the first quarter of a year corresponds to a year of his life in the future,

> that means, that by this short time or *tempus typicum*, human nature in all its parts is multiplied by 365 and through this multiplication the whole natural life, which remains imprinted in the memory, is extracted and similar to a ball of wool is unwound. In this way the whole future life, as far as it has to do with natural conditions, immediately from the first quarter of a year, is bequeathed bunched together to human nature.

In order not to misunderstand him in a materialistic sense, in the same work Kepler says, shortly before receiving one's character out of the world of the stars, that 'this character is received not in the body, for the body is much too clumsy for this, but in the nature of the soul itself, which acts like a point'. We may add that Kepler can only read from the starry script of the heavens the 'general characteristics' of the soul and 'the life, as it has to do with natural conditions'. Thus, the limits of astrological research become clear. The world at the physical level is not somehow directly influenced by the stars, still less is the spirit, the free 'I' of the human being, tightly held by the stars. It is the variety of the fashioning etheric formative forces and the whole soul-world of the astral level that can be recognized from the heavenly firmament at the moment a human being is born.

The more human beings live merely out of their urges and passions, out of their sympathies and antipathies, the more immature and inwardly bound they are, the clearer their lives and destinies will correspond to the given constellations of the firmament. The further we are removed from union with our higher 'I', which itself can never be found in a horoscope, the more we are determined by the stars. A deeper understanding of the human being, of course, helps us to recognize that this compulsive element of the stars is no outer compulsion, but for the sake of harmonizing our own being was wanted and is accepted in the pre-birth existence. The more the Logos begins to be effective in the human being, the more the free and conscious will, slumbering in each human being, emerges.

Where the path to Golgotha is inwardly followed, where crucifixion and entombment are experienced, there the freedom of the children of God in the resurrection is experienced [cf. Rom. 8:14]. The more strongly human beings are able to live out of their creative freedom, the more it is possible to make tangible prophecies according to the position of the constellations, the more they grow beyond the influence of the planetary constellations. Kepler, of the same mind as Goethe, witnesses to the overcoming of the lawfulness through the raying out, the divine will of deeds in the higher human 'I' through the 'I' power of Christian human hope, as expressed in the final verse of Goethe's *Urworte. Orphisch* (Orphic Primal Verses):

*ELPIS, Hoffnung*
*Doch solcher Grenze, solcher ehrnen Mauer*
*Höchst widerwärt'ge Pforte wird entriegelt,*
*Sie stehe nur mit alter Felsendauer!*
*Ein Wesen regt sich leicht und ungezügelt:*
*Aus Wolkendecke, Nebel, Regenschauer*
*Erhebt sie uns, mit ihr, durch sie beflügelt,*
*Ihr kennt sie wohl, sie schwärmt durch alle Zonen;*
*Ein Flügelschlag—und hinter uns Äonen!*

ELPIS, hope
Yet in such a border, such an iron wall
The highest opposing gate is being unlocked,
It but stands as long as old rocks do!
A being stirs lightly and unbridled:
From cloud cover, mist and rain showers
She raises us, with her, inspired with wings by her,

You know her well, she pulses through all regions;
One beat of her wings—and behind us aeons!

The astrology of the Arabs that degenerated into the determinism of astro-romanticism, under whose fascination Wallenstein was also drawn, repeatedly denies the above-mentioned fact. Johannes Kepler attempted to free Wallensein from this superstitious view. Kepler refrained from answering the many 'particular questions' posed by Wallenstein. For an interpretation of the birth-firmament must never concern concrete and specific events, the laying holding of a finished, fashioned form. On the contrary, it has to do with a 'fashioned form that develops in a living manner', a future of dispositions of the 'general characteristics'. 'That the heavens do something in the human being one sees clearly enough; what it does specifically, however, remains hidden' (*Antwort auf Röslins Diskurs*—'Answer to Röslin's Discourse').[324]

Through the horoscope one learns to recognize in unimaginable depths these general characteristics, the individual, typical basic traits of one's personality. By gaining a glimpse into the forces at work and how they mutual relate, one sees how one's inner character relates to one's destiny, coming apparently from outside. Human beings learn to hearken to the voice of their genius, to understand the language of their angel. In the picture of the stars the strengths and weaknesses of every personality is revealed. At the same time recognizing the ways and means to harmonize them helps the higher 'I' in the human being to break through. 'Nobody should claim it unbelievable that useful knowledge and sanctuary cannot also be found out of astrological folly and godlessness' (*Tertius interveniens*).

## Conclusion

Such an interpretation of the starry script should serve a real spiritualizing of life; it changes a depressing astral teaching of predestination into a magnificent instrument of freedom. It is an important part of the true wisdom of the stars, which in its being differs essentially from all traditional astral-romanticism. The meeting of Johannes Kepler and Albrecht Wallenstein can become for us a picture for the crisis of the spirit in this realm, for the differentiation of an Arabic astrology of the Middle-Ages from a Christian, Rosicrucian astrosophy.

The astronomer here certainly did not achieve to raise the Commander towards the clarity and profundity of his own astrosophical thinking. In 1625 Kepler wrote to Wallenstein:

> Since then I could not be moved to interpret a single birth-chart, except when I was guaranteed that my work would be taken up by somebody who understands *philosophiam*.

Moreover:

> Philosophy and also true astrology are a testament of God's works, also a sacred matter, not to be taken flippantly; this, as far as I am concerned, I do not want to dishonour.

The genial Commander did not understand *philosophiam*. The love of wisdom was not strong enough in him.

Johannes Kepler stands as a leading spirit at the beginning of the fifth post-Atlantean cultural epoch, which, according to Rudolf Steiner presents a recapitulation on a new level of the Egyptian-Babylonian era. From this it can be understood why at the present time interest in astrology and horoscope-making is increasing over wide areas of the population. Even today Kepler would have to struggle against irresponsible interpretations of the stars, against an astro-romanticism deviating into black magic. In America some large firms already employ their own astrologers in order to use the possibilities for business in the best possible way. There are medical doctors who attempt to prolong or induce birth in order to give children a most possible 'favourable' hour of birth. Wherever new impluses spring up, adversary forces are at work with tremendous busyness. It is indeed truly time to penetrate practical astrology and horoscope-making with a responsible clarity of consciousness. In no way are we helped simply through warnings concerning these things. Experience from the realm of horoscope-making clearly speaks for the actual truth of the astrological connections, which in the foreseeable future should be ever less a subject of doubt. One should never, for seemingly spiritual reasons, reject facts that are repeatedly confirmed from reliable experience. These things cannot simply be brushed aside with phrases, such as 'atavistic occultism', or 'decadent clairvoyance'. Today Kepler would again have to direct his 'warning to many theologians, medics and philosophers', not to go against their profession in ignorance with cheap rejections of a star-gazing superstition. The spirit of our time itself anticipates the rebirth of practical astrology.[325] As astrosophy, it shall prove to be a midwife for the higher 'I' in the human being.

This is only possible when within the human being there grows an ego-aware, that is, responsible, cosmic consciousness towards the starry depths of the cosmos. Without a living experience of the spirit, without a deep teaching of wisdom—which in the same way is able to embrace the dignity of the free human being and the cosmic widths of the world—any astrological activity is damaging. Such a deep teaching of wisdom, which opens to us anew the path of the spirit is given in the anthroposophy of Rudolf Steiner. It opens to contemporary people the gate to the temple of a new Johannine, cosmic Christianity. In the world-embracing greatness of this step, the wisdom of the stars of pre-Christian times can also live anew. The golden vessels out of the temples of Egypt will begin to shine anew in the blessing light of Christmas, of a Christian future—'far distant from the borders of Egypt'.

### Kurt von Wistinghausen

# *The Language of Water*[326]

The interplay of the seasons is especially eloquent in the high mountains. When winter gives way to spring it is as if after a time of contemplation and inwardness nature wants again to throw herself with new courage into the arms of teeming life. Then the great calm of the mountains is exchanged for the restless play of life—development replaces sublimity, destiny replaces heavenly stillness. But the way nature now turns to sweeter life, in the autumn turns in the reverse direction. And this coming home from autumn to winter, this transition of unrest into the rest of the mountain world, moves us especially deeply. This transition we shall discuss.

The highest peaks shine in eternal winter snow, whereas in the ravines and valleys rain and wind still pursue their wild game. In restless surging, the waterfalls swelled by rain cast themselves down; the brooks and waterways run, murmur and gurgle into the valley. Wind and water play together in unceasing noises, in driving unrest. But overnight it suddenly changes. A sublime peace has descended; the movement is arrested in a silent stillness. The almost uncontrollable waterfall is gripped and held by a cosmic power. It has frozen into greenish, glittering ice. For months its commotion is silent. The rushing brooks are also quiet, the murmuring waters are covered in abundant snow. Instead of rain that fell in torrents, now slowly and tenderly, flake by flake snow falls to the earth. The remnants of summer life, all the slight differences in the ground which brought variety to the landscape, making it restless, are now covered by shining white. A snowed-in valley in the high mountains is a classic picture of deepest peace. It has entered the tranquillity of the nature of the mountains, towards the light of the crystalline world of the snow. It is close to the eternal uninhabited peaks, the serene light of the glacier snow.

This transition of great nature from the one life into the other lays hold of the person who, with open mind experiences it deeply, because what takes place outside corresponds to a process within human nature. It is a larger picture for the transition of the soul passing over the threshold of death. The soul, too, become 'transfigured' when it approaches the calmness of eternity.

This matter of beholding nature, the pictorial character of the outer world, can suddenly become a clear insight. With a slight shock of recognition, the soul already in itself can experience something of this transition. For a flowing, moving experience of nature, 'crystallizes'—as it were, dies—within, inside, when it became 'clear', when it became thought. Thoughts are experiences that have become clear, have become 'frozen'. With each thought we 'die' a little.

The living, breathing soul feels akin to the element of water. The all-enlivening, all-penetrating water, when it is 'in its element', is in a condition of restless circulation. In the billowing ocean it arises, evaporating up to the clouds, wanders with the wind, and descends condensed at rain, runs over the earth, streams as a river into lakes and the sea, seeps into the depths, bubbles as a spring, striving upwards in all living beings. It is always changing, drawn hither and thither by the warmth of the air and by gravity, between clouds and the earth. In the cloud it lives freed and purified in its own nature; on earth it joins with [all] other material—here it becomes the water of life and is transformed into 'wine'. Only when it is laid hold by the peace of winter does it hold its breath and becomes still. Super-earthly wisdom then forms it into a crystal. We see the snow crystal as a little star, formed as a small harmonious cosmos. Ever-new divine Imagination creates in the snow innumerable starry forms. Here the beholder sees the sublime, calm, starry world of the heavens become manifest, which now in winter is, as it were, closer to the earth than in the summer— for in the long nights the stars are more apparent; their light gains in strength as opposed to the sunlight. In snow and ice water is held, it is 'fixed'. It is the eternal 'fixed stars' that in winter receive their clear counter-picture on the earth. It is as if heaven is no longer far off, but present on the earth. The glittering white of ice and snow is like captured cosmic light. The purity of fresh snow is a breath, something of the sublime world. Water has penetrated into 'heaven'.

Through the movement of water in autumn, which Goethe [1749-1832] met in 1779 in the Bernese Alps, he was moved to compose the poem 'Gesang der Geister über den Wassern'—'Song of the Spirits over the Waters'. The 'spirits' he experienced in and above the water see in the water more than only useful earthly matter. They recognize it as picturing the soul.

*Des Menschen Seele*
*Gleicht dem Wasser:*
*Vom Himmel kommt es,*

*Zum Himmel steigt es,*
*Und wieder nieder*
*Zur Erde muß es,*
*Ewig wechselnd.*

['Song of the Spirits over the Waters': 'Man's soul is like the water: it comes from heaven, it rises to heaven and must descend again to earth, ever-changing.']

In this poem Goethe pursues the changing path of water from the cloud to the lake. There in the wide expanses of water where it comes to rest, *'weiden ihr Antlitz alle Gestirne'*, 'all the stars feast their eyes'. Here, too, it is the stars, the light of which can be found with the peace at the end, when the movement of life's course comes to rest. In the same way—Goethe experiences and composes—as the water stems from the cloud, so the human soul comes from heaven, like the water going through its earthly destiny, in order (in death) to enter into the peace of the stars. It ascends again, in order to descend. The idea of repeated earthly lives was not foreign to Goethe.

In the artistic beholding of nature, he was able to understand her—but the picture of the water here may be looked at from another, also correct, viewpoint. The change of water ascending and descending in this connection may be for us a picture for the change of the human soul in falling asleep and waking up. In the awake life of day, the soul penetrates its body with consciousness; it merges with it—in the same way as the water penetrates the Earth and the living beings and becomes the water of life. The soul in the awake situation runs through the limbs of the body like water in a riverbed. But in the same way as water also evaporates, leaves the Earth and surrounds it as a cloud, so the soul withdraws from the body in sleep, casts off the earthly weight and hovers around the body, whereby consciousness is extinguished. The clouds of heaven do not for nothing remind some people of sleep and dreaming. We are indebted to anthroposophy for the knowledge that sleep is indeed an expansion and a leaving of the soul from the body that one should not imagine merely in a spatial sense—upon awakening the soul slips back into the body in order to engage in its daily work—in the same way as the rain falls to the Earth, to enable fruitful growth.

*'Ewig wechselnd'*, 'ever-changing', the soul wanders from the one situation to the other ever since it entered earthly conditions. Through birth on Earth it has dipped into the ever-moving etheric being of the water ('baptized in water') and lives throughout its earthly life in it.

Only when death enters does it find rest. There is then no more change from wake to sleep, no longer earthly bustle and activity. The soul is lovingly taken up by the forces of the spiritual realms, of the stars, purified and harmoniously fashioned. It pursues a path the water demonstrates to it when it becomes a snow crystal. It is surrounded by cosmic light and is clothed in white.

Human death is a transition over this threshold from the pulsing unrest to the rest of soul-existence, from the darkness of Earth towards the light of the spirit. That is why in the funeral service of The Christian Community through which we accompany the person who has died to his/her 'last rest': 'into the rest of soul-existence wanders the soul of our dear ... [name] who has fallen asleep. Into the light of the spirit-world enters the spirit of our dear ... [name].'

The Christian festival of death has always been a prayer through the power of Christ for peace and light for the one who has died. The Catholic ritual also begins with words expressing the same content as our ritual. The first word of the Latin text (= peace) has given the whole ritual, especially when set to music, the well-known name 'Requiem'.

With the picture of water and ice which we drew it is not meant that dying has to equate with becoming rigidified and frozen. The natural power of frost brings before our eyes here only the picture of transition, in the way 'unrest' passes over into 'rest, peace'. Warmth and cold in an earthly manner no longer touch the soul in death. That is not to say that the soul loses its soul-life. It loses its earthly consciousness, but in the calmness of soul-existence a higher, a starry life, can lay hold of the soul. Thus death becomes a higher birth. The soul no longer lives for itself alone; it allows the cosmos to live in it.

In order to be able to do this the human being has already during earthly life to carry in itself the prerequisites for starry existence, as water contains in itself the *Anlage,* the blueprint, the conditioning, to become a crystal. But, unlike water, this 'conditioning' is not given by nature. It is a task of the soul that is left to its freedom. Without this conditioning the soul in death will carry the unrest of the outer life in an unhealthy way into the spirit or fall into a dark rigidity. The task in life is to find the immortal *spirit* in the soul and to kindle it. We can also call it, with the words of the Creed of The Christian Community, the 'divine nature' of the soul, which in the unrest and darkness of dying is able to hold the soul together and to strengthen it. It is none other than the power of *love,* which leads into the peace of soul-existence, into the light of the spirit-world. In the Funeral Service we pray that the one who has died, through Christ, may find the right way into the spirit-realm: 'Eternal Spirit, may the peace of soul-existence come to him/her. May the light of the spirit-world shine for him/her.' Of Christ it says in the Creed: 'In death He became the Helper of the souls who had lost their *divine nature.*' Only insofar as Christ is in us do we die properly. He carries that cosmic starry force in Himself that can integrate our soul into the harmonies of the world out of which it has come. Light and peace are His radiant being. He is able to calm the storm of the billows, when the disciples dare to venture out with Him on to the billowing waves of the soul, not able out of their own strength to find the peace of soul-existence. According to the results of anthroposophical research, in the narration of the 'calming of the storm' on the Lake [Mark 6; Matt. 14; John 6], a real event is pictorially given that nevertheless takes place in the soul-realm of the disciples, beyond the threshold which we otherwise only cross in death or unconsciously in sleep.

The transition of an individual human being over the threshold into the 'calm of soul-existence' is always but a small picture of the great transition which one day the whole of humanity shall accomplish, and with it the Earth. And only then will death in its full extent be able definitively to lead towards sublime peace and the light, when everything earthly is transformed. The Earth, too, which for the religious person is not dead but a being related to the human being, awaits—as Paul also expresses it, redemption and transformation into a future condition of the Earth. The Earth, too, is to follow the path that water demonstrates when it freezes. One day, like a gigantic cosmic drop of water, it will crystallize. But not in the sense of a 'death of heat', as popular physics assumes for the end of the Earth. The death of heat, the outer freezing and rigidifying of the Earth that one imagines, is but the materialistic counter-picture of that which is to take place spiritually, a distorted—originally, perhaps religious—divining. Matter in our sense today will no longer exist then. The 'death of heat' would be the destiny of the Earth if it were *not* to find true crystallization, the calm of *soul-existence*. The Earth shall be transformed into a *spiritual* cryst-al ('Christ-all'), as described by the seer in the Revelation of John as the 'New Jerusalem'. The corner stone of this new world-building is laid by Christ. His body was transformed through the Resurrection into a shining star of peace. Inexpressible, as it were, 'palpable' *peace* radiates from Him. The Resurrected One appears on the evening of Easter Day amongst the disciples who had gathered in fear: 'Peace be with you' are his first words (John 20:19). Thus, the Earth's whole being shall be illuminated, rayed through by calmness, into a new 'place of peace' (the meaning of the name 'Jerusalem'). The New Jerusalem is like a crystal. 'The length and the width and the height of the city are equal' (Rev. 21:16); 'its radiance like a most rare jewel' [v. 11]. (See also Hermann Beckh's poetic piece, 'The New Jerusalem' in *John's Gospel: The Cosmic Rhythm*, Anastasi 2015, pp. 459-77, and *Alchymy*, Temple Lodge, 2019, pp. 100-13.)

In the cosmic age in which we live, the Earth is still a place of pulsing unrest. Here space and time play a turbulent game of life. Summer and winter, living and dying, blossoming and decaying rise and fall. Its essence is change and movement. And the life of civilization today shows in pictures this being of the present Earth—world-traffic celebrates its triumphs. Like the restless water running over the earth, trains run over the Earth, ships plough the waves, aircraft cross the skies, radio waves jitter. In order to be with people living at a distance, in our modern situation [written 1927] we have to be 'on the way', produce unrest. People rightly love the progress of travel; the demands of the present time are served. On the other hand, in future an earthly age will come when one rather truly reaches the other by remaining with oneself in as much stillness as possible. Outer paths to each other will become increasingly futile and meaningless. These have to be replaced by inner paths. Then one day the rushing world-traffic will be halted as the waterfall in the mountains in the transition from autumn to winter. In the bustle of the present time in which people may be fully engaged, those who know nevertheless that for the sake of the future an inner peace or stillness is needed, can become carriers for the great plan (*Anlage*), the peace of the world and the light of the stars, which the Earth needs to be transformed into the coming condition of the world. They become messengers of peace. As the individual human being in daily life requires pauses for illuminating reflection, the Earth itself seeks for sacred peaceful moments and places of light in the midst of pulsing life where she can receive the forces for her own future.

People was wish to be carriers of this future force gather in prayer around Christ, the Prince of Peace, at such places of peace. The Act of Consecration of Man gathers those who are active in life around the one thing that is necessary. Where the Service is held a point of crystallization for life and for the Earth is being created; where it sounds forth there radiates super-earthly light. It raises bread and wine, making them into starry form and starry light. It prefigures the transformation of the whole Earth. It is the blueprint for the coming condition of the world. Consequently, through this there is kindled ever anew the divining of the crystalline city of light. The Sun-castle of the New Jerusalem in which Christ is King of Heaven and Earth stands before us in the distance—in the same way as the snowy peaks of a mountain range calmly shine in glacial light, whereas in the valleys and ravines the storms still rage.

Rudolf Frieling

# Hermann Beckh's Literary Life's Work[327]

When in 1922 Hermann Beckh became a priest of The Christian Community having given up his Professorship in Berlin, he had already made a name for himself in the academic world through a work on *Buddha und Seine Lehre* [*Buddha's Life and Teaching*, Temple Lodge 2019] in two little volumes that found recognition in the well-known 'Göschen' series. What was remarkable here was a manner of approach, deviating from the norm. One could consequently see Buddha's teaching here completely under the viewpoint of the meditative life and the unique experiences connected with it. Human consciousness was looked at as changeable; the possibility to reach other forms of consciousness through inner work was taken seriously. Beckh clearly showed how Buddha was not concerned to develop a system of speculative truths, where to 'ultimate questions' answers were given that are gained through a thinking ruminating in a normal consciousness. Buddha did not want abstractly to answer abstract questions. He rather wanted to lead towards the path of certain inner experiences out of which such questions would no longer be asked or would be asked in the right way. From this point of view many things which Buddha had said—especially what he had not said—received a new light, as also the disputed concept of *nirvāṇa*. Not only scholarly knowledge speaks out of this work, but also the professional involvement in the meditative life of the Far East, which for the Westerner is at first so foreign. That he could write about Buddhism in such a way was thanks to his great teacher Rudolf Steiner, as a pupil of whom he himself also went on the path of meditative practice.

There are many specialists and appreciators of Eastern wisdom who have received wonderful impressions through which, becoming estranged from our Christian European culture, they 'emigrate' in spirit. Beckh on the one hand was protected from this, because, fully able to respect and honour the wisdom of the East, he carried the knowledge in himself of the central, incomparably sublime Mystery of Redemption of Christ and to the ego-task of Europe that is ultimately aligned to this Mystery. (For readers of our Journal, this may be said here in such a shortened form.)

Beckh, as I have mentioned, became in 1922 a Christian priest in our Movement of Religious Renewal. He was characteristically never addressed other than 'Professor Beckh'; for him the professor-line never broke down in his academic researches and teaching. It is important that his priesthood and his professorship did not run on two parallel tracks without relationship, as from time to time it does happen that a priest besides his profession works on another special subject, as for example Father Wassman S.J., the great researcher of ants. With Beckh, the Christian priest and the Oriental Professor came together in an organic manner. You stood before the phenomenon that an expert and lover of Eastern wisdom did not become lost on the way that led 'from Christ to Buddha', as with some Europeans who turn to India; rather Beckh lived in the full consciousness of what a world-historic step 'from Buddha to Christ' meant. He had taken up Buddhism, recognizing and experiencing it in all its greatness, and both distinguishing and connecting, placed it in the right relationship to the still greater redeeming Deed of Christ.

And so, he wrote in 1925 the profound little book *Von Buddha zu Christus* [*From Buddha to Christ*, complete edition, with extra material: Temple Lodge, 2019]. That it was published by The Christian Community, which was branded as a sect, was probably one of the reasons that hindered it—beyond our circles—from being recognized as an event in the history of European academic studies. But as such it certainly should be recognized.

The same year 1925 also saw the *Hingang des Vollendeten* [*The Passing of the Perfected One*, Temple Lodge, forthcoming], a new testimonial to Beckh's intimate knowledge of Buddhism. It has to do with what is the Buddhist 'gospel of death' (*Mahaparanibbana sutta*), where in a wonderfully poetic, sublime manner Buddha's entry into *nirvāṇa* is described. The solemn and rhythmically penetrated element of the original, Beckh has rendered as a re-poetizing translator in a truly genial manner, as well as his meaningful remarks on the content of the text.

To the Indian cultural realm belongs the Vedic *Der Hymnus an die Erde* [*Hymn to the Earth*, forthcoming], the translation of which Beckh published in 1934. This is certainly quite a different world from Buddhism, and by the way also from most other Indian literature. The Hymn is full of joy about earthly existence, seemingly naïve, but yet carried by deep spiritual, underground forces, 'naïve' in the sense of the originally genuine and unspoiled. His genuine connection to nature helped the translator here, in rendering this great archetypal text, breathing of the Earth, to find the right tone.

Beckh's academic interest not only belonged one-sidedly to Indology. He also turned towards the *Persian* culture in the midst of which stands the towering figure of Zarathustra. The Indian spiritual life bears above all the character of inner contemplation of a mysticism looking within (the *Hymn to the Earth* is an 'exception'). Behind the Persian culture stands a will directed more to the outer world, on working on the Earth. One could call it an impulse that is less 'mystical', more 'magical'. Especially through this interest for the Earth and its transformation, the spirituality of Zarathustra is related in a deep and sacred way to the Incarnation, understood in its cosmic greatness. Beckh wrote a little book *Zarathustra* (1927) in which he deals with this approach leading towards the Christ-Mystery. A highly interesting light falls on certain passages in Nietzsche's *Zarathustra*. As a researcher of language, Beckh at the same time introduces some unique aspects of the Avesta, allowing the reader to experience the Iranian language through a sequence of important words, especially in his book *Aus der Welt der Mysterien* (Basel: 1927) [*From the Mysteries*, Temple Lodge, 2020].

His concern with *Egypt* found a literary expression especially in the tenderly felt presentations of the secret of Isis [*From the Mysteries*]— Isis in her relationship to the Mystery of the Eternal Feminine, in her relationship to the figure of Mary.

In this way, Beckh carried in himself the great pre-Christian cultures of the Ancient Orient—India, Persia and Egypt—precisely not as a 'specialist interest' beside his Christian priesthood, but as the broad and generous spiritual landscape giving the framework within which the gospel is expressed in its whole cosmic format and its human full-sufficiency.

This view of Beckh's Orientalism would be incomplete without mentioning his work on the *Old Testament*. For him the starting point again was initially the linguistic side, as it lived revealed monumentally in the early Hebrews. Already in 1921 Beckh had written a booklet, short but rich in content, *Es werde Licht* ['Let there be Light', reprinted in *Neue Wege zur Ursprache* (1954)—*The Source of Speech*, Temple Lodge 2019], where he presents through one single sentence from Genesis certain relationships of the primal language connecting philology and esotericism.

In the first small volume that appeared by Beckh in the series *'Christus aller Erde', Der Ursprung im Lichte* (1924) [*Our Origin in the Light*, with *From the Mysteries*, Temple Lodge, 2020], he speaks about the mighty hieroglyphics of the biblical story, of prehistory from the Creation to Noah's rainbow. The rounding off of this thread of the Old Testament is with *Der 23. Psalm* (1935), translated and set to music. Outwardly not very extensive, but yet a treasure that appears like a prophecy of the unification of science, art and religion to come about one day. The 23rd Psalm translated and set to music forms the worthy conclusion to Beckh's oriental life's work.

India–Persia–Egypt–the Old Testament—how rich was the scientific world of this scholar! And yet it is not yet exhaustively described.

For the occasion of the Freiburg Conference of 1926 Beckh was led into the realm of *star-wisdom* that soon caught his ever-growing interest. He was invited to make a positive assessment of the theological endeavours of Arthur Drews on the cosmic rhythm in Mark's Gospel in its true form and its true meaning. The result of this new research was initially the book *Der kosmische Rhythmus im Markus-Evangelium* (1928) [*Mark's Gospel: The Cosmic Rhythm.* Leominster: Anastasi 2015]. What is often seen as the shortest, simplest and spiritually least demanding of all the gospels is revealed here in its majestic, elevated, stellar ordering—of course different and leading especially to quite different results from Arthur Drews. The latter, out of the stellar order draws the conclusion that the gospel is only concerned with a mere stellar myth. From the beginning Drews does not reckon with a real spiritual world that is also revealed in the signs of the zodiac, which as its culmination sends God's Son and Sun-spirit Christ to the Earth. Precisely because Christ is a cosmic being, His earthly life could not take its course other than the ordering of the stars. His life is written into the Earth with a stellar script.

In 1930 there followed *Der kosmische Rhythmus, das Sternengeheimnis und Erdengeheimnis im Johannes-Evangelium* [*John's Gospel: The Cosmic Rhythm—Stars and Stones.* Leominster: Anastasi 2015]. In this monumental work, as the title suggests, another new aspect comes to the actual contemplation of the stars—the *alchemical* aspect. No chance connection! Novalis, whose work Beckh knew deeply, had not for nothing significantly linked 'the stars' and 'the stones'. And so, as a postlude of this book on John's Gospel, in which the great question of transubstantiation, or metamorphosis, precisely in connection with

Johannine spirituality was discussed, appeared in *Vom Geheimnis der Stoffeswelt (Alchymie)* (1931) [*Alchymy: The Mystery of the Material World*. Temple Lodge, 2019].

*

More exactly, alchemy was not a 'new' nuance in Hermann Beckh's work; it can be heard earlier on. *From Buddha to Christ* ends with a reference to the *Apocalypse* and the mysteries of alchemical transubstantiation included in it, summarized in the crowning vision of the New Jerusalem.

The Apocalypse was the subject of a collaboration in the series '*Christus aller Erde*' (1925), with the title *Gegenwartsrätsel im Offenbarungslicht* ['Riddles of the present in the light of the Revelation']. Beckh agreed to write an article on the '*heavenly Jerusalem*'. To our surprise, his contribution took the form of poem (Eng. tr. in *John's Gospel*, pp. 459-77 and in *Alchemy*, pp. 100-13). Beckh's enthusiasm had broken the simple, elementary track; he could not make his contribution other than in an artistically lilting, poetic form. And with this unfortunately little-known poem, he shows his homeland is the spiritual world of Novalis.

Beckh gives an alchemical interpretation, moreover, in a beautiful article in our Journal [*Die Christengemeinschaft*] on [the Grimms' fairytale] *Snow White* [in *Alchymy*, pp. 114-26] with a fine feeling for presenting the intimacy of the fairytale sphere, while yet transmitting the conscious striving for insights of a rich content of knowledge. To go into his other valuable articles in the Journal *Die CG* [all translated in *Collected Articles of Rev. Prof. Hermann Beckh*] would overstep the limitations of this survey. At least let the choice of this atmospheric article on 'Snow White' speak for many.

Like alchemy, the motif of the 'stars' can be said to have sounded earlier, in the original booklet *Vom geistigen Wesen der Tonarten* (1922/5), Eng. tr., *The Essence of Tonality* [Leominster: Anastasi 2001/08], where the realms of spirit and soul of the various keys are related to the twelve cosmic qualities of the signs of the zodiac. Here we stand before a third spiritual province in which Beckh was productive; *music* is added to 'the ancient Orient' and 'stars and stones'.

Exactly twice seven years flowed by until Beckh wrote his great book *Die Sprache der Tonart* [in English translation as *The Language of Tonality* (Leominster: Anastasi 2015)] in the music from Bach to Bruckner, with special reference to Wagner's music dramas. Written the previous year, it appeared for Easter 1937 as his testament. The sketch of 1922 has become a fully executed, colourful painting. What previously was briefly indicated is now through an overwhelming abundance of observed examples—one might say, is demonstrated. The different musical keys are presented as individually characteristic, beings of soul and spirit. Before such a book could be written, it had to be preceded by a decades-long life in music. Beckh surveys the entire sounding work of our musical classicists, their creations great and small, from symphonies to preludes for the piano, showing his fine feeling as a player. He gained unimagined profundities from Wagner's works, in the language of tonality as well as the mythical scenes and characters recalling the Mysteries in the different music dramas from *The Flying Dutchman* to *Parsifal*. Already in 1930, in his exposition in consecrated, meditative mood *Das Christus-Erlebnis im Dramatisch-Musikalischen von Richard Wagners Parsifal* (*The Parsifal-Christ-Experience in Wagner's Music Drama*. Leominster: Anastasi 2015) he awoke a feeling for how much he discovered in Wagner.

To return to *The Language of Tonality*, the final word is not devoted to Wagner but to Bruckner's *Ninth Symphony*. It stands already in the background of the whole work, then it decisively appears at the end. It is Bruckner's 'Death-Symphony', his farewell to life. How Beckh points to the Mysteries of this symphony of death and farewell, himself no longer far from the mysterious threshold, belongs to the most impressive experiences in reading this posthumous work.

Beckh's relationship to music appears in the final years of his life in a special stage; he began to *compose* (alongside [at the time of writing] unpublished items, 'The 23rd Psalm' and 'The Roses of Damascus'). Something humanly touching lies in these creations. A soul began to sound and sing, which in its unconscious depths wants to know of the imminent homecoming into the world of its origin.

*

'*Many-sided*'—that is perhaps the first impression presented with this life's work. After a while this impression is supplemented by another: many-sided, yes; yet basically quite *unified*.

The sounding power of the words of ancient sacred languages, the harmony of the heavenly spheres, the enchanted stellar sounds in the depths of matter, the colourful variety of the musical keys—it is one and the same specific side of cosmic existence that turns towards us in Hermann Beckh's creations; a cosmic region where it sounds and sings, greatly rejoicing and monumental.

And it is always one and the same attitude of soul revealed in all these writings. They all bear the character of 'experienced knowledge'. You feel the strength of devotion, of meditation as of a tangible substance. You perceive the sonorous sound of a soul-life that in all its primeval strength and vitality *is love towards the spirit.*

\*

[*Ed. note:* To this survey (written 1937), which omits the earlier brilliant legal and Indological academic work, we can now add the *Collected Articles of Rev. Prof. Hermann Beckh,* forthcoming, also the recently discovered manuscript written on Beckh's sick-bed (1936) and now published as a full-length book: *The Mystery of Musical Creativity: Man and Music* (Temple Lodge 2019), as well as the present work on star-wisdom that he wanted to polish for publication and which can even be claimed to cap Professor Beckh's whole astonishing output.]

# Hermann Beckh, Orientalist, university lecturer, co-founder of The Christian Community, independent scholar

* 04-05-1875 D-Nuremberg
† 01-03-1937 D-Stuttgart

*Gundhild Kačer-Bock* (1924-2008)
Beckh's biographer

(http://biographien.kulturimpuls.org/detail.php?&id=48)
Tr. from the German, A.S. 2014

HERMANN BECKH, as a cultural researcher, exponent and lecturer, belongs to the exceptional figures of the Anthroposophical Movement before World War II.

He was the son of Eugen Beckh, co-owner of a factory for metal thread; his mother Marie, née Seiler [outlived her son]. His sister was twelve years his junior, to whom he was closely connected—she died already in 1929. Beckh grew up in a prosperous, sheltered situation. He was a highly gifted yet sensitive child, who possessed a fine ability to differentiate colours, musical sounds and moods of nature. At five years old in the mountains, which he greatly loved all his life, he experienced a body-free condition that convinced him that human beings live through a pre-existent existence in the supersensory world.

At school it was apparent that he possessed an exceptional memory. The teaching methods put him off all subjects so that he could not decide on a profession. Nevertheless, a brilliant *Abitur* [school finals] earned him a scholarship to the Maximilianeum in Munich, where in particular the future members of the Civil Service studied. His original plan was to study national economics, because he hoped in this subject to be able to work for the social development of humanity. Through his fellow students he was increasingly stimulated to study law—he became by chance a judge, without a real decision to enter this profession, as he himself said. He ended his studies with his prize-winning work on *Die Beweislast nach dem Bürgerlichen Gesetzbuch* ['The burden of proof according to the code of civil law'], but practising as a judge he soon saw that it was impossible for him to be a judge all his life, when he actually wanted to help human needs. So at that moment when he stood directly before a position in the Civil Service, he broke from this professional path and began again from scratch. He began to study Indian and Tibetan philology, was promoted from Berlin in 1907 with his work on Kalidasa's *Meghaduta* ('The Cloud Messenger'). With his inaugural dissertation a year later with a further work on this text, he became one of the few specialists in the Tibetan language to teach at the University of Berlin and worked on the manuscripts in the *Königlichen Bibliothek* (Royal Library).

In 14 December 1911 Beckh heard for the first time a public lecture by Rudolf Steiner (on the prophet Elijah; in GA 61. 194-220). From then on he concerned himself intensively with Rudolf' Steiner's basic books. After a personal conversation with him, he became a member of the Anthroposophical Society at Christmas 1912. A few weeks later Rudolf Steiner admitted him to the Esoteric School. During the course of 1913 he experienced a decisive climax in Steiner's career. In February the first Annual General Meeting of the newly-founded Anthroposophical Society, in August the Munich Summer Conference with Rudolf Steiner's Third and Fourth Mystery Dramas, the very first eurythmy performance, Rudolf Steiner's lecture as well as the Christmas lecture-cycle in Leipzig on *Christ and the Spiritual World* (GA 149), through which he received important impulses for the development of a renewed study of the stars. Despite the War, at Easter 1915 he could spend some days in Dornach and perceived the progress of the building of the Goetheanum.

In 1916 Beckh was called up for War-service. Shortly before, the two small volumes of *Buddha und seine Lehre* in the Göschen series were published—the climax and in a certain sense also the end of his academic activities. First, he was sent to the Balkans, after which he was called to the *Institut für Seeverkehr und Weltwirtschaft* [Institute for Shipping and World Economics] in Kiel, where he had to evaluate the economic articles in the Scandinavian newspapers. For this he had to learn the Scandinavian languages, so that he had now mastered English, French, Italian, and the Scandinavian languages, along with Greek, Latin, Hebrew, Egyptian, Syrian, Sanskrit, Tibetan and Old Persian (the language of the *Avesta*). His War-service responsibilities—from August 1918 in the Berlin Foreign Service—lasted into the post-War period.

Alongside this he began again to lecture in the University of Berlin, but he saw that his professional future no longer lay in this realm, so he searched for a possibility to work for the future of human development. He gave up his teaching post for Tibetan philology and went on leave from the University. When an extension of his leave was denied, and instead of becoming a Professor without chair, in November 1921 he wrote to have his name withdrawn from the list of private tutors. This was the end of his academic career.

Already in 1920 Beckh offered himself as an anthroposophical lecturer. He gave lectures on linguistics at the Anthroposophical Conference of 1921 and in March 1922 at the Berlin Conference, where he led the day on philology [*Sprachwissenschaft*] under the theme 'From dead philology to living philology'.

But the question of a satisfying life's task still remained open. When Beckh then learned of the preparations for the founding of the Movement for Religious Renewal, he decided there and then to join the founding group. Here the possibility was opened through the words and language of a renewed rite to find a completely new access to the word and to the sounds of speech. And he recognized that something of a future Christianity was wanting to come into being, was what he desired and intuited since as a 16-year-old he had attended a performance of Wagner's *Parsifal* in Bayreuth. Thus, he was one of the oldest of the 48 persons who in September 1922 with Rudolf Steiner's help called The Christian Community into life.

Still during the same year, Beckh moved to the newly built Urachhaus in Stuttgart. In the group of colleagues, he took a special position from the beginning. Unlike the others, he was not a priest serving a congregation, but could engage his strengths in free activity as a tutor in the Seminary, as lecturer, researcher and writer and still celebrate the sacraments at various locations. This freedom to study enabled him also to attend lectures at the Goetheanum in Dornach, Switzerland, to contribute in cultural contexts such as the Schopenhauer Society and the Astrology Association, for he was concerned to represent the aspects won out of anthroposophy wherever people wanted to hear them.

The themes on which Beckh lectured ranged widely. Initially, proceeding from his academic work, considerations on language and presentation of Eastern traditional wisdom. Soon he began to concern himself with questions of music, particularly the music of Wagner and the essence of tonality, and its connection with the forces of the stars, making his realm of study these stellar forces in the sense of a renewing of early Egyptian wisdom in astronomy and astrology. He sought to discover the cosmic lawfulness of the zodiacal influences in their various effects and reflection in all areas, in the ancient languages and their sounds, in music and the colourful circle of musical keys, in the Mystery wisdom of earlier epochs of human history, in the gospels and in human destiny. Thus his life's work did finally reveal a uniform thread.

Beckh was not a bookworm, but a human being with an impulsive temperament and a heart capable of enthusiasm. The little chores of daily life often presented obstacles, but his being and striving was always directed to the highest; thither he aimed to steer the thoughts of his listeners. With Rudolf Steiner and the Goetheanum he felt deeply connected. Experiencing the Christmas Conference 1923 in Dornach of the General Anthroposophical Society, and his presence at Rudolf Steiner's 'Last Address' to the members on 28 September 1924 (in GA 238) he felt as the climax of his life.

After he died on 1 March 1937, after a difficult period of suffering (cancer of the kidneys), Friedrich Rittelmeyer said of him, 'A singularly unique scholar, a rare wrestler for the spirit, an enthusiastic spirit-prophet has completed his rich life and has inscribed his name forever into the moving history of our time'.

# In Memoriam: Hermann Beckh
## (1875-1937)

*Alfred Heidenreich*[328]

A year ago, on March 1, 1937, Hermann Beckh, priest of The Christian Community, passed into the other world in his 62nd year. Of the forty-five original priests, who in 1922 founded The Christian Community, he was the first to cross the threshold of death. If we write in memory of him, we must describe a life that showed in a very remarkable degree along what extraordinary paths and ways someone may be led to find the spirit.

## The Scholar

In his youth he was a very brilliant lad. He had received the rare distinction of receiving his education at the 'Maxmilianeum' in Munich where the twelve best students of every year, together with a small group of specially selected sons of the old aristocratic families—at the expense of the state—were trained for a public career. Beckh specialized in law, soon acquired the degree of a Doctor of Law and, still very young, was appointed a junior judge. His office, however, increasingly became a source of great worry to him. He had to sentence when he wished to help. Eventually the tension of conscience was too great. He resigned and began to devote himself completely to a world which had increasingly become his real interest—ancient Asia. With his thoroughness of mind he started again from the beginning. He went back to University as a student, took a degree as Doctor of Philosophy, and soon his second career promised to be as brilliant as his first. He became in turn lecturer and then Professor of Oriental languages at the University of Berlin. In those years he also spent some time in England, studying Tibetan manuscripts at the British Museum, in connection with the first Tibetan dictionary that he had begun to publish. From these occasions, which were his first and last visits to England, he treasured a great interest in all that was English.

About the same time, shortly before the War, he also met Dr Rittelmeyer [the first Erzoberlenker of The Christian Community]. Rittelmeyer says of him in an appreciation which he wrote at Beckh's death in the German journal of The Christian Community [*Die Chris-tengemeinschaft*], that he found Beckh disappointed with organized Christianity and very suspicious of it.

He was, however, full of original knowledge in the most varied provinces of scholarship, a knowledge that was not so much gained on the well-trodden ways to an ambitious academic goal. But on the paths of an untiring and original search for truth and, above everything, the living spirit. This combination of recognized and acknowledged scholarship and a quite personal striving for the living spirit was characteristic of him. In this respect nobody in Germany, near and far was comparable to him. For the sake of his spiritual aims, he learned, even at an advanced age, and with an amazing energy, Persian, Egyptian, Syriac and Hebrew in addition to the languages with which he had been familiar from his student days, Latin, Greek, Sanskrit, Tibetan, French, English and Italian. Everywhere he strove for the highest—the revelation of the spirit in its earthly reflection. He followed up the traces of the light of the spirit in all races and nations.

About the same time as Rittelmeyer, he found Rudolf Steiner. He was deeply drawn into anthroposophy and became one of Steiner's personal pupils. It was through Steiner that he learned to see the meaning and reality of Christianity. 'It is quite certain,' says Rittelmeyer, 'that he would not have found Christ without Rudolf Steiner, but he found Him through him in a magnitude that made the whole world translucent.'

When the first preparations were made for the foundation of The Christian Community and Beckh heard of them, he was almost annoyed that he had not been invited from the very beginning to take part. We, on our part, did not think, of course, that 'the Professor' would come and join us. But he did, ['I belong with you,' he said. He joined] with all the zeal and enthusiasm of his character. When it became clear that the priesthood in The Christian Community required the whole of a person's work for the rest of his life, and consequently involved for him the resignation from his position at the University, he did not hesitate for a moment. It meant, of course, also a complete financial sacrifice. He had no income besides his salary as a professor, which ended with his resignation. Whatever private means he may have had he lost, as every other German, through inflation of the Mark. His resignation left him literally penniless, with an aged mother and a sister dependent on him. He took the risk, in the full confidence of the full necessity and momentous significance of the new Movement.

When the time for his resignation from the University came, he discussed with Dr Rittelmeyer the best form it should take. They both came to the conclusion that it would be the right thing for Beckh to announce a lecture at the University and give a full and public explanation for his decision. Beckh had just published a two-volume work on Buddhism, *Buddha und seine Lehre* [1916] [*Buddha's Life and Teaching*, Temple Lodge 2019], in a somewhat popular form. These volumes, which are still reckoned among the standard works on Buddhism in the German language, had considerably enhanced his esteem among his colleagues, and had also made him known, for the first time, to the general public. One should have expected, consequently, that Beckh's lecture would have attracted a great and interested if not sympathetic audience.

What actually happened was tragically typical of the academic life of Germany at the time (1922). Beckh's lecture was boycotted. *Not one* of his colleagues attended. The audience consisted of a number of students, a few casual listeners, and members of the Anthroposophical Society. To speak publicly for Rudolf Steiner in those years meant to be morally struck off the register of the intellectual society of Germany. Beckh henceforth was labelled and ostracized. Although he was not the only one who had to suffer this fact—the way in which Dr Rittelmeyer was treated was very similar—it was at times more difficult to bear than the legal prohibition of certain anthroposophical activities in recent times. And few who saw through the intolerance and conceit of the leading academic circles of Germany after the War, could doubt that sooner or later fate would wield an iron broom.

Dr Rittelmeyer writes of this event:

> Beckh's lecture was a noble and magnificent challenge to the scholars of the premiere German University. But it was as if he had been held in a desert. In the future such an event will be regarded, practically unnoticed at the time, as a great historical question, a solemn test, a kind of decisive judgement over the intellectual and spiritual life of Germany at that time. The intellectual and spiritual life of Germany has failed and must bear the consequences. From then onwards Hermann Beckh was no more listened to. For them he was dead. All the more so, as he now began to live and write entirely out of his new knowledge and no longer cared for what the reactions would be. Among the many hundreds of scholars at the time he was the only one, the solitary one, who had found the way to the new spirituality; among the followers of Rudolf Steiner he was the only scholar with an officially established reputation, and in

particular with an unparalleled authority on the spiritual wealth of ancient India. This was his historic part and will be his for all time.

## *The Man*

Those who know him only from his books may find it difficult to form a picture of the man Beckh. In his books he is the scholar and sometimes the prophet. But in his private life he had a great deal of the proverbial peculiarities of the German Professor. It was quite natural that to his death he was always known as 'Professor Beckh', even among his fellow-priests in The Christian Community, and invariably addressed as 'Herr Professor'. Shrewd as he was in the general management of life, he was at times quite oblivious of circumstances and surroundings. It has been pointed out that this is only the other side of a life of great concentration. With him this certainly was the case, but it added greatly to the—sometimes bizarre—charm of his personality. Many amusing stories were current of him. It could be rather embarrassing at times, to sit with him at a table in a restaurant or in a railway compartment where he would suddenly begin to lecture with a thunderous voice on his latest discoveries on Zarathustra. At his lectures he often had a pile of books on his desk, and those who knew his ways were always prepared for the moment when, after a sudden enthusiastic jerk, the whole pile would tumble to the floor and Beckh make frantic efforts to collect them again. I remember him coming to a lecture with considerable traces of his supper of fried eggs still on his lips and chin. When this was pointed out to him, he began to lick and wipe his face with tremendous energy completely forgetting that he was already standing on the rostrum. Rumour has it that when he once preached at Stuttgart his biretta worried him; and after several attempts to put it right he hurled it from him. Without however for a second stopping the magnificent flow of his address.

If one made deliberate fun of him, and at times this was very tempting, one would somehow regret it afterwards. He did not take offence, but he seemed curiously helpless in such moments. One loved him all the more for this because one would then suddenly have a glance into the great loneliness of his soul. He was not only a bachelor; he was at bottom a stranger almost to everyone in contemporary society. At the depths of his being, he was like one of the wise Rishis of ancient India suddenly transplanted into completely uncongenial civilization. His nearest friends were little children and the mountains. In the first house of The Christian Community at Stuttgart he occupied three tiny attic rooms, and it was deeply moving to meet him occasionally in his study, with a baby of one or two years on his arm, explaining to him in the sacred tongue of ancient India the beautiful pictures of the Himalayas that hung round the walls. He knew the mountains not only from pictures. True to his Bavarian origin he was a competent and fearless mountaineer who to the last year of his life would always go alone. After a difficult passage in the Bernese Oberland he was once overtaken by a storm and had to spend the night on a glacier. When he spoke of this experience one felt that he was happier among the giants of frost and snow than among human society.

You could receive the greatest impression of him as a lecturer when he read from the Holy Scriptures of the East in the original and in his translation. Of what is called the 'Gospel of Buddha's Death' he published a German translation of very great poetical beauty. After this translation had appeared, he went on a lecturing tour. He spoke on 'The Passing of the Perfect One' and recited the important passages in the ancient language and in his translation. I have heard once or twice in my life a cultured Indian singer recite some of the great texts of his religion. In comparison, Beckh had all the incantation and delivery of a native guru, but in addition to it also the clear vision and knowledge of the 'consciousness-soul'. To listen to him at such occasions was indeed an unforgettable experience.

## *His Work*

A short review of his literary work will show that this extraordinary man possessed still other qualities. Such a review will best take its start from his two-volume [later editions in one volume] work on Buddha's life and teaching, mentioned above, his first work outside the precincts of the ordinary specialized academic periodicals. The success of this work was due to the different treatment of Buddhism which no one could fail to notice. Buddha's teaching was revealed as proceeding from the reality of a meditative life. Beckh proved even to the critical scholar that the Buddha never intended to develop a speculative system of metaphysical truths in order to answer 'ultimate questions', but that he wished his followers to pursue a path of inward experience where such 'ultimate questions' either lose significance or can only then be rightly put. From this viewpoint many things that Buddha said become clear, and also why he did *not* say many things. Beckh's work displayed not only the competent knowledge of the scholar, but also a personal first-hand experience of meditative life which is normally strange, and even incomprehensible, to the ordinary Western mind.

After reading Beckh's *Buddha und seine Lehre* (1916, 1928³, '58, '98) one was tempted to become a Buddhist oneself. How tremendously *real* seemed the spirit of which the Buddha knew and spoke, compared with the anaemic spirituality of contemporary Christianity! But Beckh did not join the ranks of those who in despair over the decline of the West emigrated spiritually to the East. In less than seven years after the appearance of this fascinating presentation of Buddhism, Beckh became a Christian priest.

This was a representative deed. I do not know whether it ever occurred to Beckh himself, but this fact stands there in the spiritual history of our time as an opposite landmark to Annie Besant's [of the Theosophical Society] conversion to Hinduism, and to the change which the one-time Anglican priest Leadbeater made from Christianity to Buddhism. If Leadbeater later had himself again consecrated as a Bishop of the Old Catholic Church, it was not done from conviction but for other purposes. Beckh's step from the Orientalist to the Christian priest was a process in reality. He achieved in himself the development which he had recognized as the spiritual order of evolution and which *is* the spiritual order of evolution. He saw Christ as the fulfiller of the Mysteries. The essence of this progress is contained in a volume entitled *From Buddha to Christ* (1925) [complete Eng. ed. with extra material, Temple Lodge 2019]. It is a small volume but indeed full of meaning. If one reads it, one wonders at the ways of Providence. Had this book appeared in the English language, and outside the circle of what is still wrongly labelled as a 'sect', it might have become an event in the history of Oriental scholarship, and no doubt it would have had reactions in the East. One need only think of the many Christian missionaries who feel called to convert Buddhists into Christianity and are increasingly driven into the defensive, and also of the many Indians and Chinese who look with a bewildered apprehension and suspicion and yet, in spite of everything, still with a secret expectation to the West. Here is a book written by a Western scholar who not only loved the East with a true and enthusiastic love but knew its sacred writings and understood their esoteric and even occult significance. And he showed the way from Buddha to Christ which he himself had gone. Providence has ordained that it remained comparatively unknown. Perhaps The Christian Community would not yet be strong enough to deal with the practical effects it might have, and to fulfil in practice the expectations it might arouse. And surely there is no other Christian body that could do this. Beckh himself did not see the missionary side of his work, I think. This was outside his province. In that respect he was just the German professor. To him, the East-West problem was a problem of consciousness and spiritual evolution. He knew all about Buddhism as a religion, he knew a great deal about the geography and spiritual climate of the East, but he knew hardly anything of the Indian people of today. I wonder whether they even interested him. In this attitude we have a striking example of the difference of the German and English genius which so obviously need each other as mutual historic supplements.

After he had finally found his place in Christianity, Beckh turned to the study of other pre-Christian religions. He traced in them the cosmic reality of Christ in His approach to the earth and to incarnation. A monograph on Zarathustra appeared, followed by a book on Egypt, *Aus der Welt der Mysterien* (1927) [*From the Mysteries*, Temple Lodge 2020], with an especially impressive chapter on the figure of Isis and her relationship to the Virgin Mary. It was a matter of course that now he should also include the Old Testament in his studies, which until recently was the only recognized prophecy of Christ. If I remember rightly, the first public lecture which he gave, at the invitation of Rudolf Steiner, at the first public Conference in the First Goetheanum[329] was on the single sentence from Genesis: 'Let there be light.' He described certain primeval elements of sacred language, uniting philology and esoteric knowledge. Later he wrote a book on the hieroglyphic picture-language of Genesis, from the creation to Noah's rainbow, *Der Ursprung im Lichte* (1924), [*Our Origin in Light: Pictures from Genesis*, with *From the Mysteries*, Temple Lodge 2020]. His last work in connection with the Old Testament is a translation of the 23rd Psalm, done with extraordinary vision and beauty, which he himself also set to music. This little gem anticipates prophetically the future union of scholarship, art and religion.

This, however, is by no means the complete list of Beckh's works nor even a complete list of the provinces of learning in which he moved and was at home. In 1926 it was suggested to him that he speak at the International Summer Conference of The Christian Community at Freiburg on the true nature and significance of the cosmic rhythm in Mark's gospel that Arthur Drews and others had discovered. This led Beckh to an investigation of the 'wisdom of the stars' which soon became a subject of absorbing interest to him. At that period Beckh hardly spoke of anything else, even in private conversation. The result of his exploration in the new land appeared in three succeeding books, *Der kosmische Rhythmus im Markus-Evangelium* (1928) [*Mark's Gospel: The Cosmic Rhythm.* Leominster: 2015], *Der kosmische Rhythmus, das Sternengeheimnis und Erdengeheimnis im Johannes-Evangelium* (1930) [*John's Gospel: The Cosmic Rhythm—Stars and Stones.* Leominster, 2015] and *Vom Geheimnis der Stoffeswelt* [*Alchemy: The Mystery of the Material World.* Leominster, 2015]. Beckh succeeded in describing and proving down to small details how the composition of the gospels, particularly Mark's, is determined through the relationship of certain stellar constellations, in the main through the progress of the Sun through the zodiac. There are lines of indications in the New Testament which show that the sequence in which the events are described reflects the sequence of the positions of the Sun in its relationship to the signs of the zodiac. Drews had discovered the principle of it but drawn from this discovery the hasty conclusion that therefore Christ never existed historically and that the gospels were only 'astral myths'. Drews never reckoned in reality with a spiritual world which would manifest itself in the constellations and which would also as its own essence send Christ to the Earth. Beckh showed how the life of Christ was like a sacrament celebrated according to the ritual book of the heavenly constellations. Consequently, the gospels were books both of earthly *and* heavenly history, of historical *and* cosmic truth.

It may sound strange after all this that Beckh's last and most original province was music. He was not only a very good pianist who would play for hours his three great favourites, Bach, Wagner and Bruckner [as well as symphonies and other works arranged for piano duet with his friends, including Emil Bock, Rudolf Frieling and Alfred Heidenreich], but he was right when he once said, 'In all other respects I stand on the shoulders of my predecessors in scholarship, and my particular viewpoint I owe to Rudolf Steiner; but in *music*, I feel I am really breaking new ground.' Rudolf Steiner himself said of him in this respect, 'Beckh ventures into provinces which I have not yet had an opportunity of investigating myself. And there is a great deal in what Beckh says about them.' There are not many people of whom Rudolf Steiner would have made such a remark.

His first publication in the realm of music was on *Das geistige Wesen der Tonarten* (1922/25) [*The Essence of Tonality*, Leominster: Anastasi 2001/08] which soon ran into more than one edition. It was followed by *Das Christus-Erlebnis in Wagners 'Parsifal'* (1930) [*The Parsifal-Christ-Experience*, Leominster, 2015] and by his posthumous work, *Die Sprache der Tonarten* (1937/77/84) [*The Language of Tonality in Music from Bach to Bruckner*. Leominster, 2015]. This last work shows Beckh as a man who knew *all* the works of the classics, from the smallest prelude to the great symphonies. He read the proofs for this book during the last weeks of his life and said once to a friend how happy he was 'to pass over with such wonderful realities'.

During the last years he began also to write music himself. Several compositions of songs appeared, mainly of his favourite poems. Already on his sickbed he completed a series of compositions for The Act of Consecration of Man, following the seasons of the year, which can be performed either on the piano or by a small chamber group. His compositions are extraordinarily 'conscious' works, with a very deliberate use of the symbolic significance of key, interval and rhythm. They are nevertheless very 'musical' and not a bit artificial, which shows that this analysis of the essential musical elements was a discovery of realities.

Besides the scholar, he was a great 'character', who left besides his great works many small and quaint notes and jottings of a quite humorous and original nature, often found in letters to his friends. I shall venture to give a sample here which is actually contained in his last letter to me. He wrote it in the summer of 1936. The first signs of his illness appeared then, but it was not yet established as malignant. Beckh sought recovery in his beloved Bavarian Alps. From there the letter is dated. One day, he says, his mind got fixed on a quotation from Wilhelm Busch, the great humourist and cartoonist dear to every German big and small.

And one morning in bed, he hit on the idea of translating it into English. And now, this is characteristic of Beckh, he turned it over and over—he could 'ponder' over a thought—and made no fewer than seventeen translations. Here is the original German:

> *Ein Schlüsselloch wird leicht vermisst,*
> *Wenn man es sucht, wo es nicht ist.*

And here are the 17 translations:

1. A keyhole is missed easily—O great fatality—
   When it is sought where you can't find it in reality.
2. An unsuccessful man, deceived by distance,
   Looks for a keyhole there where it has no existence.

3. Who obstinately seeks a keyhole in wrong place
   A man like this remains in all his efforts lacking grace.
4. A silly man is disappointed soon
   When he for earthly things is seeking in the moon.
5. It will oftentimes for you a great distress
   When seeking nightly for a keyhole you can't find the place.
6. When after many efforts broken-hearted,
   He could not find the keyhole, he at last departed.
7. All things are ordered well in time and space
   You never find a keyhole outside of its place.
8. O stupid man, how will you ever find
   A keyhole if you are for earthly matters blind.
9. Where is the keyhole now? It's really no jest,
   To be or not to be—this the great request.
10. It is a world of tears, you never must forget,
    When you are searching for a keyhole which you cannot get.
11. There is no help against. It's really all in vain,
    When you are searching for a keyhole which you can't obtain.
12. No problem is so difficult as this,
    When you are trying for a keyhole, and you try amiss.
13. I think it is a very hopeless game
    When with the keyhole you don't reach your aim.
14. For any keyhole—mind the solemn truth—
    Will never try in vain a skilful youth.
15. The night was very cold, no keyhole could be found,
    The other morning lay a dead man on the ground.
16. The end is very sad and full of fate,
    A keyhole must be found before it is too late.
17. At last, for consolation take this principle,
    For an attentive man no keyhole is invincible.

Here you have a first-hand side-glimpse at Hermann Beckh, thoroughly thorough, even in making fun.

## His Last Days

But this is not how we should take farewell of him. We must return once more to the centre of his personality. We cannot do this better than by quoting the concluding passages of what Dr Rittelmeyer wrote about him (*Die Christengemeinschaft*), referring to the last days of Beckh's life.

An exceptionally versatile and spiritually mobile man, ever active, living entirely in his own searching and striving, though allowing his friends most willingly to share it, he had now the task to lie still under pain, and to watch slowly his own death. With a vitality and strength of mind, which was incomprehensible to us, he studied for weeks while he hardly slept more than a quarter of an hour at night, the essential books which he had come across in his life. 'Either I shall die,' he said; 'then this is the best preparation, or I remain alive, then it is also the best I can do.' If one found him groaning and restive, tossing himself about on the pillows one need only touch on a subject which interested him, and at once he would begin with a voice, completely unimpaired, to speak and to extemporize almost a small lecture—and in the end he would say that his pains are now no more there. Only in the very last days this was different. Then he lay still in his bed and had texts of Rudolf Steiner, or the ritual of The Christian Community read to him. In the depths his thoughts, however, were occupied with himself, his own being and life, his relationship to people, his relationship to Christ, and we were allowed to listen at times to words of self-criticism but also of his passionate link with the spirit. We believed we saw something of the guidance of his angel, when, after a life of indefatigable activity, these hours of inward reflection were vouchsafed to him before his transition into a higher world.

After suffering greatly for months, the passing was quiet and peaceful. When we celebrated the last rituals at his deathbed and at the coffin, it was as if a spirit full of peace filled the room. A unique scholar, a rare spiritual fighter, an inspired messenger of the spirit had finished his life and had written his name for ever into the stormy history of our time.

*

What prompted me to write this article was not only the pious duty to say at the first anniversary of his death something in memory of a fellow-priest and a great scholar. I felt that a picture of this personality, which is inseparably united with the foundation of our Movement, would show something of the compass of The Christian Community. In this country we are in some ways separated through the barrier of language and geographical isolation from the whole of The Christian Community. This is inevitable but it might lead us to form our vision of the Movement only from what we see close at hand. That would obviously be incomplete. It is right for us that we should remind ourselves at times of the potential greatness of our Movement. We find this greatness indicated, in the first place, in the spiritual content of it, but it announces itself also in a tremendous variety and wealth of human character and human destiny which has flowed and is continually flowing into it. Last summer, at the 'World Conference for Faith and Order' in Edinburgh, the thought flashed through my mind that the foundation of our Movement is like a replica, in principle and on another plane, of what was attempted there. The aim of the Conference was to prepare the way for a reunion of the many historic sections of Christianity. The historic significance of The Christian Community with a view to the future is the fact that numberless currents of historic Christianity have at its foundation flowed together into one pool, as it were, and out of this inward amalgamation the nucleus of the united church of the future has grown. Not only did the founders come together from the most varied sections of historic Christianity; it might even appear—if for once we may think in terms of repeated earth lives—that men and women have united now who in another age were themselves the protagonists of separation. Hermann Beckh added to this union another and unique reality. In him those have joined us of whom it is said in the words of The Act of Consecration of Man that God received once 'the offerings of those who had not yet Christ'. Beckh has made room for them. May what was potentially contained in his life and work, and what has become part of the being of the Movement, come to a glorious realization in the future life and activity of The Christian Community.

# Decisive Experiences through Hermann Beckh[330]

*Wilhelm Hörner*

After the death of Prof. Hermann Beckh on 1st March 1937, some students of the Priests' Seminary helped to clear his flat. Each helper was allowed to take one of his books. The secretary chose the complete edition of Grimms' Fairytales. Still today, as my wife, she reads almost daily from this volume. I chose *Geheimwissenschaft im Umriss* (*Occult Science—an Outline*) by Rudolf Steiner. The book contained an abundance of marginalia, especially astronomical and alchemical signs and symbols; in addition, many pressed Gentian flowers and rose petals.

This book accompanied me from the first day of the War 1939 in the field. I also took it with me to Crete. On the return journey of the South-East Army through the ravines and passes of the Balkans only the most essential things could be carried. In the hard winter of 1944/45 nearly all transport vehicles were inoperative. In the deep snows of the Karaula Pass, in order to be a good example I decided to lighten the load on the last transport vehicles, also to sacrifice the beloved book of Hermann Beckh's. The pressed Gentians I took out and added to my Breviary carried on my person. Then I threw *Geheimwissenschaft* into the snow as far as my strength could reach. But when I saw this unique book lying there I had quickly to pick it up again. Once more I threw it far off; again, I took it up and for the third time I threw it out of the fast-moving vehicle. The separation from the valuable piece of memory stimulated an even stronger connection to the being of Hermann Beckh and his work.

At Beckh's coffin I had an experience that was decisive for my life. Coming from a study of theology at the University, I opted to join the wake. During the night from 2nd to 3rd March I was alone for some hours with our dear departed, who was lying in his flat in Urachhaus. Around the wall the scholar's high bookshelves reached the ceiling; where there were no books pictures covered the walls so closely that the walls were completely covered. But at his head there hung in a large reproduction his favourite picture, Botticelli's *The Birth of Venus*.

In this Beckh always saw the heavenly, virginal side of Venus-Urania. Through the heavenly beauty his inner experience was akin to what Goethe puts into words at the end of his *Faust*: 'Eternal Womanhood leads us above.'

In his book *John's Gospel: The Cosmic Rhythm*, Hermann Beckh describes this as follows [p. 81]: 'Nowhere does the connection of the Mysteries of Christianity with the pre-Christian Mysteries appear more deeply and significantly than where we look from the revelation of the sea of Venus-Aphrodite to *Mary*, the *"star of the sea"*, where, in and behind the Christian Mary, the Christened Isis-Venus-Mystery is gently announced—the Mystery that in Rev. 12 has found its strongest, most revealing expression.'

With these words the whole of human becoming is indicated. The mood of this event hovered as an inexpressible, tender and deepest breath of life in the room softly lit up by peaceful candles. Carried by such a mood I dared to make two simple sketches of the sublime countenance. But the decisive element of these hours was the real experience that all existence contains its deep meaning, humanity's aim, which includes each individual person with his/her pre-birth and post-mortem existence. The decision to become a priest—concerning myself—was taken here.

As someone who still knew all the founders of The Christian Community in person, I too was graced by destiny to experience Prof. Hermann Beckh in his last seminars and lectures. He lectured with an enthusiasm appearing with almost child-like innocence and totally unencumbered. During his lectures on *Tristan and Isolde* or *Parzifal* there had to be a piano at hand. He played not only the main motifs of Richard Wagner's works, but when his own verbal explanations, when language appeared to him as an insufficient means of expression, he passed over into musical improvisation. It then served, as it were, as a continuation of the verbal lecture. 'With words one can't pursue it further, but musically somewhat like this ...' Thereby he turned his head to the audience in order to secure the undivided attention of his listeners. A spark of enthusiasm with such presentations kindled all those present.

The presentation of the cosmic rhythm in Gospels of Mark and John had struck a chord with me, the tone of which had already been stimulated by Rudolf Frieling. Consequently, with his words of Hermann Beckh's literary work I will here conclude my experiences.

'It is always one and the same attitude of soul revealed in all these writings. They all bear the character of "experienced knowledge". You feel the strength of devotion, of meditation as of a tangible substance. You perceive the sonorous sound of a full-blooded soul-life that in all its primeval strength and vitality *is love towards the spirit*.'

# Hermann Beckh's Spiritual Manner[331]

## *Emil Bock*

It was towards the end of the First World War. During the free hours my military service allowed me, I conscientiously spent time in the lecture rooms of the University of Berlin. When I once looked up what was offered on the subject of the history of religion, I discovered that two lectures were timetabled for the same afternoon, one on Islam and one on Buddhism. I nevertheless decided to attend both on the same day. So I heard the first half of the session by a Professor* who was exemplary in correctness in his figure, suit and manner of speaking—later he became for some time the democratic Cultural Minister for Prussia—who read from an intellectual and logical, thoroughly formulated manuscript on Mohammed and his teaching.

When I then joined midway in the lecture on Buddhism a completely different picture was offered to me. A mountain of papers full of notes to which he did not adhere, somebody moving about, whose fiery and at the same time childlike eyes were more important than a correct necktie, pouring forth with enthusiastic, booming voice an overabundance of content over the few listeners. A logical thread one did not expect to find. I asked myself whether it was the aim of what he wanted to offer, or whether the sudden entrance of a grey uniformed person had made the Professor lose his thread. In my case I understood only very little of what I heard. This was my first meeting with Professor Beckh and what I later learnt to love about him as a real spiritual over-abundance.

Professor Beckh was in our midst like the guest and messenger from a completely different world-order. In some things he did not quite fit into the world as it is around us. A quite elemental drive in his life made him look with strong and unceasing longing for a world where the spiritual is not rare and thin but bubbles and pours forth in abundance, working strongly into souls and also into matter. The drive for his searching and for his working was homesickness for a world once alive with magic spirit, especially the magical force of the spirit-prophesying word.

---

* Carl Heinrich Becker (1876-1933), who wrote personally to Beckh on the latter's decision to withdraw from the University of Berlin begging him to remain with an enhanced contract and increased salary.

[*1937 text*: This is why the Orient, especially the sound of the music and languages of Asia had drawn the earlier judge like a magnet of his destiny. It was the search for the real and mighty spirit which drew him to Rudolf Steiner, and which also led him as something obvious and with the inevitability of a natural event to become part of the group of original priests of The Christian Community. The spirit-word working in celebrating the rite for him was something familiar. The inner connection that he had to the hidden magical forces of the Word repeatedly led him irresistibly into the primal, archetypal heights of the snow-covered mountains, making him a lover of the stars, of flowers, crystals and children to such an extent that some thought these things his fixations. This Beloved it was who led him when he looked for the laws of the stars in the gospels—he finally allowed this Lover into his work on which he still worked on his deathbed, turning music round and round in order to come to its magic. His life stood captivated and in service to the Logos, to the creative Word.]

*[1959 text continues from the previous paragraph:]*
Many humorous anecdotes could be told which show his awkward relationship to the world of earthly things, for example, the one concerning the elegant house known for its cleanliness, where he was asked to clean his shoes. Because he had never done it for himself before, he also added polish to the soles so that afterwards large black marks revealed his footprints on the carpet. But this estrangement from the world in him was only the confused shadow of a living light. He was not quite aware of the little details of the physical plane. Consequently, he had to bear the little attacks played on him, the stranger, by the pixies of earthly matter because he was never quite in his earthly body. He remained in the sheen of the light and shimmer of colour of a pre-natal world.

From his childhood onwards he was open to the bright, primal pictorial language that approached him from the natural world. The air of our free, primal homeland wafted towards him when he found himself among animals, plants and stones. It was quite different with what came towards him from human connections. He spoke about this in his memoirs. (These, unfortunately fragmentary, appeared in the Jg. 14 Heft, 8, 12, 15 of *Die Christengemeinschaft* and are reprinted in his biography: G. Kačer-Bock, 1997): 'Here I touch on the actual dark and critical point of my childhood.' It remained like this all his life: 'All compulsion and all subservience, even if I gave myself out of freewill because of some outer circumstances, I always felt as something going against my inner being and ultimately unreal and untrue.' On the other hand, the high snow-covered mountain peaks lifted him, especially through the miracles of light and colour that played around them, above all pressure and all oppression, that is, they justified the condition in which he always found himself. He said about the evening sunset: 'Almost more than anything else these colours speak to me of a supersensory world.' And in the rainbow, he saw 'the threshold touching the spiritual world'.

A mighty visionary experience imprinted on the [five-year-old] child's soul a transport back to the origins in the spirit that he could never forget. It came to him in Einöldsbach not far from Oberstdorf [in the Bavarian Alps], within sight of the mountains where the 'sublime light' is to be found.

> The impression of mighty nature and loneliness ... was such that my consciousness was transported, was no longer in the sensory half of day-existence, but in the other half, that part which is more extensive that complements our narrow earthly existence as compared to our cosmic existence—that part close to our earthly senses but in which the kernel of our higher being originates ... on the other shore of existence ... the world of my pre-birth existence that I had forgotten in the stream of time ... I looked down from cosmic heights suddenly quite differently upon humanity ... a tremendous pain concerning humanity laid hold of me.

From his childhood onwards the wallpaper of the sensory world became transparent to him for another sphere when certain perceptions were given to him. He writes: 'Still today in spring the view of the first gentian in the high meadows awakens in me a divining of the "higher worlds".' He possessed a collection of crystals and seashells and loved the individual pieces like individual beings. The colourful butterfly over the meadow, the dragonfly over the brook, were for him spiritual impressions reminding him of life before birth. But that one could collect dead butterflies—already that thought made him break out in loud, angry protest. In the sky, Venus in particular spoke to him, the bright Evening or Morning Star. And among people, as long as he still existed, the lamplighter in the foggy evening dusk. Because of such preferences, that appeared not seldom as fixed ideas, he was often teased. But this did not annoy him. The chuckling laughter with which he reacted to this was a combination of embarrassment and enthusiasm. And something for which he was always enthusiastic, causing storms of delight in him, was when he could show his especially beloved crystals to a child and could play his favourite pieces on the piano. Then joy boomed through all the walls.

Clearly, when he entered school it meant for the boy as if he were driven out of Paradise. 'I perceived this change as an assassination of my freedom and happiness ...' He could not understand, 'why such a robbing of my freedom and violence against my whole being were necessary in order to take up knowledge that would also quite by itself would easily and playfully have flown into me.' Indeed, he learnt playfully, working still during the last phase of his life into ever-new realms of knowledge thanks to his universal memory and, connected to this, a strong auto-didactic constitution. As a child and young person, he did not need fully to concentrate; with his soul he could wander on paths of dream and yet was better in the subject than his fellow students. He should have been left in peace. That he became obtuse when something was explained to him was not the worst fate, but the attempt was made to push him into the common forms that were so foreign to him. And so it came that he lost his inner equilibrium in a most painful manner and could only continue with the greatest efforts. He became scatty in such a way that people thought it pathological. One part of his development stagnated in the time before he reached fourteen years old; it needed a sustained inner wrestling and struggle in order with his special nature nevertheless to find a turn towards freed productivity. It was fortunate that through the material given at high school, he received light and insights; the sound of the Greek language especially the divine poetry of Homer conjured forth ancient, well-known feelings of belonging.

And then the world of music, especially as it sounded in saturated over-abundance of soul and magical power from Bayreuth. At sixteen years old in 1891 he was able to hear *Parsifal* in Bayreuth. This must have given his inner development quite an unexpected jolt and incentive. Without in the usual sense of becoming a Wagnerian, throughout his life he identified and energetically inserted himself as hardly anyone else into every note of Wagner's score. To his own surprise it happened that the youth passed his school finals with the highest marks and consequently, along with very few chosen ones out of the country, earned a free place to study at the Maximilianeum in Munich.

Although this was a rare honour it must have brought heavy life-conflicts with it. In that Hermann Beckh accepted the scholarship, the question of his profession was initially decided. Confronted alone with this question he would probably not have known how to begin. 'I still had not quite finished the dream of my childhood, and with humanity ... I still had too little contact.' Many realms would have interested him. The Maximilianeum was called the 'School for Government Ministers'. When the government paid the fees for the initially gifted, then it was obvious to engage them in the Civil Service. In this way the gushing dreamer became a judge! It could not be avoided that he now had to find his way through difficult inner trials and deviations; everything that was close and would have corresponded to his being had to stand aside. In his autobiographical notes he says about this: 'My higher "I", the invisible dramatist of life, preferred the complicated, dramatic paths.'

At first the genius of childhood still holding him by the hand carries him through everything. Especially during his studies, that he himself in no way approached a life's aim in accord with his nature confirms the world-estranged hovering element in him. 'Through the whole surrounding of the Maximilianeum I was more held back in my childhood than it would otherwise have been.' The sound of the River Isar beneath his room, the wafting aroma of the mountains, a certain cosmopolitan atmosphere of the artistic city of Munich, especially with the myths and music of Wagner—where the eighteen-year-old heard for the first time *Tristan and Isolde*, which he called the 'most inspired piece of art of my life'—all this made it possible for him to pass his studies blindfold.

His first literary achievement, writing during the vacations from the Maximilianeum was for his own use: 'Fundamental thoughts and modern ideas in the *Ring of the Nibelungs.*' The second, his first printed book, was completed three years after this. It belongs to that anonymous outer world appearing to him as a blurred grey that makes him into a judge, *Die Beweislast nach dem Bürgerlichen Gesetzbuch* ['The Burden of Proof according to the Civil Code of Law'].

In 1899, the twenty-year-old doctor of both [civil and common] law is appointed judge in a suburb of Munich. Now he has to come out of his cloud that carried him down to earth. How will this be? Can there exist a greater discrepancy between the inner being of a person and his profession? Very soon the conflict comes between the world of jurisprudence and that of humanity. Beckh has to pass sentence on a couple who didn't live in poverty with their child because they stole some firewood. From the legal viewpoint the case is clear. But what of the child when the parents are in prison? Their paying the fine is out of the question where there is no money. The young judge nevertheless chooses the fine but tears up the mandate paper and gives cash to those concerned. The recorder is so moved that he too digs into his pocket. Everything seems initially to be solved. But the inner side still bothers Beckh. Despite all the encouragement of his superiors, who regard him highly, he abruptly gives up his whole career in law.

*

He begins once more from scratch. M'Lord, the assistant judge, becomes once again a student. To what will he turn now? In order to understand himself more deeply he feels compelled to go back to the sources of existence that have not only sprung from the moment of his birth; the older in years, the more he knows consciously that he is accompanied and carried by a homeland of a higher origin in the spirit. And does not there shimmer everywhere something through the transparency of the realms of creation of that sphere in which Nature itself has its pre-natal existence; something of the world of the archetypes, out of which the earthly things have been composed as bodily emblems? Is it then not obvious that to go back in the history of humanity to the primal sources, to the origins still close to the gods?

Beckh himself says that unlike Goethe he is not a visual person, but an aural person. 'Already in my early years I could hear this sound-ing of the world also sounding and singing in my soul.' The 'inner word in the world and in man' was always close to him. And his life in the mythical realm, Wagner's music pointing to far distances has awakened in him and made conscious the instrument of the Logos.

From all this it can be understood that the one-time judge approached studies of the oldest languages of humanity. Already the 'ancient languages' of Latin, Greek and Hebrew learnt in the *Gymnasium* [secondary/high school] are more full of magic substance than mod-ern languages that have absorbed much abstraction. Does one not approach more closely in the early Oriental languages the archetypal power of the Logos, which is inherent in the human word when the gods passed on the Mystery of languages to human beings?

In Kiel and Berlin Hermann Beckh studies Sanskrit, Avestan and Tibetan. Now a world opens up to him in which he is immediately happily at home, as if he came out of an unwelcoming foreign land into his homeland and to himself. Here with his being, different from other people, he finds he is in the right place. Soon he masters the Ori-ental languages from the inside as hardly anyone else. And because he belongs to the very few scholars of the Tibetan language in Europe at that time, his intention to set himself up as a tutor in this subject was very welcome and was supported. After gaining his [second] doctorate in 1907 with his dissertation on Sanskrit, also in the philosophy faculty, he begins in 1908 his teaching activities in Berlin with an inauguration publication on the problems of Tibetan grammar and soon receives an official teaching contract as special professor. It is obvious that he did not remain philologically investigating Oriental languages. The wisdom of the gods, with whom humanity in the infancy of the race still communicated, spoke to him out of the ancient sacred languages that he was now studying. World viewpoints and insights now opened up to the young scholar through which he became aware how flat and poor the spiritual life of humanity is alongside all the enormous progress of intellectual thinking and the sciences.

Indian studies soon led him to Indian theosophy. But here in particular it became clear to him that it is not possible simply to reach back to the earlier levels of humanity in order to overcome modern modes of thinking that have become abstract. The deepest laws of the development of consciousness have made it necessary that humanity, in order to attain clarity and freedom, left the older, sole bestowal of richness that was only given. The great passage through the desert began and finally will pass through the zero-point of knowledge in order on the other side of the valley out of one's own strength to begin the re-ascent, struggling to that point where the ancient wisdom is resurrected in active clarity of thought. The Indian-governed theosophy far removed from the thinking compulsion and the need for individual clarity of modern people was for Beckh only a short transition stage. It meant for him the greatest joy and fulfilment of destiny to find Rudolf Steiner who taught the spirit-knowledge suiting our modern age schooled in natural-scientific method. At the same time, through Rudolf Steiner's spiritual science, he received the true key for understanding the Indian and other Oriental texts of wisdom with which he had become so familiar.

In 1916 his two-volume work Buddhismus (*Buddha und seine Lehre*) [*Buddha his Life and Teaching*, Temple Lodge 2019] appeared in the Göschen series. It soon became recognized and famous in wider circles as the best work on this subject because of the clarity and appropriateness of the presentation. Even today it has not been superseded. In 1958 a new one-volume edition appeared (Stuttgart: Urachhaus). He could not have written it then had he not been already inspired by anthroposophy. Although some people hearing about this immediately recalled their positive opinion, these two small volumes were nevertheless for many unprejudiced people an essential recommendation for anthroposophy. Beckh himself was increasingly filled with the wish to become ever more active for anthroposophy.

*

After Friedrich Rittelmeyer changed his post as Protestant preacher from Nuremberg to Berlin and had in a certain way slowly found his feet in the spiritual life in Berlin, a group of personalities, pupils of Rudolf Steiner, gathered around him in 1918-19. They gathered for this on Sunday evenings in the 'red room' of his vicarage at Krönen Strasse 70 to exchange the results of their striving for knowledge. Besides Dr Erich Schwebsch, and Dr Hans Köster who worked in the Foreign Office, Professor Beckh and his sister also belonged to this group, who as Nurembergers were for years acquainted with Rittelmeyer; in addition to this we younger ones, Eberhard Kurras and myself, attended. In this group I now became personally acquainted with Prof. Beckh shortly after I heard him give that lecture in the University.

These evenings were blessed by a wonderful ensouled mutual exchange, each member enthusiastically reported on the fructifying and kindling that anthroposophy gave to their special field of work or research. Schwebsch led us into Bruckner's symphonies for which an overall interest was only slowly creeping over the horizon at that time. Beckh spoke in connection with his language research, of the discoveries that streamed towards him about the essence of the speech sounds and of language as such. The cosmic mystery of the musical keys and their connection to the starry heavens was a theme that concerned both of them, in particular to the constellations of the zodiac as well as the close and exact relationship to colours.

During this time Beckh could begin to breathe, as he was finally freed from the, for him, painful double life to which he was forced by the conditions of the time. During the War he served as an auxiliary soldier in Bulgaria and Romania. One can imagine in what complete helplessness this role placed him. Finally, he was called as a lawyer to the *Institut für Seeverkehr und Weltwirtschaft*—the 'Institute for sea-traffic and commerce' in Kiel (he always called it *'Institut für sehr verkehrte Weltwirtschaft'*, the 'Institute for very wrong world commerce'). Only when he was called— also as a lawyer—to the Foreign Trade Department of the Foreign Office in Berlin, could he continue his academic activities alongside. In the first years after the War, the anthroposophical movement quickly grew in the public's notice, because it was able to give concrete cultural impulses of renewal to the various realms of life, for example, to education and the ordering of the social organism. Prof. Beckh, of course, belonged to the public speakers of the numerous congresses and conferences that now took place. The abundance of thoughts and perspectives, which in his accustomed way flooded his listeners, was thoroughly stimulating even when his enthusiasm frequently made it difficult for him to reach an end. He soon gave up his teaching post at the University of Berlin for the sake of the anthroposophical activities which he regarded as more important than anything else.

At this time, too, in the group around Rittelmeyer's and with we younger ones a renewal of the religious life was sought in an increasingly concrete and active way. With what fullness of light anthroposophy opened up an understanding of the Bible and other religious streams, but especially for recognizing Christ Himself! The newly opened up book of the history of religions and the Church lay before us. In it we read not only the past, but we also divined ever more clearly how the paths would now have to proceed. At first it did not occur to us to include Professor Beckh in the conversations and planning on this theme. His manner of being and working which many of us valued very much did after all, it seemed to us, move on other paths. In 1921 the first tangible steps for the founding of The Christian Community took place. In July Dr Steiner held a first short lecture-course before a small number of younger personalities and, in September, before a considerably larger group, an extensive course in order to advise us as we had requested—without Beckh receiving any knowledge of it. But then, early in 1922 when our group met in Berlin to deal with some difficulties that wanted to hinder us, Beckh became alert to what was afoot. With elemental instinctive certainty he overviewed in one moment the meaning and extent of our endeavour. In a stormy temperamental outburst—it was on the staircase at Rittelmeyer's, in Krönen Strasse—he challenged us why we had not asked him ages ago to be involved, him, for whose whole becoming and striving the founding of a new spiritually-creative Christian culture was *the* fulfilment of his life. But his manner became even more dramatic when the positive answer was given: 'Now I am here and belong with you, and even if you do not want me, you will never get rid of me!' We were just on our way to meet with Dr Steiner, who on the occasion of a large anthroposophical Class conference was staying in Berlin and came twice to us in

Rittelmeyer's confirmation room. It was with the inevitability of a natural occurrence that Prof. Beckh immediately took part and from then on as though he had missed nothing of what had already taken place. With his whole warm temperament, he accompanied everything that led to the founding of The Christian Community and that took place within it until his death.

*

He found an active connection to our undertaking through his lectures during the Theologians Conference in Nuremberg that we had organized for Easter 1922, in order, if possible, to find similar-minded people prepared to do things. Ever more clearly, we found that he really did belong with us out of deep levels of destiny. When after this Easter Conference part of our group remained for a few weeks in Nuremberg, in order to prepare the work lying before us from the theological perspective, a warm friendly relationship grew, which soon united especially the group of us younger one with Beckh. He held a course of lectures and, perhaps what was more important, he welcomed us into the cosy environment of his parents' genuine old Frankonian house. It was unforgettable for those who were there to hear the commentary, full of inwardness, on the Grimms' fairytale 'Spindle, Shuttle and Needle' that was told not by Beckh himself but by his sister, who lived inseparably with her brother, accompanying his spiritual path in a most finely-attuned manner. A trip into the Franconian Switzerland [in Bavaria] was important for the unfolding of communal feelings. It was one of our most joyful days. Ever afresh Beckh's scattiness and his otherwise compulsive humour released our echoing laughter; but as soon he would burst in with his wonderful laugh through an exquisite joke changing the humour into something spontaneous and creative.

In the autumn of that year, as the grace of destiny allowed the sphere of the new sacramentalism and our task as priests alighted on us, we were grateful that Hermann Beckh belonged to us. He was a special and essential colour in the spectrum of our group. This rested not only on the fact that a University Professor, who had been a judge and Orientalist, had now became a priest with us. He actively took part in carrying the birth of the new ritual words; he was an expert in the mysteries of language. He had always longed that the Logos, driven to abstraction in our time, wants to resurrect in its full creative and healing power. To celebrate the spirit-word in the Service at the new altars was really the innermost fulfilment of this particular destiny. Beckh himself was always amazed at the enigmatic straight-forwardness with which, despite all apparent detours and confusion, his angel had led him to this goal.

When the centre of our expanding work was made in Stuttgart, Prof. Beckh moved into a small attic room in our house Urachstrasse 41, where Dr Rittelmeyer lived in an upper floor flat and we on the ground floor, while the first decade of our Seminary was held and where soon, too, the Urachhaus publishing house developed. You could not enter the narrow room without climbing whole mountains of books and notebooks surrounding the writing desk and piano. But the outer full-ness that wanted to burst the space was only a picture for the inner richness that strove to be realized in an untameable active urge. With an unceasing creativity Prof. Beckh made his contribution to build up a new theology. Because he who was exactly twenty years older than myself stood to me in such an expectant relationship of trust as if our ages were swapped, I was the one who received the greatest and most regular part of his constant enthusiasm and joy in discovery. An abun-dance of books came into existence whose significance perhaps will only be properly appreciated in the future.

One day we decided that we had to put something constructive from our side to face the negative theology of Arthur Drews. Drews had discovered in the gospels laws of composition that could be read in the starry sky. He concludes that the gospels would only be 'astral myths'; what they present would have no historical reality. Beckh him-self initially didn't want to be involved with it, but since in the last part of his life he was getting increasingly engaged with the stars and the connection of their constellations with earthly destiny, eventually the spark caught fire. Thus in 1928 the classic book, *Mark's Gospel: The Cosmic Rhythm*, came into existence. Much more consistently than Drews could manage, Beckh explained how the laws of the stars are present in the construction of the second gospel. He showed what a miracle arrived on the Earth through the Incarnation of Christ and the historical events of the life of Jesus. The challenge in the field against the historicity of Jesus now appeared at one stroke as the incorpora-tion of the super-historical realm in this special earthly Event. Follow-ing this, Beckh wrote a sequel on John's Gospel to continue what he had shown with Mark's Gospel.

All his reading in the rhythms and zodiacal constellations of the starry heavens belongs to Beckh's researches into the mystery of the music of the spheres, of the primal musical sound and of the primal word in the world, for the Logos, the creative Cosmic Word. A fundamental musical attitude runs through everything that he wrote on the gospels and also what he thought and wrote on what has remained alive in the East of the early wisdom of humanity. And so, the beautiful, mature book *The Language of Tonality*, the proofs of which he could correct on his deathbed, forms a wonderful concluding and summarizing cadence to his rich creative work. In it he renders his last thanks to the genius of Wagner's music and also to Rudolf Steiner, the pioneer of the new spirit-word.

# Farther Up!
# Hermann Beckh: Passing through four levels of consciousness, 1916-1931

## Neil Franklin

*'...that seemed to be the direction Aslan had meant when he cried out, "Farther up and farther in".'* C.S. Lewis, The Last Battle (1956).

On first acquaintance Hermann Beckh appears as the learned Professor and one-time judge who had given up a secure position in the Friedrich Wilhelms University in Berlin to speak for anthroposophy as a free-lance lecturer. He then became one of the elder founder-priests of The Christian Community, where he served as celebrant and teacher for fifteen years (1922-37) within the Priests' Seminary, Stuttgart.

With a little more devotion to this extraordinary man, Beckh's works on the origins of language, the structure of music and then the studies on the gospels of St Mark and St John begin to be uncovered as standing among the most erudite and perceptive publications within The Christian Community, indeed the whole anthroposophical move-ment at the time. Certainly, there was no one else who had Beckh's professorial knowledge of Tibetan, Sanskrit, Pali and Avestan (not to mention Hebrew, Latin and Greek and the nine modern languages) to bring to bear on the nature of Christ and Christianity.

However, over the last six years an ongoing project to recover, translate and edit The *Collected Works of Hermann Beckh* (including over eighty periodical articles, previously unpublished typescripts, a book-size series of articles plus a major unfinished manuscript) has provided the opportunity to consider not only the vast range of his insights, which indeed struck his contemporaries, but also to begin to approach his own developing vision. To a large extent this is beyond the reach of a single person, but the years of research have shown that a small team working closely together may make some progress.

Given what we know about Beckh's life before his ordination, both from Gundhild Kačer-Bock's biography and the first-hand memories of his colleagues,[332] there is no avoiding the observation that Beckh was never a person who rested on his laurels or made an uneasy peace with dissatisfaction. Between 1901 and 1921 (age 26-46) he made three life-changing decisions to abandon acclaimed, prestigious posts to venture into the unknown. Something similar can be discerned in his published and unpublished writings during the second part of his life. Yet these now appear not as the wandering tracks of some kind of 'restless soul', but as an indication of a determined and assured spirit who wanted to press on farther, ever more deeply into the Christian Mysteries. Moreover, there are distinct signs indicating or suggesting that Beckh's work between 1916 and 1931 reflects a recognizable spiritual lawfulness which guided his own deepening pursuits.

That said, this exploration sets out from the same point of departure as Beckh himself in 1912. Within ten years, to 1922, the judge became the Professor of Indology and then the priest serving at the altar, increasingly able to call upon Tibetan, Sanskrit, Pali, Avestan, Hebrew and Koiné Greek to support fundamental insights. On the whole Beckh became somewhat frustrated by the traditional academic approaches to ancient languages and sacred texts: comparative philology and cultural comparisons were indeed necessary but left a void. Beckh had found what he felt he had always been looking for on hearing Rudolf Steiner speak concerning the prophet Elijah on December 14, 1911.

As a member of the newly born Anthroposophical Society and soon after the First Section of the Esoteric School, Beckh read as much as he could of the publications and lectures, attended lectures when work permitted, and corresponded with Rudolf Steiner: 34 letters are still held in the Dornach Archives plus a correspondence with Marie Steiner. Without any shadow of doubt, when he was working intensively with Tibetan and Sanskrit texts for the Friedrich-Wilhelms University in Berlin, Beckh reached the conviction that the Sanskrit texts, the Pali Buddhist Canon and the Zend Avesta provided a clear testimony for the evolution of consciousness and of supersensory perception.

Yet Beckh did not want some kind of antiquarian knowledge. Sacred traditions and footprints in the snow were fine as far as they went, but what was their relevance as Europe plummeted towards the Great War? As Blake had argued in 1789,[333] if there is one humanity then there is one underlying spirituality, something that had to be founded in absolutely universal human experience, the real common ground. As with many such things (it is perhaps their most common feature) the reality was plain and simple, staring one in the face all the time, but so ubiquitous as to pass notice. For Beckh it was inescapable that there were *four states of consciousness* in addition to everyday waking thoughts and feelings. There was the borderland of waking and dreaming, full dreaming, sleeping, and also something that Beckh had personally experienced first at five years old: a pre-natal or post-mortem condition of consciousness. Given this *universal fact*, he would argue, there must be some traces in the sacred texts.

Hermann Beckh the judge would be the first to ask for some documentary evidence as background to the argument in hand. Our first testimony is St. Paul, who wrote in the second letter to the Corinthians 3:18:

> ...beholding the glory of the Lord, (we) are being changed into his likeness from one degree of glory to another, for this comes from the Lord who is the Spirit.

The Greek text has 'from glory unto glory' (ἀπὸ δόξης εἰς δόξαν) and is so expressed in the Authorised Version. Luther wrote *'von einer Klarheit zu der andern'*. Yet what the RSV translators clearly recognized was that 'from glory unto glory' is not an expression of a package trip around a series of equally interesting sites but a progression of an *intensifying experience*, ever farther in. We may not be entirely happy with 'degree' with its Masonic connotations, but the attempt at clarification in 1881-1885 RV is most welcome. Paul was clearly aware that there was more than one threshold.

Our second witness is the author (if such sources may be so expressed) of Exodus 31:3, usually presented to the public as the venerable E—the Elohist tradition. This evidence addresses the master craftsman Bezalel 'God is protection',[334] who was appointed to be the overseer or overall constructor of the Tabernacle in the desert.

> ...and I (the Lord) have filled him with the Spirit of God, with ability and intelligence, with knowledge and all craftsmanship,

It is helpful to tabulate the translations of the four qualities:

| RSV | 'ability' | 'intelligence' | 'knowledge' | 'craftsmanship' |
|---|---|---|---|---|
| Hebrew | hokhmah | tebunah | da'ath | mᵉlekah |
| | חכמה | תבונה | דעת | מלאכה |
| LXX | sophias | syneseos | epistemes panti ergo | |
| Vulgate | sapientia | intelligentia | scientia in omni opere | |
| A.V. | wisdom | understanding | knowledge | all manner of workmanship |
| Luther | Weisheit | Verstand | Erkenntnis | allerlei Geschicklichkeit |

For the craftsman who was to build the image of heaven on earth, the Spirit of God (Elohim) leads to a progression of gifts in what may be called *a descending order*, from the exalted Sophia / Wisdom / Hokhmah right 'down' to what we might call applied, practical skill, but at the same time this 'lowest' or 'outermost' gift is still seen as something supra-earthly: m<sup>e</sup>lekah also represents a feminine angelic being.[335] All four are Divine faculties *closely corresponding* to the four 'levels' of the 'descent' of the Divine Nature through the Kabbalistic Sephiroth as represented, for example, in the Zohar[336] and in the four-fold division of space with the Tabernacle.

Comparable to Bezalel in Exodus is the *precise description* of the 'Elect One'[337] in 1 Enoch 49:3:

> In him dwell the spirit of wisdom, the spirit which gives thoughtfulness, the spirit of knowledge and strength, and the spirit of those who have fallen asleep in righteousness.

The four terms can once again be tabulated:

| C'worth 1983 | the spirit of wisdom | and the spirit which gives thoughtful-ness | and the spirit of knowledge and strength | and the spirit of those who have fallen asleep in righteousness |
|---|---|---|---|---|
| Ge'ez (Ethiopic) | መንፈስ ጥበብ | ወመንፈስ ዘያሌቡ | ወመንፈስ ትምህርት ወኃይል | ወመንፈስ እለ ኖሙ በጽድቅ |
| Tr'scribed | mänəfäsä ṭəbäbə | wämänəfäsä zäyalebu | wämänəfäsä təməhərətə wäḫäyələ | wämänəfäsä who nomu bäṣədəḳə |
| 1821 R. Laurence | the spirit of intellectual wisdom | - | the spirit of instruc-tion and of power | and the spirit of those who sleep in righ-teousness |
| R.H. Charles 1912 | the spirit of wisdom | and the spirit which gives insight | and the spirit of understand-ing and of might | and the spirit of those who have fallen asleep in righteousness |

Here once again the first three terms are generic, akin to the O.T. *hokhmah* (Wisdom), *binah* (Understanding) and *da'ath* (Knowledge) in the Zohar system, but the last term is distinctive and individualizing: the consciousness that pertains to post-mortem and pre-natal consciousness. This is essentially similar to the pattern displayed with Bezalel where the fourth quality, angelic craftsmanship, is the most distinctive or personalizing.

## Preparation 1912-16: Buddhist Studies and Anthroposophy

In 1916 Hermann Beckh addressed the issue of Buddhist knowledge (*paññā*) in the Pali canon for his major (two volume) academic book, *Buddha und seine Lehre*.[338] With the aid of Gundhild Kačer-Bock's biography and a little further research, it has now become possible to appreciate the fact that Beckh was one of the very few Indologists in Germany sufficiently qualified in Tibetan, Sanskrit and Pali to undertake the demanding task for the publishers, Sammlung Göschen. The centenary of the publication has just been celebrated in the UK with an English translation, updated and expanded, to accompany the issue of a *Festschrift, Essays in Honour of Hermann Beckh*.

It is highly significant here that the translator, Dr Katrin Binder, prefaces the translation with the acute observation that Beckh's rendering of *paññā* as *Erkenntnis* poses questions for an English translator. Having worked as a lecturer for the University of Tübingen in Sanskrit studies, and being personally experienced in Buddhist meditation, Dr Binder explains that *paññā / Erkenntnis* is best expressed in English as '*realization*'. Truth here is not something downloaded from external sources but has to be *created* afresh in meditation—it is '*realized*', made real independently and originally:

> With Beckh I understand Buddhist '*Erkenntnis*' as knowledge or insight acquired in meditation. This inner process implies a 'making real' of the teachings, including the Buddhist 'truths' and imaginations. This is well illustrated by Beckh's discussion of the role of deities and supernatural beings in Buddhism. It also emerges from his discussion of the concept of '*schauendes Erkennen*'—'realizing vision (or 'seeing realization', *ñāṇadassanaṃ*). This term implies not only the gradual acquisition of supernatural powers of clairvoyance through the practice of meditation (for example with regard to the memory of previous existences). It also

carries the Buddhist image (resting on much older Indian ideas) of the 'blind' person who is made seeing by his insight, or realization, into the Buddhist truth of suffering.[339]

There can be not the slightest doubt that Beckh, having joined the new Anthroposophical Society and the Esoteric School in 1912, corresponding quite regularly with Rudolf Steiner, well understood that the older Buddhist *paññā* had a great deal in common with Imagination, Inspiration and Intuition. This should not be underestimated: we know from his biography that he was devoted between 1912 and 1916 to both *Knowledge of the Higher Worlds: How is it Attained?* and *Occult Science— an Outline.* Beckh could confirm what Steiner outlined and what the older Pali texts taught. In the simplest terms, knowledge (*paññā*) is *seeing and creating* in the supersensible for oneself. It is experiential, not learned from an outside authority.

Such personal realization, however, needs to be underwritten by the certainty of established *order.* When he left school in 1893 and won a scholarship to the prestigious Maximilianeum in Munich, Beckh took up the Law. He then became a judge within the Munich circuit, after composing a prize-winning essay on the Bavarian Code of Law for which he was awarded D. Jur. We can have no doubt that he possessed the acutest legal judgement. It is clear from his biography that he understood that 'natural law' had priority over state legislation—'positive law'—that the efforts of the French *philosophes* (Voltaire, Diderot and De Jaucourt) were not in vain. There is, absolutely, a natural law that all men and women are born free, for example, and that slavery is against such law. However, the natural law of the *philosophes* was historically a prelude to the discovery and elucidation of lawfulness in Imagination (1781-1820). From Goethe to Hegel in Germany, and from Blake to Shelley in England, the leading spirits of the time responded to a Divine call and demonstrated that '*schaundes Erkennen*' or *ñāṇadassanaṃ* realized concrete imaginations that have a universal, objective reality. A little later, in 1922, Beckh penned a fascinating article for *Anthroposophie, Zur Wandlung des Rechtsbegriffs in Menschheitsbewusstsein,*[340] where he argues convincingly that from the earliest Indian culture *lawfulness* is rooted in Sanskrit *ṛta*: the spiritual, cosmic *order* which is truly reflected in religious ritual. Within Buddhism, the perception of such lawfulness and regularity is the prerogative of the *atīndriyadraṣṭar* 'seer of the supersensible', or the one 'who saw beyond the sense-world'.

## *Threshold 1 1921-22: The Supersensible Origins of Language (Natursprache) the Borderland of Waking and Dreaming*

It is clear from Beckh's own autobiographical writing that his great divorce from a promising legal career in 1902 was the first of three such dramatic life changes. Yet even then Beckh could rely on two sources of enduring strength. The first was the fact that he had directly undergone experiences of a pre-natal existence which were undeniable (recurring at important times in his life); and secondly, especially as a student in Munich, he had heard astonishing messages in Wagner's music. As a judge Beckh found that the law punished, it did not foster human potentials. On the other hand, performances of Wagner provided a divine sustenance for those who had ears to hear. Was there a link between the experience of a pre-natal Paradisal state and the structures of richly romantic music? Was there something of cosmic lawfulness, *ṛta*, in Mozart, Beethoven, Wagner and Bruckner? The threatening gulf between his old, well-trodden career in government service, now dismissed abruptly, and a new life studying Tibetan, Sanskrit and Pali—settling down in Berlin—could be safely traversed with the aid of music.

All the same, Beckh never wanted to take short-cuts. If there was a link between the great works of music and *Erkenntnis* in the Buddhist and anthroposophical sense, then it would have to be demonstrated— almost, one might say, to the satisfaction of a global jury. How could this be achieved? The process over the seven years 1916-23, aged 41 to 48, entailed two further sacrifices of career. Beckh first gave up his university position, despite a personal request from the Minister of Culture in Prussia, and then abandoned his acclaimed work as a lecturer for Anthroposophy to become one of the founding priests of The Christian Community, joining young Emil Bock and his own contemporary Friedrich Rittelmeyer in the new Stuttgart Seminary as one of the three leading teachers. Thus it was, in 1923, that Beckh found himself in the attic rooms of Urachstrasse 41 with his piano, an iron stove, and an imposing collection of authoritative books regarding the sacred texts of India and Tibet. At the time when the Russian civil war was still in violent conflict and Mount Etna erupted, making 60,000 people homeless, Beckh composed and published *Das Geistige Wesen der Tonarten*,[341] his first major book since the Buddha study of 1916. This was not some kind of personal whim or caprice.

In the two previous years, before becoming ordained, Beckh had responded to Steiner's personal invitation that he (Beckh) should develop both the understanding that the origins of speech should be sought for in *schauende Erkenntnis*, and that distinct traces of such an origin can be found through traditional, academic philology. For two years Beckh lectured and published as much as he could to build bridges between the primordial roots of Indo-European languages, with special attention to Sanskrit, and the inner Imaginative / Inspirational experience of speech sounds. In this domain we find Professor Beckh moving fluently among the earlier sacred languages, including Avestan and Hebrew. The re-issue of *Neue Wege zur Ursprache* in 1954[342] has contributed substantially to his growing reputation and it is true that Beckh stands today as a pioneering colossus in the anthroposophical approaches to speech and eurythmy. Yet in 1923, surrounded by a good deal of acclamation for his articles and lectures on language, Beckh chose to write on music and to leave aside his professional expertise in the oriental languages. It was time to move on.

### Threshold 2 1923: Music and the Zodiac
### Entry into Dream Consciousness

For Beckh this was an enormous step forward. If in philology there was a close tie between scientific research into word roots (Novalis' *pragmatic etymology*) and the supersensory *Erkenntnis* of the primordial meanings of speech sounds (*genetic etymology*), then a corresponding connection may exist between the musical keys as played in classical compositions and a spiritual—supersensible source which we can call a 'mood', *Stimmung*.[343] Given that Rudolf Steiner consistently elaborated on the archetypal *Weltendenken* within cognition, there must also be higher *Weltenstimmungen* expressing archetypal *feelings*.

As an example, Beckh investigates, as an *atīndriyadraṣṭar*, the key of B-major and A♭-minor.[344] He describes the mood or musical key, both *Stimmung*, as:

- 'the hour before sunset'
- 'the end of summer'
- a 'mood of farewell'
- 'transfiguring'

The range of music considered here by Beckh is quite narrow in compass, with most points being consistently refurbished between 1923 and 1937:

- Isolde's *Liebestod* at the end of *Tristan and Isolde* (B-major)
- The *Karfreitagszauber* in *Parsifal* (B-major)
- The A♭-minor Arioso in Beethoven's *Piano Sonata*, op. 110
- The Funeral March movement in A♭-minor from Beethoven's *Piano Sonata*, op. 26
- Music associated with St. Elisabeth in *Tannhäuser* (B-major)
- Music associated with Midsummer's Eve in *Die Meistersinger* (B-major)

In 1923, however, Beckh had *realized*, heard for himself, that such passages, which had nourished him during many a weary hour of studying legal texts and hand-printed Tibetan characters, could not have been written in any other key. Once again, the task was to plummet universal *lawfulness*. Here the ocean was very deep and difficult to sound, but life as a Priest of The Christian Community could confirm that the rhythms of the day, the week and the year expressed ṛta, the rhythmic cosmic order. Beckh deeply reflected on the seasons of the year and the Christian festivals. The inherent lawfulness of the musical keys was rooted in the rhythms of time expressed spatially in the zodiac, and this was far more difficult to access than the sources of speech. The mystery of the musical keys belonged to an interweaving of *Weltenstimmungen* experienced in the seasons with the dark night sky becoming alive with stars. Where was the archetype of B-major and A♭-minor to be found? Beckh found that the 'mood' (*Stimmung*) of this key, especially in selected bars from *Tristan and Isolde* and *Parsifal* was that of late summer, perhaps the first week of September when light begins to fade and people gather along the coast to bid farewell to the setting sun and the end of the summer holiday. Such an experience of leave-taking, a 'mood of farewell' falls to the sign of Virgo. Some ten years later Beckh was to write in detail for the Priests' *Rundbrief* on the zodiac *signs* while Rudolf Frieling supported his findings and carefully extended the study to focus on the 12 signs and the 12 parts of The Creed, also for the *Rundbrief*. Within Beckh's contributions, however, we now find that Virgo (the archetype of Isis and Provider of Nourishment, Eucharist) is accepted as the star-guide, presiding genius, of The Christian Community.[345]

Between 1923 and 1930 Beckh was hard at work meditatively researching the starry archetypes which he encountered in music. For the time being, the emphasis moved from examples in music to the stars themselves, that is, as they are found to be in relationship to the Earth and its rhythms and seasons. There was a strong reason, or occasion, for this. When Beckh responded to Steiner's open invitation to speak about the origins of language it was understood that academic linguistics had fallen prey to the assumptions and theories of Fritz Mauthner.[346] In Mauthner's view, any observation on speech had to be supported by empirical evidence; introspection was unacceptable; there was no *psyche* as it could not be observed or measured by sense perception. Shortly after September 1920 Europe was further stirred up by the popular success of Arthur Drews' *Das Markus Evangelium als Zeugnis gegen die Geschichtlichkeit Jesu.*[347] Drews had thrown down the gauntlet: the gospel accounts of the life of Jesus were no more than a rehash of ancient myths associated with the constellations through which a non-historical, fictional Sun-God ran round his path three times in three years. There were riots outside Vienna Cathedral.

## *Expanding the Vision 1924-28: from Music to the Gospels*

The Faculty later met in Urachstrasse and concluded that someone had to reply to Drews, and it could only be Beckh. The principal problem here was that Drews had compiled an argument that had some vestige of the truth in it but had reduced the *Weltenstimmungen* of Beckh's approach to music to the crudest observations on zodiac and other constellations, not signs. Put in the simplest terms (as David Hume used to enjoy doing) Drews' argument was:

> The gospels are rooted in ancient and classical myths of the stars.
> Such myths are obviously worthless as history.
> Therefore, the gospels are worthless as history.

In these years Beckh had to contend both with Drews and with misapprehensions of astrology; while the threats from National Socialism and Communism grew apace. Neither Emil Bock nor Friedrich Rittelmeyer could take up the challenge. Yet we now find Beckh still moving on into uncharted waters, that is (still with almost unavoidable metaphors) deepening the meditative quest. The calling was now to extend earlier discoveries in the lawful structures of speech and music to the structures of the Gospels of Mark and John. Beckh found that realizations of the zodiac-signs were the essential spiritual guide to both music and the gospels, but at the same time something more profound was just beginning to make itself felt.

In the early 1920s Beckh had to cross a first threshold, from academic erudition and skillfulness to the borders of dreaming where the origins of resonant word-roots could be inwardly experienced. Here there is a certain balance between sharp fully awake consciousness and something of a waking dream which is often found to be highly attractive in his writings on language and etymology: it is a broadly accessible area. With the progression to music in 1923, however, Beckh is more deeply within a dreamlike environment where the meanings of the zodiacal archetypes begin to shine forth as actively creative beings, and this is much harder to experience truly for oneself. One can say that an evening twilight brings forth a night that is radiant with stars, radiant with new meanings. Yet as time progressed from 1924 to 1930, Hermann Beckh also took further steps in meditation: it is as though (we are always encountering metaphors) he encountered a realm where the stars, constellations and planets disappeared entirely to produce a pitch-black night sky wherein there was no orientation. Here was a third threshold, between dreaming and sleeping.

## *Threshold 3: 1924-28. Encountering the Divine Feminine Entry into Sleep Consciousness*

In the later 1920s Beckh was blessed with two sources of support for the daunting task of crossing this 'deeper' threshold. On the one hand there was the continuing publication of fine anthroposophical studies. Günther Wachsmuth's *Die ätherischen Bildekräfte in Kosmos, Erde und Mensch* appeared in 1924,[348] to which Beckh had constant recourse; and then Albert Steffen's *Mani* was published in 1930.[349] Like Beckh, Steffen was well versed in the nature or substance of Paradise and recovered the glorious old term *'terra lucida'*.[350] On the other hand there was Mozart. Probably the most heart-stopping moment here is when Tamino, within the Temple of *The Magic Flute*, finds himself in total darkness, all lights are extinguished. The musical key changes to a haunting A-minor with *'O Ew'ge Nacht'* and Tamino's tenor launches out the great question to darkness and infinity, *'Unsichtbaren, saget mir / Lebet Pamina noch?'* Almost as an echo to the question, the invisible choir replies in what must be one of the most truly magical moments in the history of Western music, redolent with profound pauses: *'Pamina – lebet – noch!'* In the deepest darkness, almost at the edge of all extinction and hope, Tamino is assured that the Divine Feminine is still alive—the choir here is usually led by high female voices. Mozart achieves the astonishing task of portraying a true Mystery on the stage, something that Beckh could profoundly appreciate.

While Beckh confronted the extinguishing of all lights and the inner darkness without stars, with consciousness penetrating from dream to deeper sleep, we too have a very important threshold to cross. Beckh found between 1924 and 1930 that the darkest night sky, bereft of signs and constellations, became radiant with the Divine Feminine. In all probability we do not have an adequate language for this: even Steiner's communications on Inspiration are only waymarks. The darkest night sky becomes radiant with the presence of, well, what language shall we use? The Divine Feminine? Pamina?

There is no lack of options. The best of recent studies on the Old Testament (Margaret Barker D.D.) elucidates the 'Queen Mother, Ashratah' or simply 'The Lady';[351] the Zohar points to a fourfold feminine from Hokhmah to Shekinah; other Kabbalist texts emphasize that Shekinah is found also to be the text of the Torah; Soloviev, and Bulgakov encountered Sophia.[352] The list of possibilities is almost endless, but one of the most helpful guides is Jakob Böhme who developed a complex theosophical system from 1612 to 1624, founded on original vision.[353]

In a sense following the pioneering work of Bulgakov on Sophia and Mary, few have achieved more today in Old and New Testament studies than Margaret Barker. She has argued convincingly that the O.T. Law was originally *vision*, and also that Ezekiel saw into the divine feminine (fourfold) that was expressed as ᶜ*hayyah*, the 'living one' of Ez. 10:17: her evidence and argument, at the highest level of Hebrew studies, are simply incontrovertible.[354] But what does all this really mean? '*Pamina lebet noch*'?

As Beckh painstakingly investigated the Divine Feminine between 1924 and 1930, he set out a vast range of metaphors and traditional images. From anthroposophical natural science he discussed Wachsmuth's four ethers and related this to the Tree of Life; he understood that the Tree and the Goddess were expressions of the same source; he investigated the hieroglyphs and the traditions of Isis; he understood the Bride of the Lamb and the New Jerusalem; he presented the story of Snow-White, Rose-Red and their Mother.[355] He explained that the Tree of Life was still with us, but is lost when we fall asleep.[356] No one else during these years did more to convey a glimpse of the radiant Divine Feminine who presided in silent secrecy beyond the 24 tones of the zodiac.

There was still a final threshold to cross. In his last years, 1930-37, aged 55-62, Beckh continued to compose music for The Christian Community, and returned to the earlier 1923 text, *The Essence of Tonality*, to expand it into *The Language of Tonality in the Music of Bach to Bruckner* (published 1937). He published two small musical compositions, *Psalm 23* and *The Roses of Damascus*, and was writing a new work on music during his final months of earthly life, *The Mystery of Musical Creativity: Man and Music*.[357] However, before these tasks he had realized that his massive studies of Mark and John required a certain clarification which we can initially simplify as: What is the *substance* of The New Jerusalem?

## Threshold 4 1930-31: The Christ Consciousness Enters the Pre-natal / Post-mortem Condition

As the distinguished Professor of Indology, Beckh applied the clearest logical thinking to what should be understood by *nirvāṇa* in the Pali Canon of Buddhist thought. The analysis in Part 2 of *Buddha's Life and Teaching* (1916) is a model of exposition. It is just here, however, that Beckh points out, with abundant evidence, that the Buddhist 'step-ladder' of meditation leads in its latter stages to an inner experience of a 'this-side' *nirvāṇa* (*diṭṭhadhammanibbāna*).[358] This is to say that in advanced meditation the subject will encounter within him / herself a true 'realization' of the post-mortem and pre-natal condition of consciousness *while still in incarnation*. It will be remembered that Beckh had three such experiences during his life, albeit involuntary. In fully awake consciousness, assisted by immense scholarly learning, the publication explained Gautama Buddha's teaching on 'this-side' *nirvāṇa* to the satisfaction of the logical intellect.

When Hermann Beckh was living in the Stuttgart seminary, we are reminded by Gundhild Kačer-Bock, her sister Rosemaria and by others who knew Beckh well that he would make a particular point of showing them Venus or Sirius in the night sky, usually above Stuttgart, and that he maintained a collection of beautiful crystals. It is not difficult to imagine the Professor pondering and meditating on them: how has supernal light come to find itself in cold, hard physical matter? The question stood before him whenever he observed snowflakes, ice-covered mountains or simply frost on the windowpanes of his attic room in Urachstrasse 41.

During the 1920s Beckh published a range of periodical articles approaching the question from a number of different angles. Among the most attractive are his contemplative verses on The New Jerusalem, his discussions of Isis, most of all his meditative findings in the story of Snow-White. More thorough analyses are then to be found in the two books on the gospels. In 1930 Beckh was completing

*John's Gospel: The Cosmic Rhythm—Stars and Stones*, but then found that something more still needed to be said. Between 1930 and 1931 Beckh continued to write extensively on the stars and astrology for the Priests' *Rundbrief* while composing what was intended to be a fairly short Appendix for *John's Gospel* and also publishing the intense study *The Parsifal=Christ=Experience in Wagner's Music Drama*. Very quickly the planned Appendix became a fully-fledged work in its own right with the title *Vom Geheimnis der Stoffeswelt (Alchymie)* in 1931. Among Beckh's works this is the text that has been most often reissued.

The 1931 *Parsifal* expresses the *realization* that the music drama progresses through four distinct stages, that it develops through deepening levels of Mystery. All of Act 1 presents the young, unknowing Parsifal 'in the region of the Grail' where he listens to Gurnemanz but has to admit that he does not know what the Grail is. Act 2 Sc. 2 presents Parsifal many years later in Klingsor's magic garden overcoming Kundry and coming to understand Amfortas' wound. Act 3, Sc. 1, is Good Friday where the death of Titurel is reported, and the music drama reaches its climax with the renewal of the Earth, the *Karfreitagszauber*, and then, Sc. 2, the unveiling of the Grail. Regarding the spring-like renewal of the Earth Beckh adds the observation: 'The earth is transformed into a shining monstrance.'[359]

In the penultimate paragraph of the study, Beckh presents his final overview:

> In the four steps of the Parsifal-path, Wagner presents in artistic images that same mystery which is enacted at the altar in The Act of Consecration of Man of The Christian Community.

These four 'steps' or stages are then summarized:

> The Liturgy of the Word or 'Proclamation of the Gospel'.
> The Offertory: 'the soul has to step through the gate of purification'.
> Transubstantiation: 'bread and wine radiate in the light of renewed purity'.
> Communion: 'the human being as *bearer of the Cup*'. (My emphases.)

As both scholar and artistic visionary, Beckh had striven through the 1920s, with publications culminating in the two gospel studies, to convey what he had experienced as the Divine Feminine as the provider of spiritual nourishment in the most defined sense, whether as Sanskrit *soma*, Avestan *huoma* or Hebrew *manna*. As we have seen above, the Divine Feminine was perceived as the one source of light and renewed life, the Tree of Life which radiates the uncreated light which is normally invisible. For Beckh this was also what is presented in the Grail vessel. But this left the question, what of the vessel itself? Beckh had to extend the gospel studies into what he had found beyond the final threshold: *Vom Geheimnis der Stoffeswelt* had to be written.

Between 1904 and 1922 Hermann Beckh had cultivated first a professorial knowledge of Buddhism and then a mature understanding of what Rudolf Steiner was presenting. It is now known that when he was called up in autumn 1916 to serve as a foot-soldier on the Eastern Front the one book that he took with him, along with the trench-digging tools, was *Occult Science—an Outline* at the very same time that *Buddha's Life and Teaching* saw publication in Berlin. The one thing that was abundantly clear to him as he took shelter in an empty house in Romania on Christmas Eve 1916[360] was that perception depends on levels of consciousness, with both Buddhism and Anthroposophy, the supersensible beings that are encountered on different levels on the Path are themselves states or expressions of the changing consciousness.

When he composed *Buddha's Life and Teaching* in 1915-16, Beckh did not oversimplify Buddhist teachings. Part 2 of the book set out, with full scholarly apparatus, an impressive analysis of the complex series of stages of meditation to be encountered by the Buddhist disciple on four levels. In due sequence we find *saddhā* (belief), *samādhi* (meditation), *paññā* (realization), and *vimutti* (liberation). Within *vimutti*, a fourth stage of exalted contemplation (*dhyāna*) is described closely following texts in the Pali canon. Beckh carefully explains that this fourth stage is the highest attainable as 'this-side' *nirvāna*.

> 'If,' thus it is said in the passage on meditation of the Dīghanikāya (SPhS 83), 'the spiritual or mental element (*cittaṃ*) has been thus concentrated, purified and filled with light, free from all impurities and earthly passion, compliant and pliable, steadfast and unmoving, then he directs this spiritual element towards the realizing vision (or 'seeing realization', *ñānadassanaṃ*).' That which presents itself first to his vision is his own body, his own being, which he then sees as if split into a duality: a physical being, constituted by the four elements which is the result of physical heredity (*mātāpettikasambhava*) and which carries the conditions of decay and dissolution in itself, and another one, a principle of spiritual consciousness (*viññāna*) which permeates that physical being in the same way as a coloured thread drawn through a pure, stainless, polished eight-sided precious stone, and it is said that he sees this his physical body which is subject to decay and traversed by the thread of the consciousness-soul as if *from the outside* like someone who takes a precious stone into his hand and

says: this is a precious stone with these particular characteristics, and here a coloured thread has been drawn through it.[361]

In this powerful image, the archetype of the physical body displays its crystalline nature, a precious stone through which the 'coloured thread' of *viññāna* is drawn. The 'eight-sided precious stone' of the Pali Sāmaññaphala Sutta 84 is *veḷuriya* from which classical Greek *beryllos* derives, i.e. beryl. Although in later publications Beckh preferred to represent this as a diamond. Part 1 of *Buddha and His Teaching*, given over to a painstaking examination of Gautama Buddha's life in history and legend, had drawn the reader's attention to a pertinent detail in the Lalitavistara account of the Buddha's birth.

Beckh tells the Sanskrit Lalitavistara story of the birth as follows:

> The gods offer Queen Māyā their abodes for her to reside in until the birth of the Bodhisattva. By way of his magically effective concentration, the Boddhisattva causes Māyā to be seen in all those divine abodes at the same time. He himself rests in the womb in the position of yoga meditation (*paryaṅka*). So that no earthly impurity may tarnish him, a shell of radiating beryl lustre surrounds him (*ratnavyūhabodhisattvaparibhoga*) which is transported into Brahmā's heaven by the gods after his birth and kept as a sacred relic there. In that night, where the Boddhisattva enters his mother's womb, a lotus grows from the earth reaching up to Brahmā's heaven. Only Brahmā himself is able to see this lotus. Whatever is available as powerful essence in the wide compass of the worlds is present as a drop of honey in this lotus. Brahmā himself offers this drop of honey in *a bowl of beryl* to the child in the womb, and the Boddhisattva accepts the refreshment in order to show himself gracious to the god. Nobody would be able to tolerate this drop of power except the Boddhisattva in his last earthly existence.[362]

The 'bowl of beryl' here is made of Skr. *vaiduryā*, beryl, the Sanskrit form of Pali *veḷuriya*.

Neither here in the 1916 *Buddha* nor at any other time does Beckh point out this extraordinary coincidence, which is more than simple philology, although he must have been fully aware of it. Certainly, the restrictive format of the publisher Sammlung Göschen limited the amount of discussion; the text studiously avoids any mention of Rudolf Steiner and Anthroposophy, apart from one fleeting footnote reference to *Riddles of Philosophy*. Nevertheless, in 1916 Beckh *realized* that in Buddhist tradition at the deepest level of meditation the physical body appears as a pure crystal formed out of beryl, and that *the same substance*—we could say hypostasis—forms the vessel which contains the divine nourishment to sustain life.

From time to time between 1922 and 1924 Beckh considered the Grail, especially in the 1923 *Das Geistige Wesen der Tonarten* (regarding Wagner) and at Christmas within The Christian Community. While central Europe had to contend with Drews' 'Christ Myth', Beckh continued to explore the realm of the twenty-four musical keys and the zodiac, as we have seen, but he was also under some pressure to make it clear that he was a Christian priest and not a Buddhist professor. The result was the publication of *From Buddha to Christ* in 1925.[363] Here was the principal opportunity to bring together the university scholarship on Buddhism and what he had heard in Wagner's *Parsifal*. Beckh reintroduces the eight-sided stone and retells the Lalitavistara story at some length immediately after explaining that a great deal of Christian esotericism is to be found in the Grail legend and then stating: 'The Holy Grail is also beheld many times as a bowl of beryl.' The persistent image recurs in the traditional story of 'the bowl of beryl or emerald' presented by the Queen of Sheba to Solomon, and the nineteenth-century story from August Schultz wherein the precious jewel that fell from Lucifer's crown becomes the Grail vessel.[364]

By 1931 Beckh had approached the Grail from many sides, most purposefully in the two large studies of Mark and John. The new publication, for Rudolf Geering Verlag, now set out to bring light into the subject of the mystery of matter itself, but for a broad readership. In consequence, the account largely moves within familiar territory. The alchemical 'Stone of the Wise' naturally finds many synonyms and closely related images: *terra lucida*, the philosopher's stone, Oetinger's thesis on the salt crystal[365] all testify to the substance or hypostasis of Paradise and the Resurrection Body, and all within Beckh's comprehensive grasp are indicative of the Eucharist and the New Jerusalem. It can easily appear that the author is spreading out *ad lib* over subjects that are dear to his heart, but this is to mistake the text.

Once again Beckh presents the octahedral *veḷuriya* from the Sāmaññaphala Sutta with reference to *Buddha's Life and Teaching*, but now adds the observation:

> These occasional echoes in Buddha in what is still retained from later ages of Indian wisdom appear to us all the more remarkable, considering the otherwise diminishing awareness of alchemy as well as the astrology connected to it. Reading between the lines of Buddhist traditional texts,

mysteries of the zodiac as well as planetary wisdom may still be discovered in which genuine primal wisdom is contained...[366]

'Beyond' or 'farther in from' sleep Beckh had three experiences of a pre-natal consciousness during his life. He felt that this was his homeland from which he been estranged at birth, and that some intimation of this could always be rediscovered in crystal formations. This was confirmed by the exalted vision of the octahedral stone, *veḷuriya*, as the realization of the ground of the physical-material body and the coloured thread of a raised consciousness that runs through its midst.

After a brief mention of the legendary jewel that fell from Lucifer's crown to become the substance of the Grail vessel, *Alchymie* presents two short observations on beryl. First, with reference to the colour-circle, the 'yellow-green' crystal conveys 'the mediating colour' which represents 'the spirit of Christ'. The second realization follows an analysis of the sequence of signs in the zodiac wherein beryl is found to correspond with the Lion. Implicit here is the notion that the primordial origin of the physical-material body is to be found in the sacrificial outpouring of Divine warmth.[367] For Hermann Beckh two associations are implicit. On one hand, his considerable knowledge and attraction to crystals could not avoid basic mineralogy: beryl is found to form some of the Earth's largest crystals (several *metres* along the axes) and is thus able to be shaped into substantial artefacts such as bowls or chalices. Then, as a consecrating priest, Beckh realized that the Christian Sacrament at Communion is precisely the 'mediating' element of divine substance.

Yet for all this, the evidence in texts and Beckh's personal fourfold path only present something of a greyscale route-map or a spider's web cast over the vibrant personality. One can imagine explaining to him the series of thresholds, the Buddhist and Biblical passages, *vaiduryā*, and *veḷuriya*, while walking along Urachstrasse in 1931 only to be met with a beaming smile and his booming voice. 'Of course! Of course!' he would say, 'Don't you see it all?' And he would point to the reddening glow of sunset, Venus as the Evening Star, and the fresh peach blossoms.

The creation of man and the archetype of the physical body called to resurrection? Lacking a diamond, Beckh would always show the two little Bock girls a piece or two of beryl which he kept in his crystal cabinet.

If ever there was a token of genius it is the natural, and then cultivated gift to *realize* the marriage of immense scholarly learning and personal spiritual insight with the simplest perceptions of everyday life.

# BOOK REVIEWS

# The Starry Mystery of Christ's Life on Prof. Beckh's book: *Mark's Gospel: The Cosmic Rhythm*[368]

Since the turn of the 19th century there have been attempts from various sides to apply the 'astral-mythological' way of observation to the gospels. During the 19th century the historical Jesus was the aim of research, where the gospel tradition was increasingly taken as having to be acknowledged as 'historically unreal'. From another side attempts were made to give this historically critical view the death blow. It was said, the gospels do not intend to be historical accounts at all; they present the myth of a Sun-god and what this Sun-god experienced going through the twelve zodiacal signs during the course of the year. According to this view the myth of the dying and resurrecting god was nothing other than the personified destiny of what the Sun has to go through each winter and new spring. It is overcome by the dark powers yet rises again out of its grave.

I recall, how in winter 1920/21 Arthur Drews [1865-1935], Professor of Philosophy from Karlsruhe, announced his new book. In well-attended public lectures, he consistently carried through the monist position to its conclusion. In his book on Mark's Gospel he attempted step by step to show how the whole path from the baptism in the Jordan to Golgotha presents a triple circuit of the Sun through the zodiac—but condensed into a lived myth. One can easily show how superficially the details of this progress through the zodiac is made by Drews. He simply has taken up old star-maps with their added pictures and seeks out all sorts of analogies between Christ's life and the various stellar images through which the Sun passes. But this method is *consistent*. It was shocking to experience how weak the objections were from the side of current theology amongst the assembly at the time. It did not weaken him; for someone who concerns himself with the manner of seeing things cosmically feels there must be something true about it.

The time indeed is ripe to uncover a new side of Christianity, to deepen and broaden the picture of Christ from the cosmic perspective.

We can also say, *we have to discover the cosmic Christ*; for at the beginning of Christianity he was already a live Presence. But before Arthur Drews published his book on Mark's gospel, some years before Rudolf Steiner in a lecture-cycle explained Mark's Gospel with individual examples showing how indeed the gospels—but Mark in the most transparent way—are built up in such a way that the earthly, human events at the same time mirror heavenly events. For example, the meeting of John the Baptist and His baptism in the floods of the Jordan, although an earthly, historical event, is also such a 'starry script'. It mirrors the entrance of the Sun into the sign of the Waterman. Steiner has shown us how we do not need to delete a single line from the gospel. We are dealing everywhere with historical, although often with spiritual, super-sensory realities, and yet in all earthly events we can find the reflection of the great laws of the stars.

For man and all human life is indeed *heavenly existence carried down into earthly existence*. It is only the fact that our earthly existence is so bound to the earth and so darkened that the mysteries of the stars are but covered in us. Here and there they clearly shine up at life's turning points; destiny then becomes symbolic. The Incarnation of Christ differs from all other human destinies in that on His earthly pathway at no moment is His heavenly origin denied. For Him at any and every moment Goethe's expression is valid, which otherwise is meant only for the highpoints of human life:

> and in the clear lake
> all the stars feast their eyes.

This viewpoint—under which one quite rightly views the whole of Christ's life without dissolving it into a mere myth or astral fantasy—Hermann Beckh has developed right into the details in his book, *Mark's Gospel: The Cosmic Rhythm* [Leominster: Anastasi Ltd, 2015], such a book seems to us a spiritual deed; however many people already initially find access to this sublime way of looking at the subject. The universal aspect of the viewpoints are here brought into a comprehensive view.

Today it depends on our understanding that materialism—and Drew's book is consistent materialism in gospel research—cannot be fought by seeking to weaken its arguments. One has to be courageous enough to agree with materialism in its sphere. It indeed penetrates, as in other realms, to cosmic mysteries that need to be recognized today. It leads towards thresholds; but it does not possess the strength to enter the new land. What Drews describes through the starry charts quite superficially as the Sun's course with a sequence of mythological, heavenly pictures becomes in Beckh's presentation a deepened path-way of the soul. The true disciple can enter this pathway of the soul by inwardly following the life of Christ and His pathway to death. Prof. Beckh shows how Mark's Gospel is built up through certain laws. It does not only want to present the outer historical sequence of events in the life of Jesus. It describes and connects the events in such a way that they become the inner steps and initiation experiences for the soul of one disciple. He is mentioned only here and there, otherwise he goes mostly unnoticed throughout the whole story. He is the favourite disciple, John; the same one who then wrote John's gospel as the only one who was able to remain faithful to the Lord right up to the hour of death. He alone was able with Him to live through Golgotha, standing under the cross, whereas all the others had already failed.

Hermann Beckh shows how John's Gospel is the true gospel of Christ. Yet what we call Mark's Gospel is actually a 'Johannine gospel'; it pres-ents the life and dying of Christ to us as mirrored in the soul of the matur-ing and developing disciple John. He shows how at first the whole group of disciples is spiritually led and in stages helped by Christ to rise to the awakening of the soul. But the group of disciples as such fails; some can only follow as chosen ones, but also these are no longer able to hold out under the power of the mighty experiences. Finally, there remains the one; he who remained faithful to the Lord.

In the picture of the 'rich young man', who asked the Lord for the conditions required of a follower—of 'the scribe', who asked about the most important commandment, and other things—this 'one' approaches us unnamed. As a personality, he steps back behind what he has to live on the *path of the soul*. His meetings with Christ, the great impressions of Christ, which worked on his soul and which led it to awaken, are what is described in Mark's Gospel. In the face of this, all the merely personal factors are unimportant—even his name. For the gospel is in fact not written as a biography, like modern memoirs, but it intends to call followers. Everyone who reads it, allowing the pictures to work on his soul, can become a 'John'. He himself becomes that disciple who follows the Lord through death to resurrection, when he is able to develop the breadth of experiences demanded by the course of the events. Whoever has not run out of breath already beforehand, before reaching the path of death in life—living and suffering through it step by step—this person is allowed at the end to feel he is the disci-ple 'whom the Lord loved'.

But spiritual experiences, which do not only shake and engage the soul in passing, need to follow the inner lawfulness of the process. They are to awaken and mature in us that part of our being that is not of this world but of heavenly origin. Consequently, it is not surprising that the great laws that we can observe in the sky—although at first only outwardly—also apply to soul-development, for the human being is a microcosm. He reproduces the cosmos in his inner life. If he finds the inner Sun, the Christ rising in the firmament of his inner being—then with this Sun he will also have to go on his own path. The outer Sun in the cosmos goes through the twelve signs of the zodiac; the Christ-'I' that wants to awaken in us and that begins its own inherent life-rhythm, goes through something like an inner, spiritual starry course.

For the more profound and more unprejudiced readers who find their way into this commentary on Mark, the more inevitable and organic the structure of the gospel appears to be. The path of the soul of the striving human being awakening to the spirit becomes a starry pilgrimage. Christ, the Sun in our spiritual firmament leads the cycle, moving from picture to picture. At some places the description in Beckh's book takes on as it were dramatic tension. Divining from the distance, we experience how Christ Himself was anxious for the souls of His disciples as he strove for their awakening, having to place them before trials of the spirit at which the strength of most of them failed. Beckh's presentation frequently with a single sentence touches psychological depths on the most sacred and deepest level in human souls that academic books on psychology could never give us, which poets seldom and only musicians here and there are able to reveal.

All the more one would have liked to see that the author had been able to give his expositions a form that a broader readership would appreciate what he has to give. For this it would have helped had the author bridged from the current concepts to be found everywhere to his purely spiritual values of the zodiacal signs as realms of spirit and spirit experience. The general reader who, more or less clearly, carries in his head the world-conception of contemporary mathematical astronomy will ask himself step by step: how can this starry world up there in the universe spiritually affect the course of destiny in human life and is pictorially mirrored so that the earthly events become symbols of the heavenly constellations? This bridge in a full sense can be established today through the anthroposophical view of the world. In a written work for contemporary educated readers one would not like to miss this constant reference to the world of real facts. For this, in this great work some things could have been sacrificed out of the sheer abundance of viewpoints. Following the main thread through the life of Christ through the main stations on this sublime path of destiny, the impression would but have been enhanced.

However, anyone who immerses himself into a study of this work, might be put off in a first reading as he cannot immediately overview the abundance of connections. One may also question whether each detail in the gospel is rightly interpreted—all this is not decisive for the importance of this book. As the author himself says (p. 328f.): 'It is not the intention immediately to press connections, as the above might suggest, into some kind of notion and theory, but far rather that one can learn in a certain inner silence to repose with them. Such an inner silence would then reveal much to the soul.'

In the above-mentioned sense such a work on the gospel can also convey strong impulses of religious deepening. It creates a breadth of view and reverence before the inexhaustible Mystery of Christ set against its *starry depths*.

If one took it in a dogmatic sense as a new body of knowledge of Christology, or so that one no longer finds any access to the gospel texts without cosmic-astronomical knowledge—this would be against the intention of the author, and obviously against the spirit of The Christian Community.

If I am to summarize the impression left by a study of such a comprehensive work, then I could only do it with the words of Christian Morgenstern. This poet has expressed the Mystery of Christ's transformation of the Earth in the following words, that have come to us from his literary estate:

*Er sprach. Und wie Er sprach erschien in Ihm*
*Der Tierkreis, Cherubim und Seraphim,*
*Der Sonnenstern, der Wandel der Planeten*
*Von Ort zu Ort.*
*Das alles sprang hervor bei Seinem Laut,*
*Ward blitzschnell wie ein Weltentraum erschaut,*
*Der ganze Himmel schien herabgebeten,*
*Bei Seinem Wort.*

He spoke, and how He spoke, there appeared in Him
the zodiac, Cherubim and Seraphim,
the Sun-star, the planets in their courses

from station to station.
That everything arose out of His speech,
Was quick as lightning beheld as a cosmic dream,
the whole of heaven appeared invited down
through His Word.

Rudolf Meyer

## *Editor's Addition*

As Rudolf Meyer indicates, Hermann Beckh's understanding of Mark's Gospel is to be most sharply differentiated from Drews' popular publications. Whereas Drews considers the visible constellations, Beckh, as he most carefully explains, is concerned with the *signs* of the zodiac as both representations of archetypal spiritual forces and *their connection to the Earth*. Drews also presents his arguments with reference to constellations outside the zodiac; hence with regard to Jesus on board a ship on the Lake of Galilee, Drews mentions the constellation Argo for no reason other than the fact that it is a ship and has connections with the Argonauts legends. In contrast, the whole of Professor Beckh's account shows a meditative and informed response to the cycle of the Signs as relating to the natural rhythms of the Earthly and Christian year.

Both Drews and Beckh observe that Mark's Gospel is structured around the Sun passing along the zodiac in three rounds. Drews considered that the cycle runs from Aries to Aries, and that the three cycles are essentially undifferentiated. He furthermore manages to include each zodiac constellation as connected to events in the gospel three times. Beckh rightly perceives that this is an inflexible and mechanical pattern.

To a more careful observer it is clear that the gospel follows a path wherein each cycle becomes smaller: we are dealing with a spiral moving downwards to Golgotha, moving through Imagination, Inspiration and Intuition. Moreover, there is evidence in Beckh's presentation that the three stages of the spiral conclude at Golgotha and *then* move into a new sphere of life. In other words, Drews presents the cycle of zodiacal constellations as an aggregate, whereas Beckh understands the signs in connection with the Earth as a living rhythm.

Following a predetermined programme of analysis Drews was keen to locate three episodes in the gospel which connect to the constellation Leo. Beckh does not share these assumptions: he discovers with some surprise that certain signs are 'missing' from the second and third cycles in Mark, they are only implicit with the appropriate acknowledgement of the other gospels, and, still more significant, Leo is not one sign in the annual rhythm through which the gospel passes. It appears to be absent because its presence—through the relationship with Mark himself—irradiates all parts of the narrative.

Finally, Drews wanted to reduce the gospel to a solar myth, a simple story of the Sun moving through the constellations. Beckh is incomparably more sensitive: Mark's Gospel is pre-eminently concerned with the story of the disciples' response to the Christ among them, their struggles, achievements and failures. Central to this is the fact, in Beckh's view, that Mark's Gospel has a very strong focus on the becoming of 'the beloved disciple' John from the earlier 'Lazarus'. Drews has no interest whatsoever in the effect that the Christ has on the circle of disciples.

It is possible to reduce Drews' argument to the kind of revelatory syllogism favoured by David Hume. In Drews' view:

*Premise 1:* = There are a number of legends in antiquity belonging to the constellations; these are simply superstitious and worthless.
*Premise 2*: the Gospel of St. Mark creates a life of Jesus Christ with these legends.
*Conclusion*: the Gospel of St. Mark is worthless as history.

It is doubtful if the conclusion is valid, and very probable that both premises are untrue.

# Mark's Gospel: The Cosmic Rhythm by Prof. Dr Hermann Beckh[369]

Beckh's most recent publication deserves special attention for several reasons. He attempts in his own way to show in detail the influence of the stars in the details of Mark's Gospel. In the figure of Christ-Jesus they are revealed in every moment from the baptism in the Jordan to the Mystery of Golgotha. Beckh follows a path indicated by Rudolf Steiner in his book, *The Spiritual Guidance of Man* (GA 15). The special interest of the present book is to observe how the anthroposophical way of spiritual-scientific knowledge inspired a personality such as Beckh's to these anthroposophical and astrosophical studies. They initially don't appear to be his professional task in the strict sense of the word. And yet if, with understanding, you inwardly sympathetically follow Beckh's development, from his professorial seat in Indology to this book, you can see the logical line of destiny allowing him in this life, especially tangibly to experience the cosmic-earthly stream of development from ancient India up to the present.

In this book—which will be followed with a sequel on John's Gospel—Beckh summarizes all his knowledge and insights in order with them to illuminate the cosmic-starry revelations brought through Christ. He accomplishes this right into the style, not only researching scientifically, but experiencing with a religious and artistic sensibility.

In the midpoint of the exposition stands the Apostles' drama of Christian initiation, the greatest drama of world-history. With strong, holy seriousness Beckh has worked out how Christ with and in the souls of the disciples struggles for the balance between cosmos and earth, between God and man, spirit-world and sensory world. With great love he immerses himself into Christ's work of initiating the souls of the twelve Apostles. With this seriousness and with this love, Beckh dares to approach the Mystery surrounding the two great figures, John the Baptist and John the Apostle and Apocalyptist. To a high degree Beckh has enriched the thoughts of each true pupil of Dr Steiner's anthroposophy, concerning in intimate consecrated hours with this great triad—John the Baptist, Christ, and John, the disciple, whom the Lord loved—in order to experience these thoughts in the centre of their concern as a seed of a new cosmic rhythm of the Christened Earth.

Mark's Gospel is written in the sign of the Lion. It is the sign in which the great cosmic Christ-Sun reigns. In the human organism it is revealed essentially at work in the heart-forces. Both Johns are impulsed by the virtue of courage, where they are pure, by the courage of 'great love'. Beckh rightly calls John the 'Disciple of Love', for his 'I' in the truest sense of the word is a child of Christ's love, engendered and brought to birth in the act of initiation, in 'the awakening, or raising, of Lazarus'.

Something of this courage of the sign of the Lion flows through Beckh's thoughts when he shows right into the details of the apostolic, Christian movements from the individual disciples to the present day. Much becomes clear as though present, experienced by each individual human soul in their way, as the '*drama of Christianity*', with regard to the quarrels of the confessions and the sects. This is shown as especially significant with the spiritual impulses of Judas and Peter. The betrayal by Judas and the threefold denial by Peter are part of the whole 'flight before the cross' by the whole group of disciples. They consequently cannot experience the Mystery of Golgotha with full consciousness. Only John is able to do so, out of the strength of the love of Christ. Thus, Beckh finally leads the reader with John, the disciple and Apostle of Love, before the three crosses on Golgotha.

This book, however, is not intended only as a religious and artistic treatment, but at the same time a special reminder to self-knowledge. This reminder is not expressly made, but certainly as the inner result of such thoughts as Beckh expresses, climaxing in the question of the reader to him/herself: 'Am I able with John to stand before the three crosses on Golgotha?'

Dr Bruno Krüger (1887-1979)

# Mark's Gospel: The Cosmic Rhythm[370]

Thanks to the dedicated work of Alan Stott, a treasure becomes available for the English reader. Professor Hermann Beckh—about whom an introductory article appeared in the previous issue of *New View*—wrote a remarkable and quite unique book on the cosmic influences in the life of Christ-Jesus as portrayed in Mark's Gospel. This was, in fact, the very first substantial publication on one of the gospels which the newly formed Christian Community inspired, and which has never been surpassed. Beckh attempts to show in great detail how the Sun of Christ spiralling inwards three times through the twelve signs of the zodiac during the three years of the Ministry incarnates ever more deeply into the body of Jesus of Nazareth, preparing the Mystery of Golgotha. In the new English edition, the reader is considerably assisted: the author's longer complex sentences become manageable, large sections of text are divided into smaller units with subtitles, and many useful notes have been included as well.

Anyone who loves occupying himself with the twelve archetypal qualities that stream down to Earth from cosmic heights and influence our daily life will find many joyful new insights. Beckh works with the signs[1] from at least four different aspects. First of all, the signs belong to the rhythm of the year with its solstices and equinoxes and the different seasons. Secondly, the same qualities can be found in the rhythm of each day, with the height of summer at midday and the depth of winter in the midnight hour. How often the gospel indicates a specific time of the day receives deeper meaning in this context. Thirdly, out of his great love for music Beckh relates the twelve signs to the twelve musical keys, relating specific events to the quality of the major major or minor keys. Fourthly, he relates the macrocosmic man to the microcosmic man, how every sign relates to a particular area and task of the human body and how the twelve senses originate from cosmic influences. Beckh's introduction to the book is already worth reading as this unity of twelve begins to become alive and audible.

Beckh not only sees Mark's Gospel as a description of the Incarnation of the Cosmic Christ. He sees this gospel as an exact description of the path of initiation trod to its end uniquely by that disciple 'whom

Jesus loved'. So, the first round through the zodiac covering Mark 1 to Mark 6:11 can be seen as the task of developing Imagination. The second round from Mark 6:12 to the end of Mark 8 describes this disciple's effort to rise to sphere of Inspiration. The trials of Intuition are described in the third round of Mark's Gospel. Beckh has no doubts that this path is a very difficult one; with great compassion he comments on the constant failings and denials of the disciples who struggle to rise to the task demanded of them.

Anyone interested in the relationship and co-working of the three Johns (John, son of Zebedee, John the Baptist and Lazarus-John)[2] will find Beckh's view quite unique and particularly interesting. In what way is Lazarus-John, the initiated disciple, present in the Garden of Gethsemane? What has he to do with the Angel that strengthens Christ and the 'young man' that flees naked?

It is indeed a book that opens new horizons to the cosmic aspect of the life of Christ. It gives unexpected insights into the gospel stories over which one has pondered many times.

The English translation not only includes forewords, one by Dr Frieling and one for the English-speaking edition, but also six appendices, relevant articles of Hermann Beckh, a perceptive contemporary review, Rudolf Steiner's 'Last Address' that inspired Beckh's researches for life, a biographical sketch and an overview of the written works of Prof. Hermann Beckh. An *enormous* 'thank-you' goes to the translators and publishers of this unique work!

Erhard Keller

## Notes

1.  Hermann Beckh takes great care in both the *Mark's Gospel* and the companion volume on *John's Gospel* (1930; Eng. tr. 2015) to distinguish between the visible constellations and the 12 zodiacal *signs.* It is the latter that are of premier importance as representing archetypal qualities, which can be found to inform the structures of musical compositions and the 24 keys in the classical tradition. Beckh had already begun his ground-breaking exploration of this with his *Vom geistigen Wesen der Tonarten*, (1922), with an English translation by Alan Stott *The Essence of Tonality*, Anastasi 2002/08. It was also clearly essential for Beckh and the young Christian Community to establish the vast gulf between the atheist analysis of Mark's Gospel by Arthur

Drews (1920), wherein the gospel is seen as a pious fabrication with relationships to the visible stars and constellations with their traditional legends, and an approach to the spiritual qualities conveyed with the signs. Beckh meditatively approaches the latter with a concern for individual signs, polar reciprocity, as well as threefold and fourfold relationships.

2.  Rudolf Steiner's Hamburg lectures on *The Gospel of St. John* (1908) are central to Beckh's presentation of the 'becoming of John' the evangelist and author of Revelation from Lazarus 'he who is sick', John 11. Steiner also considers the sacrifices of John the Baptist which further empower the becoming evangelist, and which inform the ministering angel in the Garden of Gethsemane (Mark 14). For the 'young man' uniquely presented in Mark 14, see Rudolf Steiner's Basel lectures (1912), *The Gospel of St. Mark*, lecture 9. Hermann Beckh can then address the identity of John the son of Zebedee, Mark chapter 1, in this publication.

# John's Gospel: The Cosmic Rhythm, Star Mystery and Earth Mystery by Prof. Dr Hermann Beckh[371]

Hardly two years after the appearance of the book on *Mark's Gospel: The Cosmic Rhythm*, there appears as a kind of sequel, though also understandable on its own—once again a significant book. After that first beginning, to present and appreciate Mark's Gospel with its narration of Christ's mission pre-eminently in the light of the cosmic rhythm, one can meet the announced appearance of the sequel of such a manner of exposition with a certain expectancy. How will Prof. Dr Beckh be able to achieve this task in relation to the 'I'-Mystery of Christ? With this new title he succeeds surprisingly in making a significant advance in the soul-aspect of the stellar-earthly influence and its characterising the 'I'-activity in the human being and the world.

The first thing to be emphasized is the beautiful perfecting of the style, which corresponds to the manner of exposition in rhythmic repetition, and at the same time reveals with constant inner development the path of initiation of John's Gospel in its mutual significance for the human being and the world. Although he deals with the most difficult regions of knowledge, Beckh knows how to unlock these in a manner that with a really serious study and familiarity can be available to *everyone*. The abundance of material, which Beckh offers us, is kept together through the great inner thread; the whole thing harmonizes to a tremendous composition. The attentive reader is called to co-operate in soul, able to transmit to him at the present time the urgently necessary deeper understanding of the gospels.

In a pleasant contrast to many astrological utterances, Prof. Dr Beckh avoids outer sensationalism in order to evoke something popular; and he also avoids one-sided and specialist technical terms. The whole work is traversed and glows through with an elevated enthusiasm for the sublime, world-encompassing mission of Christ in the cosmos, in the stream of time, in the world of the stars and in the earthly world.

With the anthroposophical manner of knowledge gained from Dr Steiner, the work is presented as a completely free, autonomous and self-creative achievement. As such it is a beautiful testament to the creative strengths of the human individuality through the awakening force of anthroposophy, without which this work would not have been presented to human beings to attain self-knowledge.

Out of the rich abundance of the content the great rhythm of initiation may be taken as especially important, which coming out of the pre-Christian ages of the Earth, is crystallized in John the Baptist. From him it is led through the Jordan-Baptism to the initiation of Lazarus-John, which was the first Christian initiation. The motif of the 'Johannine triangle' in the stellar realm of Waterman, Crab and Scorpion, shone over by Uranus, sounds like a basic chord through everything. And what sounds into earthly manifestation, through the great discord of the crisis of humanity through the 'Scorpion', is harmonically resolved through the initiation of John to the 'Eagle'. To recognize, to experience this as the greatest of all transubstantiations, all metamorphoses, becomes the leading-thought of the whole book. The expositions relating to this, already contributing many valuable things in the 'cosmic rhythm of Mark's Gospel', are deepened through John's Gospel. Something of the Johannine eagle's vision and eagle's flight of thought striving for the light pulses through the author's bold flight of thoughts, directed towards and working aloft to the cosmic-'I', in which he seeks with great love to place himself into the soul of John.

In the beautiful chapter on 'giving the name', Beckh has valuable things to say on the great rhythm of breathing, the starry constellation and the earthly zodiac, constellation and zodiacal signs, on human destiny and the Christ-'I' in mutual interpenetration. 'Everything that concerns the "I" as the human member that is for the future and which only exists today in seed-form, belongs to a higher world than the earthly zodiac and the planetary connections of destiny, pointing us to the real worlds of the stars' (p. 166).

The various etymological word-studies of the author with a comparison of the relationships of the languages contribute to a further enlivening of the whole and lead in the same way to yet other paths to understand the 'cosmic word'. Expositions like those on 'body' as Sun-dress, 'life' as Moon-dress, on 'light' as Star-dress, and 'love' as Cosmic-'I' (Cosmic Word) in connection with the changes of the incarnation of the Earth illuminate the tremendous Primal Word in the beginning of John's Gospel, concerning the metamorphosing creative power of the Cosmic Word that with eagle's pinions circles the universe.

With his manner of exposition, Beckh deeply illumines the connections of the Mystery of Golgotha with the Ancient Egyptian, Persian and Indian Mysteries of the past, and with the 'I'-Mystery of the future. It is very interesting to follow the development of the author of his studies in language out of the soul of the ancient epochs of the peoples to the stellar script of the cosmos. The intimate connection of both languages—the language of the divine stellar script and the human stellar language of words—as it is also shown in Wolfram's *Parzifal*, becomes especially clear through Beckh's explanations.

Right into the tangible details he points with this stellar script and the cosmic language of Christ to the possibility of cosmic-earthly prophecy, as lies before us in the Apocalypse of John in grandiose pictures, signs and symbols.

The nature of the three crosses, the physical (of the Father), the etheric (of the Son), the astral (of the Holy Spirit) in their relationships and influence to the will, the feelings and the thinking of the human soul, as well as their metamorphosis through the reception of Christ become clear in many mutual constellations of the stellar clock in the cosmos. The 'Word in the primal beginning' in the sign of the Bull and the Ram, the 'Jordan Baptism' in the sign of the Fishes, the 'Marriage in Cana' in the sign of the Waterman, the 'Conversation by night with Nicodemus' in the sign of the Goat, the 'Samaritan woman at the well' and the 'Healing of the Centurion's son' in the sign of the Archer, that of the 'invalid in Bethesda' in the sign of the Scorpion, etc., then the great crisis of humanity, 'and the darkness comprehended it not', in the further events in the signs of the oscillating Scales, which between the Virgin and the Scorpion seek the balance. Furthermore, the raising of Lazarus-John and the great Mystery of the cross with the Resurrection of Christ Himself become for us in reading the cosmic starry clock revealed as *the* rhythm, in which the inner human being walks initially unconsciously, as he awakes during the day, in the rhythm of clock-time experiences his everyday destiny.

Thus, the cosmic extent becomes humanly accessible. We experience the core of the Mystery-drama of all time, how through all the pictures and events right through John's Gospel the seed is laid and nurtured, in order in the human 'I' to un-bind the will to join Christ and therewith again to go to the Father: 'I go to the Father'; 'No one comes to the Father, but through me' (through the 'I') …

The book is raised to the highest seriousness in the presentation of the crisis of humanity in the sign of the Scorpion, which *alone* John overcomes; it is changed to the sign of the Eagle. For this reason, the Eagle is also the occult sign of John's Gospel. This crisis, before which humanity stands anew today, becomes at the same time the 'verdict' for human beings, whether they want to entrust themselves to the adversary of the depths or the divine in the height. At the division of the ways Christ stands as the 'love in the primal beginning'. Therewith Christ becomes the 'Lord of destiny'. Cf. John 3:19: 'This is the separation and the decision: Light has come into the world, but men loved darkness more than the light, because their deeds weighed on their destiny.' Beckh impressively works out the motif of 'changing destiny' through Jesus Christ in the scene with the woman taken in adultery, as the motif of the *Richten*, judging out of the '*I*', in the sense of *Aufrichten*, getting up, straightening up.

We receive strong stimuli out of the cosmic-earthly stellar constellation with the initiation of Lazarus-John which, in itself and in its relationship to the Mystery of Golgotha forms the actual culmination of John's Gospel, as the one-off, unique example of initiation of *those* human beings who decide out of free-will of love of the I-AM to become 'imitators of Christ'.

In time there came Frau Dr Steiner's worthy decision to publish Dr Steiner's lecture-cycle on John's Gospel in book form, somewhat earlier the Apocalypse of John in duplicated form. Whoever seriously works through this with the seriousness with which Beckh studied them and inwardly re-experienced them, will through both of Beckh's works with quite special deepening of the soul gain much that will contribute a deeper understanding of the lecture-cycles of Dr Steiner.

Dr Bruno Krüger

# Prof. Dr Hermann Beckh, *John's Gospel: The Cosmic Rhythm—Stars and Stones*[372]

Two years ago, Beckh's book appeared on the cosmic rhythm in Mark's Gospel. The longer one concerns oneself with this work the more the evidence of the exposition given there becomes an experience. As soon as the 'star-script' has become somewhat familiar to the reader, he notices how through it many things are confirmed the more he penetrates into Mark's Gospel. If in this way one stands under the growing impression of the remarkable significance of Beckh's book on Mark, one is especially delighted that now this monumental work now finds its continuation in a comprehensive volume on John's Gospel.

The general, basic part is this time devoted to more details. This is very welcome. It really meets an urgent request when it is clearly and scientifically exactly shown how Dr Steiner's indications on the starry worlds relate to what academic knowledge has to say about astronomy.

Beckh gives a satisfactory answer to the questions which have to arise through the 'precession of the equinoxes', through the disparity between 'star constellation' and 'sign'. In addition to this he brings extraordinarily important viewpoints. Beckh gives a satisfactory answer to the question how the 'cultural epochs' indicated by Dr Steiner and linked to the starry constellations relate to the 'official' astronomical periods (spring equinox of the Sun), why, for example, Dr Steiner gives the starting point of the age of Pisces only in the 15th century, whereas astronomically the Sun moves its spring point into Pisces during the time of Christ.

Beckh gives a satisfactory answer to the question what the 'seven planets' mean in the early occult tradition, in which—astronomers today regard it differently—Sun and Moon are also counted, whereas on the other hand Uranus and Neptune are missing. Modern astronomy is acknowledged within its limits; the understanding is opened for quite different viewpoints to justify why people still rightly speak today of the 'seven planets'. For all these basic considerations building bridges to the consciousness of other thoughtful contemporaries one is especially grateful to Beckh.

With the actual section on John's Gospel, Beckh does not fall into the error of those researchers who, for instance, have found something important and under all circumstances apply it everywhere schematically and thus ultimately discredit their discovery. In Mark's Gospel the three rounds through the twelve star-signs are evidently present. What would be more obvious than to see it in John's Gospel? But precisely here the situation is different. Beckh does justice to the unique character of this gospel and recognizes how one does not progress by 'going around the circle', but how the cosmic rhythm here unfolds its own special and intimate manner. It does not concern making circles, doing the round, but with a to-and-fro ('beat of eagle's wing') between the five 'dark' signs, upon which transformation and an imbuing with light is what concerns Johannine Christianity.

The many-sidedness so characteristic for Beckh—in which, however, the thoroughness of the 'Professor' in no way becomes lost—also comes to the light of day in a wonderful way in this new book.

As a philologist Beckh—deepening philology to a real 'love for the Logos' and with sure tact avoiding the dangerous cliffs of etymology—makes revealing remarks, among them concerning the important words in John: *monos* (the only one) and *nomos* (law), *moné* (dwellings) and *nomé* (pasture). He shows how right into the speech-sounds [*m-n* and *n-m*] the polarity of mid-point and starry periphery creates the expressions.

As an Orientalist coming from Yoga and Buddhism, Beckh places several passages of the gospel in a surprisingly new light, for example, the mysterious words 'raising the serpent'. The passages of John's Gospel become cosmically significant, where 'thirsting' is mentioned, when one knows what a depth the concept of '*tanha*', of the great thirst, has in Buddhism. The rightly understood history of religion is indeed no enemy of Christianity. It does not introduce relativity, a levelling out, but lights up from all sides the fulfilment actually achieved through Christ. As an expert of the early occult traditions of astrology and alchemy, Beckh can make us aware of the relationship so essential, especially with John, between the mystery of the stars and matter. The whole monumental greatness of Goethe's words ['Symbolum'] becomes recognizable:

*still ruh'n oben die Sterne,*
*unten die Gräber*

The stars on high are silent still;
Silent the graves, nor make reply.

[*Another translation:*
Deep slumber fill
The stars over-head,
And the foot-trodden grave.]

As a musical person, Beckh possesses a fine feeling for the 'symphonic' character of John's Gospel, for the perceiving and the development, for the 'fuguing', or sounding together, of 'motifs'. The breadths of the horizon, the ability not to be entangled 'only' in theology, are shown, for example, amongst other things, how Beckh with a sure hand introduces Dostoevsky's 'Cana' chapter in *The Brothers Karamazov*, and most beautifully allows the intuition of the great Russian poetic writer to be heard with his expositions on the mysteries of the stars in the wedding in Cana. The exposition receives an enrichment beyond the author's book on Mark, in that to the zodiacal star-signs are added the planets belonging to them. Through this the whole subject becomes more colourful; to the strict theme is added the full soul-chord. Further details will have to remain for another article; for the present, this short indication has to suffice.

If earlier as a theologian one listened to the debates on the genuineness of John's Gospel and suffered under the problem that had to arise from a theology increasingly removed from the spiritual background of the gospels, then one is grateful to one's destiny to have been allowed to look into these new worlds of a cosmically great understanding. It seems that one may say with even deeper justification than the humanists: 'O *litteras, o saeculum! juvat vivere! Es ist eines Lust zu leben!*'—'O new knowledge! O century! It is a joy to be alive!'

Rudolf Frieling

# Alchymy: The Mystery of the Material World[373] by Prof. Dr Hermann Beckh

This book of 119 pages that manages to master an over-abundance of content has to be seen in the context of a great survey on the star-script. *Mark's Gospel: The Cosmic Rhythm* (1928) shows the principle of ordering the stars in the writing of the Lion-evangelist. There the cosmic Figure appears in the earthly destiny. The earthly life of Christ exists as starry script that is written into the Earth. In 1930 there followed the book on John's Gospel, which we reviewed in the November issue of this journal. There the way of observing, which in the earthly realm follows the mysteriously revealed sound-figures of the stars, is extended to John's Gospel. Here it is shown in particular how looking at the stars demands from an inner lawfulness to be supplemented through quite a different viewpoint— through looking at the mysteries of matter of the Earth's depths. Goethe touches on this polarity of the starry heights and the depths of matter in the last chapters of *Wilhelm Meister's Journeyman Years* [1821/29]:

> Here there is the mysterious, starry transfigured figure of Makarien, in whom a sacred astrology is essentially incorporated, so that in her loosely grounded soul-organism she can follow the planetary courses in their rhythmical dances in the cosmic distances, in order to bring what was experienced there as moral impulses into earthly life. And on the other side the 'she who feels the metals', the friend of Montan, who in a similar manner, only in the opposite direction, senses the mysteries of the earthly depths (Beckh, Eng. ed. p. 82).

In the book on John's Gospel, the 'mystery of the stars' meets the 'mystery of the Earth; the latter naturally overflowed into further discussion, hence the present monograph on alchymy. In reading and overviewing Beckh's work one gains the encouraging feeling of the right inner balance, of the fully human quality, as Goethe expressed in *Wilhelm Meister*: 'To manifest the mutual qualities of both in the passing appearances of life is the highest achievement to which the human being can strive.'

This mutual relationship of the world of the stars and matter is highly interesting, in particular for someone involved in the sacramental life. In the liturgical celebration the working together of the two worlds becomes an impressive event.

Those who have perceived the divine order in the sequence of the Act of Consecration of Man, possess a key to the starry script, to the mysteries of composition of the gospels. We feel the heavenly lawfulness in the Christ-destinies which could only be played out in such a way and in no other, 'in order to fulfil the scriptures'. In the same way as the priest at the altar in what he does realizes 'what stands written' in the Missal, so Christ celebrates His earthly life, fulfilling, 'what stands written'. It is not only written in the prophets, but especially in the starry script of the heavens. This was the cosmic Missal for the holy deed of the life of Christ, which like the Sun solemnly passes from star-constellation to star-constellation. The starry element meets us in the liturgical celebration initially in everything that comprises 'order'. This order is in the most literal sense the 'heavenly daughter bestowing blessing'.

A further experience one can have during the eucharist is the 'element' which is formed from on high. Not only the 'sense and taste for the eternal' is addressed in the sacrament, but also the feeling for the mystery of matter. Hereby one may not think of 'materialism'. Is it not precisely materialism, which is most helpless facing the actual essence of matter, as Dr Steiner paradoxically formulates the situation? Experience confirms that precisely the materialist will ultimately become empty and void, because he loses reverence for its miracle. Precisely the sacramental ritual dealing with matter is one of the most effective weapons against sclerotic materialism, because it awakens the sense for the mystery of matter and keeps it alive.

If I may insert a personal recollection here, I remember the golden chalice in the rectory in which I grew up; with what feelings I observed it when it was brought out of its box for the celebration of the Lord's Supper; full of intuitive hunches, the mystery of gold passed through the soul—something resounded in the soul that later helped in finding the way to The Christian Community. In such feelings from boyhood probably old, primordial yearnings of humanity for the Sun echoed on, which die out to the extent that people become abstract and intellectual. Die out—or even undergo eerie distortion. A romantic poet speaks of *'auri sacra fames'*, and means the accursed, damned hunger for gold. But *'sacra fames'*—*sacra* originally does mean 'holy'. The cursed hunger for gold is something of a mistaken, terribly corrupt, but originally a sacred desire of the soul for Sun-filled gold.

What is popularly known about alchemy relates more to the daemonic attitude of the 'search for gold'. But there was another side to alchymy pursued by the true alchymists in whom the ancient sacred yearning still lived. These childhood hunches of the race speak an obscure language of dream in the alchymical writings that have come down to us. At most, a modern natural scientist has to regard this as 'sometimes poetic', for the rest nevertheless as nonsensical fantasy. This whole hieroglyphic world of pictures of alchymical literature would have to die out without hope of rescue before the scientific-oriented present-day consciousness, had not Rudolf Steiner's anthroposophy as a spiritual science rehabilitated these hunches within a scientifically clear conception of the world. Professor Beckh, as somebody with a scientific conscience, following the insights and stimuli of Rudolf Steiner, translates into understandable concepts what the early alchymists spoke in obscure riddles. The oracular words of thinkers and 'brooders', the flashes of intuition of the gifted artist, the 'ecstatic confessions' of visionaries, everything comes together within a surveyable world-conception. Dawning premonitions of humanity become overwhelming, insightful findings in the broad daylight of a spirit-devoted thinking.

After reading such a book, one turns again with new joy to the impressions of the sacraments. The central mystery of metamorphosis, or transformation, is seen in a new light. Precisely here is the most tremendous 'mutual relationship' of the world of the stars and that of matter. Here in particular one can approach the nature of this polarity: the shining stars above, the starry nature enchanted in a sunken, nocturnal darkness below. In the introductory words spoken each time with the metamorphosis, these are both united: Christ raising his gaze to heaven and his uniting Himself in blessing over bread and wine.

In five chapters of his very concentratedly written book, Beckh writes about inexhaustible matter:

I.   Alchymy and Man's Past. (Rosicrucianism, the Virginal Earth, the philosopher's stone.) After discussing the early hunches, there follows

II.  Alchymy and Mankind in the Present: an argument with modern science. The process which the alchymists before the forum of recent science in the first instance have lost, is taken up again with a new viewpoint. Precisely the most recent researches approach the alchymical realm.

III. Alchymy and the Bible (Old Testament). Here the most revered first chapter of Genesis is respected for its alchymical meaning. Beckh does not fall into the one-sidedness ascribing to the Bible only the alchymical meaning. The Bible is so rich that it can give something to the various viewpoints. Besides that which hitherto appeals in the Bible to devout people, there appears as a new aspect (or rather re-newed aspect): the alchymical one. The Bible becomes increasingly powerful, commanding respect.

IV. Alchymy and Mythology. Pre-Christian revelation belongs not only to the Old Testament. A primal revelation exists, which also appears in the myths of peoples. 'Isis; *The Rhinegold*; the Golden Fleece; Venus-Urania.' It would be wrong in the context of this summary to state in an even shorter manner what in Beckh's book is already presented summarily enough, which certainly some readers find a pity. One thing may be expressed: the fear that artistically fashioned pictures like the early myths would lose something through intellectual expla- nation. This happens often enough when these contents are 'laid hold of and explained away'. But here the understanding awakens feelings and deepens feelings, the inside into the hid- den truth of these often so mysterious pictures frees as it were the feeling[s] out of the soul for their beauty and magnificence. So, it can happen especially with the Uranus-Venus myth the description of which can probably be reckoned as one of the most splendid passages in the book.

V. Alchymy and Man's Future: Here the alchymical meaning of the New Testament, in particular the Johannine writings stand in the centre. As in the first chapters of the Bible, also the last chapter (the Apocalypse), the alchymical theme becomes again important with some motifs that were already touched on in John's Gospel. If one sees what American influenced sects make of the Apocalypse, how otherwise educated Christians turn away from this book in non-understanding, then one is the more grateful when the content so deep in Mysteries of this mysterious book is raised into the light of consciousness, as happens here in the valuation of anthroposophical insights.

How wonderfully there shines here the last words of Christ in the Bible: 'I am the root and offspring of David, the bright morning star!' [Rev. 22:16].

In our time of the Depression and the terrible financial crisis one loses so easily the perspective on the great tasks of humanity. Especially today when the fetters of material existence can be felt so painfully it does one good to look at the 'other side' of matter, on to the hidden mystery of the world of matter, on to the silent hope of all creatures, to be transformed by redeemed humanity. This can give us joy an enthusiasm for our earthly existence. Beckh could not have ended his book with a better ending than with Goethe's magnificent Lodge-poem ['Symbolum'], which finishes with the words: 'Wir heißen euch hoffen—we invite you to hope.'

Rudolf Frieling

# Prof. Dr Hermann Beckh. *Das Parsifal =Christus=Erlebnis* ('The Parsifal=Christ=Experience in Wagner's Music Drama')[374]

The author, who already with his booklet *The Essence of Tonality* [Anastasi 2008] extends his mythological and cultic researches on spiritual-scientific bases in the direction of the less-researched realm of the art of music, makes with the above publication a further advance with a study of the 'stage dedication festival play', Wagner's *Parsifal*. This little book recommends itself straight away through its warm red case with the golden lettering and pictorial motif drawn by Margarita Woloschin—reproduced for the English edition—in which the basic concept is meditatively concentrated.

In this work, Prof. Beckh in an impressive manner leads the reader into a deeper understanding of this final word-music drama crowning Wagner's life's work. Above all he seeks to awaken a *consciousness* of what is generally only felt, that is, the sounding drama of the musical and esoteric language of the seven scenes: the Swan, the Walk to the Grail Castle, Amfortas and the Grail, and so on. With this work, Beckh faces the light off-hand objection that with this work he has only added yet another to the many, sometimes quite good, explanations of this Christian Mystery play. Through the manner of spiritual-scientific research, he seeks with particular earnestness to fulfil Wagner's wonderful admonition to gain knowledge in the final words of Parsifal:

*Nicht soll der mehr verschlossen seen: Enthüllet den Gral, öffnet den Schrein!*

No more shall it be hidden; uncover now the Grail, open the shrine!

To meet this admonition to gain knowledge, Beckh's revelations convey important matters, originating out of meditative experience on the musical motifs and the dramatic, pictorial events of the work. Beckh does not proceed in the analytical, dissecting sense, as so often in the completely inadequate outer interpretation of the motifs and themes, whereby the spirit of the work of art is killed. But he proceeds in a synthetic, spiritually developed sense, so that in the soul of the engaged reader something can come to light of Parsifal's first experience of the Grail: 'I scarcely tread yet seem already to have come far.'

Beckh observes the progress of the Mystery play that engages with the deepest Mysteries of the world-evolution and of human development, with the leitmotif of the Christ-Impulse, of the One who loves, who suffers, and who emerges victorious. How this leitmotif is woven by the other, how the Sun is surrounded by the round-dance of the stars—to establish this is particularly well achieved with the observations on the Prelude to *Parsifal*. This portrays the inner experience of the Last Supper in musical sound, the Mystery of metamorphosis, of transubstantiation.

The particularly valuable thing about this book is the manner how for not particularly musical people it personally, individually, leads the soul of the reader in a generally understandable way, to the threshold of this change from suffering to victory, from the Mystery of Golgotha to resurrection. Beckh concentrates his presentations especially on the Redeemer's look of love sounding from within, looking full of compassion outwards. This is the leitmotif and the suffering motif of the longing of Kundry's double nature:

> *Nun such' ich Ihn, von Welt zu Welt, Ihm wieder zu begegnen …*
> Now I seek Him from world to world to meet Him once again…

'From world to world', whereby Wagner wanted slowly to prepare his age for deeper realms of experience of the searching soul, for the intuitive consciousness 'from incarnation to incarnation', from the karma of the Christ-Impulse in the pattern of re-embodiments.

With these leading thoughts and leading feelings, Beckh takes the figure of Parsifal, the human being searching, suffering, and through the power of Christ emerging victorious, in whose metamorphosis he sees man's actual task. Through the already-mentioned seven scenes from the experience with the swan to the 'Good-Friday music', we are led, accompanying Parsifal on the path of transformation, the transubstantiation of the human soul through the *will* symbolized by the Spear, in the striving to the Communion with the power of the victorious, resurrected One, the spiritually present Christ.

It lies in the essence of this work of art that it can be seen and interpreted from various sides. Beckh takes here the path into the inner realm of the human soul. The macrocosmic aspect of the starry script in *Parsifal*, which is no less great, he only touches on, although the author of *Mark's Gospel: The Cosmic Rhythm* would have had much to say.

The most important musical examples added with the sung text, give moreover an introduction to follow and check for oneself the author's explanations, and in meditation to deepen one's knowledge. The book does not intend to close off but rather to stimulate the reader's conscious deepening of the experience of *Parsifal* as a work of art, both poetically and musically. In many respects it can contribute something to reveal the present task of the consciousness-soul and its connection with Christ in the realm of aesthetic experience. For the sake of this task, the book should find its way to many souls whose hearts are set on this task.

[The English translation, *The Parsifal=Christ=Experience*, Leominster: Anastasi 2015, contains in addition three remarkable studies: Hermann Beckh's essay 'Richard Wagner and Christianity' (1933), and two articles, Emil Bock, 'Twilight of the Gods and Resurrection: Wagner's Mythological Wisdom' (1926) and Rudolf Frieling, 'King Ludwig II of Bavaria' (1956)—*Tr. note.*]

Dr Bruno Krüger

# The Works of Prof. Dr Hermann Beckh

'An abundance of books came into existence whose significance perhaps will only be properly appreciated in the future.'
(Lic. Emil Bock, 'Hermann Beckh' in *Zeitgenossen Weggenossen Wegbereiter*, Stuttgart: Urachhaus 1959. P. 132)

*

*Die Beweislast nach dem Bürgerlichen Gesetzbuch*
'The burden of proof according to the Code of Civil Law'
Prize essay, awarded distinction from the Law Faculty the University of Munich
München und Berlin 1899. Download: http://dlib-pr.mpier.mpg.de/m/kleioc/0010/exec/books/%22103926%22/

*Ein Beitrag zur Textkritik an Kālidāsas Meghadūta*
'A contribution for the text criticism of Kālidāsa's Meghadūta'
Doctorate dissertation approved by the Department of Philosophy of the University of Berlin 1907.

*Die tibetische Übersetzung von Kālidāsas Meghadūta*
'The Tibetan translation of Kālidāsa's Meghadūta'
Edited and with a German translation, Berlin 1907/2011.

*Beiträge zur tibetischen Grammatik, Lexikogaphie, Stilistik und Metrik*
Habilitationsschrift. Berlin 1908.
'Contributions to Tibetan grammar, lexicography, style and prosody'
Inaugural dissertation.

*Udānavarga*
A collection of Buddhist sayings in the Tibetan language
Berlin 1911 (also reprinted by Walter de Gruyter, 2013).

*Verzeichnis der tibetischen Handschriften*
'Catalogue of Tibetan MSS in the Royal Library in Berlin' (Vol. 24 of the Manuscript Catalogue)
First division: Kanjur (Bhak-Khgur)
Berlin 1914/2011/14.

*Buddha und seine Lehre*
'Buddha and his Teaching.' Vol. 1: The Life. Vol. 2: The Teaching
Sammlung Göschen. Berlin & Leipzig 1916. Third edition 1928.
Later one-volume editions, Stuttgart: Urachhaus 1958/98/2012. Tr.
into Dutch and Japanese.
Eng. tr. *Buddha's Life and Teaching*, Temple Lodge 2019.

*'Rudolf Steiner und das Morgenland'*
in *Vom Lebenswerk Rudolf Steiners*
Ed. Friedrich Rittelmeyer, München: Chr. Kaiser 1921
Reprint by HP, Univ. of Michigan (www.lib.umich.edu) (download:
www.archive.org).
Eng. tr. in *Hermann Beckh and the Spirit-Word*, Leominster: Anastasi
2015. 33-65; also in *The Source of Speech*, 16-71.

*Der physische und der geistige Ursprung der Sprache*
The physical and the spiritual origin of language. Stuttgart 1921.
*'Es werde Licht!'*
'Let there be light!'
The primal biblical words of creation and the primal significance of the
sounds in the light of spiritual science. Stuttgart 1921.
*Etymologie und Lautbedeutung*
Etymology and the significance of speech sounds in the light of spiri-
tual science
Stuttgart 1922/2013.

All three essays on language (above) reprinted in
*Neue Wege zur Ursprache*, Stuttgart 1954
Eng. tr. *The Source of Speech,* with all relevant essays and articles. Tem-
ple Lodge, 2019.

*Anthroposophie und Universitätswissenschaft*
'Anthroposophy and University Knowledge'
Breslau 1922. Eng. tr. in *Hermann Beckh and the Spirit-Word*, Leominster:
Anastasi 2015. 71-101; also in *The Source of Speech.* 181-207.

*Vom geistigen Wesen der Tonarten*
*The Essence of Tonality: An Attempt to view musical Problems in the Light of
Spiritual Science*. With diagrams. Breslau 1922. Third edition 1932. Eng.
tr. Leominster: Anastasi 2008.

*Der Ursprung im Lichte. Bilder der Genesis*
*Our Origin in the Light: Pictures from Genesis*. Stuttgart 1924. Eng. tr. with
*From the Mysteries*, and *Zarathustra*. Temple Lodge 2020.

*Von Buddha zu Christus*
*From Buddha to Christ*
Stuttgart 1925 (tr. in Norwegian, Oslo 1926); Eng. tr. of short digest Floris Books 1978.
New Eng. tr. of full text, with additions, Temple Lodge 2019.

*Das neue Jerusalem*
'The New Jerusalem'
A poetic work, in the collaborative work *Gegenwartsrätsel im Offenbarungslicht* ('Problems of the present in the light of revelation'), Stuttgart 1925. Eng. tr. incl. in *John's Gospel: The Cosmic Rhythm —Stars and Stones*. Leominster: Anastasi 2015. 459-77; also in *Alchymy*. 100-13.

*Der Hingang des Vollendeten*
'The Passing of the Accomplished One and His Nirvāṇa (Mahāparinibbāna Sutta of the Pali canon)'.
Translated and with an introduction. Stuttgart 1925/60. Eng. tr. *Buddha's Passing*, forthcoming.

*Zarathustra*
Stuttgart 1927
Eng. tr. with additional articles, pub. with *From the Mysteries* and *Genesis*, Temple Lodge, 2020.

*Aus der Welt der Mysterien*
*From the Mysteries*
Seven articles (reprinted). Basel 1927. Eng. tr. as triple book with *Genesis* and *Zarathustra*, Temple Lodge, 2020.

*Der kosmische Rhythmus im Markus-Evangelium*
*Mark's Gospel: The Cosmic Rhythm*
Basel 1928/60/97. Eng. tr. Leominster: Anastasi 2015.

*Der kosmische Rhythmus, das Sternengeheimnis und Erdengeheimnis im Johannes-Evangelium*
*John's Gospel: The Cosmic Rhythm—Stars and Stones*

Basel 1930. Eng. tr. Leominster: Anastasi 2015.

*Das Christus-Erlebnis in Dramatisch-Musikalischen von Richard Wagners 'Parsifal'*
*The Parsifal=Christ=Experience in Wagner's Music Drama*
Stuttgart 1930. Eng. tr. with 'Richard Wagner and Christianity' (1933) and essays by Emil Bock (1928) and Rudolf Frieling (1956), Leominster: Anastasi 2015.

*Vom Geheimnis der Stoffeswelt (Alchymie)*
*Alchymy: The Mystery of the Material World*
Basel 1931/37/42/2007/13. Eng. tr. with appendices, Temple Lodge 2019.

*Der Hymnus an die Erde*
*The Hymn to the Earth*: From the Old Indian Atharvaveda: A memorial to the oldest poem and to the early Aryans. Stuttgart 1934/60. Eng. tr. forthcoming.

*Psalm 23 aus der Heilige Schrift*
*Psalm 23*: Newly translated from the original text and set to music, op. 7. Stuttgart 1935.

*Die Rosen von Damaskus*
*The Roses of Damascus*. 'Thibaut von Champagne'. The ballad by Conrad Ferdinand Meyer. For solo high voice with piano accompaniment set to music, op. 8. Stuttgart 1937.

*Die Sprache der Tonart*
*The Language of Tonality in the Music from Bach to Bruckner with special reference to Wagner's Music Dramas*
Stuttgart 1937/87/99. Eng. tr. Leominster: Anastasi 2015.

*Richard Wagner und das Christentum*
*Richard Wagner and Christianity*
Stuttgart 1933. Eng. tr. incl. in *The Parsifal=Christ=Experience in Wagner's Music Drama*. Leominster: Anastasi 2015.

*Indische Weisheit und Christendom*
*Indian Wisdom and Christianity*

Articles: 10 reprinted and 9 from the literary estate
Stuttgart 1938. Eng. tr. forthcoming.

*Der Mensch und die Musik*
*The Human Being and Music*
A recently discovered history of music in Ms (1936):
Five chapters pub. in three articles in *Der Europäer*, Basel
09.2005/09.2006/02.2007-08.
http://www.perseus.ch/archive/category/europaer/europaer-archiv
Full restored text translated into English, Temple Lodge 2019.

*The Language of the Stars: Zodiac and Planets in Relation to the Human Being*
with a chapter on the *Anthroposophical Soul-Calendar (1911-12)* (1930-33)
by Prof. Dr Hermann Beckh
and *The Cosmic Rhythm in the Creed: for readers of Beckh's books* (1930-31)
by Dr Rudolf Frieling
with an Introduction and Reviews by Rudolf Frieling and others
translated from the German by Maren & Alan Stott
edited by Neil Franklin.
Temple Lodge Publishing 2020.

*Collected Articles of Rev. Prof. Hermann Beckh* translated into English, forthcoming.

# Three Further Publications

*Hermann Beckh: Leben und Werk*
*Hermann Beckh: Life and Work*
by Gundhild Kačer-Bock (d. 2008)
Stuttgart 1997. Eng. tr. Leominster: Anastasi 2016.

*Hermann Beckh and the Spirit-Word:*
*Orientalist, Christian Priest and Independent Scholar*
Anastasi 2015. Contents includes:
    Alan Stott, 'Hermann Beckh and the Twenty-First Century'
    H. B., 'Rudolf Steiner and the East'
    H. B., 'Anthroposophy and University Knowledge'
    H. B., 'Meeting Rudolf Steiner'
    Numerous appreciations by Beckh's colleagues and his biographer;
    introducing the *Collected Works of Hermann Beckh.*

*Festschrift in Honour of Hermann Beckh*
on the Centenary of *Buddha und seine Lehre* and the publication of the
English translation *Buddha's Life and Teaching* also the first publication
of Beckh's *The Mystery of Human Creativity: The Human Being and Music*
and the English translation of Gundhild Kačer-Bock's biography *Hermann Beckh: Life and Work.* Anastasi 2016.
Contents include:
Prof. Hermann Beckh: 'Steiner und Buddha' (1931; previously unpublished)
Prof. Hermann Beckh: 'Buddhism and its significance for humanity'
'Buddhism and its Significance for Humanity' (1928)
Prof. Hermann Beckh, 'The Little Squirrel, the Moonlight Princess and
the Little Rose', illustrated by Tatjana Schellhase
'Prof. Hermann Beckh' by Johannes Lenz (Berlin)
'Daniel Simeon and Asita the Sage' by Manfred Krüger (Nuremberg)
Oliver Heinl: 'Prof. Dr Hermann Beckh—Pioneer linguistic work in the
light of Christ'
Susana Ulrich-Alvarez Ulloa (Öschelbronn): 'The Search for the Lost Word'
Katrin Binder (Nottingham): '*Buddha's Life and Work* one hundred years on'
Alan Stott (Stourbridge): 'Hermann Beckh: Musician' (a lecture, Dornach, April 2016)
Rosemaria Bock (Stuttgart): 'Recollections' (with photos)
Gundhild Kačer-Bock (1924-2008) Memories & Appreciations.

# Notes

1.  The memoirs form the basis of his biography written (1997) by Gundhild Kačer-Bock, Eng. tr. by M. & A. Stott, *Hermann Beckh: Life and Work*, Leominster: Anastasi 2016.

2.  The article (1931) was not accepted for publication. It is published for the first time in English translation: *Festschrift: Essays in Honour of Hermann Beckh* (Leominster: Anastasi 2016).

3.  Beckh tells his own story honestly in order to explain, as fully as time allowed him, the anthroposophical contribution to Buddhist studies. Beckh loved the Buddha because he saw his great significance for humanity. The author spoke and wrote in order to share his discoveries. His voice is as contemporary as ever, if not more so today.

4.  References to important recent discoveries on Bach's cryptic, theological statements in his instrumental cycles and Chopin's musical creations in all the musical keys (the *Preludes*) are included in the Introduction to *The Language of Tonality*, Leominster: Anastasi, 2015 (Temple Lodge, forthcoming). To summarize: Beckh's description of a musical journey through all the keys on the circle of fifths is at the same time a journey through the zodiac as the creative archetypes. He takes the three 'crosses of the 12 key-centres' to reveal this journey with musical references to well-known compositions from Bach to Bruckner. The account features a detailed study of Wagner's music dramas, where the extra evidence of a libretto also guides the journey. Beckh's account, based on reasoned intuition, is acknowledged by later anthroposophical musicians who add their research (Christoph Peter, Friedrich Oberkogler, etc.). Later research has revealed Bach's hidden sub-plot for the instrumental cycles, beginning with Hans Nissen (Der Sinn des Wohltemperierten Klaviers II. Teil, *Bachjahrbuch* 1951-52, pp. 54-80. Online: https://doi.org/10.13141/bjb. v19521567

    Eng. tr. A. S. in Ms, notes some typos giving a few inaccurate numbers). Nissen's thesis was essentially confirmed by Hertha Kluge-Kahn, *Johann Sebastian Bach: die verschlüsselten theologischen Aussagen in seinem Spätwerk*, Wolfenbüttel & Zürich: Möseler Verlag 1985 (Eng. tr. forthcoming). Helga Thoene added significantly with research on the solo violin works (http://www.helga-thoene. de). Bach, amongst other things in a multi-coded approach, hid chorale tunes in free rhythms and made extensive use of gematria; the evidence suggests he was a Rosicrucian. Bach took the chromatic order of the musical keys. Chopin was the first major composer to research the alternative order of keys, the circle of fifths, as a spiritual journey in his *24 Preludes*, op. 28. From the evidence of the score, Chopin's intention to write a homage to Bach, with details of how he did it, are initially discussed by Alan Stott, 'Celebrating the Musical System—an esoteric study: Bach and Chopin', in *Festschrift: Essays in Honour of Hermann Beckh*. Anastasi, 2016, pp. 165-81.

5.  H.B.: 'I intend in any case to publish the content of this work on star-knowledge' *Contribution* No. 14; also mentioned by Gundhild Kačer-Bock, *Hermann Beckh: Life and Work*, 2016, p. 41, in the context of Beckh's final years.

6.  'Zum Geleit', Introduction to *Indische Weisheit und Christentum: Gesammelte Studien*, ed. by Lic. Robert Goebel and Rudolf Meyer. Stuttgart: Verlag Urachhaus 1938, p. 3.

7.  Hermann Beckh. *The Language of Tonality*. Leominster: Anastasi 2015; Temple Lodge, forthcoming. Tr. and with Introduction 'Hermann Beckh in the Twenty-First Century' by A. S. (pp. 15-42). Prof. Beckh would not have heard Gustav Holst's (1874-1934)—the name may sound Teutonic, but the composer was thoroughly British—orchestral suite *The Planets*, op. 32 (written 1914 & 1916; probably influenced by Alan Leo's astrological work *The Art of Synthesis*, 1912), which only later became internationally known, especially through the interpretations of Herbert von Karajan (famous recordings with the VPO 1961, and the Berlin Phil. 1981). True, Beckh did not only choose the subject of music to develop his theme. For this present Introduction, I have mentioned a few writers of English, English literature being the internationally recognized cultural achievement (an important balance for a 'nation of shopkeepers', or 'consumer society', as we would say today). Obviously other lines of enquiry exist (the visual arts, sacred sciences, and so on) beyond the references mentioned here to this and other cultural phenomena.

8.  'This attempt is the first up to now and unique' (RB 126). Beckh's life's work is all of a piece, invariably based on first-hand study of original texts in the original languages, as well as a vast knowledge of musical scores which he played on the piano—*Tr. note*.

9.  Rudolf Steiner, *Christ and the Spiritual World: the Search for the Holy Grail* (GA 149). Lectures, Leipzig 1913-14. London; Rudolf Steiner Press, 2008.

10. www.rsarchive.org is a useful site. The fate of Beckh's copy of *Geheimwissenschaft* is described by Wilhelm Hörner (see p. 488 above). During his military service during World War II, the young Wilhelm Hörner was carrying the book in his backpack. Forced to lighten his load, he faced having to ditch the volume. Reluctantly he threw it into the forest, retrieved it twice, only finally to cast it from him. A painful sacrifice! The marginalia of Beckh's copy was apparently full of 'astronomical and alchemical symbols'.

11. John 14:15 (NIV). By now that Voice is obeyed; at the same time it is recognized as our own innermost possession (cf. the final chapter of Schwartz [FN 12, below]). One is reminded of Psalm 40:6 (Heb.): 'Ears thou hast dug for me', that is, a nature 'formed for obedience' (cf. R.M. Benson, *The War-Songs of the Prince of Peace*. London: John Murray 1901. I. P. 23).

12. Michael Ward. *Planet Narnia*. Oxford: OUP 2008. Lewis' 'science fiction' trilogy is also receiving renewed interest, see: Sandford Schwartz, C.S. *Lewis on the Final Frontier: Science and the Supernatural in the Space Trilogy*, OUP 2009; all three novels, Schwartz demonstrates, use a chiastic structure. Jean Seznec, *The Survival of the Pagan Gods: The Mythological Tradition and its Place in Renaissance Humanism and Art*, Princeton Univ. Press, 1953/72, is a classic text of world mythology to stand alongside Edgar Wind, *Pagan Mysteries in the Renaissance*. Penguin Books 1967; Norton & Co. 1968, OUP 1980.

13. John Docherty. *The Literary Products of the Lewis Carroll—George MacDonald Friendship*. Lewiston, Queenston, Lampeter: Edwin Mellen Press 1997.

14. The 'consciousness-soul', alternative name 'spiritual soul': terms used in anthroposophy for that stage of spiritual development where eternal truth begins to light up—as Beckh terms it, the 'spirit in the 'I''—in the process of spiritual self-knowledge. Culturally prepared in the West by remarkable historic pioneers but appearing more widely from the fifteenth century onwards, it is individually developed particularly between the years 35-42. Shakespeare gave its development an enormous boost: see Colin Still, *The Tempest: Shakespeare's Mystery Drama* (C. Palmer 1921; Scholarly Press 1972; Kessinger 2010); the author demonstrates that Shakespeare's late play follows the authentic mystical tradition, the details of which he reconstructs from surviving texts from the ancient world; rewritten as *The Timeless Theme*, Ivor Nicholson & Watson 1936; Folcroft Library Editions 1969, reprinted several times. The poet Ted Hughes has revealed the myth/s the Bard lived and with which he worked out in detail the 'tragic equation', the origin of tragedy as well as its resolution through transmutation: Ted Hughes, *Shakespeare and the Goddess of Complete Being*, London & Boston: Faber & Faber 1992. John Vyvyan's Shakespearean trilogy (1959, '60, '61), a peak in criticism, should not be overlooked, republished (also e-books): John Vyvyan, *The Shakespearean Ethic*, London: Shepheard-Walwyn, 2011; *Shakespeare and the Rose of Love: A Study of the Early Plays in Relation to the Medieval Philosophy of Love*, Shepheard-Walwyn, 2013; and *Shakespeare and Platonic Beauty*, Shepheard-Walwyn, 2014.

15. 'The Twelve', first pub. in *The Christian Community Journal*, March/April 1948, pp. 39-43, reprinted in Kenneth Gibson, *Adam Bittleston: His Life, Work and Thought*, Floris Books, Edinburgh 2010, pp. 222-27. Bittleston's monograph on the stars—*Human Needs and Cosmic Answers: The Spirit of the Circling Stars*, Floris Books, Edinburgh 1993.

In another arrangement, Johannes Kühn suggests the two wings of the table be imagined as the zodiac circle, as it were made straight. The viewer stands between Simon (Ram) and Bartholomew (Fishes). This position, the heavenly origin of His Incarnation, was given up by Christ's free deed to come to the Earth. Christ (as the cosmic Sun) rays over the whole zodiac, He appears on Earth historically in the opposite position, between the Scales and the Virgin (between John and Thomas). Thus the zodiac order from Ram to Fishes is represented by the disciples (sitting position, not heads) from right to left of the painting. Johannes Kühn, *Die Darstellung des Abendmahls*, Columban-Verlag, Schaffhausen 1948, pp. 43-5.

16. Horst Lozynski, *Enhüllte Geheimnisse vom Abendmahl des Leonardo da Vinci*, 2 Vols., Verlag Horst Lozynski 1987. (Enquiries: Verein für Homa-Therapie e.V. E-mail address: shop@homa-hofheiligenberg.de/ Eng. tr. A. S. in MS. Lozynski, b. 1936 [today Heigl], runs a therapeutic centre and study centre in south Germany.) The disciples are arranged, with detailed explanations, according to the triune groups relating to the four elements: Simon (*Saggitarius*), Judas Thaddeus (*Leo*), Matthew (*Aries*); Thomas (*Gemini*), James the Great (*Aquarius*), Philip (*Libra*); Bartholomew (*Taurus*), James the Less (*Virgo*), Andrew (*Capricorn*); Judas (*Scorpio*), Peter (*Pisces*), John (*Cancer*). (Incidentally, a hitherto unknown chamber in the Great Pyramid, exactly described by Lozynski in 1987, found possible confirmation in 2017, but further information from Giza has not yet been made public.)

17. Rudolf Steiner, *The Inner Realities of Evolution*, GA 132, Berlin, 7 Nov. 1911.

18. Readers interested in other pioneers of a Christ-oriented astrosophy will know above all the work of Elisabeth Vreede (1879-1943) and Willi Sucher (1902-85).

19. John Henry Newman (1801-1890) (canonized in 2019) is the outstanding nineteenth-century writer of prose in the English language. Much of Newman's thought, progressive in its day, is regarded today as a main architect of Vatican II. In his day Newman dared to say: 'I want an intelligent, well-instructed laity; I am not denying you are such already: but I mean to be severe, and, as some would say, exorbitant in my demands. I wish you to enlarge your knowledge, to cultivate your reason, to get an insight into the relation of truth to truth, to learn to view things as they are, to understand how faith and reason stand to each other, what are the bases and principles of Catholicism and where lie the main inconsistencies and absurdities of the Protestant theory. I have no apprehension you will be the worse Catholics for familiarity with these subjects, provided you cherish a vivid sense of God above, and keep in mind that you have souls to be judged and to be saved. In all times the laity have been the measure of the Catholic spirit...' J.H. Newman, *Lectures on the Present Position of Catholics in England*. Birmingham 1852. London: Burns & Oates. 1885. Longmans & Green 1896. 390. Online:

    http://www.newmanreader.org/works/england/lecture9.html

20. See in *Hermann Beckh & the Spirit-Word*, Leominster: Anastasi 2015, footnote 9, p. 25f. and *Festschrift: Essays in Honour of Hermann Beckh*, Anastasi 2016.

21. A reminder that the rhythms of 7 and 12 govern artistic and social life with unlimited therapeutic and developmental applications, see, for example, Werner Barfod, *The Zodiac Gestures of Eurythmy*, Edinburgh: Floris Books 2019; the gestures are to be observed in standard, daily human work. Moreover, the independent educational organization 'Ways to Quality'® formulate

a 12-fold sequence of 'the inner and outer preconditions of quality work' (Aries to Pisces): 'Task-setting; Individual Responsibility; Ability; Freedom; Trust; Protection; Financial Considerations or Balance; Knowledge-based Responsibility; Personal Development; Initiative-taking; The Individual and the Community; Community as Destiny.' Group-development as a planetary sequence follows the days of the week (beginning with 'Saturn', Saturday): 'Finding one's place; Seeking each other; Finding a home; Meeting each other' Effective working groups; Creative team; Parting Group ('seeds'). Again, in seven words: Aims, Policy, Planning, Integration, Organization, Innovation, Evaluation. These stages are observable in every group development, from human friendships to political systems, and so on.

22. Lewis only needed to point to Jean Seznec, *The Return of the Pagan Gods: The Mythological Tradition and its Place in Renaissance Humanism and Art* (Mythos: The Princeton/Bollingen Series in World Mythology). Princeton 1953, '72, '95. See also Edgar Wind, *Pagan Mysteries of the Renaissance*. Norton 1958, rev. 1968; Penguin 1967/76, OUP 1980.

23. Elisabeth Vreede's *Rundbriefe* appeared monthly between Sept. 1927 and Aug. 1930. Two Eng. trs. are available: The American version *Anthroposophy and Astrology* Great Barrington MA: Anthroposophic Press 2001, translates the *Newsletters* as they first appeared, with the astronomical mistakes. These were corrected 1980, and this corrected version is translated, with two extra articles, by Henry Goulden: Elisabeth Vreede, *Anthroposophy and Astronomy*, Leominster: Anastasi 2001.

24. Rudolf Steiner, *Anthroposophical Leading Thoughts*, No. 1 [GA 26].

25. Hermann Beckh, *John's Gospel: The Cosmic Rhythm—Stars and Stones*, Leominster: Anastasi 2015. P. 15.

26. A planet may be taken as a significator of a person or of an event, or of affairs ruled by a (zodiacal) House—*Ed.*

27. The Dutch astrologer Roelf Takens (1862-1930).

28. Corrected here—*Tr.*

29. *John's Gospel*, Anastasi 2015, pp. 36-7. For the 'householder' and the given formative forces in Beckh's analysis of Buddhist *saṁskāra*, see H. Beckh, *Buddha's Life and Teaching*, tr. K. Binder. Temple Lodge 2019.

30. In *Human and Cosmic Thought* [GA 151] the 12 world-conceptions (Ram to Fishes) are translated into English as: 'Idealism, Rationalism, Mathematism, Materialism, Sensationalism, Phenomenalism, Realism, Dynamism, Monadism, Spiritism, Pneumatism, and Psychism.' The 'world-outlook-moods' (Moon to Saturn) are translated as: 'Occultism, Transcendentalism, Mysticism, Empiricism, Voluntarism, Logicism and Gnosis'—*Tr. note.*

31. Among the major moons of Uranus & Neptune only Triton and Nereid, belonging to Neptune, are retrograde. Triton was discovered in 1846—*Ed.*

32. Dr Wilhelm Kaiser (1895-1956). Beckh mentions Kaiser's *Die geometrischen Vorstellungen in der Astronomie*, 2 vols., with supplements. Basel: Robert Geering Verlag 1928 in his book on *John's Gospel*, p. 29, as a 'valuable and interesting' way to overcome materialistic thought. W. Kaiser joined the Anthroposophical Society at the time of The Christmas Foundation, 1923, and became a co-worker with Elisabeth Vreede. After 1928 the publication mentioned here grew to five volumes.

33. Since 2006, Pluto is now regarded as a 'dwarf planet'—*Tr. note*.

34. The typescript text has 'Astrologie'—*Tr*.

35. See previous footnote.

36. In *Galgenlieder*, 1905. *Gallows Songs and Other Poems*, selected and translated by Max Knight. Munich: Piper, 1972.

37. All eight planets in the solar system orbit the Sun in the direction that the Sun is rotating, which is counterclockwise when viewed from above the Sun's north pole. Six of the planets also rotate about their axis in this same direction. The exceptions—the planets with retrograde rotation—are Venus and Uranus—*Ed*.

38. Radium, in the form of radium chloride, was discovered by Marie and Pierre Curie in 1898. They extracted the radium compound from uraninite and published the discovery at the French Academy of Sciences five days later—*Ed*.

39. Rudolf Steiner. GA 323, Stuttgart, 1-18 Jan. 1921.

40. *The East in the Light of the West, The Children of Lucifer and the Brothers of Christ* (GA 113). 9 lectures, Munich, August 1909.

41. Alan Leo (1860-1917, born William Frederich Allan), Theosophist, Freemason, author, publisher and astrologer, who has been called 'the father of modern astrology', was presented by Rudolf Steiner with a signed portrait and date of birth (see *Contribution* XVIII). It is likely Steiner was interested in working with Alan Leo. The chart and horoscope is published in Alan Leo, *The Art of Synthesis* (1912), reissued Destiny Books. Rochester, Vermont 1989. pp. 206-11—*Tr. note*.

42. Rudolf Frieling, *Die sieben Sakramente*, '*Christus aller Erde*' Band 22, Stuttgart 1926, p. 36.

43. Although here the seven colours of the rainbow are admittedly suggested only as an analogy, it may be remarked in passing that however widely held, the concept of 'seven' colours of the rainbow derives rather from Newton's mystical preconceptions. In order to name seven colours (a number Newton found satisfying), he had to split one of them into indigo and violet. Goethe, on the other hand, speaks convincingly of six colours on his colour circle—*Tr. note*.

44. Early debate on the distribution of radium quickly followed the research and publications of Robert John Strutt FRS in the first decade of the twentieth

century. The first part of Beckh's claim was justified, but the latter was viewed sceptically on the grounds that an increase of radium in deeper levels of the Earth would cause massive over-heating—*Ed.*

45. See Gundhild Kačer-Bock, *Hermann Beckh: Life and Work*, Leominster: Anastasi 2016, for biographical details of Beckh's changes of career from prize-winning student (Munich), to Judge (Bavaria), to University Professor (Berlin), finally to Priest of The Christian Community (Stuttgart)—*Tr. note.*

46. The explosion at a mine in Alsdorf on the same day as the total eclipse was the largest German mining accident to that date, with 271 fatalities—*Ed.*

47. On Oct. 25, 1930, 99 miners lost their lives through the massive explosion at the mine at Maybach—*Ed.*

48. On 8 Oct. 1930, southern Germany was shaken by a strong quake at Magnitude 5.3 centred in northern Tyrol—*Ed.*

49. Alexander Strakosch (1879-1958), railway engineer, anthroposophical lecturer, took an active part in the development of the anthroposophical impulse in art, intimately connected to the building of the first Goetheanum, later an upper-school teacher at the Waldorf School, Stuttgart. See Alexander Strakosch, *Lebenswege mit Rudolf Steiner: Erinnerungen*, Dornach 1994 —*Tr. note.*

50. Nöhbauer, Hans F., *Ludwig II.: Ludwig II of Bavaria*. Taschen, 1998.

51. Beckh prefers the older spelling *Alchymie*, no doubt in an attempt to link to the genuine philosophical tradition rather than the transmutation of metals—*Tr. note.*

52. Vogl, Albert. (1978). *Life and Death of Thérèse Neumann, Mystic and Stigmatist.* Vantage Press, 1978. It is worth noting that Hermann Beckh shows a particularly warm interest in the affairs of Bavaria, where he felt most at home—*Ed.*

53. This was Ernst Uehli, b. 4 May 1875. He first heard Rudolf Steiner lecturing in 1905—*Ed.*

54. Quotation from *Entsprechungen zwischen Mikrokosmos und Makrokosmos. Der Mensch—eine Hieroglyphe des Weltenalls* [GA 201], lecture 11, Dornach, 2 May 1920, p. 168 (1987 ed.), however, has '*sind ja zugeflogene*'. Eng. tr. in *Man—Hieroglyph of the Universe*, London: Rudolf Steiner Press, 1972, p. 151—*Ed.*

55. See endnote 31 above.

56. From Lecture 10 in GA 110, *Geistige Hierarchien in ihrer Wiederspiegelung in der physischen Welt. Tierkreis, Planeten, Kosmos* [GA 110], lecture 10, p. 159 (1997 ed.). Eng. tr. *The Spiritual Hierarchies and their Reflection in the Physical World*, Anthroposophic Press 1970, p. 126.

57. GA 129, Munich, 25 Aug. 1911. Eng. tr. *Wonders of the World, Ordeals of the Soul, and Revelations of the Spirit*, London, Rudolf Steiner Press, 1983.

58. It is widely accepted today that the classical myth of Uranos as told for example by Hesiod in *Theogony* has its foundations in Hurrian and Iranian sources,

both probably looking to Varuna in Indian tradition. Ahead of his time, Beckh often equated Uranos with Varuna and Mitra-Varuna (the night sky), e.g. *Indische Weisheit und Christentum*. Stuttgart: Urachhaus 1938, pp. 118-22. English translation in H. Beckh, *Collected Articles*, Temple Lodge, forthcoming. Gk. *aphros* meant sea-foam.

59. *Spiritual Hierarchies*, op. cit., 18 April 1909.

60. *medium coeli* (MC) is also called the midpoint, because it is the zenith of the zodiac in the horoscope. Its counterpart is *imum coeli* (IC) the lowest point on the zodiac, below the horizon—*Tr. note*.

61. The legend of the jewel fallen from Lucifer's crown, mentioned in Lohengrin, originally imagined in San Marte (pseudonym for A. Schultz), *Parcival, Rittergedicht von Wolfram von Eschenbach, Im Auszuge mitgetheilt von San Marte*. Magdeburg, 1832—*Ed*.

62. 'I am free to taunt mortals with the frank confession that I am stealing the golden vessels of the Egyptians, in order to build of them a temple for my God, far from the territory of Egypt.' Johannes Kepler, *Harmonies of the World*, tr. Charles Glenss Wlllis (1939), available online: http://www.24grammata.com/wp-content/uploads/2014/08/Kepler-Harmonies-Of-The-World-24grammata.pdf

63. *Umwandlungsimpulse für die künstlerische Evolution der Menschheit* / Nach einer vom Vortragenden nicht durchgesehenen Nachschrift vom 29. und 30. Dezember Dornach 1914. Herausgegeben mit einem Geleitwort von Marie Steiner. Verlag: Dornach Philosophisch-Anthroposophischer Verlag, 1928.

64. Friedrich Doldinger, Ph.D. (1897-1973), poet, writer and composer, with Prof. Beckh, one of the founding members of The Christian Community.

65. *Der Vogel Gryff*. Ein Spiel nach dem gleichnamigen Märchen der Gebrüder Grimm. Julius Umbach, Lörrach 1927. (Written in German dialect, inspired by the Oberufer Mystery Plays.) The story in the Grimms' collection is called 'The Griffin' or 'The Griffin Bird'—*Tr. note*.

66. Contrary to this, today's mainline theory of accretion (smaller particles / dust join together by gravity to form larger objects, then planets) was developed in 1969 by Victor Safronov, who graduated from Moscow State University Department of Mechanics and Mathematics under Stalin, publishing *Evolution of the Protoplanetary Cloud and Formation of the Earth and the Planets*. Moscow: Nauka Press, 1969, under Brezhnev—*Ed*.

67. Rudolf Steiner, *The Agriculture Course*. GA 327. Koberwitz, 7-16 June 1924.

68. *Die CG* Jg. 4, Nr. 2, Mai 1927, pp. 37-40; Eng. tr. in *The Collected Articles of Rev. Prof. Hermann Beckh*, forthcoming.

69. The typescript has 'Uranus'. The Professor points out (*Contribution* No. 17) the influence of Uranos has to pass through the sphere of Uranus, as boundary-marker, just as by analogy to the waiting traveller a long-distance train comes from its starting city *through* some other town *en route*—*Tr. note*.

70. Eng. tr. *Our Origin in the Light*, in the triple volume *From the Mysteries*, Temple Lodge 2020.

71. This rather supports the claim that Hermann Beckh, progressing through the stages of higher consciousness, by 1930 had reached the third stage, Intuition—*Ed*.

72. See endnote 27 above.

73. The gentleman in question, to me a stranger, spoke with me once in Kanonenweg [Stuttgart], after a sermon that I had given and that he had heard. I have since visited him in his mountain village, where he initially kept from me the fact that he is an astrologer. Only when he had my book on *Mark's Gospel* (meanwhile, he had come through me to anthroposophy), it came out.

74. Arthur Schult, Christlich-rosenkreuzersche Astrosophie und arabisch-mittelalterliche Astrologie (Johannes Kepler zu seinem 300. Todestag), *Die CG*, 7. Jg. Nr. 9, Dez. 1930. Pp. 257-64. Eng. tr. see p. 447f. It appears highly significant here that Steiner's concluding lecture in the Leipzig lecture-course offered extensive quotations from Kepler—*Tr. note*.

75. Elisabeth Vreede's *Rundbriefe* appeared monthly between Sept. 1927 and Aug. 1930. Two Eng. trs. available: The American version *Anthroposophy and Astrology*, Great Barrington MA: Anthroposophic Press 2001, translates the *Newsletters* as they first appeared, with the astronomical mistakes. These were corrected 1980, and this corrected version is translated, with two extra articles by Henry Goulden: Elisabeth Vreede, *Anthroposophy and Astronomy*, Leominster: Anastasi 2001—*Ed*.

76. *verunglückt*, 'injured', even 'ruined'. Some theologians, notably Calvin, speak of human nature as utterly depraved. The redemption was necessary for we cannot help ourselves. Cf. Beckh's careful account of the first and most important Christian initiation of all time, where everything had to be relinquished, and its relation to the Mystery of Golgotha, in *Mark's Gospel: The Cosmic Rhythm*, and its sequel *John's Gospel: The Cosmic Rhythm—Stars and Stones*. Beckh also discusses at some length the 'wound' in terms of artistic *longing*, in his newly-discovered book *The Mystery of Musical Creativity: Man and Music*, Temple Lodge, 2019—*Tr. note*.

77. Werfel's trilogy first appeared in 1920, and was addressed by Rudolf Steiner in an article for *Das Goetheanum* Jg. 1 Nr. 51-2, July 1922. Reprinted GA 36, pp. 225-33.

78. Verlag der Christengemeinschaft, Stuttgart, 1930.

79. At the time of writing, Hermann Beckh was approaching his fifty-sixth birthday on 4 May 1931—*Ed*.

80. In 'Farther Up' (see p. 503f.) it is intimated that Hermann Beckh found the 'nearer' side of Saturn in dream-consciousness (mirroring, but offering the content to the higher heavens); Uranus (connected with the Sun) is found in sleep-consciousness, Neptune is the pre-natal consciousness—*Ed*.

81. See GA 128, *An Occult Physiology* (GA 128), lecture 4.

82. Note especially *The Deed of Christ and the Opposing Spiritual Powers*, RSP 1976 (GA 107, lect. 16, Berlin, 22 March 1909). A comprehensive presentation in English of Steiner's indications regarding the Asuras is available at initiativeforanthroposophy.org/wiki/asuras/Accessed 18 Sept. 2020—*Ed.*

83. Published R. Geering, Basel, 1930.

84. Thus in the original text. Usually presented as 'Sorath'.

85. Rudolf Steiner, *The Soul's Probation* [GA 14]. Sc. 1. Tr. Ruth & Hans Pusch. Toronto: Steiner Book Centre. 1973. 18f.

86. Verlag der Christengemeinschaft, Stuttgart, 1927; Band 24 of the series *Christus aller Erde*. Eng. tr. in the triple volume, *From the Mysteries, Genesis, Zarathusta*, Temple Lodge 2020, p. 112.

87. Tr. Adams 1969, p. 134; Monges, p. 141; Creeger, p. 160.

88. Rudolf Steiner. *An Outline of Esoteric Science*, tr. C.E. Creeger. Anthroposophic Press, 1997, p. 220f. Cf. tr. Monges, p. 197f., tr. Adams, p. 117f.

89. Astronomers today (2020) confirm that Jupiter emits a great deal of infra-red radiation, but not visible light—*Ed.*

90. Tr. Adams 1969, p. 144f; Creeger, p. 174f; Monges, p. 154f.

91. *The Spiritual Hierarchies and their Reflection in the Physical World* (GA 110), lecture 5.

92. Page reference to Hermann Beckh, *Mark's Gospel: The Cosmic Rhythm*, Anastasi 2015.

93. Ernst Moll had taken up the appointment as priest in Lörrach after his ordination on April 6, 1924. Beckh here refers to E. Moll, *Der Krieg in Ost und West*, Stuttgart: Die Christengemeinschaft, March 1931. (Ernst Moll published the first edition of his *Die Sprache der Laute: Buchstaben-Namen und -Zeichen alter europäischer Alphabete im Lichte geisteswissenschaftlicher Erkenntnisse* in 1950, expanding it in the ensuing years. He died in 1962. This book on the language of speech-sounds was completed as far as possible from his notes by Ludmilla Goth. Ernst Moll, *Die Sprache der Laute*, Stuttgart: Freies Geistesleben 1968)—*Ed.*

94. This conclusion is found originally with Newton. Modern astrophysics (2016) calculates that the overall density of the Earth is 5.52 g/cubic cm; the Moon is 3.34 g/cubic cm.—*Ed.*

95. In the German language and in Teutonic mythology, the Sun is feminine—*Tr. note.*

96. To simplify the writing of the Greek words, in what follows I shall keep to the Latin script—H.B.

97. *The Spiritual Hierarchies and their Reflection in the Physical World*, Düsseldorf, 1909, op. cit, lectures 3 and 4 [GA 110].

98. The Ephesian Mystery verse by Rudolf Steiner, with the Greek
    words from Rev. 5:12 and planetary signs:
    Weltensprossenes Wesen, du in Lichtgestalt
    Von der *Sonne* erkraftet (ἰσχὺς ☉)
    in der *Mond*gewalt (δύναμις ☽)
    Dich beschenke des *Mars* erschaffendes Klingen (εὐλογία ♂)
    Und *Merkurs* gliedbewegtes Schwingen (τιμὴ ☿)
    Dich erleuchte *Jupiter*s erstrahlende Weisheit (σοφία ♃)
    Und der *Venus* liebetragende Schönheit (δόξα ♀)
    Dass *Saturn*s weltenalte Geist-Innigkeit (πλοῦτος ♄)
    Dich dem Raumessein und Zeitenwerden weihe!


    Offspring of all the Worlds! Thou Form of Light,
    Firm framéd by the *Sun*, with *Luna*'s might,
    Endow'd with sounding *Mars*' life-stirring song,
    And swift-wing'd *Mercury*'s motion in thy limbs.
    Illumin'd with radiant *Jupiter*'s all-wisdom
    And grace-bestowing *Venus*' loveliness—
    That *Saturn*'s ancient memoried inwardness
    Hallow thee to the world of Space and Time!
    (Eng. tr. by George Adams)

99. The current issue of the *Newsletter*, it seems, was originally delayed for some
    reason—*Tr. note*.

100. Hermann Beckh, *John's Gospel*, p. 265 ff. (Leominster: Anastasi 2015). In the
    second of these *Contributions* Beckh has reminded us that Venus is 'at home'
    in the Scales—*Ed*.

101. Cf. Sophie's words in *Heinrich von Ofterdingen*: 'The great secret is revealed to
    all, yet remains forever unfathomable'—*Ed*.

102. Gustav Meyrink, *The Golem*, tr. Mike Mitchell, Cambridge: Dedalus 2005; tr.
    Isabel Cole, Vitalis 2005. See also Beckh's article, 'My Experience with Gustav
    Meyrink' (*Die Christengemeinschaft*. 9. Jg. 12. March 1933. Pp. 369-73. Eng. tr.
    in *Collected Essays and Articles*, forthcoming, with the essay 'Fakir paths' from
    the literary estate of Gustav Meyrink [1868-1932] published 1973 in part 2 'Das
    Zauberdiagramm' of *Das Haus der letzten Laterne*, ISBN: 3811818023; download
    available: http://literatten.bplaced.net/ap/m/Fakirpfade.php.

103. Oskar Schmitz, *Der Geist der Astrologie*. München: Georg Mueller Verlag, 1922.

104. Beckh would have had access, among other things, to Oskar Schmitz' three
    volumes of autobiography, Munich, 1926-7—*Ed*.

105. Segantini, Giovanni; 1858-1899. 'L' Amore alla fonte della vita', 1896. Oil on
    canvas, 70 × 98 cm. Milan, Civica Galleria d'Arte.

106. In the *Divine Comedy* Dante addresses this phrase to Beatrice, and then also
    states his understanding of it to St. John the Apostle in *Paradiso* 26, l.38—*Ed*.

107. Hermann Beckh expresses these observations in *John's Gospel*: Thus, from the aspect of the planets, Venus (♀) stands over the ♉, the sign of the Word and of the earth's primal beginning. In his *Divine Comedy* Dante calls her love in the primal beginning, *'il primo Amore'*—divine Love revealed in the creation. In one of his paintings of the fullness of light of the Obergadin, Segantini expressively names her as 'the love at the primal fountain of life'. Both revelations of Venus are divine. In the ♉ she 'holds sway over world-becoming', creative 'love in the primal beginning'. In ♎ she is the 'heavenly love' (Venus Urania), the redeeming love which leads back to the primal source of being (cf. Novalis, *Hymns to the Night*: 'then came eternal Love's redeeming hand—and he slept.'). Anastasi, 2015, p. 177—*Ed*.

108. Lecture 2, 5 Aug. 1908, in *Universe, Earth and Man: Their Relationship in Egyptian Myths and Modern Culture* (GA 105).

109. Almost certainly the sonnet *An eine Rose* which Rudolf Steiner pointed out in the Stuttgart speech-course, 29 March 1923 (GA 281, p. 145).

110. Rudolf Steiner, The Michael Imagination in *Das Miterleben des Jahreslaufes in vier kosmischen Imaginationen*, GA 229 (1984), Erster Vortrag, Dornach, 5. Oktober 1923, p. 12ff.

111. 'The Spiritual Individualities of the Planets', Lecture 1 of GA 228, Dornach, 27 July, 1923. An English translation is published in *The Golden Blade*, London 1988, also available online: rsarchive.org.

112. Most notably in Lecture 9 of *Man in the Light of Occultism, Theosophy and Philosophy*, Oslo, 11 June 1912 (GA 137).

113. Hermann Beckh was particularly concerned with this subject in *Vom Geheimnis der Stoffeswelt (Alchymie)* 1931, ch. 1, p. 16ff. English tr., Temple Lodge 2019, p. 13ff. The principal lecture by Rudolf Steiner is Lecture 4 of *Theosophy of the Rosicrucians*, Munich 1907. Attention is also drawn to the inclusion of the phrase 'the philosophers' stone' in the first edition of *Occult Science*, 1910, p. 352f.—*Ed*.

114. As well as the lectures collected under the title *The Karma of Anthoposophy*, London: RSP 2009, see especially the first two lectures of *Materialism and the Task of Anthroposophy*, Anthroposophic Press, 1987 (GA 204).

115. Rudolf Steiner, *Human and Cosmic Thought*, GA 151, 4 lectures, Berlin 20-23 Jan. 1914.

116. Rudolf Steiner, *Third Scientific Lecture-Course: Astronomy*, GA 323, 18 lectures, Stuttgart, 1-18 Jan. 1921.

117. 30 March 1931—Monday in Holy Week.

118. Theosophical literature, especially H.P. Blavatsky's *Secret Doctrine* (1888) and A.P. Sinnett's *Esoteric Buddhism* (1883) used 'rounds' for the seven embodiments of Earth and 'races' / 'root-races' for the first major subdivision. In later anthroposophy the latter is usually represented as 'evolutionary epochs'—an expression taken from theosophical literature for the first great division, resulting in the seven great aeons of Earth evolution—*Ed*.

119. The duplicated text has 'Uranus'. As noted (endnote 65) Beckh is using a shorthand where 'Uranus' as planetary marker stands for the entire 'Uranos' sphere—*Ed.*

120. H. Beckh, *John's Gospel*, Anastasi, 2015, p. 298f., addresses the subject in more detail.

121. Most notably in *Anthroposophical Leading Thoughts*, GA 26 (Germ. ed. 1972, p. 197), in the chapter 'What is the Earth in reality in the Macrocosm?' LT 153-55—*Ed.*

122. When Beckh was writing these *Contributions* he had just completed the little book on *Alchymie* (1931) as a supplement to his vast study of John's Gospel. *Alchymy: the Mystery of the Material World* contains particular reference (p. 23f.) to the *Geheime Figuren der Rosenkreuzer aus dem 16. und 17. Jahrhundert*. This work, originally published in Altona in 1785, has now reappeared with Hermann Barsdorf, Berlin, 1919 (Freiburg im Breisgau: Verlag Hermann Bauer, 1988. Also available, complete, in German and English in: Paul M. Allen [ed.], *A Christian Rosenkreutz Anthology*, Blauvelt, New York: Rudolf Steiner Pub., 1968. 211-328): according to Rudolf Steiner's indications in his lecture-course on Chr. Rosenkreutz 1911 (GA 130. See Lecture 7, Neuchâtel, 27 Sept. 1911, in *Esoteric Christianity*, London: Rudolf Steiner Press, 2000/05), it contains the renewal of the Christian-Rosicrucian impulse in the eighteenth century. The 'black fire' of the Rosicrucians is found in the *Geheime Figuren* in the lines devoted to the *Ignis Philosophorum* on the page headed 'Elohim Jehovah' (M. Allen, p. 266). Milton alludes to the alchemical tradition with the 'darkness visible' of the fires of Hell in *Paradise Lost*—*Ed.*

123. Described as a 'play of light' and 'flickering' in the English translation by George and Mary Adams (RSP, 1962/3), p. 122ff.—*Ed.*

124. A quotation from Christian Morgenstern's (1871-1914) poem '*Licht ist Liebe*', in *Wir fanden einen Pfad* (Piper: Munich 1914, frequently reprinted).

125. Itivuttaka, §27. Various translations differ—*Ed.*

126. Lectures 3, 4 and 5 in *The Karma of Anthroposophy* (in GA 240), Arnhem, 18-20 July 1924.

127. Mabel Collins, *Light on the Path. Through the Gates of Gold*. Pasadena, CA: Theosophical University Press 1976. Reprint of 1888 ed. with notes by the author, from *Lucifer*, Vol. 1, 1887-8. Also: *Light on the Path*, Adyar Centenary Edition 1982; the treatise is also downloadable from the internet. Mabel Collins (1851-1927) penned at least 46 books.

128. Wilhelm Kaiser (1895-1983), anthroposophist, published several books on astronomy. His two volume *Die geometrischen Vorstellungen in der Astronomie* was published in Basel in 1928, the same time that Beckh produced his study of *Mark's Gospel: The Cosmic Rhythm*… Interesting observations on Wilhelm Kaiser appear in Werner Schmötzer, *Anthroposophie, Astronomie, Astrologie: kosmische Rhythmen und Zyklen*, 2012—*Ed.*

129. In Contribution 3, above. See also H. Beckh, 'The Content of the Rig-Veda' from *Die Drei*, 3. Jg. 1923. 233-39, in *Collected Articles*, Temple Lodge, forthcoming; H. Beckh, 'Das Mysterium des Taghimmels und Nachthimmels' in *Indische Weisheit und Christentum*, Urachhaus, 1939, Eng. tr. also in *Collected Articles*— Ed.

130. Novalis, from *Hymns to the Night*, V, tr. George MacDonald.

131. *Der Geist der Astrologie*. 4. Aufl. Uranus-Verlag, Hamburg, 1937 (reprint from Hamburg 1922). Oskar Schmitz (1873-Dec. 1931) was in the last year of his life when Beckh paid this tribute. Stimulated by psychological interests, but also by his own psychological crises, Schmitz turned to psychoanalysis and psychotherapy at an early stage, in particular C.G. Jung and Alfred Adler. He also joined Count Keyserling's 'Wisdom School'. Long before psychologists referred to personality conceptions of astrology, Schmitz's *Geist der Astrologie* (1922) foresaw the development of an 'astro-psychology' that still occupies a central and current position in Western esotericism. The first edition is still readily available, München, Georg Müller (1922), reprinted Pranava Books (2019).

132. Hermann Beckh. *Alchymie: Vom Geheimnis der Stoffeswelt* (1931/ 1937/ 1987), p. 120; Eng. tr., *Alchymy: Mystery of the Material World*, Temple Lodge, 2019.

133. Dornach, 25 Nov. 1917 [GA 178]. *The Reappearance of Christ in the Etheric.* Lecture XII: Individual Spirit Beings and the Undivided Foundation of the World, Part 3.

134. In: Rudolf Steiner, *Colour.* Twelve lectures by Rudolf Steiner. Tr. John Salter & Pauline Wehrle. London: Rudolf Steiner Press, 2001. p. 188.

135. *Mark's Gospel*, Anastasi, 2015, p. 289f.

136. A neologism. Beckh is simply pointing out that even avid students prefer reading any number of Steiner's lecture-courses than face the challenge of a detailed study of the relatively very few written textbooks—he implies the gains by far compensate for the time and effort spent in reading the latter. (Similarly, people generally prefer meals prepared by somebody else than to face the chore of cooking for themselves.)—*Tr. note.*

137. Hermann Beckh points out (e.g. in *Contributions* Nos. 8 & 12) that his spiritual path was from music to the stars, evolving from his musical studies that culminated with Wagner's music dramas while still a student of law in Munich. With the most sensitive aesthetic perception he found that there is agreement between the great composers 'from Bach to Bruckner'. Composers hear their music in specific keys—the keys best able to express what is felt. The ability to create lasting music depends on the ability to draw on the creativity inherent in the musical keys, to compose out of the experience of tonality. By drawing additionally on Wagner's libretti, Beckh was able to demonstrate the composer's mastery in this realm. In *The Mystery of Musical Creativity*, chaps. 5, 6, 8 & 10 he refers to Tristan & Isolde, so dear to his

and the composer's heart. Here the *Liebestod* concluding Tristan & Isolde is written in B-major—the lawfulness of logic (*Weltendenken*) is no more absolute that the musical laws (*Weltenstimmungen*), drawn ultimately from the signs of the zodiac. For the *Liebestod*, see H. Beckh, *The Essence of Tonality*, Anastasi, 2001, p. 22f., *The Language of Tonality*, Anastasi, 2015, pp. 188-92 with the appended article 'The Mystery of the Night in Wagner and Novalis'. In both publications (1925 and 1937) Beckh presents B-major as the key of Virgo, which he recognizes as the 'sign' of 'our movement', The Christian Community. See p. 141—*Tr. note*.

138. Written, of course, before space research had revealed pictures of the far side of the Moon—*Tr. note*.

139. Rudolf Steiner, *The Michael Mystery*, GA 26, Chapter 6.

140. H. Beckh, *John's Gospel*, op. cit., p. 111f.

141. Beckh is probably recalling the term *Mondenfestung* from *Die geistigen Individualitäten unseres Planetensystems schicksalbestimmende und menschenbefreiende Planeten*, Dornach, 27 July 1923, in GA 228, CW *Science of Initiation and Knowledge of the Stars*.

142. Lecture 3 of *Human and Cosmic Thinking*, op. cit., see endnote 30.

143. Alfonso X 'the Wise' of Castile (1221-84) said, when struggling with astronomical epicycles, 'If the Lord Almighty had consulted me before embarking on creation, I should have recommended something simpler.'

144. H. Beckh, *Alchymy: The Mystery of the Material World*, Temple Lodge 2019.

145. Published tables of the calculated positions of celestial objects.

146. Beckh is also aware of the very old tradition in both Western and Eastern churches wherein 'going up the mount' refers to the 'Mount of The Holy Spirit' as depicted, for example, in Rublev's icon 'The Hospitality of Abraham'.

147. In the German edition of my book on *John's Gospel* there is a printing error: p. 166 (l. 9), not 'Regulus' but 'Aldebaran' [the English tr. is correct]—H.B.

148. 'Barbara branches', picked on December 4, St. Barbara's day, and put in the water will start blooming at Christmas. The farmer observed these flowering branches, which mostly consist of cherry, apple or pear, to see what kind of fruit he could expect next year. Dec. 4 falls within the *constellation* Sagittarius, but the *sign* Scorpio.

149. As written on the document enclosed within the foundation stone.

150. Rudolf Steiner. *Karmic Relationships. Esoteric Studies*, 8 volumes [GA 235-40], London Rudolf Steiner Press. 2nd ed. 1972.

151. *Die CG*, IV, No. 2. Eng. tr. in *Collected Articles*, Temple Lodge, forthcoming.

152. Rudolf Steiner, *The Spiritual Beings in the Heavenly Bodies and in the Kingdoms of Nature*. Helsinki 1912. GA 136.

153. C. Aqua Libra, i.e. Roelf Takens (1862-1930), see *Contribution 1*, endnote 26.

154. For Rudolf Steiner's first observations on the Breviary for the priests of The Christian Community, see GA 343, p. 586. In contrast to the R.C. Breviary, the new mediations are for morning, midday and evening.

155. The right-hand margin of the original typescript page is unclear and in places incomplete, but it can be reconstructed with some certainty. Here 'bede....' is read as 'bedecken'—*Tr. note.*

156. See endnote 25 above—*Ed.*

157. Rudolf Steiner, *The Agriculture Course.* GA 327. Koberwitz, 7-16 June 1924, Lecture 6.

158. 'The Year as Symbol of the Great Cosmic Year', 31 Dec. 1915, included in GA 165.

159. The Great Financial Crisis in Germany, summer 1931, has been repeatedly investigated as paving Hitler's way to power. The event included the closure of all financial institutions—*Ed.*

160. C. Aq. Libra (Roelf Takens), *Astrology: Its Technics and Ethics* (1917, p. 34), terms the crosses: (Ram, etc.) 'Cardinal Cross', (Bull, etc.) 'Fixed cross', (Twins, etc.) 'Mutable Cross'—*Tr. note.*

161. Friedrich Creuzer, *Symbolik und Mythologie der alten Völker*, 1810-12. Downloadable from several websites.

162. *Alchymy: The Mystery of the Material World*, Temple Lodge, 2019, pp. 86-8.

163. Both topics are fully presented in H. Beckh, *Buddhas's Life and Teachings*, Temple Lodge, 2019.

164. The Professor has not added the word 'polar' (as distinct from 'logical') to the noun 'opposite', but it is implied. See S.T. Coleridge, 'Towards a more comprehensive Theory of Life', ably expounded by Owen Barfield in *What Coleridge Thought*, Barfield Press UK, 2014—*Tr. note.*

165. Oscar A.H. Schmitz, *Der Geist der Astrologie* (München: Georg Müller 1922; Hamburg: Uranus Verlag 1936/7; Lebesweiser Verlag 1953; Tradition Classics 2012; Antigonos 2013/16). Cf. also C. Aq. Libra (Roelf Takens [1862-1930], Dutch astrologer), *Astrology its Technics and Ethics* (1917; Forgotten Books 2015), which Beckh quotes with some approval in *Contribution* No. 1—*Tr. note.*

166. Cf. my essay 'Rudolf Steiner and the East' [in *Hermann Beckh & the Spirit-Word.* Leominster: Anastasi 2015, pp. 33-65. Also in *The Source of Speech*, Temple Lodge 2019, pp. 16-42].—H.B.

167. Hubert Korsch, 1883-1942/3, the leading German astrologer at the time of writing, rising to prominence in 1926. Author of several books on astrology and founder of the principal astrological magazine in Germany, *Zenit*, in Jan. 1930. The magazine was banned by the Nazis and Dr Korsch died in a concentration camp.

168. In 1928 Beckh had published his thorough study of *Mark's Gospel* to overturn the simplistic astrology found in Arthur Drews' *Das Markus Evangelium*, 1st ed. 1920, 2nd 1928.

169. Jan. 1930 to Dec. 1938.

170. 8 July, 1927. Beckh's lecture on Buddhism for the Schopenhauer Congress is now translated and available in Hermann Beckh, *Festschrift: Essays in Honour of Hermann Beckh*, Anastasi 2016. Also in *Collected Essays and Articles*, Temple Lodge, forthcoming.

171. Karl Ernst Krafft (1900-45), author of *Typokosmie. Über Urbilder und Sinnzeichen und ihre Einordnung zum Lebenskreis. Kosmologische Symbole im Wandel der Zeiten. Vom Walten des Sprachgeistes*. Düsseldorf, Verlag des *Zenit* (Dr H. Korsch), 1934. For Krafft's later co-operation with leading Nazis, see Ellic Howe, *Astrology and Psychological Warfare During World War II*. Rider & Co., 1972 (new edition reprints the early chapters and adds more on the 1940's: *Astrology and the Third Reich*, Aquarian Press/ Thorsons Publishers 1985.

172. Curt Englert-Faye (1899-45), anthroposophist active at the time in the Rudolf Steiner School, Zürich, and later (1936) General Secretary of the Anthroposophical Society in Norway. However, Beckh may be recalling the elder Englert-Faye, the father, who was an original member of the Goetheanum (Johannes-Bau) project almost 20 years earlier—*Ed.*

173. See GA 239, lecture 9; English tr. *Karmic Relationships*, Vol. VII, lect.1, London: Rudolf Steiner Press, 1973.

174. This saying is difficult to trace exactly. In the re-issue of R. Steiner, *Lucifer-Gnosis* (GA 34, pp. 396-99), the article (Sept. 1905) 'Wie verhält sich die Theosophie zur Astrologie?' ['How does theosophy relate to astrology?'] appears. In it, amongst other things, one finds the sentence: '*Die astrologischen Gesetze beruhen nun allerdings wieder auf solchen Intuitionen, gegenüber denen auch die Erkenntnis von Wiederverkörperung und Karma noch sehr elementar ist.*' ['Astrological laws certainly touch on such Intuitions, in the face of which the realization of reincarnation and karma is still rather elementary.'] This points in the direction of the viewpoint that Beckh consistently emphasizes—*Tr. note.*

175. Dr Rolf Reißmann, Astrologie und Philosophie, in „Astrologie 1930", *Vorträge und Berichte des IX. Astrologen-Kongresses*, Dortmund 1930. http://dl.ub.uni-freiburg.de/diglit/zb_okkultismus1930 /0559?sid=99da6825e21a72f88f7689fe4425e9aa&navmode=struct

176. Daily newspaper, Berlin, 1901-34, editor August Scherl.

177. Cf. Johnnes Tautz, *Walter Johannes Stein: A Biography*. Tr. John M. Wood, London: Temple Lodge 1990.

178. The author of five major books on astrology between 1925 and 1927. After WWII Strauss maintained an interest in C.G. Jung and astrology, but only with one major publication: *Psychologie und astrologische Symbolik: eine Einführung*, Zürich, 1953.

179. *Die Astrologie des Johannes Kepler: Eine Auswahl aus seinen Schriften* (zusammen mit Sigrid Strauß-Kloebe). Oldenbourg Verlag München 1926; Bonz Verlag Fellbach 1981.

180. Fr. Sigrid Strauss-Kloebe, who became a Jungian psychotherapist.

181. Beckh is probably remembering the time in Breitbrunn, ten years previously, when he was writing Forewords for his major studies of language and etymology: summer 1921—*Ed.*

182. Theodor J. J. Ram, 1884-1961, influenced by theosophy, published *Psychologische Astrologie* in 1935, and founded the Dutch school of psychological astrology. He also proposed the existence of three planets beyond Pluto for which he offered the names Persephone, Hermes and Demeter. His earlier ideas on this are discussed by Beckh below—*Ed.*

183. H. Beckh, *John's Gospel,* op. cit., p. 73.

184. Rudolf Steiner, *The Soul's Awakening,* tr. Ruth and Hans Pusch, Vancouver: Steiner Book Centre, 1973, p. 74. Below, another tr.:

    I could see you joined with beings whose effects
    would have to be harmful to man ere they to take
    a part creatively in evolution now.
    And yet they live like seeds in human souls
    to ripen in the future for the earth.
    I could behold such seeds within your soul.
    You do not know them, this is for your good—
    they'll learn one day to know themselves through you.
    Yet still the way is closed for them that leads
    into the realm of matter.
    Rudolf Steiner, *Four Mystery Plays.* Tr. Adam Bittleston, London: Rudolf Steiner Press, 1982, p. 430.

185. Friedrich Rittelmeyer, *Wiederverkörperung im Lichte des Denkens, der Religion, der Moral.* Stuttgart: Verlag der Christengemeinschaft, 1931. Eng. tr. *Reincarnation: Philosophy, Religion, Ethics.* Edinburgh: Floris Books, 1988/90.

186. *Astrologie* 1933. Vorträge und Bericht des XII. Astrologen-Kongresses Stuttgart 1933. Herausgegeben im Auftrage der Astrologischen Zentralstelle e.V. von Dr Hubert Korsch, Düsseldorf 1933. Pp. 67-9, 69-71.

187. As of today, 2020, astronomy has located a further seven dwarf planets beyond the orbit of Neptune.

188. See pp. 328f. above.

189. In this whole paragraph Beckh is clearly speaking to his actual colleagues at a critical juncture all those years ago. He simply desired peace to allow research to unfold. He intended (as he says) to publish these *Contributions* in a polished form. Beckh's death prevented this step from being taken, as noted in the Introduction (see p. 5). Feeling his end approaching, he revisited *music* as an approachable subject enabling many readers to recognize the creative Archetypes ('my theme')—and, under ever growing painfully distressing circumstances, wrote (we now know) not one but *two* masterpieces (*The Language of Tonality* pub. by Anastasi, 2015, and *The Mystery of Musical Creativity,* Temple Lodge, 2019). Today

we are in a better position to evaluate the present unique, pioneer work. Under pressure of circumstances, the writer revealed he knew what he was attempting. Now that his colleagues, too, have all passed on without fulfilling the writer's wish to publish, it should be possible today to relate Beckh's *Contributions* to other attempts of the time, and indeed to later developments in the new star-knowledge. It might seem even more important to appreciate whether or not this present work *actually caps* the momentous achievement of Hermann Beckh's whole *oeuvre* (invariably a marriage of originality and research of, respectively, musical scores and texts in the original languages) seen in the cultural context of almost a century later. The writer's inherent humility—genuine, one feels—has served its turn, that is, if, in recognizing his genius and his avowed intentions, we take seriously Matt. 5:16—*Tr. note.*

190. Perhaps this refers to Friedrich Doldinger, Eberhard Kurras or another priest-musician. A member of a later generation, Matthaeus Reisch (8 May 1912-18 Oct. 1972), a priest-musician of The Christian Community (ordained 1946), over the years composed a wealth of service music for various instrumental combinations. Reisch worked for the most part with Beckh's tone-zodiac as well as with the mood of the Seasonal Prayers. Should Beckh's own service music prove to be irredeemably lost (at 2020 only a few pieces have been recovered) would it be (for those interested) a consolation to imagine from Reich's first compositions some possible *echo* of how Beckh's piano-cycle might have sounded? For example, an early cycle of liturgical music for piano, written by Reisch in Munich, has survived, rather different from his later characteristic style—*Tr. note.*

191. In mentioning the inspiration which starry knowledge *did* convey to the working life of one priest-musician, it seems the obvious next step would be to open the subject, thereby enriching a collaboration with all striving church musicians, and indeed all striving Christian souls whose religious needs priests and musicians attempt to serve from first to last—*Tr. note.*

192. Cf. 'The planets are exalted in certain signs …. The best explanation is based upon the esoteric idea that the planets corresponds to the principles… The Sun, ruler of the heart, life and vitality, is exalted in Aries from the standpoint of illumination, Aries, ruling the head, would be illuminated by the presence of the Sun in that sign… Mars, king of the passional, emotional and sense nature, would be exalted in the house of the lower mind, Capricorn, having more power in this sign by its saturnine nature… Venus in Pisces, this being the end of the zodiac, the sign of understanding and universal love….' Alan Leo, *The Complete Dictionary of Astrology*, Rochester, Vermont: Destiny Books, 1983, 61f.—*Tr. note.*

193. Here and subsequently Beckh's insights into the manifestations of the qualities of zodiac-signs in music can be compared with his three major books on the subject, all now available in English, *The Essence of Tonality*, Anastasi 2008; *The Language of Tonality*, Anastasi 2015; *The Mystery of Musical Creation*, Temple Lodge 2019.

194. The Dendera zodiac (a bas-relief now in The Louvre) was shown on a projected slide and discussed by Elisabeth Vreede during a lecture at Hamburg, 5 May 1926.

195. Rudolf Steiner mentions that early depictions of the Ram show the head turned to look over the shoulder—a picture of self-knowledge, also seen in many images of the Easter Lamb—*Tr. note.*

196. Eugen Kolisko (1893-1939) published 'Die zwölf Gruppen des Tierkreises' in *Gäa-Sophia*, Bd 5, 1930, contemporaneously with Beckh's studies of the zodiac as this informs *Mark's Gospel* (1928) and *John's Gospel* (1930)—*Ed.*

197. Imma Erkardstein (1871-1930). A facsimile edition of the original illustrated *Calendar 1912-13*, ed. and Intro by Christopher Bamford, is available through SteinerBooks: Great Barrington 2003.

198. Behind these simple words lies the fact of a friendship with Arthur Schult who lived in Oberstdorf—*Tr. note.*

199. Friedrich Creuzer, *Symbolik und Mythologie der alten Völker*, available online.

200. The Professor is pointing to the meaning expressed in the sounds of speech themselves, a subject he explored deeply following Novalis' differentiation of 'genetic etymology' and 'pragmatic etymology' (see H.B. *The Source of Speech* and *The Mystery of Musical Creativity*—both Temple Lodge 2019—and articles in *Festschrift: Essays in Honour of Hermann Beckh*, Anastasi 2016. The new art of eurythmy ('visible signing' and 'visible word') attracted his interest as a research method; he was present at the very first public performance and helped with the item performed in Sanskrit (Berlin, 20 & 21 Jan. 1914. See R. Steiner, GA 277a, p. 57; Gundhild Kačer-Bock, *Hermann Beckh: Life and Work*, Anastasi 2016, and 'Hermann Beckh Yearbook', forthcoming). The dictionary meanings of the words in the example are: the 'scales' and the 'wave', 'to weigh, weighing' and 'to surge', the 'wave' and 'to rock', 'to weigh'—*Tr. note.*

201. Odyssey 5, 333-53. Some of the mysteries attached to this story are displayed in Blake's Arlington Court tempera painting sometimes known as 'The Sea of Time and Space'—*Ed.*

202. The refrain of the short *Lied* 'Wie mit grimmgen Unverstand' by J.D. Falk (1768-1826).

203. 'The planets are exalted in certain signs … Saturn, the planet of the lower mind, is exalted in Libra, by reason of this sign being the house of balance and Justice.' Alan Leo, *The Complete Dictionary of Astrology*, Rochester, Vermont: Destiny Books, 1983, p. 61f. See also endnote 191 above—*Tr. note.*

204. Recalling Beckh's love of mountains, the fuller extract from Goethe may be of interest:

'… Auf einem hohen nackten Gipfel sitzend und eine weite Gegend über-schauend, kann ich mir sagen: Hier ruhst du unmittelbar auf einem Grunde, der bis zu den tiefsten Orten der Erde hinreicht, keine neuere Schicht, keine aufgehäufte zusammengeschwemmte Trümmer haben sich zwischen dich

und den festen Boden der Urwelt gelegt, du gehst nicht wie in jenen fruchtbaren schönen Tälern über ein anhaltendes Grab, diese Gipfel haben nichts
Lebendiges erzeugt und nichts Lebendiges verschlungen, sie sind vor allem
Leben und über alles Leben. In diesem Augenblicke, da die innern anzie-
henden und bewegenden Kräfte der Erde gleichsam unmittelbar auf mich
wirken, da die Einflüsse des Himmels mich näher umschweben, werde ich
zu höheren Betrachtungen der Natur hinaufgestimmt, und wie der Men-
schengeist alles belebt, so wird auch ein Gleichnis in mir rege, dessen Er-
habenheit ich nicht widerstehen kann. So einsam, sage ich zu mir selber,
indem ich diesen ganz nackten Gipfel hinabsehe und kaum in der Ferne
am Fuße ein geringwachsendes Moos erblicke, so einsam, sage ich, wird es
dem Menschen zumute, der nur den ältesten, ersten, tiefsten Gefühlen der
Wahrheit seine Seele eröffnen will. Ja, er kann zu sich sagen: *Hier auf dem ältesten, ewigen Altare, der unmittelbar auf die Tiefe der Schöpfung gebaut ist, bring
ich dem Wesen aller Wesen ein Opfer*. Ich fühle die ersten, festesten Anfänge
unsers Daseins, ich überschaue die Welt, ihre schrofferen und gelinderen
Täler und ihre fernen fruchtbaren Weiden, meine Seele wird über sich selbst
und über alles erhaben und sehnt sich nach dem nähern Himmel...'
Goethe, *Über den Granit*, Goethe-HA Vol. 13 (1962), pp. 255-56. Emphases
added.

205. Anna Katharina Emmerich (1774-1824), A German Augustinian nun. Clemens
Brentano (1778-1842), German poet and novelist, is a major figure of German
romanticism—*Tr. note*.

206. In the section on the precious stones of Paradise (Gen. 2) in *Alchymy*, Temple
Lodge 2019, Beckh also invites the attentive reader to make a connection
between Heb. *soham*, appearing in English as 'onyx', and the Sanskrit *soham*
meaning approximately the divine 'He Who Is'. The finest human mirroring
of *soham* in Indian traditions (mentioned by Beckh) is *hamso*, a swan, thereby
leading to Lohengrin the Swan Knight.

207. This echoes Rev. 22:1. Beckh points out (e.g. *Mark's Gospel*, p. 398) that this is
traditionally known as the 'heavenly Ganges' in India.

208. These are specific technical terms in anthroposophy for the stages of higher
cognition, hence the use of capital letters—see, amongst other texts, R. Steiner,
*Knowledge of the Higher Worlds: How is it achieved?* [GA 10]—*Tr.*

209. The unfortunate events at Bad Berka where the fledgling Christian Community
held a synod in the summer of 1923. The situation is briefly presented by F.
Rittelmeyer, *Meine Gespräche mit Rudolf Steiner*, Urachhaus 2016, pp. 43f. in the
section originally subtitled 'Der Irrtum einer Hellseherin'. The clairvoyant
causing havoc was Fr. Wiegand—*Ed.*

210. The missing closing quote-marks—no doubt from a remark by Rudolf Steiner,
yet certainly an echo of points discussed earlier in these *Contributions*—are
supplied here as a suggestion—*Tr. note*.

211. And as a Christian seeker, who receives the words of the Creed when taking the step to become a member of The Christian Community—*Tr. note.*

212. A few years before this *Contribution*, Emil Bock had produced and circulated his typewritten *Studies in the Gospels* (1927-29). Here the association of the name Pontius Pilate is related, following R. Steiner, to the two 'sea-pillars' of initiation. English trans., Floris Books 2011, pp. 185-86. Between 1906 and 1914 R. Steiner himself addressed candidates for the 1° initiation of the ritual order Mystica Æterna standing before these two pillars. The masonic image of a ship sailing beyond the two pillars towards a natural Sun and the Blazing Star of initiation is still to be found today, e.g. the Seal of the Masonic Quest Lodge in Paignton, Devon, UK.

213. N.T. and patristic Greek adjective meaning 'of the Lord'.

214. Beitrag zur Sankhyaphilosophie: Sattva, Rajas, Tamas und ihre Beziehung zur goetheschen Farbenlehre im Lichte der Sprachwissenschaft, in *Kultur und Erziehung*. Anthroposophischer Hochschulkurs der Freien Hochschule für Geisteswissenschaft. Goetheanum in CH-Dornach 26 Sept. – 16 Oct. 1920. Bd. III. 1921. Der Kommende Tag A.G. Verlag. Stuttgart, 57-66. Eng. tr. Indology and Spiritual Science, III. Contribution to Sankhya philosophy: Sattva, Rajas, Tamas and their relationship to Goethe's *Theory of Colours* in the light of linguistics, in *The Source of Speech*, Temple Lodge 2019.

215. GA 229, Dornach, 5-13 Oct. 1923. English tr. *The Four Seasons and the Archangels*, London: RSP 1984.

216. The work may have appeared in the 1924 typescript of the lecture—the only version available at the time. Beckh may also be recalling the series of lectures now appearing in *Mysteriengestaltungen*, GA 232—*Ed.*

217. According to Ellic Howe, *Astrology and the Third Reich*, The Aquarian Press, 1984, 108-9, Hitler's horoscope was rarely mentioned in astrological journals and predictive almanacs between 1924 and 1931. However, by 1931 it was becoming a popular topic. One of the first of these was composed by the Austrian Nazi Karl Frankenbach and appeared in *Zenit*, April 1931 where Beckh must have read it. Howe also points out that the leading Nazi astrologer Karl Krafft was taken up by the idea of 'the Uranus-laden quality of the ruling fascist hierarchy in Germany', p. 173—*Ed.*

218. R. Steiner, *Wahrspruchworte*, GA 40, 1998, p. 165. The verse is dated 22 Sept. 1924.

219. The first volume of *Karmic Relationships*, subtitled *Esoterische Betrachtungen*, had been issued by Marie Steiner in 1926.

220. Composed 7-8 Oct. 1817. Published in *Zur Morphologie*, 1820. 1st stanza, Dämon.

221. From Gäa-Sophia Bd. 6, 1932. *Goethe-Jahrbuch*. Pp. 135-161. Eng. tr. in *Collected Essays and Articles*, forthcoming.

222. GA 132, Berlin, Oct.-Nov. 1911, early English translation as *The Inner Realities of Evolution*, London: RSP, 1953.

223. See, for example, lecture 1 of GA 228, Science of Initiation and knowledge of the Stars, Dornach, 27 July 1923. Beckh has previously referred to this lecture where the late arrival of Uranus and Neptune is also mentioned.

224. Precise examples in R. Cowan, *Roman Guardsman 62 BCE-324 CE*, Osprey Publishing, 2014. It appears that the emblem was particularly found among the elite Praetorian Guard.

225. In *John's Gospel: The Cosmic Rhythm* (p. 363), the Professor speaks of the word σκορπισθῆτε in John 16:32 (from *skorpizein* 'to scatter', 'bring into isolation')— *Tr. note.*

226. Ernst Bindel (1890-1974), *Die ägyptischen Pyramiden als Zeugen vergangener Mysterienweisheit*. Stuttgart: Verlag Freies Geistesleben, 1957/79. See also *Die geistigen Grundlagen der Zahlen*. Fischer Taschenbuch, 1989/Anaconda, 2011 (Fr. tr. *Les Nombres*. Anthroposophiques Romandes 1985/1990/2006); *Die Zahlengrundlagen der Musik im Wandel der Zeiten*. Stuttgart: Freies Geistesleben, 1985. Ernst Bindel, a mathematician, was called upon by Rudolf Steiner to teach maths and physics in the first Waldorf School in Stuttgart, where no doubt Hermann Beckh made his acquaintance, especially as Bindel by the time of this *Contribution* had become a valued co-worker with Elisabeth Vreede in the mathematical-astronomical Section of the Goetheanum—*Ed.*

227. Rudolf Steiner. *Esoteric Christianity*. Neuchâtel, 1911. GA 130. Rudolf Steiner Press, 2000/05.

228. This reference to the circle of fifths probably summarizes the overuse of conventional tonic-dominant-subdominant harmony. And as an example pointing to the need to move on, the suggestion of a more adventurous use of mediant relationships is made (these particular harmonic progressions and relationships have, of course, been around for a while, already with Haydn and particularly Beethoven—Beckh cites Wagner in this respect). In the context of writing briefly for non-musicians, the point about the musical future is not gainsaid. Almost a century on, it could be clear that tonality does have a future, although (as in all realms where Beckh attempted to uncover forces of renewal) it is secured only by pro-active listening, as Beckh elsewhere makes clear. This spiritual, that is creative, activity relies on nothing merely theoretical, merely conventional, or merely aurally exotic. See H.B. *The Mystery of Musical Creativity: Man and Music* with its Introduction, and H.B. *The Language of Tonality* with the Introduction to the Eng. tr., Anastasi 2015—*Tr. note.*

229. A whole musical development is enclosed in these brief remarks. Hermann Pfrogner, *Zeitwende der Musik*, München-Wien: Langen Müller 19 (Eng. tr. 'Music's Turning Point of Time', forthcoming) argues that a new, third term be coined—derived, however, from Archytas (428-347 BCE)—for the stage beyond the diatonic and diatonic-chromatic stages in musical evolution. The 'enharmonic stage', when the twelve vibrant primes come into their own, like

*key*-centres, inspiring a free exploration of the nature of tonality, anticipated in some compositions yet still a far-off ideal, casts its shadow before in the bare (actually abstracted, 'made absolute') twelve-*notes* of tempered tuning of the atonal concept—*Tr note*.

230. Ellic Howe, op. cit. p. 102, points out that the majority of some 400 astrological books and pamphlets were printed in Germany between 1921 and 1935—*Ed*.

231. Guenther Wachsmuth, *Die Aetherische Welt in Wissenschaft, Kunst und Religion*, Dornach 1927.

232. Alan Leo, *The Art of Synthesis* (1912) includes Leo's interpretation of Steiner's horoscope (see endnote 41 above).

233. See R. Frieling, The Gospel Trigons in the Creed (I), Sentence 1.

234. Lecture 1 of the series commonly known as *Ancient Myths and the New Isis Mystery*, Dornach, 4 Jan. 1918 (GA 180, Lecture 1).

235. Hermann Beckh, *John's Gospel*, Leominster: Anastasi, 2015, p. 202ff.

236. See for example Alan Leo, *Esoteric Astrology* (1913) with several modern reprints.

237. Icarus, a figure in Greek mythology often depicted in art. With his father, he escapes from Crete flying with wings made of feathers and wax. Ignoring his father's advice to fly neither too high nor too low, he flies too high; the Sun melts the wax in his wings and he falls into the sea. Ovid narrates the story at some length in *Metamorphoses*, viii 183-235.

238. Another translation:

> *The Representative of the Air Element (Gairmanus-Belicosus)*
> Escape from heavy weight of earth existence
> which kills the being of thy self in sinking.
> Take flight from it with lightness of the air.
> *In cosmic space search for reality of brightness.*
> Bind to thy semblance that which thou does find;
> in flying, it will grant to thee existence.
> [Tr. Ruth & Hans Pusch. 104, emphases added.]

239. Guenther Wachsmuth, *The Etheric Formative Forces in Cosmos Earth and Man*, London: Anthroposophic Pub., Co./ New York: Anthroposophic Press 1932, p. 130: 'Ancient wisdom schools of the Orient and the Occident spoke of Lucifer-"Phosphorus" who brought the heavenly light down to the earth and gave it to man in a debased form.'

240. Eng. tr. included in H. Beckh, *From the Mysteries, Genesis, Zarathustra*, Temple Lodge 2020.

241. *Tristan and Isolde*, Act 3, iii. Isolde: '*Heller schallend,/ mich umwallend,/ sind es Wellen/ sanfter Lüfte?/ Sind es Wolken/ wonniger Düfte? Wie sie schwellen,/ mich umrauschen,/ soll ich atmen,/ soll ich lauschen?/ Soll ich schlürfen,/ untertauchen? /Süss in Düften /mich verhauchen? /In dem wogenden Schwall, /in dem tönenden Schall, /in des Weltatems /wehendem All, ...*'

—'Are they gentle/ aerial waves/ ringing out clearly,/ surging around me?/ Are they billows/ of blissful fragrance?/ As they seethe/ and roar about me,/ shall I breathe,/ shall I give ear?/ Shall I drink of them,/ plunge beneath them?/ Breathe my life away/ in sweet scents?/ In heaving swell,/ in the resounding echoes,/ in the universal stream/ of the world-breath...'

242. 'The Spiritual Individualities of the Planets', Dornach, 27 July 1923 in GA 228. Eng. tr. in *The Golden Blade*, 1988. Currently available online (2020).

243. Beckh had earlier published several in-depth studies of this theme. The major articles are included in the triple-volume translation, *From the Mysteries, Genesis, Zarathustra,* Temple Lodge 2020; the remainder are forthcoming in H. Beckh, *Collected Articles.*

244. Lect. 14 of GA 236 (*Karmic Relationships*), Dornach, 4 June 1924.

245. Traditionally, December 8 is celebrated as Bodhi Day by Buddhists around the world. With Beckh's understanding, this falls within the *sign* Capricorn.

246. This order of five steps is also suggested in the Professor's exposition *Mark's Gospel* (2015, p. 56f.), also in connection with the human supersensible members, yet without the additional explanation given here. Again, the twelve main events of Buddha's life may be mentioned elsewhere, but nowhere else in Beckh's *oeuvre* is it worked out in such detail as given here—*Tr. note.*

247. Rudolf Steiner, *Four Mystery Dramas* [GA 14], 'The Soul's Awakening'. Tr. Ruth & Hans Pusch, p. 104f.

248. Ernst Florens Friedrich Chladni (1756-1827), German physicist and musician, researched vibrating plates. Chladni's technique, first published in 1787 in his book *Entdeckungen über die Theorie des Klanges* ('Discoveries in the Theory of Sound'), consisted of drawing a bow over a piece of metal whose surface was lightly covered with sand. The plate was bowed until it reached resonance, when the vibration causes the sand to move and concentrate along the nodal lines where the surface is still, outlining the nodal lines. The patterns formed by these lines are what are now called 'Chladni figures'—*from wikipedia.*

249. From Christian Morgenstern's collection, *Palmström*. 'Fisches Nachtgesang' is a phonetic poem. On the page it consists solely of a pattern of repeating mute symbols, the symbols for long and short feet of metric scansion—*Tr. note.*

250. Goethe: *Faust*, Part 1, Faust's study (i) 447-453: tr. W.H. van der Smissen, 'in the original metres'. Dent/ Dutton, London/ New York, 1926.

251. *The Four Seasons and the Archangels*, lecture 5, Dornach, 13 Oct. 1923.

252. *Tr. note*: Prof. Beckh points to the wider linguistic context, witnessing to a consciousness before splits of meaning became widespread. Without reference to the Mystery traditions that show historical changes of human consciousness, and without the specific aspect here of the light-ether, we are left with the bare linguistic background (assuming 'either light or horns'). That here modern dualistic 'either-or' thinking (Owen Barfield's R.U.P., the 'residue of unresolved positivism') unwittingly projects its own inevitable

confusion, is clearly summarized in an essay available online. Barfield and Beckh, both universal scholars, were convinced the future of the race depends on overcoming dualism. Cf. the following observations—*Tr. note.*

The ancient Greek translation of Exodus 34:29 [LXX] reads, 'when he went down from the mountain, Moses knew not that the appearance of the skin of his face was *glorified'*

(καταβαίνοντος δὲ αὐτοῦ ἐκ τοῦ ὄρους Μωυσῆς οὐκ ᾔδει ὅτι δεδόξασται ἡ ὄψις τοῦ χρώματος τοῦ προσώπου αὐτοῦ). This Greek translation is not faithful to the original Hebrew, but does give the sense of the passage—Moses' face shone brightly. So, where did Michelangelo get the horns? The Hebrew of Exodus 34:29 is:

וַיְהִי בְּרֶדֶת מֹשֶׁה מֵהַר סִינַי וּשְׁנֵי לֻחֹת הָעֵדֻת בְּיַד־מֹשֶׁה בְּרִדְתּוֹ מִן־הָהָר וּמֹשֶׁה לֹא־יָדַע כִּי קָרַן עוֹר פָּנָיו

The issue is with the third to last word, the Hebrew verb קָרַן (*qaran*). The noun form of this verb, קֶרֶן (*qeren*) has as its primary meaning, 'horn', like the horns of an animal. However, this word can also refer to things that are long and cylindrical or that radiate from a common source. For instance, this noun refers to the horns of the altar in the Temple in 1 Kings 1:50 and even to rays of light in Hab. 3:4: 'His radiance is like the sunlight; He [God] has *rays* flashing from His hand.' A Bible translator might therefore understand this verb form in Exodus 34:29 much like the noun, as either referring to literal animal horns or to something like light radiating from Moses' face. Jerome decided on the former. The Latin of Ex. 34:29 is: '*et ignorabat quod cornuta esset facies*': 'and he (Moses) was ignorant that [his] face was horned' (Lat. *cornutus, -a, -um,* adj., *horned, having horns*). Thus, in their (Latin) Bible, Moses had animal horns. During the Reformation, translators removed the horns from the text of Exodus. However, according to some, Moses with horns became a common western, medieval depiction of Moses—*Vincent Bradshaw.* gracesacramento.org

253. Early Norwegian folk-song of an initiation-journey during the Holy Nights, arising out of instinctive clairvoyance. See R. Steiner, *Art as seen in the Light of Mystery Wisdom* [GA 275], lecture 4, Dornach 14 Dec. 1914. Also *The Mystery of Death* [GA 159] lectures, Hanover, 19 Feb. & Bremen 23 Feb. 1915; *The Cycle of the Year as Breathing-Process of the Earth* [GA 223], Dornach, April 4, 1923. The text is performed in eurythmy, tr. by Ingeborg Möller-Lindholm, rhyming version by Rudolf Steiner who also created the group-forms, 1921 (see Rudolf Steiner, *Eurythmieformen*, Band 1, K 23)—*Tr. note.*

254. Rudolf Steiner, *Calendar 1912-13.* Facsimile Edition, ed. and Intro., with relevant English trans. by Christopher Bamford. Great Barrington: Steiner Books 2003. The facsimile does not supply the German of the 'Oral Explanations'. Since the published translations are unfortunately not all quite accurate, we supply both the German sentences with the English revised as necessary—*Tr. note.*

255. One may provisionally infer that the design reproduced a very similar motif in comparison with both the 1912/13 Calendar and the zodiac Archer painted on the ceiling of the principal Stuttgart Theosophical Society meeting room in 1911/12 according to Dr Steiner's design—*Ed.*

256. Rudolf Steiner, *Esoteric/Occult Science.* Tr. Creeger 200f., Adams 163f., Monges p. 202f.

257. The relevant sections in the early periodical *Luzifer-Gnosis* were later issued as *Aus der Akasha-Chronic* (now GA 11). Eng. tr. *Cosmic Memory*, Rudolf Steiner Publications, 1959.

258. See endnotes 15, 16 & 17.

259. Dr Steiner's Notes, as translated in the facsimile edition, contain two sketches (which are reproduced) of the figure in the picture; the first sketch is accompanied by the words 'Mirror image of the sign', followed by a circle with a dot in the centre (the traditional symbol for the Sun) out of which in the picture the Leo-sign begins, '⊙ in hearts with chakra'—*Tr. note.*

260. *Halsgegend*, 'region of the throat', stands in the original typed text, also *eigenartige Auswüchse* 'strange growths'. In the sketch, however, the two oblong shapes surrounded by spiral swirls towards the left of the torsos are clearly in the position of the heart—*Tr. note.*

261. Arthur Schult, Christlich-rosenkreuzerische Astrosophie und arabisch-mittelalterliche Astrologie (Johannes Kepler zu seinem 300. Todestag), *Die CG*, 7. Jg. Nr. 9, Dez. 1930. Pp. 257-64. Eng. tr. see p. 447f. above.

262. In particular, Hermann Beckh, *Mark's Gospel: The Cosmic Rhythm* (Anastasi 2015, Temple Lodge forthcoming), and *John's Gospel: The Cosmic Rhythm—Stars and Stones* (Anastasi 2015, Temple Lodge forthcoming). In what follows: MG = the former book; JG = the latter book.

263. Beckh's spiritual experience as a five-year-old in the mountains convincing him of pre-existence, and which produced an overwhelming compassion for humanity, is probably the best context to mention here (see his biography, p. 66ff.). The experience is also reflected in Beckh's poetic piece 'The Heavenly Jerusalem' (Eng. tr. In JG pp. 459-77 and *Alchymy*, pp. 100-13). This profound experience was apparently a reminder of his real life's task; it was repeated at various times in his early career. Needless to say, acts inspired by compassion are, of course, ever the mark of those who aspire to 'follow the Master'. This is repeatedly practised in approaching the altar—distinctions in life, including all qualifications are beside the point; the initiate and the most simple person (as Rudolf Steiner points out) are here at one. How does this basic attitude inform everyday life that ever aspires to become a 'living sacrifice'? Beckh's own example of clarity and tact is a permanent inspiration precisely here in all 'household' ordering—involving musical contributions, insights of astrosophy, appreciating other religious movements, to mention but some of the Professor's interests and pursuits— where traditional patterns can prove themselves painfully inadequate—*Tr. note.*

264. At the time of writing, Martin Borchart (1894-1971), one of the founding priests, was living and celebrating the sacraments alongside Hermann Beckh in Stuttgart. See Rudolf F. Gädeke, *Die Gründer der Christengemeinschaft*, Verlag am Goetheanum, 1992, p. 249f.—*Ed.*

265. See Bock's *Studies in the Gospels*, op. cit.; Robert Geobel's (1900-83) major work at the time of this *Contribution* was *Die Evangelium in den vier Evangelien*, Stuttgart, 1929. He was ordained in 1925—*Ed.*

266. The tremendous thought here points to the name 'Micha-el', which (as is often noted) means 'Who is like God?' This implies—if the question mark is allowed—the answer arising out of self-knowledge, in short, we were created precisely in order that we ourselves discover why we were created—*Tr. note.*

267. A German echo of the name Pontius Pilate. See endnote 211.

268. Part of the *Isenheimer Altarpiece* (1512-16) by Matthias Grünewald (1470-1528), in the Musée d'Unterlinden, Colmar, Alsace, France.

269. For H. Beckh's acute discoveries in this area, see 'Etheric Formative Forces and Hieroglyphs', *Gäa-Sophia*, Bd. 1, p. 388f. (1926). Eng. tr in H. Beckh, *Collected Articles*, forthcoming.

270. Goethe, from '*Symbolum*', tr. Arthur John Lockhart. The German translates literally: 'Above the stars, below the graves'—*Tr. note.*

271. Frieling gracefully acknowledges Beckh's pioneering book on Genesis 1-9 that carried the title *Der Ursprung im Lichte*, 1924. Eng. tr. *Genesis*, Temple Lodge, 2020 (with *From the Mysteries* and *Zarathustra*).

272. A line from Nietzsche's *Thus spoke Zarathustra: A Book for Everyone and Nobody*, Bk. 2, 11, The Grave-Song. 'And only where there are graves are there resurrections.' Tr. Graham Parkes. OUP. 2005. P. 98; tr. R.J. Hollindale, Penguin Books, 1961. P. 136.

273. It has been pointed out, however, that the strong gesture of the Christ in Michelangelo's painting (in the Sistine Chapel, the Vatican, Rome), could also be interpreted as indicating something like a transference of virtue from the redeemed to those on the downward slope, who are in desperation, unable to help themselves—*Tr. note.*

274. Emil Bock, *Studies in the Gospels*, Vols. 1 & 2, Edinburgh: Floris Books, 2009/11.

275. See H. Beckh, JG, 2015, p. 146.

276. Literal children? George Matheson (the remarkable 'blind seer of Scotland') regards NT references to 'the little ones' rather as suggesting the sacrificial spirits in humanity who 'have attained to the nature of God ... they alone can behold like ... still rejected and despised by men' while yet on earth; they are privileged to 'behold the face of their Father who is in heaven', practicing above all pastoral care. See: George Matheson, *Studies in the Portrait of Christ*, 2 Vols., London 1899/1900, and reprint editions—*Tr. note.*

277. 'Temple theology' today, established single-handed by the outstanding researcher Margaret Barker, has opened awareness that cloud imagery in the NT recalls the cloud of the Presence, later evoked through incense and prayer. 'Heaven' *is* the cube-room itself. It consequently remains a question whether '*Himmel*' occurring in the liturgical Epistles should be translated 'sky'

or whether we are to regard the imagery ('rainbow', 'chariot', and so on) in the Temple context as well, in the sense that the Temple is all around us today. The imagery, however, is indisputably inner; is it becoming 'lost in translation'? Beckh's emphasis in almost every publication is to insist on the strength of the 'I'—that is, we adequately recognize the spirit 'out there', including cosmic contexts, *only* in so far as the awareness comes from within. Beckh did his level best to suggest the raising spatial concepts into musical categories— in the extended sense, as processes. This, Rudolf Steiner emphasizes, is the expectation, or faith, of the Archangel Michael himself (GA 219. Dornach, 17 June 1914)—*Tr. note.*

278. Karl Justus Obenauer. *Hölderlin / Novalis.* Jena: Eugen Diederichs Verlag, 1925. Obenauer (1888-1973), author of several acclaimed books on German literature, especially Goethe and Nietzsche, maintained cordial relationships with both anthroposophy and The Christian Community. Very shortly afterwards, however, he joined the SS (1934). One year later he gave his inaugural speech as the new Professor of modern German history at Bonn in his SS uniform. He was to move up the ranks quickly and participated in the progrom of Nov. 10, 1938. See de.wikipedia.org/wiki/Karl Justus Obenauer, which provides references.

279. See endnote 264 above.

280. Karl Justus Obenauer, *Hölderlin / Novalis.* Jena: Eugen Diederichs Verlag, 1925.

281. F. Rittelmeyer, *Vom Johannischen Zeitalter*, Stuttgart 1925, Chapter 3. An Eng. tr. of this chapter is included with *Letters on John's Gospel*, Temple Lodge, forthcoming.

282. Frieling quotes Luther (1545): *'der Verstorbene'*, echoed in the AV/KJV (1611) 'which had been dead'. The word is omitted in many good Ms authorities, but is nevertheless present in *Vaticanus* and *Sinaiticus* (both fourth century) and other Mss. It is omitted in the earlier T.R., the 'Received Text', also today's revisions of Luther's translation and the Zürcher Bibel; this word (or phrase in English) is also omitted in modern translations in English. If mentioned at all in the notes of commentaries, it is claimed these words in John 12:1 'do not add to the meaning of the sentence'. Frieling, however, must have felt justified to follow Luther. The phrase 'which had been dead' emphasizes the tremendous truth, and he points to Beckh (e.g. JG, p. 330): the event is not a resuscitation out of some trance-induced sleep. Lazarus died; John is 'another person'. In his outstanding explanations, Beckh uses imagery of caterpillar and butterfly to make the process graphically clear—*Tr. note.*

283. Frieling points to the line of verse in Angelus Silesius, *Cherubinischer Wandersmann*, Book 1, no. 23, 'Ich muss Maria sein und Gott aus mir gebären'.

284. T.H. Meyer, *The New Cain*, Temple Lodge, 2017.

285. John 3:8, the dialogue regarding the Holy Spirit with Nicodemus. Luther and English Bibles generally translate the Gk. *phonē* here as *Sausen*, sound.

286. From the Ephesian Verse by Rudolf Steiner, 22 April 1924 [GA 233a], tr. George Adams (also in Beckh JG 55).

287. Michael Bauer (1871-1929), teacher and writer, helped at the founding of The Christian Community. His Collected Works comprise stories, essays, a biography and study on the poet Christian Morgenstern (completed by Margareta Morgenstern and Rudolf Meyer), aphorisms & fragments, etc. The cited reflection on the time phenomenon opens up the idea that through the right distinction between the temporal and the eternal, the eternal is presented to the temporal as its actual, but never obtainable, determination. Augustine makes this concrete in the idea that eternity forms time (*Confessions* XI. 30, 40). That means: time, presence, steadiness and calmness are not attained by themselves, but by the arrival of eternity—just as the body is shaped and determined by the soul—*Tr.*

288. Erich Schwebsch (1889-1953), a good friend in Stuttgart of both Beckh and Frieling, teaching in the first Waldorf School. The quotation is from E. Schwebsch, *Anton Bruckner. Ein Beitrag zur Erkenntnis von Entwickelung in der Musik*, Kommende Tag, Stuttgart, 1921; also Bahrenreiter, 1923. Schwebsh also wrote an extensive study *Johann Sebastian Bach und die Kunst der Fuge*, latest ed. Freies Geistesleben 1987.

289. The notion is also related to the cult of Jupiter-Amon.

290. H. Beckh, MG 2015, p. 163f.

291. The patristic Latin phrase is particularly associated with the Cistercians founded by St. Bernard of Clairvaux, informing his sermons on The Song of Songs, e.g. Sermon 85—*Ed.*

292. Guenther Wachsmuth. *The Etheric Formative Forces*, Vol. 1, London & New York, 1932 (download from: https://www.scribd.com).

293. With such Italian, Frieling may be alluding to The Pontifical Institute 'S. Maria dell'Anima' which includes the church of the German-speaking Catholics in Rome with the adjacent Priests' College. The 'Anima' was founded to the glory of the Mother of God under the title 'beatae Mariae animarum' and served as a hospice for those of the German nation. C.G. Jung believed anima development has four distinct levels, which in 'The psychology of the transference' he named Eve, Helen, Mary and Sophia—*Ed.*

294. Cf. H.B. *John's Gospel*, pp. 172, 77, 79, 453 and *The Language of Tonality*, pp. 105, 244, etc.—*Tr.*

295. See H. Beckh, *From the Mysteries*, Temple Lodge, 2020.

296. Luke 11:2. ελθετω το πνευμα σου το αγιον εφ ημας και καθαρισατω ημας (May your Holy Spirit come upon us and purify us). The words are found in the N.T. Mss 162 (Vatican Library. Barb. Gr. 449) and 700 (B.M. Egerton 2610)—*Ed.*

297. H.B. *Alchymy: The Mystery of the Material World*. Temple Lodge 2019.

298. Cf. H.B. *The Origin of Speech*. Temple Lodge 2019. Pp. 157f., 172 and section 12.

299. Known as 'The Mystical Nativity' or 'The Adoration in the Forest' c.1459, now in the Gemäldegalerie, Berlin.

300. The lecture known in English as 'Whitsun: the Festival of the Free individuality', Hamburg, May 15, 1910 (Whitsunday), GA 118, lect. 13. Eng. tr in *The Festivals and their Meaning*, RSP, 1981, p. 258f.

301. 'final word' = representing Christ's last testament as in a will—*Ed.*

302. R. Frieling, *Die Sieben Sakramente*, Stuttgart, 1926. Bd. 22 of the series *Christus aller Erde*.

303. Ch. Rau, tracing the eight mealtimes in Luke, discovered the renewal of the Eightfold Path. See *Die Vier um den Einen*, Bochum 2008; Eng. tr. 'The Four around the One', forthcoming—*Tr.*

304. Probably the account now to be found in E. Bock, *Studies in the Gospels*, op. cit., Vol. 1, pp. 131-32.

305. The old tradition of aligning Jerusalem with Virgo had been confirmed by the standard work C. Aq. Libra, *Astrology, its technics and ethics*, 1917. See p. 195 of the reissue by Forgotten Books.

306. Probably as found today in E. Bock, *Studies in the Gospels*, op. cit., Vol. 2, pp. 9-26.

307. Kurt von Wistinghausen, *Von der Sprache des Wassers* ('The Language of Water'), *Die CG*, Feb. 1927, pp. 327-31; Eng. tr. see p. 458f. above.

308. Those bearing palm branches. Frieling is well aware that Latin *palma* represented Gk. *phoinikas*, palm-tree or phoenix, the symbol of rebirth.

309. This was especially the case between the seventeenth-century *Evangelaria* (liturgical biblical readings) and at the time of writing. The usage today (2020) is more in abeyance.

310. *Cherubinischer Wandersmann*, 2.30.

311. According to the medieval *Golden Legend*, the place where the magi first perceived the star.

312. Funeral service at home: Eternal Spirit (4); eternity (1); world of eternal being (1); at the place of cremation or burial: eternal Spirit (6); eternal soul (1).

313. Literally, 'undying medicine'.

314. MG 2015, p. 115f.

315. In the context of the Eucharist here, the reference is probably to lecture 12 of *The Apocalypse of St. John* (GA 104); Anthroposophical Publishing Company, London, 1958, p. 211.

316. Hermann von Skerst (1901-95), Priest of The Christian Community, ordained 1924.

317. Source: *Die Christengemeinschaft*, 7. Jg. Dec. 1930, pp. 257-64. Tr. M. & A. S. 2020, in time for Kepler's 390th—soon 400th—death anniversary.

318. Albrecht von Wallenstein (1583-1634), a Bohemian military leader and statesman, who became supreme commander of the armies of the Habsburg Emperor Ferdinand II and a major figure of the Thirty Years' War—*Tr.*

319. Short bibliography in German given. Editions in English include: *The Harmony of the World*, Create Space 2014; *The Secret of the Universe* (reprint and Engl tr. of *Prodromus Dissertationum Mathematicarum Continens Mysterium Cosmographicum*. Tübingen 1596) New York, Abaris Books, 1981; Selections from Kepler's *Astronomia Nova* (Science Classics Module for Humanities Studies), Green Lion Press 2011. Further details, see wikipedia article: Johannes Kepler—*Tr.*

320. Friedrich Doldinger (1897-1973), Priest of The Christian Community, composer, poet and writer—*Tr.*

321. *Harmonies of the World*, Tr. Charles Glenss Willis (1939), available online: http://www.24grammata.com/wp-content/uploads/2014/08/Kepler-Harmonies-Of-The-World-24grammata.pdf

322. Attributed to Ptolemy and quoted approvingly by Thomas Aquinas—*Ed.*

323. From the selection by Heinz Artur Strauss, *Auswahl aus Keplers astrologischen Schriften*, Munich 1926.

324. *Antwort Ioannis Keppleri Sae. Cae. Mtis. Mathematici auff D. Helisaei Röslini Mecici et Philosophi Discurs von heutiger Zeit beschaffenheit und wie es künfftig ergehen werde 1609*. International Edition 2020.

325. The author lists five works by three authors, founder priests of The Christian Community: Dr Friedrich Rittelmeyer, *Der Ruf der Gegenwart nach Christus* ('The call of the present day for Christ') (1928), *Theologie und Anthroposophie, eine Einführung* ('Theology and antroposophy: an introduction') (1930); Lic. Emil Bock, *Vorboten* [3rd ed. 1955: *Boten*] *des Geistes, Schwäbische Geistesgeschichte und christliche Zukunft* ('Harbingers of the spirit: spiritual history in Swabia and the Christian future') (1929)—chapters on Paracelsus, Reuchlin, Kepler, Bengel, Oetinger, Schiller, Hölderlin, Hegel, Schelling, Kerner, Uhland, Mörike, W. Hauff, D.F. Strauss and F.T. Vischer; Prof. Hermann Beckh, *Der kosmische Rhythmus der Sternenschrift im Markusevagelium* (1928) (*Mark's Gospel: The Cosmic Rhythm*) and *Der kosmische Rhythmus im Johannesevangelium* (1930) (*John's Gospel: The Cosmic Rhythm*). The last-mentioned titles have appeared in English translation (both 2015, Temple Lodge, forthcoming)—*Tr.*

326. Source: *Die Christengemeinschaft, 11. Jg. Feb 1927*, pp. 327-31. Kurt von Wistinghausen (1901-86) worked in Stuttgart, initially occupying rooms next to Prof. Beckh in Urachhaus. For many years he edited the Priests' *Newsletter*. He saw Beckh's *Die Sprache der Tonart* through the press (1937); the stock of the first edition was soon pulped by the Nazis. Author of *Der Verborgene Evangelist Studie zur Johannes-Frage*, Stuttgart: Urachhaus 1983 and two illustrated articles on representations of the Last Supper portraying thirteen disciples: 'Dreizehn Jünger', *Die CG* 1984, pp. 106-12, and 'Der geist-erfüllte Jüngerkreis', pp. 365-71.

327. From *Die Christengemeinschaft, 14. Jg. April 1937*. Pp. 23-6. Tr. A. S., in *Hermann Beckh and the Spirit-Word*, Anastasi 2015. Pp. 153-60.

328. *Source*: *The Christian Community Journal*, 1938. Pp. 65-75; ed. A. S. 2014, with additions vividly remembered from conversations with the author, London 1969. Dr Heidenreich, a founder priest of The Christian Community, brought this 'Movement for Religious Renewal' to the British Isles. The story is told in Alfred Heidenreich, *Growing Point*, Edinburgh: Floris Books 1979.

329. Beckh's biographer claims it was during a conference in Zürich—*Tr. note.*

330. Source: *Die Christengemeinschaft*, März 1987, p. 104f.

331. *Source*: Initial paragraphs from *Die Christengemeinschaft* 1937. 14. Jg. 21. Later extended in Emil Bock, *Zeitgenossen, Weggenossen, Wegbereiter*, Stuttgart: Urachhaus 1959. Pp. 122-133. Emil Bock (1895-1959), a founder priest of The Christian Community, steered the movement from 1938-1959.

332. For translated observations from friends and colleagues, see *Hermann Beckh and The Spirit-Word*, Anastasi, Leominster, 2015, p. 121 ff.

333. The early illuminated print *All Religions are One*.

334. Or 'in the shadow / protection of God'.

335. Thus understood by Margaret Barker D.D. in several publications, including *Temple Mysticism An Introduction*, SPCK, London, 2011, p. 33.

336. A reliable account is provided by Arthur Green's Introduction to *The Zohar*, Stanford University Press, Volume 1, 2004, pp. XLVI – LIII.

337. The title appears numerous times in the Books of Enoch to represent the Messiah (the anointed one) and is thus taken up by Isaiah 42:1-4 and applied to Jesus in Matthew 12:18.

338. Sammlung Göschen, Berlin, reprinted several times. See also the edition by H. Rau, Freies Geistesleben, Stuttgart, 2012. English translation by Dr K. Binder, *Buddha's Life and Teaching*, Temple Lodge 2019.

339. H. Beckh, *Buddha's Life and Teaching,* Temple Lodge 2019, p. 10f.

340. *Anthroposophie*. Nr. 46. 17 May 1923. English translation in *Collected Articles*, Temple Lodge, forthcoming.

341. Preuss & Jünger, Breslau, 1923. English translation *The Essence of Tonality*, Anastasi, 2001/08.

342. Edited with a Foreword by Rudolf Meyer, Urachhaus, Stuttgart.

343. The word encompasses a range of meanings, including 'mood', 'atmosphere', 'state of mind' as well as a musical key, pitch or tuning.

344. See also N. Franklin, 'Up the Stairs', in *Festschrift: Essays in Honour of Hermann Beckh*, Anastasi, 2016, pp. 181-212.

345. Contribution VIII (RB 120, 18 February 1931). Eng. trans. in *The Language of the Stars*, Temple Lodge, 2020.

346. See Gershon Weiler, Mauthner's *Critique of Language*, Cambridge University Press, 2009.

347. Jena, 1921, 2nd. ed. 1928.

348. Available in English as *The Etheric Formative Forces in Cosmos, Earth and Man: A Path of Investigation into the World of the Living*. Vol. 1, translated by Olin Dantzler Wannamaker, 1932, Anthroposophic Press, New York.

349. Steffen, *Mani,* Verlag für Schöne Wissenschaften, Dornach und Stuttgart, 1930.

350. Ibid., p. 51.

351. M. Barker, *Temple Mysticism*, op. cit., p. 57. For a thorough investigation into the subject of the Divine Feminine in the O.T., see the same author's *The Mother of the Lord*, Vol. 1, Bloomsbury T. & T. Clark, London and N.Y., 2012, especially p. 88ff.

352. In the French translation, *La Sagesse de Dieu*, trans. C. Andronikof, L'Age d'Homme, Lausanne, 1983, pp. 42-3.

353. See for example, J.J. Stoudt, *Jacob Boehme*, Wipf and Stock, 1957.

354. *Temple Mysticism*, op. cit., p. 65.

355. See especially H. Beckh, Ätherische Bildekräfte und Hieroglyphen, *Gäa Sophia*, Bd. 1, Beitrag 33, Oct. 1926 (Eng. tr. in *Collected Articles*, forthcoming); Das Neue Jerusalem, in *Gegenwartsrätsel im Offenbarungslicht*, Christus aller Erde, Band 16, Verlag der Christengemeinschaft, Stuttgart, 1925, pp. 105-21 (Eng. trans. in *John's Gospel: The Cosmic Rhythm*, Anastasi 2015, pp. 459-77, also *Alchymy: The Mystery of the Material World*, Temple Lodge, 2019, pp. 100-13.); Schneewittchen, *Die Christengemeinschaft* Jg. 1, Nr. 5, Aug. 1924 (Eng. tr. in *Alchymy*, pp. 114-26).

356. H. Beckh, *Aus der Welt der Mysterien*, R. Geering, Basel, 1927, p. 120. Eng. trans. *From the Mysteries*, Temple Lodge, 2020.

357. The complete text of the Ms, newly transliterated from Beckh's Sütterlin handwriting by Dr Katrin Binder and translated, *The Mystery of Musical Creativity: Man and Music*, Temple Lodge 2019. Five chapters (in German) were published in three articles in *Der Europäer*, Basel 2005/06/07-08. http://www.perseus.ch/archive/category/europaer/europaer-archiv/.

358. *Buddha und seine Lehre*, op. cit., p. 219. Eng. tr. p. 205.

359. H. Beckh, *The Parsifal-Christ-Experience*, Anastasi, 2015, p. 109.

360. G. Kačer-Bock, *Hermann Beckh: Life and Work*, Anastasi, 2016, pp. 142-43.

361. *Buddha und seine Lehre*, op. cit., p. 185. Eng. tr. p. 174.

362. Ibid., p. 39. Eng. tr. p. 38f.

363. H. Beckh, *Von Buddha zu Christus*, Verlag der Christengemeinschaft, Stuttgart, 1925. Eng. trans. of the complete text, with extra material, *From Buddha to Christ*, Temple Lodge, 2019.

364. The legends of the Queen of Sheba's bowl of beryl presented to Solomon and the jewel from Lucifer's crown had previously been brought together in H. Beckh, 'Maya. Das Weihnachtsmysterium im Indischen Blütengarten', *Die CG*, Dez., 1924. Eng.trans. in *Collected Articles*, Temple Lodge, forthcoming. The presentation of the bowl is said to depicted in an early stained-glass

window in the Church of St. Urban, Straßburg. See San Marte (pseudonym for A. Schultz), *Parcival, Rittergedicht von Wolfram von Eschenbach, Im Auszuge mitgetheilt von San Marte,* Magdeburg, 1832.

365. F.C. Oetinger, *Das Geheimnis von dem Salz,* Frankfurt and Leipzig, 1762 (reprint currently available). The unorthodox Lutheran theologian was much influenced by Böhme and Swedenborg. In all probability Beckh would have read Emil Bock's discussion of Oetinger in *Boten des Geistes,* Stuttgart, published in 1929 when Beckh was writing his principal study of the Gospel of John. Oetinger is frequently mentioned by R. Steiner as a significant pioneer for the reformation and renewal of Christianity.

366. H. Beckh, *Vom Geheimnis der Stoffeswelt,* R. Geering Verlag, Basel, 1931, p. 19; Eng. tr. p. 21.

367. R. Steiner, *The Inner Realities of Evolution,* GA 132, Berlin, 1911, lecture 1; also *Occult Science—an Outline,* Chap. 4, section on 'Ancient Saturn'.

368. *Die Christengemeinschaft,* 6. Jg. Nr. 4, Juli 1929. Pp. 116-19.

369. Source: *Das Goetheanum,* 9. Jahrgang, Nr. 3. 19 January 1930. P. 22f.

370. Written for *New View,* appearing here for the first time.

371. Source: *Das Goetheanum,* 9. Jahrgang. Nr. 42. October 19, 1930. P. 333f.

372. Source: *Die Christengemeinschaft,* 7. Jg. Nr. 8. Nov. 1930. Pp. 248-50.

373. Source: *Die Christengemeinschaft,* 8. Jg. Nr. 4, Juli 1931. Pp. 117-19.

374. Source: *Das Goetheanum.* Jg. 9, No. 21; 25. Mai, 1930. P. 166.